Modern Conveyancing

By

Ruth Annand, B.A., Solicitor,
Lecturer in Law, University of Bristol

and

Brian Cain, LL.B

London : Sweet & Maxwell : 1984

This edition published in 1984
by Sweet and Maxwell Limited
of 11 New Fetter Lane, London.
Phototypeset by Alphabyte Limited, Cheltenham
Printed in Scotland

British Library Cataloguing in Publication Data

Annand, Ruth
   Modern conveyancing.
   1. Conveyancing—England
   I. Title   II. Cain, Brian
   344.2064′38   KD979

   ISBN 0–421–32090–7
   ISBN 0–421–32100–8 Pbk

Modern Conveyancing

AUSTRALIA AND NEW ZEALAND
The Law Book Company Ltd.
Sydney : Melbourne : Perth

CANADA AND U.S.A.
The Carswell Company Ltd.
Agincourt, Ontario

INDIA
N.M. Tripathi Private Ltd.
Bombay
and
Eastern Law House Private Ltd.
Calcutta and Delhi
M.P.P. House
Bangalore

ISRAEL
Steimatzky's Agency Ltd.
Jerusalem : Tel Aviv : Haifa

MALAYSIA : SINGAPORE : BRUNEI
Malayan Law Journal (Pte.) Ltd.
Singapore

PAKISTAN
Pakistan Law House
Karachi

To
Bertie Littman
Dr. Harold Wilkinson
and Mo

Contents

Table of Cases

Table of Statutes

Table of Standard Conditions of Sale

1. Law Society Conditions

2. National Conditions

1: Introduction

"My people are destroyed for lack of knowledge."

Hosea, Chapter 4, verse 6

If solicitors wish to retain their conveyancing business in today's competitive climate, they must give the best possible service to their clients in terms of quality, efficiency, speed and cost. This book is designed to help those starting off in the profession to achieve such a service. For the total newcomer to the subject, we begin by outlining, from start to finish, the conveyancing procedure for buying and selling a house, with unregistered or registered title.

OUTLINE CONVEYANCING PROCEDURE FOR BUYING AND SELLING A HOUSE

Stage One—Preliminary

Vendor's Solicitor	*Purchaser's Solicitor*
Take instructions:	Take instructions:
(i) Obtain details of sale: names, addresses, property, price, furniture and fittings, completion date, private or agency sale. Details will be confirmed by estate agent's (if any) instructions;	(i) Obtain details of purchase: names, addresses, property, price, furniture and fittings, completion date, private or agency sale. Details will be confirmed by estate agent's (if any) instructions;
(ii) Ascertain location of deeds: vendor or vendor's bank if no mortgage, building society or bank if mortgage;	(ii) Advise joint purchasers on how property should be held;
(iii) Discuss financial matters;	(iii) Discuss financial arrangements;
(iv) Go through Enquiries before Contract form (Con 29 long) with vendor.	(iv) Advise survey;
	(v) If appropriate, inform purchaser's mortgagee that you are acting on behalf of purchaser.

1

Stage Two—Up to Exchange of Contracts

Obtain deeds. Registered land: bespeak office copies of entries on the register and filed plan (Form A44) from District Land Registry. (Explanatory leaflet No. 9.)	If land unregistered make a search of Public Index Map (Form 96).
Draft the contract. Send draft contract to purchaser's solicitor. Registered land: include office copies of entries on the register and filed plan.	Peruse draft contract (and office copies). Make Local Land Charges search (LLC1) and Enquiries of District Council or London Borough (Con 29A/D). Send Enquiries before Contract (Con 29 long) to vendor's solicitor. Check plan with site. Is a Commons Registration search or search of the Registers of Rent necessary? Receive mortgagee's instructions following offer of loan to purchaser.
Answer enquiries before contract; refer to vendor where necessary.	
	Peruse replies to search and enquiries and discuss with purchaser together with mortgage offer and surveyor's report.
Agree contract.	Agree contract.
	Make sure property is insured as from exchange of contracts.
Get contract signed, exchange parts, obtain deposit.	Get contract signed, exchange parts, pay deposit.
	Consider necessity of protecting purchaser's contract by registration.

Stage Three—Contract to Completion

Send purchaser's solicitor abstract of title, or registered land, authority to inspect the register[1] (Form 201) (if office copies of register and filed plan not sent in stage two, do so now).	Peruse abstract or office copies.

[1] This is unnecessary where the Law Society's Contract for Sale (1984 rev.) is used and the purchaser is represented by a solicitor. The authority to inspect the register is incorporated into the contract by Special Condition E. See *post*, p. 165.

Stage Three—*contd.*

Notify mortgagee about redemption and obtain redemption figure and "daily rate" in event of delay.	Send Requisitions on Title to vendor's solicitors (Con 28B). Reserve right to raise further requisitions on behalf of mortgagee.
Reply to requisitions on title.	Consider replies to requisitions on title.
Approve draft conveyance or transfer and return to purchaser's solicitor.	Draft and submit conveyance or transfer to vendor's solicitor. Send results of Local Land Charges search, Enquiries of District Council or London Borough and Enquiries before Contract with replies, contract, abstract or office copy entries and authority to inspect register, Requisitions on Title with replies and approved draft conveyance or transfer to mortgagee's solicitor (if same solicitor not acting for purchaser and mortgagee). Receive mortgagee's requisitions on title and mortgage deed.
Reply to additional requisitions on title.	Report to mortgagee (by raising further requisitions with vendor's solicitor if necessary).
Prepare and send completion statement to purchaser's solicitor.	Ask mortgagee for statement of amount they will provide on completion. Engross conveyance or transfer.
Obtain vendor's execution of conveyance or transfer. Arrange for handing over of keys.	Obtain purchaser's execution of conveyance or transfer and mortgage deed. Send executed conveyance or transfer to vendor's solicitor.

Stage Three—*contd.*

	Make Land Charges search (Form K15). Registered land: make Official search of the Register (Form 94A) and "Bankruptcy only" Land Charges search (Form K16) against purchaser if necessary.
	Check results.
	Is a search of the Companies' Register necessary.
	Send completion statement and your bill of costs to purchaser.
	Obtain completion moneys.
	Inspect property.

Stage Four—Completion

Produce deeds or Land Certificate or Charge Certificate and conveyance or transfer.	Ensure that requisite documents will be handed over.
	Check abstract against deeds or office copy entries against Land or Charge Certificate.
Produce receipts for outgoings.	Peruse receipts for outgoings.
Date conveyance or transfer.	
Obtain purchase money.	Pay purchase money.
Hand over deeds or Land or Charge Certificate, receipted mortgage deed or Form 53 or undertaking redischarge of mortgage, conveyance or transfer and keys.	Receive deeds or Land or Charge Certificate, receipted mortgage deed or Form 53 or undertaking redischarge of vendor's mortgage, conveyance or transfer and keys.
	Date mortgage deed.
Redeem vendor's mortgage.	Unless also acting for mortgagee, send mortgagee's solicitor all rele-

Stage Four—*contd.*

Send bill of costs to vendor.

Send vendor balance of purchase moneys.

Forward receipted mortgage or Form 53 to purchaser's solicitor.

vant documents (including receipted mortgage or Form 53, together with completed P.D. form (Stamps L(A)451). Mortgagee's solicitor then attends to stamping (within 30 days) and lodges application for first registration or registration of dealings with district land registry (if necessary), paying appropriate fee.

If purchaser has no mortgage attend to stamping and registration (if necessary).

Where appropriate, bespeak office copies of entries on the register and filed plan.

2: Searches

INTRODUCTION

Our modern law of conveyancing seeks to ensure that a purchaser can discover all matters relating to the title of the land he is intending to buy if he performs three tasks; if he peruses the title deeds, inspects the property and searches the appropriate registers.

The solicitor acting for the purchaser is under a duty to make "usual searches"[1] on behalf of his client and to communicate the result of those searches to him.[2] The "usual searches" to be made will vary according to the nature of the transaction. In *G. & K. Ladenbau (U.K.) Ltd.* v. *Crawley and de Reya*[3] purchasers were buying a vacant site for industrial development. Their solicitors were held liable for not making a search in the Commons Register against the land. Heed must be taken of Lord Diplock's recent statement in *Saif Ali* v. *Sidney Mitchell and Co.*[4]

> "The general trend in the policy of the law as developed by your Lordship's house in recent years has been to extend to new areas of activity the notion that a man is liable for loss or damage to others resulting from his failure to take care."

It is hoped that this chapter will provide a useful guide to the searches that should be made.

LOCAL LAND CHARGES SEARCH

Introduction

One of the major objectives of the 1925 property legislation was to simplify the buying and selling of land by creating a comprehensive register of local land charges, so that purchasers of land could discover obligations enforceable against successive owners by local authorities under the terms of various statutes. Local land charges arise because it is necessary in a society such as ours to limit an owner's use of property in the interests of the welfare of the community at large. Although they were

---

[1] J.T. Farrand, *Emmet on Title* (18th ed.) p.2; R. P. M. Jackson and J. L. Powell, *Professional Negligence* (1982), p. 169.
[2] *Lake* v. *Bushby* [1949] 2 All E.R. 964.
[3] [1978] 1 W.L.R. 266.
[4] [1980] A.C. 198 at p. 218.

originally the creation of the Land Charges Act 1925 by the mid 1950s it was obvious that the system needed reform and a Law Commission study in 1973–74 resulted in the Local Land Charges Act 1975.[5] This Act repealed the whole of the Land Charges Act 1925 in so far as it related to local land charges. The position is now entirely governed by the 1975 Act, which came into force on August 1, 1977, and the various rules made thereunder.

What is a Local Land Charge?

The definition of a local land charge is contained in sections 1 and 2 of the 1975 Act. Essentially a local land charge can be any matter of a public nature affecting land; some are charges in the ordinary sense involving an obligation to pay money, others restrict or limit the ways in which land can be used. They are usually in favour of, or imposed by, a local authority or other statutory undertaker, for example, a water authority.

The importance of these charges to a purchaser lies in section 10 of the 1975 Act which has the effect of making *any* local land charge enforceable against subsequent purchasers of the land affected, whether or not the charge has actually been registered and whether or not its existence (when registered) was disclosed in an official certificate of the result of search. As will be seen any person who suffers loss as a consequence may be able to claim compensation—but only if a search has been made. The importance of a local land charges search cannot, therefore, be understated.

A local land charges search is normally made by a purchaser's solicitor before exchange of contracts, together with his enquiries of the local authority.[6] Whereas the search will disclose matters already in existence affecting the property, the enquiries will show the local authority's future plans for the area in which that property is situate. For example, the search would show that the property was in a smoke control area[7] whereas the enquiries would show the authority's intention to create such an area. In order to appreciate more fully what the search reveals the actual contents of the register must be looked at.

The Register of Local Land Charges

Section 3 of the Act provides that a register of local land charges and an index must be kept by every district council, London borough council and the common council of the City of London—"registering authorities." Recently provision has been made for the computerisation of all such registers and indices though it will be some time before this takes place.[8] The body who brings the charge into existence is known as an "originating authority." The "originating authority" is not necessarily the registering

---

[5] Report on Local Land Charges, Law Comm. No. 2.

[6] See *post*, p. 73.

[7] See *post*, p. 81.

[8] Local Government (Miscellaneous Provisions) Act 1982, s.34. Lancaster is now computerised.

authority concerned, it could be Bristol Waterworks Company, and in this case the originating authority is under a duty to apply for registration in the appropriate register whereupon the registering authority must register it. Where the registering authority is itself the originating authority it must register the charge in the appropriate register.[9] No matter where the originating authority is, the charge must be registered with the council responsible for the area in which the affected land is situate.

The register is divided into 12 parts, each part containing different types of charge.

PART 1: GENERAL FINANCIAL CHARGES

Various statutes such as the Public Health Acts or the Highways Act 1980 give local authorities power to recover the expense of executing certain types of work from the owners or occupiers of property. Suppose a local authority repairs a private road. It is entitled to recover the cost of so doing from the persons living in the street. Such expenses become a charge on the property which a local authority may enforce in the same way as if it was the owner of a charge by deed expressed to be by way of legal mortgage.[10] Until the final costs have been ascertained and apportioned between the frontagers the charge will be registered in part 1 of the register. This gives a prospective purchaser warning that as soon as the final adjustments have been made a specific charge will be registered in part 2 of the register. Within 15 months of the specific charge being created the general charge must be cancelled. A specific charge may only be registered if the general charge has been cancelled. In practice very few registrations of specific financial charges are preceded by a registration in part 1, as the cost of executing the works is assessed and apportioned immediately they are completed.

PART 2: SPECIFIC FINANCIAL CHARGES

These arise and are enforceable in the manner outlined above. Other examples of specific financial charges include expenses incurred by a local authority in removing a rubbish tip on private property which has become a danger to health (Public Health Act 1936) or those incurred in repairing a house which is unfit for human habitation (Housing Act 1957) or for the destruction of rats and mice in an infested property (Prevention of Damage by Pests Act 1949).

The importance of finding out about such charges is illustrated by the case of *Payne* v. *Cardiff R.D.C.*[11] A local authority carried out streetworks under the Private Street Works Act 1892 and a charge was taken over the house of a frontager payable by seven annual instalments. The owner defaulted on the first three instalments and it was held that the local authority was entitled to sell the house and recover the amount of the charge with interest and costs.

---

[9] Local Land Charges Act 1975, s.5.
[10] Ibid. s.7.
[11] [1932] 1 K.B. 241.

PART 3: PLANNING CHARGES

In general a planning charge is one that arises under the mass of planning legislation which controls the use and development of land.

Under the Town and Country Planning Act 1971 local planning authorities have the power to control development[12] to preserve amenity. A landowner must usually obtain planning permission to carry out any development. The permission may contain certain conditions, for example, to build a car park adjoining the development, and this is registrable as a planning charge. Enforcement notices issued by a planning authority for breach of a planning permission were formerly registered in this part of the register. Notices served on or after November 27, 1981 are more likely to appear in the new register of enforcement and stop notices kept by local planning authorities.[13] The new form of Enquiries of District Councils have a question specifically designed to reveal the existence of such notices.

Under the Town and Country Planning (Control of Advertisements Regulations) 1984, a local planning authority may also control the display of advertisements. Again an "enforcement notice" may be served for breach and again the charge is registrable as a planning charge.

In future certain regulations made under the Wildlife and Countryside Act 1981 will be registrable as planning charges. They may restrict an owner's enjoyment of his property insofar as the Act was introduced to preserve the countryside and certain species of our animal and plant life.

PART 4: CHARGES NOT REGISTRABLE ELSEWHERE

This comprises a variety of charges ranging from listing as a "scheduled monument" under the Ancient Monuments and Archaeological Areas Act 1979[13a] to notices served under the Weeds Act 1959 requiring a landowner to stop the spread of injurious weeds. Matters more likely to concern a purchaser include closing orders, that is orders preventing occupation of houses unfit for human habitation[14] and orders designating smoke control areas.[15]

A recent example is the Housing (Right to Buy) (Designated Rural Areas and Designated Regions) (England) Order 1982 which designates parts of Norfolk as a rural area for the purposes of section 19 of the Housing Act 1980. The general effect of this is that a council may restrict the sale of council houses to those who have lived or worked in the area for three years.

PART 5: FENLAND WAYS MAINTENANCE CHARGES

These charges relate to expenses incurred by county councils in maintain-

---

[12] Town and Country Planning Act 1971, s.22, defines development as "the carrying out of building, engineering, mining or other operations in, on, over or under land, or the making of any material change in the use of any buildings or other land."

[13] Local Government and Planning (Amendment) Act 1981.

[13a] See the guide to the Act printed in (1983) L.S. Gaz. 270 at the request of the Department of the Environment.

[14] Housing Act 1957, ss.17, 18, 26 and 35.

[15] Clean Air Act 1956, s.11 as amended by Local Government, Planning and Land Act 1980.

ing private ways in fenlands. A charge may only be registered against land, the value of which has increased as a result of work done.

PART 6: LAND COMPENSATION CHARGES

Part 6 is confined to certain matters relating to compensation arising under the Land Compensation Act 1973. Two types of charge are registrable:

(1) When land has been compulsorily acquired from a landowner. If the landowner retains part of the land, particulars of it may have to be registered as a local land charge in respect of "injurious affection." For example, part of A's garden is acquired by the local authority to build a new road. The values of A's house depreciates because of the noise, vibration and dust from the flow of traffic. The house has been caused injurious affection and A can claim compensation for his loss.

(2) When an advance payment of compensation is to be made in connection with a compulsory acquisition. Particulars of the advance payment (including the date on which it would be paid) and the balance of the compensation are registered against the property. If your purchaser is buying land subject to a compulsory purchase order it is important for him to know whether or not any compensation has been paid.

PART 7: NEW TOWNS CHARGES

The first step in the building of a new town is for an order to be made by the Secretary of State for the Environment designating an area of land as the site of a proposed new town. The next step is for a compulsory purchase order to be made by a development corporation (the members of which are appointed by the Secretary of State) and confirmed by the Secretary of State in accordance with the procedure laid down under the New Towns Act 1981.[16] Both steps are registrable as charges.

PART 8: CIVIL AVIATION CHARGES

To carry out its functions effectively the Civil Aviation Authority has statutory powers[17] to make various orders and directions which must be registered under this head in the appropriate registering authority's register. Under these powers orders may be made creating easements or other rights, over or in land, enabling the authority to install and maintain equipment. Orders may also be made restricting the nature of development near a civil airport and agreements can be made with individual landowners permitting the authority to enter onto their land and maintain installations, for example power cables.

PART 9: OPENCAST COAL MINING CHARGES

Under the Opencast Coal Act 1958 the National Coal Board may by order compulsorily acquire the land or the right to occupy and use the land temporarily. These orders are registrable as local land charges.

PART 10: LISTED BUILDINGS

The Secretary of State may draw up a list of buildings of special

---

[16] New Towns Act 1981, ss.1 and 10.
[17] Civil Aviation Act 1982, Pt. II.

architectural or historic interest or approve such a list where it is made by
"other persons or bodies of persons."[18] The part of this list which relates
to a county district must be placed with the registering authority (treated
for this purpose as the originating authority)[19] and a copy of the list must
be registered in Part 10.

Once a building is listed it is unlawful for any person to change the
character of the building without having first obtained a listed building
consent from the local planning authority. Listing can have a drastic effect
on the value of the property. In *Amalgamated Investment & Property Co
Ltd.* v. *John Walker & Sons Ltd.*[20] a group of companies contracted
to buy a warehouse in Commercial Road, London for £1,710,000 with a
view to development. The day after contracts were exchanged the
warehouse was listed. The group would have had to apply for listed
building consent before they could develop the property. The evidence
showed that if consent was refused the value of the warehouse would have
fallen by over £1,500,000, all within one day.

PART 11: LIGHT OBSTRUCTION NOTICES

This is the only type of charge registrable on the application of an
individual. An individual applies for such a notice to be registered when
he wishes to prevent a neighbour from acquiring a right to light by
perscription. Section 3 of the Prescription Act 1832 provides that the
actual enjoyment of the access of light to any building for 20 years shall
make the right absolute. A right to light does not accrue, however, if its
enjoyment has been interrupted or granted by a written consent or
agreement. "Interruption" in this context would mean the landowner
building so as to block his neighbour's access of light.

A problem arose during the last war when buildings were destroyed by
bombing. If the owner of bombed land did not reconstruct the building
within 20 years his neighbour could acquire an easement of light which
would effectively stop the owner building on the land in the future. To
counteract this problem some owners put up hoardings or screens. In
1959[21] an owner of vacant land was given an alternative choice of
registering a charge against his neighbour's land provided that the
neighbour was given prior notice in writing inviting him to challenge this
obstruction of his light.

Light obstruction notices are now registrable in part 11 of the register
on payment of a fee of £32.00.

If a purchaser buys land subject to a light obstruction notice it is possible
that building operations are being contemplated on the next door
property. The purchaser may therefore be involved in proceedings in the
Lands Tribunal to preserve his right to light.

PART 12: DRAINAGE SCHEME CHARGES

Expenses incurred by a water authority in implementing certain drainage

---

[18] Town and Country Planning Act 1971, s.54.
[19] Local Land Charges Act 1975, Sched. 1.
[20] [1977] 1 W.L.R. 164.
[21] Rights of Light Act 1959, s.2.

schemes under the Land Drainage Act 1976, for example constructing sewers, are recoverable from the several owners of the land which the scheme benefits. The land is made subject to a charge which operates in the same way as financial charges.[22]

The Effect of Registration or Non-Registration of a Local Land Charge

Since 1975 the registers of local land charges operate as notice registers. The enforceability of a local land charge against a purchaser or other person dealing with the land does not depend on registration or non registration. Assuming that the charge is enforceable against him according to the general law (apart from the 1975 Act) he will be bound by the charge irrespective of whether or not he makes a search and even if he does search, irrespective of the fact that the charge is not disclosed by the official certificate of search.[23] In the case of unregistered land where the charge is registered that registration "is deemed to constitute actual notice [of the charge] and of the fact of such registration, to all persons and for all purposes connected with the land affected. . . ."[24] A local land charge affecting registered land is capable of protection as a minor interest by the entry of a notice or restriction on the register.[25-26] Most charges are not entered on the title register for in the absence of such registration they constitute "overriding interests" under section 70(1)(i) of the Land Registration Act 1925. A search of the local land charges register is therefore equally important whether the vendor's title is registered or unregistered.

WHEN TO MAKE THE SEARCH

A purchaser's solicitor should (and in fact does) make his search before exchange of contracts. On a sale of land the general rule is that a buyer enters into the contract at his own risk. The vendor is, however, under a duty to disclose any latent defects in title. Some local land charges must be disclosed by a vendor before contract, for example financial charges. However, the case of *Re Forsey and Hollebone's Contract*[27] shows that a vendor is under no duty to disclose certain types of land charge which may be of great importance to a purchaser, here a resolution by the local planning authority to prepare a town planning scheme which was registered in the local land charges register. If the search is not done until after contract the purchaser, on discovering such a charge, would have no right to rescind the contract or claim damages from the vendor.

An official certificate of search obtained in reply to a requisition for a local land charges search speaks only for the date on which the certificate

---

[22] See *ante*, p. 9.

[23] Local Land Charges Act 1975, s.10.

[24] Law of Property Act 1925, s.198, as amended by Sched. 1 to Local Land Charges Act 1975.

[25-26] A financial charge must be so entered before realisation of the property to enforce the charge.

[27] [1927] 2 Ch. 379.

of search was issued. It confers no priority period, that is it does not guarantee that a purchaser will not be bound by a charge registered within a set period from the issue of the certificate. Therefore, ideally the purchaser's solicitor should make his application for search at such a time as to ensure that he receives the official certificate as near as possible to the date set for exchange of contracts.

WHO CAN SEARCH?

Any person may search in any local land charges register on paying the prescribed fee.[28]

WHERE TO SEARCH

The search should be made with the appropriate district council, or for property in the Greater London area, with the appropriate London borough council. A search may be made in person or by means of a written application. The power to make a personal search is rarely used in practice partly owing to its inconvenience (coming from the personal experience of an articled clerk who has made a personal search at Eastbourne Town Hall) and also because on a personal search it is easy to miss charges that have been registered. The fee for making a personal search is £1·05.

POSTAL SEARCHES

A postal application for search is made on form LLC 1—"Requisition for search and official certificate of search." Form LLC 1 has a printed duplicate attached to be torn off and retained by the local council, the original only being sent back with the signed certificate on it. Both parts must be filled in.

The register is divided into 12 parts and a search may be made only in those parts with which the purchaser is concerned. However, it is almost universal practice to apply for a search of the whole register. Where a purchaser is buying land in separate occupation or separately rated then a requisition for search must be made for each separate part. As local land charges are registered against the land affected a description of the land sufficient for it to be identified must be inserted on the form. In most cases the full postal address will suffice, but if necessary a plan of the property should be sent with the requisition. The plan need not be in duplicate unless the applicant requires a copy to be sent back with the official certificate of search. The fee payable is £2·65 where a search of the whole register is applied for, and for a search of any one part of the register it is £1·05.

The search usually takes the local authority 14 days to process (in London they are currently taking about three to four weeks). The certificate, when received, will state whether or not there are any subsisting entries affecting the property and if there are, a schedule detailing these will be attached. Office copies of documents relating to an entry can be obtained on payment of a reasonable fee.

---

[28] Local Land Charges Act 1975, s.8.

PURCHASER'S RIGHT TO COMPENSATION

Where a purchaser has made a local land charges search before contract and at a time when the charge existed but was not registered, then under section 10 of the 1975 Act he will be entitled to compensation from the registering authority for any loss suffered as a result of non registration. Where the charge was registered but not disclosed by the official search certificate the same right to compensation arises.[29] Where a personal search was made a purchaser will not be entitled to compensation if he overlooked an entry properly recorded by the registering authority. "Purchaser" for the purposes of section 10 includes a lessee or mortgagee.

Any purchaser who has suffered loss within section 10 should claim the sum that he considers that he has lost from the registering authority in whose area the land affected is situate. If his claim is not met he may take proceedings in the County Court; if the claim exceeds £5,000,[30] proceedings are taken in the High Court. The compensation received by a successful litigant will be his loss and legal costs. Initially the registering authority is liable to pay the compensation but they may recover the sum from the originating authority (where not the registering authority themselves) where it has failed to apply for registration of the charge in the proper time.[31]

VALUE OF THE OFFICIAL CERTIFICATE OF SEARCH

As has been seen, the only value that an official certificate of search has for a purchaser is that it gives him "notice" of the charge. However, a solicitor or other person in a fiduciary position such as a trustee or personal representative is protected in so far as section 13 of the 1975 Act provides that he "shall not be answerable in respect of any loss occasioned by reliance on an erroneous official certificate of search or an erroneous office copy of an entry in a local land charges register."

CANCELLATION

Section 5(5) of the 1975 Act provides that the registration of a local land charge may be cancelled pursuant to an order of the court. This subsection can only be used where it is beyond doubt that a registration should not be or remain on the register. The subsection cannot be used to question the validity of the charge.[32]

PUBLIC INDEX MAP SEARCH

As part of the system of land registration introduced by the Land Registration Act 1925 maps are kept at the Land Registry showing the

---

[29] See (1976) 40 Conv. 106 for a detailed discussion of the purchaser's right to compensation.

[30] County Courts Act 1959, s.39 as amended.

[31] Local Land Charges Rules 1977, r.5.

[32] *Re Engall's Agreement* [1953] 1 W.L.R. 977, where a purchaser of land unsuccessfully tried to use this procedure to question the validity of an estate contract registered as a C(iv) land charge.

extent of all registered estates. Together with the list of pending applications for first registration they form the Public Index Map. Unlike the register of title itself the Map is made available for public inspection without the need to obtain the prior consent of the landowner concerned.

If a vendor deduces title on the basis that his land is unregistered a purchaser's solicitor should make sure that neither the land, nor a part of it, is registered with a title adverse to the unregistered documentary title shown by the vendor. The title to the land may have been registered voluntarily[33] some time ago, yet subsequently dealt with as unregistered land. The legal estate would be vested in the person registered as the proprietor. A search of the Public Index Map would reveal the earlier voluntary registration and prevent a purchaser from taking a conveyance from somebody who did not have the legal estate.[34]

A search of the Public Index Map should be made by a purchaser's solicitor at the earliest opportunity, that is as soon as he has a sufficient description of the property. There is no need to make a search when the purchaser is buying (or a mortgagee is lending money on the security of) a registered freehold title. In every other conveyancing transaction a search should be made to see whether the superior title is registered. For example, on grant of a lease for a term of over 21 years the search will reveal whether it is necessary to register the lease because the freehold is already registered.[35] Searches of the Public Index Map may also be made on behalf of an intending incumbrancer so that his interest or right in the land may be protected in the appropriate manner, that is, by registration of a notice, caution or restriction (registered land) or land charge (unregistered land).

Application for an official search of the Index Map should be made on Form 96.[36] The Land Registration Rules 1925[36] state that a plan describing the land in question should be furnished with all applications. However, the Chief Land Registrar has said[37] that any description which establishes the identity of the property will be acted upon. A plan is only likely to be needed when the application relates to land situated in an area where registration of title is not compulsory. In all other cases the usual postal address may be used. A fee of £2·00[38] is payable for each property in respect of which a search is required. When applying for a search the applicant may request that the land registry issue a plan of the property with the official certificate of search. This plan can later be used as the basis of a plan for a deed in the transaction leading to first registration. It may also be compared with the contract plan to ensure that there are no discrepancies as to the extent of the land to be sold. A fee of 50p (in addition to the search fee)[38] is payable for this service which is only available in connection with the built up land in areas of compulsory registration.

The official certificate of the result of search will disclose the following matters:

---

[33] See *post*, p. 306.
[34] See further *Claridge* v. *Tingey* [1967] 1 W.L.R. 134.
[35] Land Registration Act 1925, ss.19(1) and 22(1).
[36] Land Registration Rules 1925, r. 286.
[37] Registered Land Practice Notes (1982/83 ed.) Note E.1.
[38] Land Registration Fee Order 1981 (S.I. 1981 No. 54), Sched. 5.

(i) Whether the land is registered or not, and if so whether with freehold or leasehold title, and the title number. In the case of leasehold land, brief particulars of the lease will be given. This will include the parties, the term and the date the grant was made.

(ii) Whether the land is affected by a caution against first registration or a priority notice. A caution against first registration is registered by somebody who has some claim against the property in question. Notice then has to be given to the cautioner of any application for first registration of the title to the property so that he may assert his claim against the person so applying. The cautioner has 14 days within which to produce to the Registrar conclusive evidence of the correctness of his claim, after which time he may lose his right to object. A priority notice against first registration is registered by a person entitled to apply for registration as proprietor of the land. Provided that he lodges his application for first registration within 14 days of the notice nobody else can be registered as owner in the meantime.

(iii) Whether the land is in an area where registration of title is compulsory. This tells a purchaser's solicitor whether or not an application for first registration will have to be made after completion has taken place.[39]

In contrast with an official certificate of search of the register,[40] the official certificate of search of the Public Index Map gives no protection to a purchaser against a subsequent registration. However, if a search is incorrectly made by the land registry the purchaser may be entitled to statutory compensation for any loss suffered as a result of his reliance on the certificate of search.[41]

LAND CHARGES SEARCH

Introduction

In the case of any transfer of property with unregistered title, of which there are still many millions, the purchaser's solicitor needs to make one or more searches in the now computerised[42] office of the Land Charges Department of H.M. Land Registry at Plymouth. Whereas the Registers of Local Land Charges record public matters affecting the ownership of property,[43] this office keeps records of matters of a private commercial nature which might affect the property, such as bankruptcies, deeds of arrangements, agreements for sale, or a wife's right to occupy the matrimonial home.

---

[39] For the occasions when a transaction necessitates registration see *post*, p.309.

[40] See *post*, p. 37.

[41] Land Registration Act 1925, s.83(3).

[42] As from September 9, 1974 when the dispersal of the organisation from Kidbrooke, London to Plymouth was completed.

[43] See *ante*, p. 7.

A system of registration of third party rights did exist before 1925, but was extended by the Land Charges Act 1925 and the Law of Property Act 1969 and is presently maintained under the Land Charges Act 1972[44] and the Land Charges Rules 1974. Two fundamental principles govern the system. Registration is deemed to constitute actual notice of the matter registered and the fact of such registration to all persons and for all purposes connected with the land affected[45]; a purchaser is bound by a registrable interest if it is registered, whether or not he searches the register. But failure to register renders the interest void against a purchaser;[46] in general a purchaser is not bound by a registrable interest that is unregistered even if he actually knows about it. Thus in *Midland Bank Trust Co.* v. *Green*[47] a father granted his son an option to purchase his farm at a favourable price. The son failed to register his option as a land charge. The father then sold the farm to his wife in order to defeat the son's option. The House of Lords held that the wife took free of the son's option, even though she knew all about it; the option was statutorily void against her for non-registration.

Where someone is buying land with title registered as absolute,[48] there is no need to make a search in the Land Charges Department, with the exception perhaps of a "bankruptcy only" search.[49] Where the title is registered with possessory, qualified or good leasehold title[50] there could be charges affecting the land which are not entered on the land certificate, and a land charges search is desirable. Usually, however, this is impossible as the details necessary to facilitate such a search are unavailable, and the purchaser will have to decide whether to take the risk. It follows from this that in practice searches in the Land Charges Department are mainly done in connection with unregistered title to property.

It will help emphasise the importance of a land charges search if a brief look is taken at the volume of work handled by the Land Charges Department. The office currently holds approximately 5,250,000 records of matters affecting property, registered against the names of about 3,500,000 landowners. Every working day, just over 1,000 new charges are recorded and some 20,000 searches are made at the request of solicitors.

What Matters are Registrable? What will a Search Reveal?

Section 1(1) of the Land Charges Act 1972 places on the Registrar an obligation to keep the following registers, namely:

(a) a register of land charges;

---

[44] Replacing the Land Charges Act 1925 with effect from January 29, 1973.
[45] Law of Property Act 1925, s.198(1).
[46] Ibid. s.199.
[47] [1981] A.C. 513.
[48] For the effect of registration with title absolute see *post*, p. 326.
[49] See *post*, p. 35 and Land Charges Act 1972, s.14.
[50] See *post*, p. 328.

  (b) a register of pending actions;
  (c) a register of writs and orders affecting land;
  (d) a register of deeds of arrangement affecting land;
  (e) a register of annuities.

The Registrar is also required to keep an index of all the entries made in the registers. Entries in all five registers are made against the names of estate owners and grouped according to the county in which the land affected by the entry lies.[51] The land charges register is perhaps the most important of the registers to everyday conveyancing, hence the use of the term "a land charges search." In fact the same search covers all five registers, so that only one application for a search need be made.

THE REGISTER OF LAND CHARGES

Section 2 of the 1972 Act provides that certain classes of charges or obligations may be registered in the register of land charges. It should be noted that the charge or obligation must relate to land.[52] In *Georgiades* v. *Edward Wolfe & Co. Ltd.*[53] it was held that a charge on the proceeds of sale of land for payment of an estate agent's commission was not a charge on land capable of registration, nor in *Thomas* v. *Rose*[54] was an agreement for the division of the proceeds of sale. The different classes of land charges are as follows:

    Class A. Comprises charges on land imposed by statute, but which only come into existence on the application of someone. For example, where a landlord who is not entitled to the land for his own benefit has to pay compensation to an agricultural tenant, the landlord may apply to the Minister of Agriculture, Fisheries and Food for a charge on the land for the amount of the compensation.[55] Class A charges are registrable whenever created.

    Class B. Comprises land charges similar to those in Class A, except that they do not arise only on the application of someone, they are imposed automatically by statute. Few charges are registered in this class as most are charges in favour of public authorities and registered as local land charges. One example of a Class B charge is a charge in favour of the Law Society to secure unpaid contributions of a legally-aided litigant to the legal aid fund.[56] A Class B charge created before January 1, 1926 can only be registered if acquired by the person seeking registration, under a conveyance made on or after that date.[57]

    Class C. There are four categories:

C(i) *A puisne mortgage.* This is a legal mortgage which is *not* protected by deposit of the title deeds with the mortgagee. It is included as a

---

[51] For the precise contents of each register see the Land Charges Rules 1974, Sched. 1.
[52] Defined in Land Charges Act 1972, s.17(1).
[53] [1965] Ch. 487.
[54] [1968] 1 W.L.R. 1797.
[55] Agricultural Holdings Act 1948, s.82.
[56] Legal Aid Act 1974, s.9(6).
[57] Land Charges Act 1972, s.2(8).

registrable land charge, even though it is legal, to ensure that a purchaser can discover its existence; normal lack of title deeds providing no evidence.

C(ii) *A limited owner's charge.* This is an equitable charge acquired by a tenant for life of settled land or other limited owner, when he personally pays capital transfer tax or other liabilities in respect of settled land. The charge, if registered, secures the right of the limited owner to reimbursement out of the land of the money paid by him to the Inland Revenue, in the same way as if he had lent money to the estate on mortgage.

C(iii) *A general equitable charge.* This is a residuary class and covers the many odd non-legal charges which people create unwittingly. It is defined by exclusion, that is, a charge which is *not* protected by title deeds, *not* arising under a trust or settlement[58] and *not* included in any other class of land charge. Most important of the charges it includes are equitable mortgages of a legal estate if not protected by title deeds, for example a charge securing a bank overdraft. An unpaid vendor's lien is another example. It does not include a charge on the proceeds of sale of land.[59-60]

C(iv) *An estate contract.* This is defined as, "a contract by an estate owner or by a person entitled at the date of the contract to have a legal estate conveyed to him, to convey or create a legal estate including . . . [the grant of] a valid option to purchase, a right of pre-emption or any other like right."
Provided that the estate owner has some sort of legal estate in the land, it seems to be irrelevant that it is not the same as the estate he has agreed to create or convey. Thus in *Sharp* v. *Coates*[61] a yearly tenant agreed that if he acquired the reversion he would grant his sub-tenant a 10-year lease. This was registrable as an estate contract. The definition of estate contract includes ordinary contracts of sale and purchase, sub-sale, lease and mortgage, a contract to make a settlement of land entered into by an estate owner and in certain cases by persons who are not yet estate owners,[62] and options to purchase, to take a lease and to renew a lease.[63] In *Greene* v. *Church Commissioners for England*,[64] a clause in a lease requiring the tenant to first offer surrender of his lease to the landlord before applying for consent to assign was registrable as an estate contract, as being "any other like right." And in the recent case of *Haselmere Estates Ltd.* v. *Baker*[65] Sir Robert Megarry V.-C. stated that he was of the view "that a conditional contract relating to land is registrable as an

---

[58] Such an interest is overreachable, *i.e.* attaches to the purchase moneys on sale.
[59-60] *Georgiades* v. *Edward Wolfe & Co. Ltd.* [1965] Ch. 487.
[61] [1949] 1 K.B. 285.
[62] Settled Land Act 1925, s.11(1).
[63] *Taylor Fashions Ltd.* v. *Liverpool Victoria Trustees Co.* [1981] 2 W.L.R. 576.
[64] [1974] 3 W.L.R. 349.
[65] [1982] 1 W.L.R. 1109.

estate contract if the condition is one that is to be satisfied not by the parties but by some extraneous person or event."

There has long been a doubt whether a right of pre-emption (sometimes called a right of first refusal) is an interest in land at all[66] capable of protection as an estate contract, although the legislation clearly proceeds on the basis that it is.[67] There is a case law authority for the proposition that it is a purely contractual right creating no interest in land at all,[68] unless for example it is a statutory right which is clearly intended by the statute to bind successors in title to the land to which it relates.[69] In the most recent decision on this point, the majority of the Court of Appeal were of the opinion that a right of pre-emption may have the status of an interest in land but only when the right becomes exerciseable[70] (usually when the grantor decides to sell). This view can operate unfairly to the owner of the right of pre-emption where for example the grantor then grants an option to purchase to someone else and it is registered before he decides to sell, so before the right becomes exerciseable. When the grantor does sell, the option can be exercised free from the right of pre-emption as it has priority.[71]

To qualify for registration all Class C land charges must have been created on or after January 1, 1926 or must have been acquired by the person seeking registration under a conveyance made on or after that date.[72]

The Law Commission, in their recent report "Transfer of Land – The Law of Positive and Restrictive Covenants"[72a] recommend the creation of a new interest in land, the "Land Obligation."[72b] They propose that such an obligation (positive or negative) should, like an easement, run with the benefited and burdened land so as to be directly enforceable by and against the *current* owners of each. Whether legal (if equivalent to an estate in fee simple or a term of years absolute and created by deed) or equitable (if created in writing), a land obligation affecting unregistered land should be registrable as a Class C (v) land charge.

Class D. These consist of three categories:

D(i) *Death duties*. A charge acquired by the Inland Revenue under any enactment for death duties arising on a death after 1925. For deaths

---

[66] See, for example, Megarry and Wade, *Law of Real Property* (4th ed.), p. 578; Gibson's *Conveyancing* (21st ed.), p. 258.
[67] Land Charges Act 1972, s.2(4)(iv).
[68] *Manchester Ship Canal Co.* v. *Manchester Racecourse Co.* [1901] 2 Ch. 37 followed in *Murray* v. *Two Strokes Ltd.* [1973] 1 W.L.R. 823 and see (1974) 38 Conv. 8.
[69] *First National Securities Ltd.* v. *Chiltern District Council* [1975] 1 W.L.R. 1075.
[70] *Pritchard* v. *Briggs* [1980] Ch. 338.
[71] This actually happened in *Pritchard* v. *Briggs*. See [1980] 44 Conv. 433 and (1980) 130 New L.J. 795.
[72] Land Charges Act 1972, s.2(8).
[72a] 1984, Law Com. No.127.
[72b] This will be of two types; neighbour obligations and development obligations.

after March 12, 1975 only a charge to capital transfer tax in respect
of a transfer on death can give rise to the charge.[73] In practice the
sanctions available to the Inland Revenue Commissioners for
enforcing death duties are so powerful that they rarely, if ever,
register such a charge.

D(ii) *A restrictive covenant.* This is a covenant or agreement restricting the
uses to which land may be put. Only those restrictive covenants not
in leases[73a] are registrable. If the Law Commission's proposals for the
creation of "land obligations" (mentioned above) are enacted, only
those restrictive covenants not in leases, and created before the new
Act, will be registrable under this head.

D(iii) *An equitable easement.* This is defined as "an easement, right or
privilege over or affecting land . . .being merely an equitable
interest." Examples of interests registrable as equitable easements
are a mere agreement for an easement[74] or an easement for life.[75]
It was held in *Lewisham Borough Council* v. *Maloney*[76] that
the words "right or privilege" must be construed *euisdem generis*
with the term "easement". It is thought that the following are
therefore not registrable as equitable easements; an equitable right
to re-enter land,[77] interests protected by proprietary estoppel,[78] a
right to remove fixtures[79] and a licence to occupy land.[80] Unfortunately for the purchaser this means that whether or not he buys land
subject to certain informal arrangements may depend on whether or
not he has notice.[81] Class D charges to be registrable must have been
created after 1925.[82]

Class E. Comprises annuities (defined by section 17 of the 1972 Act)
created before 1926 and not registered before 1926 in the register of
annuities.[83] This class is small and dying out.

Class F. Section 1(1) of the Matrimonial Homes Act 1983[84] gives a
spouse with no interest in the matrimonial home certain rights of
occupation, where the legal estate is vested in the other spouse or held by
trustees for that other spouse, under trusts where no-one but the spouses

---

[73] Finance Act 1975, s.22, Sched. 4, paras. 20 and 21; Sched. 12, para. 1.
[73a] Covenants in leases are unaffected by the Law Commissions proposals on the law of
positive and restrictive covenants (Law Com. No. 127).
[74] Lacks formality, Law of Property Act 1925, s.52(1).
[75] Falls outside, Law of Property Act 1925, s.1.
[76] [1948] 1 K.B. 50.
[77] *Shiloh Spinners Ltd.* v. *Harding* [1973] A.C. 691.
[78] *E.R. Ives Investment Ltd.* v. *High* [1967] 2 Q.B. 379; see [1981] Conv. 347.
[79] *Poster* v. *Slough Estates Ltd.* [1969] Ch. 495 and see (1963) 27 Conv. 30.
[80] (1953) 17 Conv. 464, [1983] Conv. 50.
[81] See *post*, p. 28.
[82] Land Charges Act 1972, s.2(5).
[83] Ibid. s.2(6).
[84] This Act replaces the Matrimonial Homes Act 1967 (as amended). The Matrimonial
Homes Act 1983 consolidates the various statutory provisions relating to a spouse's right to
occupy the matrimonial home. It came into force on August 9, 1983.

are possible beneficiaries.[85] The rights are not to be evicted or excluded from occupation and if not in occupation, to enter and occupy the home with the leave of the court.[86]

Initially the rights are rights *in personam* against the spouse owner (or trustee) but when accompanied by registration as a Class F land charge bind third parties who acquire the land thereafter.[87] Section 1(11) of the 1983 Act extends these registrable rights to a spouse who has an equitable interest in the home but who is not the legal owner.[88] Basically the effect of registering the charge is that the spouse cannot be evicted without an order of the court. Therefore, the spouse-owner cannot give vacant possession to a purchaser unless the non-owner spouse voluntarily removes the charge or the court orders its removal.[89]

The problem with the Class F charge is that the Land Charges Department is under no duty to inform the owner-spouse of the registration and does not do so. A vendor can therefore contract to sell with vacant possession in complete ignorance of the charge. Furthermore a Class F charge can be registered for the first time after contract,[90] the registration conferring retrospective priority[91] over the purchaser's equitable interest under the contract (so that registration of an estate contract is useless). The practical solution to this is for a purchaser's solicitor to make a land charges search before contract and if no charge has been registered by then,[92] require the vendor's spouse to release her rights of occupation so that no charge can be registered thereafter.

A Class F charge cannot be registered by a spouse to freeze proceeds of sale of the home in the hands of the owner spouse; the reason for the registration has to be to protect the spouse's rights of occupation.[93-94]

Companies. Section 95 of the Companies Act 1948 requires most charges on land created by a company for securing money to be registered at the Companies Register within 21 days of their creation. In the case of floating charges and land charges created before January 1, 1970 registration of the Companies Registry is sufficient.[95] After that date charges must be registered in both registers.[96]

---

[85] Matrimonial Homes Act 1983, ss.1(8) and 2(3).

[86] Ibid. s.1(1), replacing s.1(1) of the Matrimonial Homes Act 1967. See *Watts* v. *Waller* [1973] Q.B. 153, the right is registrable before the leave of the court has been obtained.

[87] Matrimonial Homes Act 1983, s.2, replacing s.2 of the Matrimonial Homes Act 1967.

[88] Replaces s.38 of the Matrimonial Proceedings and Property Act 1970 passed as a result of the decision in *Caunce* v. *Caunce* [1969] 1 W.L.R. 286.

[89] Matrimonial Homes Act 1983, s.2(4), replacing s.2(2) of the Matrimonial Homes Act 1967.

[90] *Wroth* v. *Tyler* [1974] Ch. 30 discussed at (1973) 123 New L.J. 123.

[91] To January 1, 1968 or date of marriage or the date of the house purchase, whichever is the later. Matrimonial Homes Act 1983, s.2(1), replacing Matrimonial Homes Act 1967, s.2(1).

[92] The priority period conferred by the official search certificate will ensure no charge is registered before exchange of contracts. See *post,* p. 35.

[93-94] *Barnett* v. *Hassett* [1981] 1 W.L.R. 1385.

[95] *Property Discount Corpn. Ltd.* v. *Lyon Group Ltd.* [1981] 1 W.L.R. 300.

[96] Land Charges Act 1972, s.3(7).

THE REGISTER OF PENDING ACTIONS

Two types of matter are covered by this register, pending land actions and petitions in bankruptcy.[97]

A pending land action means "any action or proceeding pending in court relating to land or any interest in or charge on land."[98] In *Calgary & Edmonton Land Co Ltd.* v. *Dobinson*[99] a shareholder in a company registered a pending land action prior to the determination of an action in the Companies Court for an order restraining the company from disposing of its land. This was an improper registration, since, although the action was to impede a sale, the shareholder had no interest in the land capable of protection by the registration. Again in *Taylor* v. *Taylor*[1] a wife's application under section 17 of the Married Women's Property Act 1882 for a declaration of her share in the matrimonial home and for an order of sale was not capable of registration as a pending land action because it represented a claim to a share of the proceeds of sale, not the land. However, a claim for the transfer of land under section 24 of the Matrimonial Causes Act 1973 is a *lis pendens*,[2] as is a landlord's application under the Leasehold Property (Repairs) Act 1938 for leave to commence an action intended to lead to forfeiture of the lease.[3] Registration of the action ensures that a purchaser will be bound by the claim. A purchaser may proceed with his purchase if he wishes, but would only be wise to do so if satisfied that the opponent's claim has no substance or possibly if the vendor gives an indemnity.

Bankruptcy petitions are automatically registered whether or not the debtor is known to own any land. Where a bankruptcy petition is registered, the legal estate remains in the debtor but a purchaser would be extremely unwise to take a conveyance from such a person since if an adjudication order is made against him, the title of the bankrupt's trustee in bankruptcy relates back to the date of the act of bankruptcy on which the petition was based[4] and the purchaser's title can be upset.

A registration in this register lasts for five years only.[5] If the case continues it can be re-registered for another five years.

THE REGISTER OF WRITS AND ORDERS AFFECTING LAND

In this register may be registered[6]:

   (i) any writ or order affecting land or made by any court for the purpose of enforcing a judgment or recognisance; this includes a court order charging a judgment debtor's land with payment of the money due;
   (ii) any order appointing a receiver or sequestor of land;

---

[97] Ibid. s.5(1).
[98] Ibid. s.17(1).
[99] [1974] Ch. 102.
[1] [1968] 1 W.L.R. 378.
[2] *Whittingham* v. *Whittingham* [1978] Fam. 9.
[3] *Selim Ltd.* v. *Bickenhall Engineering Ltd.* [1981] 3 W.L.R. 1318.
[4] Bankruptcy Act 1914, s.37.
[5] Land Charges Act 1972, s.8.
[6] Ibid. s.6(1).

(iii) any receiving order in bankruptcy made after 1925 whether or not it affects land.

As opposed to the last mentioned register, this is a register of orders *enforcing* judgments and orders of the court.

Where a writ or order other than a receiving order is registered a purchaser can acquire good title to the land subject to the provisions of the judgment on which the writ or order is based, but in practice this will rarely occur. Where a receiving order in bankruptcy is registered, the legal title remains in the bankrupt but he cannot dispose of the land (his assets are "frozen"). A purchaser must not proceed with the purchase in this case because when the adjudication order is finally made, his title can be upset by the bankrupt's trustee.

Section 2 of the Charging Orders Act 1979 now enables the court to make a charging order against the interest of someone who is concurrently entitled to land as a joint tenant or tenant in common[7] (for example a husband or wife). Section 3 of that Act provides that these orders are registrable under the Land Charges Act 1972 in the same way as other orders or writs issued or made for the purpose of enforcing judgments.

Registration in this register must be renewed every five years.[8]

THE REGISTER OF DEEDS OF ARRANGEMENT

Basically a deed of arrangement[9] is any document whereby control over a debtor's property is given for the benefit of his creditors. If the deed conveys an interest in land, it may be registered in this register.[10] Where a deed of arrangement is registered the debtor will not be able to convey the legal estate; the power to do this will be vested in the person who took the legal estate under the deed. Registration must be renewed every five years.[11]

THE REGISTER OF ANNUITIES

This register was opened in 1855 and closed in 1925. Few registered annuities remain.

Against Whom is Registration Made?

LAND CHARGES

A land charge must be registered against the name of the estate owner whose estate is to be affected.[12] Care must therefore be taken when acting for a sub-purchaser. Where A contracts to sell his legal estate to B who then contracts to sell it to C, it is against A that C must register his estate contract. Registration against B is ineffective even though he later acquires the legal estate.[13] Since a sub-purchaser may often not know of

---

[7] *National Westminster Bank Limited* v. *Stockman* [1981] 1 W.L.R. 67.
[8] Land Charges Act 1972, s.8.
[9] Deeds of Arrangement Act 1914, s.1.
[10] Land Charges Act 1972, s.7(1).
[11] Ibid. s.8.
[12] Ibid. s.3(1).
[13] *Barrett* v. *Hilton Developments Ltd.* [1975] Ch. 237.

the identity or existence of the vendor a special condition should be inserted in the contract requiring the name of the estate owner to be made known immediately contracts are exchanged.

As will be seen later, care should also be taken to register the charge in the correct name of the estate owner.[14] The name appearing on the title deeds can be taken to be the correct version.[15] One question asked[16] which has never arisen in practice is: can a land charge effectively be registered against the name of a deceased person? The books on the subject give a negative answer. Wolstenholme and Cherry state[17]: "Registration against a deceased person is not authorised; he is no longer an estate owner." However it has been pointed out[18] that the Land Charges Department might think otherwise where for example an estate owner dies suddenly in between creating the charge and its registration.[19] It is recommended that the chargee re-register his charge against the name of the new estate owner as soon as he discovers the death.

Registration of a land charge against oneself may be necessary in the following situation. Suppose A contracts to sell his legal estate to B who agrees to lease the property back to A on completion. If B is completing his purchase with the aid of a mortgage A must register his lease-back agreement as an estate contract against himself (the estate owner) to ensure priority over the mortgagee.[20]

REGISTRATION IN THE OTHER REGISTERS

Pending actions and writs and orders affecting land are registrable in the name of the estate owner or other person whose estate or interest is intended to be affected.[21] Deeds of arrangement are registered in the name of the debtor.[22] Again registration should be made in the correct name.

When is a Purchaser Bound by a Registrable Interest?

WHERE THE INTEREST IS REGISTERED

Section 198(1) of the Law of Property Act 1925 provides that registration under the Land Charges Act "shall be deemed to constitute actual notice of such instrument or matter, and of the fact of such registration, to all persons and for all purposes connected with the land affected. . . . "If the interest is registered the purchaser will be bound by it and section 198 stops him from claiming to be a purchaser without actual knowledge of the registered interest. However in circumstances outlined later[23] he may

---

[14] See *post*, p. 31.
[15] *Oak Co-operative Building Society* v. *Blackburn* [1968] Ch. 730.
[16] [1979] Conv. 249.
[17] *Conveyancing Statutes* (13th ed.), Vol. 2, p. 22.
[18] (1971) 35 Conv. 155.
[19] This affects the recommended search period, see *post*, p. 30.
[20] Pointed out in Precedent Editor's Notes [1980] Conv. 170.
[21] Land Charges Act 1972, ss.5(4) and 6(2).
[22] Ibid. s.7(1).
[23] *Post*, p. 30.

be able to claim statutory compensation[24] or rescind[25] the contract of sale if he discovers a charge not known at the date of the contract.

WHERE THE INTEREST IS NOT REGISTERED

It was said in the introduction to this section that in general the effect of non-registration is to make the registrable interest void against the purchaser. Unfortunately the position is not quite as simple as this. A chart followed by some explanatory notes will show precisely what happens.

REGISTER	CLASS		INTEREST	IF NOT REGISTERED BEFORE COMPLETION OF THE PURCHASE WILL NOT BIND
LAND CHARGES	A		Charge imposed by statute on application of someone	A purchaser for value of the land or any interest therein. If created before 1889 void if not registered within one year from the first conveyance of it after 1888.
	B		Charge imposed by statute auto-matically	A purchaser for value of the land or any interest therein. If created before January 1, 1926 will be void unless registered within one year of the first conveyance of it after that date.
	C	(i)	Puisne Mortgage	A purchaser for value of the land or any interest therein.
		(ii)	Limited Owners Charge	A purchaser for value of the land or any interest therein.
		(iii)	General Equit-able Charge	A purchaser for value of the land or any interest therein.
		(iv)	Estate Contract	A purchaser of the legal estate for money or money's worth. Any class C charge created before January 1, 1926 void unless registered within on year of the first conveyance of it after that date.
	D	(i)	Inland Revenue Charge	A purchaser of the legal estate for money or money's worth.
		(ii)	post 1925 Restric-tive Covenant	A purchaser of the legal estate for money or money's worth.
		(iii)	post 1925 Equit-able Easement	A purchaser of the legal estate for money or money's worth.
	E		Pre 1926 Annuity	A purchaser for value of the land or any interest therein.
	F		Spouse's rights of occupation	A purchaser for value of the land or any interest therein.
PENDING ACTIONS			Pending land action	A purchaser for value of the land or any interest therein, provided he has no express notice of it.
			Bankruptcy petition	A bona fide purchaser of the legal estate for money or money's worth without notice of an available act of bankruptcy, i.e. one not more than three months old.

[24] Law of Property Act 1969, s.25.
[25] Ibid. s.24.

WRITS AND ORDERS AFFECTING LAND	Those other than receiving orders	A purchaser for value of the land or any interest therein.
	Receiving orders	A bona fide purchaser of the legal estate for money or money's worth without notice of an available act of bankruptcy, *i.e.* one not more than three months old.
DEEDS OF ARRANGEMENT		A purchaser for value of the land or any interest therein.
ANNUITIES	Those created before and registered before 1926.	A purchaser for value of the land or any interest therein.

Some Explanatory Notes

(1) The effect of failing to register a registrable interest is contained in sections 4, 5, 6 and 7 of the Land Charges Act 1972.

(2) The word "purchaser" includes a mortgagee or lessee.[26]

(3) With the limited exceptions of pending land actions, bankruptcy petitions and receiving orders it is irrelevant that the purchaser buys with actual knowledge of the unregistered interest.[27] "Bona fides" is also irrelevant[28] with the exception of bankruptcy petitions and receiving orders.

(4) It is important to note that the crucial time for determining whether or not a purchaser is bound by the registrable interest is completion of the purchase.[29] An interest that is void for non-registration at the time of purchase cannot be revived by a subsequent registration.[30]

(5) Most of the interests are void for non-registration against a purchaser for value of any interest in the land. "Value" includes marriage consideration[31] but excludes nominal consideration and the purchaser can take either a legal or equitable interest in the land, and still be protected.

(6) However a land charge within Class C(iv) (estate contract) or Class D created after 1925, bankruptcy petitions and receiving orders are only void for non-registration if the purchaser buys a legal estate and gives money or money's worth. On this latter requirement the House of Lords has held that it will not enquire into the adequacy of the consideration.[32]

(7) No provision appears to have been made governing the validity of the following interests vis à vis a purchaser:

(i) interests created before 1926, for which no provision for registration has been made, for example restrictive covenants;

(ii) registrable interests which are not necessarily void against that *particular* purchaser for non-registration either because (a) for the

---

[26] Land Charges Act 1972, s.17(1).

[27] Law of Property Act 1925, s.199(i); *Hollington Bros. Ltd.* v. *Rhodes* [1951] Ch. 578.

[28] *Midland Bank Trust Co.* v. *Green* [1981] A.C. 513.

[29] Land Charges Act 1972, ss.4, 5, 6 and 7.

[30] *Kitney* v. *M.E.P.C. Ltd.* [1977] 1 W.L.R. 981 discussed at (1978) 128 New L.J. 5. The result of this is that prior official search certificates can be relied on.

[31] Law of Property Act 1925, s.205(1)(xxi).

[32] It may be nominal, *Midland Bank Trust Co.* v. *Green* [1981] A.C. 513.

purposes of note (5) he is a donee of the legal or equitable interest or (b) for the purposes of note (6) he is a purchaser of the legal estate for marriage consideration, or he is a purchaser of an equitable interest for money or money's worth (nominal or otherwise).

In these situations the purchaser must rely on the old law. If he is a bona fide purchaser of the legal estate for value (including marriage consideration) then he will be bound by the interest if he has actual, constructive or implied notice[33] of it, but not otherwise. In all other cases the rule is that where the equities are equal (that is in the absence of fraud or negligence) the first in time prevails.[34]

The Priority Notice

A search may show the registration of a priority notice. The priority notice was introduced to cope with a rapid series of transactions, for example the creation of a restrictive covenant followed by the creation of a mortgage in the same purchase. Section 11(1) of the Land Charges Act 1972 provides that a person intending to apply for the registration of a contemplated charge, instrument or other matter may give a priority notice, in Form K6[35] at least 15 days before the substantive registration is to take effect. The notice is entered in the register to which the intended application relates. If the application for substantive registration is made within 30 working days after the date of registration of the notice, the registration of the charge or matter takes effect as if it had been made at the time when the charge instrument or matter was created, entered into, or arose[36]; so in our example giving the restrictive covenant priority over the mortgage. The fee for entering a priority notice is 50p per name.[37]

If the search certificate discloses a priority notice which is less than 30 working days old the purchaser should be warned that if he completes he runs the risk that a substantive registration may be made with priority over him.

The Search of the Registers

WHEN TO SEARCH

At one time it was thought prudent practice for a purchaser's solicitor to make a search of the registers before contracts were exchanged. This practice stemmed from a decision of Eve J. in *Re Forsey and Hollebone's Contract*[38] and the rule that a purchaser who discovers a latent defect in his vendor's title after contract may rescind the contract or claim damages,

---

[33] Law of Property Act 1925, s.199(1)(ii).
[34] *McCarthy & Stone Ltd.* v. *Hodge* [1971] 1 W.L.R. 1547 discussed at (1974) 124 New L.J. 286.
[35] Land Charges Rules 1974, r.4.
[36] Land Charges Act 1972, s.11(3).
[37] Land Charges Fees Order 1975, Sched. 1.
[38] [1927] 2 Ch. 379.

but if he knows of the defect before he enters the contract then he waives his right to object and must take subject to it.[39]

Eve J. was of the view that since section 198(1) of the Law of Property Act 1925 says that the registration of any instrument or matter under the Land Charges Act constitutes actual notice, both parties must be deemed to have entered the contract with actual notice and therefore the existence of a registered matter would not entitle the purchaser to rescind. However, the practice of making pre-contract searches often presented difficulties. To make a search the purchaser has to know the names of prior estate owners and in unregistered conveyancing this information is given after exchange of contracts, when the abstract of title is handed over.

Section 24 of the Law of Property Act 1969 was introduced to remedy this situation. It preserves the purchaser's right to rescission or damages in this situation, unless he has actual or imputed[40] knowledge (not s.198 "deemed" knowledge) of the registered charge before entering the contract. Therefore pre-contract searches are now theoretically unnecessary. Most purchaser's solicitors make their land charges search just before completion. The object of this is to take advantage of the priority which an official search gives. Where a purchaser obtains an official certificate of search he will take free of any interest registered against the vendor after the date of the certificate provided that he completes his purchase before the end of the fifteenth working day after the date of the certificate (unless there is a registration made pursuant to an effective priority notice).[41]

Despite this, it is still wise to make a search before contract whenever possible. It avoids possible disappointment and delay if a purchaser is informed of any incumbrance on the property he is purchasing before contracts are exchanged. Where a purchaser is selling as well as buying he may be forced to proceed with the purchase even if the incumbrance is unacceptable to him, because although he can rescind his purchase contract he has no corresponding right to rescind his contract of sale. Finally it can avoid the problems created by Class F land charges, outlined earlier.[42]

HOW FAR BACK SHOULD YOU SEARCH?

One of the problems with the land charges system is that of "names behind the root of title." The statutory period of title a vendor must prove is 15 years and back beyond that to a good root.[43] Yet interests may have been registered against estate owners of the land right back to January 1, 1926. The purchaser will be bound by such interests even though he is not entitled to demand the information[44] necessary to enable him to discover them. Section 25 of the Law of Property Act 1969 provides rather an unsatisfactory solution to this problem. Basically this states that where a

---

[39] *Per* Jenkins L.J. in *Timmins* v. *Moreland Street Property Co. Ltd.* [1958] Ch. 110.
[40] *i.e.* knowledge acquired in the course of the transaction by his solicitor counsel or agent.
[41] Land Charges Act 1972, s.11(5).
[42] See *ante*, p. 23.
[43] Law of Property Act 1969, s.23.
[44] *i.e.* the names of the estate owners.

purchaser searches for the statutory period and then completes his purchase, if after completion he learns for the first time of the existence of an incumbrance which was registered outside the statutory period, then he has a right to compensation. The compensation is payable by the Chief Land Registrar out of public funds. The solution is unsatisfactory because the purchaser might not want compensation; he might never have bought the property in the first place had he known of the interest or incumbrance. Therefore it is advisable (although rarely done in practice) to search back as far as possible.

For reasons outlined earlier[45] it is safe to rely on old certificates of search, although for this purpose it should be remembered that the period of protection afforded by official certificates of search has been altered several times since 1925. Up until November 25, 1940 the search certificate gave two days protection, up until March 1, 1972 14 days protection and after February 29, 1972 15 days protection.

It is important to ensure that the correct particulars were entered on the application for search.

As an added precaution the purchaser's solicitor could ask for a list of the full names of all estate owners of the property since 1925 other than those for whom clear search certificates were obtained within the relevant periods, in his enquiries before contract. However, quite often the vendor's solicitor will not have this information either.

WHO TO SEARCH AGAINST?

It has already been seen that one application for search covers all five registers and that an index of the names of all persons against whom any charge or other matter is registered is kept in the Land Charges Department. The purchaser should always make a search against his vendor. In addition he should search against all former estate owners during the period of title under investigation except those for whom an official certificate of search was obtained and is produced.

It is essential that the application for an official search is (or was when relying on a prior certificate) made in the correct name of the estate owner or other person. Two cases illustrate this. In *Oak Co-operative Building Society* v. *Blackburn*[46] the vendor, whose correct name was Francis David Blackburn but who was commonly known as "Frank," contracted to sell his house and an estate contract was registered against the name of "Frank David Blackburn." Before completion of the sale he granted a legal mortgage over the property to the Society. The Society applied for and obtained a clear certificate of search in the name of "Francis Davis Blackburn." Was the Society bound by the estate contract? The Court of Appeal held that the certificate of search was a nullity and gave the Society no protection. Two guidelines emerge from the case. First (*per* Russell L.J.) a registration in one version of the correct full names (here Frank as opposed to Francis) will be valid against a purchaser who does not search at all or who (as here) searches in the wrong name. Secondly (*per curiam*) if a search is requested in the correct full names and the purchaser obtains

[45] *Ante*, p. 26.
[46] [1968] Ch. 730.

a clear certificate of search he is not bound by the registration; in this case it is the chargee who runs the risk if he does not register his charge in the correct full names.Thus in *Diligent Finance Co. Ltd.* v. *Alleyne*,[47] a husband was known to his wife as "Erskine Alleyne" but the title deeds bore the name "Erskine Owen Alleyne." The wife registered a Class F land charge against "Erskine Alleyne." Before taking a legal charge on the property the finance company obtained a clear certificate of search in the name of "Erskine Owen Alleyne." They were not bound by the wife's Class F charge.

When acting for a sub-purchaser it is important to remember to search against both the original and immediate vendor.[48]

It is equally important to describe the land correctly, although as will be seen it is not now essential to include a description of the land in the application form. In *Du Sautoy* v. *Symes*[49] an application for search was made in the correct name of the estate owner but the land was incorrectly described. A clear search certificate did not protect the purchaser against correctly registered prior estate contract.

SEARCHES BY A LESSEE

A special problem presents itself to a solicitor acting for an intending lessee.

Section 44(2) of the Law of Property Act 1925 provides that under an open contract to grant a lease, the lessee is not entitled to investigate the freehold title. Where a lease is granted in consideration of a lump sum payment, the lessee will usually insist on a term being included in the contract, entitling him to investigate the lessor's title, but where a lease is granted at a rack rent such a term is rarely included. However, there may well be matters registered against the freehold, for example post 1925 restrictive covenants, which are not disclosed in the lease. An intending lessee can search against the name of the lessor but if he has not contracted for investigation of the lessor's title, he will not be able to find out or search against the names of prior estate owners. Yet he will be deemed to have notice of any registered interest[50] and must take subject to it.[51] Furthermore he will not be entitled to compensation under the statutory scheme.[52]

When acting for a lessee, the right to investigate the lessor's title should be stipulated for and the necessary searches made.

SEARCHES BY A MORTGAGEE

Under section 8(3) of the Matrimonial Homes Act 1983,[53] a mortgagee of a dwelling-house who brings an action for enforcement of his security must serve notice of the action on a spouse whose rights of occupation are

---

[47] (1972) 23 P. & C.R. 346.

[48] *Barrett* v. *Hilton Developments Ltd.* [1975] Ch. 237.

[49] [1967] 1 Ch. 1146.

[50] Law of Property Act 1925, s.198(1). This prevails over Law of Property Act 1925, s.44(5).

[51] *White* v. *Bijou Mansions Ltd.* [1938] Ch. 351.

[52] Land Charges Act 1972, s.16.

[53] Replacing the Matrimonial Homes Act 1967, s.7A(3) (which was inserted by s.2 of the Matrimonial Homes and Property Act 1981).

protected by the registration of a Class F land charge. Such a mortgagee may apply for an official certificate of search of Form K15. The certificate of search will ensure that no Class F charge can be registered for 15 days.

WHO MAY SEARCH?

Anyone may make a search in the registers maintained by the Land Charges Department.

WHERE TO SEARCH

The Land Charges Department at Burrington Way, Plymouth PL5 3LP.[54-56]

The office provides four services:

(i) official searches based on written applications delivered by post;
(ii) official searching by telex;
(iii) official searching by telephone;
(iv) searches by applicants who personally attend the office.

In addition the office provides an excellent general information service which can be reached by telephoning Plymouth 779831.

SEARCHES BY POST

An application for an official search by post should be made on;

> Form K15 for a search in all the registers,
> Form K16 for a "bankruptcy only" search.

The official search is done by computer. It only "reads" the information it is given, therefore special care must be taken when filling in the particulars required by the form.

Each name to be searched must be entered on the form. This should be the correct full name. The computer searches all entries in the name given on the form, all initials as given and the surname alone. Thus an application for a search against the name Ruth Elaine Annand will reveal entries against Ruth Elaine Annand, R.E. Annand, and Annand. So an entry against Ruth Annand will not be revealed. If the purchaser is uncertain of the exact name of an estate owner it is best to try all possibilities, treating each as a separate name. The task of searching against a company is made easier by the acceptance of common abbreviations which make it unnecessary to specify alternative versions of a company's name. For example, for the word "Limited" the computer also searches against Ltd, Ld and the Welsh equivalents Cyfyngedig and Cyf. Further information on the variants the computer searches can be obtained from the Land Charges Department.

Although the registers are kept primarily according to the names of estate owners, entries are grouped according to the county named in the application to register. The search form therefore requires information as to the present county in which the land is situated. Where there has been a boundary or name change in the county during the period to be

---

[54-56] The Land Charges searching facilities at Croydon were discontinued as from September 1, 1980 and transferred to Plymouth.

searched, the name of any former county in which the land was situated should be stated.

The period in respect of which the search is to be made for each estate owner must be shown. The dates are given in complete calendar years. Most solicitors search for the period the estate owner owned the land. However to cover the problem of a registration against a deceased owner being valid[57] it is a good idea to add one year to each side of the period of ownership. The form also invites the applicant to give a description of the property, but it is not essential to supply this. An incorrect description could lead to the official certificate of search being a nullity,[58] so unless an accurate description can be given it is best to leave this part of the form blank.

The name and address of the applicant (or his key number), the address for despatch of the certificate and the date should be inserted in the form.

The fee payable for a written application for an official search is 50p[59] per name. This should be prepaid by means of land registry adhesive stamps. The Registrar may authorise any firm or person to open a credit account[60] at the Department, in which case the fee payable is debited to the account, which must be settled monthly.

The average processing time of a postal application is three to four days.

TELEX SEARCHES

Only applicants with credit accounts can apply for a search by telex. Teleprinters receive the application which should give the same details as a postal application. The result of the search is not telexed. The applicant receives a full printed result of the search, usually within 24 hours. The fee for a telex application is 70p[61] per name.

TELEPHONE SEARCHES

Again an application can only be made by a person who has a credit account with the Department, and it can only be made for a full search (not a "bankruptcy only" search). The service operates between the hours of 10.00 a.m. to 4.00 p.m. from Monday to Friday and the telephone number is Plymouth 701171. The operators have visual display units through which they interrogate the computer and give the result of the search over the telephone. The applicant then receives a full printed result of the search, usually within 24 hours. The fee payable for a telephone search is 80p per name.[62]

PERSONAL SEARCHES

Anyone can make a personal search on payment of the fee (80p per name)[63] in cash or by land registry stamps. The applicant fills in a Form

---

[57] See *ante*, p. 26.
[58] *Du Sautoy* v. *Symes* [1967] 1 Ch. 1146.
[59] Land Charges Fees Order 1975, Sched. 1.
[60] Ibid. Sched. 3.
[61] Ibid. Sched. 1.
[62] *Ibid.*
[63] *Ibid.*

K15 in the normal way and the result is given on a visual display unit so that he can judge it himself. A full printed result of the search is then sent to the applicant within 24 hours. A "bankruptcy only" search cannot be made personally.

Under section 10(6)(*b*) of the Land Charges Act 1972, the registry accepts no responsibility for information given otherwise than in the official certificate of search. In the case of telephone and personal searches reliance should only be placed on the full printed result of the search.

"BANKRUPTCY ONLY" SEARCHES

A "bankruptcy only" search can be applied for by any person interested in the solvency of another, whether or not that other person is an estate owner. A building society contemplating lending money to a proprietor of registered land will often make a "bankruptcy only" search against its borrower. The application must be made on Form K16[64] and cannot be done by telephone or in person. A "bankruptcy only" search reveals details of petitions in bankruptcy, receiving orders in bankruptcy and deeds of arrangement.

The fees are the same as for a full search.

The Value of an Official Certificate of Search

By virtue of section 10(4) of the Land Charges Act 1972 an official certificate of search is conclusive in favour of a purchaser or an intending purchaser whose application for search was made correctly. If therefore an entry is properly registered against an estate owner but is not disclosed on the official certificate of search then the purchaser takes free from it. It is thought that damages for negligence can be obtained by the chargee against a negligent registry employee and the Crown may be vicariously liable[65] except where the loss arises from a discrepancy between the particulars in the search application and the particulars shown in the official search certificate as being the particulars in respect of which the search was made.[66]

The result of giving an incorrect name or description of the land on the application for search has already been discussed.[67]

The official search certificate also gives the purchaser the protection of a "priority period."[68] If he completes his purchase before the expiration of the fifteenth working day after the date of the certificate he is not bound by any entry in the registers made after the date of the certificate and before completion, unless the entry is made pursuant to a priority notice[69] entered on the register before the certificate was issued. The date on which the priority period expires is shown in the box on the top right hand side of the official certificate of search.

---

[64] Land Charges Rules 1974, r. 16(1).
[65] *Ministry of Housing and Local Government* v. *Sharp* [1970] 2 Q.B. 223.
[66] Land Charges Act 1972, s.10(6)(*a*).
[67] See *ante*, p. 31.
[68] Land Charges Act 1972, ss.11(5) and 11(6).
[69] See *ante*, p. 29.

Finally section 12 of the 1972 Act provides that a solicitor or a person in a fiduciary position (for example a trustee or personal representative) is not answerable for any loss that may arise from an error in an official certificate of search.

"Subsisting Entries"

If the official search certificate reveals an entry which might affect the property then it is wise to obtain an office copy of the instrument of registration. Office copies can be obtained from the Department by postal application (Form K.19),[70] or requested by telex or over the telephone. The fee payable in all cases is 50p per copy.[71] If the entry does relate to the land in question the purchaser's course of action will obviously depend on the nature of the entry.

How to Cancel an Entry

An application to cancel an entry on the register is made on Form K11 (except for Class F charges). It must be accompanied by "sufficient evidence of the applicant's title to apply for cancellation" unless it is made by the owner of the benefit of the entry, or such office copies of orders of the court or the Lands Tribunal as would justify cancellation. The Registrar may then cancel the entry in whole or in part if he is satisfied that the application was properly made.[72] An entry may also be removed by court order.[73]

An application to cancel a Class F land charge must be made on Form K13 and unless it is signed by the person who made the application for registration, must be accompanied by a written release of the spouse's rights of occupation, or a certificate that either spouse is dead, or an official copy of a court decree terminating the marriage or an official copy of a court order terminating the spouse's rights of occupation.[74] In the case of a spouse's death or a decree terminating the marriage the Registrar will not cancel the entry if the court has made an order directing that the charge shall not come to an end on the termination of the marriage and the registration was renewed thereafter.

The fee payable for cancellation is 50p.[75]

Is the System "Watertight"?

We have seen that if an interest is registrable under the Land Charges Act then in general it is void against a purchaser who completes his transaction before that interest is registered; notice and good faith are irrelevant.

---

[70] Land Charges Rules 1974, r. 19(1).
[71] Land Charges Fees Order 1975, Sched. 1.
[72] Land Charges Rules 1974, rr. 9 and 10.
[73] Land Charges Act 1972, s.1(6).
[74] Land Charges Rules 1974, r. 11; Matrimonial Homes Act 1983, s.5.
[75] Land Charges Fees Order 1975, Sched. 1.

Harman J. said in *Hollington Bros. Ltd.* v. *Rhodes*,[76] "it was the policy of the framers of the legislation of 1925 to get rid of equitable interests of this kind unless registered . . . . I do not see how that which is void and which is not to prejudice the purchaser can be validated by some equitable doctrine." And in *Midland Bank Trust Co.* v. *Green*,[77] Lord Wilberforce expressed the view that it is not a fraud to rely on legal rights conferred by statute.

However "equitable doctrines" have been used in two recent first instance decisions to disturb the certainty that was hitherto thought by conveyancers to exist in this area. *Taylor Fashions Ltd.* v. *Liverpool Victoria Trustees Co.*,[78] shows that in certain circumstances a purchaser will be prevented from denying the existence of an interest (here an unregistered option to renew a lease) which is otherwise statutorily void against him for non-registration by the doctrine of proprietary estoppel. The other more startling decision of *Lyus* v. *Prowsa Developments Ltd.*[79] seems to say that such an interest may be validated by the court imposing a constructive trust on a purchaser with actual knowledge whenever it feels that not to do so would cause injustice.[80]

The exact width of these "equitable doctrines" is at present unclear. However if the courts follow this trend in the future, a purchaser who knows of an unregistered interest before he completes his transaction will be robbed of much of the protection given by the system.

OFFICIAL SEARCH OF THE REGISTER

Introduction

A vendor's only proof of title to registered land is the actual register kept[81] at H.M. Land Registry. His evidence[82] of title is the Land Certificate. This is an accurate copy of the register when last compared by the Land Registry.[83] On the registration of most dealings with the land, the certificate must be produced to the Registrar and will be updated to reflect the dealing.[84] However, certain entries may be made in the register without the certificate being produced, so rendering it an inaccurate record of the register. Cautions,[85] entries relating to the impending

---

[76] [1951] Ch. 578.

[77] [1981] A.C. 513.

[78] [1981] 2 W.L.R. 576; M. Clements (1981) 131 New L.J. 1001.

[79] [1982] 1 W.L.R. 1044. Although the case concerned registered land the principle seems equally applicable to unregistered land.

[80] For a more detailed discussion see M. Duggan (1983) 127 S.J. 166; D. Hayton (1983) 133 New L.J. 188; C.T. Emery and B. Smythe (1983) 133 New L.J. 798.

[81] Pursuant to Land Registration Act 1925, s.1.

[82] *Ibid.* s.68.

[83] *Ibid.* s.63.

[84] *Ibid.* s.64(1) and (2).

[85] Land Registration Rules 1925, r. 215.

bankruptcy of the registered proprietor, charges to capital transfer tax[86] and notices protecting a spouse's rights to occupation under the Matrimonial Homes Act 1983[87] may, *inter alia* all be registered without the production of the Land Certificate.

A vendor is required to give the purchaser a copy of any restrictions or interests affecting the property before contracts are exchanged. Since these will normally be noted on the register, and in part fulfillment of his statutory[88] duty to prove his title after contract, a vendor will often send the purchaser a complete copy of his title with the draft contract. Most vendor's solicitors following an oft repeated Council of the Law Society recommendation,[89] send an office copy of the entries on the register and the filed plan. Unlike a photocopy of the Land Certificate an office copy is warranted to be accurate at its date of issue.[90]

A fundamental principle of registered conveyancing is that a purchaser acquires the land subject to interests noted on the register and existing overriding interests, but free from all other interests whatsoever irrespective of notice, as soon as his application to be entered on the register as the new registered proprietor is received by the Land Registry, and he is so registered.[91] An official search of the register serves two vital purposes:

1. It enables the purchaser to ascertain whether or not any entries have been made in the register since the date on which the office copies supplied by the vendor were issued, or the Land Certificate last compared with the register; and

2. It ensures that the state of the register cannot change to the purchaser's disadvantage, if his transfer is presented for registration within a set time limit. Ruoff and Roper state: "It would be the height of folly for a solicitor acting for a proposing purchaser of registered property to omit to make an official search of the register. . . . "[91a]

Making the Search

WHO MAY SEARCH?

The register is secret. Subject to certain exceptions, only the registered proprietor of the land or of a charge and such persons who are authorised by the proprietor may inspect the register or any document referred to on it and kept at the Land Registry.[92] Inspections that are allowed without

---

[86] Land Registration Act 1925, s.64(1)(*c*) as amended by Finance Act 1975, Sched. 12.

[87] Replaces Matrimonial Homes act 1967 s.2(7). A spouse's right of occupation can now only be protected by a notice. The Matrimonial Homes Act 1983, s.2 states that a spouse is no longer entitled to lodge a caution under s.54 of the Land Registration Act 1925 to protect the rights of occupation.

[88] Land Registration Act 1925, s.110(1).

[89] This recommendation is endorsed by H.M. Land Registry and given recognition in the Law Society General Conditions of Sale (1984 rev.) Cond. 12(1)(*b*)(i).

[90] Land Registration Act 1925, s.113.

[91] *Ibid.* ss.20(1) and 23(1); Land Registration Rules 1925, r.83(2); Land Registration (Official Searches) Rules 1981 r. 5; see Lord Wilberforce in *Willams & Glyn's Bank Ltd.* v. *Boland* [1981] A.C. 487.

[91a] Ruoff and Roper, *Registered Conveyancing* (4th ed.), p. 329.

[92] Land Registration Act 1925, s.112.

the authority of the registered proprietor broadly speaking fall within the following categories[93]:

1. searches by Government Departments;
2. searches authorised by court order;
3. searches by the Director of Public Prosecutions or senior police officers in connection with a criminal offence;
4. searches by judgment creditors[94];
5. searches by mortgagees.[95] A mortgagee of a dwelling-house who brings an action for the enforcement of his security must serve notice of the action on a spouse whose rights of occupation are currently protected by the registration of a notice or caution. The mortgagee may apply (without the authority of the registered proprietor in the case of a charge protected by notice or caution) for an official search of the register to find out if a spouse's rights are so protected.[96] In this special case the official search certificate only confers 15 days priority.

THE AUTHORITY TO INSPECT THE REGISTER

Unless the search is made by the registered proprietor of the land or of a registered charge or in one of the exceptional circumstances outlined above, the applicant must hold an authority to inspect the register signed by the proprietor of the land or charge.[97] Under section 110(1) of the Land Registration Act 1925, a vendor is under a duty, out of which he cannot contract, to furnish the purchaser with an authority to inspect the register, as part of his duty to prove title after the contract is made. However, this duty only extends to a purchaser. If the purchaser is completing with the aid of a mortgage and the same solicitor is not acting for both the mortgagee and the purchaser (in which case one search is sufficient protection for both) the vendor should be asked to extend the authority to the mortgagee. Under an open contract for the grant of a lease out of the freehold the lessee is not entitled to see the freehold title[98] and cannot require an authority to inspect the register thereof.[99] As there may be matters registered against the freehold[1] affecting the property, the lessee should ensure that the contract provides for an authority for him to search the register.

It is clear from the wording of the statute[2] that the authority to inspect

---

[93] *Ibid.* ss.112 and 112A, as amended by Administration of Justice Act 1982, s.67.

[94] Judgment creditors can make an application for production of title, etc., to registered land by way of *ex parte* application in the proceedings in which judgment was obtained. Where the creditor wishes to enforce a High Court judgment by way of charging order in the county court, an application for inspection should be made to the county court. *Practice Direction (Land Register Inspection)* [1983] 1 W.L.R. 150.

[95] Land Registration Act 1925, s.112B, inserted by Matrimonial Homes and Property Act 1981, s.4(4).

[96] Matrimonial Homes Act 1983, s.8(3) (replacing s.7A(3) of the Matrimonial Homes Act 1967); Land Registration (Matrimonial Homes) Rules 1983, r. 6.

[97] Land Registration Rules 1925, r. 287.

[98] Law of Property Act 1925, s.44.

[99] Land Registration Rules 1925, r. 287.

[1] *White* v. *Bijou Mansions Ltd.* [1938] Ch. 351.

[2] Land Registration Rules 1925, r. 112.

can only be given by the "registered proprietor." Thus if A, the registered proprietor, contracts to sell to B who then contracts to sell to C, B cannot authorise C to inspect the register. A should be requested to authorise both B and C to make a search.

An authority to inspect the register is usually given on Form 201 but may be by way of letter addressed to the Chief Land Registrar.

WHEN TO SEARCH

An official search of the register should ideally be made four or five days before the completion to ensure that full advantage can be taken of the priority protection afforded by the official search (discussed later). This leaves ample time to stamp the transfer, before lodging it with the application for registration at the Land Registry.

WHERE TO SEARCH

There are 13 district land registries in England and Wales, apart from the central administration office of the Land Registry at Lincoln's Inn Fields, London.[3] The search should be made with the district land registry in whose area the property lies. The Land Registration (District Registries) Order 1980 created the new Peterborough registry and transferred responsibility for the registration of titles in connection with the other registries, as from April 1, 1981. It is vitally important that the search be sent to the correct office, because no priority can be obtained until this is done.[4] A map showing the areas of responsibility of the district land registries appears on the following page. Alternatively, details can be obtained from Explanatory Leaflet No. 9, available free of charge from any office of H.M. Land Registry.

At present most of the work handled by H.M. Land Registry is done manually. Extension of compulsory registration of title and registrations under the Housing Act 1980 "right to buy" provisions[5] have increased the volume of work enormously and have led the Chief Land Registrar to look towards computerisation.[6] At present this is only at an experimental stage (mainly concentrated on the Plymouth and Harrow district land registries) but it is hoped that within four to five years computers will handle all the district registries' more menial tasks, such as searches. Statutory provisions have already been introduced to pave the way to computerisation, for example permitting records of title to be held by computers.[7]

Three types of official search are possible[8]:

1. a written application for an official search;

---

[3] This office has an excellent information service. Tel. 01–405 3488.

[4] Press Release Chief Land Registrar May 5, 1982.

[5] Housing Act 1980, s.20(1). It is estimated that 15,000 applications (of all varieties) are received each month.

[6] Report of E. J. Pryer (present Chief Land Registrar) (1983) 127 S.J. 46. Computerisation is now surely a 'must' following the recent government announcement that it is hoped that by 1987 compulsory registration will cover areas containing 85 per cent. of the population [February 17, 1984].

[7] Administration of Justice Act 1982.

[8] Land Registration (Official Searches) Rules 1981.

DISTRICT LAND REGISTRIES IN ENGLAND AND WALES

showing their areas of responsibility as from April 1 1981

NOTTINGHAM
Derbyshire
Nottinghamshire
South Yorkshire
Staffordshire
West Yorkshire

PETERBOROUGH
Cambridgeshire
Leicestershire
Lincolnshire
Norfolk
Northamptonshire
Suffolk

DURHAM
Cleveland   Northumberland
Cumbria   North Yorkshire
Durham   Tyne and Wear
Humberside

STEVENAGE
Barking and Dagenham
Bedfordshire
Buckinghamshire
Essex
Havering
Hertfordshire
Newham
Redbridge
Waltham Forest

Durham ○

LYTHAM
Greater Manchester
Lancashire

○ Lytham

BIRKENHEAD
Cheshire
Merseyside

TUNBRIDGE WELLS
East Sussex
Kent
Surrey

○ Birkenhead

Nottingham ○

○ Peterborough

GLOUCESTER
Berkshire
Gloucestershire
Oxfordshire
Warwickshire
West Midlands

Stevenage ○

○ Gloucester

○ Swansea

○ Harrow

SWANSEA
Hereford and Worcester
Shropshire
All the counties in Wales

○ Croydon

Tunbridge Wells ○

PLYMOUTH
Avon   Dorset
Cornwall   Somerset
Devon   Wiltshire

Weymouth ○

HARROW
The City of London   Hammersmith
The Inner Temple and   and Fulham
   the Middle Temple   Haringey
Barnet   Harrow
Brent   Hillingdon
Camden   Hounslow
City of Westminster   Islington
Ealing   Kensington
Enfield   and Chelsea
Hackney   Tower Hamlett

CROYDON
Bexley   Lewisham
Bromley   Merton
Croydon   Richmond
Greenwich   upon Thames
Kingston   Southwark
   upon Thames Sutton
Lambeth   Wandsworth

Plymouth ○

WEYMOUTH
Hampshire
Isle of Wight
West Sussex

2. an application for a search by telex or telephone;
3. a personal search.

There is no charge for making a written application for an official search. A fee of £3 is payable for an application for a search by telex or telephone and a fee of £1 for a personal search by someone other than the registered proprietor. The fees may be paid in cash, by Land Registry adhesive stamps, by postal order, by cheque (H.M. Land Registry) or debited to a credit account where applicable.[9]

POSTAL SEARCHES

Printed Form 94A should be used where the whole of the land in the title is being purchased; Form 94B where only part of the title is being dealt with. The official certificate of search is returned on Form 94D or E (printed on the back of the Form 94A or 94B for convenience). The particulars of the land to be searched must be identified by reference to the County and district (or London borough) the title number and the name of the registered proprietor. Application is then made for an official search of the register of the title quoted, to ascertain whether any adverse entry has been made in the register since a specified date. Here should be inserted the date on which the office copy entries were issued by the Land Registry or the date when the Land or Charge Certificate was last compared with the register. The applicant or his solicitor must certify that he intends to purchase, or take on lease, or accept a charge over the land comprised in the title. Finally the applicant's solicitor is required to state that he either also acts for the registered proprietor or that he holds a written authority of the registered proprietor to inspect the register.[10] Where the application relates to part only of the land comprised in the title the land must be sufficiently described and accompanied by a plan if necessary. No plan is required where the land forms a numbered plot on an estate lay-out plan approved by the Land Registry; the applicant need only refer to the plot number. Form 94A or B should be sent in duplicate (with any plan in duplicate) to the appropriate district land registry. Provided it is received before 11.00 a.m. on any working day and is in proper order the official certificate of search will be despatched on the same day. "Purchaser" for the purposes of the official search procedure is defined[11] as any person (including a lessee or chargee) who in good faith and for valuable consideration acquires or intends to acquire a legal estate in land. It is unclear what "good faith" means in the context of the application for a search. It seems to have more relevance to the question of whether or not a purchaser, who has completed his purchase and lodged his application for registration, can take advantage of the priority protection afforded by the official certificate of search. In this latter context Plowman J. said in *Smith* v. *Morrison*[12] that a purchaser acts in good faith if he acts honestly and without ulterior motive.

---

[9] Land Registration Fee Order 1981.
[10] When a solicitor is not acting for the applicant this must accompany the application.
[11] Land Registration (Official Searches) Rules 1981, r. 2(1).
[12] [1974] 1 W.L.R. 659.

The Land Registration (Official Searches) Rules 1981 seem to envisage that someone other than a purchaser or intending purchaser may wish to apply for an official search of the register.[13] Provided the applicant has the written authority of the registered proprietor he may apply on Form 94C for a search. In this case the certificate of official search will confer no priority. Presumably this procedure is aimed at donees or purchasers of an equitable interest and so on. The Rules can surely not be interpreted as encouraging purchasers in bad faith. The fee for a Form 94C search is £1.

Mortgagees wishing to search the register to see if a notice or caution has been registered to protect a spouse's rights of occupation should apply for a search on Form 106.[14] The search is free of charge.

SEARCHES BY TELEPHONE OR TELEX

A person who has an authority to inspect the register may apply by his solicitor for a search by telephone or telex.[15] Where the search is applied for by telex the particulars required are similar to those required by Form 94A or B,[16] except that an undertaking to forward a written application for an official search must be given. If the application is made by telephone the following procedure should be followed[17]:

  (i) an undertaking should be given that an application for an official search on Form 94A, B or C will be sent forthwith to the proper office accompanied by the appropriate Land Registry fee;
  (ii) the following particulars should be supplied:
    (a) the title and a short description of the property;
    (b) the full name of the proprietor who has authorised the inspection of the register;
    (c) the name, address and telephone number of the solicitor making the application together with the name of the person for whom he is acting;
    (d) the date from which search is to be made.

The result of search is then returned by telex or telephone but does not take account of any pending applications.[18] Furthermore a mistake made by the Land Registry in the case of a telephone or telex result of search will not entitle the applicant to be indemnified[19] for any loss and confers no priority protection on the applicant.[20] A purchaser should therefore only rely on the official certificate of search received in pursuance of his subsequent written application for search.

PERSONAL SEARCHES

Although possible these are rarely made. A personal search confers no protection whatsoever.

---

[13] Land Registration Rules (Official Searches) 1981, r. 9.
[14] The Land Registration (Matrimonial Homes) Rules 1983, r. 6.
[15] Land Registration (Official Searches) Rules 1981, r. 7.
[16] *Ibid.* Sched. 2.
[17] *Ibid.* r. 7(2).
[18] *Ibid.* r. 8(1).
[19] Under Land Registration Act 1925, s.83.
[20] Land Registration (Official Searches) Rules 1981, r. 8(4).

Certificate of the Result of an Official Search

The certificate (on Form 94D or E) will give the result of the search as at the time and date when the application is deemed to have been delivered.[21] It may disclose that since the date from which the search was requested:

(1) No adverse entries have been made. This is the most common result of a search.

(2) Cancelled entries. The Registry is under no obligation to show that an entry has been cancelled but frequently does.

(3) Entries made in the register since the date specified in the application form for the commencement of the search and particulars of any applications pending in the Land Registry which affect the land and which have not yet been entered on the register. These could comprise cautions, notices, restrictions or inhibitions. Cautions and notices in general protect the same type of interests which are registrable as land charges under the Land Charges Act 1972.[22] If the entry is protected by a caution it means that no dealings can be registered without notice being given to the cautioner, so that he can assert his right to object to the registration.[23] Cautions often protect money charges, such as a general equitable charge, and the purchaser will usually proceed with his purchase on the vendor's assurance that the charge will be paid off on or before completion. If the caution protects a continuing interest, like an equitable easement, then the purchaser will normally know of it and be willing to be registered subject to it. If, however, the caution protects a pending action relating to the land or a deed of arrangement, or (registered before February 14, 1983)[24] a spouse's right to occupy the matrimonial home, the purchaser should insist on cancellation of the caution or rescind the contract. A notice[25] reveals the exact nature of the interest and ensures that thereafter all dealings take subject to the interest. If the notice protects a spouse's rights of occupation the vendor should be asked to have the notice withdrawn and, or provide on completion, a declaration signed by the spouse releasing his or her rights in the home. If the search reveals a creditor's notice, then the purchaser should not complete (unless the notice is cancelled) as this constitutes notice of an available act of bankruptcy by the vendor[26] and the purchaser's title may be upset.

Inhibitions are very rare and the most likely example would be a bankruptcy inhibition.[27] In this case the purchaser must not complete

---

[21] *Ibid.* r. 2(3).

[22] They are precluded from registration under the Land Charges Act 1972 if they relate to registered land, by s.14 of that Act.

[23] Land Registration Act 1925, ss.53 and 54.

[24] A spouse's right to occupation cannot be protected by a caution after February 14 1983, which was the date s.4(2) of the Matrimonial Homes and Property Act 1981 came into effect. See s.2(9) of the Matrimonial Homes Act 1983. Cautions lodged before February 14, 1983 for this purpose are not prejudicially affected.

[25] Land Registration Act 1925, ss.48–52.

[26] *Ibid.* s.61(2) and (3).

[27] *Ibid.* s.61(3).

because the Chief Land Registrar must refuse his application for registration.[28]

Restrictions[29] in general protect overreachable interests, that is those arising under a trust for sale or a settlement. They restrict the registered owner's powers of disposition. In the case of property held by co-owners beneficially as tenants in common, the Registrar must enter a restriction to the effect that a sole survivor cannot execute a disposition involving capital money. In this case the purchaser must ensure that he takes his transfer from two registered proprietors, or if one has died, that another trustee of the legal estate is appointed. Again in the case of a restriction relating to settled land, the purchaser must ensure that the tenant for life is acting within his statutory powers[30] and that the purchase money is paid to two trustees of the settlement. A more unusual restriction is one entered by a local authority restricting the persons to whom a council tenant, who has exercised his "right to buy," can sell where the house is in a National Park or place of historic interest.[31]

(4) Current certificates of search. Where another official certificate of search has been issued and the period of it has not expired, brief details will be given.

(5) The certificate of search will always show the date on which it was made and the date on which the period of protection expires.

The duplicate application form and duplicate official certificate of search are kept by the registry and are open for public inspection during the priority period the certificate confers.[32]

Value of the Official Certificate of Search

As well as enabling a purchaser to determine the exact state of the register before he completes his purchase, the official certificate of search affords him the valuable protection of a priority period. Thus if he delivers his application for registration as the new registered proprietor before 11.00 hours on the thirtieth working day after the application for an official search was received by the land registry, any entries made during the priority period affecting the land will be postponed.[33] However, he will not be protected against such an entry if his application for registration is not lodged before the priority period expires.[34] It is irrelevant that the purchaser's application is not in "proper order" when received by the land registry. As long as the registration takes place he can claim the priority protection of his official certificate of search.[35] It should be noted that the priority period cannot be extended. A new search must be applied for if completion is delayed. A solicitor who obtains an official certificate of

---

[28] *Ibid.* s.61(4).
[29] *Ibid.* s.58.
[30] Settled Land Act 1925.
[31] Housing Act 1980, s.19(10).
[32] Land Registration (Official Searches) Rules 1981, r. 4.
[33] *Ibid.* rr. 5 and 2(1).
[34] *Watts* v. *Waller* [1973] 1 Q.B. 153.
[35] Land Registration (Official Searches) Rules 1981, r. 5.

result of search is not liable for any loss sustained by his client if the
certificate turns out to be incorrect.[36]

"Good Faith"

We have seen that a purchaser of registered land buys the land subject to
entries on the register and overriding interests, but otherwise free from all
other interests whatsoever. "Purchaser" is however defined in the
statutory provisions as being a person acting in good faith. Can a
purchaser with actual knowledge of an unprotected minor interest be a
purchaser in "good faith"? There is weighty authority in favour of the view
that such a purchaser takes free of the interest.[37] However, recently, by
employing the doctrine of constructive trust, purchasers were held to be
bound by unprotected minor interest because to find otherwise would be
"against good conscience."[38] This had led conveyancers to suspect that the
register may not any longer be everything.

Incorrect Search

It is clear from the case of *Parkash* v. *Irani Finance Co. Ltd.*[39] that where an
interest in registered land has been correctly protected by an entry on the
register but does not appear on the official certificate of search the
purchaser is bound by the interest. If the purchaser suffers loss as a result
his only claim is for compensation from the insurance fund.[40]

Certificate of Inspection of Filed Plan

A person may apply on Form 101 for a certificate of official inspection of
a filed plan which he has authority to inspect. This is of particular use to
a solicitor whose client is buying a plot of land in a large development for
which the Land Registry has approved an estate lay-out plan. The
inspection counts as an official search for the purposes of compensation
for an error in the result, and the protection of a solicitor.[41] The fee is £1.[42]

---

[36] Land Registration Rules 1925, r. 295.
[37] *De Lusignan* v. *Johnson* (1973) 230 E.G. 499; *Hodges* v. *Jones* [1935] 1 Ch. 657;
Williams & Glyn's Bank Ltd. v. *Boland* [1981] A.C. 487.
[38] *Peffer* v. *Rigg* [1977] 1 W.L.R. 285; *Lyus* v. *Prowsa Developments Ltd.* [1982] 1 W.L.R.
1044; see D.J. Hayton (1983) 133 New L.J. 188.
[39] [1970] Ch. 101.
[40] Land Registration Act 1925, s.83(3).
[41] Land Registration (Official Searches) Rules 1981, r. 10.
[42] Land Registration Fee Order 1981, Sched. 5.

THE COMMONS REGISTER

THE COMMONS REGISTRATION ACT 1965

According to its short title the aim of the Commons Registration Act 1965 was "to provide for the registration of common land and of town or village greens in England and Wales . . . ." This would simplify for purchasers the complicated problem of ascertaining what land was subject to rights of common, requiring in many cases investigation of medieval land law, quite apart from the real difficulty of establishing the necessary facts.

Local authorities were required to establish and maintain two separate registers[43]; a register of common land and a register of town or village greens. Here they would enter details of applications to register (i) any common land or a town or village green (the "lands section"), (ii) any rights of common thereover (the "rights section"), and (iii) the ownership of such land (the "ownership section").[44] The two registers were to be open to public inspection at all reasonable times.[45] A "commoner" could apply to his local authority for registration of his rights and, or common land from January 2, 1967 to January 2, 1970, after which date his right to register was lost. A local authority could itself register rights of common and common land until August 1, 1970.[46] By a combination of the 1965 Act[47] and sections 193 and 194 of the Law of Property Act 1925 after July 1970 no land capable of being registered under the 1965 Act was to be deemed to be common land (or a town or village green) unless so registered and any rights of common not registered under the Act or previously registered under the Land Registration Acts 1925 to 1936 were extinguished.[48] A purchaser can therefore safely ignore pre-1970 unregistered common land or rights of common.

When a purchaser buys land affected by a pre-1970 registration there is a chance that he may find himself involved in a dispute as to its validity. Initial registration under the 1965 Act was provisional only.[49] If no objection was made within two years[50] of the registration it became final and final registration was stated by section 10 to be conclusive evidence of the matters registered at the date of registration, except ownership of the fee simple. There can be no doubt that many bogus claims may have achieved validity in this way. Where an objection was made in time to a registration the local authority was required to refer the matter to the Commons Commissioners for their decision.[51] Appeals from such

---

[43] Commons Registration Act 1965, s.3(1).

[44] *Ibid*. s.1(1).

[45] *Ibid*. s.3(2).

[46] *Ibid*. s.4(1); Commons Registration (Time Limits) Order 1966 (S.I. 1966 No. 1470), as amended by S.I. 1970. No. 383.

[47] Commons Registration Act 1965, s.1(2).

[48] *Central Electricity Generating Board* v. *Clwyd County Council* [1976] 1 W.L.R. 151.

[49] Commons Registration Act 1965, s.4(5).

[50] *Ibid*. s.5(2).

[51] *Ibid*. s.5(6).

decisions could be made on a point of law by way of case stated to the Chancery Division of the High Court[52] and where land registered under the Act ceased to be common land an application could be made to the local authority for an amendment[53] of the register. Where such an amendment was made there was again provision for appeal to the Chancery Division.[54] On February 20, 1980 it was reported to the House of Commons that some 8,500 disputed registrations and 4,800 claims of ownership remained to be heard by the Commissioners; it was predicted that this could take four to five years. Of late there has been a flurry of commons appeals[55] in the Chancery Division, in one of which[56] Lord Denning M.R. expressed regret that due to poor drafting the 1965 Act had sadly failed to achieve its purpose of preserving the commons.

Provision has been made for the registration of new commons. Where after January 2, 1970 any land becomes common land or a town or village green application may be made for inclusion of the land in the registers and for the registration of rights of common over the land and persons claiming to be owners.[57] In this case there is no time limit within which applications must be made and the land does not cease to be common land nor do the rights of commons cease to be exercisable if not registered. The procedure for objections and appeals is the same. New commons can arise, *inter alia* by grant or by prescription.[58]

What is a Right of Common and Common Land?[59]

Many kinds of rights of common exist, some only in certain parts of the country. They can be defined as rights of a person (usually together with others including the owner of the land) to take part of the natural produce of another person's land. Common examples are rights to graze animals and take fish from a river. More unusual rights of common successfully claimed have included a right to cut bracken for litter for pigs and gorse for breadovens[60] and a right to take peasticks and leafmould from land.[61] Specifically included by the 1965 Act as rights of common are cattlegates or beastgates (found generally in the north) and rights of sole or several vesture and herbage or sole or several pasture.[62] These are different types of grazing rights. Rights of way (public or private) and rights to water cattle or horses or other animals are not rights of common. Rights held

---

[52] *Ibid.* s.18.

[53] *Ibid.* s.13.

[54] *Ibid.* s.14.

[55] See, for example, *Re Sutton Common, Wimborne* [1982] 1 W.L.R. 647; *Re Tillmire Common, Heslington* [1982] 2 All E.R. 615.

[56] *Corpus Christi College* v. *Gloucestershire County Council* [1982] 3 W.L.R. 849.

[57] Commons Registration Act 1965, s.13(*b*); Commons Registration (New Lands) Regulations 1969 (S.I. 1969 No.1843).

[58] Commons Registration (New Lands) Regulations 1969 (S.I. 1969 No. 1843).

[59] For a detailed account of Commons see *Halsbury's Laws of England* (4th ed.), Vol. 6.

[60] *Re Snelsdon Common, Cheshire*, Decision of Commons Commissioner (34/D/15).

[61] *Re Shottisham Poor's Common, E. Suffolk*, Decision of Commons Commissioner (5/D/12); (1974) 118 S.J. 434.

[62] Commons Registration Act 1965, s.22(1).

for a term of years or from year to year are not registrable under the Act. "Common land" does not fulfil its popular image of wide open spaces. It is defined by the Act[63] as (a) land subject to rights of common or (b) waste land of a manor not subject to rights of common.[64] Land has been found to be common land where villagers had a right to erect a maypole on it to dance round[65] and where children from adjoining houses habitually played on it.[66]

WHEN SHOULD A SEARCH BE MADE?

Where a purchaser is buying a vacant piece of land, he normally has development in mind. The existence of rights of common or claims to ownership of common land would obviously defeat the purpose of his purchase. In *New Windsor Corpn.* v. *Mellor*,[66a] a local authority was forced to discontinue use of a piece of land in the middle of New Windsor as a car park because a "customary right" had been established by the "Bachelors of Windsor" to play cricket on the land. If there is any possibility of the land (or part) being common land or of rights of common existing over the land then a search of the commons registers should be made. This is so whether the vendor's title to the property is registered or unregistered. Claims to ownership of common land cannot be registered under the 1965 Act where the freehold title is registered at H.M. Land Registry.[67] However, rights of common over registered land are registrable in the commons register not against the title.[68]

An added consideration is the question of whether a solicitor may render himself liable in negligence if he fails to make a search and a registration is not discovered, as in *G. & K. Ladenbau (U.K.) Ltd.* v. *Crawley & de Reya*.[69] Mocatta J. said in that case: "This decision does not mean that a solicitor is in peril of an action for negligence unless he searches the register in every case in which he is retained on behalf of a purchaser of land. There is clearly room for some discretion . . . ."[70] Plainly if one were dealing . . . with the sale of a large office block near the Bank of England one could safely ignore the possibility of there being any rights of common involved."[71]

The search should be made before contracts are exchanged. This is not only to avoid causing a purchaser unnecessary frustration and delay but to ensure that a purchaser can exercise his full contractual remedies. Although a vendor is under a duty to disclose latent rights affecting the property of which he is (or should be) aware, it seems that in the case of

---

[63] *Ibid.* s.22(1).

[64] For meaning of this see *Box Parish Council* v. *Lacey* [1980] Ch. 109; *Baxendale* v. *Instow Parish Council* [1981] 2 W.L.R. 1055; *Corpus Christi College* v. *Gloucestershire County Council* [1982] 3 W.L.R. 849.

[65] *Re The Village Green Shillingstone, Dorset* (10/D/21).

[66] *Re the Village Greens Waddingham, Lincs.*; (1973) 117 S.J. 537.

[66a] [1975] 3 All E.R. 44.

[67] Commons Registration (New Land) Regulations 1969, reg. 3; Commons Registration Act 1965, s.4(3).

[68] Commons Registration Act 1965, s.1(1).

[69] [1978] 1 W.L.R. 266.

[70] *Ibid.* at p. 289.

[71] *Ibid.* at p. 278.

applications for provisional registration of commons before 1970, local authorities were not bound to inform owners of the land in question of the application and did not do so.[72] These provisional registrations have long since become final and conclusive (unless objected to within the proper time) and presumably there may still be owners who are unaware that their property is burdened by a commons registration.[73] The situation is unlikely to arise in connection with the registration of new commons. Local authorities must on receipt of an application to register send a notice to the owner of the land or other person likely to object, publicise the notice and affix it in a conspicuous part of the land when vacant.[74]

HOW TO MAKE A SEARCH

Any person may make a search of the registers by filling in a requisition for an official search on Form 21 and delivering it personally or by post to the appropriate registration authority. The authority must make a search and issue an official certificate of search. The registration authority for land in Greater London is the Greater London Council and for land elsewhere is the council of the county in which the land is situated. Form 21 must be submitted in duplicate and be accompanied by a plan in duplicate and by a sufficient verbal description of the land to enable the authority to identify it. Where land is in separate occupation or separately rated a requisition must be made in respect of each separate part. The new Form 21 provides for a compulsory search of both the register of common land and the register of town or village greens.[75] The fee payable for an official search and certificate is £3·00. A further charge of 25p is made for each additional parcel of land included in the requisition. Certified copies of relevant entries may be obtained on payment of a reasonable fee.

Value of the Official Certificate of Search

Note 4 on the back of Form 21 warns the applicant that "A certificate of official search includes registrations made up to and including the date of issue, but takes no account of pending applications and confers no protection on a purchaser or intending purchaser." Presumably this will not exempt the registration authority from tortious liability for making a negligent search.[76]

COMPANY SEARCHES

Where a purchaser is intending to buy land from a company it is important

---

[72] See "Council Notes." (1971) 68 L.S. Gaz. 132, 195.

[73] This occurred in *G. & K. Ladenbau (U.K.) Ltd.* v. *Crawley & de Reya* [1978] 1 W.L.R. 266.

[74] Commons Registration (New Land) Regulations 1969, reg. 5.

[75] Commons Registration (General) Regulations 1966 (S.I. 1966 No. 1471) as amended by S.I. 1980 No. 1195 (New Form 21 and fees).

[76] By analogy with *Coats Patons (Retail) Ltd.* v. *Birmingham Corpn.* (1971) 115 S.J. 757.

to ascertain whether or not that land is subject to a charge created by the company. Similarly he must be sure that the company is not being put into liquidation as this will limit the company's power to sell the property.[77] Additional searches may have to be made to discover this information but first a brief look will be taken at the types of charge a company may create.[78]

Charges a Company May Create

A company, like an individual, may create a fixed charge on a specific asset; it may mortgage its factory to a bank. A fixed charge limits the company's powers to deal with the factory. Unlike an individual a company may also create a "floating charge." This is a charge on some (or all) of the present and future property of the company. The company is free to deal with the property currently forming the subject matter of the charge in the normal course of its business. If the company breaks the terms of the charge, defaults on repayments for example, and the chargee takes steps to enforce his security or proceedings are brought to put the company into liquidation the floating charge "crystallises". It becomes a fixed charge on the relevant assets.

Registration of Company Charges on Land

AT THE COMPANIES REGISTRY

Section 95 of the Companies Act 1948 states that particulars[79] of charges on land created by a company for securing money must be registered at the Companies Registry within 21 days of their creation. If particulars of a registrable charge are not delivered within this period the charge is void against a liquidator and any creditor of the company (including a mortgagee)[79a] in so far as the land is concerned. Section 95(1) provides that in this event money lent under the charge becomes repayable immediately but if the company goes into liquidation a chargee could lose both money and his security. In view of the importance to a chargee of having his charge duly registered, it is provided that he may effect registration of the charge personally.[80] Therefore in most cases the charge will be registered.

In *Williams* v. *Burlington Investments Ltd.*[81] a debtor company did not have to register an agreement which provided for the future creation of a legal mortgage over such land as the company then owned. The agreement was not a charge on land within the terms of section 95(2)(d) of the Act

---

[77] Companies Act 1948, s.281 (voluntary liquidation) and s.227 (compulsory liquidation).

[78] For a detailed analysis see W. J. Gough, *Company Charges*.

[79] The instrument creating the charge itself is sent (to be returned after registration) with particulars detailed on Form 47, Companies (Forms) Regulations 1979 (S.I. 1979 No. 1547).

[79a] *Re Ashpurton Estates Ltd.* [1982] 1 W.L.R. 964; *Re Resinoid and Mica Products Ltd.* [1982] 3 W.L.R. 979.

[80] Companies Act 1948, s.96(1).

[81] (1977) 121 S.J. 424; Brightman L.J. in *Property Discount Corpn. Ltd.* v. *Lyon Group Ltd.* [1981] 1 W.L.R. 300.

and did not fall within any of the other categories of charge requiring registration under the sub-section. Section 106 of the Companies Act 1948 extends the operation of the registration provisions of section 95 to a foreign company which creates a charge over land owned by it in this country, if at the time the charge is created, the company has an established place of business here. Section 407 of the same Act provides that a foreign company which has assets and an established place of business in Great Britain, should enter details of itself in what is known as "the Slavenburg Index," kept at the Companies Registries. A purchaser buying land here from a foreign company should theoretically be able to discover whether or not that company is under an obligation to register any charges, by making a search of the "Slavenburg Index." But it has been held[81a] that registration in the Index is not compulsory and a search is therefore not conclusive.

AT THE LAND CHARGES DEPARTMENT

A charge created by a company over unregistered[82] land must be registered under the Land Charges Act 1972 as well as under section 95 of the Companies Act 1948. There are two exceptions to this rule; in the case of floating charges (whenever created) and fixed charges created before January 1, 1970, Section 3(7) of the Land Charges Act 1972 provides that registration under section 95 of the Companies Act 1948 "shall be sufficient in place of registration under this Act and shall have effect as if the land charge had been registered under this Act."[83] A purchaser cannot discover the existence of these from his land charges search and must make a search at the Companies Registry.

A problem can arise where a company contracts to buy land, charges its interest under the contract and only registers the charge under the Companies Act. If the charge is floating or in the unlikely event of the charge (and the contract) being created before 1970, it would not be registrable as a land charge and would not be revealed by a purchaser's land charges search against the owner of the land, his vendor. Yet he would be deemed to have actual notice of the charge[84] and must take the land subject to it.[85]

AT H.M. LAND REGISTRY

All charges created by a company affecting registered land must be protected by the entry of a notice or caution on the register of title. If a charge on registered land is registered *only* at the Companies Registry it will not bind a purchaser.[86] It may, therefore, be thought unnecessary for a purchaser of registered land from a company to make an additional

---

[81a] *N. V. Slavenburg's Bank* v. *Intercontinental Natural Resources Ltd.* [1980] W.L.R. 1076; and see (1981) 78 L.S. Gaz. 921.

[82] A charge on registered land is excluded from registration here by Land Charges Act, 1972, s.14.

[83] For an example in relation to a pre-1970 fixed charge, see *Property Discount Corpn. Ltd.* v. *Lyon Group Ltd.* [1981] 1 W.L.R. 300.

[84] By the combined effect of Land Charges Act, 1972, s.3(7) and Law of Property Act 1925, s.198.

[85] (1980) *Company Lawyer* 144.

[86] Land Registration Act 1925, s.60.

search at the Companies Registry. However, his official search of the register will not disclose whether a resolution[87] has been passed to put the company into voluntary liquidation, nor will it disclose whether the company has been struck off the register of companies under section 353 of the Companies Act 1948. Search facilities are also offered by the Companies Registration Office, 55 City Road, London E.C.1. In this latter event a purported transfer by the company would be invalid. A non-existent company cannot validly execute such a transfer.[88]

Summary of Reasons for Making a Companies Search

1. In the case of unregistered land to ensure that no pre-1970 fixed charges or floating charges have been created by the company.
2. In all cases (registered or unregistered land)

(a) to ensure that no resolution has been passed to put the company into voluntary liquidation; and
(b) to ensure that it has not been removed from the register.

The Search

Ideally a search at the Companies Registry should be made on the day of completion. No priority period is conferred by the result of the search. It may be advisable to make an earlier search as well. If a floating charge is revealed by the search the purchaser needs proof that the charge has not crystallised. The only conclusive proof consists of letters from both the company and the chargee stating that this has not occurred. Obtaining the letters may take some days necessitating a delay in completion if an earlier search has not been made.[89]

WHO TO SEARCH AGAINST

A search should be made against the name of the company concerned. Since the enactment of the Companies Act 1980 companies have been classified as either public limited companies (public companies) or limited companies (private companies). Provision is made in the 1980 Act for the registration of new companies and re-registration of existing companies.[90] When searching at the Companies Registry the fact that an old company may have re-registered under a slightly different title should be borne in mind. Wherever possible the company's registered number should be obtained to ensure a correct search.

WHO MAY SEARCH

The Companies Registry is open to the public and any company's file may be inspected for details of charges created by the company without the need to obtain any prior consent.

---

[87] Such a resolution must be registered at the Companies Registry; Companies Act 1948, s.143.
[88] For a more detailed discussion see (1976) 120 S.J. 75.
[89] See "Correspondence" (1970) 67 L.S. Gaz. 107; (1977) 74 L.S. Gaz. 132.
[90] Companies Act 1980, ss.2–13.

WHERE TO SEARCH

For companies whose registered office is in England and Wales a search
should be made at the Companies Registration Office, Crown Way,
Maindy, Cardiff, CF4 3UZ. For companies whose registered office is in
Scotland the search should be made at the Companies Registration Office,
102 George Street, Edinburgh, 2.

HOW TO SEARCH

Particulars of registered charges can be obtained by making a personal
search of the company's file. No facilities exist for making official searches
at the Companies Registry. An applicant (or his agent) should attend at
the appropriate Companies Registry and give the clerk at the searches
counter details of the company against which the search is to be made.
The registered number of the company can be obtained (if not already
known) from the index of companies kept at the Registry free of charge.
A search ticket should be purchased, the current fee being £1.00.[91] The
clerk will then hand you the company file. Since 1976 all documents sent
to the Companies Registry have been filmed and are therefore available
on microfiche which may be viewed on the facilities available. Documents
sent before 1976 will be contained in the company's documentary file
which is made available in appropriate cases.

Compulsory Liquidation

A search at the Companies Registry will not disclose the fact that
proceedings have been started to have the company compulsorily wound
up. Such proceedings commence once a petition has been filed at the
Company's Court. Any disposition made of company property after the
presentation of a petition is void unless the court orders otherwise.[92] There
are several ways to check whether or not a petition has been presented. A
search may be made of the *London Gazette* in which details of petitions
must be advertised. Alternatively enquiry may be made at the Companies
Court, Thomas More Building, Royal Courts of Justice, Strand, London,
WC2A 2LL. This must be done in person. A court official will check the
records of petitions filed and inform the enquirer of the result. Perhaps
easiest—there is now a register of winding-up petitions, and telephone
enquiries will be answered free of charge by ringing 01–405 7641.

MORE INFORMATION

The foregoing searches will reveal many of the matters (public and
private) which a purchaser needs to know about the property he is
intending to buy. He will be able to glean more information from the
answers to his solicitor's preliminary enquiries of the vendor and the local
authority and from his own periodic inspection of the property. These are
discussed in the next chapter.

All that remains here is to mention a few additional searches that a
purchaser's solicitor might want to make in special cases.

---

[91] Company (Fees) Regulations 1980 (S.I. 1980 No. 1749).
[92] Companies Act 1948, s.227.

National Coal Board Searches

The National Coal Board have the right under the Coal Industry Act 1975[93] to withdraw support from surface land in order to work coal seams. To inform landowners, in areas where mining is to take place, that subsidence may occur a notice is served on them by the National Coal Board. This notice is also published in the *London Gazette* and local newspapers. A purchaser of land in a coal mining area should make enquiries of the local Regional Office of the National Coal Board to find out if the land is in an area where subsidence may occur. If the land is liable to subsidence he may wish to buy land elsewhere. The enquiries should therefore be made before contracts are exchanged. Application is made by letter addressed to the relevant Regional Office preferably enclosing a plan of the land.[94] A fee is payable which varies according to the amount of work involved in answering the particular enquiry.

Searches of the Registers of Rent

Whenever a purchaser is buying property which is subject to a tenancy falling within the rent control provisions of the Rent Act 1977[95] his solicitor should make a search of the registers of rent kept pursuant to sections 66 and 79 of that Act.

In the cases of "regulated tenancies"[96] and "restricted contracts"[97] it is possible that a fair rent has been registered in respect of the property. This is a rent fixed by the rent tribunal as a proper rent to be charged in respect of the property. Once registered no landlord may charge in excess of this amount unless an application is made to the rent tribunal to allow the increase or a period of two years has elapsed since the last registration.

Searches in respect of "regulated tenancies" should be made in the register kept by the rent officer for the area in which the property is situate. A certified copy of any entry on the register can be obtained on payment of a fee of 50p.[98] Recently the responsibility for keeping the register of fair rents in respect of dwellings let on "restricted contracts" has been transferred from local authorities to the various Rent Assessment Panels which serve different areas of the country.[99] A standard form (Conveyancing 29E) has been drawn up to allow solicitors to make enquiry of the Rent Assessment Panels by post on payment of a fee of £2·00. The form contains a clause limiting the liability of the Presidents of the Rent Assessment Panels in terms similar to that on the Enquiries of District Council (Form Conveyancing 29A).[1] Again a certified copy of any entry on the register may be requested on payment of 50p.

---

[93] Coal Industry Act 1975, s.2.
[94] There is as yet no agreed form of enquiry.
[95] As amended by the Housing Act 1980.
[96] Rent Act 1977, s.18, as amended.
[97] *Ibid.* s.19, as amended. Basically a "restricted contract" tenancy is one where the landlord lives on the property.
[98] S.I. 1980 No. 1967.
[99] Rent Act 1977, s.79, as amended by the Housing Act 1980, Sched. 25, para. 43.
[1] See *post*, p. 94.

Railway Fences Search

Records are kept by the British Rail Property Board of all land in respect of which the Board has a subsisting obligation to maintain fences. Some of these obligations were created many years ago when the land was first acquired to build a railway line. A purchaser buying land adjacent to a railway may wish to know whether a fence on the land is maintainable at the Board's expense. His vendor may not be sure of the position. Enquiry can be made in the regional office of the Board. Application is by way of letter and a plan should also be sent to identify the land in question. The Board will then inform the purchaser whether or not the fence is maintainable at their expense. A reasonable fee may sometimes be charged for this service.

3: Pre Contract Tasks

INTRODUCTION

In recent years conveyancers have witnessed a violent change of emphasis from post to pre-contractual matters. This is due to a combination of several factors: first, the vendor's limited duty of disclosure; secondly, the vast increase of public legislation controlling private ownership of property; thirdly, the opening of the "floodgates"[1] of the tort of professional negligence; fourthly, the passing of the Misrepresentation Act 1967 and fifthly the House of Lords' decision in *Williams and Glyn's Bank Ltd.* v. *Boland*[2].

"Normal conveyancing practice" dictates that in the purchase of both registered and unregistered land the purchaser's solicitor attend to certain matters before contracts are exchanged. These matters are described in the following pages. The result of not attending to these tasks could be liability to the purchaser for negligence.[3] If time is such that these matters cannot be done before contract, they should be carried out as soon as possible thereafter and the contract made conditional on the outcome being satisfactory to the purchaser.

PRELIMINARY ENQUIRIES OF THE VENDOR

Introduction

A sale of land inherently produces a conflict of interests. The purchaser wants to find out all that he can about the property, whereas the vendor, albeit keen to sing its praises, may well wish to conceal its faults.

The Vendor's Duty of Disclosure

At common law a vendor is under a duty to disclose any latent defect in his title, a restrictive covenant[4] for instance, but not a patent defect in title, that is one which a purchaser could reasonably discover himself by inspecting the property, for example an obvious right of way.[5] Where the

---

[1] *Hedley Byrne & Co. Ltd.* v. *Heller & Partners Ltd.* [1964] A.C. 465.
[2] [1981] A.C. 487.
[3] *Midland Bank Trust Co.* v. *Hett, Stubbs & Kemp* [1979] Ch. 384, *G. & K. Ladenbau (U.K.) Ltd.* v. *Crawley & de Reya* [1978] 1 W.L.R. 266.
[4] *Re Stone & Saville's Contract* [1963] 1 W.L.R. 163.
[5] *Yandle & Sons* v. *Sutton* [1922] 2 Ch. 199.

sale is governed by the Law Society's General Conditions of Sale (1984 revision) a vendor must disclose any patent easements and other rights of which he knows or ought to know other than those known to the purchaser at the date of the contract, or which a prudent purchaser would have discovered by that date, by making the usual searches and enquiries.[6-7] A vendor is under no obligation to tell a purchaser about any physical defects in his property, latent or patent, although if he is the original builder or has done any do-it-yourself work to the property he may be liable to the purchaser for resultant defects in the tort of negligence. In *Hone* v. *Benson*,[8] "amateur builder"–vendors owed a duty of care to their purchasers in respect of an allegedly faulty central heating system which they had constructed themselves and installed in the property.

The limited obligation on the vendor to give the purchaser information about the property he is selling is commonly referred to as the rule of "caveat emptor"—"purchaser beware!"

Frequently vendors and their agents do make statements about the property concerned. Since the passing of the Misrepresentation Act 1967, they run the risk that if their statements are untrue, and whether they made them negligently or innocently (or, of course, fraudulently) the purchaser may be entitled to rescind the contract or claim damages[9] even after the sale has been completed. As will be shown, today we may be witnessing the age of "caveat vendor."

Enquiries Before Contract

The "caveat emptor" rule long ago led to purchasers' solicitors presenting vendors' solicitors with a list of questions about the property before contracts were exchanged, but it is only in recent decades that preliminary enquiries on the purchase of property have become the rule,[10] evidencing the shift of emphasis in conveyancing from post to pre-contractual matters.

In fact there is little authority on the duty of a solicitor to make these enquiries and advise his client on the replies, although failure to do so (unless expressly instructed) would be unlikely to be "in accordance with the best conveyancing practice accepted by the profession"[11] and may render a solicitor liable for negligence.[12] In *Goody* v. *Baring*[13] a purchaser bought property subject to tenancies. He successfully sued his solicitor in negligence for not obtaining information as to the terms of the tenancies and whether or not they were subject to rent control, in addition to making his standard preliminary enquiries.

Primarily the object of making preliminary enquiries of the vendor is to ensure that the purchaser has as much information as possible about

---

[6-7] Law Society Condition 5(1).

[8] (1978) 248 E.G. 1013.

[9] The Misrepresentation Act 1967, ss.1 and 2.

[10] P. H. Kenny (1982) 126 S.J. 407.

[11] J.T. Farrand, *Emmet on Title* (18th Ed.) p.2.

[12] *G. & K. Ladenbau (U.K.) Ltd.* v. *Crawley & de Reya* [1978] 1 W.L.R. 226; P. H. Kenny (1982) 126 S.J. 387.

[13] [1956] 1 W.L.R. 448; see also *Hill* v. *Harris* [1965] 2 Q.B. 601.

the property he is interested in before he signs the contract and commits himself to the purchase. More recently it has been observed[14] that they have been "reduced to an attempt to extract actionable representations from a party unwilling to make even a hint of a statement of fact."

It should be noted that neither a vendor or his solicitor is under any obligation to answer pre-contractual enquiries. However, the current trend amongst vendors' solicitors is to be as helpful as possible towards purchasers, and to consult their clients on matters within their own personal knowledge, taking care of course to avoid giving any incorrect information. To refuse to answer enquiries would provide ammunition for those who attack the profession's conveyancing monopoly and could lead to sales being lost.[15]

The Standard Form

A standard form of Enquiries before Contract has been in use by solicitors since 1944. Since then the form has undergone several revisions largely due to criticisms by writers and the profession that the questions were long-winded, clumsily drafted, often irrelevant and that the information sought by them could be found by the purchaser more appropriately elsewhere, from the local authority, by commissioning an independent survey or by personally inspecting the property. In 1976 the questions were described as "a series of time-honoured rhythmic inanities"[16] and in 1980, the replies as "no more informative than an official communique."[17]

The form has been revised again. The questions are shorter and more direct (although overlap with the purchaser's other enquiries still occurs) and additions have been made to cover recent developments in the law. A new disclaimer has also been included. Purchasers' solicitors should therefore now make their preliminary enquiries on form Con 29 LM (Revised) (long version) or form Con 29 SM (Revised) (short form) introduced by Oyez on September 1, 1980. The back of the forms bear the distinguishing mark "8/80,"[18] "1/81"[19] or "4/83."[19]

It is proposed to go through in detail the long form of Con 29, as this is the form most frequently used in practice. The short form covers basically the same ground as the longer version but each question is shorter and there are only 13 general enquiries.[20] Whether the long or short version is used, it should be submitted in duplicate to the vendor's solicitors. It is usually sent once the draft contract has been received, so that additional enquiries can be drafted and made if necessary. The replies should be read together with the replies to the purchaser's Enquiries of the Local Authority, and further enquiries made of the vendor if necessary before contracts are exchanged.

---

[14] P. H. Kenny (1983) L.S.Gaz. 326; and see J.E.Adams (1970) 67 L.S.Gaz. 318.

[15] J. E. Adams (1970) 120 New L.J. 610 and 630; and (1970) 34 Conv. 224.

[16] M. Joseph, *The Conveyancing Fraud.*

[17] H. W. Wilkinson (1980) 130 New L.J. 1215.

[18] "Printerese" for August 1980.

[19] Reprint dates.

[20] The last two are omitted.

CON.29 LM (REVISED): "ENQUIRIES BEFORE CON-TRACT"

The form is divided into two sections; General Enquiries and Leasehold Enquiries. A space is left at the end of each section where additional enquiries relevant to the particular transaction in hand may be inserted. Enquiries which are inappropriate in any case should be deleted.

Each Enquiry will be commented on in turn.

General Enquiries

BOUNDARIES

This question asks the vendor for information as to the ownership of boundary walls and fences and the upkeep of them. It is interesting to note that once the contract has been made the purchaser cannot demand an answer to this question. At common law *Dawson* v. *Brinckman*[21] seems to say that the vendor is under no duty to define the ownership of boundary walls and fences and both sets of standard conditions of sale confirm this expressly.[22] Therefore, if the purchaser needs such information he must acquire it at this stage of the transaction. The vendor's solicitor will normally reply to the question by reference to the title deeds. It should, however, be remembered that Land Registry filed plans indicate general boundaries only, unless they are noted as fixed, and cannot be used in boundary dispute.

DISPUTES

Enquiry 2 asks if the vendor is aware of any disputes regarding boundaries, easements, covenants or other matters. The reply is of considerable importance to a purchaser who will usually not wish to buy himself into a legal wrangle. In its Final Report the Royal Commission on Legal Services remarked that "one of the most fruitful sources of dispute and litigation relates to boundaries,"[23] and in the Fifth Annual Report[24] of the Lay Observer, Major General J. C. R. Allen said "I have been surprised by the frequency of these disputes and I have been appalled by the extreme bitterness which they so often generate."

As the case of *Wilson* v. *Bloomfield*[25] illustrates, vendors' solicitors should be wary of answering this enquiry without direct reference to their clients. There, solicitors replied to enquiries before contract that their client was not aware of any boundary disputes. There were such disputes and they were sued by the purchaser on the basis that they knew he would rely on their replies being accurate and therefore owed a duty of care to him. The Court of Appeal held that this was an arguable point of law and refused to strike out the action against the solicitor/defendants.

---

[21] (1850) 3 M. & G. 53.
[22] National Conditions of Sales (20th ed.) Cond. 13(2) and Law Society Conditions of Sale (1984 rev.) Cond. 13(1).
[23] 1979.
[24] 1979.
[25] (1979) 123 S.J. 860.

NOTICES

The vendor is asked to give details of any notices relating to the property which he has given or received.

If the local authority has served a notice on the vendor, for example a closing order[26] or an abatement notice,[27] the replies to the purchaser's Enquiries of District Councils (or London Boroughs) will state that the notice has been served and where it may be inspected, but may not give further details. The notice will have already been served on the vendor, so here the purchaser is really asking the vendor in advance if he has received a notice and if so for a copy, so that he can discover the details of it. In the last resort he will have to inspect the document at the relevant local authority office.

The enquiry also embraces notices relating to private actions. Examples might be a writ served by or against a neighbour for private nuisance or a notice of claim served on the National House-Building Council for a defect covered by the scheme.

GUARANTEES, ETC.

Enquiry 4 consists of two sections, (A) and (B). Section (A) has five parts. Part (i) asks for copies of the agreement and certificate or insurance policy with notice of insurance cover where the property is covered by the National House-Building Council scheme. The scheme is described fully later in the book. Basically it applies to houses, bungalows, maisonettes and flats, built and sold with the benefit of the scheme by builder-vendors who are registered with the Council. It gives 10 years protection to the original and subsequent purchasers against certain defects which may subsequently develop in the property. The main drawback of the pre 1979 scheme was that the insurance cover given by the Council was not inflation-linked. The first purchaser could counteract this problem by buying "top-up cover" but this was not available to a second or subsequent purchaser. Solicitors acting for the latter therefore had to check the extent of insurance cover in their preliminary enquiries. Great changes were made to the scheme in 1979,[28] one of which was that insurance cover is now inflation-linked. Thus if the property is being sold with the benefit of the new 1979 agreement (H.B.5 (1979)) the extent of cover need not be checked.[29] Express assignment of the benefit of an N.H.B.C. agreement to a subsequent purchaser is unnecessary.[30] It has recently been announced that the N.H.B.C. scheme is to be extended to cover properties which have undergone major conversion by registered builders.

Part (ii) of enquiry 4 (A) asks whether insurance has been taken out to cover any defect in the title offered by the vendor or against the risk of an old restrictive covenant being enforced against the property, and if so requests a copy be produced. Title insurance has been common in

---

[26] Housing Act 1957, s.17.
[27] Public Health Act 1936, s.93.
[28] J. E. Adams (1980) 130 New L.J. 171, 195 and 219.
[29] Insurance cover must be checked when dealing with pre–1979 agreements.
[30] *Marchant* v. *Caswell & Redgrave Ltd.* (1976) 240 E.G. 127; cl.10, H.B.5 (1979).

America for quite some time, but has only recently gained favour here. It is usually effected by a single premium payment.

Part (iii) is aimed at finding out what guarantees, certificates, and so on the vendor has relating to the fabric of the property, for example woodworm or dry rot treatment guarantees. The benefit of any such agreements must generally be expressly assigned to the purchaser.

Part (iv) asks for a copy of any agreement or covenant by some third party to maintain any of the property's access roads or footpaths.

Part (v) relates to road maintenance and to the upkeep of any private sewer. It will be seen in the next section[31] that in the case of new housing developments the builder generally agrees with the local authority and water authority to construct necessary roads and sewers respectively and maintain them until taken over by the relevant authority. This agreement is nearly always supported by a bond; a guarantee. The purchaser's Enquiries of the Local Authority will reveal the existence of any such agreement or bond. The purchaser is now asking for copies so that he can ensure that the bond is adequate should the builder default on his obligations under the agreement. If this happens the purchaser must know that he will be able to recover from the bondsman any charges he has to pay towards completing the work. Part (v) will reveal any agreements with neighbours relating to the maintenance of any private sewer or road, and details of any road charges that must be paid, where the property abuts a private road which is about to be taken over by the local authority.

Part (B) asks for particulars of any claims that have been made under any of the Part (A) agreements and whether or not the claims have been settled.

SERVICES

Enquiry 5 is similar to number 1 because it seeks information which the vendor is under no duty to disclose once contracts have been exchanged. 5(A) asks if the property is connected to the usual mains services; water, gas, electricity and drainage. The purchaser will usually have found this out from the estate agent or the vendor himself. 5(B) and (C) are more important in that they ask whether the services pass through any land not included in the sale and their route. Although the vendor is under a duty to disclose burdens he is under no duty to reveal benefits; easements necessary for the enjoyment of the property. The purchaser's solicitor should discover if any easements are necessary and ensure that they are included in the description of the property in the draft contract.[32] This will in due course entitle him to investigate title to them.

Country properties are not always connected to the mains water supply. Sometimes a licence is required to extract water from a local stream or river. Under the Water Resources Act 1963 a licence may lapse unless notice is given to the water authority within one month of a change of ownership.[33] In appropriate cases an additional enquiry should be made asking for details of the licence (if any) or copy of it.

---

[31] See *post*, p. 75.

[32] Omission is not fatal, as the conveyance will pass all existing easements without express mention. Law of Property Act 1925, s.62.

[33] The Water Resources Act 1963, s.32.

EXCLUSIVE FACILITIES

This asks if the property enjoys any exclusive facilities over land belonging to someone else, such as the right to go onto neighbouring land to repair an outside wall of the property, and if so, whether there are any restrictions on the exercise of the right and whether any payment has to be made for its use.

SHARED FACILITIES

Enquiry 7 asks whether the vendor has the right to use any roads, paths, drains and so on in conjunction with the owners or occupiers of other property, and if so, for details of any agreement regulating the use of the right or upkeep of the facility. An example might be a row of houses served by a private sewer leading into a public sewer.

ADVERSE RIGHTS

Enquiry 8 could be said to be the most important to the purchaser of all the enquiries on the form, especially when he is buying land with registered title. It is divided into three parts.

Part (A) asks if the vendor is aware of any rights or informal arrangements affecting the property. These rights are unlikely to be referred to in the title deeds, do not therefore appear on the draft contract, and are not usually apparent on inspection of the property. Perhaps the most famous of these rights is the equitable interest in land protected by estoppel illustrated by the cases of *E.R. Ives Investment Ltd.* v. *High*[34] and *Crabb* v. *Arun District Council*[35] both of which concerned informally created rights of way. To date the cases in this area have related to unregistered land. Being outside the categories of registrable interests under the Land Charges Act 1972, their validity against subsequent purchasers depends on notice. Making this enquiry of the vendor is probably the only way a purchaser's solicitor can ensure that his client will not unwittingly be fixed with constructive notice of the right and be bound by it.

In the context of registered land these rights are not registrable interests. It seems that they are protectable by a caution under section 54 or a notice under section 49(1)(*f*) of the Land Registration Act 1925, despite the obiter dicta of Cross J. in *Poster* v. *Slough Estates Ltd.*[36] Even if these rights are not so protected they may possibly be overriding interests or bind a purchaser with notice under the doctrine that Equity will not permit a statute to be used as an instrument of fraud.[37] Again it is important for a purchaser to know of the existence of any such rights before he signs the contract.

Part (B) of Enquiry 8 was introduced in the wake of the House of Lords' decision in *Williams and Glyn's Bank Ltd.* v. *Boland*[38] where

---

[34] [1967] 2 Q.B. 379.
[35] [1976] Ch. 179.
[36] [1969] 1 Ch. 495.
[37] *Lyus* v. *Prowsa Developments Ltd.* [1982] 1 W.L.R. 1044.
[38] [1981] A.C. 487.

it was decided that the interest of a person who is in actual occupation and who has acquired a beneficial interest in a registered property (by contributing to the purchase money for example) is protected as an overriding interest and binds a purchaser "save where enquiry is made of such person and the rights are not disclosed."[39] It is important to note that the decision is not confined to spouses and can encompass a wide range of persons, hence the enquiry asks for details of anyone over 18 in occupation, other than the vendor and for the nature of their rights, if any, in the property. There has been no equivalent decision concerning unregistered land,[40] but it is highly likely that the same principle will be applied and that the purchaser will be bound by such an interest if he makes no enquiries under the doctrine of constructive notice.[41] It is, however, arguable that a person's presence on property sufficient to constitute "actual occupation" within section 70(1)(g) may not be sufficient to fix a purchaser with constructive notice. In a completely different context occupation of property at weekends and during holidays was sufficient to constitute "occupation"[42] for the purpose of entitlement to owner-occupier's supplementary compensation on the acquisition of an unfit house.[43] Would it be sufficient to fix a purchaser with constructive notice? If the enquiry reveals that there is a person in occupation who has or is likely to have acquired an interest in the property, then the purchaser's solicitor should ask that they be joined as a party to the contract of sale, or that a special condition be inserted into the draft contract, to the effect that the vendor will ensure that they sign a document releasing any rights that they have in the property and that such document will be delivered to the purchaser on or before completion. In the case of a spouse in occupation, it is also a convenient method of ensuring that the spouse does not register any rights of occupation after contracts are exchanged.

In registered land, conveyancers' problems with equitable interests are not confined to those illustrated by *Boland*. The cases show that the following interests when coupled with actual occupation are, *inter alia*, overriding interests; an option to purchase contained in a seven year lease[44] (which lease cannot be registered or noted on the register), a vendor's lien for unpaid purchase money where the vendor was in occupation of the property under a lease back to him,[45] the interest of a beneficiary under a bare trust,[46] and a right to have the register rectified.[47]

Part (C), although appearing last in Enquiry 8, is also of importance to

---

[39] Land Registration Act 1925, s.70(1)(g).

[40] The case of *Midland Bank Ltd.* v. *Farmpride Hatcheries Ltd.* (1981) 260 E.G. 493 could be regarded as such a case but it is submitted that it was wrongly decided. See R. E. Annand [1982] Conv. 67.

[41] Preserved by Law of Property Act 1925, s.199(1)(ii); *Hunt* v. *Luck* [1902] 1 Ch. 248.

[42] *Heron* v. *Sandwell Metropolitan B.C.* (1980) 255 E.G. 65. The case shows how inspection of the property may be insufficient in the case of registered land.

[43] Housing Act 1969, Sched. 5.

[44] *Webb* v. *Pollmount Ltd.* [1966] Ch. 584.

[45] *London and Cheshire Insurance Co. Ltd.* v. *Laplagrene Property Co. Ltd.* [1971] Ch. 499.

[46] *Hodgson* v. *Marks* [1971] Ch. 892.

[47] *Blacklocks* v. *J. B. Developments (Godalming) Ltd.* [1981] 3 W.L.R. 554.

a purchaser. This requires the vendor to disclose whether he is aware of any other overriding interests under section 70(1) of the Land Registration Act. Examples would be, legal easements and profits,[48] public rights, squatters' rights,[49] local land charges,[50-51] and short leases. Obviously Part (C) is only relevant in the case of registered land.

RESTRICTIONS

This enquiry will reveal whether there has been a breach of any restrictive covenant affecting the property. Sometimes where part of an estate is sold off, the original vendor's consent and approval of plans is necessary before building work can be carried out on that part. Enquiry 9 asks whether this is the case and for written evidence that consent or approval of plans has been obtained. A purchaser does not wish to be saddled with the task of later obtaining them himself.

PLANNING

We can again compare Enquiry 10 with Enquiries 1 and 5. Under an open contract of sale the vendor need not show that the existing use of the land is an authorised one or that any buildings have been erected in accordance with planning restrictions.[52] If it is important for a purchaser to have information on these matters, he must obtain it at this stage of the transaction. Enquiry 10 is designed to extract this information from the vendor and is sufficient in most cases of residential conveyancing. It asks when the present use of the property began and whether the use has been continuous since then and for details of any alterations or additions to the property (for example an extension) or other building operations during the past four years and whether any conditions attached to planning permissions have been complied with. It also requests the vendor to supply a copy of any planning permission for the present use and building.[53]

If the vendor's replies indicate that building operations have taken place on the property within the past four years, then the purchaser's solicitor should satisfy himself that the requisite permissions were obtained and their terms complied with. Where building work is carried out in breach of planning control a local authority can issue an enforcement notice (described fully in the next section) at any time until four years have elapsed from when the work was done,[54] and this is not prevented by a subsequent purchase of the property. At worst a purchaser may have to pull the building down.

In some transactions it may be necessary or useful to delve back into the property's planning history further than the past four years. The following are examples. A local authority does not lose its right to issue an enforcement notice by lapse of time if there has been any unauthorised

---

[48] These are usually unimportant as overriding interests as they are usually created by deed and noted on the register of title.

[49] *Re Chowood's Registered Land* [1933] Ch. 574.

[50-51] These would also be revealed by the purchaser's Local Land Charges Search Certificate.

[52] *Edler* v. *Auerbach* [1950] 1 K.B. 359. But see National Condition 15(3) and 3, and Law Society Condition 4.

[53] This follows a Council of the Law Society Opinion. See (1966) 63 L.S.Gaz. 21.

[54] Town and Country Planning Act 1971, s.87.

"material change of use" since 1963.[55] Thus where a property's use became authorised under the provisions of the Town and Country Planning Act 1947 (because this was its use on July 1, 1948) the exact nature of the use in 1948 must be ascertained to ensure that no "unlawful" change of use has occurred since 1963. This information will also be useful to the purchaser in determining how far he will be able to alter the nature of his user of the property without obtaining planning permission. The General Development Order 1977[56] permits certain increases in the size of a building without the need for planning permission. If the purchaser is hoping to extend the property, then he will need to ascertain the size of building for which the original permission was granted.

On rare occasions it may be necessary for the purchaser's solicitor to request copies of other documents, a caravan site licence or an industrial development certificate for instance.

FIXTURES, FITTINGS

The law relating to fixtures is vague and rarely litigated. Yet in practice the subject often generates a considerable amount of aggravation. Many solicitors will have had to placate angry purchasers complaining that their vendors have removed items from the house or garden. Enquiry 11 is designed to avoid this problem. The vendor is required to confirm that "removable" items at present on the property, such as garden sheds, T.V. aerials, power switches and shrubs are included in the sale. These items all lie on the fixture/chattel borderline. It will be remembered that a fixture is part of the land and so passes to the purchaser, whereas a chattel remains the vendor's personal property and he may take it with him. Further any fixture (kitchen units for example) not included in the sale must be listed and finally in the case of property with oil-fired central heating, the vendor is asked whether he intends to sell his remaining stock of oil to the purchaser.

A recent case which shows the care that must be taken when answering Enquiry 11 is *Hamp* v. *Bygrave*.[57] Included in the particulars of sale of a house for £150,000 were eight outside light fittings, five stone flower urns, a stone statue, a pond ornament and a lead garden trough. The purchaser made an offer of £130,000 which was refused. During subsequent negotiations it was suggested by the vendor that the sale price could be lowered if the garden ornaments were excluded from the sale. This idea was rejected. Eventually the parties agreed on a price of £147,500. The vendor's replies to Enquiries before Contract indicated that the ornaments were included in the sale,[58] but they were not mentioned in the contract itself. On taking possession the purchaser found that they had been removed and brought proceedings for their recovery. Boreham J. applying the twofold test for fixtures, purpose and degree of annexation, found that the ornaments were chattels. However, he said it was clear from the particulars, subsequent negotiations, and the Enquiries before Contract,

---

[55] *Ibid.* s.87(4).
[56] As amended.
[57] (1983) 266 E.G. 720.
[58] It was not stated that they were excluded.

that the vendor regarded them as included in the sale and as part of the land, and for this reason they were fixtures and passed to the purchaser. Alternatively he said that the vendor was estopped from denying that they were included in the sale.

OUTGOINGS

This asks for the rateable value of the property and whether any work has been carried out which might increase this, and whether any periodic payments have to be paid other than general and water rates. Ground rent would be an example. The purchaser will probably already know this information from the estate agent's particulars.

COMPLETION

This asks when completion will take place. In most cases the parties will have already agreed a date. Otherwise it is usually four weeks after exchange of contracts.

DEVELOPMENT LAND TAX

This is a very specialised question and will usually only be relevant in commercial transactions. Development Land Tax charges the development value of land to tax and leaves any other increase in value of the land to be subject to other taxes. If the purchaser is buying land situate in the United Kingdom from a non-resident vendor he is under a duty[59] to deduct 40 per cent.[60-62] of the consideration and send it to the Development Land Tax Office. "Development Land" is land which has the benefit of planning permission for material development which has not been started at the time of the disposal. "Material development" is basically any development within section 22(1) of the Town and Country Planning Act 1971, with certain exemptions, for example dwelling houses, and buildings on agricultural or forestry land which are to be used for that purpose.

No duty is cast on the purchaser if his normal searches do not show that the land is development land or if the *purchaser* is non-resident himself.

NEW PROPERTIES

Enquiry 15 is relevant to new properties only. It asks for information about the cost of linking the property to the main services and for details of responsibility for fencing boundaries, levelling and clearing the garden, and laying paths.

After Enquiry 15 there is a space on the form where the purchaser's solicitor may insert additional enquiries relevant to the particular transaction. Common enquiries include the following; that an apportionment of the price be made between chattels and the property (to lessen liability to stamp duty), that the interest rate specified in the draft contract be lowered, that a special condition be inserted in the draft contract that the vendor will make good any damage incurred in the removal of fixtures, and that the vendor confirm that the central heating is in good order. A few less common additional enquiries have already been mentioned. One

[59] Development Land Tax Act 1976, s.40.
[60-62] From August 6, 1983.

more could perhaps usefully be added. In the exceptional case of a solicitor acting for a purchaser buying vacant land with caravans on it, in addition to asking whether a site licence is required and, if so, whether it has been obtained and its terms, the vendor should be asked for details of those persons who have the right to park their caravans on the site. The Mobile Homes Act 1983 gives security of tenure to caravan "occupiers" comparable to that given by the Rent Acts.[63] This security of tenure does not depend on continuous occupation, so that inspection of the site will not necessarily bring an "occupier's" rights to light.

Leasehold Enquiries

Con.29 (Long) also contains five enquiries which are only relevant where the purchaser is buying leasehold property. Enquiry I is a general enquiry. It asks if the lease is a head lease or underlease. The reply to this enquiry could be important to a purchaser's solicitor in deciding the title he should stipulate for in the contract. Under an open contract for sale a purchaser of an underlease is not entitled to see the headlease[64] and although he is not bound by restrictions contained in the headlease,[65] he may find himself unwittingly implicated in forfeiture proceedings against the headlessee. The contract should therefore be worded so as to entitle the purchaser to see the headlease. Then details of the lessor and any superior lessors and their respective solicitors are requested together with copies of any licences obtained other than licences to assign. An example might be a licence by the lessor consenting to some alteration. Finally it is asked what steps have been taken to obtain the lessor's consent to the assignment (if necessary) and for the supply of a copy of any licence already granted. Where a lease prohibits assignment without the consent of the lessor, the purchaser lays himself open to forfeiture proceedings if he completes without such consent being obtained.

Enquiry II relates to covenants and asks whether the lessor has complained of any breach of covenant. It particularly asks whether the repair covenants have been complied with. The purchaser (or his solicitor) should ensure that the property is in a proper state of repair, for he may be compelled to do the work himself once he completes his purchase. If repair work has not been done, a special condition should be included in the contract requiring the vendor to remedy the situation before completion or a reduction in the purchase price should be agreed.

Enquiry III is a short question requiring details of service charges. Enquiry IV is about insurance. The reply to this question is particularly important where the lease contains a covenant that the lessee must insure with an insurance office approved by the lessor. The lessor can refuse his approval[66] even if the office is of good repute. Where the purchaser is buying with the aid of a mortgage, his mortgagee may also require him to insure at a certain office. If the two offices differ the purchaser's solicitors

---

[63] See T. M. Aldridge (1983) 127 S.J. 399.
[64] Law of Property Act 1925, s.44(3).
[65] *Ibid.* s.44(8)—unless he actually knows of them.
[66] *Tredegar (Lord)* v. *Harwood* [1929] A.C. 72.

should ask the mortgagee for his consent. Lastly Enquiry V asks if there is with the deeds a marked abstract or office copy of the freehold title or any superior lease. We have already seen why it is important for the purchaser to see any superior lease. It is also important to be able to investigate the freehold title as there may be restrictive covenants against it which could affect the purchaser's proposed enjoyment of the property. Under an open contract for a lease the lessee is not entitled to see the freehold title, so that these documents may well not be in the vendor's possession. If they are the purchaser should stipulate for a right in the draft contract to peruse them.

Again there follows a space for additional enquiries relevant to the purchase.

Buying Property Subject to Tenancies

The draft contract will normally state whether the sale is with vacant possession or subject to tenancies, particulars of which are given. If there is no express provision it is usually implied that the sale is with vacant possession. In any event occupation by a tenant may be notice to the purchaser of his rights,[67] in the case of unregistered property or in the case of property with registered title may be an overriding interest. Obviously the purchaser needs to have full details of the terms of any tenancies he is buying the property subject to and whether or not they have statutory protection, before he can decide whether to proceed with the purchase. Both the National and Law Society's Conditions of Sale envisage that copies or particulars of all leases and tenancies will be supplied to the purchaser before contracts are exchanged. In addition Oyez have produced a form of very comprehensive General Tenancy Enquiries (Con 291) which the purchaser's solicitor can submit along with his Enquiries before Contract. The first section contains a list of questions relevant to tenancies generally, requiring details of the tenant, the terms of the lease or tenancy agreement, rent, particulars of any underlease and so on. Section 2 then deals with business tenancies and the applicability of the Landlord and Tenant Act 1954.[68] Section 3 relates to residential tenancies and will elicit information as to whether the tenancy is a regulated tenancy or restricted contract or covered by the provisions of the Leasehold Reform Act 1967.[69] Additional enquiries will have to be drafted where the tenancy has been granted by a housing association or the Crown Estate Commissioners. Where the property is subject to an agricultural tenancy, form Con 292 should be used.

The Disclaimer

The Enquiries before Contract contain this disclaimer of responsibility:

> "These replies are given on behalf of the proposed vendor and without responsibility on the part of his solicitors their partners or

---

[67] *Hunt* v. *Luck* [1902] 1 Ch. 428.
[68] As amended by the Law of Property Act 1969.
[69] As amended by the Housing Act 1980.

employees. They are believed to be correct but their accuracy is not guaranteed and they do not obviate the need to make appropriate searches, enquiries and inspections."

The disclaimer consists of two parts each of which serve a different purpose. For the sake of clarity the second part will be commented on first.

"THEY (THE REPLIES) ARE BELIEVED TO BE CORRECT BUT THEIR ACCURACY IS NOT GUARANTEED AND THEY DO NOT OBVIATE THE NEED TO MAKE APPROPRIATE SEARCHES, ENQUIRIES AND INSPECTIONS"

This part of the disclaimer is aimed at relieving the *vendor* of liability for misrepresentation.

A misrepresentation is a false or misleading statement of fact, whether made fraudulently, negligently or innocently which induces someone to enter into a contract. At one time damages could only be obtained where the misrepresentation, was made fraudulently. For non-fraudulent misrepresentation rescission was the only remedy and it was generally too late if the contract had been completed by conveyance. After the Misrepresentation Act 1967, where a misrepresentation is made negligently (that is the representor has no reasonable grounds for believing it to be true) the purchaser has the choice of rescission or damages[70] even after conveyance. An innocent misrepresentation also entitles the purchaser to rescind the contract, but does not give him the alternative right to claim damages. The court can award damages in lieu of rescission in both aforementioned cases.

If the vendor, or his solicitor or other agent makes a misrepresentation, innocently or negligently, in his replies to the purchaser's Enquiries before Contract, for example regarding the existing of boundary disputes as in *Walker* v. *Boyle*,[71] how far will the disclaimer protect him against the purchaser's remedies for misrepresentation? The clause must be read in the light of section 3 of the Misrepresentation Act 1967 (substituted by section 8 of the Unfair Contract Terms Act 1977), which provides:

"If a contract contains a term which would exclude or restrict—

(*a*) any liability to which a party to a contract may be subject by reason of any misrepresentation made by him before the contract was made; or

(*b*) any remedy available to another party to the contract by reason of such misrepresentation that term shall be of no effect except in so far as it satisfies the requirement of reasonableness as stated in section 11(1) of the Unfair Contract Terms Act 1977. . . . "

It is for the vendor to show that the clause is reasonable. It has been argued that the disclaimer on Con 29 is not caught by section 3 as the preliminary enquiries are not part of the contract. This argument was effectively annihilated by Bridge L.J. in *Cremdean Properties Ltd.* v.

---

[70] The Misrepresentation Act 1967, s.2.
[71] [1982] 1 W.L.R. 495.

Nash[72] where he said of a similar disclaimer that if it was not contractual it could not help the vendor and if it was contractual it would offend section 3.[73]

Section 11(1) of the Unfair Contract Terms Act 1977 provides that "reasonableness" means that "the term shall have been a fair and reasonable one to be included, having regard to the circumstances which were, or ought reasonably to have been, known to or in the contemplation of the parties when the contract was made." It seems that there is no clear test of what is "fair and reasonable"[74] and that whether or not the disclaimer will protect the vendor will depend on the facts of each case.[75] It is clear, however, that liability for misrepresentation will not be avoided by this part of the disclaimer or any other exclusion clause, even though the accuracy of replies is not guaranteed, the purchaser is advised to make his own enquiries and the parties are both represented by solicitors using a common form clause.[76] The House of Lords[77] have recently said in connection with "fair and reasonable" that an appellate court should not interfere with an original decision unless "it proceeded upon some erroneous principle or was plainly and obviously wrong."

It is thought[78] that the words "so far as the vendor knows" are now unlikely to relieve the vendor of liability for misrepresentation despite the older authority of *Gilchester Properties* v. *Gomm*.[79]

One way a vendor could avoid liability would be "by channelling every statement through the disinfecting medium of (his) agent."[80] In *Overbrooke Estates Ltd.* v. *Glencombe Properties Ltd.*[81] it was held that it was permissible and not contrary to section 3 for a vendor, by means of sale particulars to limit the ostensible authority of his agent to make representations about the property being sold. However, as has been said, to allow this means "a veritable convoy of coach and fours can trundle through the 1967 statute."[82] The idea is unlikely to draw much favour from the profession.

What is clear in this area, is that the vendor's solicitor should ensure that any statements he or his client makes are accurate. Furthermore it may well be that losses suffered by others in the purchase and sale chain, of whom the vendor knows (perhaps even ought reasonably to have known of) might be recoverable from him as damages in negligence if the loss of his own sale through misrepresentation causes them to lose their contracts.[83]

---

[72] (1977) 244 E.G. 547.
[73] Discussed by H. W. Wilkinson (1978) 128 New L.J. 79.
[74] "Exemption clauses in land contracts," H. W. Wilkinson [1984] Conv. 12.
[75] *South Western General Property Co. Ltd.* v. *Marton* (1982) 263 E.G. 109.
[76] *Walker* v. *Boyle* [1982] 1 W.L.R. 495; and see K. Hodkinson [1982] Conv. 236.
[77] *George Mitchell (Chesterhall) Ltd.* v. *Finney Lock Seeds Ltd.*, [1983] 2 A.C. 803 and see R.T.H. Stone (1984) New L.J. 155.
[78] By the writers.
[79] [1948] 1 All E.R. 493.
[80] J. E. Adams [1981] Conv. 326 at 327.
[81] [1974] 1 W.L.R. 1335.
[82] J.E. Adams [1981] Conv. 326 at 327.
[83] *Wadsworth* v. *Lydall* [1981] 1 W.L.R. 598; T. M. Aldridge (1981) 125 S.J. 732.

Finally it should be noted that where it is the vendor's solicitor who makes a negligent misrepresentation, it is clear from the recent decision of *Resolute Maritime Inc.* v. *Nippon Kaiji Kyokai*[84] that the purchaser cannot sue the *solicitor* directly for damages under section 2 of the Misrepresentation Act. Of course the solicitor will be liable to his client if the purchaser rescinds the contract or recovers damages from the vendor. However, if the solicitor makes the misrepresentation innocently and the purchaser rescinds the contract, the vendor has no come back.

"THESE REPLIES ARE GIVEN ON BEHALF OF THE PROPOSED VENDOR AND WITHOUT RESPONSIBILITY ON THE PART OF HIS SOLICITORS THEIR PARTNERS OR EMPLOYEES"

This part of the disclaimer purports to shield the *vendor's solicitor* from liability in tort to the purchaser for negligent misstatements. The first point to note is that if the vendor's solicitor makes a reply fraudulently he will be liable to the purchaser in the tort of deceit.[85] Secondly if he has reasonable cause to believe his statement to be true he attracts no liability. Only where he has no such reasonable cause can he be guilty of negligence.

The clause was introduced into the disclaimer, on the advice of the Council of the Law Society, as a result of the decision in *Wilson* v. *Bloomfield*.[86] The purchaser was told, in replies to Enquiries before Contract that there were no boundary disputes. There were. The purchaser, *inter alia*, sued the vendor's solicitors for damages in negligence; they knew he would rely on their replies being accurate, they should have known of the boundary dispute and they therefore owed a duty of care to him. The solicitors were unsuccessful both at first instance and in the Court of Appeal in getting the claim against them struck out of the purchaser's action; he had an arguable point in law. The decision has led to the fear that a vendor's solicitor may be liable to a purchaser (even though represented by his own solicitor) in negligence if he knows or ought reasonably to have foreseen[87] that the purchaser would rely on his careless statement. Presumably this duty of care could be owed to others in the conveyancing chain.

Does the disclaimer effectively protect the vendor's solicitor? It is thought that it falls within the reasonableness test of section 2 of the Unfair Contract Terms Act 1977 because it is a notice purporting to exclude liability in negligence so it will depend on the circumstances of the case. Professor J. E. Adams feels that the clause is justified because "it seeks to avoid asking the solicitor to shoulder liability which should not fairly be his."[88] This is fair enough where the misstatement is made by the vendor himself in reply to a question on the form that is only within his knowledge. However, there are questions on Con 29 which only a solicitor

---

[84] [1983] 1 W.L.R. 857.
[85] *Derry* v. *Peek* (1889) 14 App.Cas. 337.
[86] (1979) 123 S.J. 860.
[87] *Anns* v. *Merton London Borough Council* [1977] 2 W.L.R. 1024 *per* Lord Wilberforce; followed in *J.E.B. Fasteners Ltd.* v. *Marks, Bloom & Co.* [1981] 3 All E.R. 289; and see T. I. Bailey (1982) 132 New L.J. 679.
[88] J.E. Adams [1982] Conv. 236.

can answer, for example Enquiry 8 (C), overriding interests. Furthermore, where a vendor's solicitor replies to preliminary enquiries himself, without referring them to his client, he cannot have reasonable grounds for believing his replies to be true and cannot use the disclaimer to cloak his fault.[89]

ENQUIRIES OF LOCAL AUTHORITIES

Introduction

The need for these enquiries is a direct result of the huge body of public legislation affecting private ownership of property. A vendor is under no duty to disclose to his purchaser the impact of this legislation on his property.

Each local authority has access to an enormous amount of this information. Only part of it is revealed by making a search of the register of local land charges as described in the previous chapter.[90] Matters not registrable as local land charges, for example the details of a scheme of registration for houses in multiple occupation[91] and the local authority's future proposals for the property will only be revealed by making direct enquiry of the appropriate local authority. The procedure for making these enquiries and the topics dealt with in them is outlined below.

Submitting the Enquiries

The enquiries are made by submitting a standard form questionnaire drawn up by the Law Society and the Associations of Local Authorities. This form should be sent in duplicate to the appropriate local authority along with the Requisition for Search and Official Certificate of Search of the register of local land charges. For district councils in England and Wales (excluding London) form Con 29A "Enquiries of District Councils" should be used. A special form, Con 29D, is used to obtain information from local authorities in London, the questions being in a slightly different form to cater for the special provisions which apply to the London area.

A new edition of the form was introduced in June 1982. This superseded the 1977 edition and has been revised to avoid, as far as possible, any overlap with the official search of the register of local land charges. Care should be taken to use the "1982 Edition" as enquiries submitted on old forms will not be answered. As an alternative to using the full forms (Con 29A and Con 29D consist of eight pages of questions) a single sheet form (Con 29AX or Con 29DX) can be used, which requests replies as though the full form had been submitted. In view of the possibility that something will be overlooked should the replies be read without direct reference to

---

[89] H. W. Wilkinson (1980) 130 New L.J. 1215.
[90] See *ante*, p. 17.
[91] See *post*, p. 92.

the actual enquiries themselves, forms Con 29A and Con 29D should be used if available.[92]

The form is divided into two parts. Part I contains the standard enquiries. These will be answered on payment of the fee which is currently £9·65p for one parcel of land. A further fee of £2·40p must be paid for each additional parcel.[93] Part II contains optional enquiries which will only be answered if the applicant initials the questions to indicate he wants a reply to those questions. A fee of 75p for each optional question answered is charged whether the enquiry relates to one parcel of land or more. A purchaser or his solicitor may ask "home made" questions but the local authority retains the right to refuse to answer such questions. Should they be willing to answer a fee of £1·80p per question is payable.

Whenever possible a plan of the property should be sent in duplicate to accompany the form. This will enable the local authority to identify the boundaries of the property and so give more accurate replies, for example as to whether any public path abuts on or crosses the property. In any case the local authority reserves the right to call for a plan in duplicate before furnishing replies. If a plan is to be sent with the request for a local land charges search the local authority will use this and no further plan is necessary.

In the panel on the front of the form the applicant should describe the property. As well as the road mentioned in the address of the property details of any roads, paths and footways over which the property has rights should be included, for example rear entrances. These details will be obtained from the draft contract.

As a matter of convenience the questions will be described by reference to their subject matter. The numbers of the questions are given in each case.

Roads and Paths

Part I—Enquiries 1 and 2
Part II—Enquiries I and II
When buying land a purchaser will want to know whether he will have to incur expense in maintaining or constructing a road or path which fronts the property or gives him access to it.

The highway authority, usually the county council,[94] is under a duty to keep a register of highways maintainable at the public expense.[95] The replies[96] will indicate whether all the roads and paths referred to in the panel on the front of the form are so maintainable. The highway authority will be responsible for the upkeep of roads and paths in the majority of cases.

If the roads and paths are not maintained at the public expense three

---

[92] See the comments in (1982) 126 S.J. 319 and 401.

[93] If the fee would exceed £100 an arrangement can be made with the local authority to fix the amount to be charged.

[94] Highways Act 1980, s.1.

[95] *Ibid.* s.36.

[96] Part I—Enquiry 1.

problems arise for the prospective purchaser. The first is whether or not the purchaser will have a right of way over the road or path. Enquiry 7 on form Con 29[97] will give the answer to this. Secondly, to what extent will he be asked to contribute towards the repair of the roads and paths? Again Enquiry 7 will give the reply. The third problem is the council's power by resolution under section 205 of the Highways Act 1980 to make up to their own satisfaction any road not "sewered, levelled, paved, metalled, flagged, channelled or made good and lighted" properly. Once any works have been executed the cost will be apportioned between the frontagers and becomes a charge on their property.[98] The replies will indicate whether such a resolution has been passed by the council.[99]

The council may also resolve to adopt a road or path as maintainable at the public expense without cost to the frontagers under section 37 of the Highways Act 1980. Usually this is done only if the road or path has been dedicated as a public highway, made up and satisfactorily maintained for a period of at least 12 months. Again in appropriate cases such a resolution would be revealed by Enquiry 1(B).

NEW HOUSING DEVELOPMENTS

Particular care must be taken over liability for the construction and maintenance of roads on newly built housing estates. Usually the builder will covenant with a purchaser to make up the roads on the estate at his own expense (the price of the house reflecting the cost to the builder). This covenant will not avail the purchaser if the builder subsequently goes into liquidation. Should this happen the council can make up the roads and charge the expense to the frontagers.

A purchaser should ensure that the builder has made an agreement with the council under section 38 of the Highways Act 1980 and that this is supported by a bond. The agreement usually details standards to be observed by the builder when constructing a new road and the period during which the builder must maintain the road in order to see if any faults in its construction develop. After this period that road is adopted without cost to the frontagers. A bond given by a bank, an insurance company or other institution will support the agreement in most cases. This allows purchasers to recover from the bondsman any expenses they incur as a result of the council making up the road. Note that the council cannot look directly to the bondsman but must recover its expenses from the frontagers. A footnote on the form reminds the enquirer that he should satisfy himself that the bond is adequate. Should it prove insufficient to cover the cost of making up the estate roads the frontagers, including any subsequent purchaser, would be liable for the shortfall. The value of a bond, given some years ago when the development began, may have been eroded by the effects of inflation and so further investigation may be required by a purchaser or his solicitor.

FUTURE PROPOSALS FOR ROAD CONSTRUCTION OR IMPROVEMENT

The purchaser having visited the property before deciding to purchase it

[97] See *ante*, p. 63.
[98] See *ante*, p. 9.
[99] As to the frontager's rights to object see the Highways Act 1980, s.228.

will be aware of the general layout of roads around the property. It is in his interests to find out whether there will be any significant change in the near future. If, for example, he is proposing to buy a cottage in the country to retire to he will want to know before exchange of contract whether a motorway is about to be built through his garden. Question 2 of Part I will show this. The reply will show whether proposals exist for the construction of any new roads, including plans by the Secretary of State to construct a new trunk road or motorway or to improve roads or construct subways, underpasses, flyovers, footbridges, elevated roads or dual carriageways. The information is limited in that it only relates to proposals involving work being carried out within 200 metres of the property. It would also show the impending compulsory acquisition of the property to build a new road.

An optional enquiry[1] also requests information regarding the stopping up or diversion of any of the roads referred to on the form. Under the Highways Act 1980 and the Town and Country Planning Act 1971 various provisions exist allowing a local authority, magistrates court or the Secretary of State to stop up or divert a road or path.[2] This may affect access to the property on a permanent or temporary basis, and the solicitor should inform his client immediately. An order under one of the above statutes does not affect any private right of way which may have been granted before the road or path was dedicated.[3]

Finally, on the subject of roads and paths if the purchaser is buying property in a rural area he may wish to know whether or not there is any public path crossing the property. Again an optional question[4] can be asked of the local authority requesting details of any path abutting on or crossing the property. Such path may be shown on a "definitive map and statement" prepared by the council under the Wildlife and Countryside Act 1981 or the National Parks and Access to the Countryside Act 1949. Evidence of a public path on such map is conclusive proof of the public's right to use the path. However, the absence of a map showing a path does not prove that no public right of way exists over the land. An owner of land crossed by a public path must not interfere with its enjoyment. For example he must not permit a bull to be at large in a field crossed by a path[5] or permanently plough up the surface of the path (with certain exceptions).[6]

Sewers

Part I—Enquiry 5
The importance of making adequate enquiries as to the status of and

---

[1] Part II—Enquiry II.
[2] See Town and Country Planning (Public Path Orders) Regulations 1983 (1983 S.I. 83/22), Public Path Orders and Extinguishment of Public Right of Way Orders Regulations 1983 (1983 S.I. 83/23).
[3] *Walsh* v. *Oates* [1953] 1 Q.B. 578.
[4] Part II—Enquiry I.
[5] Wildlife and Countryside Act 1981, s.59.
[6] *Ibid.* s.61.

liability to repair the sewers serving the property should not be overlooked.[7] If a sewer is private a heavy financial burden may be cast upon the purchaser who must contribute towards its repair and maintenance. Indeed, if the length of an enquiry is any measure of its importance this must be by far the most important matter dealt with on the form!

By way of introduction it may help the uninitiated to define a few terms. A "drain" is "an underground pipe or open channel for carrying off water, soil, etc. from one building or premises within the same curtilage into a cesspool or sewer."[8] A sewer is "any trench, channel or pipe through which water or sewage flows."[8] A public sewer is a sewer vested in a water authority[9] or occasionally a highway authority. A private sewer is one owned by one or more persons and serving their property, which leads usually, to a public sewer.

The reply should show the method by which both surface water and foul drainage is carried from the premises. If it is indicated that a private sewer serves the premises enquiry should be made of the vendor to establish the likely cost of its maintenance. It may be that surface water drains from the property into a public sewer owned by a highway authority (as opposed to the water authority).[10] Alternatively an agreement under section 38 of the Public Health Act 1936 may be disclosed. Under such agreement the local authority may require that two buildings (at present not connected to the mains) be drained in combination. A private sewer is constructed and the costs apportioned between the owners of the buildings and in some cases the authority itself.[11] Thereafter it is maintained at the expense of the two properties.

The council is asked whether it is aware of any agreement under section 18 of the 1936 Act for the adoption of a private sewer or drain. The agreement is made between a water authority and a builder of a new housing estate and the procedure is similar to the making of an agreement to adopt a road, described earlier.[12] If the council is not aware of any such agreement enquiry can be made of the water authority itself. Another point to watch in connection with the construction of new premises is the power given to the local authority to insist that the premises be drained into an existing public sewer, if there is one within 100 feet of the property, at a level such as to make the connection possible.[13] The expense of carrying out such works could be considerable.

Under provisions of the Public Health Acts 1936 and 1961 the water authority may recover certain expenses from the owners of premises served by one of its sewers. Under section 24 of the 1936 Act the cost of maintaining, renewing or improving a public sewer may be recovered if that sewer was on October 1, 1937;

---

[7] See Letters (1980) 77 L.S.Gaz. 600.

[8] Jowitts, *Dictionary of English Law* (2nd ed.).

[9] Public Health Act 1936, s.20 (as amended by the Water Act 1973, Sched. 8).

[10] *Ibid.* s.21(1)(*a*).

[11] Usually when the nearest possible connecting public sewer is more than 100 feet from the property.

[12] See *ante*, p. 75.

[13] Public Health Act 1936, s.37 (as amended by the Water Act 1973, Sched. 8.). This power does not apply to the Inner London area.

(a) vested in the local authority but lying under private premises,
(b) a combined drain (a drain serving several premises) which the local authority was not under a duty to maintain.

Sections 12 and 13 of the 1961 Act allow the water authority to reclaim the expense of constructing a public sewer in a highway maintainable at the public expense (or when a street is laid out on land under which there runs a public sewer). The presence of the public sewer must have increased the value of the properties fronting the highway before any apportionment of cost is made. The power to recover expenditure under section 12 and 13 of the 1961 Act is now exercised by the water authority. Should a negative reply to the question dealing with this matter be received from the council it may be thought appropriate to confirm the position with the relevant water authority itself.

Conservation

Part I—Enquiries 12, 13 and 16
Part II—Enquiries IV, V, VII, X

CONSERVATION AREAS

Every district council in performance of its functions as a local planning authority must consider whether any part of their area should be designated a conservation area.[14] Once created measures are taken by the planning authority to preserve the character and appearance of the area.

Designation of a conservation area has a number of consequences for anybody proposing to buy property in the area. Any building operations or change of use likely to affect the character and appearance of the area may be curtailed. Applications for planning permission relating to such development must be advertised by notice in the local press and on or near the site of the development itself. A period is then allowed for the public to make representations. One such notice in the Clifton area of Bristol related to the installation of two replacement windows and the alteration of a bathroom interior. That is not to say that all development in the area will be prohibited, but a purchaser who intends to buy a site for development within a conservation area would be well advised to seek planning permission before he enters into a binding contract. The demolition of buildings within the area is strictly controlled. No building can be demolished without first obtaining listed building consent (with certain exceptions, for example small buildings of less than 115 cubic metres).[15] However, consent to demolition may be granted especially if the retention of a building would detract from the appearance of the area in general or if the cost of refurbishing the building would be unduly high.[16] Special provisions may also exist within a conservation area as to the type of advertisement which may be displayed.

---

[14] Town and Country Planning Act 1971, s.277 (as substituted by the Town and Country Amenities Act 1974).
[15] Town and Country Planning Act 1971 s.277A (introduced by the Town and Country Amenities Act 1974).
[16] See (1983) 266 E.G. 894.

Conservation areas designated on or after August 31, 1974 are registrable as local land charges and will appear in the official certificate of search.[17] If the property is in a conservation area designated before that date it will be disclosed by the reply to Enquiry 12 (Part I).

LISTED BUILDINGS

A building may be listed as being of special architectural or historic interest.[18] The annual report of the Historic Buildings Council for England 1980/81 stated that as at March 31, 1981, 275,750 buildings had been listed. Whether or not a particular property has been listed will be revealed by the search of the local land charges register. Once listed it is an offence to alter the character of the building in any way without first obtaining listed building consent (in addition to any planning permission that may be required).[19]

A purchaser of a listed property will want to know whether any alterations made to the building by its owner were authorised by a listed building consent. There is an optional enquiry[20] which asks the local authority whether any listed building consents have been granted or refused in respect of the property. By checking these consents he will be able to assure himself that no breach of planning law has taken place.

Should a building of special architectural or historic interest be demolished or altered without consent, or in breach of a condition attached to a consent the local planning authority may serve a "listed building enforcement notice"[21] requiring that the building be restored to its former condition. Any such notice already served on the owner or occupier of the building will be revealed on searching the local land charges register. However, the replies on the form[22] given by the local authority will indicate whether or not they have *resolved* to serve such an enforcement notice in the near future and also whether any notice already served has been complied with. A purchaser may then be spared the expense or disappointment involved in having to comply with any listed building enforcement notice (the notice would be binding on him should he purchase the property).

If the owner of a listed building allows it to fall into a state of disrepair the local planning authority may serve him with a "repairs notice" under section 115 of the Town and Country Planning Act 1971. This will set out the works considered necessary by the local planning authority to put the building into a reasonable state of preservation. The local authority is asked[23] whether service of a notice has been authorised. Should one have been served in respect of the property the purchaser's solicitor should warn his client that this could be a first step towards compulsory

---

[17] Notice must also be given in the *London Gazette* and the local press.

[18] Town and Country Planning Act 1971, s.54. See also *ante*, p.12.

[19] *Ibid*. s.55. Also, if it is proposed to demolish a listed building, notice must be given to the Royal Commission on Historical Monuments.

[20] Part II—Enquiry IV.

[21] Town and Country Planning Act 1971, s.96 (as substituted by the Local Government and Planning (Amendment) Act 1981).

[22] Part II—Enquiry IV.

[23] Part II—Enquiry V.

acquisition of the property by the local authority. Under section 114 of the 1971 Act either the Secretary of State or a local authority may compulsorily acquire a listed building which has not been kept in a reasonable state of preservation provided that a repairs notice has been served at least two months before the initiation of the procedure to acquire. If, therefore, a repairs notice has been served a prospective purchaser will have to comply with the notice (or ensure his vendor does) or run the risk of losing the property altogether.

The council, as local planning authority, may already have authorised the making of a compulsory purchase order in respect of the property, if a repairs notice served some time ago on the vendor has not been complied with to their satisfaction. The information[24] given by a local authority to an applicant will disclose this and also whether it is intended to include in that compulsory purchase order a "direction for minimum compensation."

There are two bases of compensation for calculating the amount to be paid to the owner of a listed building which is being compulsorily acquired. Under the usual basis the compensation is assessed as either the site value of the property as it stands or the value of the site on the assumption that listed building consent would be granted for demolition or any other works, except where such development has been refused already or was granted subject to conditions.[25] The value of the site and the amount of the compensation may therefore be increased because these assumptions are made. However, where the owner of a listed building deliberately lets it fall into disrepair, for example to justify its demolition so that he may develop an adjoining plot of land, a direction for minimum compensation may be included in the compulsory purchase order. This brings the second basis of calculating the compensation payable to the owner of the building into operation. Again the amount payable may be equal to the bare site value of the property as it stands. Under this basis, however, it is assumed that the site has no development potential, that is that the only listed building consents which would be granted would be those for works to restore the building to a reasonable state of repair. The amount of compensation may not, therefore, be as high as it would have been had the "usual basis" been used. The basis of compensation might affect the purchaser's decision to buy the property.

A procedure exists to ensure that any building of special architectural or historic interest, although not included in a list prepared by the Secretary of State, is protected, whilst consideration is given to the question of whether to list it or not. Section 58 of the Act of 1971 provides that a "building preservation notice" may be served on the owner of a building or in cases of urgency affixed to the building itself. The building is then to all intents and purposes treated as if it were a listed building. The notice remains in force for six months or until the Secretary of State includes the building in a list prepared by him under section 54. If the notice lapses or it is decided not to list the building the local planning

---

[24] *Ibid.*

[25] In practice it is usually assumed that planning permission would be granted only for development within the terms of the Town and Country Planning Act 1971, Sched. 8.

authority is liable to pay compensation to the owner for loss suffered as a result of the building preservation notice being made.[26] This may consist for example of damages for breach of contract paid by the owner of a building to a developer who had to discontinue work. The replies[27] will reveal whether the council have authorised the service of a building preservation notice. A purchaser may not want to buy a property which will be listed in the very near future.

AREAS OF OUTSTANDING NATURAL BEAUTY

Under section 87 of the National Parks and Access to the Countryside Act 1949 the Countryside Commission may designate an area as one of outstanding natural beauty. This may be a preliminary step towards the creation of a national park if the area is not too small.

If the property is situated in a predominantly rural area an optional enquiry[28] may be asked as to whether an order under section 87 has been made. In such areas planning control may be stricter, in that the local planning authority may refuse planning permission to a development which detracts from the appearance of the area. For example, it may impose conditions on planning permissions for new houses that they be constructed out of a stone only to be found in that locality, which has been used for building in the area in the past. Special grants are available in these areas to those who undertake projects which enhance the natural beauty of the area.

POLLUTION CONTROL

The council may resolve to make an order declaring either a noise abatement zone or a smokeless zone.[29] In a noise abatement zone the owners of specific types of building may be required to keep the noise emanating from those buildings below a certain level. A register is kept of the required levels which may be inspected free of charge.[30] The replies[31] will show whether the property is within such an area and, if so, where the register may be inspected. Under section 65 of the Control of Pollution Act 1974 the local authority may give consent to the owner of a building within the zone allowing him to exceed the required noise level.

In a smokeless zone it is an offence to emit smoke from a chimney. Grants are available to help householders, etc., to adapt fireplaces to enable them to comply with the order. The order itself may contain exceptions and limitations allowing some smoke to be emitted from specified buildings. If the property is found to be within a smokeless zone the vendor should be asked to confirm that all heating appliances and so on comply with the order.

---

[26] Town and Country Planning Act 1971, s.173.
[27] Part I—Enquiry 13.
[28] Part II—Enquiry VII.
[29] Control of Pollution Act 1974, s.63 (Part II—Enquiry X) and Clean Air Act 1956, s.11 (Part I—Enquiry 16).
[30] Control of Pollution Act 1974, s.64.
[31] Part II—Enquiry X.

Urban Renewal

Part II—Enquiries XI, XII and XIII
The three optional enquiries referred to above all deal with special statutory provisions introduced within the last few years to rejuvenate the increasing number of industrial wastelands appearing over the country. How successful these measures will be time alone will tell.

The Secretary of State may designate an area by statutory instrument as an "urban development area."[32] For example, Merseyside and the London Docklands have already been designated urban development areas.[33] Once designation has taken place an urban development corporation (usually the local authority) is established whose job it is to secure the regeneration of the area. To achieve this the corporation may make grants and loans, for example to enable buildings to be brought into effective use or to encourage industry and commerce. The urban development corporation may also have delegated to it such functions as enforcing planning control or carrying out the work of the housing authority. A prospective purchaser of property within an urban development area may wish to enquire further as to any grants which may be available to him or alternatively seek the corporation's views as to a proposed development.[34]

Enterprise zones, basically small versions of urban development areas, may be designated by order of the Secretary of State.[35] By a general relaxation of many laws which discourage industrial growth and the provision of financial inducements it is hoped that such areas may be encouraged to develop. For example, no development land tax is payable and rates are generally not levied on industrial and commercial buildings. A positive reply to this question[36-37] may be of interest to a corporate purchaser intending to set up in business within such a zone.

A council may resolve to define an area as one which it wishes to improve, under section 4 of the Inner Urban Areas Act 1978. Once this has been done the council may then make loans and grants towards the improvement of buildings used for industrial or commercial purposes.

Planning Matters

Part I—Enquiries 4, 6, 7, 8, 9, 10 and 11
Part II—Enquiries III, VI and VIII

THE STRUCTURE PLAN

A structure plan is a document, consisting of a written statement, illustrated by maps and diagrams, prepared by a county council and approved by the Secretary of State. It sets out in very broad terms the

---

[32] Local Government, Planning and Land Act 1980, s.134.
[33] See, *e.g.* (S.I. 1981 No. 560).
[34] Part II—Enquiry XI.
[35] Local Government, Planning and Land Act 1980, Sched. 32.
[36-37] Part II—Enquiry XII.

general planning policy which will be followed in the future for the area. For example, the plan would indicate proposals to encourage developments which added to the recreational facilities or the stock of housing resources in the area. The future planning policy towards such matters as the transportation network, the establishment of new shopping centres and the expansion of industry for the locality would be dealt with in the plan.

The structure plan is supplemented by a series of local plans prepared usually by the district councils for the area covered by the structure plan. The local plans relate to precise areas of land and elaborate the broad policies and proposals contained in the structure plan. Whereas a structure plan may relate to an area spanning two counties, a local plan may cover only part of a district. The local plan contains more detail than its larger counterpart and would for instance identify the primary use to which an area of land is to be put.

The two types of plan described above are gradually replacing what used to be known as "development plans," except in London where the Greater London Council still prepares a development plan. In some areas, however, the old style (development) plans are still in force and the enquiries[38] are drafted to take account of this fact.

The preparation of all these types of plan involves surveys being carried out, draft plans being prepared and copies being made available to the public, so that they may make their views known to the planning authorities. The procedure is very lengthy and all the plans are subject to constant revision.

The information[39] furnished by the local authority will include the following; the stage reached in the preparation of each type of plan, whether any proposals to alter an approved plan have been made public, and in the case of local and development plans whether the area which includes the property has been allocated a primary use, such as residential or industrial.

The long term planning policy for an area is unlikely to be of great importance to the purchaser of a dwelling-house who will prefer to rely on his own knowledge of the local environment. However, a property developer or commercial client may wish to inspect the structure or local plans for an area in detail. Local planning authorities will usually be more than willing to make copies of the plans available and answer any further enquiries which may arise.

Sometimes a planning proposal implies that land is going to be compulsorily acquired in the future. If this happens the land in question becomes difficult to sell at a worthwhile price. This is known as "planning blight." Generally speaking the owner of blighted land may serve a purchase notice on the local authority or other body likely to acquire the property.[40] The notice requires the local authority or other body to take

---

[38] Part I—Enquiry 7.

[39] *Ibid.*

[40] See Town and Country Planning Act 1971, ss.192 and 193; and A. E. Telling, *Planning Law and Procedure* (6th ed.), pp. 168–174.

the land from the owner as though proceedings had already been started to purchase the land compulsorily.[41]

A purchase notice may be served in respect of land falling within one of the categories specified in section 71 of the Land Compensation Act 1973. This is land which has been set aside by either the local authority or Secretary of State as possibly required for the purposes of any government department, local authority or statutory undertaker. The replies[42] will disclose whether or not the property which the purchaser intends to buy falls within these categories. The purchaser is thereby warned that he may be taking a blighted property which may be difficult to sell in the future.

PLANNING PERMISSIONS

A full explanation of the need for planning permission and the procedure involved in applying for it is outside the scope of this book.[43] It is enough for our purposes at present to understand that if any building or other operations or any material change of use is to be carried out on the property, planning permission may be needed.

Under section 34 of the Town and Country Planning Act 1971, every local planning authority must keep a register of planning applications and decisions. The information contained in the register will be of interest to a prospective purchaser for two reasons. First, it will reveal the local planning authority's attitude towards the development and use of the property. Secondly, and perhaps more importantly, it will allow the purchaser to assess the development potential of the site more realistically. Answers to Enquiry 11, Part I will reveal any entries in the register relating to the property and where the register can be inspected, usually the district council's offices. The register itself is divided into two parts. Part One contains details of all pending applications for planning permission together with any plans and drawings which may have been submitted. Part Two relates to applications[44] which have already been determined, and in addition to any relevant plans and drawings, shows the date the decision to grant or refuse permission was taken.

Although the enquiries of the local authority will only reveal entries relating to the property in question, the register, which is open to inspection free of charge, may contain valuable information as to the proposed future development of neighbouring land. By making a search of the register in respect of neighbouring land a purchaser may be forewarned of any future development which could have an adverse effect on his enjoyment of the property he proposes to buy.

The entries in the register will only reveal details of development where an express application for planning permission had to be made. The General Development Order 1977[45] obviates the need to make an express application for planning permission in a large number of cases. For

---

[41] The local authority have the right to refuse to take the land in certain circumstances.

[42] Part I—Enquiry 7.

[43] See E. Telling, Planning Law and Procedure (6th ed.).

[44] Including applications for a determination under the Town and Country Planning Act 1971, s.53.

[45] Town and Country Planning General Development Order 1977 (S.I. 1977 No. 289) as amended, art. 3.

example class I of that order permits the enlargement, improvement or other alteration of a dwelling-house so long as the cubic content of the original dwelling-house is not exceeded by 70 cubic metres or 15 per cent. (in the case of a terraced house the limits are respectively 50 cubic metres and 10 per cent.). There are several important restrictions on the nature of the alterations which can be made, relating to the height of the original building and the area of curtilage covered by any buildings already on the property.[46] Twenty-two other classes permit various types of development to be carried out without obtaining express planning permission. Existing industrial buildings may be added to,[47] certain changes of use are permitted[48] and the erection of fences and walls is allowed provided they do not exceed two metres in height.[49] Reference should be made to the order itself in any particular case, to find out the restrictions and limitations imposed on the proposed development.

In some areas the benefit of having a "deemed" planning permission under the General Development Order 1977 has been withdrawn. Article 4 of the order empowers the Secretary of State or local planning authority to direct that the provisions of the General Development Order shall not apply either to a specified area, for example a conservation area, or to a particular case. Such directions are commonly referred to as "Article 4 directions."

The effect of such a direction is to withdraw the permission granted by the General Development Order and restore the need to apply for planning permission for *any development*. Obviously a purchaser who was intending to extend the property would wish to know whether an "Article 4 direction" had been made which affected the property. The replies[50] to the Enquiries of the District Council will tell him whether the council has resolved to make such a direction thus making him aware that he may need to apply for planning permission to build his extension in the future.

Once granted, a planning permission (including one granted by the General Development Order) attaches to the land for its benefit, subject to any conditions in the permission. However, the local planning authority may make an order either revoking or modifying a permission already granted as long as the development in question has not been completed.[51] A similar order may be made where the development has been completed, requiring the discontinuance of a lawful use of property or the alteration or demolition of lawfully erected buildings.[52]

Compensation is payable to the owner of the land in either case[53] and if after the order has been made the land is not capable of reasonably

---

[46] See *North-West Leicester D.C.* v. *Secretary of State for the Environment* (1984) 4 Property Law Bulletin 59.

[47] Class VIII General Development Order 1977.

[48] *Ibid.* Class III.

[49] *Ibid.* Class II: one metre in the case of a wall or fence which abuts onto a road.

[50] Part I—Enquiry 8.

[51] Town and Country Planning Act 1971, s.45; such an order must be confirmed by the Secretary of State.

[52] *Ibid.* s.51; again confirmation by the Secretary of State is needed.

[53] *Ibid.* ss.164 and 170.

beneficial use, the owner may serve a purchase notice on the council requiring them to take the land.[54] The amount of the compensation will be calculated having regard to any depreciation in the value of the land, any loss of rights by the owner and any expenditure incurred by him in reliance on a planning permission before it was revoked or modified.

Enquiry 9, Part I asks whether the local authority has resolved to make any order such as those described above. The same enquiry also asks if a tree preservation order[55] is to be made which will affect the property. This order once made is a local land charge and will be disclosed by the official certificate of search. The order makes it an offence to cut, top, lop or wilfully destroy any tree covered by it and may also provide for the replanting of trees felled in the course of forestry operations allowed by it. It is not an offence to cut or otherwise destroy the tree if it is dead or dying, in a dangerous state, or the consent of the local planning authority has been obtained in advance.

COMPLETION, ENFORCEMENT AND STOP NOTICES

Occasionally an authorised development is started, but the builder involved then does nothing for some considerable period of time. The result can be the creation of an eyesore and the tying up of valuable development-ripe land. If this happens the local planning authority may serve a "completion notice" under section 44 of the 1971 Act. The notice will state that any planning permission relating to the uncompleted development will cease to have effect, if the project is not finished within the specified period (which must be at least a year). Should the builder not comply with the notice the local planning authority may ask the Secretary of State to confirm it and so bring it into effect. Before he does this the Secretary of State will give both the person upon whom the notice was served and the local planning authority involved an opportunity of appearing at a public inquiry.

An optional enquiry[56] will reveal whether the council have resolved to serve a completion notice and thereby terminate any existing planning permissions pertaining to the property. A positive reply to this question could spell disaster for a purchaser intending to buy land with the benefit of a planning permission in order to develop it.

Where there has been a breach of planning control the local planning authority may issue an "enforcement notice" under section 87 of the 1971 Act. A breach occurs if any development is carried out contrary to any condition in a planning permission or without obtaining permission at all. If the breach involves a material change of use the enforcement notice may be issued at any time after the breach has taken place. An enforcement notice relating to unlawful building or other operations may only be issued within four years of the breach having occurred.[57]

---

[54] *Ibid.* s.188.

[55] *Ibid.* s.60.

[56] Part II—Enquiry VI.

[57] Exceptionally the four year rule also applies in the case of an unauthorised change of use of a building, to use as a single dwelling-house.

A copy of the notice must be served on the owner or occupier of the land and any other person having an interest in the land who would be materially affected.[58] The notice must state the following matters; first, the alleged breach of planning control; secondly, the steps to be taken to remedy the breach, for example the demolition of a building; thirdly, the date on which the notice is to take effect; fourthly, the period, beginning with the date on which the notice takes effect, for complying with the steps required to be taken to remedy the breach.

Failure to comply with an enforcement notice is a criminal offence.[59] It can also lead to the local planning authority exercising its powers to enter onto the land and carry out any remedial works itself. The expense of these works is then recoverable from the current owner of the land whether he is responsible for the unauthorised development or not.

It is important that an intending purchaser is aware of any enforcement notice affecting the land he is to buy. If he completes his purchase and the vendor fails to comply with an enforcement notice he may be named as a party in any proceedings taken against the vendor.[60] Similarly he may himself be guilty of an offence if he uses the land (or permits it to be used) in contravention of an enforcement notice prohibiting an unauthorised change of use.

Enforcement notices issued by a local planning authority were formerly registrable as local land charges. However, such notices issued or served on or after November 27, 1981 are more likely to appear in the register of enforcement and stop notices kept by the local planning authority under section 92A of the 1971 Act.[61] The register contains all the information included in the notice itself and in addition the date on which the local planning authority became satisfied that the notice had been complied with.[62]

The applicant will be told[63] if any enforcement notice has been authorised for issue or service by the local planning authority. If the notice was issued after November 27, 1981 he will also be told of any entries in the register and where that register can be inspected. In appropriate cases the fact that the enforcement notice has been complied with will also be disclosed.

If an enforcement notice relating to the property is disclosed whether in the official certificate of search or in the replies to the enquiries, it is imperative that details of the notice be given to the purchaser. These details will have already been requested from the vendor on form Con 29. The purchaser should be informed that if he completes he must be prepared to comply with the notice which could prove expensive and inconvenient. In the last resort a search of the register should be made to obtain details of the works necessary to restore the land to its original state. The register will usually be kept available for inspection (free of charge) at the district councils planning offices.

---

[58] Town and Country Planning Act 1971, s.87(5).
[59] *Ibid.* s.90, and see C.M. Brand and D.W. Williams (1983) 80 L.S. Gaz. 1471.
[60] *Ibid.* s.89.
[61] Added by the Local Government and Planning (Amendment) Act 1981, s.1.
[62] S.I. 1981 No. 1569.
[63] Part I—Enquiry 6.

Sometimes a person upon whom an enforcement notice has been served may appeal against its issue to the Secretary of State.[64] The lodging of an appeal suspends the operation of an enforcement notice until the validity of the notice is finally determined. During the period of appeal it would therefore be possible for operations to be carried out on the land which would later be declared unlawful. To prevent this the local planning authority may serve a "stop notice."[65] The stop notice prevents the continuance of operations pending the outcome of the appeal against the enforcement notice.

A stop notice can only be served after the issue of an enforcement notice. It may only be used to prevent an activity complained of in that enforcement notice. It can be served upon the owner, occupier or any other person interested in the land and in addition upon any person carrying out the activity complained of. For example, the owner of a site may be served or a contractor employed by the owner to build a house in breach of planning law. In cases of real urgency a stop notice can even be put up in a prominent position on the site to which it relates.[66]

Again failure to comply with a stop notice is an offence. However, if the enforcement notice is quashed on appeal (or withdrawn earlier) the local planning authority may be liable to pay compensation to owners and occupiers of the land for any loss attributable to that notice.[67] Commonly this will include paying an owner of land compensation for damages he has been forced to pay a contractor, because the service of the stop notice made it impossible to carry out their contract.

The replies[68] will reveal whether the council have authorised the issue of a stop notice in addition to any enforcement notice. A search of the register of enforcement and stop notices may again be appropriate should the purchaser's land be affected and details not be available from the vendor.

COMPENSATION PAYABLE UNDER SECTION 169 OF THE TOWN AND COUNTRY PLANNING ACT 1971

Compensation is payable under this section when the Secretary of State refuses planning permission (or grants it subject to conditions) for development which falls within Part II of Schedule 8 to the Act of 1971. This the Secretary of State may do either on appeal to him by an applicant refused planning permission by his local planning authority, or under section 35 of the Act which allows him to "call in" applications for planning permission to decide the matter in the first instance.

The type of development within Part II of Schedule 8 may broadly be described as development incidental to the existing use of the land. For example, the owners of a block of flats (existing use residential) may wish to add a storey to the building. If planning permission was refused on appeal by the Secretary of State (or granted subject to conditions) the

---

[64] See C.M. Brand and D.W. Williams (1984) 81 L.S. Gaz. 26; and I. Gatenby (1983) L.S. Gaz. 1706.

[65] Town and Country Planning Act 1971, s.90.

[66] *Ibid.* s.90(5).

[67] *Ibid.* s.177.

[68] Part I—Enquiry 6.

owners would be able to claim compensation from the local planning authority.[69]

The amount of compensation payable under section 169 is the difference between the value of the land with planning permission for the development and the value without the permission.[70] It must be emphasised that compensation, although payable by the local planning authority, is not given under the section for a refusal of planning permission by the authority even if the development falls within Part II of Schedule 8.

Once compensation has been paid under section 169 in respect of a refusal of planning permission further compensation will not be paid to a subsequent owner of the land, who makes a similar application which is refused. However, should a subsequent owner of the land successfully apply for planning permission he will not be under an obligation to repay any of the compensation received by his predecessor.

The local authority will disclose details of any compensation already paid under the section.[71] Apart from the fact that no further compensation will be paid in respect of a refusal for similar development, the purchaser should be advised that on a subsequent compulsory purchase of the property the compensation then payable may be reduced to take account of a payment already made under section 169.[72]

ADVERTISING CONTROL

The consent of the local planning authority is now required for the display of any outdoor advertisement. The definition of advertisement in section 290 of the 1971 Act is couched in extremely wide terms. It will cover virtually any device used to convey information to the public at large. A trade name painted over the window of a shop is clearly covered as are doorplates and posters advertising consumer products.

The Control of Advertisements Regulations 1969[73] as amended and consolidated by the Town and Country Planning (Control of Advertisements) Regulations 1984[73a] contain the relevant law on the subject. Regulation 3 exempts the following from the regime of control; advertisements on enclosed land not readily visible to the public, advertisements on vehicles or articles for sale, advertisements forming part of the fabric of the building, and those displayed inside a building unless visible from the outside.

The local planning authority is not to act as a censor in relation to advertising carried out within its area. When considering whether to give consent regard should only be given to matters of public safety and amenity. For example a large advertisement on a balloon carrying a picture of a scantily clad female (or male) could not be refused consent solely on the ground that it was contrary to the moral views of the members of the planning authority. It could be refused consent however

---

[69] *Peaktop Properties Hampstead Ltd.* v. *Camden L.B.C.* [1982] J.P.L. 453, now affirmed on the question of eligibility within s.169 by the Court of Appeal.

[70] Town and Country Planning Act 1971, s.169(2).

[71] Part I—Enquiry 10.

[72] Land Compensation Act 1961, s.15.

[73] S.I. 1969 No. 1532.

[73a] S.I. 1984 No. 421.

if it was thought that it would be such a distraction to motorists in the area as to be a danger to public safety. It might also be possible to refuse consent on the ground that the balloon introduced alien commercial features into an otherwise serene and rural area.[74]

It is an offence to display an advertisement without first obtaining any required consent,[75] punishable by a fine of up to £200, and £20 for each day the breach of the regulations continues.

A register of applications for consent to display advertisements is kept by the local authority in a similar form to that pertaining to applications for planning permission.[76] This register is open to inspection free of charge.

The replies[77] will indicate whether any entry in the register has been made which affects the property. If there should be an entry, the register should be inspected to ascertain the exact details of any consent. This matter will be of especial importance to a commercial client or purchaser intending to use premises for the purposes of his business. Purchasers of this nature will be eager to know the extent to which they can advertise.

The enquiries[78] also ask for information on a number of other matters relating to advertising control. Regulation 14 allows certain advertisements to be displayed without consent. These may then be challenged by the local planning authority who can require their removal. Such advertisements include professional nameplates, church notice boards and temporary advertisements with regard to the sale or letting of premises. Under regulation 16 the local authority may serve a discontinuance notice requiring the removal of an advertisement displayed by virtue of a deemed consent under the Regulations. Again the replies would reveal an intention of the council to authorise service of such a notice in the near future.[79] Compliance with the notice will be disclosed in appropriate cases unless this would necessitate an inspection being carried out by the council's agents. Under regulation 15 the Secretary of State may direct that the provisions of regulation 14 shall no longer apply to a property. This is similar to the "Article 4 direction" described earlier. Any such direction would be revealed by the enquiries[80] of the local authority.

Regulation 26 provides that the local planning authority, with the approval of the Secretary of State, may designate an area as one of special control. In such areas the local planning authority can only grant consent to the display of certain types of advertisement. These consist of notices relating to certain local activities, for example a summer fête, signposts to nearby buildings, for example public conveniences, advertisements promoting public safety and permitted advertisements under regulation 14.[81] The replies will indicate whether the council has resolved to make an order

---

[74] But see Civil Aviation (Aerial Advertising) Regulations 1983. S.I. 83/1885, and also reg. 3(1)(d).

[75] S.I. 1984 No. 421, reg. 8.

[76] *Ibid.* reg. 31.

[77] Part II—Enquiry III.   [78] Part II—Enquiry III(c).

[79] A notice already served would appear on the official certificate of search of the local land charges register.

[80] Part II—Enquiry III(c).

[81] Advertisements within reg. 14 will still not require express consent in an area of special control.

defining the area in which the property is situate, as an area of special control.

PIPELINES

Enquiry 8 in Part II asks if any map has been deposited under section 35 of the Pipelines Act 1962 or section 39 of the Gas Act 1972 showing a pipeline within one hundred feet of the property. Maps will be deposited pursuant to these provisions when it is proposed to construct or divert a pipeline.

The maps only give an indication as to the route to be taken by the pipeline, they do not show its exact location on the property.

Before any construction work is commenced on surface land within 10 feet of a pipeline, the consent of the Secretary of State must be obtained. Any building erected in default may be required to be demolished, if it is not possible to execute other works to safeguard the pipeline.[82] The Secretary of State may also order that any such building be vacated beforehand.

Clearly if a positive reply is received to this enquiry steps need to be taken to ensure that the purchaser is aware of the need to obtain consent before he begins to build or add to the property. The authority which owns the pipeline will have to be contacted, if the exact location of the pipeline is to be ascertained.

If this question is to be asked of the local authority it is essential that a plan be sent with the form to enable them to give as accurate replies as possible.

BUILDING REGULATIONS

The local authority is asked if it has authorised any proceedings in respect of an infringement of the Building Regulations.[83] These Regulations set down minimum standards to be complied with when constructing a new building or making any alteration or improvement to a new one. A full discussion of the provisions contained in the Regulations is outside the scope of this book. However, standards are laid down as to such matters as damp-proofing, the depth of foundations and materials used in the construction of buildings. For example a recent addition to the Regulations, controls the use of formaldehyde in cavity wall insulation because it can, under certain conditions, produce noxious fumes.[84] Contravention of the Regulations constitutes a criminal offence and it is obviously in a purchaser's interests to find out if proceedings have been started in respect of the property before contracts are exchanged. If he completes the purchase he will have to remedy the breach of the Regulations if his vendor has not done so, and this may prove expensive.

Compulsory Registration of Title

Part I—Enquiry 18
The local authority will tell the purchaser whether the property is in an

---

[82] Pipe-lines Act 1962, s.27.
[83] In the Inner London boroughs the Building Regulations are replaced by the London Building Acts.
[84] Building (3rd Amendment) Regulations 1983 (S.I. 1983 No. 195).

area where registration of title is compulsory and if so the date upon which the registration of title in the area became compulsory. This information should already have been obtained by a purchaser's solicitor by completing a search of the Public Index Map on form 96.[85]

Rates

Part I—Enquiry 17
The levying of general rates is regarded as a tax on the occupation of premises. For this reason no rates are charged where property is unoccupied. However, it is socially undesirable that property should be left unoccupied for prolonged periods. To discourage what may somewhat loosely be termed the "Centrepoint phenomena" a rating authority may resolve, under Schedule 1 to the General Rate Act 1967, to levy rates on unoccupied premises.

The replies will indicate whether such a resolution has been passed, the date it became effective, and the categories of property affected. When Schedule 1 is in force, premises which have been unoccupied for more than three months are charged to rates, usually at 50 per cent. of the full rate. The rates so payable become the liability of the person entitled to occupy the premises, usually the owner.

Similar provisions apply in London under various statutes[86] although a tenant entitled to possession is allowed to deduct any rates payable under these provisions from the rent he pays to the owner of the building.

Housing and Related Matters

Part I—Enquiries 3 and 15
Part II—Enquiry IX
Houses in multiple occupation may be required to register with the local authority for the area.[87] A local authority may refuse to register such a house on the grounds that it is not in a fit state or the person having control of the house is not a fit and proper person.[88]

A house is in multiple occupation when it is lived in by the members of more than one family. It is usually lodging-houses and hostels which are required to register. The basic amenities in such houses (water supply, drainage, gas and electricity, lighting and heating) must conform to a minimum standard. The local authority may also require the person in control of the house to provide adequate fire escapes, proper storage for refuse and to keep the common parts of the house clean and free from obstruction. Grants may be made to bring a property up to standard.

The replies will indicate whether the property has been registered under these provisions. If a purchaser intends to use the property in the future

---

[85] See *ante*, p. 15.
[86] City of London Sewers Act 1848 and 1851; City of London (Union of Parishes Act) 1907.
[87] Housing Act 1961, s.22(1).
[88] Housing Act 1969, s.64(4), control provisions.

for multiple occupation he should enquire further of the council whether registration will be necessary.

Enquiry 15 asks the council if the property is in either a slum clearance area or a General Improvement Area.

If the property is in a slum clearance area it is highly likely that at some time in the future the council will compulsorily acquire the property. This it must do before it decides to demolish the property and redevelop the site. The purchaser's interest in discovering whether the property is in a slum clearance area is obvious. Furthermore he would not be granted a mortgage advance.

A General Improvement Area is declared under section 28 of the Housing Act 1969. These are areas of poor housing where the council has shown a commitment to rehabilitation. Various powers allow the council to make grants to encourage owners of houses within the area to improve their properties. For example a grant may be made to help a home owner to install a fixed bath or shower in his house. Compulsory purchase powers may also be used by the council in such areas to acquire property which is in a serious state of disrepair.

Finally on this subject Part I contains a question [89–92] asking the council if there are any outstanding statutory or informal notices which have been issued by the council in relation to the property under the Public Health, Housing or Highways Acts. The kind of notice disclosed by this enquiry will vary from region to region along with the particular *modus operandi* of each council. However, the sorts of things which will be revealed may include the following; informal notices requiring the abatement of a statutory nuisance (for example defective guttering), compulsory repair notices under the Housing Acts, notices prescribing improvement lines where development is taking place along a highway[93] and informal notices relating to road widening schemes. Note that it is only notices issued under the aforementioned Acts which the council is asked to reveal. If the purchaser or his solicitor is aware of any other provision which may affect the property he should consider adding an additional enquiry.

Compulsory Acquisition

Part I—Enquiry 14
This enquiry will reveal any proposals by the council still capable of implementation to compulsorily acquire the property. A positive reply to this enquiry will put an end to most conveyancing transactions especially those involving residential properties. A full discussion of the statutes which authorise a local authority to purchase land compulsorily is outside the scope of this book and reference should be made to other works.[94]

The Local Authority's Liability for Negligent Replies

Headnote (3) on the front of the form reads as follows:

[89–92] Part I—Enquiry 3.
[93] Highways Act 1980, s.188.
[94] Davies, *Law of Compulsory Purchase and Compensation.*

"The replies below are furnished after appropriate enquiries and in the belief that they are in accordance with the information at present available to the officers of the respective councils but on the distinct understanding that neither the District Council nor the County Council, nor any officer of either council, is legally responsible therefor, except for negligence. Any such liability for negligence shall extend . . . to a person (being a purchaser for the purposes of s.10(3) of the Local Land Charges Act 1975) who or whose agent had knowledge . . . of the Replies to these Enquiries."

This disclaimer was introduced after the case of *Coats Patons (Retail) Ltd.* v. *Birmingham Corpn.*[95] In that case the defendant corporation had approved the construction of a subway for pedestrians opposite a shop, which the plaintiff company proposed to purchase. In the course of their precontractual enquiries the plaintiff submitted a form of enquiry to the corporation. One question on the form asked whether any proposals had been approved by the corporation for the construction of a subway or underpass within the highway immediately opposite the property. A clerk answered this question incorrectly, without making appropriate enquiries within the corporation, and the plaintiffs suffered loss as a result. The disclaimer on the form read as above without the words "except for negligence." It was held that the defendants were liable in tort for negligently failing to take reasonable care in answering the enquiry. The disclaimer failed to protect them if they did not make appropriate enquiries. In the aftermath of the case many local authorities tried to disclaim any legal responsibility whatsoever for the replies furnished in response to the Enquiries. Clearly this position was intolerable and after negotiations between the Council of the Law Society and the Associations of Local Authorities the present disclaimer was agreed upon.

The authority will be liable in tort. It will also be liable in contract as a fee is payable for the enquiries. This could make a difference to the limitation[96] period governing any cause of action which may accrue against the local authority. If the suit is brought in contract the six year time limit runs from the date of the breach, that is the date the replies are given. If the action is brought in negligence the six years will run from the date the damage occurs which could be considerably later. It would seem that the exclusion clause would be subject to the reasonableness test contained in section 3 of the Misrepresentation Act 1967.[97]

Liability to prospective purchasers is admitted to the same extent as liability for defective searches of the register of local land charges.[98]

Finally headnote (4) points out that "so far as the Replies may relate to proposals they may yet change." This limitation on the value of any replies given must be appreciated. As with local land charges an element of arbitrariness is introduced in that replies given today may be radically different from those which would be given tomorrow.

---

[95] (1971) 115 S.J. 757.
[96] Limitation Act 1980.
[97] As amended by the Unfair Contract Terms Act 1977, s.8.
[98] See *ante*, p. 15.

PERSONAL INSPECTIONS

In the preceding sections we have explained when and why certain personal inspections may have to be made by the purchaser and/or his solicitor, before contracts are exchanged. Here is a checklist of those inspections.

I. INSPECTING THE PROPERTY

What to Look for	Why
(A) RESIDENTIAL PROPERTIES	
(i) Persons (over 18) in occupation. Primarily members of vendor's family especially spouses. Also look for tenants and squatters and contractual licencees, *e.g.* mistresses[99] and old ladies.[1]	(i) (a) Unregistered land; interest may bind purchaser with notice (actual, imputed or constructive). (b) Registered land, interest could constitute an overriding interest within section 70(1) of the Land Registration Act 1925.
Note: In this case inspection is important up until the purchaser becomes the owner of the property, *i.e.* (a) unregistered land, date of conveyance (usually completion) (b) registered land, date of registration of purchaser with title absolute.[2]	
(ii) Make sure property corresponds to contractual description and plan, especially boundaries.	(ii) To avoid disputes, delay and disappointment.
(iii) Recent improvements to the property.	(iii) Planning permission may have been necessary. Conditions? Possible rate increases.
(iv) Extensions	(iv) Has the extension used up the permitted increase in cubic content under the General Development Order 1977. Possible rate increases.

[99] *Tanner* v. *Tanner* [1975] 1 W.L.R. 1346.
[1] *Binions* v. *Evans* [1972] Ch. 359.
[2] *Re Boyle's Claim* [1961] 1 W.L.R. 339.

What to Look for	Why
(v) Newly built houses. Cracks, etc.	(v) Possible claim against the builder or the N.H.B.C. (surveyor should report).
(vi) Cavity wall insulation	(vi) May infringe Building Regulations and be a danger to health.
(vii) Mains Services	(vii) Obvious.
(viii) Fixtures and fittings	(viii) To ascertain what the vendor is taking, and ensure he makes good any damage in removing items. To agree price of items vendor is selling separately. To apportion purchase price.

(B) COMMERCIAL PROPERTY

What to Look for	Why
(i) Persons (over 18) in occupation, especially tenants, squatters, contractual licencees[3] and service occupants.	(i) To ascertain whether they have an interest which may be binding on the purchaser (see residential (i) above).
(ii) Stock in trade	(ii) Apportionment of purchase price.
(iii) Building operations	(iii) Breach of planning control and–or change of use?
(iv) Present user	(iv) Does it conform with the planning permission. Can the purchaser use premises for his contemplated purpose without there being a material change of use.
(v) Present display of advertisements	(v) Are they permitted? Will the purchaser be using the same kind of advertisement? If not further permission may be needed.

II. INSPECTIONS AT THE OFFICES OF THE LOCAL AUTHORITY

What to Look for	Why
(A) RESIDENTIAL PROPERTIES	
(i) Register of Planning Applications and Decisions	(i) To ascertain details of those relating to this and neighbouring property. Shows

---

[3] *Midland Bank Ltd.* v. *Farmpride Hatcheries Ltd.* (1981) 260 E.G. 493 (Managing Director of an egg farm).

What to Look for	Why
	planning authority's present attitude towards development.
(ii) Local Plan	(ii) Shows present and future proposals for the development of the immediately surrounding area. May be of special importance to purchaser in relation to schools, for example.
(iii) Register of Enforcement and Stop Notices	(iii) Recent breach of planning control. Purchaser may have to remedy breach if proceeds with purchase.
(iv) Register of Listed Buildings	(iv) Possible specifications regarding external decoration and repair.
(v) Register of Advertisements	(v) May be a public sign attached to property, or private advertisement paid for by arrangement. Is it permitted?
(B) COMMERCIAL PROPERTIES	
(i) Structure Plan	(i) Long term policies for the area. Future designation of area as Urban Development Area or Enterprise Zone.
(ii) Local Plan	(ii) Short Term policies, *e.g.* construction of new trunk roads would ease transportation.
(iii) Register of Planning Applications and Decisions	(iii) Details of planning permission for site and user. Council's attitude towards future development of site.
(iv) Register of Advertisements	(iv) Is it adequate for the purchaser's needs?
(v) Register of Enforcement and Stop Notices	(v) Recent breach of planning control.
(vi) Register of Listed Buildings (if appropriate)	(vi) Extra controls.

SURVEY

We have already seen that the vendor is under no duty to disclose any defects in the physical state of the property, whether they be patent, a missing chimney, or latent, a damaged flue. Therefore the purchaser should satisfy himself as to the condition of the property. One way in which he can do this is to instruct a surveyor to make a report. The survey should be carried out before the purchaser exchanges contracts with the vendor.

A survey is an inspection of the property carried out by a qualified surveyor to determine its condition. A report of the inspection is made and presented to the client. The extent of the inspection will vary according to the particular premises and the purposes for which it is made. For example the owner of property may be worried about subsidence and a survey would be carried out limited to this one aspect. A building society preparing to make an advance to a mortgagor will have a survey made to find out if the property will form adequate security for the loan.[4] This would deal only with factors affecting the building society's decision on whether to make the loan and is often referred to as a "mortgage valuation." The most extensive survey possible is the full structural survey which provides for a thorough and detailed examination of every aspect of the property, its structure and internal decorative state.

The surveyor's report should be given full consideration by the purchaser before he decides to go ahead with the transaction.

Should the Purchaser's Solicitor Advise a Survey?

There are two views on the correct answer to this question. The first suggests that a solicitor is under no duty to advise on the need for a survey.[5] The second view held by the Council of the Law Society states that normal conveyancing practice dictates that a solicitor should advise his client on the desirability of instructing a surveyor.[6]

The purchaser's solicitor should be wary of giving advice on the physical condition and value of the property. Such matters are the province of another profession and any advice given by a solicitor would have to be judged in the light of the standard of care applicable to that profession. So judged, a solicitor's "off the cuff" advice to his client may take on the guise of an actionable negligent misstatement.

Can a Purchaser Rely on his Building Society's Survey?

The recent case of *Yianni* v. *Edwin Evans & Sons*[7] suggests that in certain circumstances a purchaser/mortgagor may rely on the results of his building society's mortgage valuation survey. If this is performed negligently and he suffers loss as a result he may sue the surveyor in the tort of negligence and recover damages.

In *Yianni* the purchaser decided to buy a house with the aid of a building society mortgage. The building society instructed the defendants to inspect

---

[4] Building Societies Act 1962, s.25.
[5] *Buckland* v. *Mackesey* (1968) 112 S.J. 841.
[6] Memorandum No. 3, Pt. I; Council of the Law Society's written evidence to the Royal Commission on Legal Services.
[7] [1981] 3 W.L.R. 843.

the house and value it. In their instructions to the defendant the society named the purchaser and gave details of the purchase price and the amount of the proposed loan. The defendant negligently reported that the property was adequate security for the loan. In fact the house suffered from subsidence and distortion in the foundations. Despite receiving the usual warning to have their own independent survey carried out the purchaser/mortgagor went ahead with the purchase and completed in reliance on the society's valuation. It was found as a fact that this practice of relying on valuation surveys was common knowledge to the defendant. Ten months after they moved in the purchasers discovered cracks in the foundations. They sued the surveyors in negligence claiming damages for loss, suffered as a consequence of relying on the negligently prepared report. It was held that the surveyor owed the purchaser/mortgagor a duty of care. This he had broken. He was liable to pay damages to the plaintiff. It was further held that the purchaser/mortgagor had acted reasonably in relying on the building society's report and not having instructed his own independent surveyor. As Park J. stated:

> "[it is] said a decision in favour of the plaintiffs would encourage applicants for a mortgage to have no independent survey of the house they wished to buy. I can see nothing objectionable in a practice which would result in a house being surveyed once by one surveyor."[8]

Despite the *Yianni* decision a purchaser/mortgagor should not rely on his building society's valuation report. It is not a full survey. An independent survey should always be commissioned.

OTHER SOURCES OF INFORMATION

Frequently the enquiries described above will reveal all the information a purchaser requires. However, where property is to be developed, some further enquiries may be necessary to discover the existence or location of equipment put onto or under the land by a statutory undertaker. For instance, the replies to the enquiries of the vendor and the local authority will reveal the existence of a sewer running under the property. If the purchaser proposes to build on the land it is important that the position of the sewer be pin-pointed in order that arrangements can be made to safeguard the sewer and the building from damage in the future.[9] Therefore, reference must be made to the district council who hold maps showing the exact position of all sewers vested in the water authority.[10] Similar considerations of safety apply to land on which gas or water pipes have been laid. The Regional Water Authority or Area Office of the British Gas Board will answer enquiries relating to the existence of their equipment on land with a view to preventing it from being damaged unintentionally. The Area Boards of the Central Electricity Generating

---

[8] *Ibid.* at p. 859.
[9] Public Health Act 1936, s.25.
[10] *Ibid.* s.32 (as amended by Water Act 1973).

Boards keep records of the location of all their cables and installations.[11] These records are open to inspection and copies of any maps may be taken away. A small fee is payable for this service. Area Offices of British Telecom will deal with any enquiries that may arise in connection with their equipment. For example, the construction of a factory may necessitate the removal of telegraph poles which stand on the property. It may be possible to reach an agreement with British Telecom regarding the relocation of such poles.

These types of enquiry are often answered purely as a matter of grace without charge. In appropriate cases it may be of assistance to the authority in question if the applicant provides them with a plan of the property.

---

[11] Electric Lighting (Clauses) Act 1899, s.60.

4: Conditional Agreements

Introduction

Agreements relating to the sale and purchase of land are frequently made subject to some qualification. The most commonly occurring example is an agreement made "subject to contract." Where the agreement is qualified it is always a question of construction as to whether or not the qualification precludes the existence of a binding contract. On the one hand, the insertion of the words "subject to contract" into the opening negotiations will prevent the parties from inadvertently concluding a contract. They remain in a state of negotiation until the qualification is removed. On the other hand, the qualifying phrase may not preclude the existence of a binding contract. The qualifying words serve merely to suspend the enforceability of the contract until such time as the condition has been fulfilled.[1] Such agreements may truly be called "conditional contracts." If the latter is the case the parties are not free to resile from the contract pending the fulfilment of the condition.[2] An example of this type of case is where the contract is made conditional upon planning permission being obtained by the purchaser.[3]

Another way of expressing the distinction between qualifying phrases which preclude the existence of a contract and those which do not, is to say that some conditions are precedent to contract, others being precedent to performance of the contract. For example, in *Aberfoyle Plantations Ltd.* v. *Cheng*[4] a contract for the sale of certain property contained the following clause; "The purchase is conditional on the vendor obtaining [the renewal of certain leases] . . . to be in a position to transfer the same to the purchaser and if for any cause whatsoever the vendor is unable to fulfil this condition this agreement shall become null and void." The Privy Council held that until the condition was fulfilled there was no concluded contract.[5] The Privy Council treated the clause as having the same effect as "subject to contract." However, in *Hinderer* v. *Weir*[6] a condition that the contract was subject to a valuation and to satisfactory references being obtained by the purchaser was held to be precedent to performance of an already binding contract. When the references and valuation had been completed the parties would be obliged to perform the contract.

---

[1] Or if possible waived; see *post*, p. 114. See also *Ee* v. *Kakar* (1980) 40 P. & C.R. 223.

[2] *Smallman* v. *Smallman* [1971] 3 W.L.R. 588.

[3] *Batten* v. *White* (1960) 12 P. & C.R. 66, see *post*, p. 108.

[4] [1960] A.C. 115.

[5] See however the judgment of Danckwerts J. in *Property & Bloodstock Ltd.* v. *Emerton* [1968] Ch. 94 and Lord Atkinson in *New Zealand Shipping Co. Ltd.* v. *Société des Ateliers et Chantiers de France* [1919] A.C.1.

[6] (1953) 161 E.G. 156.

In *Wood Preservation Ltd.* v. *Prior*[7] Goff J. classified conditional agreements under four heads:

"The first is where the arrangement between the parties, which would otherwise be a contract, is subject to a condition precedent to the making of an agreement at all. The second class of case is where there is a contract under which one party assumes a unilateral obligation to purchase from another in a certain event and there is no obligation on the other to bring that event about.

[The] third case is where you have a bilateral contract of sale subject to a condition precedent with an immediate obligation on one of the parties to perform the condition or to use his best endeavours to perform it. There is . . . an immediate obligation but the bilateral obligations of the contract for sale are nonetheless subject to a condition precedent and there is no sale until the condition is performed.

[The] fourth class is where you have an immediate contract of sale but on the basis or term that one of the parties, say the vendors, would obtain some particular information or assurance or something of that sort . . . the contract of sale is nonetheless immediate and not subject to any condition precedent."

Within the first class fall the "subject to contract" cases.[8] The second class of cases would include option agreements, for example, to purchase the freehold or renew a lease.[9] The third class would include many of the common conditional phrases described below, for instance "subject to survey."[10] The fourth class comprises those cases where the contract contains a provision that the contract is to become void or voidable in the future on the occurrence of some specified event. A common example of this type of conditional contract is where there is a contract to assign a leasehold interest with a term that the vendor is to obtain the reversioner's consent.[11]

The courts have not been consistent in their approach to conditional agreements. Some of the cases are difficult to reconcile and sometimes clauses which appear to be very similar have been held to have different effect.[12] In view of this a review of the case law on some of the more commonly occurring conditional phrases may be found helpful.

"Subject to Contract"

In *Winn* v. *Bull*[13] the defendant agreed to take a lease of a dwelling house. The agreement was "subject to the preparation and approval of a formal contract." No formal contract was ever drawn up and the defendant withdrew from the agreement. The plaintiff sued to enforce the agreement. It was held that there was no binding contract to enforce. Since this case

---

[7] [1969] 1 W.L.R. 1077.
[8] *Sherbrooke* v. *Dipple* (1980) 255 E.G. 1203; *Cohen* v. *Nessdale Ltd.* [1982] 2 All E.R. 97.
[9] *Smith* v. *Morgan* [1971] 1 W.L.R. 803; *Brown* v. *Gould* [1972] Ch. 53.
[10] See *post*, pp. 106–107.
[11] See *post*, Chap. 6, p. 178.
[12] See, *e.g.* the cases on "subject to finance" *post*, p. 112.
[13] (1877) 7 Ch. D. 29.

it has been accepted that an agreement "subject to contract" has the effect of leaving the parties in a state of negotiation until a formal contract is drawn up and exchanged.[14]

As any student of contract law knows, it is an essential part of the formation of a contract that the parties intend to create legal relations. By expressly making the agreement "subject to contract" the parties indicate that they have no intention to create a contractually binding relationship. Whilst negotiations continue both parties are at liberty to withdraw from the agreement. The purchaser is entitled to have repaid to him any deposit he may have paid to the vendor[15]; he is not entitled to recoup from the vendor any wasted expenditure he may have incurred in employing solicitors or surveyors and so on. The vendor, for his part, will be entitled to the return of any papers he may have sent to the purchaser such as office copies of the entries on the register of title or the draft contract. Other expressions have been held to prevent the formation of a binding contract in a similar fashion. These include *inter alia*; "subject to a suitable agreement being arranged between your solicitor and mine"[16]; "we are instructed to accept and have asked solicitor to prepare contract"[17]; and "formal contract to be signed when approved"[18]; In every case it was held that there was no contract in existence. The question of the enforceability of "the contract," therefore, did not arise.

The Law Commission, in its Report on "Subject to Contract Agreements,"[19] has stated that the procedure whereby negotiations are, in the first instance, conducted "subject to contract," "is one which has been evolved in order to ensure that those buying and selling houses do not find themselves irrevocably committed to a sale or purchase before being given the chance of taking advice, of making proper enquiries, searches and inspections and of making their financial arrangements." There can be no doubt that this is a laudable intention. However, because parties who agree "subject to contract" are bound in honour only it is open for intending vendors to abuse their position. As Oliver Goldsmith once wrote "honour sinks where commerce long prevails."[19a] The practice of "gazumping" developed in the rising property market of the 1960s. An intending vendor, having agreed to sell (subject to contract) at one price would continue to raise the purchase price before entering into a formal contract. This led Sachs J. to observe,[20] "this hybrid type of 'subject to contract' transaction, which is so often referred to as a gentleman's agreement . . . is only too often a transaction in which each side hopes the other will act like a gentleman and neither intends so to act if it is against

---

[14] *George Trollope & Sons* v. *Martyn Bros.* [1934] 2 K.B. 436; *Eccles* v. *Bryant & Pollock* [1948] 1 Ch. 93.

[15] *Chillingworth* v. *Esche* [1924] 1 Ch. 97.

[16] *Lockett* v. *Norman-Wright* [1925] Ch. 56.

[17] *Bonnewell* v. *Jenkins* (1878) 8 Ch. D. 70.

[18] *Bartlett* v. *Greene* (1874) 30 L.T. 553; see also *Clark* v. *Robinson* (1903) 51 W.R. 443; *Rouse* v. *Ginsberg* (1911) 55 S.J. 632; *Raingold* v. *Bromley* [1931] 2 Ch. 307; *Edgewater Developments Co.* v. *Baily* (1974) 118 S.J. 312.

[19] Law Comm. No. 65, (1975).

[19a] *The Traveller*.

[20] *Goding* v. *Frazer* [1967] 1 W.L.R. 286 at 293.

his material interests." As yet no effective method of countering gazumping has been devised.[21]

Removing the "Subject to Contract" Qualification

Although the vendor and purchaser may commence negotiations "subject to contract" they may decide at some stage to remove that qualification. This happened in *Griffiths* v. *Young*.[22] A solicitor sent some correspondence regarding the sale to the other party's solicitor. The correspondence was expressed to be "subject to contract." Subsequently in a telephone call an unconditional offer was made and accepted. The Court of Appeal held that the telephone conversation had effectively removed the suspensive "subject to contract" qualification. From the moment the telephone conversation was made there was a binding contract. The contract in this case was held to be enforceable because it was supported by sufficient written memoranda as required by section 40 of the Law of Property Act 1925.[23] Some doubt has been cast upon the latter aspect of *Griffith's* case in a later Court of Appeal decision[24] but the case remains authority for the proposition that the parties may orally remove the "subject to contract" qualification. It is not open to one party to a "subject to contract" agreement to unilaterally remove the suspensive condition and so create a binding agreement. To permit this would be to allow a person, in effect, to force a binding contract onto another, possibly without that other party's agreement as to all the material terms. In *Tevanan* v. *Norman Brett* (*Builders*) *Ltd.*[25] Brightman J. in an instructive passage stated; "when the parties started their negotiations under the umbrella of the "subject to contract" formula, or some similar expression of intention, it was really hopeless for one side or the other to say that a contract came into existence because the parties became of one mind notwithstanding that no formal contracts had been exchanged . . . they were only of one mind on the footing that all the terms and conditions of the sale and purchase had been settled between them, and even then the original intention still remained intact that there should be no formal contract in existence until the written contracts had been exchanged." Brightman J. continued, stating that the "parties could get rid of the qualification of 'subject to contract' only if they both expressly agreed that it should be expunged or if such an agreement was to be necessarily implied." This passage was cited with approval by Templeman L.J. in a subsequent Court of Appeal decision *Sherbrooke* v. *Dipple*.[26] The facts of the case were as follows. Miss H. owned a house with a garden of nearly one acre. Miss H. let Mr. and Mrs. Dipple use a fenced-off corner of her

---

[21] See (1975) 39 Conv. 229 for a discussion of various proposed methods. See also *Pateman* v. *Pay* (1974) 232 E.G. 457; *Damn* v. *Herrtage* (1974) 234 E.G. 365.

[22] [1970] Ch. 675.

[23] See *post*, Chapter 5 for formalities in relation to contracts for the sale of land.

[24] *Tiverton Estates Ltd.* v. *Wearwell Ltd.* [1975] 1 Ch. 146.

[25] (1972) 223 E.G. 1945 at 1947.

[26] (1980) 255 E.G. 1203.

garden as a site for their caravan.[27] Miss H. died leaving the property to a Miss B., who thinking she was acting in accordance with Miss H.'s wishes negotiated for the sale of the corner of the garden to the Dipples. Miss B.'s solicitors wrote a letter to the Mr. Dipple on January 22, 1975 offering to sell him the site for £200 "subject to contract." Nothing was done about this offer and it was found as a fact that the "first phase of the negotiations" concluded on November 15, 1975. In March, 1976 Mr. Dipple suddenly appeared in Miss B.'s solicitors office offering them £200. A further written offer of sale was made by the solicitors acting for Miss B. This was orally accepted by Mr. Dipple. Mr. Dipple argued that an oral contract had been made between the parties when he had accepted this later offer. He sued to enforce the alleged contract. The Court of Appeal applied the approach laid down by Brightman J. in *Tevanan's* case. They held that the negotiations between the parties were *all* conducted under the umbrella of the "subject to contract" condition contained in the opening letter of January 22, 1975. All the subsequent negotiations were subject to that overriding initial condition. There had been no express or implied removal of the suspensive condition contained in the opening letter despite the gap in negotiations of some four and one half months. In *Cohen* v. *Nessdale*[28] on somewhat similar facts the Court of Appeal held that a gap of eight months was not sufficient *per se* to imply a removal of the subject to contract qualification. In the absence of an express removal of the condition they held that there was no binding contract. It is clear from these two cases that the courts are trying to restrict the circumstances in which an oral waiver of the "subject to contract" condition can operate. In this respect *Griffiths* v. *Young*[29] must be looked upon as being confined to the particular facts of that case. In practice however, it may be desirable to ensure that all negotiations are expressly carried on "subject to contract," especially if there is an appreciable gap between them. The court might hold that the later discussions were new negotiations rather than a continuation of the old ones. In this case even though the first set of negotiations were "subject to contract" the later negotiations (in the absence of any express reassertion of the "subject to contract" qualification) would not be protected and a binding oral contract might inadvertently be concluded. This contract could then become enforceable, for example if there was a sufficient act of part performance.[30]

Finally, the case of *Michael Richards Properties Ltd.* v. *Corporation of Wardens of St. Saviour's Parish, Southwark*[31] should be noted. The defendant charity offered certain property for sale by tender. The plaintiffs' tender was accepted by the defendants who duly sent them a letter informing them that their tender had been accepted. Unfortunately there was a clerical error and the words "subject to contract" were typed below the signature to the letter. The charity later received information

---

[27] Subject to conditions regarding fencing and removal of huts from the land both of which were accepted by Mr. Dipple.

[28] [1981] 3 All E.R. 118.

[29] [1970] Ch. 675.

[30] As to which see *post*, p. 140.

[31] [1975] 3 All E.R. 416 noted at 40 Conv. 437.

that the local authority were probably going to acquire the property compulsorily. The purchasers sought to withdraw from the transaction and sued to recover their deposit. They argued, *inter alia*, that there was no concluded contract because the words "subject to contract" left the matter in a state of negotiation. Goff J. whilst accepting, that if the words "subject to contract" stood there would be no contract held that on the facts the words should be rejected as meaningless. He later pointed out[32] that this decision was based on its peculiar facts and was not to "throw any doubt upon the well established and well settled sanctity of the words "subject to contract."

"Subject to Survey"

The construction of contracts expressed to be "subject to survey," has given rise to a diversity of judicial opinion. In some cases the phrase has been treated as having a similar effect to the "subject to contract" qualification discussed above.[33] For example, in *Marks* v. *Board*[34] the parties made an agreement for the sale and purchase of a house. The agreement was expressed to be "subject to surveyor's report." The vendor refused to perform the agreement and the purchaser sued for damages. The purchaser argued that the words "subject to survey" did not prevent the formation of a binding contract. Rowlatt J. disagreed, observing that the purchaser had an absolute and unqualified right to say whether he liked the surveyor's report. He held that there was not a binding contract "because the buyer was not yet bound and, therefore, the seller was not bound either." However, despite holding that there was no contract Rowlatt J. seems to have assumed that the purchaser was bound to have a survey carried out before deciding whether or not to withdraw from the contract. If this is correct, and the purchaser was required to have a survey made, presumably he was bound to do so because there was a concluded contract. In this respect the decision seems to be contradictory.

Later cases[35] on conditional phrases moved away from the restrictive approach adopted by Rowlatt J. in *Marks* v. *Board*.[36] In *Astra Trust Ltd.* v. *Adams and Williams*[37] there was an agreement to sell a yacht "subject to satisfactory survey." The prospective purchaser commissioned a survey and after studying it, decided not to go ahead with the purchase. The vendor, who held a deposit paid by the purchaser, refused to repay it. The purchaser successfully brought an action for the recovery of the deposit. There were two grounds for the court's decision. Firstly, Megaw J. held that on the facts there was no contract binding the parties. Alternatively

---

[32] *Munton* v. *G.L.C.* [1976] 1 W.L.R. 649, 656.
[33] See *ante*, p. 102. *Marks* v. *Board* (1930) 46 T.L.R. 424; *Graham and Scott* v. *Oxlade* [1950] 2 K.B. 257 (a case on whether an estate agent had effected an introduction when the contract was made "subject to survey").
[34] (1930) 46 T.L.R. 424.
[35] *Astra Trust Ltd.* v. *Adams and Williams* [1969] 1 Lloyd's Rep. 81; *Batten* v. *White* (1960) 12 P. & C. R. 66.
[36] (1930) 46 T.L.R. 424.
[37] [1969] 1 Lloyd's Rep. 81.

he held that, *assuming there to be a contract*, the purchaser could withdraw because he was not satisfied with the survey. Megaw J. stated that on the facts of the case he did not have to decide whether the test to be applied in determining whether the survey was satisfactory was subjective or objective, because using either test, the purchaser could validly withdraw from the agreement. This left unsettled the question as to whether the purchaser had to act in good faith, when considering the results of the survey or whether he could withdraw once the survey had been made for any reason, no matter how arbitrary.

The cases on the "subject to survey" point were recently reviewed in *Ee* v. *Kakar*.[38] The plaintiff agreed to sell a property to the defendant "subject to survey of the property." The defendant tried to withdraw from the agreement and the purchaser, who wished to proceed, sought specific performance of what he argued was a binding contract. Walton J. after reviewing the previous decisions held:

(i) The use of the words "subject to survey" did not prevent a binding contract from being formed. The words were a "simple suspensory condition" merely holding the parties' other obligations under the contract in abeyance;

(ii) The purchaser was under an obligation to obtain a survey within a reasonable time. If he did not do so he waived his right to have a survey made and he could not withdraw from the contract on that ground. Presumably as part of the obligation to have a survey made the prospective purchaser is required to employ somebody with the appropriate professional skills; and

(iii) The purchaser was required to act bona fide in considering the results of the survey and whether or not to proceed with the transaction. Generally speaking, if a reasonable man would be satisfied with the results of the survey the purchaser would not be acting bona fide if he refused to proceed.

If an agreement is made "subject to survey" the vendor must not dispose of the property elsewhere until he is certain that the purchaser is withdrawing from the agreement, or alternatively has failed to obtain a survey (and is, therefore, in breach of contract). The proposed vendor must also provide the purchaser with an opportunity to carry out his survey.[39]

"Subject to Planning Permission"

Development potential is a major factor in determining the value of most pieces of land. Unfortunately, in any particular case, there is no sure way of knowing that planning permission will be forthcoming for a project of development. For example, a property development company, which hopes to buy up small plots of land to form one large site on which

---

[38] (1980) 40 P. & C.R. 223 noted at [1980] Conv. 446, J.E. Adams. See also H. W. Wilkinson (1981) New L.J. 771; H. Marksen (1980) 124 S.J. 871.

[39] *The Merak* [1976] 2 Lloyd's Rep. 250.

to build an office block, often cannot be sure that a satisfactory[40] planning permission will be granted for the development. The value of the individual plots with such permission would be greatly enhanced. Their value to the developer without such permission may well be nothing.[41] This type of factor leads to contracts for sale being made conditional upon planning permission being obtained.[42] As with other conditional agreements the effect of the clause will depend upon its construction. In drafting the clause the following considerations might usefully be borne in mind.[43]

WHAT TYPE OF PLANNING PERMISSION WILL SATISFY THE CONDITION?

As with other conditions the "subject to planning permission" qualification must be sufficiently certain. If it is not the condition will be void for uncertainty. This point arose in *Batten* v. *White*.[44] A vendor agreed to sell land to a builder "subject to planning permission and satisfactory drainage." Before the local planning authority had made any decision on the builder's application the vendor withdrew from the agreement. He subsequently argued that the agreement was void for uncertainty. It was held that during the course of negotiations the vendor had been made aware of the purchaser's intentions to build houses on the land. This knowledge was relevant in deciding whether the condition was sufficiently certain. As the vendor knew the general type of planning permission required, the condition was held valid. In practice details of the planning permission required by the proposed purchaser should be inserted in the contract and an obligation imposed upon him to apply only for that permission. This prevents a purchaser from applying for a planning permission different from that originally envisaged which has much less (or no) chance of success—a possible escape route for an unwilling purchaser.

Planning permissions come, in as many shapes and sizes as the buildings to which they relate.[45] A planning permission may be "outline" only in which case it deals with the basic structure of the proposed development alone. A detailed permission must be obtained before the development can begin (such a permission would relate to the actual design of the proposed building and the materials to be used in its construction). Furthermore a planning permission may be granted subject to such conditions as the local planning authority think fit.[46] The contract should expressly stipulate the circumstances in which the "subject to planning permission" condition is to be considered as satisfied.

---

[40] Outline planning permission may not be sufficiently detailed for the purposes of the development company.

[41] For an example see *Amalgamated Investments & Property Co. Ltd.* v. *John Walker & Sons* [1977] 1 W.L.R. 164 *ante*, p.12.

[42] For a precedent see *Precedents for the Conveyancer* Vol. 1 No. 16–3, p. 8011.

[43] See also H. W. Wilkinson [1974] Conv. 77.

[44] (1960) 12 P. & C.R. 66.

[45] See A. E. Telling, *Planning Law and Procedure* (6th ed.).

[46] Town and Country Planning Act 1971 s.29(1)—such conditions must however serve some useful planning purpose. See *Fawcett Properties Ltd.* v. *Buckingham C.C.* [1961] A.C. 636.

In *Hargreaves Transport Ltd.* v. *Lynch*[47] the contract for sale was expressed to be subject to the purchaser obtaining planning permission to use the property for the purposes of a transport depot.[48] The local authority granted outline planning permission for that use, but subsequently revoked the grant because there was a public outcry. The purchaser sought to withdraw from the arrangement. The vendor argued first, that the condition had been satisfied by the grant of the outline permission and secondly, that the purchaser should not be allowed to withdraw until he had exhausted every possible avenue of appeal against the revocation of planning permission. The court held that as the outline planning permission by itself did not permit the applicant to carry out any development (detailed permission was necessary) it could not be said that any planning permission had been obtained, so as to satisfy the condition. On the second point the court considered it was unreasonable to require a potential purchaser to run through the appeals procedure. The time and cost involved in taking an appeal could be disproportionate to any eventual benefit the purchaser might obtain if he succeeded in restoring the original grant of planning permission.

Is a conditional planning permission sufficient to satisfy the condition? Some conditions attached to planning permissions can involve the applicant in having to carry out expensive works, or otherwise affect the profitability of the development. For instance, a developer may obtain planning permission to build a shopping centre. If a condition was attached to that permission restricting the type of retail operations allowed in the centre he may decide that the project would not be profitable and wish to withdraw.[49] Problems have occurred where a contract for sale is made "subject to planning permission" and the permission obtained is conditional. In *Richard West and Partners (Inverness) Ltd.* v. *Dick*[50] a contract for the sale of certain property in Scotland was made conditional "upon planning consent being granted by the local authority following upon the application already lodged for use of the subject of sale as a hotel." The contract went on to provide that in the event of planning consent not being obtained the purchaser would be entitled to withdraw from the contract. Planning permission was granted subject to two conditions:

(i) the access from the property to a nearby trunk road was improved (to cope with the increased flow of traffic which would occur because of the nature of the proposed use of the property); and

(ii) that any alterations to the property were carried out only after the consent of the local building inspector had been first obtained.

The building inspector insisted that extensive work was carried out to make the property comply with fire protection regulations. The purchasers argued that no planning permission had been obtained within

---

[47] [1969] 1 W.L.R. 215.

[48] The contract also stated that the condition would not be satisfied if the planning permission contained unsatisfactory conditions.

[49] *E.g.* if he could not ensure that he could let all the retail units in view of the restrictions imposed by the planning authority.

[50] [1969] 2 Ch. 433.

the terms of the condition because of the imposition of these conditions. The court stated that the test to be applied in such cases was, whether or not there had been granted a true planning permission for the proposed development. On the facts of the case planning permission had been granted, because the conditions imposed were not of such an onerous nature that it could be said that no "substantial" consent had been forthcoming. The case also highlights the need for precision in drafting this type of conditional clause. The purchasers had objected to the local building inspector's requirements regarding fire protection—they would have proved costly. The court held that quite apart from anything else the imposition of conditions as to fire protection was not within the scope of the clause. Fire regulations were nothing to do with the planning application and so the contractual right of withdrawal did not apply. The contract should be made conditional not only on the purchaser obtaining planning consent, but also to any other appropriate circumstance, for example his obtaining a licence to sell alcoholic drinks.[51] In practice it might also be advisable for the condition to be further qualified so that the planning permission is "to the entire satisfaction" of the applicant.[52] Certainly the parties rights in the event of a conditional planning permission being granted should be considered when drafting the clause.

WHO MUST APPLY FOR PLANNING PERMISSION?

Unless the contract expressly provides to the contrary it is the responsibility of the purchaser to apply for any planning permission he requires. The contract may stipulate that the purchaser is to apply for planning permission within a specified period. If the purchaser does not apply within this time limit he will be in breach of contract. If the contract is silent on the matter the purchaser must submit his planning application to the local authority within a reasonable time. This was established in *Re Longlands Farm, Alford* v. *Superior Developments Ltd.*[53] The defendant company contracted to purchase some 57 acres of land for £114,000 on April 2, 1964. The contract was "subject to [the] Company obtaining planning permission to its entire satisfaction for the development of [the] land." Completion was to take place not later than 8 weeks after the condition was satisfied. The company paid a deposit—the princely sum of £5. On April 9 they protected their interest under the contract by registering a Class C(iv) land charge.[54] They failed to apply for planning permission because they felt the time was not ripe for such a permission as they required to be granted.[55] The vendor, who could not deal with the land, applied for the land charge to be vacated in December, 1967. Cross J. held that the company had a reasonable time within which to obtain planning permission. As they had not even applied for permission within a reasonable time the plaintiff was entitled to

---

[51] *Brickwoods Ltd.* v. *Butter & Walters* (1970) 23 P. & C.R. 317.
[52] *Tesco Stores Ltd.* v. *William Gibson & Son Ltd.* (1970) 214 E.G. 835.
[53] [1968] 3 All E.R. 552 noted at [1969] 34 Conv. 54.
[54] *Ante*, p. 20.
[55] As matters turned out they were absolutely right, consent being refused on July 24, 1967. See also *Aberfoyle Plantations Ltd.* v. *Cheng* [1960] A.C. 115.

terminate the contract. The defendants had argued that time should only begin to run against them from a date when they first had a reasonable prospect of success in having the planning application approved. This argument was rejected, it being held that time begins to run as from the date of the contract.

In some circumstances the purchaser may be entitled to withdraw from the contract without having applied for planning permission.[56] This occurred in *Tesco Stores Ltd.* v. *William Gibson & Son Ltd.*[57] The contract stated that the property was sold "on the footing that the purchasers obtain planning permission for the total development of the site in accordance with their requirements and this contract is subject to such consent being obtained." The purchasers subsequently found that the property was not sufficiently large enough for their requirements, so they did not apply for planning permission. The vendors who had resold the property at £30,000 less than the purchase price agreed with Tesco, sued for damages for breach of contract. It was held that Tesco, in the particular circumstances of the case, were under no obligation to apply for planning permission; they had acted in a bona fide fashion throughout. They would not be compelled to apply for permission to use the property for some purpose which, in view of the size of the property could not possibly be to Tesco's "entire satisfaction."

Sometimes a vendor will already have applied for planning permission when contracts are exchanged. In these circumstances the vendor is obliged not to withdraw his application without first consulting (and presumably obtaining the consent of) the purchaser.[58] The obligation is imposed upon the vendor as part of his trustee-like duty of care[59] in relation to the property after contracts have been exchanged.[60]

"Subject to Preliminary Enquiries and Searches"

In *Smith and Olley* v. *Townsend*[61] contracts were exchanged through the post. The plaintiffs' solicitor's covering letter stated that exchange was "subject to answers to preliminary enquiries and to searches." The preliminary enquiries subsequently revealed that the property was zoned for residential purposes. The proposed purchasers sought to withdraw from the contract and recover their deposit because they wished to use the property as a saw mill and timber factory. The vendor counterclaimed for a declaration that the deposit was properly payable by the plaintiffs. Roxburgh J. held that the purchasers could recover the deposit. He stated,[62] "[it] might be that the condition was void for uncertainty, and accordingly there was no contract at all. Or it might be that the condition

---

[56] The contract should state that the purchaser is to "use his best endeavours" to obtain the permission.

[57] (1970) 214 E.G. 835.

[58] *Sinclair-Hill* v. *Sothcott* (1973) 26 P. & C.R. 490.

[59] *Clarke* v. *Ramuz* [1891] 2 Q.B. 456.

[60] See *post*, p. 245.

[61] [1949] 1 P. & C.R. 28.

[62] *Ibid.* at p. 29.

was capable of construction and meant that the contract was subject to the answers to preliminary inquiries and local searches being satisfactory to a reasonable man or woman." Roxburgh J. did not choose between these two grounds because on the facts the answers could reasonably be considered unsatisfactory and so the result of the case would be the same whether or not the condition was void for uncertainty.

In considering whether the replies to the enquiries or the results of the local search are satisfactory, Roxburgh J. suggested that the test to be applied was an objective one. This was confirmed by the Court of Appeal in *Aquis Estates Ltd.* v. *Minton*.[63] In this case the contract was made subject to the "property being found free from adverse entry on the purchaser's local land charge and land registry searches." The purchaser intended to demolish the building. It transpired that the building had been listed as being of special architectural or historic interest.[64] The purchaser would not, therefore, be able to demolish the building. If the test to be applied in determining whether or not the results of the searches and so on was subjective, there would have been no doubt that the purchaser could have repudiated the contract. The purchaser's intention to redevelop the building could have been taken into account. However, the court reaffirmed that the test was objective and the intentions of the particular purchaser in relation to the property should not be taken into account. The correct approach was to see whether it could reasonably be said that the entry revealed by the search substantially restricted the use to which the property could be put, or substantially diminished the value of the property. On the facts listing did constitute an adverse entry. The court, however, found for the vendor on other grounds.[65]

Both sets of standard conditions of sale incorporate conditions which can be used to make the contract conditional. National Condition 3 and Law Society Condition 4 allow exchange of contracts to take place before the purchaser has completed all his pre-contractual searches and enquiries. Both allow the purchaser to withdraw in certain circumstances, should the searches or enquiries prove unsatisfactory. The operation of these conditions is discussed in more detail later in the book.[66]

"Subject to Finance"

Contracts for the sale of land which are made conditional on the purchaser obtaining a mortgage (or other source of finance) to assist in the purchase are rare in England.[67] The reason for this is that the practice of making negotiations "subject to contract" in the first instance allows the prospective purchaser to make the appropriate financial arrangements. When the courts have been asked to construe "subject to finance"

---

[63] [1975] 1 W.L.R. 1452.

[64] See *ante*, p. 11.

[65] The purchaser had waived his right to repudiate by continuing negotiations after becoming aware of the adverse entry.

[66] See *post*, pp. 157 and 165.

[67] Brian Coote (1976) 40 Conv. 37.

agreements they have not approached the question in any consistent manner.

In *Lee-Parker* v. *Izzet*[68] the sale was conditional upon the vendor arranging "a satisfactory mortgage for the purchaser within twenty-eight days." The question arose as to whether the contract was void for uncertainty. Goff J. held that the words "a satisfactory mortgage" were sufficiently certain because they meant a mortgage to the satisfaction of the purchaser acting as a reasonable man. The decision of Goff J. was distinguished in *Lee-Parker* v. *Izzet* (No.2).[69] Mrs. B. was in occupation of the property in dispute under a prior written contract. The contract was "subject to the purchaser obtaining a satisfactory mortgage." The plaintiff, an equitable mortgagee, sought possession of the property. Mrs. B. argued that as the land was registered she had an overriding interest under section 70(1)(g) of the Land Registration Act 1925[70]; this it was argued bound the equitable mortgagee. The mortgagee successfully argued that the contract under which Mrs. B. held the property was void for uncertainty.

Goulding J. thought that, "the concept of a satisfactory mortgage is too indefinite for the court to give it a practical meaning.[71] Everything is at large, not only matters like rate of interest and ancillary obligations on which evidence might establish what would be usual or reasonable, but also those two most essential points—the amount of the loan and the terms of repayment."[72] The mortgagee obtained an order giving him possession of the premises. However, in the later case of *Jan Mohamed* v. *Hassan*[73] a contract expressed to be subject to a "mortgage *satisfactory to the purchaser*" was held to be valid. The italicised words apparently made all the difference. A term could be implied that the purchaser should act reasonably in considering the mortgage and the clause could, therefore, be given effect. This last case shows that the courts will try to give effect to bona fide commercial agreements whenever this is reasonably possible.[74]

When drafting a "subject to finance" clause the following points should be borne in mind:

(i) Provision should be made for a time limit within which the proposed purchaser is to obtain the requisite finance. Consideration should be given as to whether time is to be of the essence of the clause.

(ii) The amount of the loan should be stated. A formula such as the purchaser obtaining "an advance of not less than £x" may conveniently be used.

(iii) Who is to determine whether the finance obtained is satisfactory? By analogy with the cases on "subject to planning permission"[75] it might be in the proposed purchaser's best interests to state that the mortgage shall be "to the entire satisfaction of the purchaser."

---

[68] [1971] 1 W.L.R. 1688, more fully reported at [1971] 3 All E.R. 1099.
[69] [1972] 1 W.L.R. 775—the case concerned different parties.
[70] See *post*, p. 305.
[71] Following *Re Rich's Will Trusts* (1962) 106 S.J. 75.
[72] [1972] 1 W.L.R. 775 at p. 779.
[73] (1977) 241 E.G. 609.
[74] See *Brown* v. *Gould* [1972] Ch. 53 at p. 56.
[75] See *ante*, p. 107.

(iv) The rate of interest and ancillary terms (period of repayment and so on) should be specified in the clause. In view of the fact that the rate of interest chargeable on mortgages is variable (and the period of repayment may vary with the size of the loan) a range of interest rates initially chargeable and so on could be stipulated for.

(v) The proposed purchaser should be obliged to use his "best endeavours" to find the finance. This stops the purchaser from sitting back and waiting for the time limit to expire and then terminating the agreement.

Time for Performance of the Condition

In *Aberfoyle Plantations Ltd.* v. *Cheng*[76] the House of Lords laid down three guidelines as to when a condition must be performed:

(a) If the contract for sale specifies a completion date the condition must be satisfied by that date. In the case cited the contract was subject to the vendor obtaining the renewal of certain leases. Completion was required by the contract to take place "on or before April 30." When the vendor had failed to obtain renewal of the leases by that date the purchaser was held to be entitled to terminate the contract. The effect of the decision is to make time of the essence of completion dates in conditional contracts.[77]

(b) If the contract stipulates a time within which the condition has to be performed the condition must be performed within that time limit. The time limit cannot be extended by reference to equitable principles.

(c) If no time limit is fixed, performance must take place within a reasonable time. What amounts to a reasonable time will depend upon the particular facts of the case.[78]

Waiving a Condition

Where a provision of a contract is for the sole benefit of one party, that party may waive the provision and enforce the contract without it.[79] Where there is a conditional contract, and the condition is for the benefit of one party only, that party can waive compliance with the condition and enforce the contract. For example, in *Batten* v. *White*[80] a contract for the sale of certain land was conditional upon the purchaser obtaining planning permission. Whilst the local planning authority were considering the purchaser's application the vendor tried to back out of the contract. The court held that the purchaser was entitled to enforce the contract and

---

[76] [1960] A.C. 115.
[77] This is not normally the case for a completion date; see *post* p. 155.
[78] *Re Longlands Farm, Alford* v. *Superior Developments Ltd.* [1968] 3 All E.R. 552.
[79] *Hawkesly* v. *Outram* [1892] 3 Ch. 359; *Morrell* v. *Studd and Millington* [1913] 2 Ch. 648; *Batten* v. *White* (1960) 12 P. & C.R. 66. *Chitty on Contracts* (1977, 24th ed.), p. 654.
[80] *Ibid.* See also, *Usanga* v. *Bishop* (1974) 232 E.G. 835.

obtain a decree of specific performance because he had waived the condition which had been included in the contract for his sole benefit.

In certain circumstances a condition is not capable of being waived even if it benefits only one party to the contract. Waiver will not be permitted if it would result in the contract becoming incomplete. In *Boobyer* v. *Thornville Properties Ltd.*[81] the contract was again conditional upon planning permission being obtained. However, the contract also stated that completion was to take place within six weeks of the grant of planning permission being obtained. The purchaser sought to waive the condition and enforce the contract without it. He was not allowed to do so. If the condition had been waived there would have been no completion date—rendering the contract incomplete. (The open contract rule that completion should take place within a reasonable time was ousted by the original inclusion of the express term that completion was to be within six weeks of the grant of planning permission).

If performance of the condition to which the contract is subject would benefit both parties to the contract it can only be waived by mutual consent. In *Heron Garage Properties Ltd.* v. *Moss*[82] the vendors contracted to sell part of their land to the purchaser. The retained land was to be used by them as a car showroom. The contract for sale was conditional upon the purchasers being granted planning permission to use the land as a garage. The purchasers sought to waive the condition and enforce the contract. Brightman J. held that it was not obvious on the face of the contract that the condition was for the exclusive benefit of the purchaser. He could not waive the condition unilaterally. Clearly in this case the vendors stood to benefit from performance of the condition. Use of the property sold as a garage would have increased trade in the showroom the vendors intended to build on the retained land.

---

[81] (1968) 19 P. & C.R. 768.
[82] [1974] 1 W.L.R. 148.

5: Formal Requirements for Making the Contract—Law of Property Act 1925, Section 40

Section 40(1) of the Law of Property Act 1925, provides:

"No action may be brought upon any contract for the sale or other disposition of land or any interest in land, unless the agreement upon which such action is brought, or some memorandum or note thereof, is in writing, and signed by the party to be charged or by some other person thereunto by him lawfully authorised."

Section 40(1) is an evidential section, not a substantive one; unless a contract relating to land is evidenced by some writing, then oral evidence is inadmissible to prove the terms of that contract in an action to enforce it.

Section 40(1) reproduces in modern language the provisions of section 4 of the Statute of Frauds 1677 concerning "any contract for sale of lands, tenements or hereditaments or any interest in or concerning them." The 1677 Statute, aimed at "the prevention of many fraudulent practices which are commonly endeavoured to be upheld by perjury and subordination of perjury" required that a wide variety of contracts be supported by signed writing as a matter of evidence. The requirement now only applies to two types of contract, the most important being the one in hand.[1] One of the main criticisms levelled at the old section 4 and now at section 40 is that it allows a man to break his bargain with impunity.[2] Should this insistence on form, introduced at a time when the parties themselves could not give evidence and theoretically juries still decided cases on their own knowledge, be continued in the 20th century? The question will be debated at the end of the chapter.

Nowadays most people who contemplate buying or selling land consult a solicitor. A proper formal contract, probably embodying either the National Conditions of Sale (20th ed.) or the Law Society General Conditions of Sale (1984 rev.) will be drawn up, whether the land is registered or unregistered. The risk of non-compliance with section 40 is minimal. However, parties do make oral contracts. An oral contract for the sale of land is perfectly valid, but if either party needs to enforce it by action then the formal requirements of section 40 become all-important. In fact the vast majority of cases under section 40 have involved contracts made by parties on their own (often as anti-gazumping devices) or at

---

[1] Law Reform (Enforcement of Contracts) Act 1954.
[2] See, for example, *Timmins* v. *Moreland Street Property Co. Ltd.* [1958] Ch. 110.

auctions or under the influence of estate agents. The cases where a solicitor is involved in a question of validity are relatively rare.[3]

Section 40 governs the enforceability of the contract. But before any question of enforceability can be considered it must be shown that a contract has been made. This involves a final and complete agreement between the parties on at least the essential terms, namely, the parties, the property, the price and in the case of the grant of a lease, the commencement and the period of the lease. In *Harvey* v. *Pratt*[4] the defendant failed to show that he had a valid agreement for a lease of the plaintiff's garage, which he could properly register as an estate contract. The written agreement under which he was claiming did not state the date on which the lease was to commence. In *Courtney and Fairburn Ltd.* v. *Tolaini Brothers (Hotels) Ltd.*[5] parties agreed in writing "to negotiate fair and reasonable contract sums." No price had been agreed, there was no binding contract. An agreement to negotiate was too uncertain to have any binding force at law.

Where a concluded contract is shown to exist, then compliance with the requirements of section 40 may be relevant. The section neatly splits itself into self-contained parts.

1. "No Action May be Brought"

Non-compliance with section 40 does not render a contract void but it does deprive the plaintiff of his important right to bring an action on it. In *Delaney* v. *T. P. Smith Ltd.*[6] the plaintiff had to rely on an oral agreement for lease as an essential part of his cause of action against the defendant–freeholders for trespass. He could not show that the agreement was within section 40 or that circumstances existed (sufficient acts of part performance) to take it outside the ambit of the section. His claim failed.

As the section is really just a procedural bar, a defendant may waive its requirements, but if he wishes to rely on lack of them, then this must be specifically pleaded in his defence.[7] Thus in *North* v. *Loomes*[8] the defendant pleaded the Statute of Frauds generally but did not plead that the memorandum relied on by the plaintiff, omitted an essential term of their agreement. He was ordered specifically to perform the contract. However, the court does have a discretion to allow the pleadings to be amended so that the defendant can take advantage of the section,[9] where for instance there has been an innocent mistake or a new matter has come to the defendant's knowledge since the pleadings were drawn up.

Section 40 does not prevent an oral contract being enforced by means other than action. In *Low* v. *Fry*[10] there was an oral agreement for the sale of a house. The purchaser gave a cheque in part payment of the

---

[3] *Lovesy* v. *Palmer* [1916] 2 Ch. 233; and *Smith* v. *Webster* (1876) 3 Ch.D. 49 are examples.
[4] [1965] 1 W.L.R. 1025.
[5] [1975] 1 W.L.R. 297.
[6] [1946] 1 K.B. 393.
[7] Rules of the Supreme court 1981, Ord. 18, r. 8.
[8] [1919] 1 Ch. 378.
[9] *Re Gonin, decd.* [1979] Ch. 16.
[10] (1935) 152 L.T. 585.

purchase price, but before it was presented changed his mind about the purchase and stopped the cheque. The vendor successfully brought an action to recover on the cheque even though there was no written evidence of the contract. Again, in *Monnickendam* v. *Leanse*[11] the vendor was allowed to forfeit the deposit when his purchaser defaulted, even though it had been paid under an oral contract for sale. It seems that an oral contract can also be used as a defence. Viscount Dilhorne said (*obiter*) in *Steadman* v. *Steadman*[12] that "while section 40 of the Law of Property Act 1925 and section 4 of the Statute of Frauds both prohibit the bringing of an action on such a contract, neither Act prohibits it being relied on as a defence."[13] An oral contract of sale between joint tenants, although it is unenforceable between them, may result in a severance of their beneficial joint tenancy.[14] Finally brief mention should be made here of the maxim of Equity that it will not allow a statute "to be used as an instrument of fraud"[15] and of the law relating to part performance (specifically preserved by section 40(2)) which will be explored a little later on.

2. "Any Contract for the Sale or Other Disposition"

Only contracts disposing of land or an interest in land are required to be evidenced in writing in accordance with the section. The contract may transfer an existing interest in land; for example a contract to assign a lease, or it may create a new interest in land; for example the grant of a new lease. In the vast majority of transactions it will be obvious that an interest in land is to be disposed of. The parties will then ensure that they comply with section 40. Problems arise, when two parties enter into contractual arrangements not realising that they have in fact either created or transferred an interest in land.

Disposition is defined[16] as including a mortgage, charge, lease, disclaimer or release, as well as a devise or appointment of property by will. This definition is not exhaustive. The case of *Grey* v. *I.R.C.*[17] decided that "disposition" should be given its normal wide meaning. When making agreements which are in some way connected with land the provisions of section 40 should be remembered.

Cases where the parties unknowingly dispose of an interest in land frequently arise in connection with family arrangements. In *Re Gonin*[18] a daughter was promised her parents' house if she looked after them in their old age. The promise was made orally and could not therefore be enforced by action in the absence of part performance.[19] Agreements made on divorce between spouses also commonly lead to one party disposing of an interest in land (the matrimonial home) to the other. To be enforceable by action, some note or memoranda should be kept.[20]

---

[11] (1923) 39 T.L.R. 445.   [12] [1976] A.C. 536.
[13] *Ibid.* at p. 551.   [14] *Burgess* v. *Rawnsley* [1975] Ch. 429.
[15] *Rochefoucauld* v. *Boustead* [1897] 1 Ch. 196; *Hodgson* v. *Marks* [1971] Ch. 892.
[16] Law of Property Act 1925, s.205(1)(ii).
[17] [1960] A.C. 1, a case on Law of Property Act 1925, s.53(1)(*c*).
[18] [1979] Ch. 16.   [19] See *post*, p. 140.
[20] See, for example, *Steadman* v. *Steadman* [1976] A.C. 536 and *Liddel* v. *Hopkinson* (1974) 233 E.G. 512.

It is not only in the area of family arrangements that there is a failure to realise that a disposition within the section is being made. For instance in *Daulia Ltd.* v. *Four Millbank Nominees Ltd.*[21] a vendor orally agreed with a purchaser that he would exchange contracts for the sale of some land if the purchaser came to his offices with a draft contract (in the terms already agreed) and a bankers draft for the deposit. The purchaser duly attended but the vendor, having found a buyer willing to pay a higher price elsewhere, refused to exchange. The purchaser tried to enforce the contract and the vendor in his defence pleaded section 40 and that the purchaser having no memoranda of the agreement signed by the vendor could not enforce the contract by action. The Court of Appeal upheld this argument, confirming that the oral agreement was for the disposal of an interest in land. Buckley L.J. explained how this arose:[22]

> "Such an agreement it seems to me would be specifically enforceable, for the common law remedy of damages would be inadequate . . ..
> The performance of the contract for an exchange of agreements would bring a contract of sale into existence. The latter contract would confer an equitable interest on the purchaser."

One type of disposition is not affected by the section.[23] This is the sale of land by the court. Obviously the mischief which the section was enacted to prevent would not arise in dealings in which the court was involved. In practice some written evidence of the contract is usually kept.

3. "Of Land or any Interest in Land"

Land is defined by the Act of 1925[24] as including *inter alia* land of any tenure, buildings, minerals, incorporeal hereditaments, easements and other rights and benefits in, on or over land.

Some problems have been encountered in the past in relation to the exact meaning of the words "interest in land."

LEASES AND LODGINGS

A contract for the grant or assignment of a lease is clearly within the section.[25] In *Biss* v. *Hygate*[26] an oral agreement for the grant of a six year lease of a nursery garden was held to be unenforceable by action in the absence of sufficient written memoranda or part performance. It makes no difference that the premises let are furnished.[27] Less obviously within the section are contracts to procure the transfer of a lease. In *Horsey* v. *Graham*[28] A orally agreed to procure for B the transfer of a lease of land belonging to C. A had no title to the land. Brett J. decided that as the

---

[21] [1978] Ch. 231.
[22] *Ibid.* at p. 246.
[23] Law of Property Act 1925, s.40(2).
[24] *Ibid.* s.205(1)(ix).
[25] *Thursby* v. *Eccles* (1900) 70 L.J.Q.B. 91.
[26] [1918] 2 K.B. 314.
[27] *Inman* v. *Stamp* (1815) 1 Starkie 12.
[28] (1869) L.R. 5 C.P. 9.

subject matter of the agreement was a lease of land section 4 of the Statute of Frauds applied. Although leases not exceeding three years in length may be granted orally[29] a contract to grant such a lease much be evidenced in writing.[30]

Contracts for board and lodgings require no formalities as they do not fall within the ambit of section 40. They do not create any interest in land. Hence an action brought on an oral agreement for the price of board and lodgings has been held to be maintainable.[31]

MORTGAGES

Contracts relating to the mortgage of land fall within the section.[32] In *Driver* v. *Broad*[33] a limited company issued debentures charging the whole of the company's undertaking and property. A debenture holder orally agreed to sell his debenture. The contract was unenforceable; the debenture constituted a charge on the land owned by the company and was therefore an interest in land. Even if the charge on a company's property is floating, some land may eventually be taken as security. A sale of such a charge should therefore be evidenced in writing so as to comply with the section.

UNDIVIDED SHARE IN LAND

An undivided share in land is excluded from the definition of land in section 205 of the Law of Property Act 1925. Nevertheless Jenkins L.J. held in *Cooper* v. *Critchley*[34] that a beneficial interest in the proceeds of sale of concurrently owned property is an interest in land within section 40. Therefore a contract by one of two joint tenants holding on trust for sale for themselves as tenants in common, to sell his interest to the other had to be evidenced in writing. The decision has received the approval of both the Court of Appeal and the House of Lords on a number of occasions.[35]

RIGHTS OF PRE-EMPTION AND CONTRACTUAL LICENCES

A right of pre-emption or first refusal may have the status of an interest in land but only when the right becomes exercisable.[36] An agreement to grant a right of pre-emption therefore falls outside the section.

There is still some doubt as to whether or not a contractual licence can be regarded as an interest in land. The Court of Appeal in *Midland Bank Ltd.* v. *Farmpride Hatcheries Ltd.*[37] proceeded on the assumption that a contractual licence did create an equitable interest in land. If this is

---

[29] Law of Property Act 1925, s.54.
[30] *Rollason* v. *Leon* (1861) 7 H. & N. 73.
[31] *Wright* v. *Stavert* (1860) 2 El. & El. 721.
[32] *Mounsey* v. *Rankin* (1885) 1 Cab. & E. 496; *Pattle* v. *Anstruther* (1893) 69. L. T. 175.
[33] [1893] 1 Q.B. 744.
[34] [1955] Ch. 431.
[35] See *Steadman* v. *Steadman* [1976] A.C. 536; *Irani Finance Ltd.* v. *Singh* [1971] 1 Ch. 59 at 79 and also *Elias* v. *Mitchell* [1972] 2 All E.R. 153.
[36] See *ante*, p. 21, *Pritchard* v. *Briggs* [1980] Ch. 338.
[37] (1981) 260 E.G. 493 noted by R. E. Annand [1982] Conv. 67.

followed a contract for the grant of a contractual licence must be evidenced in writing.

BUILDING AGREEMENTS

An agreement to build on land belonging to another is not within the section. A licence to go onto the land to carry out the work will be implied into the agreement, but is not an interest in land for these purposes.[38] Often building agreements provide for the leasing of the land to the developer. If this is the case the contract is for the disposition of an interest in land and within section 40.

In *Lavery* v. *Pursell*[39] a vendor agreed to sell the building materials of a house on condition that all the materials were to be taken down and cleared off his land within two months. This was held to be a contract for the sale of land and unenforceable by action because of the lack of adequate written evidence.[40]

SALE OF LAND WITH CHATTELS

The basic rule is that agreements for the sale of land and chattels together, need to be evidenced in writing. Such an agreement which is unenforceable in relation to the land because of the lack of writing will not be enforceable in so far as it relates to chattels.[41] Thus in *Hawkesworth* v. *Turner*,[42] A orally agreed to buy from B a business. The sale included the goodwill, stock in trade and the premises of the business. After failing to complete the transaction A argued that section 40 applied, rendering the contract unenforceable against him. It was held that section 40 did apply. The whole of the contract including the terms as to the sale of the goodwill and stock in trade was unenforceable by action.

In certain circumstances the agreement may be enforced in so far as it relates to chattels. This is only permissible when the contract is divisible, the agreements as to land and chattels being capable of forming distinct contracts on their own.[43]

FIXTURES

Fixtures form part of the land to which they are attached and therefore a sale of fixtures constitutes a disposition within the section. However, in the case of an agreement by a tenant to sell fixtures to his landlord no writing is required. Such an agreement amounts to no more than a renunciation by the tenant of his right to remove those fixtures. So in *Lee* v. *Gaskell*[44] where a trustee in bankruptcy sold tenant's fixtures to a person, who then orally sold on to the landlord, it was held that no interest

---

[38] Subject to what has been said above regarding contractual licences see *Jameson* v. *Kinmell Bay Land Co.* (1931) 47 T.L.R. 593.

[39] (1888) 39 Ch.D. 508.

[40] The memorandum did not describe the vendor.

[41] *Ram Narayan* v. *Rishad Hussain Shah* [1979] 1 W.L.R. 1349.

[42] (1930) 46 T.L.R. 389.

[43] *Bigg* v. *Whisking* (1853) 14 C.B. 195; *Morgan* v. *Griffith* (1871) L.R. 6 Exch. 70; *De Lasalle* v. *Guildford* [1901] 2 K.B. 215.

[44] (1876) 1 Q.B.D. 700.

in land was transferred or created and so the lack of writing did not affect the enforceability of the contract.

SALE OF CROPS

It is important to realise that the sale of vegetable produce still standing in the soil may be a sale of land within the section. An important distinction is made between natural crops (fructus naturales) and cultivated crops (fructus industriales).

Natural crops are regarded as land, and therefore contracts to sell them fall within section 40. So a contract for the sale of a growing crop of grass to be mown down by the purchaser has been held to be unenforceable because it was not evidenced in writing.[45] Similarly in *Rodwell* v. *Phillips*[46] a contract to sell "all the crops of fruit and vegetables of the upper part of the garden from the large pear trees, for £30" was held to be unenforceable for want of written memoranda. If the title in the crop is not to pass until it has been severed from the land, or the goods will derive no benefit from remaining in the soil after the making of the contract it is likely that the contract will be outside the scope of section 40.[47]

Cultivated crops such as potatoes,[48] wheat and turnips, etc., are always regarded as goods and contracts to sell these are therefore enforceable even though made orally.

Contracts to sell the soil or earth actually making up the land are within the section.[49] Whether or not a separate pile of earth resting on the land yet not forming part of it is to be regarded as land is still to be settled definitively.

ARBITRATION

Finally it should be noted that an agreement to submit to arbitration a dispute relating to land or an interest in land must be evidenced in writing.[50] The same is true of an agreement concluded in the course of arbitration relating to an interest in land. In *Walters* v. *Morgan*[51] the parties agreed that an arbitrator should determine the contents of a lease. It was held that the agreement fell within section 4 of the Statute of Frauds.

4. "Unless the agreement . . . or some memorandum or note thereof"

There are several points which fall to be considered here.

FORM

The contract itself need not be in writing. Section 40(1) merely requires written evidence of it, "some memorandum or note thereof." It is

---

[45] *Crosby* v. *Wadsworth* (1805) 6 East 602.
[46] (1842) 9 M. & W. 501.
[47] See Hudson (1953) 22 Conv. 137 and *Smith* v. *Surman* (1829) 9 B. & Cr. 561.
[48] *Parker* v. *Staniland* (1809) 11 East 362.
[49] *Morgan* v. *Russell & Sons* [1909] 1 K.B. 357.
[50] *Rainforth* v. *Harmer* (1855) 25 L.T.(o.s.) 247.
[51] (1792) 2 Cox Eq.Cas. 369.

irrelevant that the writer did not intend his document to be used as a memorandum. In *Re Hoyle*[52] a testator's will was held to be a sufficient memorandum. Bowen L.J. said "the question is not one of intention of the party who signs the document but simply one of evidence against him. The court is not in quest of the intention of parties, but only of evidence under the hand of one of the parties to the contract that he has entered into it. Any document signed by him and containing the terms of the contract is sufficient . . . ."[53] Thus no special form of memorandum is necessary. In *Hill* v. *Hill*[54] a tenant wrote "Renewed lease Dec. 25, 1941" in his rent book and the landlord initialled it to acknowledge receipt of rent. An adequate memorandum existed. Case law illustrates that the most common forms of inadvertent memoranda which have been held to be within section 40(1), are receipts[55] and letters.[56] A point to watch is that a letter repudiating a prior oral contract may be a sufficient memorandum to support it,[57] although a letter denying the very existence of the contract would not.[58] More worrying is the view expressed in *Griffiths* v. *Young*[59] and followed in *Law* v. *Jones*,[60] that the words "subject to contract" on a letter (showing an intention that the letter is not to be binding) can be removed by a subsequent oral contract between the parties, with the result that the letter will supply a prematurely binding memorandum. However, there is equally weighty authority[61] for the view that such a letter cannot be a memorandum within section 40(1) and that to remove the "umbrella protection" of the words "subject to contract" from negotiations, there must be an express agreement between the parties to expunge the words "subject to contract" or that this agreement must be necessarily implied.[62]

The written memorandum of the contract must have come into existence before the action begins[63] but apart from this it can be made at any time after the contract has been made—even 14 years later.[64] There is an old line of cases[65] which establish the rule that an adequate memorandum can be made before the contract, where one party makes an offer in writing which is subsequently accepted by the other party by words or conduct. It is interesting that these cases were decided at a time when the common law knew nothing of the doctrine of part performance, and as Lord Denning M.R. said in *Tiverton Estates Ltd.* v. *Wearwell Ltd.*[66] "these

---

[52] [1893] 1 Ch. 84.
[53] *Ibid.* at p. 99.
[54] [1947] Ch. 231.
[55] *Auerbach* v. *Nelson* [1919] 2 Ch. 383; *Davies* v. *Sweet* [1962] 2 Q.B. 300.
[56] *Smith-Bird* v. *Blower* [1939] 2 All E.R. 406; *Smith* v. *Mansi* [1963] 1 W.L.R. 26.
[57] *Dewar* v. *Mintoft* [1912] 2 K.B. 373.
[58] *Thirkell* v. *Cambi* [1979] 2 K.B. 290; *Law* v. *Jones* [1974] Ch. 112.
[59] [1970] Ch. 675.
[60] [1974] Ch. 112, C.A.
[61] *Tiverton Estates Ltd.* v. *Wearwell Ltd.* [1975] 1 Ch. 146, C.A.
[62] *Cohen* v. *Nessdale Ltd.* [1982] 2 All E.R. 97. This could explain the decision in *Griffiths* v. *Young*. See [1981] Conv. 165–167.
[63] *Re Holland* [1902] 2 Ch. 360.
[64] *Barkworth* v. *Young* (1856) 4 Drew 1.
[65] *Warner* v. *Willington* (1856) 3 Drew. 523; *Smith* v. *Neale* (1857) 2 C.B.(N.S.) 67; *Reuss* v. *Picksley* (1866) L.R. 1 Exch. 342.
[66] [1975] 1 Ch. 146 at p. 156.

decisions . . . were very necessary to meet the justice of the case." It has also been observed[67] that they "pushed the literal construction of the Statute of Frauds to a limit beyond which it would perhaps be not easy to go . . .,"[68].Where a plaintiff can establish that a memorandum has been lost or destroyed, oral evidence is admissible (but treated with caution) to prove that it did satisfy section 40(1).[69]

CONTENTS

The general rule is that for a contract for the sale of land to be enforceable, it must contain all the terms which have been agreed by the parties.[70] A contract which is itself in writing (for example one drawn up and the parts exchanged by solicitors) will rarely fall foul of this rule.[71] Where the writing relied on is a note or memorandum of the parties prior oral agreement, it must normally be a true record of that agreement.

To constitute an enforceable contract the writing must specify:

  (i) The names of the vendor and the purchaser (parties);
 (ii) The subject matter of the sale or other disposition (property);
(iii) The consideration for the sale (price);
(iv) Any other terms agreed between the parties (provisions).

By way of preliminary it should be mentioned that the terms of the contract will be sufficiently stated if they fall within the rule "id certum est quod certum reddi potest"—"that is certain which can be made certain."

   (i) **Parties.** Obviously there can be no contract if the parties are not known. However, neither the vendor nor the purchaser need be specifically named, provided they are described in such a way that there can be no dispute as to their identity, because oral evidence can be admitted to complete their identification.[72]

Identification held to be sufficient. In *Sale* v. *Lambert*[73] property was described in auction particulars as being sold "by direction of the proprietor," but the vendor was not named in the contract. Sir George Jessel M.R. held that the vendor was sufficiently described. He explained this decision a few weeks later in *Potter* v. *Duffield*.[74] In the former case there was only one person who satisfied the description of "proprietor." "Proprietors" was also a good description of the vendors in *Rossiter* v. *Miller*.[75]

Apparently "mortgagee" is also sufficient.[76] In *Allen & Co. Ltd.* v. *Whiteman*,[77] one of two mortgagees agreed through estate agents to sell

---

[67] Bowen L.J., in *Re New Eberhardt Co., ex p. Menzies* (1889) 43 Ch.D. 118 at 129.
[68] Although the C. A. seemed to have managed it in *Law* v. *Jones* [1974] Ch. 112.
[69] *Barber* v. *Rowe* [1948] 2 All E.R. 1050.
[70] *Beckett* v. *Nurse* [1948] 1 K.B. 535.
[71] *Hutton* v. *Watling* [1948] Ch. 398.
[72] *Carr* v. *Lynch* [1900] 1 Ch. 613.
[73] (1874) L.R. 18 Eq. 1.
[74] (1874) L.R. 18 Eq. 4.
[75] (1878) 3 App.Cas. 1124.
[76] *Jarrett* v. *Hunter* (1886) 34 Ch.D. 182.
[77] (1920) 123 L.T.R. 773.

land. The agents agreed to sell for "our client" but did not name her. In correspondence they said that a Mr. Whiteman was the vendor's husband and in the auction particulars that the sale was "by order of the mortgagees." All these factors meant that the vendor was identifiable and bound by the agreement. In *Catling* v. *King*[78] the conditions of sale stated that "The vendor is a trustee selling under a trust for sale," but did not mention the vendor by name. In deciding that this was a good description, the Court of Appeal said that a trustee for sale could often be more easily identified than, say a Mr. Jones. A trustee for sale necessarily derives his title from a written document. For similar reasons a description of the vendor as "the legal personal representative" also sufficed in *Fay* v. *Miller, Wilkins and Company*.[79]

It has been argued (unsuccessfully) that the process of looking for identifying factors outside the name was appropriate to identify a personal vendor but inappropriate to identify a limited company, which has no physical characteristics. In *F. Goldsmith (Sicklesmere) Ltd.* v. *Baxter*[80] the plaintiff-vendors were innocently misnamed in the contract as Goldsmith Coaches (Sicklesmere) Ltd. Stamp L.J. held that the error was not fatal to the plaintiff's claim for specific performance. The registered office given in the contract was the same as the true owner's, the property was correctly described and the name of the director who signed the contract was correctly stated and was the same as that of the director of the true owner company. These elements effectively identified the vendors. In so holding Stamp L.J. was following the earlier decision of *Commins* v. *Scott*[81] where the company-vendor's name did not appear in the contract at all. However, it was clear from other clauses in the contract that what was being sold was land on which the company was carrying on its business. This was enough to render the vendors ascertainable.

If the agreement or memorandum states the names of two parties who are contractually bound to one another, then section 40(1) is satisfied even if it is known at the time, or later discovered, that one of the parties is an agent for either the vendor or the purchaser.[82] In *Basma* v. *Weekes*[83] Mr. Wright, a solicitor, agreed in writing to buy two houses in Freetown from three ladies. The ladies knew at the time of the agreement that Mr. Wright was acting as an agent for Mr. Basma, the purchaser, but he was not named in the agreement. The Privy Council held that the purchaser could sue on the contract; Mr. Wright was contractually bound by the agreement and could sue on it, therefore so could his principal, Mr. Basma.

Identification held insufficient. It is not sufficient to describe the vendor as "vendor" or for a solicitor to describe either party as "my client." Supposedly anyone could come within this description.

In *Potter* v. *Duffield*[84] the particulars and conditions of sale of property

---

[78] (1877) 5 Ch.D. 660.
[79] [1941] 1 Ch. 360.
[80] [1970] Ch. 85.
[81] (1875) 20 L.R. Eq. 11.
[82] *Davies* v. *Sweet* [1962] 2 Q.B. 300.
[83] [1950] A.C. 441.
[84] (1874) L.R. 18 Eq. 4.

by auction described the seller as "the vendor" and sometimes "vendors." The memorandum of sale, signed by the purchaser and auctioneers, stated that the sale was "confirmed on behalf of the vendor." He was nowhere stated by name. Sir George Jessel M.R. held that there was no binding contract as the seller was not so described by the word "vendor" that his identity was clear. It could be argued that just as only one person could answer the description of "proprietor" so only one could answer that of "vendor," but the courts have not taken this view.[85]

In *Lovesy* v. *Palmer*[86] a solicitor acting for an intending lessee mentioned only "my clients" when agreeing heads of agreement for a lease. Lovesy was his client but he intended to form a company to take the lease, which is why the solicitor referred to "my clients." Lovesy failed to obtain specific performance of the agreement because "my clients" was not a good description of him.

The fact that the defendant knows who the vendor is, does not render the contract enforceable if the vendor is insufficiently described in the contract.[87] Further, if a condition of sale refers to a conveyance or other document of title relating to the property, and the name or description of the vendor is not in the contract, it is not sufficient to import its contents into the memorandum even if the document of title shows who the vendor is.[88]

(ii) **Property.** Again obviously, the subject-matter of the contract must be clear. The same sort of considerations apply to the description of the property as to the description of the parties. In other words, even though the description is vague, provided it is clear enough to enable the property to be ascertained, then oral evidence is admissible to complete the identification.[89] Thus in *Cowley* v. *Watts*[90] "my house" was sufficiently certain because the evidence showed that the vendor only owned one house. It seems that the word "my" or other equivalent adjective is not essential. In *Auerbach* v. *Nelson*[91] the memorandum relied on was a receipt which included the words "House being sold for 500.*l.* from Mr. Nelson . . . ." Astbury J. applying the principle that "the court assumes that a man is selling his own property . . . ." accepted evidence to show that only one house could satisfy that description—Mr. Nelson's. The memorandum was enforceable. However, oral evidence cannot provide a description where there is none in the contract. Suppose that X contracts to sell "my property in AB street." If X has more than one property in AB street then the description is uncertain.[92]

The following are examples of descriptions that have sufficed. In *Ogilvie*

---

[85] See also *Jarrett* v. *Hunter* (1886) 34 Ch.D. 182; *Coombs* v. *Wilkes* [1891] 3 Ch. 77.
[86] [1916] 2 Ch. 233; "my principal" would also not suffice: *Rossiter* v. *Miller* (1878) 3 App.Cas. 1124.
[87] *Jarrett* v. *Hunter* (1886) 34 Ch.D. 182; *Lovesy* v. *Palmer* [1916] 2 Ch. 233.
[88] *Jarrett* v. *Hunter* (1886) 34 Ch.D. 182.
[89] *Shardlow* v. *Cotterell* (1881) 20 Ch.D. 90; see Jessel M.R. at p. 92.
[90] (1853) 17 Jur. 172.
[91] [1919] 2 Ch. 383.
[92] Given as an example in *Plant* v. *Bourne* [1897] 2 Ch. 281.

v. *Foljambe*[93] oral evidence was allowed in to identify "Mr. Ogilvie's house" and in *Shardlow* v. *Cotterell*[94] to identify "property purchased at 420.*l.* at Sun Inn, Pinxton, on the above date, Mr. George Cotterell, Pinxton, Owner." In *Plant* v. *Bourne*,[95] Plant agreed to sell "twenty-four acres of land, freehold . . . at Totmonslow in the parish of Draycott, in the County of Stafford." The Court of Appeal admitted oral evidence to show that Plant only had 24 acres of land at Totmonslow. And in *Davies* v. *Sweet*[96] the property was described in the memorandum as "land on which Evans Row houses previously stood (bottom of New Road, Pennydarren)." The description was adequate because the purchaser stated in evidence that she was buying "the demolished part of Evans Row."

The property need only be described physically. The estate or interest being sold need not be specifically mentioned as this is governed by the implied terms.[97] Where however the contract is for the grant of a lease the duration and commencement date of the lease must be stated.[98]

(iii) **The Price.** The contract or memorandum must contain the consideration for the sale. In the absence of express agreement no term will be implied by law that the purchaser will pay a reasonable price.[99]

The contract will be valid if the parties give a formula for ascertaining the price, provided that it can be assessed by the court objectively. "The court is reluctant to hold void for uncertainty any provision that was intended to have legal effect."[1] Thus an agreement to sell at a "fair price" or a "fair valuation" is sufficiently precise.[2] And in *Brown* v. *Gould*,[3] Megarry J. held valid and enforceable an option to renew a lease "at a rent to be fixed having regard to the market value . . . ."

However, if the formula involves making a subjective decision the contract will fail for uncertainty. In *Kings Motors (Oxford) Ltd.* v. *Lax*[4] a lease contained an option for the grant of a further term "at such rental as may be agreed upon between the parties . . . ." The option was void for uncertainty. And as mentioned earlier, in *Courtney and Fairburn Ltd.* v. *Tolaini Brothers (Hotels) Ltd.*[5] an agreement "to negotiate fair and reasonable contract sums" was too indefinite to be binding.

Until very recently the contract would also fail if the parties included machinery for determining a price and for some reason it failed to work. The court could not substitute machinery of its own to cure the problem, because "a price fixed in any other way does not execute any agreement of (the parties) but makes an agreement for them."[6]

---

[93] (1817) 3 Mer. 53.   [94] (1881) 20 Ch.D. 90.

[95] [1897] 2 Ch. 281.

[96] [1962] 2 Q.B. 300.

[97] *Timmins* v. *Moreland Street Property Co. Ltd.* [1958] Ch. 110.

[98] *Harvey* v. *Pratt* [1965] 1 W.L.R. 1025.

[99] *Morgan* v. *Milman* (1853) 3 De G.M. & G. 24.

[1] Per Megarry J. in *Brown* v. *Gould* [1972] Ch. 53 at p. 56.

[2] *Milnes* v. *Gery* (1807) 14 Ves. 400; *Talbot* v. *Talbot* [1968] Ch. 1.

[3] [1972] 1 Ch. 53.

[4] [1969] 1 W.L.R. 421.

[5] [1975] 1 W.L.R. 297.

[6] *Milnes* v. *Gery* (1807) 33 All E.R. 574 at 577.

The law as it stood in this area on March 18, 1981 was ably summarised by Templeman L.J. delivering the judgment of the Court of Appeal in *Sudbrook Trading Estate Ltd.* v. *Eggleton*.[7] The case involved an option to purchase at a valuation price. Each side (lessor and lessee) had to appoint valuers and in the event of their being unable to agree a valuation, the valuers were to appoint a valuer. The lessors refused to appoint a valuer. The Court of Appeal, constrained by previous authority decided, "regretfully because this option was clearly intended to be effective and was at the time thought to be effective"[8] that the option was invalid. Templeman L.J.'s summary explains why:

> "First, in ascertaining the essential terms of a contract, the court will not substitute machinery of its own for machinery provided by the parties, however defective that machinery may prove to be. Secondly, where machinery is agreed for the ascertainment of an essential term, then until the agreed machinery has operated successfully, the court will not decree specific performance, since there is not yet any contract to perform. Thirdly, where the operation of the machinery is stultified by the refusal of one of the parties to appoint a valuer or an arbitrator, the court will not, by way of partial specific performance, compel him to make an appointment. All three of these principles stem from one central proposition, that where the agreement on the face of it is incomplete until something else has been done, whether by further agreement between the parties or by the decision of an arbitrator or valuer, the court is powerless, because there is no complete agreement to enforce . . . ."[9]

As he went on to explain two great inroads had already been made into these rules. The first is where an agreement has already been partly performed: "where an agreement which would otherwise be unenforceable for want of certainty or finality in an essential stipulation has been partly performed so that the intervention of the court is necessary in aid of a grant that has already taken effect, the court will strain to the utmost to supply the want of certainty even to the extent of providing a substitute machinery."[10] Thus in *Beer* v. *Bowden*[11] a lease for 10 years provided for a rent of £1,250 per annum for the first five years and then for a rent to be agreed between the parties, taking no account of tenant's improvements. The lease was later extended by agreement from 10 to 14 years. After the first five years the parties failed to agree a new rent. It was held that a fair rent was to be implied otherwise the tenant would pay either the same rent or no rent at all for the second period. In *Thomas Bates & Son Ltd.* v. *Wyndham's Lingerie Ltd.*[12] the Court of Appeal had to deal with an almost identical set of facts, but it decided that the revised rent should be a market rent.

---

[7] [1981] 3 W.L.R. 361.
[8] *Ibid.* at p. 376.
[9] *Ibid.* at p. 373.
[10] *Ibid.*
[11] (1976) [1981] 1 W.L.R. 522.
[12] [1981] 1 W.L.R. 505; and see R. Pearce and D. Tomkin (1981) 131 New L.J. 859.

The second inroad has been made where the valuation provisions relate to a subsidiary part of a wider contract, which is itself valid and enforceable. For example in *Smith* v. *Peters*[13] there was an agreement for the sale of a house at a fixed price and for the fixtures and furniture to be valued by a specified valuer, Mr. Lounds, who was ready to act. The vendor would not let him into the house to make his valuation. Jessel M.R. made a mandatory order forcing the vendor to let the valuer into the house and for specific performance. The vendor was under an implied obligation to allow a valuation to be made. It was noted that the value of the fixtures and fittings was expected to be low in relation to the price of the house.

The decision of the Court of Appeal in *Sudbrook Trading Estate Ltd* v. *Eggleton* has now been reversed by the House of Lords,[14] and an even greater inroad made into the rules (if they have not been completely overturned). Overruling prior authorities, which they said were inconsistent with modern commercial practice, the Lords held that the breakdown of the valuation machinery should not defeat the contract unless that machinery was expressly or impliedly of the essence. In other words they said that the court can normally substitute its own machinery for machinery agreed by the parties which has not worked. They also held that the description "valuer" necessarily implied that the price to be fixed should be "fair and reasonable."

So how does the law stand now assuming no fixed price appears in the contract?

1. If the parties provide an objective formula for ascertaining the price (without adding machinery) this will satisfy section 40(1).

2. If the parties provide a subjective formula simpliciter (for example "a price to be agreed between the parties") then this will be void for uncertainty, unless the contract has already been partly performed or the formula relates to a subsidiary part of a wider contract which is itself valid and enforceable.

3. Where the parties provide machinery for determining the price and that machinery does not work the court will substitute its own, provided that the machinery is not an essential term of the contract. It may well be an essential term where an agreement is made to sell at a price to be fixed by a named valuer, who for some reason refuses or is unable to do so.[15] In this case the contract will fail for uncertainty (although presumably the "partly performed" and "subsidiary part of a wider contract" exceptions will apply).

4. In *Sudbrook* the lessees waived their right to have the price fixed according to the agreed machinery and were willing to allow the court to determine it. Therefore the House of Lords did not have to consider whether or not they could force the lessor to appoint a valuer. Lord Diplock suggested in his judgment that the court would have this power. He said[16] "I do not accept as fit for survival in a civilised system of law

---

[13] (1875) L.R. 20 Eq. 511.
[14] [1982] 3 W.L.R. 315.
[15] *Ibid*. See Lord Diplock's and Lord Fraser's judgments.
[16] *Ibid*. at p. 322.

any of the three principles extracted from the authorities that are summarised in the passage . . . from the judgment of Templeman L.J."[17]

5. It is suggested that to avoid litigation solicitors acting for parties who wish to leave the price to be fixed at some future date should use a precedent which does not allow either party to refuse to appoint his valuer. It should be expressly provided that in this event, a third party can be appointed by the other party and that he can make a binding valuation.[18]

6. For the sake of completeness it should be mentioned that where the contract is for the sale of land at a price to be fixed by an agreed valuer, both parties will be bound by an honest valuation notwithstanding that other valuers may produce different figures.[19] If the valuation is wrong and negligently carried out, the valuer may be liable for damages.

(iv) **Provisions.** Section 40(1) requires the *agreement*, "or some memorandum or note *thereof*" to be in writing. Therefore where the plaintiff is relying on a memorandum to enforce an oral agreement, the memorandum must record the terms of *that* agreement. If not then it will not satisfy the section even though at face value it shows a valid contract. In *Ram Narayan* v. *Rishad Hussain Shah*[20] there was an oral agreement for the sale of land and chattels—two farms, two bullocks, two ploughshares and one tractor, but the written memorandum only referred to the land. The whole contract was unenforceable, the memorandum did not accurately reflect the parties' bargain.

If the parties have agreed terms other than the parties, property and price, they should be included. Where a statute requires a contract to be evidenced in writing and the contract itself is in writing, the rule is that it cannot be contradicted, varied or added to by oral evidence, although as we shall see the remedy of rectification may provide a way round this. Where the contract is oral and the plaintiff alleges a sufficient memorandum within section 40(1), the rule does not apply. The defendant may produce evidence to show that the memorandum does not contain all the terms orally agreed between himself and the plaintiff and in so doing resist an action for specific performance.[21] *Johnson* v. *Humphrey*[22] is an example. In an oral agreement for the sale of a bungalow the parties agreed that the vendor need not give vacant possession until she had found herself somewhere else to live. Roxburgh J. held that the memorandum of sale was insufficient because it omitted the term. In *Tweddell* v. *Henderson*[23] the memorandum did not satisfy section 40(1) because it made no reference to the vendor's promise to make up the road, nor to certain variations in the plans, nor to payment of the purchase price in instalments.

Exceptions to the "All Terms" Rule

(A) *Implied terms.* Terms which have not been expressly agreed between

---

[17] Set out *ante*, p. 129.
[18] H. W. Wilkinson (1982) 132 New L.J. 260.
[19] *Campbell* v. *Edwards* [1976] 1 W.L.R. 403.
[20] [1979] 1 W.L.R. 1349.
[21] *Beckett* v. *Nurse* [1948] 1 K.B. 535.
[22] [1946] 1 All E.R. 460.
[23] [1975] 2 All E.R. 1096.

the parties but which are implied by law into their agreement, need not be mentioned.[24] In *Farrell* v. *Green*,[24a] a carpet salesman with other activities orally agreed to buy a Georgian mansion. He obtained the vendor's signature to an informal note of the sale "to avoid a gazumping operation." The vendor refused to proceed with the sale. In resisting the carpet salesman's action for specific performance he alleged that the memorandum was ineffective because no reference was made to vacant possession on completion. Pennycuick V.-C. held that this did not matter because the law implied, in the absence of express provision, completion within a reasonable time and vacant possession on completion. The case is also authority for the further rule that section 40(1) is not offended if an expressly agreed term which exactly coincides with an implied term is omitted from the memorandum.

(B) *Waived terms.* If the missing term solely benefits the plaintiff, he may waive the term and enforce the contract as evidenced by the memorandum. Thus in *North* v. *Loomes*[25] the plaintiff was allowed to waive an undertaking by the defendant to pay the plaintiff's legal costs in the sale and enforce the contract. However the term must be solely for the benefit of the plaintiff and it seems, not be of such importance as to be a material term of the contract. *Hawkins* v. *Price*[26] concerned an oral agreement to sell a house and orchard. The parties agreed that completion should take place on March 30, when vacant possession of the orchard should be given, but that the vendor should be allowed to stay on in the house for another one or two months. The memorandum was defective for omitting this term; it was for the benefit of both parties and a material term of the contract.

Of course it must be remembered that no question can arise of plaintiff waiving a term for his benefit unless he can first show a concluded contract.

(C) *Terms submitted to.* Where the missing term is solely to the detriment of the plaintiff, it was unclear whether the plaintiff could agree to perform the term and enforce the contract. In *Martin* v. *Pycroft*[27] the tenant sued for specific performance of a written agreement for lease. The agreement omitted a term that the tenant would pay a premium of £200. The Court of Appeal in chancery allowed the tenant to pay the premium and enforce the contract. On this authority the rule was accepted in *Williams on Vendor and Purchaser*.[28] However later in *Burgess* v. *Cox*[29] Harman J. held that the plaintiff could not submit to a term which was for the benefit of the defendant so as to cure its omission from the memorandum. Megarry J. criticised this later decision in a note in the *Law Quarterly Review*[30] where he concluded that "neither on principle nor on

---

[24] *Timmins* v. *Moreland Street Property Co. Ltd.* [1958] Ch. 110.
[24a] (1974) 232 E. G. 587.
[25] [1919] 1 Ch. 378.
[26] [1947] 1 Ch. 645.
[27] (1852) 2 De G.M. & G. 785.
[28] 1939, 4th ed. Vol. 1, p. 5.
[29] [1951] Ch. 383.
[30] (1951) 67 L.Q.R. 300.

authority does *Burgess* v. *Cox* appear to promise great longevity . . . ." More recently *Martin* v. *Pycroft* and *Williams* were followed in *Scott* v. *Bradley*,[31] where the plaintiff was awarded a decree of specific performance on agreeing to submit to a missing term to pay one half of the defendant's legal costs.

(D) *Rectification.* There is a fourth exception to the "all-terms" rule where the equitable remedy of rectification is available. Where any of the terms of the oral contract are omitted from the memorandum of it due to a mistake common to both parties, then the court may, in one action, rectify the memorandum and decree specific performance of the real agreement.[32]

Due to a recent development in the law, the equitable remedy of rectification may also be an exception to the rule that where the contract is wholly in writing, oral evidence is inadmissible to contradict, vary or add to its terms. It used to be thought that the court only had jurisdiction to rectify where a concluded contract was shown to exist prior to the written agreement in hand. In *Joscelyne* v. *Nissen*[33] the Court of Appeal rectified an agreement for the transfer of a business from father to daughter to reflect a prior understanding that she would thereafter be responsible for her parents' household bills. The Court said that it was not necessary to find a concluded contract antecedent to the agreement, they had jurisdiction to rectify on the basis of a common continuing intention of the parties, "with the qualification that some outward expression of accord is required."[34] *Emmet on Title* comments[35]: "Consequently considerable inroads into the 'all terms' rule of Section 40(1) could be achieved with sales of land where negotiations customarily proceed throughout on a basis of various common continuing intentions expressed in correspondence up to a formal exchange of contracts."

SEVERAL DOCUMENTS

It is possible for two or more documents to be read together to form a memorandum sufficient to satisfy the section. The process, often referred to as joinder of documents, may be carried out in two situations.

The first arises when all the documents sought to be joined are signed by the party to be charged. If when laid side by side they clearly point to the same transaction they may be read together to form a complete memorandum.[36]

The second situation in which joinder of documents may take place is when one document, again signed by the party to be charged, refers to some other document or transaction. The reference may be express or implied, in which case oral evidence can be given to identify the other

---

[31] [1971] 1 Ch. 850.
[32] *Craddock Bros.* v. *Hunt* [1923] 2 Ch. 136.
[33] [1970] 2 Q.B. 86.
[34] *Per* Russell L.J. [1970] 2 Q.B. 86 at p. 98.
[35] (18th ed.), p. 66.
[36] *Burgess* v. *Cox* [1951] Ch. 383; *Sheers* v. *Thimbleby & Son* (1879) 76 L.T. 709.

document referred to or to explain the other transaction and identify any document relating to it.[37]

An express reference to another document may clearly identify that document. However, it is not necessary for the reference in the signed document, to unequivocally identify the other document. For example in *Jones* v. *Victoria Graving Dock Co.*[38] it was held that oral evidence was admissible to identify "the agreement" referred to in a minute book of a company which had been signed by the defendant to the action. Once the identity of "the agreement" had been established it was joined with the minute book to form an adequate memorandum of the contract.[39] Further if the first document refers only to something which could either be written or oral, for example "instructions," parol evidence can be given to establish that the reference is in fact to a written document.[40] Thus in *Long* v. *Millar*[41] it was accepted that if A wrote to B offering to buy B's estate on stated terms and B wrote back saying, "I accept your offer," it would be open to A to prove orally that the "offer" referred to by B was written and so capable of being joined with B's letter to form a written memorandum of the contract.

The reference to another document or transaction may be implied. For example in *Stokes* v. *Whicher*[42] a purchaser signed the top copy of a written memorandum which failed to name the purchaser. The vendor's agent refused to sell. The purchaser was able to join his top copy with the carbon copy signed by the vendors agent, thereby completing the memorandum. The existence of a carbon copy implied the existence of a top copy and therefore joinder was permissible.[43] In *Timmins* v. *Moreland Street Property Co. Ltd.*,[44] T. verbally agreed to sell to M. a property for £39,000. M. paid a deposit of £3,900 by cheque and T. gave M. a signed receipt setting out full particulars of the agreement. When M. decided to withdraw from the transaction T. tried to enforce the sale. T. had a document signed by M. (the party to be charged)—the cheque. However, to have a complete memorandum T. had to be able to join the cheque with the receipt (containing the terms of the agreement). It was held that the cheque did not contain any reference express or implied to the receipt allowing T. to joint it and complete the memorandum. M. could have given T. the cheque for any number of reasons, entirely unconnected with the payment of the deposit. In what has become the leading judgment on the subject Jenkins L.J. stated "that two or more documents may only be read together if, starting with the document signed by the party to be charged, a reference, express or implied, is found to another document dealing with the same transaction."[45]

---

[37] *Timmins* v. *Moreland Street Property Co. Ltd.* [1958] Ch. 110.
[38] (1877) 2 Q.B.D. 314.
[39] See also *Morris* v. *Wilson* (1859) 33 L.T.(O.S.) 56.
[40] *Oliver* v. *Hunting* (1890) 44 Ch.D. 205; *Ridgeway* v. *Wharton* (1857) 6 H.L.C. 238. *Baumann* v. *James* (1868) 3 Ch.App. 508; *Cave* v. *Hastings* (1881) 7 Q.B.D. 125.
[41] (1879) 4 C.P.D. 450.
[42] [1920] 1 Ch. 411.
[43] See also *Studds* v. *Watson* (1884) 28 Ch.D. 305; *Fitsmaurice* v. *Bayley* (1860) 9 H.L.C. 78 (*c.f.* *Pierce* v. *Corf* (1874) L.R. 9 Q.B. 210).
[44] [1958] 1 Ch. 110.   [45] [1958] Ch. 110 at 130.

This test was recently applied by the Privy Council in *Elias* v. *George Sakely & Co. (Barbados) Ltd.*[46] The parties had orally agreed on the sale of business premises and the buyer's lawyer wrote to the seller's lawyer setting out the essential minimum terms and enclosing a cheque for 10 per cent. of the agreed price. The seller's lawyer did not reply by letter but sent a receipt setting out the names of the parties, the amount of the payment and the fact that it was a deposit on a property to be sold by the seller to the buyer. The buyer was able to join the receipt with the letter to form a memorandum of the contract. The receipt pointed to the existence of another document—the letter—and when laid side by side the receipt and the letter contained all the terms of the contract to satisfy the requirements of section 40.

Finally it should be noted that a document, signed by the defendant to an action, cannot be treated as referring to a document not in existence at the time when the first document was signed.[47] This does not mean that the court will involve itself in minute investigations to discover the order in which documents were signed, if they were, more or less, contemporaneously executed.[48]

ACKNOWLEDGMENT OF THE CONTRACT

A note or memorandum which denies the existence of a contract or disputes its terms cannot constitute sufficient written evidence within the section.[49] A denial that a contract exists must be distinguished from a repudiation of liability under an existing contract. The case of *Bailey* v. *Sweeting*[50] was the first in a long line of cases[51] which decided that if a letter or other note, distinctly admitted the contract and all its terms, but denied liability for some reason connected with the performance of the contract, then the letter or note was sufficient to satisfy the section.

It used to be a clear rule that written evidence of an oral contract for the sale of land had itself to recognise the existence of a concluded contract between the parties.[52] This is because section 40 states that if the contract itself is not in writing it must be evidenced by "some memorandum or note *thereof*." Oral evidence cannot be adduced to prove that the parties have actually made a contract. However in *Law* v. *Jones*[53] the Court of Appeal decided that a memorandum which did not acknowledge the contract's existence, but did record all the terms agreed by the parties was sufficient to satisfy section 40. Only when the memorandum denied liability under the alleged oral contract was an acknowledgment required.

---

[46] [1982] 3 All E.R. 801, *per* Lord Scarman at p. 807.
[47] *Turnley* v. *Hartley* (1848) 3 New Pr.Cas. 96.
[48] *Timmins* v. *Moreland Street Co. Property Ltd.* [1958] Ch. 110.
[49] *Goodman* v. *Griffiths* (1857) 1 H. & N. 574; *Archer* v. *Baines* (1850) 5 Exch. 625; *Thirkell* v. *Cambi* [1979] 2 K.B. 590.
[50] (1861) 9 C.B.(N.S.) 843.
[51] *Wilkinson* v. *Evans* (1866) L.R. 1 C.P. 407; *Buxton* v. *Rust* (1872) L.R. 7 Exch. 279; *Dewar* v. *Mintoft* [1912] 2 K.B. 373 are just three examples. See also *Tiverton Estates Ltd.* v. *Wearwell Ltd.* [1975] 1 Ch. 146 *per* Lord Denning at p. 157.
[52] *Societe Capa Societe a Responsabilite Limitee* v. *Acatos & Co. Ltd.* [1953] 2 Lloyds Rep. 185.
[53] [1974] Ch. 112.

Less than a year later a differently constituted Court of Appeal decided, in *Tiverton Estates Ltd.* v. *Wearwell Ltd.*,[54] that the section required a note or memorandum to acknowledge the existence of a contract in all cases, in addition to recording all the terms of that contract. It was further held that correspondence headed "subject to contract" amounted to a denial of the existence of a contract and could not constitute memoranda within the section. The two cases are undoubtedly in conflict on the acknowledgment.[55] This conflict awaits definitive resolution by the House of Lords. However two first instance decisions[56] have followed the view taken in *Tiverton Estates.* In *Cohen* v. *Nessdale*, Kilner Brown J.[57] stated; "In the light of well established authority it is clear beyond argument that the use of the term 'subject to contract' in a letter means that it indicates that there was no acknowledgment of a binding agreement and therefore it cannot be a sufficient note or memorandum." In the meantime one commentator has suggested that in future correspondence should be headed "contract denied" in preference to "subject to contract."[58]

5. "is in writing"

"Writing" is widely defined as including "typing, printing, lithography, photography, and other modes of representing or reproducing words in a visible form."[59] So, Russell J. had no difficulty in remarking "en passant" in *Aquis Estates Ltd.* v. *Minton*[60] that "the plaintiff . . . a developer . . . contracted, by telex to buy and the defendant to sell the defendant's interest for £50,000." However whether or not a contract by telex is "signed" is not so clear. As we shall see, in principle it should be alright, for a signature need not be handwritten but may be a printed name inserted with intent to authenticate the contract. A parallel may perhaps be drawn from the case of *McBlain* v. *Cross*[61] where the signing of a telegram form by an agent was sufficient to enforce the contract contained in the telegram.

6. "signed by the party to be charged, or by some other person thereunto by him lawfully authorised"

SIGNED

This requirement has been liberally interpreted by the courts. It is clear that the document must be signed somewhere, and the signatory must sign

---

[54] [1975] 1 Ch. 146.

[55] Buckley L.J. (one of the majority in *Law* v. *Jones*) in *Daulia Ltd.* v. *Four Millbank Nominees Ltd.* [1978] 2 W.L.R. 621 at p. 635.

[56] *Jones* v. *Morgan* (1974) 231 E.G. 1167, Brightman J. (as he then was) held that the memorandum must contain "an express or implied recognition that the contract was entered into." *Cohen* v. *Nessdale* [1981] 3 All E.R. 118. See also *Mulhall* v. *Haren* (1981) I.R. 364.

[57] [1981] 3 All E.R. 118 at 126. The Court of Appeal confirmed his decisions on other grounds. They did not comment on this point see [1982] 3 All E.R. 97.

[58] J. T. Farrand, *Contract and Conveyance* (4th ed.), p. 36.

[59] Interpretation Act 1978, s.5, Sched. 1.

[60] [1975] 1 W.L.R. 1452 at p. 1454.

[61] (1871) 25 L.T. 804.

in recognition of the contract alleged. Otherwise the signature may be hand-written, typed, printed or in any other form and need not appear at the end of the document. Thus it was held early on that a document beginning "I, A.B. agree"[62] would satisfy the Statute. This was followed in *Saunderson* v. *Jackson*.[63] The vendor's printed name on a bill of parcels for 1,000 gallons of gin was an adequate signature. The signature may even by inserted before the contract is made. In *Leeman* v. *Stocks*[64] the vendor's name was written by the auctioneer into the memorandum of sale before the auction took place. This was held to be an effective signature. And in *Cohen* v. *Roche*[65] a firm of auctioneers circulated an auction catalogue bearing their printed name to advertise a forthcoming furniture sale. The auctioneers conducted the sale by means of a "day book"; pages from the catalogue were pasted in the book and a space left at the side for entering details of the purchases. A set of chairs, belonging to the auctioneers was sold to the plaintiff and the details entered in the day book. The auctioneers tried to resist the plaintiffs action for specific performance by saying that there was no signed memorandum; their name did not appear in the day book. It was held that the printed name on the catalogue was sufficient for this purpose. McCardle J. pointed out that so common was the "day book" practice, that to hold otherwise would result in many purchasers at auctions having unenforceable contracts.

A name inserted into a document will not suffice if it is clear that the parties intended further signing to make the contract binding. In *Hubert* v. *Treherne*[66] the words "As witness to our hands . . ." at the end of the agreement were found to indicate such an intention. However these or similar words are not conclusive. The memorandum of sale in *Leeman* v. *Stocks*[67] had an attestation clause but the evidence showed that both the purchaser and the auctioneer considered that the purchaser's signature was all that was necessary to conclude the contract. Absence of further signature by the vendor (or the auctioneer on his behalf) did not render the contract unenforceable.

Alterations. Where the contract is reduced to writing and signed, must it be resigned if alterations are made to it? The law relating to alterations is well-settled though perhaps illogical[68]:

(a) if the signed document is altered to correct a mistake in the written statement of an existing contract[69] or is altered before the parties are contractually bound to one another[70] then the altered document is sufficiently signed by the original signature.

(b) if alterations are made to a concluded contract after it has been

---

[62] *Knight* v. *Luckford* (1794) 1 Esp. 190.

[63] (1800) All E.R. 126.

[64] [1951] Ch. 941.

[65] [1927] 1 K.B. 169.

[66] (1842) 3 M. & 9G. 743.

[67] [1951] Ch. 941.

[68] See C. T. Emery (1975) 39 Conv. 336 and *New Hart Builders Ltd.* v. *Brindley* [1975] Ch. 342, *per* Goulding J.

[69] *Buck* v. *Gompertz* (1852) 7 Exch. 862.

[70] *Koenigsblatt* v. *Sweet* [1923] 2 Ch. 314.

signed, then the alterations are treated as creating a new agreement for the purposes of section 40(1) and the document must be resigned.[71] This has led to the practice of solicitors getting their clients to initial all alterations.[72]

"BY THE PARTY TO BE CHARGED"

The document only has to be signed by the defendant. The plaintiff, provided of course he is willing to perform his part, can obtain specific performance of the agreement even though he has signed nothing.[73] The idea of one party being able to enforce an agreement which is unenforceable against him may seem unjust to the reader. Indeed in *Farrell* v. *Green*[74] Pennycuick V.-C. criticised the rule as being "distasteful to one's idea of fairness" but at the same time accepted the rule as beyond dispute.

"OR BY SOME OTHER PERSON THEREUNTO BY HIM LAWFULLY AUTHORISED"

The defendant does not have to sign the contract himself; he can authorise someone else to sign on his behalf.

(a) **Signature by an auctioneer**. An auctioneer has implied authority to sign the contract for both the vendor and the purchaser. In the case of the vendor, his authority lasts for as long as he has authority to sell, and it is not dependent on his receiving deposit from the purchaser.[75] By way of contrast his authority to sign on behalf of the purchaser (the highest bidder) is limited to the time of sale. What counts as "the time of sale" will depend on the facts of the case. In *Chaney* v. *Maclow*[76] the purchaser refused to sign the memorandum at the auction. The auctioneer returned to his offices and signed on the purchaser's behalf about two hours later. He explained that his reason for waiting was that he thought the purchaser would change his mind and come to the offices to sign the memorandum and pay the deposit. The purchaser was bound. The signature could reasonably be said to be part of the sale transaction. However in *Bell* v. *Balls*[77] signature one week later was ineffective. This latter case also establishes the rule that the auctioneer's implied authority to sign the contract does not extend to his clerk. The clerk must be expressly authorised to do so.

(b) **Signature by a solicitor.** "A solicitor has no ostensible or apparent authority to sign a contract of sale on behalf of a client so as to bind him when there is no contract in fact . . . (the plaintiff) has to prove that the solicitor has authority in fact to sign it."[78] In deciding whether such

---

[71] *New Hart Builders Ltd.* v. *Brindley* [1975] Ch. 342.

[72] See *Earl* v. *Mawson* (1974) 232 E.G. 1315.

[73] *Auerbach* v. *Nelson* [1919] 2 Ch. 383.

[74] (1974) 232 E.G. 587.

[75] *Phillips* v. *Butler* [1945] Ch. 358.

[76] [1929] 1 Ch. 461.

[77] [1897] 1 Ch. 663.

[78] *Per* Lord Denning M.R. in *H. Clark (Doncaster) Ltd.* v. *Wilkinson* [1965] Ch. 694 at p. 702.

authority exists in the particular circumstances the court draws a distinction between cases where the solicitor signs the actual contract, and those where he signs a memorandum evidencing a contract which has already been made. In the former case the solicitor probably needs express authority, whilst his authority to sign a memorandum may be implied. Thus in *Smith* v. *Webster*[79] instructions to prepare a draft contract whilst the parties were still negotiating, did not authorise the solicitor to conclude or sign the contract. Contrast *North* v. *Loomes*[80] where the defendant instructed his solicitor to "carry out" the contract which he had already made with the plaintiff. A letter signed by the solicitor in the following terms: "I need not trouble you to send me another contract as the one which your client has signed is, I think, quite sufficient" constituted sufficient signature of the memorandum on the defendant's behalf.

It seems that litigation may provide an unintentional signed memorandum. In *Grindell* v. *Bass*[81] counsel signed a defence in an action which recognised as existing, and contained, the terms of an oral contract. The defence constituted a sufficient memorandum for the purposes of the statute; the defendant had clearly authorised her counsel to sign it. Russell J. commented that "it matters not that the fact that a memorandum within the Statute of Frauds would thereby be brought into existence was not present to the minds of either counsellor or client."[82]

Finally it has been held[83] that where a solicitor is authorised to sign, it is irrelevant that he has accepted the deposit as a stakeholder rather than as an agent for the vendor.

(c) **Signature by any Other Agent.** The agent must have authority to sign the contract. Section 40(1) does not prescribe how the authority must be given and therefore written authorisation is unnecessary.[84] The test for deciding whether an agent has authority to sign the contract is whether he is acting within the usual scope of his authority. If he is, the signature is valid.[85]

Instructing an estate agent to sell property does not authorise him to sign the contract on behalf of the proposed vendor. The estate agents job is to introduce possible purchasers to the owner.[86] It was said in *Keen* v. *Mear*[87] that if the agent is definitely instructed to sell at a certain price, then those instructions involve authority to make a binding contract and sign an agreement, although this is limited to signing an open contract for sale, not one with special conditions. However Lord Greene M.R. said in *Wragg* v. *Lovett*[88] "we must not be understood as suggesting that when a

---

[79] (1876) 3 Ch.D. 49.
[80] [1919] 1 Ch. 378 and see *Horner* v. *Walker* [1923] 2 Ch. 218.
[81] [1920] 2 Ch. 487; and see *Daniels* v. *Trefusis* [1914] 1 Ch. 788.
[82] *Ibid.* at p. 492.
[83] *Elias* v. *George Sakely & Co. (Barbados) Ltd.* [1983] 3 A.C. 646.
[84] *Daniels* v. *Trefusis* [1914] 788.
[85] *John Griffiths Cycle Corporation Ltd.* v. *Humber & Co. Ltd.* [1899] 2 Q.B. 414.
[86] *Keen* v. *Mear* [1920] 2 Ch. 574.
[87] [1920] 2 Ch. 574 following *Rosenbaum* v. *Belson* [1900] 2 Ch. 267.
[88] [1948] 2 All E.R. 968. However *Rosenbaum* v. *Belson, supra*, was not cited.

vendor merely authorises an estate agent to sell at a stated price he must be taken to be authorising the agent to do more than agree with an intending purchaser, the essential . . . term, *i.e.* the price. The making of a contract is no part of an estate agent's business, and although, on the facts of an individual case, the person who employs him may authorise him to make a contract, such an authorisation is not lightly to be inferred from vague or ambiguous language."

Where someone signs a contract without express or implied authority, a principal (but not an undisclosed principal[89]) may ratify the signing subsequently so as to bind himself to the contract.[90] Further a principal may be estopped from denying that the contract was entered into by a person without his authority if by his conduct he leads the plaintiff to believe that such person did have the authority to enter a binding contract on his behalf, and the plaintiff has acted to his detriment in reliance on this representation.[91]

An interesting question arises in connection with concurrently owned real property. Since 1925 all concurrent ownership of land must exist behind a trust for sale. Can one co-trustee (a wife for example) appoint the other (the husband) to be his or her lawful agent to sign a contract within section 40(1)?

Despite the affirmative answer suggested to this question in *Watts* v. *Spence*[92] and the not uncommon practice of signing contracts "for self and co-owner," it is submitted that the correct view is that stated by P. W. Smith in his article "Co-owners and Agency,"[93] namely that one co-owner cannot appoint the other as his agent for this purpose. Signing a contract for the sale of trust property is a discretion which a trustee cannot delegate to an agent under section 23(1) of the Trustee Act 1925.

7. "This section . . . does not affect the law relating to part performance"—section 40(2)

Section 40(1) owes its existence to section 4 of the Statute of Frauds 1677 but by 1686,[94] Equity had invented the doctrine of part performance which robs the provision of many of its terrors. The doctrine (now given statutory recognition by section 40(2)) seems to rely on the long established rule that Equity will not allow a statute to be used as an instrument of fraud. If a party to an unenforceable contract has acted on the assumption that the contract would be performed, he may acquire equities against the other party. If the acts performed themselves provide cogent evidence of the alleged contract it would be absurd to allow a statutory provision, intended to prevent false allegations of contractual

---

[89] *Spiro* v. *Lintern* [1973] 1 W.L.R. 1002.
[90] *Keen* v. *Mear* [1920] 2 Ch. 574.
[91] *Spiro* v. *Lintern* [1973] 1 W.L.R. 1002.
[92] [1976] 2 Ch. 65.
[93] [1980] Conv. 191.
[94] *Butcher* v. *Stapely* (1685) 1 Vern. 363.

liability, to stop the court from recognising a contract that was clear from the evidence.

For many years the leading authority on the doctrine of part performance was *Maddison* v. *Alderson*[95] which laid down various rules with which the acts relied on had to conform. One of these was that the acts had to be "unequivocally referrable" to the alleged contract; in other words, there could be no explanation for the acts other than that they were made in performance of the alleged contract. However, it was soon appreciated that this test, if applied strictly would exclude almost all cases, since it is difficult to conceive of any act which can only have one explanation. For example most acts in part performance of a contract to sell a freehold would be equally consistent with a contract to sell a long leasehold.

Thus in subsequent cases the courts displayed a more relaxed attitude and the doctrine would be applied if "the acts in question be such as must be referred to some contract and may be referred to the alleged one; that they prove the existence of some contract and are consistent with the contract alleged."[96] In *Kingswood Estate Co. Ltd.* v. *Anderson*[97] a widow moved out of her rent-controlled house into a flat provided by the landlord under an oral agreement that she could remain there for the rest of her life. The oral agreement was a successful defence against his claim for possession. And in the later case of *Wakeham* v. *Mackenzie*[98] a widow of 67 agreed to move in with and act as housekeeper for B. a recently widowed friend aged 72, on B.'s oral promise that she could have his house and its contents on his death. She agreed to pay for her own food and coal. P. gave up her council flat, moved into B.'s house and looked after it and him until his death. He did not leave his house or its contents to her. P. successfully obtained specific performance of the oral agreement; her giving up her flat, moving in and looking after B. and his house, and her paying for her own food and coal were acts of part performance sufficiently referrable to the contract she alleged.

In most cases, the acts of part performance relate to a change of possession but this is not a requirement. In *Rawlinson* v. *Ames*[99] the landlord of a flat made certain alterations to the premises in accordance with the wishes of the defendant, who had orally agreed to take a lease of the flat. Specific performance was granted.

One point that all the books and cases agreed on was that the payment of money was not by itself a sufficient act of part performance, for there can always be innumerable reasons for that. So Lord Selborne said in *Maddison* v. *Alderson*[1]: "It may be taken as now settled that part payment of purchase money is not enough; and judges of high authority have said the same even of payment in full." This and the foregoing observations

---

[95] (1883) 8 App.Cas. 467.
[96] Fry, *Specific Performance* (6th ed.), p. 278 quoted by Stamp J. in *Wakeham* v. *Mackenzie* [1968] 1 W.L.R. 1175 at p. 1181.
[97] [1963] 2 Q.B. 169.
[98] [1968] 1 W.L.R. 1175; [1968] 2 All E.R. 783.
[99] [1925] Ch. 26.
[1] (1883) 8 A.C. 467 at p. 479.

must now be read in the light of the House of Lords decision in *Steadman* v. *Steadman*.[2]

A wife had brought her ex-husband before the magistrates for non-payment of maintenance but, before they went into court they agreed that the husband would buy out the wife's interest in the matrimonial home for £1,500 and she would agree to a variation of the maintenance order if he paid her £100 on deposit. Both parties went before the magistrates where the arrangement was explained and, having obtained the wife's confirmation that this was something she wanted to do, the magistrates amended the maintenance agreement. The husband duly paid the £100 and his solicitors sent a draft form of transfer to the wife's solicitors but the wife refused to proceed. Since the whole transaction had been explained by the parties to the magistrates, there was no shadow of doubt that a contract had been made, but the wife sought to rely on section 40(1). The House of Lords held (Lord Morris of Borth-y-Gest dissenting) that there were sufficient acts of part performance.

The facts of Steadman are obviously exceptional and unlikely to re-occur in exactly the same combination. Nonetheless the House of Lords undertook an extensive, if divergent, examination of the nature of the acts which may be relied on within the doctrine of part performance and their pronouncements must therefore be noted.

The one general principle that can be extracted from the decision, is that it is no longer true to say that the mere payment of money is not a sufficient act of part performance. However, the House of Lords did not state the converse; presumably whether or not payment of money will suffice will depend on the surrounding circumstances in each case. Lord Salmon and Lord Reid[3] suggested that payment of a deposit or part payment of the purchase price would only suffice if the vendor could not repay the purchaser (if he was bankrupt for example). This suggestion has been criticised as "illogical and impractical."[4] Furthermore the majority of the Law Lords were of the opinion that in the ordinary circumstances of a contract for the sale of land, a sufficient act of part performance could be found in the fact of a purchaser instructing his solicitors to prepare and submit a draft conveyance or transfer.[5] However one question on which the majority was equally divided was whether the acts of part performance had to be referrable to some contract between the parties, or to some contract concerning land. In the later case of *Re Gonin*[6] Walton J. therefore felt free to follow the traditional view that the act need refer to some contract concerning land.

The principles laid down in *Steadman* were applied in *Re Windle*[7] which concerned an oral agreement between a husband and wife as to the transfer of property. Goff J. held that payment of mortgage arrears and instalments would not suffice as an act of part performance, but that instructing solicitors to prepare the transfer and payment of their costs and

---

[2] [1976] A.C. 536; and see Wade 90 M.L.R. 433.
[3] [1976] A.C. 536 at 571 and 541 respectively.
[4] J. T. Farrand, *Emmet on Title* (18th ed.), p. 68.
[5] For the practical effect of this see (1974) 38 Conv. 388.
[6] [1979] Ch. 16.
[7] [1975] 1 W.L.R. 1628.

disbursements did. In *Sutton* v. *Sutton*[7a] a wife's consenting to the divorce as agreed (which included an oral promise by the husband to transfer the home to her) was a sufficient act of part performance; "the term about the house was in the petition which must have been posted to her when her formal consent was sought under the postal procedure which was followed. That means that her consent to the petition was in itself, in the circumstances, tied to the contract about the house."[7b]

Lastly, reference should be made to two instances where the acts where insufficient to bring the case outside the ambit of section 40(1). In *Daulia Ltd.* v. *Four Millbank Nominees Ltd.*[8] procuring a banker's draft for the deposit and attending at the vendor's offices with the purchaser's signed copy of the contract were found not to be acts of part performance of an existing contract but acts done in contemplation of making a contract. For the same reason the purchaser's application for planning permission was an insufficient act of part performance in *New Hart Builders Ltd.* v. *Brindley*.[9]

Should Section 40 be Retained?

In their crusade to prevent section 40(1) being used as an instrument of fraud, the courts have been generous in its interpretation and have admitted oral evidence on numerous grounds. Therefore it has been argued[10] that there is no longer any need for a contract of the sale of land to be evidenced in writing and that the courts are more than able to determine whether or not a concluded contract exists from the available evidence.

In 1937 the Law Revision Committee on the Statute of Frauds and the Doctrine of Conversion, produced a report[11] which resulted in the repeal of most of the residue of section 4 of the Statue of Frauds and section 4 of the Sale of Goods Act 1893. Section 40 was not within their terms of reference but five of their criticisms of the aforementioned provisions are relevant:

(1) The requirement for signed written evidence of a contract originated over 300 years ago, when parties could not give evidence and in theory juries could decide cases on their own knowledge.

(2) The requirement may stop perjury but it may also stop the truth.

(3) It is out of line with how business is conducted; often informally.

(4) It can operate unfairly. For example if A and B make a contract which is evidenced by writing and A only signs the writing, B can sue but not A.

(5) The contract is not void for non-compliance merely unenforceable by action.

But the Committee did recognise that formality could be justified by the subject-matter of the contract. Land has always formed the tangible basis of our social, political and economic life and has in the past been accorded

---

[7a] [1984] 1 All E.R. 1680.
[7b] *Ibid.* Per John Mowbray Q.C. at p. 172.
[8] [1978] Ch. 231.
[9] [1975] Ch. 342.
[10] H. W. Wilkinson (1967) 31 Conv. 182.
[11] Cmd. 5449 (1937).

a "special" status in our law. However recently the House of Lords[12] indicated that perhaps the distinction between real and personal property had been overplayed. So why should a contract for the sale of land still be in writing, when a contract for the sale of a yacht need not be? Further if land is really so important is that not a reason for dispensing with formalities?

Several counter-arguments can be levelled at these criticisms. First, because section 40 has accumulated such a vast body of case law, new principles are unlikely to arise and practitioners should have little trouble in advising clients.[13] Secondly, although it is true that some sales of personal property involve large sums of money, they are few in comparison with land sales. Thirdly, land *is* unique; a third party cannot have a right of way over a car. And for most people, buying a house will be the single most important purchase they make in their lifetime—the contract should be formal. Indeed it is[14] thought by some that one standard form of contract should be introduced by Parliament for general use. One standard form contract was also recommended by the Royal Commission on Legal Services, as part of their overall plan for the improvement and simplification of conveyancing in England and Wales.[15]

---

[12] *National Carriers Ltd.* v. *Panalpina (Northern) Ltd.* [1981] A.C. 675.
[13] But see *Sudbrook Trading Estate Ltd.* v. *Eggleton* [1982] 3 W.L.R. 315.
[14] H. W. Wilkinson (1967) 31 Conv. 254.
[15] Cmnd. 7648 (1979) Chap. 21, Annex 21.1.

6: The Contract

PART I. GENERAL

Once the parties have made a binding agreement, a contract for the sale of land is valid, whatever its size, shape or form and whether it is oral or in writing. But its enforceability by action depends on whether it also satisfies the requirements of section 40 of the Law of Property Act 1925.[1] Hence the normal practice of the vendor or his solicitor preparing and submitting to the purchaser, a formal written contract.

Particulars and Conditions

A contract for the sale of land traditionally consists of two parts: the particulars and the conditions. The best way to distinguish between the two is to refer to a statement of Malins, V.-C. in *Torrance* v. *Bolton*[2]: "The proper office of the particulars is to describe the subject-matter of the contract, that of the conditions to state the terms on which it is sold." The Council of The Law Society[3] have amplified this statement by making the following observation: "The proper description of the subject-matter involves not only a physical description, but also a description of the exact estate or interest sold and of every charge upon it or right restricting the purchaser's absolute enjoyment of it; these matters should appear in the particulars and not merely in the conditions. Reference should accordingly be made in the particulars to onerous covenants, easements and the like, whether or not they are also mentioned in the conditions."

Mention an agreement for the sale of land to a lawyer and nine times out of ten he will conjure up a standard form contract incorporating either the Law Society's General or National Conditions of Sale. Most forget that *every* agreement for sale is made on the terms of an open contract. Standard conditions may seek to modify or supplement the position under an open contract, but they never displace it entirely; the common law still regulates the basic rights and duties of the vendor and purchaser. In fact the current Law Society's General and National Conditions historically owe their existence first to vendors and later to purchasers not wishing to enter into an open contract of sale "but to modify by express stipulation the legal incidents of the bargain."[4]

---

[1] See Chap. 5.
[2] (1872) L.R. 14 Eq. 124 and Warrington J. in *Blaiberg* v. *Keeves* [1906] 2 Ch. 175 at p. 184.
[3] (1952) 49 L.S.Gaz. 29.
[4] *Williams on Vendor and Purchaser* (1st ed.), p. 15; and see J.T. Farrand, *Contract and Conveyance* (4th ed.), pp. 3–82.

Note should also be taken of Wilberforce, J.'s statement in *Re Hewitt's Contract*[5]: "In approaching the question of the construction of the conditions of sale, it is well established that the court should have regard to the normal rules of equity as regards the respective rights of vendor and purchaser." Let us suppose, for example, a contractual provision exists in a contract that no misdescription shall annul a sale. The provision may be inoperative because of the rule laid down in *Flight* v. *Booth*[6], that if the misdescription is substantial the purchaser will be able to avoid the contract at law and in equity and recover his deposit with interest and costs.

We shall start by looking at the position under an open contract for as Professor J.T. Farrand[7] has pointed out: "Any discussion of the terms of contracts for the sale of land must have much in common with the house that Jack built: that is the agreement that incorporates the special conditions that refer to the general conditions that modify the statutory provisions that vary the equitable principles that mitigate the rules of common law."

Open Contracts

An open contract is one which states the names of the parties, the property and the price but nothing else. The rights and duties of the parties are governed by the general law; part statutory[8] part judge-made. A comprehensive list of the terms implied into open contracts can be found in *Emmet on Title* (18th ed.), pages 70 to 71. Here are some of the more "well-worn" ones:

(1) That the vendor is selling an estate in fee simple free from incumbrances.

(2) That the vendor will show good title. In the case of unregistered land the vendor has to show title for at least 15 years.[9] A purchaser of registered land is not concerned with the history but with the "state guarantee" of the vendor's title. Section 110 of the Land Registration Act 1925 prescribes how title should be deduced on the sale of registered land and with one exception[10] cannot be contracted out of.

(3) That vacant possession will be given on completion. This presumption may be rebutted if the property was occupied by someone other than the vendor when the purchaser inspected it, or if the contract states that the sale is subject to tenancies.

(4) That completion of the sale and purchase shall be within a reasonable time.

(5) Under section 41 of the Law of Property Act 1925 time is not to be "of the essence of the contract" unless the contract itself so provides, or the surrounding circumstances show that the parties intended it to be so.

---

[5] [1963] 1 W.L.R. 1298 at p. 1301.
[6] (1834) 1 Bing N. C. 370.
[7] J. T. Farrand, *Contract and Conveyance* (4th ed.), p. 76.
[8] Law of Property Act 1925, ss.41 *et seq.*
[9] *Ibid.* s.23.
[10] Land Registration Act 1925, s.110(2), see *post*, p. 311.

(6) Finally it is implied[11] that certain expressions shall have the following meanings unless the context otherwise requires:

(i) "month" means calendar month;
(ii) "person" includes a corporation;
(iii) the singular includes the plural and vice versa;
(iv) the masculine includes the feminine and vice versa.

Void Conditions

Statute renders the inclusion of certain contractual provisions impossible. The following are examples of void conditions most likely to be met in practice.

(1) A provision that a purchaser of a legal estate in land shall accept a title made with the concurrence of a person entitled to an equitable interest, if a title can be made discharged from the equitable interest without such concurrence:

(i) under a trust for sale; or
(ii) under the Law of Property Act 1925 or the Settled Land Act 1925.[12]

(2) A provision barring the purchaser from objecting to lack of stamping on a document forming part of the title or requiring the purchaser to pay for the proper stamping of that document.[13]

(3) A provision that a purchaser shall not be entitled to inspect a power of attorney affecting the title, or be supplied with a copy of it, free of charge.[14]

(4) A provision preventing a purchaser from employing a solicitor of his own free choice, or a provision that the conveyance to or the registration of the title of the purchaser shall be prepared or carried out at the expense of the purchaser by the vendor's solicitor. It is expressly provided that this does not affect any right reserved to the vendor to furnish the purchaser with a form of conveyance from which the draft can be prepared, and to charge a reasonable fee for it.[15] The Council of the Law Society have said[16] that "what is a reasonable fee will depend on the circumstances, but should not, it is considered, exceed the out-of-pocket expenses of the vendor's solicitors for providing the form . . . The practice of providing a form of conveyance in estate development is normally to assist the vendor by ensuring conformity and therefore high charges cannot be justified. In the Council's view, subject as above-mentioned the practice is unobjectionable, but would not generally be appropriate on the sale of a single property."

A lessee or underlessee is protected in a similar way but if the contract does contain such provisions which are rendered void, an alternative

---

[11] The Law of Property Act 1925, s.61, which applies to "all deeds, contracts, wills, orders and other instruments . . .made . . .after the commencement of this Act."

[12] Law of Property Act 1925, s.42(1).

[13] Stamp Act 1891, s.125(2).

[14] Law of Property Act 1925, s.125, as amended by the Law of Property (Amendment) Act 1926 and Powers of Attorney Act 1971, s.11(3).

[15] Law of Property Act 1925, s.48(1).

[16] (1965) 62 L.S.Gaz. 184.

provision is implied that "the lessee or underlessee shall register with the lessor or his solicitor within six months of the date thereof, or as soon after the expiration of that period as may be practicable, all conveyances and devolutions (including probates or letters of administration) affecting the lease or underlease and pay a fee of one guinea in respect of such registration, and the power of entry (if any) on breach of any covenant contained in the lease or underlease shall apply and extend to the breach of any covenant so to be implied."[17]

Statute does not prevent a vendor from stipulating in the contract that the purchaser shall pay his solicitor's conveyancing costs.

Standard Conditions of Sale

Individual standard conditions covering a wide variety of topics have been put forward by authors of precedent books for hundreds of years.[18] Today most solicitors prefer to use a standard form of contract for the sale of land incorporating *a set* of conditions, either the Law Society's General or National Conditions of Sale. The choice lies with the vendor's solicitor; both sets enjoy approximately equal popularity. The first edition of the National Conditions was published around 1902. The Law Society's Conditions were introduced to ease conveyancing under the 1925 property legislation and were used from January 1, 1926. Both sets have since undergone close scrutiny and have been revised and updated several times. The current Law Society's General Conditions are the 1984 revision (of the 1980 edition); the current National Conditions, the twentieth edition published on December 1, 1981.[19]

Both sets of conditions cover basically the same areas, although on occasions differently. It will be useful at this stage to look very broadly at some of the things the conditions do:

(1) They incorporate common law decisions and adapt them where necessary. For example the conditions dealing with concluding the contract (Law Society 10, National 1(6)) are a result of the decision in *Domb* v. *Isoz*.[20])

(2) They correct the deficiencies of the common law. For example where a vendor sells part of his land, the rule in *Wheeldon* v. *Burrows*[21] gives the purchaser certain benefits over the vendor's retained land, but gives no benefits to the vendor over the land sold (unless expressly reserved). Law Society 5(3) now gives mutual benefits to both parties but National 20 is more favourable to the vendor.

(3) They try to avoid statute. Both sets of conditions contain different provisions aimed at excluding liability for misrepresentation under the Misrepresentation Act 1967.

---

[17] Law of Property Act 1925, s.48(2)
[18] Thomas Martin, *Practice of Conveyancing* (1837); T.W. Williams, *Original Precedents in Conveyancing* (1780). Modern equivalents are the *Encyclopaedia of Forms and Precedents*, the *Conveyancer Precedents*, etc.
[19] Reproduced in the Appendix.
[20] [1980] 1 All. E.R. 942.
[21] (1879) 12 Ch.D. 31.

(4) They use statutory provisions. Law Society 2 uses section 196 of the Law of Property Act 1925 in relation to service of notices and delivery of documents; National do not.

(5) They dispense with statutory provisions. For example Section 47 of the Law of Property Act 1925 deals with insurance of the property after exchange. Law Society 11 excludes section 47 altogether and substitutes a new provision. National 21, leaves section 47 to operate but mitigates its effect by stating that the vendor need not insure the property after exchange.

(6) They follow current practice. Both set time-limits for the steps in the transaction after exchange, geared towards completion within 20 working days; four weeks. They also require completion by the early afternoon so that completion monies can be banked. Law Society Conditions 2(1) and 10(1) give recognition to the growing use by solicitors of document exchange services.

It should be mentioned that a third "rival" set of Conditions of Sale were published in 1978. They are entitled "The Conveyancing Lawyer's Conditions of Sale"[22] and were drafted by Ernest Scamell, but do not seem to be used. It has been said that the draftsman and publishers misjudged their market.[23] Practitioners have enough trouble familiarising themselves with the Law Society and National Conditions without having to master a third, more intricate and much lengthier, set. The demand is for one set of standard conditions only.

Contracts by Correspondence

Where an open contract is made "by correspondence" (that is, no standard set of conditions have been expressly incorporated) then the Lord Chancellor's Statutory Form of Conditions of Sale[24] will apply. Although out of date, they do mitigate some of the inconveniences of an entirely open contract; *inter alia* they provide a time-table for the steps from contract to completion and give the vendor contractual remedies of rescission and re-sale.[25] The problem is that no-one seems to know the exact meaning of "by correspondence." It has not been defined by statute or by the courts. Professor J.T. Farrand suggests[26] that "since the statutory form resulted from an intention to relieve the inconveniences of an open contract, the widest possible relief should be given." It probably covers a contract made by the parties by an exchange of letters through the post or by hand, or by an exchange of telegrams. It also probably applies where an offer is made orally and accepted by letter delivered through the post or by hand (and vice versa.) Telex or telephone communications are more doubtful.

---

[22] Described fully in [1981] Conv. 38 "Legal Eagle".
[23] [1981] Conv. 38 at p.54.
[24] S.R. & O. 1925 No. 779, made under s.46 of the Law of Property Act 1925.
[25] Conds. 7 and 9 respectively.
[26] J. T. Farrand, *Contract and Conveyance* (4th ed.), p. 81.

Incorporation of Standard Conditions

The desired set of standard conditions must be adequately incorporated for them to become terms of the contract. Where a printed standard form of contract is used, either the Law Society's or the National Contract for Sale, this is obviously achieved. But these are not always used in practice. In *McKay* v. *Turner*[27] the first special condition in some auction particulars stated that the property was sold "subject to the general conditions printed within . . . ." Nothing was printed within, but the intention had been to incorporate the Law Society's Conditions of Sale (1973 edition). Fox J. said that the special condition could only be construed on its actual wording in the light of any admissible surrounding circumstances, of which the vendor's intention was not one. No general conditions were *incorporated*. However in *Smith* v. *South Wales Switchgear Co. Ltd.*[28] a contract of sale was made "subject to . . . our general conditions . . . obtainable on request." The evidence showed that the vendors had at the time of the contract, three different versions of their general conditions of sale, revised at different dates, and if asked, would have sent whichever version came to hand. The argument that none of the versions were incorporated by the reference, was rejected by the House of Lords because "its logical result would seem to be that there was no contract at all." They held that the reference to general conditions must be taken to incorporate the version current at the date of the contract. How far *Smith's* case affects the decision in *McKay* v. *Turner* is uncertain. It should be mentioned that the contract in *Smith's* case did not relate to land. A motor manufacturing company, the purchaser, contracted with an electrical company, the supplier, for maintenance work to be carried out at its factory "subject to our general conditions of contract obtainable on request."

Construction of Conditions

Vendors' solicitors should bear in mind that the courts are likely to construe vague or ambiguous conditions in favour of the purchaser, in accordance with the *contra proferentem* principle. Knight-Bruce V.C. said in *Symons* v. *James*[29]: "If a vendor means to exclude a purchaser from that which is a matter of common right he is bound to express himself in terms the most clear and unambiguous. And if there be any chance of reasonable doubt, or reasonable misapprehension of his meaning, I think that the construction must be that which is rather favourable to the purchaser than to the vendor." This view was recently repeated by Slade J. in *Leominster Properties Ltd.* v. *Broadway Finance Ltd.*[30] where he stated that if the words of a condition were ambiguous (here Condition 10 of the National Conditions of Sale (19th ed.)) they should be construed against the vendor because "it was the grantor, and the rights of the plaintiff as purchaser were thereby restricted."

---

[27] (1975) 120 S.J. 367.
[28] [1978] 1 W.L.R. 165.
[29] (1842) 62 E.R. 983.
[30] (1981) 42. P. & C.R. 372 at p. 387.

How the conditions will be dealt with

In the remainder of this part of Chapter 6 it is proposed to describe both the National and Law Society's printed forms of Contract for Sale, and to take the reader through some of the more general standard conditions. The information that must be included in the contract is governed by the law relating to the vendor's duty of disclosure, as varied by the conditions. This, together with the purchaser's remedies in the event of default will be looked at in Part II. Part III will concentrate on exchange of contracts and Part IV the position of the parties after exchange. Conditions relating to deducing title and completion will be left for discussion in the chapters on these topics.

THE STANDARD FORMS OF CONTRACT

The National Contract for Sale (20th ed.) (Reproduced on Pages 152–153)

Two forms (both pale green) are available differing only as regards what is printed on the back page under the heading "Special Conditions of Sale." One form on the back page simply leaves a space for special conditions headed with the letter "A," to show that special conditions should be lettered not numbered, to avoid confusion with the general conditions. The other form of back page (reproduced overleaf) contains Special Conditions A–F and leaves a space for other special conditions. The front page is headed "Contract for Sale" because the new National Condition 1(6) refers to a "document . . . in the form of a contract for sale."

PARTIES

The correct names and addresses of the vendor and purchaser should be typed in here. Sometimes the vendor of land is not the owner of the legal estate and a land charges entry against him will not protect the purchaser's interest against the estate owner.[31] A special condition might be thought desirable asking the vendor to give details of the estate owner, if it is not the vendor himself.

REGISTERED LAND

If the land is registered enter the appropriate District Land Registry and title number.

AGREED RATE OF INTEREST

If a figure is inserted here it will be the "prescribed rate" of interest under the National Conditions. If not the "prescribed rate" will be the rate payable by an acquiring authority on entry under compulsory powers. The

---

[31] *Barrett* v. *Hilton Developments Ltd.* [1975] Ch. 237.

[Front of form]

CONTRACT OF SALE
The National Conditions of Sale, Twentieth Edition

Vendor

Purchaser

Registered Land		
District Land Registry:	Purchase Price	£
Title Number:	Deposit	£
Agreed rate of interest:	Balance Payable	£
	Price fixed for chattels or valuation money (if any) £	
	Total £	

Property and interest therein sold

Vendor sells as   Completion date:

AGREED that the Vendor sells and the Purchaser buys as above, subject to the Special Conditions endorsed hereon and to the National Conditions of Sale Twentieth Edition so far as the latter Conditions are not inconsistent with the Special Conditions.

* *Signed*

Date   19

[*Back of form*]

Re: : to

SPECIAL CONDITIONS OF SALE

A. Condition 3 of the National Conditions of Sale shall [not] have effect [But it shall not apply to a matter or matters affecting the value of the property by less than £   or to the following:—

]

B. Title shall be deduced and shall commence as follows:—

C. The sale is with vacant possession/subject to the existing tenancy of which details have been supplied to the Purchaser/subject to the following tenancies:—

D. The property is sold on the footing that the authorised use thereof for the purposes of the Planning Acts is the use (if any) specified in the particulars of sale/use as

E. The sale includes the chattels fittings and separate items specified in the inventory annexed which are to be taken by the Purchaser for a sum (additional to the purchase price of the property) of £   /to be ascertained by a valuation to be made by
at the expense of

F. The property is sold subject so far as they are subsisting and capable of being enforced or of taking effect to the restrictions and stipulations

---

rate at the time of writing is 10¾ per cent. per annum.[32] The rate as it changes is published in the *Solicitors' Journal*.

The "prescribed rate" is important to both parties as it governs the amount of interest the purchaser must pay to the vendor on the outstanding balance of the purchase price in certain circumstances, for example if there is a delay in completion. The fall-back "prescribed rate" will generally be lower than most vendors' solicitors will want to have as a contract rate. In domestic conveyancing a figure of 3–4 per cent. above the base rate of one of the major clearing banks is normally agreed.

PURCHASE PRICE, DEPOSIT, CHATTELS

National Condition 2 provides that the purchaser shall pay a deposit of 10 per cent. of the purchase price to the vendor's solicitor on the date of the contract. A reduced deposit may be acceptable to the vendor in exceptional circumstances, and if this is the case it should be provided for in a special condition. Any preliminary deposit paid to the vendor's estate agent should be deducted. In domestic conveyancing it is quite useful and normal practice to agree and state separately the value of chattels the vendor is leaving on the property. This reduces the purchase price and consequently the amount of stamp duty the purchaser eventually has to pay. Stamp duty can only be saved in this way if the price for the chattels bears a reasonable approximation to their true value.[33]

PROPERTY AND INTEREST THEREIN SOLD—THE PARTICULARS

The perfect particulars should state:

(i) the physical extent of the land, accurately;
(ii) the estate or interest in the land sold;
(iii) the rights the benefit of which are to pass with the land sold;
(iv) the rights the burden of which the land is subject to. This will include any charges, easements, restrictive covenants and so on.

Although the existence of benefits and burdens should be referred to in the particulars, full details are usually given in the special conditions.

The particulars are more conveniently dealt with in Part II of this chapter, but it can usefully be mentioned here that care should be taken in drafting the particulars because of the possibility of misdescription. In the case of unregistered land a physical description of the land can usually be gleaned from the title deeds, but "it is the duty of the conveyancer in framing a description upon sale not to take it for granted that he is to follow the exact terms of the description of the existing title but to make full enquiry into the facts in order that he may be able to describe correctly the subject intended to be disponed."[34] It is particularly important to check the accuracy of any plan referred to, in order to identify the property.[35] Registered land is sufficiently described by following the

---

[32] Acquisition of Land (Rate of Interest after Entry) (No. 3) Regulations 1983 (S.I. 1983 No. 1735).

[33] *Alexander* v. *Rayson* [1936] 1 K.B. 169.

[34] *Gordon–Cumming* v. *Houldsworth* [1910] A.C. 537 at p. 574.

[35] *Scarfe* v. *Adams* [1981] 1 All E.R. 843; *Spall* v. *Owen* (1982) 44 P. & C.R. 36.

description on the property register of the title and by referring to the filed plan and title number.

If part only of the vendor's land is being sold a new description and plan will have to be made. Recently in *Scarfe* v. *Adams*[36] the Court of Appeal issued a reminder to conveyancers that where part of property is being sold it may be insufficient to describe the part generally and by reference to an Ordnance Survey map on a small scale. It should be described with such particularity and precision that there is no room for doubt about its boundaries, and if a plan is intended to control the description, an ordnance map on a scale of 1:2,500 is worse than useless.

VENDOR SELLS AS

Here there will be a statement of the capacity in which the vendor is selling the property. The alternatives include beneficial owner (where the vendor owns the whole legal and equitable interest), trustee (for example trustees for sale or a tenant for life of settled land), personal representative, mortgagee, settlor or under an order of the court. The capacity in which the vendor sells is important to the purchaser as it dictates which covenants under section 76 of the Law of Property Act 1925[37] will be implied into the conveyance or transfer to him.

Where the vendors are concurrent owners they should strictly sell as trustees. However if between them they own the whole beneficial ownership, the purchaser's solicitor should require them to convey as beneficial owners, as the covenants for title given will be more extensive.[38]

COMPLETION DATE

Under an open contract for sale the law implies that completion will take place within a reasonable time. This is a question of fact in every case depending on the remaining legal business to be carried out; investigating title, preparing the conveyance and the like.[39] Usually the parties will agree a date for completion and it should be inserted here. If not National Condition 5(1) states that it shall be "the 26th working day after the date of the contract or the date of delivery of the abstract of title whichever be the later." In *Marks* v. *Lilley*[40] a contract expressed to be governed by the National Conditions (16th ed.) contained no agreed completion date, so the conditions supplied a date five weeks from the delivery of the abstract.

The contract should not provide that completion shall take place when possession of the property is given, if no date is fixed for the giving of possession. On these facts, it was held in *Johnson* v. *Humphrey*[41] that the implication of common law that completion was to take place within a reasonable time was excluded by the express term that completion was to be determined by reference to possession and in turn had excluded any implied term as to when possession should be given. The contract was unenforceable.

---

[36] [1981] 1 All E.R. 843.   [37] See *post*, p. 375.
[38] For an argument that they should convey as trustees. See A.O. and P. Kenny, (1983) 80 L.S. Gaz. 1473.
[39] *Johnson* v. *Humphrey* [1946] 1 All E.R. 460.
[40] [1959] 1 W.L.R. 749.   [41] [1946] 1 All E.R. 460.

Neither should the parties state a date for completion "to be agreed between the parties." In *Gavaghan* v. *Edwards*[42] the county court judge held that no concluded and binding contract could be found in an agreement to agree, and that the special condition eliminated the general condition that otherwise completion should take place within seven weeks. The Court of Appeal upheld the appeal on other grounds and unfortunately did not comment on this point. There were two earlier cases[43] which favoured the view that even though the parties specified a completion date to be agreed in the future, the court would imply a term that completion should take place within a reasonable time, thus validating the contract.

The latest case, *Walters* v. *Roberts*[44] concerned a contract for the sale of a sheep farm, a flock of sheep and additional farm land. The contract was governed by the National Conditions (19th ed.). The contractual date for completion passed and the parties agreed that "a completion date . . . will have to be agreed." Nourse J. actually decided that the parties had not made an agreement to agree. On the facts they had agreed that completion would take place after the lambing season. But he did express the view that if the parties had left the date for future agreement, the court would have implied a reasonable time in default of agreement: "Both parties must be taken to intend that completion will take place sooner or later."

Thus it would seem safer to put nothing at all in the contract if the parties wish to agree a completion date in the future. The standard "fall-back" condition (a must) will then be able to operate in default of agreement and any "reasonable implications" will be excluded.

AGREEMENT FOR SALE

This formally recites that an agreement for sale and purchase has been made as above subject to the Special Conditions on the back page and the National Conditions insofar as they are not varied by the Special Conditions. There then follows a space for signing and dating the contract. If no date is inserted, the day on which the contract is made is governed by National Condition 1(7).[45]

THE SPECIAL CONDITIONS

Special Condition A. Special Condition A relates to the new optional National Condition 3: "Purchaser's short right to rescind." The condition was designed to meet considerable demand from the profession for a condition that would allow the purchaser to make a contract in a hurry without, for example, waiting for searches to be made.

National Condition 3 only applies if the special conditions so provide (3(1)). Broadly, it gives the purchaser a right to rescind the contract by serving notice on the vendor within 16 working days of the contract (time being of the essence) if he discovers any matter materially affecting the value of the property except a matter not existing or subsisting at the date of the contract, or (essentially) a matter of which the purchaser on

---

[42] [1961] 3 Q.B. 220.
[43] *Simpson* v. *Hughes* (1897) 76 L.T. 237; *Fowler* v. *Bratt* [1950] 2 K.B. 96, C.A.
[44] (1981) 258 E.G. 965; discussed [1981] Conv. 168.
[45] See Pt. III.

entering into the contract had knowledge, excluding knowledge imputed by virtue of statute or the other National Conditions (3(3) and 4). Thus the purchaser would not be able to rescind if the property is greatly reduced in value by reason of being listed under the Planning Acts after contract as occurred in *Amalgamated Investment & Property Co. Ltd.* v. *John Walker & Sons.*[46] The purchaser's notice must expressly refer to Condition 3 and to the matter for which he claims he is entitled to rescind (3(2)).

Condition 3(5) states that the purchaser's short right to rescind is additional to National Condition 15, which provides that the purchaser can rescind later if a special condition states that the property is sold on the footing of a specified authorised use which turns out not to be so authorised under the Planning Acts. Rescission under either Condition 3 or 15 is governed by National Condition 10(2): "the vendor shall return the deposit, but without interest, costs of investigating title or other compensation or payment, and the purchaser shall return the abstract and other papers furnished to him." "Abstract" includes the documents listed in Section 110 of the Land Registration Act 1925.

Rescission under National Condition 3 (and 15) is only available to the purchaser. The purchaser therefore knows that the property cannot be sold to someone else unless he decides to rescind, but the vendor really cannot be sure until 16 working days after the contract that he has a sale (later in respect of condition 15). Furthermore National Condition 3 is very wide. It is certainly not confined to matters normally revealed by searches. It could for example cover survey matters. There are also likely to be disputes over what matters "materially affect the value."[47] It seems that the draftsman forsaw that condition 3 was not for everyday use. First it must be incorporated by Special Condition A and secondly its effect can be limited by the addition of the words "But it shall not apply to a matter or matters affecting the value of the property by less than £— or to the following: . . . ."

Special Condition B. In Special Condition B the vendor states how he intends to prove his title.

(a) *Unregistered land.* Since the National Conditions are silent on the matter, the open contract rule applies. The vendor must show a good root of title at least 15 years old and all subsequent dealings.[48] A good root of title is an instrument which deals with or shows title to the whole legal and equitable interest, contains a recognisable description of the property and does nothing to cast doubt on the title. It will normally be a conveyance on sale. If the Special Condition gives less than 15 years good root, the vendor must fully disclose the nature of the root. In most cases the purchaser would be unwise to accept such a title.

---

[46] [1977] 1 W.L.R. 164.

[47] See H.W. Wilkinson, *Standard Conditions of Sale of Land* (3rd ed.), p. 209.

[48] Law of Property Act 1925, s.44(1), as amended by Law of Property (Amendment) Act 1969.

(b) *Registered land.* Construction (11) says that title to registered land shall be deduced in accordance with section 110 of the Land Registration Act 1925. By section 110 the vendor must supply to the purchaser:

(i) a copy of the entries on the register;
(ii) a copy of the filed plan;[49]
(iii) an authority to inspect the register;
(iv) an abstract or other evidence of matters as to which the register is not conclusive, for example overriding interests.

The Council of the Law Society have recommended[50] that copies furnished under section 110 should be office copies. Words such as, "Title shall be deduced in accordance with section 110 of the Land Registration Act 1925 except that copies supplied should be office copies," will therefore normally be typed into Special Condition B.

Finally the vendor should take care to disclose any defects in his title at this stage, because of the possibility of misdescription or non-disclosure.[51]

Special Condition C. Here the vendor should state either that the sale is with vacant possession or subject to tenancies. If the contract is silent as to vacant possession it is implied that vacant possession will be given.[52] This is so even where the contract is silent as to a tenancy to which the property is subject.[53] The vendor must therefore disclose the existence of any tenancy and supply the purchaser with the relevant details.

If the property is sold with vacant possession section 4(1) of the Matrimonial Homes Act 1983 implies a term into the contract, that the vendor will secure the cancellation of any registration of rights of occupation against it.

"Vacant Possession" has a dual meaning: (i) "physical" vacant possession; and (ii) "legal" vacant possession.

(i) *"Physical" vacant possession.* The duty to give vacant possession may be broken if the vendor leaves the property in a physically non-vacant state; if he leaves excess rubbish for instance. In *Cumberland Consolidated Holdings Ltd.* v. *Ireland*[54] a contract for the sale of a warehouse provided that vacant possession would be given on completion. The vendor left the cellars of the warehouse filled to about two-thirds of their height with hardened cement and empty drums. After completion the purchaser was able to compel the vendor to remove the rubbish. The Court of Appeal said that the term "vacant possession" included freedom from any physical "impediment which substantially prevents or interferes with the enjoyment of the right of possession of a substantial part of the property."[55]

As a result the following special condition is sometimes found: "The Purchaser shall accept that vacant possession is given of the whole

---

[49] (i) and (ii) cannot be contracted out of.
[50] Opinion of the Council of the Law Society 316(*i*).
[51] See Pt. II, p. 229.
[52] *Cook* v. *Taylor* [1942] Ch. 349.
[53] *Farrell* v. *Green* (1974) 232 E.G. 587.
[54] [1946] K.B. 264 and see *Norwich Union Insurance Society* v. *Preston* [1957] 1 W.L.R. 813.
[55] [1946] 1 All E.R. 284 at p. 287 (Lord Greene).

notwithstanding that there may be furniture fittings or effects remaining therein and shall not be entitled to require the removal of any such furniture fittings and effects or object to taking the same on the ground that the presence thereof prevents the giving of vacant possession." On occasions an indemnity for any claims to such chattels and a disclaimer of any implication of the vendor's title to any item, are added. Obviously it would be unwise for a purchaser to accept these variants. Furthermore it should be noted that the presence of a third party's belongings might constitute occupation so as to produce an overriding interest in registered land or notice in unregistered land.

(ii) *"Legal" vacant possession.* The purchaser is entitled to an interest in possession not reversion, neither the vendor nor anyone else with legal rights (a tenant for example) can be in occupation.[56]

The entitlement to "legal" vacant possession was highlighted by the case of *Topfell Ltd.* v. *Galley Properties Ltd.*[57] A "closing" order on the untenanted part of property prevented vacant possession of the ground floor being given. The purchaser successfully got a reduction in the purchase price of the property; from £3,850 to £2,050. This was despite the fact that a general condition of the contract for sale provided that the purchaser should buy subject to any notices, whether registered or not. Templeman J. held that the general condition could not contradict the vendor's contractual obligation to give vacant possession. The contrary case of *Korogluyan* v. *Matheou*[57a] (where the notice was of compulsory purchase and entry) was not cited in *Topfell.*

Again the decision has produced special conditions. One example is as follows: "The Purchaser shall accept that vacant possession is given of any part offered with vacant possession notwithstanding that if a dwelling house it cannot legally be used for immediate residential occupation by reason of any matter"—again, unlikely to gain much favour with purchasers' solicitors.

Special Condition D. Under National Condition 15(2) the purchaser is entitled to raise requisitions concerning the authorised use of the property for the purposes of the Planning Acts (as defined by construction (8)). But where the use is specified in Special Condition D, the purchaser has to accept it as the authorised use. On the other hand putting the use in here, activates National Condition 15(3) and the purchaser can rescind the contract if it later turns out that this is not the authorised use.

Special Condition E. This is for use where chattels and fittings are included in the sale. If they are not included in the purchase price the extra sum payable for them should appear here. A valuation is normally only relevant in a sale of commercial property. As was shown in *Hamp* v. *Bygrave*[58] it will avoid the possibility of later dispute if precise details of chattels included in the sale are listed here.

---

[56] *Cumberland and Consolidated Holdings Ltd.* v. *Ireland* [1946] K.B. 264; [1946] 1 All E.R. 284.

[57] [1976] 239 E.G. 650.

[57a] (1975) P. & C.R. 309.

[58] (1983) 266 E.G. 720.

Special Condition F. In the absence of any contrary stipulation in the contract, it is implied that the vendor sells free from incumbrances. Therefore the vendor must use Special Condition F to inform the purchaser of incumbrances that will not be discharged on completion (a mortgage for example would be, a restrictive covenant would not). Most incumbrances affecting registered land will be mentioned in the charges register of the title. The vendor will simply state in Special Condition F that the sale is subject to the entries on the charges register, excluding those relating to mortgages.

National Condition 19(5) states that: "where the property is sold subject to legal incumbrances, the purchaser shall covenant to indemnify the vendor against actions and claims in respect of them." National Condition 19(6) provides that the purchaser shall covenant in the conveyance to *observe and perform* any stipulations, restrictive or other covenants which the property is sold subject to and to indemnify the vendor against any actions and claims in respect thereof. This gives the vendor the valuable right to obtain an injunction to restrain the purchaser from breaking the covenants.[59] At common law where the property is sold subject to covenants there is an implication that the purchaser will covenant in the conveyance to perform the covenants and indemnify the vendor but only "with the object and intention of affording to the vendor, his heirs, executors and administrators a full and sufficient indemnity . . . ." Here the vendor's only remedy is by way of indemnity, useless if the purchaser becomes insolvent, and the vendor must wait until he is sued by the covenantee.[60] National Condition 19(6) will to a certain extent become redundant if the Law Commission's proposals on "land obligations" are accepted.[60a] No more restrictive covenants as we know them will be capable of being created and no longer will there be any need to use artificial means to make the burden of a positive covenant run with the land. Vendors will not remain liable for breach of "land obligations" they have given; the benefit and burden of the obligations, whether positive or restrictive, will any be enforceable between the current owners of the land. However the Law Commission do not recommend retrospective changes. Therefore National Condition 19(6) will still be pertinent to many sale and purchase transactions.

Where a leasehold interest is sold section 77 of the Law of Property Act 1925 (unregistered land) and section 24 of the Land Registration Act 1925 (registered land) imply into the conveyance or transfer covenants that the assignee will henceforth duly pay the rent, perform the covenants and observe the conditions affecting the land and indemnify the vendor against any action arising out of his failure to perform and observe the covenants and conditions. National Condition 19(7) states that 19(5) and (6) operate without prejudice to these statutory provisions and that the vendor may not insist on an express covenant from the assignee to cover the same

---

[59] *Re Poole & Clarke's Contract* [1904] 2 Ch. 173. This makes it unnecessary to provide for it by special condition.

[60] *Reckitt* v. *Cody* [1920] 2 Ch. 452.

[60a] "Transfer of Land. The Law of Positive and Restrictive Covenants." Law Com. No. 127.

matters as the implied statutory covenant does. However it is uncertain[61] whether sections 77 and 24 allow the vendor to sue on the implied covenant unless he himself is sued by the person he is responsible to. It may be thought desirable to cure this uncertainty by means of a special condition.

The Law Society's Contract for Sale (1984 rev.) (reproduced on pages 162–163)

The Law Society's contract (bright pink) is available in one form only, with standard special conditions printed on the back. Area Law Societies do sometimes produce their own contract forms incorporating the Law Society's General Conditions but varying the Special Conditions to suit the area.

Although the Law Society's contract differs in appearance to the National Contract, its content is basically the same. To avoid repetition only the differences will be dealt with in detail.

FRONT PAGE

The agreement for sale and purchase and the names of the parties appear at the top of the contract and are separated from the signature box. This separation does not matter as the signature is clearly intended to govern the whole document. The particulars and details of the purchase price should be stated in the manner already mentioned. Either the word "freehold" or "leasehold" should be deleted from the particulars as appropriate. At the bottom of the form the names and addresses of the vendor's and purchaser's solicitors and the relevant local authorities should be given.

The Law Society's contract deals with the interest rate and completion date by Special Condition.

THE SPECIAL CONDITIONS

Special Condition A. This incorporates the Law Society's General Conditions so far as not inconsistent with the Special Conditions "but general condition 8(5) shall apply in any event." These extra words were designed to counter a suggestion made in the *Conveyancer* in 1974.[62] Law Society Condition 8(5) applies to leasehold property and provides that the implied covenants of title (Law of Property Act 1925, s.76(1), unregistered land; Land Registration Act, s.24, registered land) shall not operate so as to make a vendor liable for any breach of repairing covenants and it is stated that: "This sub-condition applies notwithstanding that a special condition provides for the vendor to convey as beneficial owner." The 1974 suggestion was that modifications of the implied covenants where there are breaches of repairing obligations might be precluded where the vendor sells as beneficial owner, hence the extra words in Special Condition A. However it has since been pointed out that the suggestion

---

[61] For further discussion see H.W. Wilkinson, *Standard Conditions of Sale of Land* (3rd ed.).

[62] (1974) 38 Conv. 312.

[Front of form]

THE LAW SOCIETY'S CONTRACT FOR SALE (1984 REVISION)

AGREEMENT made the   day of   198

BETWEEN

Vendor

Purchaser

IT is agreed that the Vendor shall sell and the Purchaser shall purchase in accordance with the following special conditions the property described in the particulars below at the price of

PARTICULARS—ALL THAT freehold/leasehold property

SPECIAL CONDITIONS OF SALE—SEE BACK PAGE

Purchase money
less deposit paid

SIGNED

Chattels, fittings etc.

Balance

Vendor/Purchaser

Vendor's Solicitors   Ref.

Purchaser's Solicitors   Ref.

Local Authorities

[Back of form]

SPECIAL CONDITIONS

A.   The property is sold subject to The Law Society's General Conditions of Sale (1984 Revision) ("general conditions") printed within so far as they are not varied by or inconsistent with these special conditions but general condition 8(5) shall apply in any event.

B.   For the purposes of the following general conditions—

    1(*b*)   the contract rate is   % per annum above the base rate from time to time of

    1(c)   contractual completion date is   198
    21(2)(*b*) the specified bank is
    21(5)(a) the latest time is   am/pm
    1(g)   the following are not working days

    5(3)   the retained land is

C.   General condition 4 shall not apply. [For the purposes of general condition 4(2) the period shall be from the date hereof and for the purposes of general condition 4(3)(*b*) the specified use is   .]

D.   The Vendor shall convey as

E.   The Vendor's title is registered with   title under Title No.
     in the   District Land Registry.
     The Vendor authorises the Purchaser's solicitors to inspect the register and to obtain office copies thereof.

(or)   E.   The abstract of title shall begin with

F.   The property is sold with vacant possession on completion.

(or)   F.   The property is sold subject to the following leases or tenancies

G.   The property is sold subject to

was unfounded in view of the decision in *Butler* v. *Mountview Estates Ltd.*[63] A purchaser tried to sue the vendor on the implied covenants for past breaches of repairing covenants. He failed because, a condition in the contract (Law Society's 1934 ed.), that the purchaser bought the property with full notification of its state and condition, was held to modify the implied covenants. This was so even though the vendors sold as "beneficial owners." The words "general condition 8(5) shall apply in any event" in Special Condition A merely confirm the *Butler* decision. They do not mean that the parties cannot alter 8(4) by special condition if they wish.[64-67]

Special Condition B. This expands on some of the terms in the Law Society's general conditions.

(a) *Contract rate.* This is the equivalent of "the agreed rate of interest" on the front page of the National contract form. If no contractual rate of interest is agreed between the parties and specified here, the fall-back rate of interest under the Law Society's general conditions is the same as under the National Conditions, that is the rate prescribed from time to time under section 32 of the Land Compensation Act 1961 for interest payable thereunder, at present 10¾ per cent. per annum.

(b) *Completion date, specified bank, and time.* If no completion date is specified, Law Society Condition 21(1) provides that it shall be the twenty-fifth working day after the date of the contract. Purchase moneys are usually paid by banker's draft and Law Society Condition 21(2)(*b*) limits the range of banks whose drafts are acceptable on completion, but does allow a purchaser's solicitor to include within the range, an otherwise "unauthorised" bank by inserting its name in Special Condition B. The contract also gives the parties an opportunity to specify the actual time of completion. Where no time is agreed, Condition 21(5)(*a*) says that if the completion moneys are not paid before 2.30 p.m. on the day set for completion, then completion does not take place until the next working day, thus rendering the purchaser liable to pay interest for delay in completion.

(c) *Working days.* The definition of non-working days may be extended in Special Condition B to cover days other than those defined in Condition 1(*g*).

(d) *Retained land.* By Law Society Condition 5(3)(*b*) the conveyance of the land to the purchaser will contain certain reservations (for example a right of way or rights of drainage) in favour of "retained land." "Retained land" means "land retained by the vendor (i) adjoining the property, or (ii) near to the property and designated as retained land in a special condition." (5(3)(*a*)) It is obviously important that a vendor selling only part of his land should have the benefit of these reservations. Since the word "adjoining" is not defined by the general conditions, vendors' solicitors are advised to designate in Special Condition B all relevant land

[63] [1951] 2 K.B. 563.
[64-67] H.W. Wilkinson, *Standard Conditions of Sale of Land* (3rd ed.), p. 78.

retained(adjoining or nearby) and to complete its identification with a plan. On the other hand purchasers' solicitors should ascertain what land adjoins the property, since if it belongs to the vendor it need not be designated in the Special Condition.

Special Condition C. This concerns Law Society Condition 4, which like National Condition 3 gives the purchaser a right to rescind the contract if adverse matters are found. It too was introduced to meet demand for such a clause from the profession. Condition 4 only applies if expressly incorporated by Special Condition C. (4(1)) To rescind, the purchaser must serve notice on the vendor within 20 working days from the date of the contract unless the special condition sets a different time limit. Time is of the essence. The notice must state the ground on which the purchaser is rescinding. The grounds justifying rescission are (4(3)): if the property is subject to a financial charge that the vendor cannot or will not discharge, if it is subject to a statutory prohibition adversely affecting the continued use of the property for the pre-sale purpose or the purpose mentioned in the special condition, or if it turns out that there is something likely to reduce the open market value of the relevant interest in the property, that the purchaser did not know about when contracting. Condition 4(4) states that the purchaser's knowledge includes everything in writing that came to the knowledge of his solicitor, counsel or other agent in the course of the transaction leading to the contract, but "does not include anything solely because a statute deems that registration of a matter constitutes actual notice of it." The last ground for recission is very wide. Like National Condition 3 it gives the purchaser a large bolthole, but means that the vendor cannot count on the sale until four weeks have elapsed from the date of the contract. For this reason most vendors will wish to exclude Condition 4 altogether. Vendors who are desperate for a sale and are forced into accepting Condition 4 sometimes insert an amount as a lower limit for matters likely to reduce the property's market value.

Special Condition D. This condition will contain a statement of the capacity in which the vendor is selling.

Special Condition E. Here the vendor will inform the purchaser how he intends to prove his title. The special condition is printed in the alternative; one for registered land (which includes the vendor's authority for the purchaser's solicitor to inspect the register and obtain office copies of it) and one for unregistered land. The inappropriate alternative should be deleted.

Special Condition F. Special Condition F is also printed in the alternative. It requires the vendor to state whether the sale is with vacant possession or subject to tenancies, details of which are given. Again the inappropriate condition should be deleted.

Special Condition G. The vendor should disclose in this special condition any incumbrances that the property is subject to, which will not be discharged on completion.

Law Society Condition 17(4) provides that the purchaser shall in the conveyance covenant to *indemnify* the vendor against all actions claims and liability for breach of any covenant, stipulation provision or other matter which the property is sold subject to. It should be noted, in comparison to National Condition 19(6)[68] that this is a covenant for indemnity only. Unless and until the vendor is sued by the covenantee for breach of covenant, he has no action against the purchaser. Vendors' solicitors may wish to add a special condition to the effect that the purchaser shall additionally covenant in the conveyance "to observe and perform" the covenants. This will give the vendor the power to restrain any breach of covenant regardless of whether he himself is being sued for breach thereof.[69] A special condition of this nature is normally quite acceptable to purchasers' solicitors.

The Standard Conditions—General

DEFINITIONS

Both sets of standard conditions contain a definition section; the National Conditions under a separate introductory heading "Construction of the Conditions," the Law Society Conditions in Condition 1. Some of the definitions have already been met, for example "prescribed rate" (National) and "contract rate" (Law Society). Others require no explanation: "The "vendor" and the "purchaser" include the persons deriving title under them respectively" (National Construction 1(1)), for instance.

The following are deserving of specific comment:

(i) "**Solicitor.**" National Construction 1(5) gives a new definition of "solicitor" to include a barrister who is employed by a corporate body to carry out conveyancing on its behalf and is acting in the course of his employment. The Law Society Conditions do not define "solicitor."

(ii) "**Designated bank.**" Both the National and Law Society Conditions provide methods by which a purchaser can pay money due on completion. By National Condition 5(3) these include bankers drafts and guaranteed cheques drawn on a "designated bank." "Designated bank" means a bank designated from time to time under section 59 of the Building Societies Act 1962. (National Construction (7)). This covers most high street banks.[70] A current list of "designated banks" is published by the *Solicitors' Journal* from time to time. If in doubt a check can be made at the Registry of Friendly Societies, 17 North Audley Street, London W1Y 2AP (telephone 01–629–7001). The equivalent provision in the Law Society conditions is found not in the definitions but in condition 21(2)(*b*). This gives a narrower choice of banks than that given by the National conditions; "a settlement bank for the purposes of the Clearing House Automated Payments System." (CHAPS). The sub-committee responsible for revising the 1980 edition of the conditions gave two reasons for the

---

[68] See *ante*, p. 160.
[69] *Re Poole & Clarke's Contract* [1904] 2 Ch. 173. The reader should bear in mind the previous comments on the proposals for "land obligations".
[70] See list (1981) 125 S.J. 799.

restriction.[71] "First . . . it is essential for the bank upon which a completion draft is drawn to have arrangements with the Committee of London Clearing Bankers for immediate clearance of its drafts without further formality and, secondly . . . when a draft is presented upon completion, the recipient should be able to recognise at once that it is drawn on a bank that has the clearing facilities referred to above." CHAPS, a new electronic funds transfer service introduced on February 9, 1984 satisfies both these requirements. It boasts, *inter alia*, "non-stoppable" payments and immediate clearance of funds. Present CHAPS settlement banks are: Bank of England, Bank of Scotland, Barclays Bank plc, Central Trustee Savings Bank Ltd., Clydesdale Bank plc, Co-operative Bank plc, Coutts & Co., Lloyds Bank plc, Midland Bank plc, National Girobank, National Westminster Bank plc, Royal Bank of Scotland plc, Williams & Glyn's Bank plc.[72]

(iii) "**Working day.**" National Construction (6) defines "working day" as a day on which clearing banks in the City of London are open for business (or would be but for a strike, lock-out, or other stoppage affecting particular banks or banks generally), except that for the purposes of National Condition 19(4) it means a day on which the Land Registry is open to the public.

Law Society Condition 1(g) defines "working day" as any day from Monday to Friday inclusive except Christmas Day, Good Friday, any statutory bank holiday and any other day specified in a special condition.

The periods under the National and the Law Society Conditions governing the procedural steps from contract to completion are all calculated by reference to working days.

Neither set of conditions state when the time limits laid down by them start, therefore the common law rule applies. Where a person must do an act within a period of days the day from which the period starts to run is not counted against him.[72a] For instance by National Condition 9(3), a purchaser must deliver his requisitions on title 11 working days after delivery of the abstract. If the abstract is delivered on Monday, time begins on Tuesday.

As the time limits are set by reference to working days, they can only run out on a working day.

(iv) "**Normal deposit.**" For the first time Law Society Condition 9(1) makes provision for a reduced deposit to be paid where this is agreed between the parties. To emphasise that a deposit of less than 10 per cent. of the purchase price is the exception rather than the rule, Condition 1(f) contains a new term, "normal deposit" which is defined as "the sum which, together with any preliminary deposit paid by the purchaser, amounts to ten per centum of the purchase money (excluding any

---

[71] See Sub-committee's Notes on the Law Society's General Conditions of Sale (1984 revision).

[72] For a description of "CHAPS" see P. J. Purton (1984) 81 L.S.Gaz. 181.

[72a] *Blunt* v. *Heslop* (1838) 8 Ad. & El. 577.

separate price to be paid for any chattels, fixtures or fittings)." The National Conditions do not provide for a deposit of less than 10 per cent. to be paid.

SERVICE AND DELIVERY OF DOCUMENTS

Section 196 of the Law of Property Act 1925 lays down regulations respecting notices required or authorised to be served under that Act and "notices required to be served by any instrument affecting property . . . unless a contrary intention appears."[73] Basically it provides that a notice in writing, sent by registered post or recorded delivery to the person to be served at his last known place of abode or business, and not returned through the Post Office undelivered, is deemed to be served at the time when the registered or recorded delivery letter would in the ordinary course of post be delivered.[74]

Law Society Condition 2(1) utilises and extends section 196. It provides that section 196 shall apply to any notice served under the contract save that: (i) service on a party or his solicitor is valid service, (ii) any reference to a registered letter in section 196 includes a first class ordinary letter, (iii) there is only to be deemed service under section 196(4) on a working day, (iv) service by telex or telegraphic facsimile is effective on that day but if transmitted after 4 p.m. on the next working day and (v) service by document exchange[74a] is deemed to be made on the working day after that on which the document would, in the ordinary course be available for collection by the addressee. In connection with the use of document exchange services it should be noted that the inclusion of a reference to a document exchange in a solicitor's letterhead shall be conclusive evidence of his membership thereof. By Condition 2(2) the same provisions apply to the service of any documents under the conditions (for example requisitions).

Condition 2 only applies to the service of notices and delivery of documents. It is suggested that other communications made pursuant to the conditions, for example a letter authorising the purchaser to go into possession of the property before completion (Condition 18), are "served" when received.[75]

The National Conditions are silent on the question of the method and deemed time of service of notices and delivery of documents. It is probable that none of the notices referred to in the National Conditions fall within section 196. Words like "notice to . . . " show an intention contrary to the "deemed" service provisions of section 196.[76] Such words are also inconsistent with, and displace, the rule that the mere posting of a letter can be acceptance of an offer if the parties contemplate such a method of acceptance, acceptance taking place at time of posting.[77] Thus,

---

[73] Law of Property Act 1925, s.196(5).
[74] *Ibid.* s.196(4). Read in the light of *Re 88 Berkeley Road, London N.W.9.* [1971] Ch. 648.
[74a] For a description of the British Document Exchange Service see (1980) 80 L.S.Gaz. 398.
[75] By analogy with *Rightside Properties Ltd.* v. *Gray* [1975] 1 Ch. 72.
[76] *Holwell Securities Ltd.* v. *Hughes* [1974] 1 W.L.R. 155.
[77] *Henthorn* v. *Fraser* [1892] 2 Ch. 27.

in the absence of a special condition along the lines of Law Society Condition 2, service and delivery of documents under the National Conditions takes place at the time of actual receipt.[78-79]

AUCTIONS

Where property is sold by auction, the contract (prepared in advance by the auctioneer and the vendor's solicitor and often attached to the auctioneer's particulars) will usually incorporate either the National or the Law Society's Conditions of Sale.

In *New Zealand Shipping Co. Ltd.* v. *Satterthwaite*[80] Lord Wilberforce gave the auction as one example of a contractual situation which is difficult to analyse in traditional terms of "offer and acceptance." The contractual position of a "normal" auction (one subject to a reserve price) was established by the courts over a century ago.[81] A few clouds however still lurk around the auction "without reserve."

When a vendor, or auctioneer on his behalf, advertises property for sale by auction, he makes an invitation to treat. He invites people to attend the auction and make their bids. An auctioneer's call for bids is a repetition of this invitation; neither creates any binding obligations. The bids themselves are the offers and when one is accepted by the fall of the hammer an agreement is made. To comply with section 40 of the Law of Property Act 1925, the agreement must be recorded in writing and signed by the parties.

The problem with an auction that is advertised "without reserve" is how to hold the auctioneer to his implied promise to sell to the highest bidder without upsetting this framework. Apart from *obita dicta* in *Warlow* v. *Harrison*[82] and *Harris* v. *Nickerson*[83] to the effect that the auctioneer should be bound in contract to sell to the highest bidder, the question remains judicially unresolved. It has been suggested[84] that the answer lies in treating the advertisement as doing two things; advertising that the auction will take place, which creates no binding obligations and making an implied promise that the auctioneer will sell to the highest bidder. This implied promise is unilateral in intent, like the famous advertisement offer to pay £100 to anyone who should walk from London to York. Once a person starts out on his course to make himself the highest bidder, the auctioneer cannot retract his promise.

To return to the standard conditions, both the National and Law Society conditions contain similar provisions governing sales by auction and in the main repeat the general law.

(i) **Reserve price.** Section 5 of the Sale of Land by Auction Act 1867 provides that "the particulars or conditions of sale by auction of any land shall state whether such land will be sold without reserve or subject to a

---

[78-79] *Sun Alliance and London Assurance Co. Ltd.* v. *Hayman* [1975] 1 W.L.R. 177.
[80] [1975] A.C. 154.
[81] *Payne* v. *Cave* (1789) 3 T.R. 148; *Harris* v. *Nickerson* (1872–73) L.R. 8 Q.B. 286.
[82] (1859) 1 E. & E. 309 at pp. 314 and 318.
[83] (1872–73) L.R. 8 Q.B. 286.
[84] C.G. Cox, (1982) 132 New L.J. 719.

reserve price, or whether a right to bid is reserved." Where the sale is at a reserve price (but not otherwise) and the vendor reserves a right to bid, the vendor or any person acting on his behalf may bid.[85]

National Condition 1(2) and Law Society Condition 25(2) state that the property and each lot, where the property is sold in lots, is subject to a reserve price (unless otherwise stated in the special conditions). If the auctioneer accepts a bid lower than the reserve then there is no concluded contract.[86] A right for the vendor or his agent to bid up to the reserve price is expressly reserved. (National Condition 1(2), Law Society Condition 25(3)(b)).

(ii) **The auctioneer's control of bidding.**

(a) *Refusing bids.* National Condition 1(3) and Law Society Condition 25(4)(a) provide that the auctioneer may refuse to accept any bid. This probably merely restates the general law.[87]

(b) *Fixing amounts of bids.* National Condition 1(3) further provides that no person shall at any bid advance less than the amount fixed for that purpose by the auctioneer. This appears to conflict with National Condition 1(5) that the highest bidder shall be the purchaser unless 1(5) is read subject to 1(3) so that the "highest bidder" is the one who bids the highest in the amounts fixed by the auctioneer.[88] The Law Society Conditions contain no similar provision.

(c) *Determining Disputes.* Both sets of conditions give the auctineer power to determine any dispute that arises,[89] but a little differently. Both give the auctioneer a choice. He can either:

   (i) decide the dispute in favour of one party or the other; or
   (ii) (a) under National Condition 1(4), "the property may at the vendor's option, either be put up again at the last undisputed bid or be withdrawn." If the vendor is not present at the sale, presumably the auctioneer has implied authority to make the choice;
       (b) under Law Society Condition 25(4)(b) put the property up at the last undisputed bid.

(iii) **The highest bidder.** National Condition 1(5) says that the highest bidder shall be the purchaser. Read in the light of the decision in *Johnston* v. *Boyes*[90] this means the highest bidder who has complied with all the conditions of sale. In *Johnston* v. *Boyes* property was auctioned on terms that the highest bidder would be the purchaser and the purchaser should pay a deposit immediately after the sale. The plaintiff's husband made the highest offer and this was accepted by the auctioneer. He tried to give a cheque for the deposit but was refused as he was known to be financially

---

[85] Sale of Land by Auction Act 1867, s.6.
[86] *McManus* v. *Fortescue* [1907] 2 K.B. 1.
[87] *Payne* v. *Cave* (1789) 3 T.R. 148.
[88] *Johnston* v. *Boyes* [1899] 2 Ch. 73 supports this interpretation.
[89] For an example see *Richards* v. *Phillips* [1969] 1 Ch. 39.
[90] [1899] 2 Ch. 73.

unsound. In fact the husband was buying the property for his wife who had ample funds to cover the purchase. She sued for breach of contract. It was held that the contract would have been specifically enforceable had all the conditions of sale been complied with. Here they had not because of the implied requirement that at auctions deposits should be paid in cash.

(iv) **Deposit and signature.** By National Condition 1(5) with 2(1), and Law Society Condition 25(5) the purchaser shall forthwith complete and sign the contract and pay the deposit. "Forthwith" is not defined in the conditions but probably means at the end of the auction or a short time thereafter.

Both National Condition 2(1) and Law Society Condition 25(5) require a 10 per cent. deposit to be paid. (Although Law Society Condition 9(1) allows for a lesser deposit to be paid on a sale by private treaty, a "normal deposit" must be paid on a sale by auction). Neither condition says how the payment is to be made. The common law therefore applies. In *Johnston* v. *Boyes*[91] it was said that deposits at auctions should be paid in cash, but in the earlier case of *Farrer* v. *Lacy, Hartland & Co.*[92-93] it was held that payment by cheque was acceptable.

It will be remembered from Chapter 5[94] that an auctioneer has an implied authority to sign the contract on behalf of both parties. This authority cannot be revoked before the hammer has fallen. The auctioneer's implied authority to sign on behalf of the vendor lasts for the period for which he is expressly made the vendor's agent.[95] His authority to sign on behalf of the purchaser naturally only arises when the hammer falls and is confined to the time of sale.[96] Signature by an auctioneer on behalf of a purchaser two hours after the sale, was however effective in *Chaney* v. *Maclow*,[97] because on the facts it could reasonably be said to be part of the sale transaction.

National Condition 1(5) states that the date of the contract shall be the date of the auction. This is presumably to cover the type of situation which occurred in *Chaney* v. *Maclow*, where the contract is validly signed after the auction. There is no equivalent provision in the Law Society Conditions.

(v) **Additional provisions in the Law Society Conditions.** Condition 25(3)(*a*) reserves to the vendor the right to divide the property into lots and to rearrange the lots. Condition 25(3)(*c*) reserves the right to withdraw any property from the sale. This merely restates the right which exists at common law.[98]

THE DEPOSIT

Under an open contract for the sale of land there is no implied term that the purchaser shall pay a deposit.[99] In practice the contract will invariably contain an express clause requiring a deposit to be paid.

---

[91] [1899] 2 Ch. 73.
[92-93] (1886) 31 Ch.D. 42.
[94] See *ante*, p. 138.
[95] *Leeman* v. *Stocks* [1951] Ch. 941.
[96] *Bell* v. *Balls* [1897] 1 Ch. 663.
[97] [1929] 1 Ch. 461.
[98] *Harris* v. *Nickerson* (1872–3) L.R. 8 Q.B. 286; *Payne* v. *Cave* (1789) 3 T.R. 148.
[99] *Doe d. Gray* v. *Stanion* (1836) 1 M. & W. 695.

National Condition 2(1) provides that the purchaser shall pay a 10 per cent. deposit, "on the date of the contract."[1]

By Law Society Condition 9(1) the purchaser has to pay a deposit of 10 per cent. or in the case of a sale by private treaty "such lesser sum as the vendor shall have agreed in writing," "on or before the entering into the contract." The provision for payment of a reduced deposit is a novel feature of the revised Law Society Conditions. If however the vendor in such a case serves a completion notice[1a] on the purchaser, the purchaser must pay to him any amount necessary to make up the full 10 per cent. deposit.

The deposit is calculated on the purchase price of the property unless otherwise stated. The National Conditions impliedly exclude any sum payable in respect of chattels by separating "chattels or valuation money" from "purchase price" in the "box" on the front of the form. Law Society Condition 1(f) does so expressly. The National Conditions do not comment on how the deposit should be paid. Cash or banker's draft are the only forms of payment the vendor can be certain of, although it is common for the deposit to be paid by solicitor's clients' account cheque. Law Society Condition 9(1) says that: "on a sale by private treaty, payment shall be made by banker's draft or by cheque drawn on a solicitors' bank account."

Litigation concerning the non-payment of a deposit is rare; contracts are not exchanged if the purchaser does not pay a deposit. Furthermore in *Morris* v. *Duke-Cohan & Co.*[2] solicitors who did not obtain a deposit from a prospective purchaser before exchanging contracts and who did not properly advise their clients of the risk involved were held liable for professional negligence.

Litigation has however arisen where a cheque for the deposit "bounced" (*Myton Ltd.* v. *Schwab-Morris*[3]) where it was stopped (*Pollway Ltd.* v. *Abdullah*[4]) where part only of the deposit was paid (*Johnson* v. *Agnew*[5]) and where the purchaser simply forgot to pay the deposit (*Millichamp* v. *Jones*[6]). All raised the problem of the status of the deposit.

Myton's[7] case left open the question of whether payment of the deposit was a condition precedent to the formation of the contract or a fundamental term of a contract which had been formed, although Goulding J. preferred the former view. The difference between the two is crucial. If the deposit is a condition precedent, the contract never comes into existence. The vendor cannot enforce it and more importantly cannot forfeit the deposit (by suing for it or for the unpaid balance) because the

---

[1] Defined by National Condition 1(7). See Pt. III, *post*, p. 236.
[1a] See Chap. 8 *post*, p. 415.
[2] (1975) 119 S.J. 826.
[3] [1974] 1 W.L.R. 331.
[4] [1974] 1 W.L.R. 493.
[5] [1979] 2 W.L.R. 487.
[6] [1982] 1 W.L.R. 1422.
[7] Considered by H. W. Wilkinson (1974) 124 New L.J. 811.

right to forfeit depends on the contract being there. Also the purchaser who has yet to pay the deposit is put in the unsatisfactory position of being able to choose whether to bring the contract into existence (by paying) or withdraw. If payment of the deposit is a fundamental term of the contract the vendor is in a better position. He can proceed with the sale (if he thinks it worthwhile) or terminate the contract, in which case he can forfeit any part of the deposit already paid and sue for the balance.[8] *Pollway's* case (in which *Myton* was not cited) and *Johnson* v. *Agnew* gave oblique support for the view that payment of the deposit was a fundamental term of the contract because the decisions in both proceeded on the basis that the contract was in existence.

The uncertainty raised by *Myton*, now seems to have been settled beyond doubt by *Millichamp* v. *Jones*. On the question of the status of a deposit Warner J. said[9]: "The weight of authority is in favour of the view that a requirement, in a contract for the sale of land, that a deposit should be paid by the purchaser does not constitute a condition precedent, failure to fulfil which prevents the contract from coming into existence, but is in general to be taken as a fundamental term of the contract, breach of which entitles the vendor, if he so elects to treat the contract as at an end and sue for damages including the amount of the unpaid deposit." This statement of the law was followed and applied by Leggatt J. very recently in *Damon Cia Naviera S.A.* v. *Hapag-Lloyd International S.A.*[10] Also applied was the view[11] that a vendor is entitled to sue for the unpaid deposit and claim damages for breach of contract. Furthermore, the unpaid deposit is recoverable even though (as in *Damon*) it exceeds the vendor's actual loss.

However although *Millichamp* v. *Jones* clarified the status of a deposit at common law it has created further problems for the vendor and has highlighted an important omission in the standard conditions, which has only been cured in part by the 1984 revision of the Law Society's Conditions.

Both sets of standard conditions[12] anticipated the decision in *Millichamp* v. *Jones* regarding the status of a deposit.

National Condition 2(2) provides:

> "In case a cheque taken for the deposit (having been presented, and whether or not it has been re-presented) has not been honoured, then and on that account the vendor may elect
> either (i) to treat the contract as discharged by breach thereof on the purchaser's part

---

[8] *Johnson* v. *Agnew* [1979] 2 W.L.R. 487 casts doubt on the former rule to the contrary laid down in *Lowe* v. *Hope* [1970] Ch. 94. *Lowe* v. *Hope* was not followed in *Damon Cia Naviera S.A.* v. *Hepag-Lloyd International S.A.* [1983] 3 All E.R. 510.

[9] [1982] 1 W.L.R. 1422 at p. 1430.

[10] [1983] 3 All E.R. 510.

[11] Supported by *Dewar* v. *Mintoft* [1912] 2 K.B. 373, *Johnson* v. *Agnew* [1979] 2 W.L.R. 487 and *Millichamp* v. *Jones* [1982] 1 W.L.R. 1422. The decision to the contrary is *Lowe* v. *Hope* [1970] Ch. 94.

[12] The National Conditions (20th ed.), the Law Society's Conditions (1984 rev.)

or (ii) to enforce payment of the deposit as a deposit, by suing on the cheque or otherwise."

No limit is placed on the time within which the vendor must make his election. He will doubtless have a reasonable time and his conduct will be relevant. He may waive his right to insist on payment of the deposit if he proceeds with the sale in the normal way.[13]

Since the status of a deposit is now known at common law, the new Law Society Condition 9(3) contains no reference to fundamental breach. It states: "If any draft, cheque or other instrument tendered in or towards payment of any sum payable under this condition is dishonoured when first presented the vendor shall have the right by notice to the purchaser within seven working days thereafter to treat the contract as repudiated."

It will be noted that the vendor is not given the chance to represent the cheque or other instrument, although it is probable in the light of what is said below that he would have the right to terminate the contract at common law if the cheque or other instrument was not met on second presentation.[13a]

The omission in the conditions is as follows. National Condition 2(2) does not deal with the situation where the purchaser pays none or only part of the deposit. Law Society Condition 9(3) covers part payment of the deposit but not complete failure to pay it. Where the conditions are inapplicable the vendor is forced back on his position at common law. In *Millichamp* the facts were rather unusual but basically the purchaser had simply forgotten to pay the deposit. The vendor refused to perform the contract. We have seen that Warner J. held that payment of the deposit was a fundamental term of the contract. He then went on to consider whether or not there had been a breach of this fundamental term. (To most lawyers there would have been; the deposit was not paid on time). He decided that on the facts there was no breach. In previous cases the purchaser was at fault; he had either refused to pay the deposit (*Pollway*) or the cheque for the deposit had been dishonoured (*Myton*). Here there was "a mere oversight," not a "sufficient breach of the term to entitle (the vendor) to treat the contract as discharged." The judge said that before the vendor could treat the purchaser's breach as a repudiatory breach of the contract he should have given the purchaser notice saying that he would so regard the failure to pay the deposit and requiring the purchaser now to pay. Then he said a fundamental breach would only occur if the purchaser's conduct was such as to show he was unable or unwilling to pay the deposit.

The decision poses two problems to a vendor under an open contract or in the above situations where the standard conditions cannot operate: (1) How long must he wait for the purchaser to pay once he has served a notice requiring payment of the deposit, and (2) he is put in the unenviable position of having to decide when the breach by the purchaser has become fundamental enough to entitle him to terminate the contract. In *Damon Cia Naviera S.A.* v. *Hepag-Lloyd International S.A.,* failure by the

---

[13] *Johnson* v. *Agnew* [1979] 2 W.L.R. 487.

[13a] Although his failure to give notice under Condition 9(3) after the cheque is dishonoured on first presentation may constitute a waiver of his right to terminate the contract.

purchasers to pay the deposit on being given three days notice by telex within which to do so, was a sufficiently fundamental breach of their contract to buy three ships to entitle the vendor to terminate the deal.

To avoid these problems it is suggested[14-16] that National Condition 2(2) be extended to cover non-payment of part or all of the deposit; Law Society Condition 9(1) to cover failure by the purchaser to pay any of the deposit at all.

Agent or stakeholder. The deposit is normally paid to a third party; the vendor's solicitor, an estate agent or auctioneer. The third party can hold the deposit in any one of three capacities:
  (i) as agent for the purchaser; or
  (ii) as agent for the vendor; or
  (iii) as stakeholder.
The capacity will usually be expressly agreed. Thus National Condition 2(1) provides that the deposit shall be paid "on a sale by auction, to the auctioneer, or on a sale by private treaty, to the vendor's solicitor and, in either case, as stakeholder." Law Society Condition 9(1) says the deposit shall be paid to the vendor's solicitors as stakeholders. In the absence of express provision the following rules apply. A vendor's solicitor holds a deposit as agent for the vendor.[17] An auctioneer holds a deposit in the capacity of stakeholder.[18] An estate agent does not take a deposit as agent for the vendor. In *Sorrell* v. *Finch*[19] it was stressed that where an estate agent is instructed to find a purchaser, he has no implied or ostensible authority to receive a pre-contract deposit from a prospective purchaser. The vendor is not liable, even if he knows that a deposit has been taken.

A stakeholder is the agent of both parties. Unless and until the purchase is completed, when he must hand the deposit to the vendor, or the deposit becomes returnable to the purchaser, he may not pay it to either party without the other's consent.[20] A stakeholder is entitled to keep the interest earned by the deposit pending payment to the appropriate party.[21] In *Potters* v. *Loppert*[22] this rule was extended to an estate agent expressly holding a pre-contract deposit as "stakeholder" and even though the contract was never concluded. Under the Estate Agents Act 1979 (part of which came into force on May 3, 1982) pre-or post-contract deposits received by estate agents in whatever capacity, are "clients' money." (s.12(1)). "Clients' money" must be paid into a "client account," (s.14) and where the amount belonging to any one client exceeds £500 interest on it must be paid to the client[23] (that is the vendor or purchaser as appropriate).

[14-16] See P. H. Kenny (1983) 80 L.S.Gaz. 82.
[17] *Edgell* v. *Day* (1865) L.R. 1 C.P. 80.
[18] *Harrington* v. *Hoggart* (1830) 1 B. & Add. 577.
[19] [1977] A.C. 728, H.L.
[20] *Collins* v. *Stimson* (1883) 11 Q.B.D. 142; *Harrington* v. *Hoggart* (1830) 1 B. & Ad. 577 at 586.
[21] *Harrington* v. *Hoggart* (1830) 1 B. & Ad. 577 at pp. 586–587.
[22] [1973] Ch. 399.
[23] reg. 7 of the Estate Agents (Accounts) Regulations 1981 (S.I. 1981 No. 1520) which came into force May 3, 1982.

If for some reason the deposit is lost, for example the stakeholder has gone bankrupt, the vendor must bear the loss once contracts have been exchanged.[24] If no concluded contract has been made the purchaser bears the loss.[25] By section 13 of the Estate Agents Act 1979 stake money held by an estate agent is trust money and not available to the trustee in bankruptcy.

Where after contract the deposit is held as agent for the vendor, the deposit-holder may hand it to the vendor.[26] Any action by the purchaser to recover the deposit must be brought against the vendor. The agent must account to the vendor for any interest the deposit has earned.[27] If the contract has not become binding the purchaser is entitled to repayment of the deposit on demand and cannot sue the vendor for it if the agent has defaulted.[28]

The main reason why a vendor would want the purchaser to pay the deposit to his solicitor as his agent is so that he can use the deposit as part of the deposit on his own purchase. The dangers in the purchaser allowing this are discussed by H.W. Wilkinson in (1975) 72 *Law Society's Gazette* 184, updated at (1981) 78 *Law Society's Gazette* 1128. To prevent the purchaser losing his money (he is an unsecured creditor) his lien for it should be registered as an equitable charge against the property the vendor is buying (a class C (iii) land charge in the case of unregistered land, a notice or caution for registered land). To be absolutely safe Professor J.E. Adams has suggested[29] that the purchaser should take and register an equitable charge against both the vendor's present property and the one he is buying.

Preliminary deposits. Nowadays it is quite common for estate agents to ask a prospective purchaser for a preliminary deposit, "earnest money," pending negotiation of the contract. The purchaser is not obliged to pay this and it affords him no protection whatsoever. In the absence of express authority from the vendor, the estate agent has no implied or ostensible authority to take a preliminary deposit and the purchaser has no recourse if the agent defaults with it. Disappearing preliminary deposits along with defaulting estate agents, were among the more important reasons for the passing of the Estate Agents Act 1979. We have already seen that under section 12 such deposits are clients' money and must be paid into a clients' account (section 14). However those sections in the act which were designed to ensure that purchasers did not lose their deposits, were left to be brought in at a later date. Sections 16 and 17 were to introduce compulsory "bonding" (insurance) for clients' money and by section 19 the Government was to have the power to limit the size of preliminary deposits that could be taken. In April 1983, Dr. Gerald Vaughan, Minister of Consumer Affairs, announced that (at least for the time being) the

---

[24] *Rowe* v. *May* (1854) 18 Beav. 613.
[25] *Sorrell* v. *Finch* [1977] A.C. 728.
[26] *Ellis* v. *Goulton* [1893] 1 Q.B. 350.
[27] *Harrington* v. *Hoggart* (1830) 1 B. & Ad. 577.
[28] *Sorrell* v. *Finch* [1977] A.C. 728.
[29] (1970) 120 New L.J. 1128.

remaining provisions of the Estate Agents Act were not to be implemented. Purchasers have therefore been deprived of any meaningful protection against "rogue" estate agents.

CHATTELS

National Condition 4 states: "If the sale includes chattels, fittings or other separate items, the vendor warrants that he is entitled to sell the same free from any charge, lien, burden, or adverse claim." The Law Society do not include a printed condition to the same effect.

Where the parties apportion the purchase price there are in fact two contracts; one for the sale of the land and one for the sale of the chattels. The latter is a contract for the sale of goods to which the Sale of Goods Act 1979 applies. Section 12 of that Act implies a condition that the vendor will have the right to sell the goods at completion and an implied warranty that they are and will remain free from any charge or incumbrance not disclosed or known to the purchaser at the date of the contract. The vendor also warrants that the purchaser will enjoy quiet possession of the chattels except for claims under incumbrances that were disclosed.

If the purchase price is not apportioned the Sale of Goods Act cannot apply. But where the sale includes chattels the same statutory condition and warranties are implied into the contract by section 2 of the Supply of Goods and Services Act 1982. The contract for the sale of the land includes a "contract for the transfer of goods" within section 1 of the Act.

Liability under the implied terms of section 12 of the Sale of Goods Act and section 2 of the Supply of Goods and Services Act cannot be contracted out of (s.6 of the Unfair Contract Terms Act 1977). National Condition 4 is therefore strictly unnecessary and the omission of a similar provision from the Law Society Conditions is not fatal to the purchaser.

The vendor has no title to transfer chattels that are subject to a hire-purchase agreement, and the purchaser cannot prevent the third party repossessing the goods. If this happens after completion the purchaser must seek redress from the vendor under National Condition 4 or the implied statutory terms. The case of *Butterworth* v. *Kingsway Motors*[30] shows that if the vendor pays all the outstanding payments under a hire-purchase agreement after completion he perfects the previously defective title of the purchaser and makes him the owner of the chattel.

A question of importance to a purchaser who is buying property and chattels is, when does the risk in relation to the chattels pass to him. Does it pass upon exchange of contracts as it does in the case of the land? Where the purchase price is apportioned, section 20 of the Sale of Goods Act 1979 states that "the goods remain at the seller's risk until the property is transferred to the purchaser." Sections 17 and 18 contain implied rules for determining when the property is transferred. For present purposes the net effect of these implied rules is that if chattels are itemised in the contract, title passes to the purchaser at the date of the contract. If the Sale of Goods Act does not apply, it is suggested that the courts would

---

[30] [1954] 1 W.L.R. 1286.

follow the same principles, with the result that the title to chattels would pass on exchange of contracts. The implied rules give way to contrary intention.

Law Society Condition 24 excludes the implied rules by stating: "The property in any chattels agreed to be sold shall pass to the purchaser on actual completion." The purchaser need not insure them until completion. The National Conditions are silent on the question of title to chattels. The purchaser should therefore insure them from exchange of contracts.

None of the foregoing applies to fixtures, which constitute part of the land.[31]

LICENCE TO ASSIGN

This section is only relevant to the sale of an existing lease. A lease often contains a qualified covenant against assignment without the landlord's prior consent. Where this is the case National Condition 11(5) and Law Society Condition 8(4)(a) place an obligation on the vendor to "use his best endeavours to obtain such consent," at his own expense.

In *Pips (Leisure Productions) Ltd.* v. *Walton*[32] Sir Robert Megarry said that "best endeavours" means "something less than efforts which go beyond the bounds of reason but are considerably more than casual and intermittent activities."

Qualified covenants against assignment are subject to certain statutory controls. Section 144 of the Law of Property Act 1925 provides that in the absence of contrary provision, the landlord may not demand a fine or sum of money in the nature of a fine for giving his consent to assign, although he may claim any reasonable legal expenses thereby incurred. More important is section 19(1)(a) and (b) of the Landlord and Tenant Act 1927, which applies to all land except agricultural holdings and cannot be "contracted" out of. Section 19(1)(b) says that in building leases of more than 40 years, an express requirement for consent is deemed to be subject to the proviso that no consent is needed for assignment at least until such time as the lease has only seven years to run. Much wider is section 19(1)(a) of the Act, that where a covenant in a lease imposes the need for the landlord's consent to an assignment, it is implied by section 19(1)(a) that such consent shall not be unreasonably withheld. The subsection does not remove the need to apply for consent.[33] If the landlord refuses consent unreasonably the vendor has two choices; he can proceed with the assignment regardless[34] or seek a declaration from the court that the purchaser is a suitable assignee.[35] The latter is the correct course. The vendor may well be wrong in thinking that the refusal was unreasonable, and the assignment would be a breach of covenant entitling the landlord to forfeit the lease. The risk is increased by the fact that the landlord may rely on reasons for his withholding consent advanced by him for the first

---

[31] For a modern discussion of the difference between fixtures and chattels see *Hamp* v. *Bygrave* (1983) 266 E.G. 720; discussed by H.W. Wilkinson (1983) 80 L.S.Gaz. 1773.

[32] (1981) 260 E.G. 601.

[33] *Eastern Telegraph Ltd.* v. *Dent* (1899) 1 Q.B. 835.

[34] *Treloar* v. *Bigge* (1874) L.R. 9 Exch. 151.

[35] *Young* v. *Ashley Garden Properties Ltd.* (1903) 2 Ch. 112.

time at the hearing.[36] However the vendor is not bound to go to the length of court proceedings to obtain consent to assign[37] and once he has used his best endeavours to obtain consent and failed, he may use his powers of rescission under the contract.

For parties who wish to proceed with their assignment where the landlord will not give his consent, it may help to summarise the law as it now stands on what constitutes unreasonable refusal.

1. Following the decision in *West Layton* v. *Ford*[38] the court will "look . . . at the covenant and construe that covenant in order to see what its purpose was when the parties entered into it; what each party, one the holder of the reversion, the other the assignee of the benefit of the relevant term, must be taken to have understood when they acquired the relevant interest on either side."[39]

2. There is no rigid rule governing the type of reasons which the court may or may not take into account when deciding the question of "what is reasonable refusal." For example considerations of proper estate management[40] may constitute a valid reason.

3. No refusal, on whatever grounds, can be reasonable if its sole purpose is to secure to the landlord a new advantage uncontemplated by the terms of the lease.[41]

4. Finally, the case of *West Layton Ltd.* v. *Ford* cast doubts on the existence or helpfulness of the principle of "abnormal" assignment (one relating to the "fag end" of a lease and made to obtain statutory protection) and "normal" assignment (one not so relating) in the Rent Act cases.

Covenants against assignment are further subject to the provisions of sections 21 and 24 of the Race Relations Act 1976 and section 31 of the Sex Discrimination Act 1975, which declare the withholding of consent to an assignment on the grounds of colour, race, nationality, ethnic or national origins or on the grounds of sex or marital status, "an unlawful act of discrimination." The Acts give a remedy to the person discriminated against[42] here the purchaser, but it seems that the vendor would still have to show the refusal of consent unreasonable.

Where the landlord's consent to assign is necessary the purchaser may expect to be asked to supply suitable references. National Condition 11(5) and Law Society Condition 8(4)(*b*) state that the purchaser shall supply such information and references as may be reasonably required of him by the landlord. If the purchaser deliberately refuses to give any references

---

[36] *Sonnenthal* v. *Newton* (1965) 109 S.J. 333; *Welch* v. *Birrane* (1974) 29 P. & C.R. 102; but the reason must have affected the mind of the landlord at the time he refused his consent; *Lovelock* v. *Margo* [1963] 2 Q.B. 786.

[37] *Wroth* v. *Tyler* [1974] Ch. 30.

[38] [1979] Q.B. 593.

[39] *Per* Roskill J. in *West Layton* v. *Ford* [1979] Q.B. 593.

[40] *e.g. Norfolk Capital Group* v. *Kitway Ltd.* [1976] 3 W.L.R. 796.

[41] *Bromley Park Garden Estates Ltd.* v. *Moss* [1982] 1 W.L.R. 1019 recently followed in *Anglia Building Society* v. *Sheffield County Council* (1983) 266 E.G. 311; and see R.E. Annand (1983) 127 S.J. 247.

[42] Race Relations Act 1976, ss.53 and 57; Sex Discrimination Act 1975, ss.62 and 66.

asked for, the purchaser is in breach of contract and the vendor can forfeit any deposit paid and sue for damages. If the purchaser supplies the requisite references and some or all are unacceptable to the landlord, the contract may be rescinded in the manner outlined below. The conditions oblige the purchaser to supply reasonable information and references only. In *Elfer* v. *Beynon-Lewis*[43] it was held that the obligation did not extend to the purchaser having to attend for interview by the landlord's agent.

Rescission. National Condition 11(5) places no time limit within which the vendor must obtain the landlord's licence to assign. "The sale is subject to the reversioner's licence being obtained" (11(5)), so it must be before completion, although the purchaser can agree to extend the completion date. If the licence cannot be obtained the vendor can rescind the contract, irrespective of whether or not the reversioner's refusal of consent was reasonable[43a]. Rescission is governed by Condition 10(2) in that any deposit must be returned and each party must bear their own expenses. However the provision in Condition 10(1) that 10 working days notice must be given does not apply.[44] The vendor may rescind without giving notice.

Law Society Condition 8(4)(c) provides that the licence to assign must be obtained at least five working days prior to the contractual completion date. If it is not, or is subject to any condition to which the purchaser reasonably objects, either party may rescind the contract by notice to the other (8(4)(c)). The condition has been criticised on the grounds that it gives too short a time for consent to be obtained,[45] and that as drafted the vendor can apparently rescind the contract even if the purchaser is willing to proceed without consent or grant an extension of time for completion.[46] No period of notice is needed under 8(4)(c). Rescission is governed by Condition 16(2):

> "(a) the vendor shall repay to the purchaser any sums paid by way of deposit or otherwise under the contract, with interest on such sums at the contract rate from four working days after rescission until payment
>
> (b) the purchaser shall forthwith return all documents delivered to him by the vendor and at his own expense procure the cancellation of any entry relating to the contract in any register."

THE CREATION OF EASEMENTS AND RESERVATIONS ON A SALE OF PART

Where A the owner of land does something on one part of his land for the benefit of the other part which could be an easement if the land was in separate ownership, the act is called a quasi-easement. It is not a full easement because A's entitlement to do the act is attributable to his ownership of the land[47]; he cannot have rights against himself. When A

---

[43] (1972) 222 E.G. 1955.

[43a] See *Bickel* v. *Courterly Investments (Nominees) Ltd.* [1984] 1 All E.R. 657.

[44] *Lipmans Wallpaper Ltd.* v. *Mason & Hodghton Ltd.* [1968] 1 All E.R. 1123 at p. 1130.

[45] [1982] Conv. 89.   [46] H.W. Wilkinson (1980) 130 New L.J. 1015.

[47] *Bolton* v. *Bolton* (1879) 11 Ch.D. 968.

subsequently sells off part, are full easements created corresponding to the quasi-easements which existed when A owned the whole? On a sale of part, easements are sometimes created expressly and provision for this will be made in the special conditions. In the following circumstances easements may be implied by common law or statute.

1. **Implied reservation.** If a vendor wishes to reserve an easement over land he is selling he must do so expressly[48] because of the rule that a grant (the conveyance) is construed against its maker. To this rule there are two exceptions:

(a) *Way of Necessity.* The vendor may acquire a way of necessity if he sells off land which provides the only means of access to the land he has retained.[49] The right of way so acquired is limited to allowing the vendor to use his retained land for the purposes for which it was used at the time of the grant.[50] The right to a way of necessity is not based on public policy and will yield to a contrary intention shown in the conveyancing documents.[51]

(b) *Intended Easements.* This is where both parties intended that the vendor should have an easement and its omission from the deed was a mere error. The rule is simple to state but the authors have not been able to find an example of a claim that has succeeded under this head, presumably because of the difficulty of proving common intention.[52]

2. **Implied grant.** The purchaser is also entitled to ways of necessity and intended easements. The rules are the same as for implied reservation, except that the court is more willing to imply easements in favour of the purchaser, because the grant is construed in his favour anyway. In practice the purchaser would rarely rely on the implied grant of an easement. He will prefer to base his claim on one or both of the following.

3. **The rule in Wheeldon v. Burrows.**[53] It was laid down in *Wheeldon v. Burrows* that on a grant of part of the property there will pass to the purchaser as easements, all quasi-easements over the land retained by the vendor which:

(i) are continuous and apparent,[54]
(ii) are necessary for the reasonable enjoyment of the land granted,[55] and
(iii) had been and are at the time of the grant used by the vendor for the benefit of the part granted.

The rule in *Wheeldon v. Burrows* applies to all "dispositions" including devises in wills and simultaneous sales off to different purchasers. Section 62 of the Law of Property Act 1925, considered below, applies to

---

[48] *Wheeldon v. Burrows* (1879) 12 Ch.D. 31.
[49] *Hansford v. Jaqo* [1921] 1 Ch. 322.
[50] *London Corporation v. Riggs* (1880) 13 Ch. D. 798.
[51] *Nickerson v. Barraclough* [1981] Ch. 246.
[52] *Re Webb* [1951] Ch. 808.
[53] (1879) 12 Ch. D. 31.
[54] See, for example, *Suffield v. Brown* (1864) 4 De G.J. & S. 185.
[55] See, for example, *Goldberg v. Edwards* [1950] Ch. 247.

"conveyances"[56] only, not agreements or contracts.[57] Therefore the rights impliedly granted in the contract are determined by the rule in *Wheeldon* v. *Burrows*.

4. **Section 62 of the Law of Property Act 1925.** The alternative way a purchaser can acquire as full easements those rights previously enjoyed by the vendor is under "the general words" of section 62 of the Law of Property Act 1925. Section 62 was intended as a word-saving section and merely saves the necessity of specifying what buildings, fixtures, easements and so on are to pass with the land on conveyance. However amongst its verbose ramblings are the words "or privileges, rights and advantages whatsoever enjoyed with the land or any part thereof—or reputed to be." These words are identical to words in the Conveyancing Act 1881 (s.6) and have been held[58] to convert into easements any rights in fact enjoyed at the time of the conveyance, provided of course that they are capable of existing as easements.[59] Section 62 is thus much broader than the rule in *Wheeldon* v. *Burrows* as the right does not have to be reasonably necessary for the enjoyment of the property.[60] However it has now finally been settled[61] that for section 62 to apply there must have been some diversity of occcupation of the vendor's land immediately before the conveyance. Alternatively the right must be continuous and apparent, like the right to light.[62] The "general words" of section 62 can be excluded or limited in the contract.[63] *Wheeldon* v. *Burrows* and section 62 operate in favour of the purchaser only.

National Condition 20 says: "Where the property and any adjacent or neighbouring property have hitherto been in common ownership, the purchaser shall not become entitled to any right to light or air over or in respect of any adjacent or neighbouring property which is retained by the vendor and the conveyance shall, if the vendor so requires, reserve to him such easements and rights as would become appurtenant to such last-mentioned property by implication of law, if the vendor had sold it to another purchaser at the same time as he sold the property to the purchaser." National Condition 20 is very vendor-orientated and the purchaser's solicitor should consider amending it or excluding it altogether. The first half of the condition is effective to limit the operation in favour of the purchaser of the rule in *Wheeldon* v. *Burrows* and "the general words" of section 62. This was confirmed in *Squarey* v. *Harris-Smith*,[64] where the Court of Appeal had to consider a similar condition in the 1934 Law Society Conditions, that the purchaser "shall not become entitled to" any easement or right which would restrict or interfere with the free use

---

[56] Defined by the Law of Property Act 1925, s.205(1)(ii).

[57] *Borman* v. *Griffith* [1930] 1 Ch. 493.

[58] *International Tea Stores* v. *Hobbs* [1903] 2 Ch. 165.

[59] *Grigsby* v. *Melville* [1974] 1 W.L.R. 80.

[60] *Goldberg* v. *Edwards* [1950] Ch. 247; *Ward* v. *Kirkland* [1967] Ch. 194.

[61] *Long* v. *Gowlett* [1923] 2 Ch. 177, approved by the House of Lords in *Sovomots Investments Ltd.* v. *Secretary of State for the Environment* [1979] A.C. 144.

[62] *Broomfield* v. *Williams* [1897] 1 Ch. 602.

[63] *Re Walmsley and Shaw's Contract* [1917] 1 Ch. 93.

[64] (1981) 42 P. & C.R. 118.

of the vendor's adjacent or neighbouring land for building or any other purpose. Oliver L.J. delivering the judgment of the court said that the condition had a dual effect; "First it ousts from the contract any implication of any right under the *Wheeldon* v. *Burrows* doctrine which might interfere with the vendors free use of his own land . . . Secondly, it enables the vendor to insist, if he wishes to do so, upon the exclusion from the conveyance of the general words which are implied under section 62."[65] The present condition only prevents the purchaser from acquiring rights to light or air over the vendor's retained land. The acquisition of other rights, for example drainage and support, are not excluded.

The second half of National Condition 20 reserves to the vendor "such easements and rights as would become appurtenant to" the retained land had the vendor been buying rather than selling it, and he is entitled to insist that these reservations be inserted in the conveyance. Thus the vendor gets the full benefit of the operation of the rule in *Wheeldon* v. *Burrows* and "the general words" of section 62, but the purchaser's entitlement is limited to those rights other than light or air.

"Adjacent or neighbouring property which is retained by the vendor" is not defined by Condition 20. To avoid later disputes, land retained by the vendor should be expressly designated in the special conditions.

Law Society Condition 5(3)(*b*) operates much more fairly between the parties, and makes provision for the grant as well as reservation of easements in respect of the vendor's retained land. It embodies the rule laid down for simultaneous sales-off in *Swansborough* v. *Coventry*,[66] appropriately modified to benefit the vendor. Condition 5(3)(*b*) states: "The conveyance of the property shall contain such reservations in favour of the retained land and the grant of such rights over the retained land as would have been implied had the vendor conveyed both the property and the retained land by simultaneous conveyances to different purchasers." In other words, both the vendor and purchaser are entitled to the benefit of the rule in *Wheeldon* v. *Burrows* and "the general words" of section 62.

It will be remembered that Condition 5(3)(*a*)(ii) requires land retained by the vendor "near to the property" to be designated in Special Condition B.

TIMETABLE OF EVENTS

To conclude our consideration of the more general of the standard conditions, we have included a timetable of the steps to be taken under the Law Society and National Conditions in a normal conveyancing transaction. The timeable serves the added purpose of highlighting the differences between the two sets of conditions. We are indebted to Professor J.T. Farrand on whose *Stately Saraband*[67] our timetable was based.

---

[65] *Ibid.* at p. 128.
[66] (1832) 2 M. & Sc. 362.
[67] [1980] Conv. 397.

TIMETABLE OF EVENTS UNDER THE STANDARD CONDITIONS

Law Society Condition	No.	Time	National Condition	No.	Time
A. BEFORE CONTRACT V disclose:—			A. BEFORE CONTRACT V disclose:—		
(i) Written communications received or known to vendor on or before the working day preceding date of contract, relating to any relevant matter	3(3)a	——	(i) Charge, notice, etc., under Planning Acts of which vendor knows	15(4)	——
(ii) All easements rights privileges etc. of which V knows or ought to know	5(1)	——	(ii) All latent easements and latent liabilities known to V.	14	——
(iii) Full particulars of all leases and tenancies	6(2)	——	(iii) Abstracts or copies of all leases and agreements in writing	18(1)	——
(iv) Leasehold title; copy of lease and superior lease	8(3)b	——	(iv) Leasehold title; copy of lease or underlease	11(2)	——
P obtain:—			P obtain:—		
(i) Written confirmation of statements	7(5)	——	(i) No equivalent	—	
(ii) Usual searches and enquiries	3(2)c	——	(ii) Planning enquiries	15(4)	——
(iii) Survey of state and condition of property	5(2)a	——	(iii) Survey of state and condition of property (except where to be constructed or converted by V)	13(3)	——

Law Society Condition	No.	Time	National Condition	No.	Time
B. CONTRACT P pay deposit	9	On or before the date of the contract	B. CONTRACT P pay deposit	2(1)	On the date of the contract
V and P exchange contracts	10	—	V and P exchange contracts	1(7)	—
V deliver abstract (or registered land equivalent)	12(1)	"Forthwith upon exchange of contracts"	V deliver abstract (or registered land equivalent)	9(1)	Not later than 11 working days after date of contract
V apply for licence to assign	8(4)a	"Forthwith"	V apply for licence to assign	11(5)	—
C. CONTRACT TO COMPLETION V elect re dishonoured cheque for deposit	9	Within 7 working days of first presentation	C. CONTRACT TO COMPLETION V elect re dishonoured cheque for deposit	2(2)	—
P rescind under special condition C	4	Within 20 working days from date of contract (time is of the essence)	P rescind under special condition A	3	Within 16 working days of date of contract (time is of the essence)
P insure property (except leasehold property and V obliged to insure)	11(4)	—	P insure property unless V so obliged by a third party (chattels should also be insured)	21(1)	—

Law Society Condition	No.	Time	National Condition	No.	Time
P supply information and references as may reasonably be required by reversioner	8(4)b	"Forthwith"	P supply information and references as may reasonably be required of him (for licence to assign)	11(5)	——
P deliver requisitions	15(2)	Within 6 working days of delivery of abstract or contract whichever is the later (time is of the essence)	P deliver requisitions	9(3)	Within 11 working days after delivery of abstract (time is of the essence)
No equivalent	—	——	P deliver requisitions on authorised use of property under Planning Acts	15(2)	With requisitions on title
V deliver replies	15(2)	Within 4 working days of delivery of requisitions (time of essence)	No equivalent	—	——
P deliver observations on replies	15(3)	Within 4 working days of receipt of replies (time of essence)	P deliver observations on replies	9(3)	Within 6 working days of delivery of replies (time is of the essence)

Law Society Condition	No.	Time	National Condition	No.	Time
V give purchaser notice to withdraw requisition (specifying reason for his inability or ground of his unwillingness to comply)	16(1)	—	V require purchaser to withdraw objection to title, he is unable or unwilling on reasonable grounds to remove	10(1)	—
Either— P Withdraw requisition	16(1)	Within 7 working days of V's notice	Either— P withdraw objection	10(1)	Within 10 working days of being required to do so
or— V or P rescind contract	16(1)	"Thereafter"	or— V recind the contract	10(1)	If purchaser does not withdraw objection within above time
[V repay deposit+interest and P return documents]	16(2)	[Interest from 4 working days after recission and "forthwith"]	[V return deposit without interest costs, etc. P return abstract and other documents]	10(2)	["Upon such recission"]
V produce evidence of boundaries	13(1)	—	No equivalent	—	
P require statutory declaration re boundaries (at V's expense)	13(2)	—	P require statutory declaration re boundaries (at P's expense)	13(1)	—

Law Society Condition	No.	Time	National Condition	No.	Time
V disclose—			V disclose—		
Further written communications of relevant matters	3(3)c	"Forthwith"	Requirements of local authority	16(2)	"Forthwith"
Changes in terms of tenancies	6(4)	——	No equivalent	—	——
Termination of tenancy (for P's directions and indemnity)	6(5)	——	No equivalent	—	——
V authorise P to occupy before completion	18	——	V authorise P to occupy before completion	8	——
(Limited to agreed decoration, repair or improvement)	18(1)b	——	(Limited to agreed works or installations)	8(4)	——
V or P terminate licence to occupy by giving notice	18(5)c	5 working days notice	V terminate licence to occupy	8(2)	7 working days notice
P give up occupation	18(5)c	"Thereupon" on expiry	P give up occupation	8(2)	"Forthwith" on expiry
D. PREPARING FOR COMPLETION			D. PREPARING FOR COMPLETION		
No Equivalent	—	——	P inform V of intent to execute mortgage or conveyance to third party to enable V to lodge priority notice of registration of intended covenants (unregistered land only)	19(4)	At least 15 working days before completion

Law Society Condition	No.	Time	National Condition	No.	Time
P deliver draft conveyance	17(1)	At least 12 working days before contractual completion date	P deliver draft conveyance	19(3)	At least 6 working days before completion date.
V deliver it back approved or revised	17(1)	Within 4 working days of delivery of draft	No equivalent	—	—
V insist on conveyance subject to rights	5(2)b	——	No equivalent		——
V or P insist on implied reservation or grant of right in respect of retained land	5(3)b	——	V insist on implied reservation of rights in respect of land retained by him	20	——
V insist on modification of implied covenant (leasehold)	8(5)	——	V insist on modification of implied covenant (leasehold)	11(7)	——
V insist on indemnity covenant (unless implied by statute)	17(4)	——	V insist on covenant to indemnify, observe and perform (unless implied by statute)	19(5) &(6)	——
V refuse sub-conveyance on reasonable grounds	17(6)	——	No equivalent	—	
P deliver engrossed conveyance (duly executed)	17(2)	At least 5 working days before contractual completion date	P deliver engrossed conveyance	19(3)	Within 3 working days of return of draft approved

Law Society Condition	No.	Time	National Condition	No.	Time
V or P rescind if no licence to assign	8(4)c	At least 5 working days before contractual completion date	V rescind if no licence to assign	11(5)	—
V require completion at mortgagees office	21(1)	At least 5 working days before actual completion	V's solicitor reasonably require venue for completion	5(4)	—
P obtain V's agreement to alternative method of payment	21(2)d	Before actual completion	V's solicitor request or agree to telegraphic or other direct transfer or other method of payment	5(3) iv & vi	—
No equivalent	—	—	P require possession on or immediately before time of completion	5(4)	Giving "reasonable notice"
E. DELAY IN COMPLETION V or P (if in default) liable to pay compensation to other for loss due to delay or	22(2)	After contractual completion date	E. DELAY IN COMPLETION P pay interest (except where V or mortgagee in default or property construction or conversion unfinished) or	7(1) 7(2)	From completion date
V or P opt for interest instead of compensation (by notice) or	22(3)	Before actual completion or within five working days thereafter (time is of the essence)	V by notice opt to take income instead of interest or	7(1)i	Before actual completion

Law Society Condition	No.	Time	National Condition	No.	Time
V opt by notice for income instead of compensation	22(4)	Before actual completion	P (delay not caused by his neglect or default and not in occupation) opt by notice to place completion money on deposit at designated bank and pay V interest produced by deposit instead of income or interest	7(1)ii	deposit interest payable from notice
V or P serve completion notice	23(2)	After contractual completion date	V or P serve special notice to complete	22(1)	On or after completion date
P pay any balance of 10% deposit	9(2)	On service of V's completion notice			
V or P seek extension V or P reinvoke	23(7)	—	No equivalent	—	—
V or P comply with completion notice	23(3)	Within 15 working days of service, or 7 working days of reinvocation (time is of the essence)	V or P comply with completion notice	—	Within 16 working days after service (excluding day of service) (time is of the essence)

F. COMPLETION
V—

F. COMPLETION

Law Society Condition	No.	Time	National Condition	No.	Time
Endorse sale to P on retained documents of title	20	At completion	No equivalent	—	—
Hand over statutory declaration re boundaries	13(2)	At completion	No equivalent	—	—

Law Society Condition	No.	Time	National Condition	No.	Time
P—pay by 2.30 p.m	21(5)a	Day of actual completion (contractual completion date = 25th working day after contract, or as otherwise stated (21 (1))	P—pay by 2.15 p.m if Friday	5(5)i	Day of actual completion (contractual completion date= 26th working day after contract or delivery of abstract, whichever is later, or as otherwise stated (5(1))
—by approved method	21(2)	—	—by stated method	5(3)	—
G. AFTER COMPLETION V notice claiming compensation in respect of payment after 2.30 p.m	21(5)c	Within 5 working days after completion (time is of essence)	G. AFTER COMPLETION No equivalent	—	—
P pay compensation	21(5)c	Due 5 working days after receipt of notice	No equivalent	—	—
V or P notify/pay delayed apportionments	19(6)b	"Forthwith"/"thereupon"	V or P notify/pay balance due of actual amount of service charge underlease	6(5)	—/within 15 working days of being informed
H. AFTER NON-COMPLETION If P does not comply with completion notice— P—return all documents, cancel	23(4)a	"Forthwith"	H. AFTER NON-COMPLETION If P fails to comply with special notice to complete— V—forfeit deposit	22(3)	—

Law Society Condition	No.	Time	National Condition	No.	Time
all entries in any register					
V—forfeit deposit	23(4)b	—			
—resell	23(4)(5)	Within 1 year after completion date	—resell	—	within 12 months of expiry of 16 working days from service of notice.
If V fails to comply with completion notice —					
P give V notice to repay deposit with interest	23(6)	—	No equivalent	—	
V pay interest on deposit	23(6)	From 4 working days of notice			
P return documents, etc.	23(6)	"Forthwith" on re-payment			
P's licence to occupy ends	18(5)b	"Upon termination of the contract"	No equivalent	—	
P vacate	18(5)	"Thereupon"	P vacate property	8(2)	"Upon discharge or recission of the contract"

PART II.

I. THE VENDORS DUTY OF DISCLOSURE UNDER AN OPEN CONTRACT AND UNDER THE STANDARD CONDITIONS

The basic position in the law of contract is that there is no general rule requiring contracting parties to disclose relevant facts to each other, relevant facts being those which would affect the course of negotiations between the parties. As Lord Atkin commented in *Bell* v. *Lever Brothers Ltd.*[68]: "The failure to disclose a material fact which might influence the mind of a prudent contractor does not give the right to avoid the contract." This tenet of the common law finds its most important manifestation in the rule of *caveat emptor* ("buyer beware").[69]

The rule of *caveat emptor* must not be taken to mean the vendor has no duty of disclosure. He must show good title which involves:

(i) identifying the property, and
(ii) explaining to the purchaser the nature of his title.

(1) Identifying the Property

The vendor's obligation to identify the property consists of two parts. First he must correctly state the interest in the property he proposes to sell; "the legal description." Secondly he must establish the physical extent of the property; "the physical description." In describing the physical extent of the property the parties will necessarily be concerned with the ownership of boundaries.

"THE LEGAL DESCRIPTION"

In the particulars of sale the vendor will specify whether he is selling the freehold or merely a leasehold interest in the property. Additionally he must state certain other factors qualifying the interest in order not to mislead the purchaser. For example, in *Re Brine and Davies' Contract*[70] the vendor agreed to sell a "registered freehold house." Unknown to the purchaser the title was possessory. Although what was said was true, the description was misleading as the purchaser understood from it that the property was registered with absolute freehold title. The purchaser was entitled to rescind. If leasehold property is being sold the vendor must say whether he holds under a lease or a sub-lease.[71] The length of the term should be stated to ensure that the purchaser is aware, from the start, of the duration of the interest being sold.

---

[68] [1932] A.C. 161 at p. 227.
[69] *e.g. Keates* v. *Cadogan* (1851) 10 C.B. 591. The rule was briefly mentioned earlier, *ante*, p. 58.
[70] [1935] Ch. 388.
[71] *Re Russ and Brown's Contract* [1934] Ch. 34 (*c.f. Becker* v. *Partridge* [1966] 2 Q.B. 155).

The complete legal description would set out rights which the property enjoyed and incumbrances which burdened it. Failure to state easements and the like which benefit the property is not fatal. Incumbrances should be stated in the particulars but often appear elsewhere in the contract. Unlike benefits certain burdens *must* be detailed in the contract.[72]

"THE PHYSICAL DESCRIPTION"

It is essential that the vendor is able to convey all the property he contracts to sell, otherwise the purchaser will have a claim for rescission or compensation.[73] The vendor must therefore be able to prove that the land he describes in the particulars of sale corresponds with the description of the land in the title deeds. As a result of this the practice has developed, in unregistered conveyancing of describing the property in the contract by reference to the description in the conveyance to the vendor. As long as the vendor's solicitor has confirmed beforehand that this description is accurate no problem will arise where the vendor is selling the whole of his property. Carelessly copying the description of the property from the vendor's title deeds will, however, lead to problems. For example, suppose a vendor has already disposed of part of his land. When he comes to sell his retained part to a prospective purchaser, if his solicitor merely copies the description from the original conveyance to the vendor (as the description of the retained land) then he would in effect be saying that his client was selling a part he no longer owned.[74] Further suppose, the description of the land in the conveyance to the vendor is inaccurate.[75] Later he agrees to sell the property and the same description is incorporated into the contract (in the hope of ensuring that the vendor only contracts to sell the land which was conveyed to him). If the purchaser's solicitor on investigating the title discovers the inaccuracy the vendor may lose the sale or be forced to compensate the purchaser. In every case the vendor's solicitor should examine all the facts to ensure that the contract description of the property is suitable.[76]

If a written description is too uncertain or unreliable the property should be described by means of a plan. As Brightman J. pointed out in *Lloyd v. Stanbury*,[77] where the vendor is selling part of his property the need for a plan is accentuated: "If there is a moral to this unfortunate story it is the danger of dispensing with a plan to a contract of sale particularly where natural boundaries are not obvious and the vendor is selling part only of his land."

A plan used to control the description of the property being sold must be on a scale large enough for it to be of practical use. In *Scarfe* v. *Adams*[78] purchasers at an auction each bought part of a property known as "The

---

[72] See *post*, p. 199.

[73] See *post*, p. 229.

[74] Similarly new property may have been acquired by the vendor necessitating a fresh description in the contract for sale, see, *e.g. Wallington* v. *Townsend* [1939] Ch. 588.

[75] *Spall* v. *Owen* (1982) 44 P. & C.R. 36, noted at (1983) 127 S.J. 263 (Aldridge).

[76] *Gordon-Cumming* v. *Houldsworth* [1910] A.C. 537 at p. 547.

[77] [1971] 1 W.L.R. 535 at p. 544.

[78] [1981] 1 All E.R. 843.

Coach House." The plan in the contract was an Ordnance Survey Map on a scale of 1: 2,500. It showed a dotted line running through the grounds but not the house itself. If the line had been completed it would have divided the house not along an existing party wall, but along the middle of a tenanted flat in the house. A dispute arose as to the true extent of each of the purchasers' property. It was held that the division should follow the party wall. In delivering the judgment of the Court of Appeal, Brightman J. criticised the use of small scale plans in conveyancing transactions where the boundaries have to be defined with precision.[79] A map on a scale of 1: 1,250 should be adequate for most purposes.[80] For a review of some particular problems relating to the sale of flats and maisonettes reference may usefully be made to H.W. Wilkinson's article *Mysterious Parcels.*[81]

Where the title to the vendor's property is registered describing it in the contract for sale is easier. As one writer has suggested,[82] "when on the register, do as the registrar does." Therefore, if the registered proprietor is selling the whole of his property a reference in the contract to the title number is a sufficient description.[83] However, the parties may want to use a plan to govern the description and again the Land Registry can be of assistance. They keep detailed maps of all registered estates and the "filed plan" may be incorporated into the contract. Once again the "filed plan" should be examined by the vendor's solicitor to ensure its accuracy. Mistakes have been known to occur even in these plans.[84]

On a sale of part of a registered estate a plan must be used.[85] As in unregistered conveyancing the parties must be in no doubt as to the physical extent of their properties. Additionally rule 79 of the Land Registration Rules 1925 requires an instrument dealing with part of a registered title to be accompanied by a plan; this matter should be dealt with at the contract stage. The Land Registry has a special procedure facilitating the description of plots being sold on a registered building estate.[86]

FURTHER EVIDENCE OF IDENTITY

The property identified in the vendor's documents of title will usually comprise the property he has agreed to sell. The vendor is therefore able to fulfil his obligation to show good title to the property as described in the contract.

Under an open contract where the contract description materially differs from that in the title deeds the purchaser has a right to call for further evidence of identity.[87] Contractual conditions which try to exclude this right are strictly construed by the courts. Thus in *Flower* v. *Hartopp*[87]

---

[79] See also *Mayer* v. *Hurr, The Times*, April 23, 1983.
[80] *Norwich City Council* v. *Secretary of State for the Environment* [1982] 1 All E.R. 737.
[81] (1981) 131 New L.J. 438.
[82] J. T. Farrand, *Contract and Conveyance* (4th ed.), p. 148.
[83] Registered Land Practice Notes (1982/3 ed.), p. 15.
[84] *Lee* v. *Barrey* [1957] Ch. 251.
[85] Registered Land Practice Notes, (1982/3 ed.), p. 15.
[86] *Ibid.* at pp. 7–15.
[87] *Flower* v. *Hartopp* (1843) 6 Beav. 476.

where the description of the property in the title deeds differed from that in the contract the vendor could not enforce the contract, despite a condition, that "no further evidence of identity was to be required than was afforded by the abstract and documents therein." In effect such a condition amounts to a term stating that the title deeds will show a sufficient identification of the property described in the contract.[88]

Both the National and Law Society Conditions contain provisions dealing with the vendor's obligation to establish the identity of the property. National Condition 13 reads as follows:

"(1) The purchaser shall admit the identity of the property with that comprised in the muniments offered by the vendor as the title thereto upon the evidence afforded by the descriptions contained in such muniments, and of a statutory declaration, to be made (if required) at the purchaser's expense, that the property has been enjoyed according to the title for at least twelve years.

(2) The vendor shall not be bound to show any title to boundaries, fences, ditches, hedges or walls, or to distinguish parts of the property held under different titles further than he may be able to do from information in his possession."

Its Law Society equivalent (Law Society Condition 13) reads:

"(1) The vendor shall produce such evidence as may be reasonably necessary to establish the identity and extent of the property, but shall not be required to define exact boundaries, or the ownership of fences, ditches, hedges or walls, nor, beyond the evidence afforded by the information in his possession, separately to identify parts of the property held under different titles.

(2) If reasonably required by the purchaser because of the insufficiency of the evidence produced under sub-condition (1), the vendor shall at his own expense provide and hand over on completion a statutory declaration as to the relevant facts, in a form agreed by the purchaser, such agreement not to be unreasonably withheld."

National Condition 13(1) was considered in *Re Bramwell's Contract.*[89] In this case the property described in the contract was *probably* identified by the vendor's title deeds. Despite National Condition 13(1) the vendor was unable to force the property on the purchaser. Law Society Condition 13(1) provides that the vendor shall produce such evidence as may be reasonably necessary to establish the identity of the property. Again it would not enable the vendor to force the property on the purchaser if it was not adequately identified by reference to the former's title deeds.

If the title deeds prove inadequate, both Conditions give the purchaser the right to call for further evidence of identity in the form of a statutory declaration. Under National Condition 13(1) the declaration shall state that the property has been enjoyed consistently with the title for at least 12 years. Law Society Condition 13(2) is similar although no 12 year limit

---

[88] *Curling* v. *Austin* (1862) 2 Drew. & S. 129.
[89] [1969] 1 W.L.R. 1659.

is imposed and unlike the National Condition it is the vendor who must pay for the declaration. The purchaser may require a person other than the vendor to make the declaration under both Conditions.[90]

Under an open contract the vendor may be obliged to distinguish parts of the property held under different titles.[91] Both Conditions relieve him of this duty (if it exists) when he cannot distinguish the different parts from the information in his possession.

BOUNDARIES

Under an open contract it is doubtful that the vendor is under a duty to define the ownership of the boundaries to the property.[92] National Condition 13(2) resolves this doubt in favour of the vendor by providing that he is not required to define boundaries. Law Society Condition 13(1) is less favourable to the vendor. It provides that he is not "required to define *exact* boundaries." He must produce some evidence of the identity of boundaries though this need not be conclusive. A purchaser should investigate the position and ownership of boundaries to the property prior to making the contract.[93]

Boundary disputes are the source of much acrimonious litigation between neighbouring landowners. In the absence of conclusive evidence of the position and ownership of boundaries in the vendor's title deeds, the following rebuttable presumptions will apply.[94]

(i) **Dividing walls.** These are often referred to as "party walls." They are divided down the middle vertically. The owner of the properties on either side of the wall has rights of support and user over the rest of the wall.[95] There is no obligation on either of the owners to keep the wall in good repair, though if repairs are made they must contribute towards the cost in equal shares.

(ii) **Hedges, Banks and Ditches.** The boundary is presumed to run along the edge of the ditch furthest from the hedge or bank. The presumption only arises where there is a single ditch which is man made.[96] If an Ordance Survey Map is used to describe the property the boundary line is prima facie the centre of the hedge or ditch.[97]

(iii) **Rivers.** Where land is bordered by a non-tidal river the boundary is the middle of the river bed. If the river suddenly changes course drastically the boundary remains where it was before the change.[98] Changes in the course of the river over a prolonged period will result in the alteration of boundaries.

---

[90] *Hobson* v. *Bell* (1839) 2 Beav. 17.
[91] *Monro* v. *Taylor* (1852) 2 M. & G. 713.
[92] *Dawson* v. *Brinckman* (1850) 3 M. & G. 53.
[93] See *ante*, p. 60.
[94] See T.M. Aldridge, *Boundaries, Walls and Fences* (5th ed.) for a fuller discussion.
[95] Law of Property Act 1925, s.38.
[96] *Marshall* v. *Taylor* [1895] 1 Ch. 641.
[97] *Davey* v. *Harrow Corporation* [1958] 1 Q.B. 60. This follows Ordnance Survey practice.
[98] *Ford* v. *Lacey* (1861) 7 H. & N. 151.

(iv) **Highways.** The owner of land adjacent to a road is presumed to own half of the subsoil of the road. On building estates developers will retain ownership of the subsoil of the estate roads in order to complete construction. Where the road is bordered by fences or hedges, the boundary is presumed to be the fence or hedge itself unless the circumstances indicate to the contrary.

(v) **Fences.** If the fence is maintained by the vendor the presumption is that it belongs to him. There is no legal basis for the common presumption that a fence belongs to the owner of the land on which the supporting posts stand. It is possible that a fence may be declared a "party fence." The owners rights are the same as with "party walls."

Commonly "T" marks are placed on plans to indicate ownership of fences. However, if the plan is not supported by a reference in the deed or transfer relating to their presence, they are not conclusive evidence of ownership.

(vi) **Registered Land.** Except where it is noted on the Property Register that the boundaries have been fixed the filed plan will indicate general boundaries only. This means that a filed plan cannot be used to resolve boundary disputes.[99] The exact line of the boundary is left undertermined even if the whole or a part of any ditch, wall, fence, road, stream or other boundary is expressly included or excluded from the title.[1]

Boundaries may be fixed by the Land Registry. An official measures out the boundaries exactly from a fixed point, using measurements provided by the owner. As this process necessarily "fixes" neighbouring owners boundaries it has proved unpopular and rare in practice.

(2) Explaining the Nature of his Title

FREEDOM FROM INCUMBRANCES: THE OPEN CONTRACT RULE

In an open contract the common law implies a term that the vendor is selling the fee simple in the land free from all incumbrances.[2] No such implication will arise if the purchaser is aware, at the time the contract is made that "some lesser interest or some encumbered interest was to be the subject of the sale."[3] The purchaser is deemed to be aware of all patent defects in title affecting the property to be sold whether he actually knew of them or not. So, the vendor (in the absence of an express term in the contract to the contrary) impliedly contracts to sell subject only to those latent defects in title of which the purchaser knows.

A vendor has a duty to disclose all latent defects in title. Failure to disclose latent defects results in the vendor being in breach of the term implied into the contract at common law, and gives the purchaser the right to rescind the contract and/or claim damages depending upon the

---

[99] *Lee* v. *Barrey* [1957] Ch. 251. Land Registration Rules 1925, r. 278.

[1] *Ibid.* r. 278(4).

[2] *Purvis* v. *Rayer* (1821) 9 Price 488; *Ogilvie* v. *Foljambe* (1817) 3 Mer 53. *Doe d. Gray* v. *Stanion* (1836) 1 M. & W. 695; *Hughes* v. *Parker* (1841) 8 M. & W. 244.

[3] *Timmins* v. *Moreland Street Property Co. Ltd.* [1958] Ch. 110.

seriousness of the vendor's non-disclosure.[4] As Stirling J. remarked[5]: "we cannot but observe that there is great practical convenience in requiring the vendor, who knows his own title, to disclose all that is necessary to protect himself rather than in requiring the purchaser to demand an inspection of the vendor's title deed before [contract]."

(i) **Is the Defect Patent or Latent?** A defect is latent if it is not reasonably capable of discovery on inspection of the property. A restrictive covenant burdening the property to be sold is obviously a latent defect and therefore must be disclosed.[6] Other examples are notices increasing the rent served under a rent review clause,[7] unusually onerous covenants contained in a lease,[8] and some overriding interests, as defined by section 70 of the Land Registration Act 1925.

A defect is patent if it is discoverable by a reasonably careful inspection of the property. The classic statement of the law on this point is that of Sargent J. in *Yandle & Sons* v. *Sutton*[9]: "a patent defect, which can be thrust upon the purchaser, must be a defect which arises either to the eye, or by necessary implication from something which is visible to the eye." The case concerned the existence of a right of way over property which the plaintiff was buying. He claimed that the vendor had broken the contract by failing to disclose this incumbrance affecting his land. The vendor argued that the right of way, being evidenced by a path, was discoverable by inspection and therefore not latent. It was held that the existence of an unmetalled path did not necessarily imply that the property was subject to a right of way. The path could merely be indicative of the owner's use of the property. Only if a road or path unequivocally points towards the existence of a right of way, public or private, could such an easement be regarded as patent. A path travelling from the doorstep of a neighbouring house, over a vendor's land, to a public highway would constitute a patent defect, because it would be obvious that the neighbour (at least) had a right of way over the property.[10] Again, in *Re Leyland and Taylor's Contract*[11] it was held that the fact that a street, fronting the property was unpaved should have given the purchaser notice that the local authority might ask him to contribute towards the expense of making up the street in the future. The incumbrance on the property did not require disclosure by the vendor.

A vendor, who is unsure whether a defect in title is patent or latent, would be well advised to disclose it to prevent litigation in the future.

(ii) **Purchaser's Knowledge of Defects.** It has been said that a purchaser's knowledge of a defect in the vendor's title will preclude the common law

---

[4] See *post*, p. 233.
[5] *Re White and Smith's Contract* [1896] 1 Ch. 637 at p. 641.
[6] *Re Stone and Saville's Contract* [1963] 1 W.L.R. 163; *Rudd* v. *Lascelles* [1900] 1 Ch. 815.
[7] *F. & H. Entertainments Ltd.* v. *Leisure Enterprises Ltd.* (1976) 120 S.J. 331.
[8] *Re White and Smith's Contract* [1896] 1 Ch. 637.
[9] [1922] 2 Ch. 199 at p. 210.
[10] *Ashburner* v. *Sewell* [1891] 3 Ch. 405; *Bowles* v. *Round* (1800) 5 Ves 508.
[11] [1900] 2 Ch. 625.

implication that the vendor is selling the unencumbered fee simple, to the extent of the known defect.[12]

An important distinction must be made between removable[13] and irremovable defects. It is only when the purchaser is shown to have been aware of an irremovable defect in title prior to the contract, that he may be prevented later from objecting to the property being sold subject to it. A purchaser who is aware of a removable defect in title is entitled to assume that it will be removed by the vendor before completion.[14] A common example of this is the purchaser's assumption in residential conveyancing transactions that a vendor will redeem his mortgage on completion. Again there is authority for the view that a breach of a repairing convenant in a lease is a removable defect.[15] The vendor can usually remedy the breach easily by repairing and the purchaser is entitled to assume that he will do so. Under an open contract he may, therefore, be able to object to a vendor's title on this basis. Sales incorporating either set of standard conditions expressly vary the open contract position.[16]

If the contract expressly provides that good title shall be shown the purchaser is entitled to insist on this notwithstanding that he knew of an irremovable defect in the vendor's title before execution of the contract. In *McGrory* v. *Alderdale Estate Co. Ltd.*[17] Lord Finlay said: "The law is clear that, if there is a written agreement of sale which expressly provides that a good title is to be made it is not open to the vendor to prove that at the time of the contract the purchaser knew of a defect in the title for the purpose of leading to the inference that a good title was not to be shown in that particular. This would be to vary a written contract by parol evidence. But, if the contract is open, the obligation which the law would import into it to make a good title in every respect may be rebutted by proving that the purchaser entered into the contract with knowledge of certain defects in the title. The inference in such a case is that he was content to take a title less complete than that which the law would otherwise have given him by implication."

The case of *Cato* v. *Thompson*[18] provides an example of the operation of this rule. The defendant agreed to sell land to the plaintiff on the basis he would "make a good marketable title." The land was burdened by a restrictive covenant which made it unmarketable. The plaintiff knew of the restrictive covenant, and the almost certainty that it would not be released, when he made the contract. He later refused to complete and brought an action for the return of his deposit. The court decided the vendor must return the deposit. Jessel M.R. considered the agreement amounted to no more than the purchaser saying, "I know that there is a serious defect in your title, but I will buy if you can make it marketable." The vendor could not so the purchaser was able to rescind.

---

[12] *Timmins* v. *Moreland Street Property Co. Ltd.* [1958] Ch. 110.
[13] A defect is removable if it lies within the power of the vendor to compel its removal.
[14] *Re Gloag and Miller's Contract* (1883) 23 Ch.D. 320.
[15] *Re Highett and Bird's Contract* [1903] 1 Ch. 287 may be explained on this basis.
[16] National Condition 13(3); Law Society Condition 5(2)(*a*); see *post*, p. 211.
[17] [1918] A.C. 503 at p. 508.
[18] (1882) 9 Q.B.D. 616.

Finally, section 24 of the Law of Property Act 1969 expressly preserves the vendor's common law duty of disclosure in respect of latent defects in title registrable as land charges. The section was explained earlier.[19] To recap, it allows a purchaser to rescind unless he has actual knowledge (not "deemed" knowledge under section 198 of the Law of Property Act 1925) of such a defect before making the contract.

(iii) **Covering Defective Title in the Contract.** Neither set of standard conditions expressly provide for covering a latent defect in the vendor's title. Under an open contract a vendor cannot force a purchaser to take a defective title unless he first makes full and frank disclosure of the defect and the purchaser then agrees to take the title offered. In *Re Haedicke and Lipski's Contract*[20] the vendor of leasehold land failed to reveal some unusually onerous covenants to his buyer. The agreement for sale contained a term stating that "the vendor's title is accepted by the purchaser." Despite the condition the purchaser was entitled to rescind the contract and recover his deposit. And in *Bousfield* v. *Hodges*[21] the court laid down this principle: "a purchaser is only bound by his acceptance of the title, so far as he is made cognisant of it and . . . if anything is kept back by the vendor, he is not, as to that bound by his acceptance."

In practice where a vendor has a flaw in his title he will disclose it to the purchaser in the special conditions and then state that the purchaser is not allowed to raise objections or requisitions on it. By revealing the defect he ensures that the purchaser cannot later back out of the contract. The disclosure by the vendor must be of a nature that can be readily understood by a reasonable person. It cannot be vague or couched in terms which only a "trained equity conveyancer"[22] can understand.

One situation where a purchaser does bind himself to take property subject to a latent defect in title (if any) is where he agrees to accept "such title as the vendor has." The purchaser is taking a gamble; once he contracts on this basis he cannot object if the title subsequently proves defective in some respect.[23]

SPECIFIC MATTERS WHICH THE VENDOR MUST DISCLOSE UNDER AN OPEN CONTRACT AND THE STANDARD CONDITIONS

(i) **Easements Rights and Other Liabilities.** Any latent easements, rights, privileges or other liabilities, to which the property is subject, should be disclosed to an intending purchaser. Rights of way, light and water are common examples. Perhaps less frequently encountered will be rights allowing neighbours to hang clothes on a line passing over the vendor's

---

[19] See *ante*, p. 30.
[20] [1901] 2 Ch. 666.
[21] (1863) 33 Beav. 90 at p. 94.
[22] *Faruqi* v. *English Real Estates* [1979] 1 W.L.R. 963 at p. 967; *Re Marsh and Earl Granville* (1883) 24 Ch.D. 11, Re. Fry J. at p. 17.
[23] *Re Haedicke and Lipski's Contract* [1901] 2 Ch. 666; *Gordon* v. *Turner* (1851) 51 E.R. 453.

land,[24] or even permitting them to enter onto the land to repair buildings on adjoining property.[25]

At common law a vendor's lack of knowledge of a latent incumbrance does not affect his duty to inform the purchaser of its existence prior to the contract.[26] This clearly puts a heavy burden on the vendor because he will not always know that his property is subject to such rights. The case of *E.R. Ives Investments Ltd.* v. *High*[27] affords a well known example. Law Society Condition 5(1) limits the common law duty of the vendor. The vendor only warrants that "he has disclosed to the purchaser the existence of all easements, rights, privileges and liabilities affecting the property, of which the vendor knows or ought to know, other than the existence of those known to the purchaser at the date of the contract or which a prudent purchaser would have discovered by that date." But in another respect the condition extends the vendor's duty. It was noted above that a vendor need not bring a patent defect in title to the attention of the purchaser. Under Condition 5(1) the vendor is dutybound to reveal patent easements, rights and so on if the purchaser has no knowledge of them, or could not have discovered them by making the usual pre-contractual searches and enquiries.[28] A vendor's solicitor may consider it desirable to return to the position under an open contract and amend Condition 5(1) accordingly. National Condition 14 merely restates the rule as to latent defects in title and puts the vendor under no duty to disclose patent ones.

Both sets of standard conditions state that the property is otherwise to be sold (Law Society Condition 5(2)(*b*) and "if the vendor so requires conveyed") subject to all rights of way, water, light, drainage and so on.

(ii) **Existing Leases.** In the absence of an express contractual term to the contrary,[29] the common law implies a term into the contract that vacant possession will be given on completion. As a result the vendor must disclose all tenancies affecting the property to be sold.[30] The fact that a lease was granted prior to the contractual root of title does not detract from a purchaser right to call for particulars of it.[31] A vendor who fails to disclose these matters runs the risk that his purchaser will be able to rescind the contract. Although a purchaser of property, who knows it to be subject to an existing tenancy, cannot complain that vacant possession is not given[32], as a matter of good conveyancing practice, the vendor should still send details of the tenancies to him to prevent disputes arising in the future.

---

[24] *Drewell* v. *Towler* (1832) 3B. & Ad. 735.
[25] *Ward* v. *Kirkland* [1967] Ch. 194.
[26] *Heywood* v. *Mallalieu* (1883) 25 Ch.D. 357; *Re Brewer and Hankin's Contract* (1899) 80 L.T. 127.
[27] [1967] 2 Q.B. 379.
[28] For a discussion of the 1980 version of Condition 5(1) see H.W. Wilkinson, *Standard Conditions of Sale of Land* (3rd ed.) p. 25; see also T. Aldridge (1980) 124 S.J. 798.
[29] For example Special Condition C (National Conditions) or F (Law Society Conditions).
[30] *Farrell* v. *Green* (1974) 232 E.G. 587.
[31] Law of Property Act 1925, s.45.
[32] *Timmins* v. *Moreland Street Property Co. Ltd.* [1958] Ch. 110.

A vendor landlord should also reveal the fact that he has either served or received a notice to quit. Failure to do so will be an actionable non-disclosure.[33] On the other hand there is no duty on the vendor at common law to disclose a tenant's intention to bring the tenancy to an end where the tenant has informally notified his landlord but not yet served notice as required by the lease.[34]

If it is intended to sell property subject to a tenancy full details of it must be given in the contract. To avoid misdescription care must be taken to ensure that all particulars are stated accurately. A statement in the contract that the property is sold subject to a tenancy under which rent of £1,500 per annum is recoverable when in fact the rent payable is only £1,000 per annum will result in the vendor being in breach of contract.

Commonly, details of tenancies are revealed by giving the purchaser an opportunity to inspect the leases or some written evidence of their terms.[35] In practice it is usual to send copies of the tenancy agreements to the purchaser along with the draft contract. Both sets of standard conditions contain provisions designed to give the purchaser notice of the existence, and terms, of leases subject to which the property is sold. Special conditions (National Condition "C" and Law Society Condition "F") on the back of the two forms will declare the sale to be subject to existing tenancies.[36]

National Condition 18(1) provides that: "Abstracts or copies of the leases or agreements (if in writing) . . . having been made available, the purchaser (whether he has inspected the same or not) shall be deemed to have notice of and shall take subject to the terms of all existing tenancies and the rights of the tenants." It would be grossly negligent for a purchaser's solicitor not to inspect a lease having been given an opportunity to do so.[37] Although this condition does not deal with oral tenancies affecting the property, the vendor's solicitor should give the purchaser a written account of the terms and conditions of such a tenancy to avoid possible arguments arising in the future as to what was or was not disclosed at the time the contract was made. The same applies to Law Society Condition 6(2) which merely provides for "copies or full particulars" of all leases to be furnished to the purchaser.

Once the requisite information has been supplied to the purchaser, he is deemed to have full knowledge of the tenant's rights under the lease or arising out of it, for instance a right to a statutory tenancy under the Rent Act 1977 or compensation for improvements made during the currency of the term.

The standard conditions both attempt to preclude a purchaser from objecting to a contractual misdescription relating to any tenancies (National Condition 18(1), Law Society Condition 6(1)). These provisions will only protect the vendor if he makes full disclosure of the leases. It

---

[33] *Dimmock* v. *Hallet* (1866) 2 Ch. App. 21.
[34] *Davenport* v. *Charsley* (1886) 54 L.T. 372.
[35] If for example the lease is oral.
[36] See *ante*, pp. 158 and 165.
[37] *Becker* v. *Partridge* [1966] 2 Q.B. 155.

could not be relied upon by a vendor who had not afforded his purchaser an opportunity to inspect the leases prior to the formation of the contract.

What is the position if a tenant vacates the property before completion? Between contract and completion the vendor is a qualified trustee of the property with a duty to use reasonable care to preserve it.[38] The purchaser, who in the eyes of equity owns the property at this stage, takes the benefit of any increase in the value of the land. If the property is vacated by a tenant and its value rises, because vacant possession can be given, the vendor must not deprive the purchaser of his windfall without prior consultation.[39] On the other hand if leaving the property untenanted would lead to a diminution in the land's value, as for example where agricultural land is taken out of cultivation, the vendor is under a duty to relet the property reasonably quickly.[40] The National Conditons do not deal expressly with this eventuality. The common law therefore applies. Law Society Condition 6(5) merely restates the common law adding that the vendor, having informed the purchaser of the termination of any tenancy affecting the propety, shall act as directed by the purchaser, subject to being indemnified by him against all consequential loss, expenditure and liability. As one commentator has suggested, Condition 6(5) could be usefully amended to require the vendor landlord to inform the purchaser of the tenancy's end immediately he learns of it.[41]

Under an open contract a vendor–landlord's power to alter the terms and conditions of a tenancy is curtailed once contracts have been exchanged for the sale of his reversion. He can do so only in so far as his duty to preserve the property allows.[42] Law Society Condition 6(4) requires the vendor to inform the purchaser of any change in the disclosed terms and conditions of any lease or tenancy. If for instance the vendor were to increase the rent under a review clause (the review date falling between contract and completion) he would have to notify the purchaser. However, in view of the fact that no sanction is prescribed if the vendor fails to inform the purchaser in accordance with the Condition, the purchaser's interests may be better served if the vendor's power to alter the terms and conditions of any relevant tenancy is made conditional on obtaining the approval of the purchaser. A special condition could be added to the contract in appropriate cases. The National Conditions contain no provision equivalent to Law Society Condition 6(4).

Law Society Condition 6(3) says: "The vendor gives no warranty as to the amount of rent lawfully recoverable from any tenant, as to the effect of any legislation in relation to any lease or tenancy or as to the compliance with any legislation affecting the same." The Condition will not protect the vendor if he makes an inaccurate statement regarding the amount of rent recoverable by law, prior to (or in) the contract. In such

---

[38] *Clarke* v. *Ramuz* [1891] 2 Q.B. 456; see *post*, p. 245.
[39] *Abdullah* v. *Shah* [1959] A.C. 124.
[40] *Earl of Egmont* v. *Smith* (1877) 6 Ch.D. 469; but now the protection afforded by the Agricultural Holdings Act 1948 to agricultural tenants may change the vendor's duty.
[41] [1981] Conv 1.
[42] *Raffety* v. *Schofield* [1897] 1 Ch. 937.

a case the purchaser's remedies for misrepresentation and misdescription would be available.[43] It will protect him if he merely states that £X per week is paid by the tenant. The onus of discovering whether £X is more or less than the lawfully recoverable rent (in most cases the rent which would be fixed on an application to have the rent registered under the Rent Act 1977) is placed firmly on the purchaser.[44] In relation to *written communications* received by a vendor landlord it should be remembered that a wide ranging duty of disclosure is placed on the vendor by Law Society Condition 3.[45] Matters such as applications by a tenant for registration of his rent which are notified to a landlord, should come to the prospective purchaser's attention by this route.

Under Law Society Condition 6(3) the vendor does not give any warranty as to the effect of any legislation in relation to any lease subject to which the property is sold. Where for example, a purchaser buys in the mistaken belief that the Rent Act 1977 does not apply to the tenancy because he wrongly assumes the rateable value to be in excess of the prescribed limit,[46] he would have no complaint against a vendor who proffered no view on the matter. The National Conditions contain no condition similar to Law Society Condition 6(3). Where the National Conditions are used a special condition could be added to clarify the vendor's position on such matters.

(iii) **Restrictive Covenants.** As part of the general duty to disclose third party rights, the vendor must disclose the existence of any restrictive covenant, the burden of which will bind the purchaser. In *Re Higgins and Hitchman's Contract*[47] a semi-detached house was being sold. The vendor failed to reveal the existence of a restrictive covenant, entered into by his predecessor in title, not to use the property as, or for the erection of, a public house. This was held to be a fatal defect entitling the purchaser to resist specific performance.

Restrictive covenants are usually disclosed by the vendor by referring to them in the contract particulars and special conditions.[48] The purchaser is then given an opportunity to inspect the document creating the incumbrance and so cannot complain of non-disclosure.

Only the National Conditions expressly deal with disclosure of restrictive covenants. Condition 12(2) provides that in cases where the property is sold subject to a restrictive covenant, the deed imposing the same, or a copy of it, having been made available to the purchaser, he shall be deemed to purchase with full knowledge of it's terms. By sub-condition (3) the vendor is not required to produce such a document if he cannot

---

[43] See *post*, p. 215 et seq.

[44] For the availability of this information see *ante*, p. 55.

[45] See *post*, p. 214.

[46] *i.e.* £1,500 (London) or £750 (elsewhere) on the appropriate day (broadly speaking March 23, 1965 or when first entered on the valuation list if later).

[47] (1882) 51 L.J. (N.S.) 772.

[48] Registered restrictive covenants will be revealed by searches of the Central Land Charges Register or on the office copy entries of the register of title supplied by the vendor and the purchaser's official search of the register.

obtain it, because he cannot trace the person currently in possession of it for example. The purchaser's right to raise requisitions on the covenant is not affected.[49]

(iv) **Leasehold Property.** Deduction of title to leasehold property is dealt with later in the book.[50] Here it is proposed to look in more detail at some matters, peculiar to leasehold property, which a vendor is required to disclose in the contract.

(a) *Headlease or underlease?* Whether or not the standard conditions of sale are used, care must be taken to ensure that the leasehold interest is described accurately in the contract. The purchaser should be told whether he is buying a headlease or an underlease. In *Re Russ and Brown's Contract*[51] a vendor contracted to sell "eight leasehold dwellinghouses." The properties were in fact underleasehold. The purchaser was able to resist the vendor's claim for specific performance. Underleasehold property carries with it the risk of forfeiture for acts commited by the underlessor; property held under a headlease does not. Describing a "sub-underlease" as an "underlease" is not a sufficiently serious misdescription as to justify a purchaser rescinding the contract.[52]

(b) *Unusually onerous covenants.* Under an open contract a purchaser who has knowledge of a lease is bound by all the covenants in it except those which are considered to be unusually onerous.[53] Unusually onerous covenants must be disclosed for them to bind the purchaser. As Tomlin J. stated in *Melzak* v. *Lilienfeld*[54]: "It is, I think, plain that a contract for the sale of a lease must be treated as a contract for the sale of a lease with the usual covenants, unless the grantee has been given full opportunity of ascertaining what the covenants in the lease are, and has been made acquainted, in fact, with the existence of any unusual restrictive covenants."

The rule operates both on contracts for the assignment of leasehold property[55] and for the grant of an underlease.[56] In each case the test to be applied in determining what is unusual is the same.[57] No general principle can be discerned from the cases as they all turn on their own particular facts.[58] The factors which the court takes into account include inter alia, the nature of the premises and their location, the purpose for which the premises are let, the length of the term (and in appropriate cases the fact

---

[49] As to which, see *post*, p. 353.
[50] See *post*, p. 283.
[51] [1934] Ch. 34.
[52] *Becker* v. *Partridge* [1966] 2 Q.B. 155.
[53] *Re Haedicke and Lipski's Contract* [1901] 2 Ch. 666; *Molyneux* v. *Hawtrey* [1903] 2 K.B. 487; *Flexman* v. *Corbett* [1930] 1 Ch. 672.
[54] [1926] Ch. 480.
[55] *Re White and Smith's Contract* [1896] 1 Ch. 637.
[56] *Becker* v. *Partridge* [1966] 2 Q.B. 155; *Melzak* v. *Lilienfeld* [1926] 1 Ch. 480.
[57] *Chester* v. *Buckingham Travel Ltd.* [1981] 1 W.L.R. 96.
[58] *Flexman* v. *Corbett* [1930] 1 Ch. 672.

it may be extended by statute),[59] the evidence of conveyancers and precedent books. So, what amounts to a usual covenant in the lease of a dwelling house in a rural area may be considered unusual in London and vice versa. Premises let for the purposes of trade will be judged diferently from residential lettings.

In *Hampshire* v. *Wickens,*[60] decided in 1878, Jessel M.R. suggested that the court's view of what were unusual covenants would change in line with current conveyancing practice. Recognition of this fact was given in the recent case of *Chester* v. *Buckingham Travel Ltd.*[61] and yet suprisingly an unqualified covenant against alienation and a proviso for re-entry if a receiving order in bankrutpcy was made against the tenant was held to be unusual[62] Failure to disclose unusually onerous covenants may entitle a purchaser to rescind or claim damages. For example, where a musician contracted to take an underlease, and was not shown particulars of the headlease, which contained unusual covenants preventing music lessons being given on the premises, he was held entitled to an underlease with only the usual covenants. His vendor was obliged to refuse to grant such a lease as it would inevitably have led to him being in breach of covenant himself. The musician was awarded damages for breach of contract.[63]

A vendor may fulfil his duty to disclose this type of covenant by expressly revealing it to the purchaser, for instance including details in the contract, or by giving him an opportunity to inspect the lease himself, as where the contract states that a copy of the lease may be viewed at the vendor solicitor's offices. A reference to the existence of a lease without more is not sufficient disclosure of unusually onerous covenants.[64]

National Condition 11(2) and Law Society Condition 8(3), which apply only on the sale of existing leasehold property, state that once a copy of a lease or underlease has been supplied or made available to the purchaser, he shall be deemed to buy with full knowledge of the contents thereof, whether or not he actually inspects it. He will, therefore be fixed with notice of any unusually onerous covenants. Note that neither condition applies on the grant of a new lease when the common law position outlined above applies. The conditions will not protect a vendor who positively misdescribes the property. In *Charles Hunt Ltd.* v. *Palmer*[65] leasehold property was subject to a covenant not to use the premises otherwise than for carrying on the business of a ladies outfitter.[66] At an auction the particulars (mis)described the premises as "valuable business premises." A purchaser, not knowing of the restrictive user covenant, was able to resist the vendor's claim for specific performance of the contract despite a contractual term deeming him to have bought with full notice of the contents of the lease.

---

[59] *e.g.* Landlord and Tenant Act 1954, Pt. II (business premises); Rent Act 1977 (residential premises).

[60] (1878) 7 Ch.D. 555.

[61] [1981] 1 W.L.R. 96.

[62] R.E. Annand [1981] Conv. 233.

[63] *Melzak* v. *Lilienfeld* [1926] Ch. 480.

[64] *Reeve* v. *Berridge* (1888) 20 Q.B.D. 523; *Re White and Smith's Contract* [1896] 1 Ch. 637.

[65] [1931] 2 Ch. 287.

[66] Restrictive user covenants generally reduce the value of premises.

(c) *Covenants in superior leases.* Under an open contract the purchaser of an underlease may object to the vendor's title on the ground that the covenants in it do not correspond to those in the headlease.[67]

By section 44 of the Law of Property Act 1925[68] the purchaser of an underlease is not entitled to call for the superior title and so is unable to discover such discrepancies for himself. He can only hope that the vendor will provide him with this information. However, the vendor may have been in the same position as the purchaser when he bought the underlease. He may not know what covenants the headlease contains. Therefore, the purchaser is often in the unsatisfactory position of being unsure whether the headlease contains covenants preventing him from using the property as he wishes.

The standard conditions do not provide a solution to the purchaser's problem. National Condition 11(4) amends the common law in favour of the vendor by providing that: "No objection shall be taken on account of the covenants in an underlease not corresponding with the covenants in any superior lease." Whilst not dealing with the matter specifically the effect of Law Society Condition 8(2) is to allow the purchaser of an underlease to call for the superior title if, (a) the underlease was granted less than 15 years before the date of the contract to assign it; (b) it was originally granted for a term of more than twenty one years; and (c) it is *not* registered with leasehold title absolute. Having exercised the right given by Condition 8(2) the purchaser may then compare the covenants in the headlease to those in the underlease and note the discrepances. Even where the superior title can be called for the purchaser's position is not improved if the vendor is unable to produce it. This will be the case where the vendor bought without inspecting the reversionary title. In this situation the vendor should exclude Condition 8(2). Where Condition 8(2) does not apply the common law regulates the parties' rights.

(d) *Additional matters.* The case of *Becker* v. *Partridge*[69] illustrates two other matters requiring disclosure by a vendor of leasehold land. Here a purchaser agreed to buy an underleasehold flat in a converted house. He later objected to his vendor's title on the grounds, *inter alia*, that the property sold was comprised with other property (the rest of the house) in a headlease,[70] and that breaches of covenants in the headlease made the vendor's title defeasible should the head landlord exercise his right of re-entry. The vendor had revealed none of this information to the purchaser.

The first ground failed because, on the facts, it should have been obvious to the purchaser that his flat, being part of a house, was included in a headlease of the whole house. A vendor of underleasehold property need only disclose the fact that more property is included in the headlease

---

[67] *Darlington* v. *Hamilton* (1854) Kay. 550.

[68] See *post*, p. 283.

[69] [1966] 2 Q.B. 155.

[70] Disclosure is necessary to warn the purchaser that his lease may be subject to forfeiture on breach of covenant relating to other property in the headlease, over which he has no control.

if it is not reasonably apparent on inspection. Good conveyancing practice would dictate such disclosure in all cases.

The second ground succeeded and the purchaser was allowed to rescind. A vendor of leasehold property is under a duty to disclose breaches of covenant in his own or any superior lease rendering the interest being sold liable to forfeiture.

Where land sold is held by lease or underlease section 45(2) and (3) of the Law of Property Act 1925 apply. On production of the last receipt for rent due before completion the purchaser must assume, unless the contrary appears,[71] that all the covenants and provisions of the lease, underlease and where appropriate superior leases, have been duly performed. This greatly reduces the burden put on the vendor of leasehold land to positively show that no breach of covenant has occurred.

Under the common law it is probable, though by no means certain,[72] that a purchaser must also assume the person giving the receipt to be the reversioner, or his duly authorised agent. Both sets of standard conditions resolve this doubt by expressly requiring the purchaser to assume the receipt is so given; National Condition 11(3) and Law Society Condition 8(7).

(v) **Local Land Charges.** These were considered in detail in Chapter 2.[73] Some local land charges constitute latent defects in title. Where this is the case the vendor must disclose them. One type of local land charge requiring diclosure, frequently encountered in practice, is a financial charge registered by a local authority to recoup the expense of making up a road from the frontagers.

Where the contract for sale incorporates the Law Society Conditions of Sale, Condition 3(3)(a) imposes a wide duty of disclosure on the vendor relating to written communications received by, or known to, him before contract.[74] Compliance with this Condition may result in the purchaser being made aware of other local land charges besides those falling within the scope of the common law duty of disclosure. Similarly, where the sale is governed by the National Conditions certain local land charges will be brought to the purchaser's attention by the vendor. National Condition 15 requires the vendor to disclose any local land charges registered under the "Planning Acts"[75] of which he knows. These must be mentioned in the special conditions in the contract.

THE PHYSICAL CONDITION OF THE PROPERTY

On the sale or lease of land the common law does not imply into the contract any warranty on the part of the vendor, regarding the condition of the property. The vendor is, therefore, under no duty to disclose defects

---

[71] *Re Highett and Bird's Contract* [1903] 1 Ch. 287.
[72] *Williams on Title* (4th ed.) p. 557 citing *Turner* v. *Marriot* (1867) L.R.3 Eq. 744; *c.f. Pegler* v. *White* (1864) 55 E.R. 423 at p. 425.
[73] See *ante*, p. 7.
[74] See *post*, p. 214.
[75] *i.e.* "enactments from time to time in force relating to town and country planning" Construction Condition National (8).

in its condition whether they are patent or latent. Thus in *Robbins* v. *Jones*[76] Erle C.J. said: "fraud apart, there is no law against letting a tumble-down house." Furthermore it makes no difference that the quality of the land is affected by some matter not readily visible on a personal inspection of the property. In *Greenhalgh* v. *Brindley*[77] a vendor's land did not enjoy an easement of light over some adjoining property. The purchaser took the property subject to the right of the neighbour to obstruct his light.

In 1970 the Law Commission,[78] in its Report on the *Civil Liability of Vendors and Lessors for Defective Premises*, recommended the retention of the rule of *caveat emptor* because it encouraged purchasers to seek professional advice on the condition of the property and make the requisite searches and enquiries.[79] They suggested that the implication of a warranty by the vendor as to the condition of the property would only promote litigation between purchasers and vendors.

Both the Law Society and National Conditions of Sale contain terms stating that the purchaser shall buy with full notice of the actual state and condition of the property except where it is to be constructed or converted by the vendor (Law Society Condition 5(2)(*a*) and National Condition 13(3)). These conditions merely confirm the common law position. It should be noted that neither the conditions (nor the common law) protect the vendor if he is guilty of negligence. In *Hone* v. *Benson*[80] a vendor negligently constructed and installed a heating system in his property. After completion the purchaser discovered the defect and sued the vendor in negligence. The purchaser sought to rely on Law Society Condition 5(2)(*a*) as excluding any liability he might have incurred. It was held that the Condition did not affect the vendor's liability in negligence.[81]

These Conditions will prevent the vendor of a leasehold interest from being liable to pay damages for breach of his implied covenant that any repairing covenant in the lease has been performed (should it not in fact have been observed). The purchaser who is later required by the landlord to pay for repairs will not be able to obtain an indemnity from his vendor.[82] The purchaser is deemed to know of the failure to repair because it is reflected in the state and condition of the property when it was bought.

Note that a defect in the condition of the property may in certain circumstances amount to a latent defect in title. The vendor must disclose the defect or risk the purchaser claiming rescission of the contract or compensation. Some of the cases on this point have involved the vendor's failure to inform a purchaser that a sewer on the property was vested in somebody else; the local authority.[83]

---

[76] (1863) 15 C.B.N.S. 221 at p. 240.

[77] [1901] 2 Ch. 324; *Turner* v. *Green* [1895] 2 Ch. 205; *Smith* v. *Colbourne* [1913] 2 Ch. 533.

[78] Law. Com. No. 40.

[79] See Chaps. 2 and 3.

[80] (1978) 248 E.G. 1013.

[81] Had the National Conditions applied, the decision would almost certainly have been the same.

[82] *Butler* v. *Mountview Estates Ltd.* [1951] 2 K.B. 563.

[83] *Pemsel and Wilson* v. *Tucker* [1907] 2 Ch. 191; *Re Belcham and Gawley's Contract* [1930] 1 Ch. 56.

FITNESS FOR PURPOSE

Neither the National nor the Law Society Conditions deal with fitness for purpose, therefore, the common law applies. Under an open contract the vendor does not warrant that his property is fit for any particular purpose. The purchaser must satisfy himself that the property is fit for his intended purpose.[84]

In *Bottomley* v. *Bannister*[85] the purchasers of a house had been let into possession as tenants at will. Owing to a defective boiler, carbon monoxide fumes filled the house and the purchasers were killed. It was held that the vendor was not liable; he gave no warranty that the premises were fit to live in.[86] Again, in *Sutton* v. *Temple*[87] pasture land was let to a tenant. He grazed some cattle there which later died. The cause of death was found to be poisoning due to the cattle eating grass which had been contaminated. The contamination had occurred prior to the commencement of the tenancy. This had made the land unsuitable for grazing cattle. The tenant's action against his landlord failed.

However, there are certain exceptions to this rule, at common law and under statute. When a landlord lets a furnished house the common law does imply a term that the house is initially fit for human habitation.[88] In *Smith* v. *Marrable*[89] where a landlord let furnished premises he was held liable for breach of this implied term when the tenant discovered that the house was infested with bugs, making it unfit to live in. Similarly there is an implied term at common law that a new house when built will be habitable[90]; see now the Defective Premises Act 1972, s.1.

Although there is no implied warranty regarding fitness for purpose on the sale or lease of property, it has recently been decided that there is no reason why the same rule should apply to a contractual licence giving the licensee the right to occupy premises. In *Wettern Electric Ltd.* v. *Welsh Development Agency*[91] the defendants made a contract with the plaintiff company for a one year licence relating to some industrial premises on terms, all of which, were favourable to the defendant.[92] A few months after occupying the premises the building began to disintegrate because the foundations were defective. The plaintiff company sued the Agency in damages for, *inter alia,* loss of production and expenditure incurred in relocating. The company claimed that the licence contained an implied term that the premises were of sound construction and reasonably fit for its purposes. Judge Newey Q.C. accepted that if the defendants had leased the premises no such term would be implied. He then went on to hold that

---

[84] *Hill* v. *Harris* [1965] 2 Q.B 601; *Edler* v. *Auerbach* [1950] 1 K.B. 359.

[85] [1932] 1 K.B. 458.

[86] But see *Hone* v. *Benson* (1978) 248 E.G. 1013.

[87] (1843) 12 M. & W. 52.

[88] The warranty does not extend to keeping the house habitable; *Sarson* v. *Roberts* [1895] 2 Q.B. 395.

[89] (1843) 11 M.& W. 5; *cf. Hart* v. *Windsor* (1843) 12 M. & W. 68.

[90] *Hancock* v. *Brazier (Anerley) Ltd.* [1966] 1 W.L.R. 1317.

[91] [1983] 2 All E.R. 629, discussed by H.W. Wilkinson (1983) 80 L.S.Gaz. 2195.

[92] The object of granting a licence, as opposed to a lease, was to avoid the operation of Pt. II of the Landlord and Tenant Act 1954.

such a term should be implied into the licence to give business efficacy to the parties agreement.[93] Thus the seeds of *caveat licensor* were sown. Where a sale is governed by the National or Law Society Conditions of Sale and the property turns out not to be fit for the purchaser's intended purpose, then the purchaser has no recourse against his vendor. If, however, he is allowed into occupation pending completion National Condition 8(1) or Law Society Condition 18(2) states that he occupies the property as a licensee of the vendor.[94-95] Following *Wettern* could the court not imply into this licence a term that the premises are fit for the purposes of the purchaser, so giving him a remedy.

The warranty implied on the part of the licensor in these circumstances could be expressly excluded by a term in the contract granting the licence. However, as no estate or interest in land is created, the Unfair Contract Terms Act 1977 will operate to curtail the efficacy of such a provision insofar as it is unreasonable.[96]

PLANNING

Under an open contract the vendor is not under a duty to disclose planning matters which affect the enjoyment of the property provided they do not amount to latent defects in title. For example, where a building being sold was erected under a temporary planning permission and had to be demolished at a future date it was held that the vendor was required to disclose the fact to his purchaser because it was a latent defect in his title.[97] Furthermore in the absence of a term in the contract specifying an authorised use, that is one to which the property may be put without infringing planning law, the vendor does not warrant that the purchaser's intended use of the property is authorised by planning law.[98] The purchaser must make the appropriate searches and enquiries to satisfy himself on this matter.[99]

Both the National and Law Society Conditions amend the common law in favour of the purchaser by obliging the vendor to disclose certain planning matters affecting the property. National Condition 15(4) provides: "Save as mentioned in the Special Conditions, the property is not to the knowledge of the vendor subject to any charge, notice, order, restriction, agreement or other matter arising under the Planning Acts, but . . . the property is sold subject to any such charges, notices, orders, restrictions, agreements and matters affecting the interest sold."

The Condition relates to a wide range of matters arising under legislation dealing with town and country planning,[1] for example enforcement notices, building preservation notices, planning agreements made

---

[93] *The Moorcock* (1889) [1886–90] All E.R. Rep. 530; see *Liverpool City Council* v. *Irwin* [1976] 2 W.L.R. 562.

[94-95] See *post*, p. 250.

[96] Unfair Contract Terms Act 1977, s.11.

[97] *Sidney* v. *Buddery* (1949) 1 P. & C.R. 34.

[98] *Mitchell* v. *Beacon Estates (Finsbury Park) Ltd.* (1949) 1 P. & C.R. 32.

[99] *Edler* v. *Auerbach* [1950] 1 K.B. 359; *Hill* v. *Harris* [1965] 2 Q.B. 601.

[1] *e.g.* Town and Country Planning Act 1971; Local Government, Planning and Land Act 1980.

between the vendor and the local planning authority, and conditions in planning permissions which have been granted. If the vendor is aware of any matter falling within the scope of the Condition he must give details in the special conditions in the contract. The Condition only requires the vendor to disclose planning matters of which he is aware but states that the property is sold subject to any charges, notices and so on which exist. Since the vendor will not always be aware of planning matters affecting his property the purchaser should make his own local land charges search to ensure that he obtains the most complete information available. The purchaser is deemed to buy with "knowledge in all respects of the authorised use of the property" for the purposes of planning law; National Condition 15(5). Despite Conditions 15(2) (reserving a right to the purchaser to requisition on matters concerning the authorised use of the property) and 15(4) the purchaser should not rely on the information given by the vendor but should in every case make the appropriate searches and enquiries.[2] However, where the vendor sells on the footing that the use specified in Special Condition D is the authorised use of the property for planning purposes, Condition 15(3) applies. If the purchaser discovers before completion that the specified use is not an authorised use under the Planning Acts he may give written notice to the vendor rescinding the contract. In this event National Condition 10(2) will regulate the parties rights. It provides that the vendor must return the deposit without interest and the purchaser's costs of investigating title or any other payment. The purchaser is required by Condition 10(2) to return all of the vendor's documents in his possession. Rescission cannot be claimed under Condition 15(3) once completion has taken place.

Law Society Condition 3 places the vendor under a duty to inform the purchaser of the contents of any written communications relating to any "relevant matter" received by or known to the vendor, before exchange of contracts. The definition of "relevant matter" is wide. It will include written communications relating to planning matters but could also include many other things affecting the property. The Law Society Conditions thus provide for a wider ranging duty of disclosure than the National Conditions, but limits the duty to written communications.

"Relevant matters" are defined by Law Society Condition 3(2) as:

(a) A requirement[3] of, or matter capable of registration by, a "competent authority." A "competent authority" means[4] a local authority or other body exercising powers under statute or Royal Charter, for example government departments, the National Coal Board or the Civil Aviation Authority.

(b) All matters disclosed or reasonably to be expected to be disclosed by searches and as a result of enquiries formal or informal, and whether made in person, by writing or orally by or for the purchaser or which a prudent purchaser ought to make. This category would include local land

---

[2] See *ante*, Chaps. 2 and 3.

[3] By Condition 3(1)(*b*) a " 'requirement' includes (whether or not subject to confirmation) any notice, order or proposal."

[4] Law Society Condition 3(1)(*a*).

charges, local authority proposals relating to the property and matters covered on the standard form of Enquiries before Contract.

(c) All notices served by or on behalf of a reversioner, a tenant or sub-tenant, or the owner or occupier of any adjoining or neighbouring property. Falling within this category would be notices to quit served by a tenant or a writ served by a neighbour regarding a boundary dispute.

It should be noted that although the vendor's duty is to disclose written communications of relevant matters it is not limited to those which he has actually received; he must also disclose the existence of such written communications if he knows about them. No time limit is imposed and it would seem that the vendor would have to disclose such written communications no matter how old they may be.[5]

If the vendor fails to disclose a matter falling within the ambit of Condition 3(3)(a) before the contract is made he is deemed to have made "an omission in a statement in the course of negotiations leading to the contract." The purchaser is entitled to compensation from the vendor for this non-disclosure under Law Society Condition 7.[6] Compensation is available to the purchaser for a breach of Condition 3(3)(a) even though he did not bother to make the usual searches or enquiries. No compensation is payable by the vendor where the purchaser has a right to compensation from a local authority, government department or other "competent authority." By Law Society Condition 3(3)(c) the vendor must continue to inform the purchaser of written communications relating to relevant matters between contract and completion. In other words the purchaser has to take the property subject to undisclosed relevant matters even though in appropriate cases he might be able to obtain compensation from the vendor.

If an authorised use is specified by special condition in the Law Society contract the purchaser still has to verify through his own enquiries that this is in fact the authorised use. The Law Society conditions contain no equivalent to National Condition 15(3).

II MISREPRESENTATION: PURCHASERS REMEDIES

(1) Introduction

A party to a contract may be able to claim relief if he was induced to enter into it by a statement which was misleading. Earlier it was explained how this rule operates with regard to replies given by a vendor to the Enquiries before Contract.[7] Here it is proposed to look in more detail first at the types of misrepresentation, the remedies available at common law and under the Misrepresentation Act 1967, and secondly at the way in which attempts have been made to exclude, or limit, the availability of a purchaser's remedies, particularly under the National and Law Society Conditions.

---

[5] See (1981) 78 L.S.Gaz. 149.

[6] See *post*, p. 228.

[7] See *ante*, p. 70.

To have a claim for relief the purchaser to whom a (mis)representation was made must show: (a) the representation was of a kind the law recognises as giving rise to liability; (b) it was material; and (c) he relied upon it when making the contract. Once he has shown all these factors are present the purchaser may be entitled to rescind the contract and/or claim damages. In practice it is usually the purchaser who sues for misrepresentation. However, if the purchaser makes a misrepresentation to the vendor it is equally possible for the vendor to bring an action for damages or rescission. In the following discussion it is only for the sake of convenience that the purchaser is treated as the party bringing the action.

REPRESENTATION OF A KIND THE LAW RECOGNISES

An actionable misrepresentation can only consist of a misleading statement of fact. Statements of opinion, intention or of law cannot themselves ground an action for misrepresentation.

(i) **Opinion.** "Eulogistic commendation of the *res vendita* is the age old device of the successful salesman."[8] A vendor's indiscriminate praise of his property is not recognised as being a representation of fact. For example a description of land as "uncommonly rich water meadow"[9] did not ground an action. Today the courts are less ready to allow a vendor to escape liability for misrepresentation if his praise of the property turns out to be unfounded.[10] A vendor of a farm, who having no special knowledge, wrongly stated that he thought the land would support 2,000 sheep was not liable for misrepresentation.[11] A vendor who makes a statement of opinion may, if he is in a position to know the full facts, be held liable. The vendor impliedly states that he knows facts which justify his opinion. So where the vendor of a house described it as "let to a most desirable tenant" when in fact the tenant was in lengthy arrears with the rent, he was held to have made (impliedly) an actionable (mis)representation.[12]

(ii) **Intention.** A vendor's promise to do something in the future can never ground an action for misrepresentation whether the promise is by nature contractually binding (for example a promise to repair the roof) or not. If the purchaser is to have a remedy for such a promise then he must insist on the vendor stating his intention in the contract.[13]

(iii) **Law.** If during negotiations the vendor makes a representation of law, which induces the purchaser to enter the contract, and it later transpires that the representation was wrong, the purchaser cannot claim relief for misrepresentation. In practice statements of law are difficult to

---

[8] *Cheshire and Fifoot: Law of Contract* (10th ed.), p. 239.

[9] *Scott v. Hanson* (1829) 1 Russ. & M. 128.

[10] *Erven Warnink B.V. v. J. Townsend & Sons (Hull) Ltd.* [1979] A.C. 731, *per* Lord Diplock at p. 743.

[11] *Bisset v. Wilkinson* [1927] A.C. 177.

[12] *Smith v. Land and House Property Corpn.* (1884) 28 Ch.D.7.

[13] *Maddison v. Alderson* (1883) 8 App. Cas. 467.

distinguish from statements of fact; no satisfactory test has yet been devised by the courts.[14]

MATERIAL

The purchaser generally[15] has to prove the representation was material. A representation is material if it would affect the judgment of a reasonable man in deciding whether or not to enter into the contract. Also material, are statements which induce the purchaser to contract on terms other than those he would have had the statement not been made, or without making full enquiries. For example, a vendor who tells his purchaser that he has made a local land charges search revealing no entries, when in fact no search has been made, may later find that the purchaser can rescind the contract and claim damages.

RELIANCE

If the purchaser does not rely on the vendor's erroneous representations when deciding to contract he will not be able to sue the vendor for misrepresentation. However, the vendor's (mis)representations need not be the decisive factor inducing the purchaser to enter into the contract. For instance, if the vendor states that the house he is selling is sound the fact that the purchaser relied (perhaps to a large extent *but not conclusively*) on a surveyor's report will not prevent him from bringing an action for misrepresentation against the vendor, if his words were not true.

Once the purchaser proves the vendor's representation was material the law rebuttably presumes it induced entry into the Contract.[16]

(2) Types of Misrepresentation and Remedies

FRAUDULENT

A fraudulent misrepresentation is one "made (1) knowingly, or (2) without belief in its truth, or (3) recklessly, careless whether it be true or false."[17] An absence of honest belief on the part of the person making the representation is essential to establish the element of fraud.

At common law the purchaser has a right both to rescind the contract and claim damages in the tort of deceit for a fraudulent misrepresentation. Alternatively, damages for breach of contract could be claimed where the fraudulent misrepresentation has been incorporated as a contractual term. The Misrepresentation Act 1967 has not altered the remedies available for fraudulent misrepresentation.

NEGLIGENT

At common law a negligent misrepresentation is one made in breach of a duty to take reasonable care that the statement made is accurate.[18]

---

[14] *Solle* v. *Butcher* [1950] 1 K.B. 671; *Eaglesfield* v. *Marquis of Londonderry* (1876) 4 Ch.D. 693.

[15] Not if fraud is alleged or the contract stipulates that the representation is material.

[16] See *Redgrave* v. *Hurd* (1881) 20 Ch.D. 1 *per* Jessel, M.R.; but there is no inference of law; *Smith* v. *Land and House Property Corporation* (1884) 28 Ch.D.7.

[17] *Derry* v. *Peek* (1889) 14 App. Cas. 337, *per* Lord Herschell at p. 374.

[18] *Hedley Byrne & Co. Ltd.* v. *Heller & Partners Ltd.* [1964] A.C. 465.

Broadly speaking, if, when making a statement, the vendor or his agent purports to have some special knowledge and knows, or ought to know, that the purchaser is going to rely on it the duty of care arises.[19] If the duty is broken the purchaser who suffers loss as a result may sue for damages in the tort of negligence. For example, in *Esso Petroleum Co. Ltd.* v. *Mardon*[20] the plaintiff[21] company let a garage to M. One of the company's agents, an experienced salesman, told M. that the turnover would be approximately 200,000 gallons a year. In the event, it was found to be less than half of that. It was held that the plaintiffs owed a duty of care to M. since they knew he would rely on their estimates in deciding to take a lease of the garage. The advice was clearly inaccurate because the salesman had negligently failed to take into account all the relevant factors. The plaintiffs were liable to pay damages for M.'s loss.

Where the vendor (or his agent) makes a negligent misrepresentation, statute now gives the purchaser a more valuable remedy. Section 2(1) of the Misrepresentation Act 1967 provides:

> "Where *a person has entered into a contract after a misrepresentation has been made* to him *by another party thereto* and as a result thereof he has suffered loss, then, if the person making the misrepresentation would be liable to damages in respect thereof had the misrepresentation been made fraudulently, *that person shall be so liable* notwithstanding that the misrepresentation was not made fraudulently, *unless he proves that he had reasonable ground to believe and did believe up to the time the contract was made that the facts represented were true."*[21a]

It does not matter that the misrepresentation has become a term of the contract; the right of action is expressly preserved by section 1 of the Act. Even if the contract has been performed and a conveyance or transfer executed the purchaser may still pursue his remedies under the Act. Two advantages accrue to a purchaser suing under the Act rather than common law. The first is the lack of need to prove that a duty of care is owed. The second is the reversal of the onus of proof; under the Act the vendor or his agent must prove he had reasonable grounds to believe (and did believe) that the facts represented by him were true. In practice these advantages mean that a purchaser will pursue his remedies under the Act rather than at common law.

At one time the only remedy available for any non-fraudulent[22] misrepresentation was rescission of the contract. This was available in Equity not at common law. Now, the right to rescind for a non-fraudulent misrepresentation is given by section 2(2) of the Act of 1967 which provides:

---

[19] *Mutual Life and Citizens Assurance Co. Ltd.* v. *Evatt* [1971] A.C. 793; *Esso Petroleum Co. Ltd.* v. *Mardon* [1976] Q.B. 801; *Howard Marine and Dredging Co. Ltd.* v. *A. Ogden and Sons (Excavations) Ltd.* [1978] 2 W.L.R. 515.

[20] [1976] Q.B. 801.

[21] The defendant was counterclaiming to the company's claim for arrears of rent under the lease.

[21a] Italics supplied.

[22] *i.e.* What is now negligent or innocent misrepresentation.

"Where a person has entered into a contract after a misrepresentation has been made to him otherwise than fraudulently, and he would be entitled by reason of the misrepresentation to rescind the contract, then, if it is claimed in any of the proceedings arising out of the contract that the contract ought to be or has been rescinded, the court or arbitrator may declare the contract subsisting and award damages in lieu of rescission, if of the opinion that it would be equitable to do so, having regard to the nature of the misrepresentation and the loss that would be caused by it if the contract were upheld as well as the loss that rescission would cause to the other party."

If the court thinks it equitable to do so it may declare the contract subsisting and award damages instead of ordering rescission.

Although a purchaser suing under the Act may obtain damages both under section 2(1) and 2(2) the award is not cumulative. Section 2(3) requires that a court, in assessing damages under section 2(2), take into account damages awarded under section 2(1).

If the misrepresentation is repeated in the contract the vendor may be liable for breach of contract. The purchaser may prefer to sue for damages on the contract as an alternative to suing for misrepresentation.[23]

INNOCENT

An innocent misrepresentation is one made without any degree of fault on the part of the person making it. Before the Act of 1967 was passed, rescission was the only remedy available for this type of misrepresentation. The right is now statutory and set out in section 2(2) of the Act (above). Again the court's discretionary power to award damages in lieu of rescission may be exercised. It is not possible to both rescind and claim damages for innocent misrepresentation. Damages will, however, be available should the innocent misrepresentation become part of the contract.

(3) Examples of Misrepresentation

In *Chesneau* v. *Interhome Ltd.*[24] the defendant induced the plaintiff to rent a holiday villa by carelessly stating that it was "in a quiet location." In fact it was part of a busy commercial complex. The plaintiff recovered damages under section 2(1) of the Act.

The case of *Lawrence* v. *Lexcourt Holdings Ltd.*[25] shows that, the fact that a purchaser of land has an opportunity to discover the true position, for instance, by making searches and enquiries, will not avail a vendor who misleads him. In 1974 the plaintiff offered to let the first and second floors of a property to the defendant for 15 years. During the course of negotiations the plaintiff stated that the building could be used as offices. The true position, later discovered by the defendant, was that only part

---

[23] He would not be awarded damages for both.
[24] *The Times*, June 9, 1983.
[25] [1978] 1 W.L.R. 1128.

of the first floor had planning permission for use as offices.[26] The court ordered that the contract be rescinded.

A misrepresentation may be made by conduct.[27] Thus where the vendor of a house papered over cracks in a wall to conceal defective foundations, he was held to have made a fraudulent misrepresentation and his purchaser was accordingly entitled to relief.[28]

More important to a vendor is the decision in *Watts* v. *Spence.*[29-30] Graham J. held, that one of two joint tenants, who alone contracted to sell a house, made a representation, by his conduct (negotiating and subsequently making the contract), that he was the owner and so able to sell the property. He further held that this misrepresentation was made carelessly and so fell within the scope of section 2(1) of the Misrepresentation Act 1967. Substantial damages were therefore recoverable. The later case of *Malhotra* v. *Choudhury*[31], distinguished *Watt's* case and suggested that the courts would in future be less ready to hold that entering into a contract, by itself, constituted an actionable representation of fact. The case concerned the enforceability of an option to purchase, granted by one partner to another, allowing the other to purchase the partnership practice and premises. The Court of Appeal endorsed[32] Blackett-Ord V.-C.'s statement at first instance that: "this option itself cannot I think be treated as a representation, otherwise every contract would imply a representation and every vendor would be warranting his title." However, as the recent case of *Errington* v. *Martell-Wilson*[33] shows, these words may have gone unheeded. The plaintiff wanted to buy a site to use as a builder's yard. The defendant (aged 82) offered to sell what she mistakenly believed to be her property to him for £500. In fact she had sold the property some five years earlier. The plaintiff claimed substantial damages for fraudulent, or alternatively, negligent misrepresentation within section 2(1) of the Act of 1967. He succeeded with the latter claim, the judge finding as in *Watt's* case, that there had been a false representation of ownership implicit in everything the defendant did. The obvious inference to be drawn from this case and the earlier decision in *Watt's* case is: "that it must now be greatly in the interests of purchasers to obtain express pre-contract statements from vendors about their good titles free from incumbrances. This practice would not merely be a matter of securing substantial damages in lieu of completion but would also add a fine leg and third man to support the somewhat uncertain longstop constituted by the implied covenants for title, i.e. damages or rescission despite completion under sections 1(*b*) and 2(1) of the Misrepresentation Act 1967."[34]

---

[26] A temporary planning permission lasting for two years was later obtained by the defendants relating to the whole of the premises.

[27] *Horsfall* v. *Thomas* (1862) 1 H. & C.90; *Schneider* v. *Heath* (1813) 3 Camp. 506; *Bodger* v. *Nicholls* (1873) 28 L.T. 441.

[28] *Ridge* v. *Crawley* (1959) 173 E.G. 959.

[29-30] [1976] Ch. 165; noted (1975) 39 Conv. 361.

[31] [1979] 1 All E.R. 186.

[32] [1979] 1 All E.R. 186 at p. 198.

[33] (1980) 130 New L.J. 545.

[34] (1975) 39 Conv. 381.

It has been said that remaining silent on a matter can constitute a misrepresentation, in that it distorts a positive statement already made about the property.[35] Likewise a vendor of land who reveals only half the truth may be guilty of misrepresentation.[36] In *Nottingham Patent Brick and Tile Co.* v. *Butler*[37] a vendor's solicitor stated that he was not aware of any restrictive covenants burdening the land to be sold. He did not reveal that he had not looked at the title deeds. Restrictive covenants did burden the land and would have prevented the plaintiff company from practising its trade. The vendor's solicitors statement though true was held to be sufficiently misleading to allow the purchaser to rescind.[38]

(4) Agents and Misrepresentation

In most conveyancing transactions the vendor will employ an agent to act on his behalf (*e.g.* solicitors and estate agents).

In the recent case of *Resolute Maritime Inc.* v. *Nippon Kaiji Kyokai*, (*The Skopas*)[39] the following question of law was considered as a preliminary issue: "If an agent, acting in his express or ostensible authority, makes a statement which is untrue in circumstances where he did not have reasonable ground to believe that it was true, can he (*i.e.* the agent) be held liable under section 2(1) of the Misrepresentation Act 1967." Mustill J. answered "no." He held that the purpose of the Act was to fill the gap in the remedies available to a contracting party before 1967; he could not claim damages from the other for a non-fraudulent misrepresentation whether made by that other or his agent. Agents were already liable for their own negligent statements under the principle laid down in *Hedley Byrne & Co. Ltd.* v. *Heller & Partners Ltd.*[40]

The importance of the case is that if a purchaser wishes to pursue his remedies under the Misrepresentation Act 1967 for a non-fraudulent misrepresentation made by the vendor's agent (innocent or negligent) then he must proceed directly against the vendor. The vendor who is thus subjected to liability will be able to gain compensation from the agent in the tort of negligence but only where the misrepresentation was made by his agent negligently. Where the misrepresentation was made by the agent innocently the vendor has no recourse at all.

(5) Rescission for Misrepresentation

Once a (mis)representation has been made the purchaser may elect to treat the contract as subsisting or rescind the contract. If the purchaser

---

[35] *With* v. *O'Flanagan* [1936] Ch. 575; *Traill* v. *Baring* (1864) 4 D.J. & S. 318 (failure to correct a statement which had later become untrue).

[36] *Dimmock* v. *Hallet* (1866) 2 Ch. App 21; see also *Curtis* v. *Chemical Cleaning and Dyeing Co.* [1951] 1 K.B. 805.

[37] (1886) 16 Q.B.D. 778.

[38] See also *South Western General Property Co. Ltd.* v. *Marton* (1982) 263 E.G. 109.

[39] [1983] 2 All E.R. 1.

[40] [1964] A.C. 465.

rescinds, the contract terminates. The parties are restored to the position in which they stood before the contract was entered into.[41] In all cases the purchaser should communicate his intention to rescind to the vendor.[42]

Rescission is available at common law for fraudulent misrepresentation. However, in the case of negligent and innocent misrepresentation the 1967 Act governs the position. In any action in which rescission is claimed the court is given a discretion by section 2(2) of the Act to award damages instead. This power to award damages in lieu of rescission may put severe limitations on the availability of the remedy. The discretion may be exercised for example, where the vendor has bought a new house with the proceeds of sale. To require repayment of the whole purchase price would in most cases cause him severe hardship.

The right to rescind for misrepresentation (fraudulent, negligent or innocent) is not lost because the contract for sale has been performed and a conveyance or transfer executed (Misrepresentation Act 1967 s.1(b)). This is of importance to a purchaser whose vendor has made a misrepresentation prior to the contract which is repeated in the contract. The purchaser has the choice of suing under the Misrepresentation Act 1967 or treating the inaccuracy as a misdescription and claiming rescission or damages for breach of contract. However, a remedy for misdescription is only available before completion. But even though the contract has been completed the purchaser can still claim rescission or damages under the Misrepresentation Act.

Although performance of the contract is no bar to rescission for misrepresentation certain other factors may result in the purchaser losing the right.

THIRD PARTY RIGHTS

The right to rescind is lost if an innocent third party acquires rights in the land before the election to terminate the contract is made. A purchaser buying with the aid of a mortgage will, therefore be unable to rescind the contract once his lender has acquired a charge over the property. In practice this happens almost immediately the transaction is completed as both conveyance and mortgage are executed simultaneously.

RESTITUTION IMPOSSIBLE

An essential element of rescission is the restoration of the parties to the position they were in before the contract was made. If it is not possible to substantially return to the status quo ante, rescission is not available. Thus in *Clarke* v. *Dickson*[43] it was held that a purchaser of shares in a mining company could not rescind for misrepresentation because he had exhausted the mine.

---

[41] *Redgrave* v. *Hurd* (1881) 20 Ch.D.1; *Abram S.S. Co.* v. *Westville Shipping Co.* [1923] A.C. 773.

[42] He need not do so if the vendor has dissappeared; *Car and Universal Finance Co. Ltd.* v. *Caldwell* [1965] 1 Q.B. 525.

[43] (1858) El., Bl. & El. 148.

LAPSE OF TIME

This is not strictly a bar to rescission. It is merely evidence of affirmation of the contract. Time does not begin to run until the purchaser discovers the truth.[44] However, where innocent misrepresentation is concerned it seems that time may begin to run even before the purchaser discovers the truth.[45]

(6) Damages for Misrepresentation

The purchaser will be entitled to such damages as will put him in the position he would have been in had the misrepresentation *not been made*.[46] This is not the same as the contractal method of calculating the amount of damages. The contractual method puts the purchaser in the position he would have been in if the statement in the contract *had been true*. An example will show the difference between the two rules. A buys a house from B for £10,000. B induces A to enter the contract by making a misrepresentation. If the misrepresentation had actually been true the house would have been worth £15,000. As it is the house is worth only £8,000. If A sues for misrepresentation under the Act he can only recover £2,000. On the other hand if the misrepresentation has become a term of the contract, A will be able to recover £5,000 for "loss of bargain." Clearly the purchaser will want to bring a claim for breach of contract if the representation has become a term of the contract.

The first basis described (the tortious basis) applies to claims for fraudulent and negligent misrepresentation, both at common law (on the *Hedley Byrne* principle) and under section 2(1) of the Act of 1967.[47] Damages under section 2(2), given in lieu of rescission, are unlikely to exceed those which would be awarded using the tortious basis of assessment; the precise basis of assessment is uncertain.

(7) Avoiding the Rule in Bain v. Fothergill

The general rule is that a vendor in breach of his contract to sell is liable to pay damages for "loss of bargain." However, a distinction is made between those cases in which the contract is broken because of the vendor's inability to make good title and those where it is due to the vendor's failure to do all he could to complete the conveyance. Only in the latter case will damages be recoverable by a disappointed purchaser for "loss of bargain."

When a vendor is in breach of contract because he cannot make good title the rule in *Bain* v. *Fothergill*[48] limits the damages recoverable by a

---

[44] *Aarons Reefs Ltd.* v. *Twiss* [1896] A.C. 273; *Armstrong* v. *Jackson* [1917] 2 K.B. 822.
[45] *Leaf* v. *International Galleries* [1950] 2 K.B. 86.
[46] *Winfield and Jolowicz on Tort* (12th ed.), p. 270.
[47] Treitel, *The Law of Contract* (6th ed.) p. 264; *Cheshire and Fifoot: Law of Contract* (10th ed.) p. 264.
[48] (1874) L.R. 7 H.L. 158; the rule originated in *Flureau* v. *Thornhill* (1776) 2 Wm.Bl. 1078.

purchaser to the return of any deposit paid (with interest) and any expenses incurred in investigating the vendor's title.[49] Thus in *J.W. Cafés* v. *Brownlow Trust*[50] the defendant failed to perform his contract to grant a lease because of restrictive covenants preventing use of the premises as a "milk bar." It was held that the failure being due to a defect in title, the plaintiff could only recover his deposit and expenses. Other cases in which the rule has been applied are, failure to obtain a head landlord's consent to the grant of an underlease,[51] failure to obtain a partner's consent to a sale,[52] and failure to make title owing to loss of deeds.[53]

The modern cases[54] show a less liberal approach is being adopted by the courts towards vendors who claim that the rule in *Bain* v. *Fothergill* applies. Unless the vendor has done his utmost to make a good title the courts will hold that damages for "loss of bargain" can be recovered by a purchaser. As Cumming-Bruce L.J. stated in *Malhotra* v. *Choudhury*[55]: "the vendor who seeks to avail himself of the protection afforded by what is described as the rule in *Bain* v. *Fothergill* must go to the length of satisfying the court that he has done all that he reasonably can to mitigate the effects of his breach of contract by trying to remove such fault on the title as appears." The rule is to be regarded as exceptional and applicable only to cases where the vendor is unable, through no fault of his own, to carry out his contractual duty to make good title. For instance, where a wife registered a Class F land charge after the contract had been made and the vendor was consequently unable to give vacant possession the purchaser recovered substantial damages for "loss of bargain."[56] The wife's rights did not create a defect in title within the meaning of the rule.

As has been explained:[57] "it is the steep rise in prices that the decade has seen that has provided a new eagerness on the part of the courts, epitomised by *Wroth* v. *Tyler, Watts* v. *Spence* and *Malhotra* v. *Choudhury,* to limit the operation of the rule in *Bain* v. *Fothergill* as far as, by one means or another, they possibly can . . . an appeal on suitable facts only needs to be taken to the House of Lords and it should be gone."

Mention has already been made of the case of *Watts* v. *Spence*.[58] This case shows a more devious route for circumventing the rule in *Bain* v. *Fothergill*. Here Mr. and Mrs. S. owned a house as joint tenants. Mr. S. contracted, without his wife's knowledge, to sell the house to the plaintiff. He could not make good title because his wife refused to convey when she found out what he had done. As no fraud or bad faith was alleged, the rule in *Bain's* case operated to limit the damages for breach of contract.

---

[49] Other loss may be recoverable, *McGregor on Damages*, p. 477.
[50] [1950] 1 All E.R. 894.
[51] *Vangeen* v. *Benjamin* (1976) 239 E.G. 647.
[52] *Keen* v. *Mear* [1920] 2 Ch.574.
[53] *Browning* v. *Handiland Group Ltd.* (1976) 35 P. & C.R. 345.
[54] *Re Daniel* [1917] 2 Ch.405; *Wroth* v. *Tyler* [1974] Ch.30; *Errington* v. *Martell-Wilson* (1980) 130 New L.J. 545.
[55] [1979] 1 All E.R. 186 at p. 204.
[56] *Wroth* v. *Tyler* [1974] Ch. 30.
[57] *McGregor on Damages* (14th ed.), Preface.
[58] [1976] Ch. 165.

However, the vendor by his conduct made a negligent (mis)representation that he was owner of the house and able to sell on his own. The plaintiff's claim for damages under section 2(1) of the Act of 1967 was not limited by the rule in *Bain* v. *Fothergill*. He was entitled to recover substantial damages.[59]

(8) Excluding Liability for Misrepresentation

It was once said that a contracting party who attempted to limit his liability took "a very ordinary business precaution."[60] Those seeking to rely on exclusion clauses today may well view this statement with a certain amount of scepticism. In the last two decades Parliament has revolutionised this area of the law. Begun by the passing of the Misrepresentation Act 1967, the revolution was completed by the addition to the statute books of the Unfair Contract Terms Act 1977. These two Acts severely limit the extent to which a party to a contract may exclude or restrict his liability both for breaches of contract and misrepresentation. It is with the latter aspect, the restrictions upon a contracting party's freedom to limit his liability for misrepresentation, that we are now concerned. In particular the extent to which National Condition 17 and Law Society Condition 7 are effective to exclude a vendor's liability for misleading statements will be considered.

SECTION 3, MISREPRESENTATION ACT 1967

Section 3 (as substituted by section 8 of the Unfair Contract Terms Act 1977) provides:

"If a contract contains a term which would exclude or restrict:
(a) any liability to which a party to a contract may be subject by reason of any misrepresentation made by him before the contract was made or
(b) any remedy available to another party to the contract by reason of such misrepresentation that term shall be of no effect except in so far as it satisfies the requirement of reasonableness as stated in section 11(1) of the Unfair Contract Terms Act 1977 . . . ."

Section 11(1) of the 1977 Act provides that

"reasonableness" means that "the term shall have been a fair and reasonable one to be included, having regard to the circumstances which were, or ought reasonably to have been, known to or in the contemplation of the parties when the contract was made."

The person seeking to rely on the clause must establish its reasonableness. Because the court in each case must have regard to the circumstances

---

[59] Doubt exists as to whether damages were *assessed on a contractual or tortious basis*. *McGregor on Damages* (14th ed.), p. 1000; *Treitel op.cit.* p. 268; *Cheshire and Fifoot op.cit.* p. 264.

[60] *Cellulose Acetate Silk Co. Ltd.* v. *Widnes Foundry (1925) Ltd.* [1933] A.C. 20, *per* Lord Atkin at p. 25.

in which the contract was made[61] the same exclusion clause may be held reasonable in one case and unreasonable in another. The only guidance given by the courts so far is more in the nature of a warning to those who are aggrieved at a first instance decision that an exclusion clause is unreasonable. In *George Mitchell (Chesterhall) Ltd.* v. *Finney Lock Seeds Ltd.*[62] the House of Lords warned that appellate courts would only interfere with the original decision if it was based on some incorrect principle or "plainly and obviously" wrong.

One type of clause used by vendors to try to escape liability for misrepresentation purports to deny that any representation has been made. In *Cremdean Properties Ltd.* v. *Nash*[63] particulars of sale at an auction stated that they were for the convenience of purchasers but that "their accuracy is not guaranteed and any error, omission or misdescription shall not annul the sale . . . any intending purchaser . . . must satisfy himself as to the correctness of each of the statements contained in these particulars." The vendor contended that the clause effectively denied any (mis)representation was made and that therefore the Misrepresentation Act 1967 could not apply. The court did not agree. They decided that such a clause could not protect the vendor. The clause was in effect saying that the vendor was making a representation which the purchaser was invited to verify. Another type of exclusion clause is one in which the purchaser states he "has not been induced to enter into the contract by any representation made orally or in writing by any person." This kind of clause will not protect a vendor either, because the court will always enquire whether the purchaser did, or did not, in fact rely on the representation.[64] Furthermore it is very unlikely that it would pass the fair and reasonable test of section 11 of the Unfair Contract Terms Act 1977.

There is one way of avoiding the section and that is by channelling all statements about the property through an agent. In *Overbrooke Estates Ltd.* v. *Glencombe Properties Ltd.*,[65] Brightman J. held that a clause, providing that auctioneers had no authority to make or give any representations or warranty in relation to the property, effectively protected the vendor from liability, when the auctioneers made statements about the property which misled the purchaser. The Act of 1967 did not alter the vendor's ability to publicly limit the scope of his agent's authority. The purchaser was taken to have bought knowing that anything the auctioneer said could not bind the vendor. The decision has been criticised as allowing a vendor to "put into circulation facts about the property which can only be intended to affect the minds of potential purchasers," without the risk of incurring liability for misrepresentation.[66] The vendor must not, however, give his

---

[61] *South Western General Property Co. Ltd.* v. *Marton* (1982) 263 E.G. 109.

[62] [1983] 2 All E.R. 737.

[63] (1977) 244 E.G. 547.

[64] *Lowe* v. *Lombank Ltd.* [1960] 1 W.L.R. 196; *Cremdean Properties Ltd.* v. *Nash* (1977) 244 E.G. 547; Bridge, L.J. at p. 551.

[65] [1974] 1 W.L.R. 1335, followed in *Collins* v. *Howell-Jones* (1980) 259 E.G. 331; see also H.W. Wilkinson (1967) 117 New L.J. 975; J.E. Adams (1970) 67 L.S.Gaz. 257 and 318; R.G. Lawson (1982) 79 L.S.Gaz. 1114.

[66] H.W. Wilkinson [1984] Conv. 12; J.E. Adams [1981] Conv. 326.

agent authority to put these statements into circulation. Once he does this the clause will not protect him; the agents representations will be binding on him.

EXCLUDING LIABILITY UNDER THE STANDARD CONDITIONS

(i) **National Condition** 17. National Condition 17 provides:

"(1) Without prejudice to any express right of either party, or to any right of the purchaser in reliance on Law of Property Act 1969, s.24, to rescind the contract before completion and subject to the provisions of paragraph (2) of this condition, no error, mis-statement or omission in any preliminary answer concerning the property, or in the sale plan or the Special Conditions, shall annul the sale, nor (save where the error, mis-statement or omission relates to a matter materially affecting the description or value of the property) shall any damages be payable, or compensation allowed by either party, in respect thereof.

(2) Paragraph (1) of this condition shall not apply to any error, mis-statement or, omission which is recklessly or fraudulently made, or to any matter or thing by which the purchaser is prevented from getting substantially what he contracted to buy.

(3) In this condition a 'a preliminary answer' means and includes any statement made by or on behalf of the vendor to the purchaser or his agents or advisers, whether in answer to formal preliminary enquiries or otherwise, before the purchaser entered into the contract."

Condition 17(1) entitles the purchaser to compensation for any misrepresentation, made by or on behalf of the vendor (17(3)), which materially affects the value of the property. Sub condition (2) gives the purchaser a right to rescind in any case where the vendor or his agent mislead him fraudulently or recklessly. A right of rescission is also reserved to the purchaser where the misrepresentation leads the purchaser to believe he is buying property fundamentally different from that which he in fact contracts to buy. The purchaser's right to rescind on discovery of an undisclosed land charge, given by section 24 of the Law of Property Act 1969,[67] is unaffected.

The misrepresentation may be contained in the contract itself,[68] a plan sent with the contract or answers given by the vendor or his agent to any enquiries before the purchaser entered into the contract; written or oral.

The Condition was drafted in its present form following the decision in *Walker* v. *Boyle*.[69] The vendor misled his purchaser by stating that there was no current boundary dispute affecting the property. In fact there was a dispute with a neighbour over the position of a fence. The sale was subject to the National Conditions of Sale (19th ed.), Condition 17 of which was similar to the current Condition 17, except that it stated that

---

[67] See *ante*, p. 30.
[68] See also remedies for misdescription *post*, p. 229.
[69] [1982] 1 W.L.R. 495.

damages were only available for a misrepresentation made in writing which materially affected the description or value of the property. Dillon J. giving judgment for the purchaser, held that (the old) Condition 17 did not meet the requirements of fairness and reasonableness contained in section 11 of the Unfair Contract Terms Act 1977. The fact that the Condition had been in use for many years and that both parties were independently advised did not "entitle it to the automatic accolade of fairness and reasonableness." Dillon J. also commented unfavourably on the fact that the Condition purported to exclude compensation for any oral mistatement, fraudulent or otherwise, no matter how serious it might be. It was this *obiter* comment which prompted the inclusion of the present sub-condition(2).

As redrafted Condition 17 now only attempts to exclude the purchaser's remedies for misrepresentation (whether oral or written) in cases where it is not material or substantial in its effect and is not made recklessly or fraudulently. Whether the Condition as redrafted will satisfy the require-ments of Section 3 of the Misrepresentation Act remains to be seen; this will depend upon the particular facts of the case.[70]

(ii) **Law Society Condition** 7. Law Society Condition 7 provides:

"(1) No error, omission or misstatement herein or in any plan furnished or any statement made in the course of the negotiations leading to the contract shall annul the sale or entitle the purchaser to be discharged from the purchase.

(2) Any such error, omission or misstatement shown to be material shall entitle the purchaser or the vendor, as the case may be, to proper compensation, provided that the purchaser shall not in any event be entitled to compensation for matters falling within conditions 5(2) or 6(3).

(3) No immaterial error, omission or misstatement (including a mistake in any plan furnished for identification only) shall entitle either party to compensation.

(4) Sub-condition (1) shall not apply where compensation for any error, omission or misstatement shown to be material cannot be assessed nor enable either party to compel the other to accept or convey property differing substantially (in quantity, quality tenure or otherwise) from the property agreed to be sold if the other party would be prejudiced by the difference.

(5) The purchaser acknowledges that in making the contract he has not relied on any statement made to him save one made or confirmed in writing."

Again the purchaser has a right to rescind, for a misrepresentation which results in him getting property; "differing substantially . . . from the property agreed to be sold." This result is achieved by reading sub-condi-tion (1) with sub-condition (4). Compensation is given to the purchaser if the misrepresentation is shown to be material. In *Re Fawcett and Holmes'*

---

[70] *South Western General Property Co. Ltd.* v. *Marton* (1982) 263 E.G. 109.

Contract[71] the vendor agreed to sell a house, builders yard and stables. He stated that the area of the property was 1,372 square yards. The true figure should have been 1,033 square yards. When the purchaser sought rescission it was held that the misrepresentation was material not substantial and therefore only entitled him to compensation. No compensation is payable for misstatements relating to matters of which the purchaser is deemed to have knowledge by Condition 5(2)[72] (state and condition, easements and so on). Similarly a misrepresentation as to matters within the scope of Condition 6(3)[73] (rent lawfully recoverable from a tenant and so on) does not carry a right to compensation.

Condition 7(5) attempts to prevent the purchaser from obtaining relief on the basis of any oral misrepresentation made by the vendor before contract. The courts have shown a willingness to go behind statements like this and enquire whether a representation was relied on.[74] If so the exclusion will be ineffective, unless it passes the "reasonableness" test. Despite this and despite Dillon J.'s criticism in *Walker* v. *Boyle*[75] of the former and similarly drafted National Condition 17, no change to Law Society Condition 7 was recommended in 1984. Presumably it was not thought profitable to try and predict what the courts would find reasonable in any particular case. As drafted the clause seems "to put a duty on a purchaser's solicitor to find from his client what representations have been made to him and either warn his client not to rely on them or insist that the vendor puts them into writing."[76] Finally, it should be noted that the Condition does not expressly give a purchaser the right to rescind for a fraudulent mis-statement unless it is substantial.

(9) Misdescription

Misdescription is merely a form of misrepresentation. It is a statement of fact, relating to the description of the property, contained in the contract. The particulars of sale form part of the contract and if the vendor cannot convey the property therein described he will be in breach of contract.

The misdescription may relate to the physical extent of the property, the nature of the interest sold or the quality of the land. Under an open contract the parties rights depend whether the error is trivial, material or substantial. The standard conditions mainly reflect the common law position but do make changes in places.

TRIVIAL ERRORS

Falling within this category would be cases where the purchaser obtains almost exactly that which he paid for. For example in *Vartoukian* v. *Daejan Properties Ltd.*[77] a number of flats were sold. The contract

---

[71] (1889) 42 Ch.D. 150.
[72] See *ante*, p. 203.
[73] See *ante*, p. 206.
[74] *Lowe* v. *Lombank Ltd.* [1960] 1 W.L.R. 196.
[75] [1982] 1 W.L.R. 495.
[76] H.W. Wilkinson [1980] Conv. 404 at p. 406.
[77] (1969) 20 P. & C.R. 983.

described them as being held on long leases. In fact one of the tenants held under a short lease. Soon after the contract was made the vendor remedied the position by granting that tenant a long lease. It was held that the purchaser, having obtained substantially all he agreed to buy, could only recover nominal damages. Trivial errors do not allow a purchaser to rescind the contract.

The standard conditions of sale both contain provisions dealing with the parties rights in the event of a slight misdescription. National Condition 17(1) provides that no compensation or damages shall be payable for an error, which did not materially affect the description or value of the property.[78] This exclusion does not apply to slight errors if they are made recklessly or fraudulently; National Condition 17(2). Similarly Law Society Condition 7(3) precludes either party from claiming compensation for "immaterial" errors.

MATERIAL ERRORS

(i) **Purchaser's Position.** This category comprises those cases where the purchaser receives a different property from that which he bargained for but not drastically different. In *Belsworth* v. *Hassell*[79] there was an agreement to assign "the unexpired term of eight years" remaining under a lease. The remainder of the term was actually seven years and seven months. Lord Ellenborough decided that the purchaser was obliged to complete as he received more or less that which he had agreed to pay for. A misdescription relating to the physical extent of the property would be dealt with in the same way.[80]

A material error will generally not allow a purchaser to rescind the contract; he can only claim damages.[81] However, he is entitled to seek specific performance of the contract with an abatement of the purchase price. Where the price of property is reached not on the basis of area, but on its value for some other reason, for example it gives the purchaser access to previously isolated property, this can be of considerable advantage to the purchaser. By being given an abatement he is in effect being allowed to pay a lower price for something he thought more valuable.[82]

The purchaser will not be able to specifically enforce the contract with an abatement in the price if the error cannot fairly be assessed in monetary terms. In these circumstances he is given the right to rescind. In *Rudd* v. *Lascelles*[83] L. agreed to sell some property to R. for £3,500. The land, unknown to R. when he contracted, was subject to restrictive covenants limiting the uses to which it could be put. R. claimed specific performance with an abatement in the price of £1,000. The action was dismissed on the

[78] *Pagebar Properties Ltd.* v. *Derby Investment Holdings Ltd.* [1972] 1 W.L.R. 1500.
[79] (1815) 4 Camp. 140.
[80] *Watson* v. *Burton* [1957] 1 W.L.R. 19.
[81] *Dyer* v. *Hargrave* (1805) 10 Ves. 505; *Re Fawcett and Holmes' Contract* (1889) 42 Ch.D. 150.
[82] *Hill* v. *Buckley* (1811) 17 Ves. 394; *Whatley* v. *Slade* (1830) 4 Sim. 127; *McKenzie* v. *Hesketh* (1877) 7 Ch.D. 675.
[83] [1900] 1 Ch. 815; see [1981] C.L.J. 47 for a criticism of the case.

ground *inter alia*, that compensation for such an error could not be assessed. R. was left to his remedies for breach of contract and he rescinded.

The National and Law Society Conditions reflect the common law giving the purchaser a right to compensation in respect of any misdescription shown to be material. Law Society Condition 7(4) also takes into account the decision in *Rudd* v. *Lascelles* by giving the purchaser the opportunity to rescind where compensation cannot be assessed. The National Conditions leave the common law to apply.

Under an open contract the purchaser has to claim compensation for a material misdescription before completion.[84] After completion the contract merges into the conveyance and no action can be brought on it. The purchaser can sue on the implied covenants for title but only if the misdescription is repeated in the conveyance. However, if on the construction of a contract for the sale of land any of its provisions are intended to be effective after a formal conveyance has been executed those provisions "survive" the conveyance and remain operative.[85] This is the case where the contract contains a term giving a right to compensation for any misdescription. National Condition 17 and Law Society 7 are examples of such provisions and will allow the purchaser to claim compensation even after completion has taken place.

Law Society Condition 7(2) provides that no compensation can be claimed by the purchaser for matters falling within the ambit of Condition 5(2) (state and condition, easements and so on) or Condition 6(3) (matters affecting a subsisting tenancy subject to which the property is sold).[86]

(ii) **Vendor's Position.** A vendor who innocently misdescribes his property is able to specifically enforce the contract, subject to giving the purchaser proper compensation for the deficiency. Equity looks to the substance of the transaction rather than the form and will not permit a purchaser to avoid a contract because of some insubstantial error which would not have altered his decision to buy.[87]

The misdescription may be to the prejudice of the vendor, for example where he contracts to sell more property than he intended to. At common law he has no implied right to increase the price. It is the vendor's responsibility to ensure that he describes the property accurately.[88] However if the misdescription means that the vendor will suffer extreme hardship, as where the acreage of land contracted to be sold is far in excess of the intended acreage, the court may refuse specific performance and order a purchaser to pursue his remedies for breach of contract.[89] In

---

[84] *Joliffe* v. *Baker* (1883) 11 Q.B.D. 255 *cf. Clayton* v. *Leech* (1889) 41 Ch.D. 103 (misdescription not discoverable before completion).

[85] *Palmer* v. *Johnson* (1884) 13 Q.B.D. 351.

[86] See *ante*, p. 203.

[87] *Bowyer* v. *Bright* (1824) 13 Price 698; *Cato* v. *Thompson* (1882) 9 Q.B.D. 616; *Shepherd* v. *Croft* [1911] 1 Ch. 521.

[88] *Lloyd* v. *Stanbury* [1971] 1 W.L.R. 535.

[89] *Rudd* v. *Lascelles* [1900] 1 Ch. 815.

Manser v. *Back*[90] property was put up for sale at auction. The particulars omitted to reserve the vendor a right of way. Although the auctioneer subsequently amended the particulars the purchaser signed an agreement which through some oversight, again omitted to reserve the right of way. The purchaser claimed specific performance of the contract for sale free from the right of way. The court held that to grant the decree would cause great hardship to the vendor. They, therefore, gave the purchaser a choice; specific performance subject to a right of way and proper compensation, or damages for breach of contract.[91]

Both the National and Law Society Conditions of Sale greatly improve the position of the vendor. National 17(1) and Law Society 7(2) give the vendor a right to compensation for material or substantial errors.

SUBSTANTIAL ERRORS

Whether the sale is under an open contract or the standard conditions of sale a vendor cannot force on a purchaser property which differs substantially from that which he has agreed to buy. The rule at common law was developed in *Flight* v. *Booth*.[92] A purchaser bought a market stall in Covent Garden at an auction. The particulars gave details of restrictive covenants preventing use of the premises for, any offensive trade, the business of a working hatter or as a coffee shop. The contract contained a term saying that errors should not vitiate the sale, but that there should be an allowance in price to either party in the event of a misdescription. After the auction the purchaser discovered other covenants preventing use for various trades including *inter alia*, butcher, tripe seller, distiller, dyer, dealer in old iron and fruiterer. In view of the location of the property, the purchaser objected. He was allowed to rescind and recover his deposit despite the clause in the contract forbidding him to do so. In the course of his judgment Tindal C.J. said that a purchaser can rescind despite a contractual clause to the contrary if the misdescription; "although not proceeding from fraud was in a material and substantial point, so far affecting the subject matter of the contract that it may be reasonably supposed, that, but for such misdescription, the purchaser might never have entered into the contract at all."[93] The vendor is not given the option of specific performance even if he is willing to pay the purchaser compensation.

The following have been held to be substantial misdescriptions allowing the purchaser to rescind. Describing a factory as having an area of 3,920 square yards when it only had 2,360 square yards[94]; describing a house as 58 Pall Mall when it had no frontage to Pall Mall[95]; stating a property is connected to a mains water supply and that water rates are payable when water is supplied by a private company and is paid for annually according

---

[90] (1848) 6 Hare 443; *Earl of Durham* v. *Legard (Sir Francis)* (1865) 34 Beav. 611.
[91] See also *Thomas* v. *Dering* (1837) 1 Keen. 729.
[92] (1834) 1 Bing. N.C. 370; see also *Re Belcham and Gawley's Contract* [1930] 1 Ch. 56.
[93] *Ibid.* at p. 377.
[94] *Watson* v. *Burton* [1957] 1 W.L.R. 19.
[95] *Stanton* v. *Tattersall* (1853) 1 Sm. & Griff. 529.

to their scale of charges[96]; and more recently describing a freehold house as sold with "entire vacant possession" when part of the first floor is completely blocked off and rented as a storeroom by the owners of adjoining property.[97]

Whether a misdescription is substantial is a question of fact to be decided by the court in every case. No general rule can be stated other than the quote of Tindal C.J. given above. However, the more particularity with which the property is described the smaller the margin of error allowed to a vendor before the purchaser is allowed to rescind.[98]

The purchaser does not have to rescind. He is given the choice of enforcing the contract and taking the vendor's property as it is with compensation.[99] As with material errors the purchaser's right to compensation and specific performance is limited to cases where the loss is assessable[1] and the grant of a decree would not cause the vendor undue hardship. Again under an open contract the purchaser must pursue his remedies before completion.

The rule in *Flight* v. *Booth*[2] is expressly incorporated into the current editions of both forms of standard conditions. National Condition 17(1) provides that "no error . . . in the sale plan or the Special Conditions, shall annul the sale." This is subject to Condition 17(2) which goes on to state that 17(1) shall not apply if the misdescription is made "recklessly or fraudulently . . . or to any matter . . . by which the purchaser is prevented from getting substantially what he contracted to buy." Law Society Condition 7(1) read with 7(4) is of similar effect. However, the Law Society Condition adds that a party seeking rescission must be prejudiced by the error even if it is substantial. It is arguable that this requirement is in conflict with the rule in *Flight* v. *Booth* where there is no need for a purchaser to prove the prejudicial effect of a substantial error. Despite this, the requirement in the Condition was accepted without question in *Watson* v. *Burton*.[3] In practice a purchaser receiving property fundamentally different from that described in the contract would almost certainly be prejudiced in some respect.

(10) Remedies for Non-Disclosure

A purchaser's remedies for non-disclosure of a latent defect in title are exactly the same as those available to him where the vendor has misdescribed the property in the contract. Under an open contract a substantial non-disclosure will entitle a purchaser to either rescind the

---

[96] *Fisher* v. *Andrews* [1955] J.P.L. 452.
[97] *Mustafa* v. *Baptist Union Corporation Ltd.* (1983) 266 E.G. 812.
[98] *Jacobs* v. *Revell* [1900] 2 Ch. 858.
[99] *Rutherford* v. *Acton-Adams* [1915] A.C. 866.
[1] See the note at [1983] Conv. 1 suggesting that loss is now nearly always capable of assessment. Also *Re Chifferiel* (1880) 40 Ch.D. 45; *Aspinalls to Powell and Scholefield* (1889) 60 L.T. 595; [1981] C.L.J. 47.
[2] (1834) 1 Bing. N.C. 370.
[3] [1957] 1 W.L.R. 19.

contract or specifically enforce it with an abatement in the purchase price.[4] A material non-disclosure will entitle the purchaser to compensation only.[5] The vendor will be able to enforce the contract subject to giving the purchaser proper compensation. A trivial non-disclosure does not entitle the purchaser to relief.

National Condition 17 and Law Society Condition 7 apply to non-disclosure ("omissions") in the same way as they apply to misdescription and misrepresentation.

PART III. CONCLUDING THE CONTRACT

As long as parties continue to make contracts for the sale of land, cases will arise where one party to the transaction wishes to withdraw before the matter has been concluded. Two questions then become relevant:

(i) Have the parties made a binding contract?
(ii) Have the formal requirements of section 40 of the Law of Property Act 1925 been complied with?

Part III looks at the first question.

Intention to Exchange

In *Eccles* v. *Bryant*[6] Lord Greene M.R. said:

"When parties are proposing to enter into a contract, the manner in which the contract is to be created so as to bind them must be gathered from the intentions of the parties, express or implied."[7] In most conveyancing transactions the parties intend that the contract will only become binding on "exchange." A formal contract is drawn up in duplicate by the vendor's solicitor and approved by the purchaser's solicitor. Each party signs one part of the contract and the parts are physically exchanged. Neither party is bound until the exchange is made. Thus in *Eccles* v. *Bryant & Pollock* the vendors' solicitors wrote to the purchaser's solicitors stating that the vendors had signed their part of the contract and were ready to exchange. A week later the purchaser's solicitors wrote: "We enclose herewith the contract signed by our client, and shall be glad to receive in exchange the part signed by your clients." This letter crossed in the post with a letter from the vendors' solicitors repudiating the contract. The purchaser failed in his action for specific performance; no contract was formed until the parts were exchanged. It was argued by counsel for the vendors that exchange was a mere matter of machinery, having in itself no particular importance or significance. To

---

[4] *Carlish* v. *Salt* [1906] 1 Ch. 335; *Phillips* v. *Caldcleugh* (1868) L.R. 4 Q.B. 159. Again specific performance will not be granted if it would cause the vendor extreme hardship.
[5] *Rudd* v. *Lascelles* [1900] 1 Ch. 815 – if compensation can be assessed.
[6] [1948] 1 Ch. 93.
[7] *Ibid.* at p. 99.

this Lord Greene M.R. replied that where parties contemplate (as here) that a binding contract will only come into existence on exchange, "it is not right to say of exchange that it has no significance, it is the crucial and vital fact which brings the contract into existence."[8] He went on to explain that exchange has become the accepted way to conclude a contract because it ensures that three requirements, essential in a sale of land, are satisfied:

(i) on exchange the parties can be sure that a contract exists;
(ii) there can be no dispute as the terms of the contract because both parties have identical parts in their possession; and
(iii) both have a document signed by the other. This is "a document of title" which enables either party to enter into further transactions, a sub-sale for instance.

Where the parties use either the National or Law Society's form of contract it is clear that an exchange is intended. Lord Greene M.R. indicated in *Eccles* v. *Bryant & Pollock* that if a solicitor takes it upon himself (without authority) to agree a method for concluding the contract, other than exchange, he may well be in breach of duty to his client and liable for heavy damages for negligence. It is suggested that his Lordship was referring to the situation where the client has expressly or impliedly instructed his solicitor to conclude the contract by exchange. In other words he was referring to the question of whether or not the solicitor was acting within his actual authority. In *Domb* v. *Isoz*[9] the Court of Appeal made it clear that the client who instructs a solicitor to act for him in a disposition of land impliedly and ostensibly authorises him to make the contract binding "in such manner and by such agents as the solicitor may think fit."[10]

In *Eccles* v. *Bryant* the parties' intention to exchange was derived from the fact that their prior correspondence was stated to be "subject to contract." However these words are not an essential pre-requisite to an intention to exchange. If the correspondence clearly shows that the parties contemplate approval and exchange of formal contracts, the words "subject to contract" are implied into the correspondence, even though they were not expressly used.[11]

Furthermore even though the parties originally intended exchange, if their intent changes, they can bind themselves to a contract without physical exchange. In *Griffiths* v. *Young*[12] a purchaser wrote offering to buy land "subject to contract." The following day his solicitors agreed by telephone with the vendor's solicitors that the matter should become binding immediately and the vendor's solicitors sent a letter agreeing the terms set out in the first letter. The Court of Appeal held that the effect

---

[8] *Ibid.* at p. 99.
[9] [1980] 1 All E.R. 942.
[10] *Ibid., per* Templeman L.J. at p. 952; *North* v. *Loomes* [1919] 1 Ch. 378; and see A. Waite (1980) 130 New L.J. 774.
[11] *Tevanan* v. *Norman Brett (Builders) Ltd.* (1972) 223 E.G. 1945.
[12] [1970] Ch. 675.

of the telephone conversation was to waive the words "subject to contract" so that an informal but binding contract had been created. (Evidenced by the letters). But in *Sherbrooke* v. *Dipple*[13] and *Cohen* v. *Nessdale Ltd.*[14] the Court of Appeal re-emphasised[15] the principle that if correspondence is initially made "subject to contract," those words qualify all subsequent correspondence (the intent to exchange remains) unless the parties expressly or impliedly "take down the umbrella" of the "subject to contract" provision.

Personal Exchange

What has been described as "the ceremonial form of exchange"[16] occurs when the parties' solicitors meet, usually at the vendor's solicitors office, and the two signed engrossments are passed across the table. This method of exchange is now dying out, especially where the respective firms of solicitors are in different parts of the country.

Exchange by Post

Where contracts are exchanged by post it is not clear[16] whether exchange takes place when the second part to be forwarded is put in the post[17] or when it is actually received by the other party.[18] The standard conditions would seem to render this problem academic. National Condition 1(7)(ii) provides that the date of the contract shall be "on an exchange of contracts by post (unless the parties' solicitors otherwise agree) the date on which the last part of the contract is posted." Law Society Condition 10(1) is in the same terms. The latter Condition also allows for the use of document exchanges. In this case exchange of contracts takes place when the second part of the contract is delivered to the document exchange, not when it is available for collection by the addressee.[18a]

It has however been pointed out that these conditions may be terms of a non-existent contract,[19] unless they are viewed as an expression of the intention of the parties, in which case the conditions are effective. If the former view was to be preferred, the common law position, with all its uncertainties (document exchanges?) would apply. The moral is for the parties to agree and insert the date of the contract.

Exchange by Telephone or Telex

Today chain bargains are the norm rather than the exception. They require simultaneous contracts for sale and purchase all the way down the

---

[13] (1980) 255 E.G. 1203.

[14] [1982] 2 All E.R. 97.

[15] *Tiverton Estates Ltd.* v. *Wearwell Ltd.* [1975] 1 Ch. 146.

[16] *Eccles* v. *Bryant & Pollock* [1948] 1 Ch. 93.

[17] The normal rule laid down in *Adams* v. *Lindsell* (1818) 1 B. & Ald. 681.

[18] *Holwell Securities Ltd.* v. *Hughes* [1974] 1 W.L.R. 155.

[18a] By contrast to Condition 2(1). See *ante*, p. 168.

[19] [1981] Conv. 163.

chain and this cannot be achieved by the traditional means of personal or postal exchange. The recent case of *Domb* v. *Isoz*[20] tested the efficacy of exchange by telephone, a practice becoming extremely popular with solicitors. At first instance[21] the judge labelled the practice "bad" and held that it was an ineffective method of exchanging contracts unless expressly authorised by the client. On appeal all three judges (Buckley, Templeman and Bridge L.JJ.) agreed that telephonic exchanges were both authorised and effective. The practice did not dispense with exchange. "The client confers power to exchange but is not interested in the machinery or method of exchange which are matters for the solicitor and the general law."[22] In *Domb* v. *Isoz* itself the two parts of the contract were in the possession of the vendor's solicitor when the exchange by telephone was made, but the principle applies equally to the case where each solicitor retains his client's part and gives an undertaking on the telephone to hold it to the other's order. Although the contract becomes binding at the time of the telephone conversation, the process of exchange is completed in the normal way by posting the relevant part or parts of the contract to the other side. There are risks involved in constructive exchanges, the main ones being the inability to check the signature and contents of the contract. Further the decision raises the question of who in a solicitors office may make a telephonic exchange. Buckley and Bridge L.JJ. spoke in general terms of the authority of solicitors to make exchanges by telephone. Templeman L.J. thought that they should only be made by partners and that a short formula for attendance notes should be used. This latter suggestion has been followed up by the Council of the Law Society which has produced two alternative formulae for telephone exchanges, accompanied by notes of guidance.[23]

Exchange of contracts by telephone or telex is provided for in National Condition 1(6) and Law Society Condition 10(2). National Condition 1(6) authorises "a solicitor" to make a constructive exchange. By National Construction (5) "solicitor" includes an employed barrister acting in the course of employment. Law Society Condition 10(2) is couched in similar terms but "solicitor" is undefined.

In *Aquis Estates Ltd.* v. *Minton*[24] it was assumed that an exchange of contracts by telex was effective, although as mentioned earlier[25] there may be a problem as to whether or not the telex message is sufficient evidence of signed writing to satisfy section 40 of the Law of Property Act 1925. The House of Lords decision in *Brinkibon Ltd.* v. *Stahag Stahl mbH*[26] indicates that there may be other difficulties involved in telex exchange. Their Lordships held that where a contract is made by instantaneous communication, like telex, the general rule applies that the contract is made when and where acceptance is received. However Lord Wilberforce

---

[20] [1980] 1 All E.R. 942; H.W. Wilkinson [1980] Conv. 227.
[21] (1978) 248 E.G. 783.
[22] [1980] 1 All E.R. 942, *per* Templeman L.J. at p. 952.
[23] See (1980) 77 L.S.Gaz. 144; republished in (1984) 81 L.S. Gaz 1891.
[24] [1975] 1 W.L.R. 1452.
[25] See *ante*, p. 136.
[26] [1983] 2 A.C. 34.

was of the opinion that the rule may only apply where the vendor and purchaser make the telex contract themselves and he added that the rule may be affected by a variety of other factors.

As a final point, it should be noted that National Condition 1(6) and Law Society 10(2) are really terms of an unmade contract; the contract is only made on exchange. It is arguable that *Domb* v. *Isoz* regulates the conduct of constructive exchanges, not the conditions.

Identical Parts

In *Harrison* v. *Battye*[27] the vendor agreed, subject to contract, to sell his house to the purchasers for £8,250. The draft contract stated that the deposit was £825. The parties' solicitors later agreed to reduce the deposit. The purchasers' solicitor amended the purchasers' part of the contract by altering the amount of the deposit to £100 and sent the amended draft signed by the purchasers to the vendor's solicitor. The vendor's solicitor failed to amend the vendor's part and by mistake sent back to the purchasers' solicitor the purchasers' own signed part with a covering letter: "We enclose part contract signed by our client to complete the exchange." The vendor refused to proceed. The Court of Appeal unanimously thought that if the vendor's part of the contract had been amended there might well have been a binding contract. Sir Erich Sachs was "much impressed with the view that on the posting (of the letter sent with the wrong part of the contract) there was communicated to the purchasers an unequivocal appropriation of the counterpart signed by the vendor . . . (the purchasers) became entitled to possession of that document and an effective exchange . . . occurred despite the clerical error in the vendor's solicitors' office."[28] The point was left open. The case was decided on the ground that the two parts could not be exchanged as they differed from each other in a material respect (the deposit). Lord Denning said: "When two people sell a house "subject to contract" the contract is not concluded until the two parts are exchanged. These two parts must be in identical terms. If they differ in any material respect there is no contract".[29]

That the parts must be identical is further illustrated by the case of *Earl* v. *Mawson*.[30] The purchaser signed the top copy and the vendor the carbon of a typed contract, but whilst the purchaser had initialled some obvious alterations the vendor had not. Although the parts were formally exchanged, they were not the same and therefore there was no binding contract between the parties.

In *Domb* v. *Isoz*[31] the two parts of the contract were also not identical; the vendor's part contained a clause about the apportionment of part of the purchase price as between land and fixtures, but the purchaser's part did not. The Court of Appeal held that this did not affect the purchaser's right to enforce the contract because "there could in my judgment be no

[27] [1975] 1 W.L.R. 58.
[28] *Ibid.* at p. 61.
[29] *Ibid.* at p. 60.
[30] (1974) 232 E.G. 1315.
[31] [1980] 1 All E.R. 942.

doubt whatever that the remedy of rectification would be available, for it is common ground that both parties intended that the sale should include the fixtures and fittings referred to and the apportionment of the price was purely a matter of conveyancing and not of contract and would be of no significance."[32] *Harrison's* case was distinguished on the ground that rectification was not available because the discrepancy was due to the amount of the deposit and resulted from the vendor's solicitor without authority accepting a smaller deposit.

Intention to Create a Contract by other Methods

One example of when the parties will not intend an exchange of contracts is where the same solicitor acts for both parties. In *Smith* v. *Mansi*[33] Danckwerts L.J. stated the point succinctly: "Where there is only one document as the contract and only one solicitor, acting for both parties, the idea of exchange, in my opinion, can only be described as artificial nonsense. It is impossible to carry out. Once a complete contract has been signed by both parties there is nothing more to be done."[34] Evidence that the vendor did not intend to be bound at the time of signing was held to be inadmissible, although Russell L.J. said that evidence that neither party intended to be bound would have been admissible. The same solicitor acting for both parties would now be a rare occurrence. The general rule is that one solicitor may no longer act for both parties to a conveyancing transaction.[35]

Two cases involving the sale of council houses by Manchester City Council, show that the parties may negate an intention to exchange by their words and conduct. The facts of *Storer* v. *Manchester City Council*[36] were briefly as follows. The Council instructed the town clerk to devise a simple form of agreement for the sale of council houses, aimed at dispensing with legal formalities. Mr. Storer applied to buy his council house with the aid of a council mortgage. The town clerk wrote to him saying: "I understand you wish to purchase your council house and enclose the Agreement for Sale. If you will sign the Agreement and return it to me I will send you the Agreement signed on behalf of the council in exchange." Mr. Storer signed the Agreement and returned it. Due to a change in policy the Council refused to proceed with the sale. The Court of Appeal held that a binding contract had been created. The town clerk's letter comprised the offer and acceptance was made by Mr. Storer signing and returning the Agreement. The Council's instructions to the town clerk to devise a simple form of agreement and the clerk's letter were evidence of the Council's intention to dispense with exchange.

With Storer should be contrasted *Gibson* v. *Manchester City Council*.[37] This again involved the Council's sale of council houses but Mr. Gibson

---

[32] *Ibid. per* Buckley L.J. at p. 968.
[33] [1963] 1 W.L.R. 26.
[34] [1963] 1 W.L.R. 26 at p. 32.
[35] "New Practice Rule 2" (1972) 69 L.S.Gaz. 117.
[36] [1974] 1 W.L.R. 1403.
[37] [1979] 1 W.L.R. 294.

had only got as far as applying for details of the purchase price of his house and of a mortgage. The Council sent him an application form which he completed and signed. The House of Lords analysed the correspondence in terms of offer and acceptance and came to the conclusion that the parties had never made a binding contract. The Council had merely stated that they might be prepared to sell and invited Mr. Gibson to make an application. This was not an offer capable of acceptance, it was an invitation to treat.

Solicitor's Duty on Exchange[38]

A client who is selling one property and buying another, will often instruct his solicitor to act on the basis that the sale and purchase are to be simultaneous. If the solicitor fails to synchronise the transaction and loss results, he will be liable to his client in damages.[39] In the absence of express instructions, in a sale and purchase transaction the solicitor should still try to synchronise the exchange, unless he has been instructed that he may make a unilateral exchange after the risks have been explained to the client. The Council of the Law Society in its evidence to the Royal Commission on Legal Services (1977) said that it was part of a solicitor's duty to his client (vendor or purchaser) to ensure the synchronisation of exchange of contracts and completion dates.

Contract Races

The Council of the Law Society has issued the following ruling on the sending out of more than one draft contract.[40]

> "*Vendor's solicitor submitting forms of contract to more than one prospective purchaser.*"
>
> 1. The Council recognise that a solicitor acting for a vendor may sometimes be instructed by his client to deal with more than one prospective purchaser at the same time.
>
> 2. The Council have accordingly directed that where a vendor instructs his solicitor to submit (whether simultaneously or otherwise) forms of contract to more than one prospective purchaser, the following steps by the solicitor are obligatory:
>
> (A) WHERE SOLICITOR IS ACTING FOR VENDOR
> The solicitor (with his client's authority) must at once disclose the vendor's decision direct to the solicitor acting for each prospective purchaser or (where no solicitor is acting) to the prospective purchaser(s) in person and such disclosure, if made orally, must at once be confirmed in writing. If the vendor refuses to authorise disclosure, the solicitor must cease acting for the vendor forthwith.

---

[38] See H. W. Wilkinson (1978) 128 New L.J. 191.
[39] *Buckley* v. *Lane Herdman & Co.* [1977] C.L.Y.B. 3143.
[40] (1977) 74 L.S.Gaz. 834.

(B) WHERE SOLICITOR IS ENTITLED TO ACT FOR BOTH VENDOR AND
PURCHASER

Notwithstanding the exceptions contained in para (2) of Rule 2 of the
Solicitors Practice Rules 1936–72, a solicitor cannot act for both
vendor and purchaser if a conflict of interest arises. Where there is
more than one prospective purchaser, the Council consider that the
danger of a conflict of interest is greatly increased. The Council are
reluctant to issue a general prohibition against acting in such cases
and they therefore warn all solicitors concerned to consider most
carefully whether, and if so to what extent, they can properly act in
these cases. If in an exceptional case a solicitor decides that he can
properly act for both vendor and one of the prospective purchasers,
then (in addition to the steps he must take under paragraph A above)
the solicitor must at once disclose his decision direct to those two
clients and also to the solicitor acting for every other prospective
purchaser or (where no solicitor is acting) to the prospective
purchaser(s) in person and such disclosure, if made orally, must at
once be confirmed in writing.

(C) WHERE SOLICITOR IS ASKED TO ACT FOR MORE THAN ONE
PURCHASER

Where forms of contract are submitted to more than one prospective
purchaser, a solicitor must not accept instructions to act for more than
one prospective purchaser.

In 1979 the Council's ruling was republished with the following
important notes[41]:

> 3. For the avoidance of doubt the Council wish to emphasise that
> the Direction applies to all sales and purchases of freehold and
> leasehold property.
> 4. The Council also wish to emphasise to the profession that the
> Direction is mandatory upon all solicitors and that any solicitor who
> is found to be in breach of the Direction in future is liable to face
> proceedings before the Solicitor's Disciplinary Tribunal.

It has been suggested[42] that in sending out several copies of the draft
contract the vendor makes an implied agreement to enter into a contract
for the sale of the land with the first person to tender the deposit with his
part of the contract signed. If so, paragraph 2(A) of the Council's ruling
may create a trap for the unwary vendor's solicitor. In *Daulia Ltd.* v. *Four
Millbank Nominees Ltd.*[43] the vendor orally agreed with the purchaser,
that if the purchaser attended his offices before 10 o'clock the following
day with a banker's draft for the deposit and a signed copy of the contract
then he, the vendor, would enter into a formal written contract for the sale
of the property. The Court of Appeal held that the oral agreement
(referred to as a "unilateral contract") was a contract for the disposition

---

[41] 76 L.S.Gaz. 1177.
[42] J.T. Farrand [1978] Conv. 87.
[43] [1978] Ch. 231.

of an interest in land (it would result in the purchaser acquiring an equitable interest in the property) and unenforceable for non-compliance with section 40 of the Law of Property Act 1925. The inference of the decision is that had the vendor's oral agreement been evidenced in writing, then it would have been enforceable. Paragraph 2(A) of the Council's ruling requires the vendor's solicitor to inform each prospective purchaser *in writing* that several contracts have been sent out. Might this writing not provide a memorandum (signed on behalf of the party to be charged) sufficient to enable the first purchaser who tenders the deposit and a signed contract, to force the vendor to enter into a contract for the sale of the land to him?

Registration of the Contract

UNREGISTERED LAND

A contract by an estate owner or by a person entitled at the date of the contract to have a legal estate conveyed to him to convey or create a legal estate is registerable as an estate contract in the register of land charges.[44] Registration must be in the name of the estate owner whose estate is intended to be affected.[45] Failure to register renders the contract void against a subsequent purchaser for money or money's worth[46] of a legal estate in the land.[47]

REGISTERED LAND

The purchaser's contract is a minor interest[48] capable of protection by entering a notice, restriction or caution on the register.[49] If the purchaser goes into occupation under the contract he has an overriding interest under the Land Registration Act 1925, s.70(1)(g) which will bind third parties.[50] As a general rule if the contract is not protected on the register or as an overriding interest, the purchaser's rights will be overridden by a subsequent registered disposition for valuable consideration.[51] However in *Lyus* v. *Prowsa Developments Ltd.*[52] a purchaser's contract was held to bind a subsequent purchaser, despite the fact that it was unregistered and not an overriding interest (the purchaser was not in occupation), by virtue of the doctrine that Equity will not allow a statute to be used as an instrument of fraud. Purchasers' solicitors very rarely protect their client's contracts by registering an estate contract or by entering a notice, caution or restriction on the register unless:

(i) the good faith of the vendor is doubted;
(ii) a dispute arises between vendor and purchaser;

---

[44] Land Charges Act 1972 s.2(4); see Chap. 2, p. 20.
[45] Land Charges Act 1972 s.3; *Barrett* v. *Hilton Developments Ltd.* [1975] Ch. 237.
[46] *Midland Bank Trust Co.* v. *Green* [1981] A.C. 513.
[47] Land Charges Act 1972, s.4(6).
[48] Land Registration Act 1925, s.3(xv).
[49] *Ibid.* ss.49, 58 and 54.
[50] *Bridges* v. *Mees* [1957] Ch. 475.
[51] Land Registration Act 1925, ss.20(1) and 23(1).
[52] [1982] 1 W.L.R. 1044.

(iii) the vendor delays completion; or

(iv) the purchase price is to be paid by instalments with a conveyance to be made after the last payment.

Emmet on Title (18th ed.) advocates protection by the appropriate means in all cases and cites a statement of Megarry J. in *Wroth* v. *Tyler*[53]:

> " . . . this case may serve as a warning to conveyancers to reconsider their practice. . . . Can conveyancers safely continue this practice of not registering a contract for the purchase of land as an estate contract (or by a notice on the Land Register) except in a case of suspicion or delayed completion?"

Part IV. The Position of the Parties After Exchange of Contracts

(1) Vendor's Rights

THE VENDOR MAY RETAIN POSSESSION

The vendor has the right to retain possession of the property until actual completion takes place and the purchaser pays the balance of the purchase price.[54] Sometimes the contract will allow the purchaser to take occupation of the property pending completion by agreement with the vendor; for example National Condition 8 and Law Society Condition 18.[55]

UNPAID VENDOR'S LIEN

Until the purchaser pays the full price the vendor has a lien over the property for the balance of the purchase price. The lien comes into existence immediately the contract becomes binding.[56] If it becomes necessary for the vendor to protect his lien (because he will be parting with the title deeds before obtaining the full purchase price) he may register a general equitable charge if the land is unregistered[57] or apply for a notice to be entered on the register if the land is registered. In the latter case, if the vendor fails to lodge a notice but remains in occupation of the land his lien is adequately protected as an overriding interest.[58]

If the purchaser does not pay the balance of the purchase price the vendor may enforce the lien by seeking a court order for the sale of the property or allowing him to regain possession.

The vendor has no lien over the property if he agrees to leave the whole, or part, of the purchase price outstanding on a mortgage even if his security later proves to be unenforceable.[59]

---

[53] [1974] Ch. 30 at p. 64.
[54] *Lysaght* v. *Edwards* (1876) 2 Ch.D 499.
[55] See *post*, p. 250.
[56] *Re Birmingham* [1959] Ch. 523.
[57] Land Charges Act 1972, s.2(4).
[58] *London and Cheshire Insurance Co. Ltd.* v. *Laplagrene Property Co. Ltd.* [1971] Ch. 499.
[59] *Capital Finance Co. Ltd.* v. *Stokes* [1969] 1 Ch. 261.

THE VENDOR KEEPS RENTS AND PROFITS

The vendor is entitled to keep the rents and profits accruing from the land between contract and the contractual completion date (or if no date is fixed for completion the time he shows good title).[60] After that date the rents and profits belong to the purchaser.

The outgoings of the property must be paid by the person for the time being entitled to the rents and profits. However, both sets of standard conditions alter the open contract position by placing the burden of certain expenses in respect of the property on the purchaser, whether he is receiving the rents and profits or not.

National Condition 16(1) provides:

> "If after the date of the contract any requirement in respect of the property be made against the vendor by any local authority, the purchaser shall comply with the same at his own expense, and indemnify the vendor in respect thereof: in so far as the purchaser shall fail to comply with such requirement, the vendor may comply with the same wholly or in part and any money so expended by the vendor shall be repaid by the purchaser on completion."

By National Condition 16(2) the vendor is obliged to inform the purchaser of any such requirement immediately he receives notice of it. The Condition does not state when the requirement of the local authority is deemed to be made. Difficulties may, therefore, arise when a notice is served on the vendor before contract but the works specified in the notice are carried out after contract. Is the requirement "made" when the notice is served or when the work is actually done? It has been suggested[61] that the purchaser should foot the bill in this situation because the works will be in the nature of a permanent improvement to the property and so he will be the one to benefit from them. No such problem arises in sales governed by the Law Society Conditions. Law Society Condition 3(4) requires the purchaser to indemnify the vendor in respect of any liability incurred as a result of a "requirement"[62] of a "competent authority" whether it is made before or after contract. The scope of Condition 3(4) is further enlarged, in comparison to National Condition 16(1), by the wide definition given to "competent authority" which includes not only local authorities but government departments, statutory undertakers and so on.[63]

Both Conditions allow the vendor to comply with the requirement of the local authority (or "competent authority") and later recover the expense from the purchaser, if the purchaser does not carry out any necessary steps himself. Under the National Conditions the money expended by the vendor is recoverable on completion. The Law Society

---

[60] *Cuddon* v. *Tite* (1858) 1 Giff. 395.

[61] H.W. Wilkinson, *Standard Conditions of Sale of Land* (3rd ed.) p. 22.

[62] A requirement is defined by Condition 3(1)(*b*) to include "(whether or not subject to confirmation) any notice, order or proposal."

[63] Law Society Condition 3(1)(*a*); "competent authority" means a local authority or other body exercising powers under statute or Royal Charter.

Conditions allow the vendor to recover not only the cost of actually complying with the requirement but also other reasonable costs, for example solicitor's fees should advice be sought as to the legality of the requirement. Any sum recoverable by a vendor under Law Society Condition 3(4) must be paid by the purchaser on demand.

(2) The Vendor's Duty of Care

Immediately a binding contract for the sale of land is made the purchaser becomes the owner of the property in the eyes of Equity.[64] The remedy of specific performance may be available to enforce the contract and if so equity regards the contract as performed.[65] The vendor retains the legal estate in a position similar to that of a trustee holding the property for the purchaser, who is the beneficial owner. Unlike an ordinary trustee he retains a personal and substantial interest in the property which he is entitled to protect.[66] The property is his security for the purchase price and there is also the possibility of the sale going off and the beneficial ownership reverting to him. Nevertheless the vendor's rights of ownership are qualified by the imposition of a trustee-like duty to take care of the property. In *Clarke* v. *Ramuz*[67] Lord Coleridge C.J. said:

> "It appears to be well established in equity that, in the case of a contract for the sale and purchase of land, although the legal property does not pass until the execution of the conveyance, during the interval prior to completion the vendor in possession is a trustee for the purchaser, and as such has duties to perform towards him, not exactly the same as in the case of other trustees, but certain duties, one of which is to use reasonable care to preserve the property in a reasonable state of preservation, and, so far as may be, as it was when the contract was made."

The vendor must neither carelessly allow the property to be damaged nor intentionally damage it himself. In *Phillips* v. *Lamdin*[68] the vendor was held liable to the purchaser in damages when he removed an ornate door and replaced it with a plain white wood door after contract. Again in *Ware* v. *Verderber*[69] a purchaser arrived at his new house to find packing materials all over the floor, the phone torn from the wall, doors hanging off their hinges and a spiral staircase damaged. He was able to recover damages on the ground *inter alia*, that the vendor had failed to exercise reasonable care to keep the property in the state it was in when the contract was made. The vendor is not liable for what may reasonably be regarded as fair wear and tear during the interval between contract and

---

[64] *Musselwhite* v. *C.H. Musselwhite and Son Ltd.* [1962] Ch. 964; *Hillingdon Estates Co.* v. *Stonefield Estates Ltd.* [1952] Ch. 627.

[65] P.H. Pettit (1960) 24 Conv. 47.

[66] *Shaw* v. *Foster* (1872) L.R. 5 H.L. 321.

[67] [1891] 2 Q.B. 456 at p. 459.

[68] [1949] 2 K.B. 33.

[69] (1978) 247 E.G. 1081.

completion. The case of *Sinclair-Hill* v. *Sothcott*[70] shows that the vendor's duty is not confined to preserving the physical state of the premises. The purchaser, a property developer, agreed to buy land from the vendor. The vendor had an application for planning permission already before the local planning authority. This made the land more valuable to the purchaser because planning permission for his development could be granted more quickly than if he had to submit a fresh application. Consequently there would be less delay in completing the development and the profit margin would be higher. After contract, and without consulting the purchaser, the vendor withdrew the application. The purchaser's argument that the vendor had broken his trustee-like duty of care was upheld by the court. The vendor had caused the value of the land to fall and the purchaser was entitled to be compensated.

The vendor's duty continues as long as he retains the right to possession of the property. He cannot relieve himself of the obligation to take reasonable care of the property merely by moving out. Thus in *Lucie-Smith* v. *Gorman*[71] a vendor vacated the house he had contracted to sell in the middle of winter. He failed to turn off the mains water supply. Owing to the severe cold weather a water pipe burst causing damage to the property. The purchaser, who had not been given possession, was able to recover damages from the vendor. Only if the purchaser is allowed into occupation of the property pending completion will the vendor be relieved of his obligation to look after the property.[72]

The vendor is not entitled to an indemnity from the purchaser in respect of expenditure he incurs in fulfilling his duty to preserve the property.[73] The expense is regarded as an outgoing and as long as the vendor is entitled to the rents and profits he must meet the cost himself.

If the contract is not specifically enforceable for some reason the vendor is not under any duty towards the purchaser to preserve the property.[74] Similarly, if the transaction eventually falls through the purchaser will not be entitled to any relief from the vendor if after contract the vendor had allowed the property to deteriorate.[75]

The National and Law Society Conditions of Sale do not alter the common law position outlined above.

(3) The Purchaser's Position Pending Completion

INCREASES IN THE VALUE OF THE LAND

Under an open contract if the value of the land increases between contract and completion the vendor is not allowed to increase the purchase price to take this into account. The purchaser is the owner of the land in Equity and any gains accruing to the land during that period belong to him.[76]

---

[70] (1973) 26 P. & C.R. 490.
[71] [1981] C.L.Y. 2866.
[72] See *post*, p. 250.
[73] *Re Watford Corporation's and A.S. Ware's Contract* [1943] Ch. 82.
[74] *Howard* v. *Miller* [1915] A.C. 318.
[75] *Plews* v. *Samuel* [1904] 1 Ch. 464.
[76] *Harford* v. *Purrier* (1816) 1 Madd. 532.

Thus, if the purchaser buys the reversion to a life interest and the tenant for life dies before completion takes place it is the purchaser who reaps the benefit.[77] Again, if the property is rezoned for planning purposes between contract and completion and consequently becomes more valuable it is the purchaser who stands to gain not the vendor. Furthermore, in *Monro* v. *Taylor*[78] it was held that a vendor who spent money on improving the property, after he had agreed to sell it, could not look to the purchaser for a contribution towards the cost. The purchaser is not entitled to any financial benefit received by the vendor if it does not relate to the property which forms the subject matter of the contract. Thus in *Re Lyne-Stephens and Scott-Miller's Contract*[79] where land was sold with vacant possession on completion, the vendor was allowed to retain a sum of money, paid by the outgoing tenant in respect of dilapidations. The money received by the vendor related to the lease, in which the purchaser had no interest. Had the contract been for the sale of the property, subject to and with the benefit of, the lease the purchaser may have recovered some or all the money from the vendor. If the financial accretion can fairly be said to relate to the property in the contract it seems that the court will only regard the vendor as a trustee of the money for the purchaser, if on construing the contract the conclusion is reached that the sale included the right to receive the money.[80]

THE RISK OF LOSS IS ON THE PURCHASER

The risk of any loss or damage to the property occurring between contract and completion, falls on the purchaser unless it is occasioned by a breach of the vendor's duty to take reasonable care to preserve the property. If the property is consumed by fire,[81] damaged by an earthquake[82] or blown up by a terrorist's bomb[83] it is the purchaser who must suffer the loss. In *Robertson* v. *Skelton*[84] the vendor's premises collapsed damaging neighbouring property. The purchaser had to indemnify the vendor in respect not only of the cost of repairing the property but also in respect of a neighbour's successful claim against the vendor for damages.

It is a moot point whether the doctrine of frustration can ever apply to a contract for the sale of land.[85] Recently in *National Carriers Ltd.* v. *Panalpina (Northern) Ltd.*[86] the majority of the House of Lords held that it could apply to a lease or an agreement for a lease. Previously it was argued that the doctrine was inapplicable to leases for two reasons. First, the object of the granting of a lease is to vest an estate in the lessee and

---

[77] *White* v. *Nutts* (1702) 1 P. Wms 61; *Ex p. Manning* (1727) 2 P.Wms 410.
[78] (1848) 8 Hare. 51.
[79] [1920] 1 Ch. 472.
[80] *Re Hamilton-Snowball's Conveyance* [1959] Ch. 308.
[81] *Paine* v. *Meller* (1801) 6 Ves. 349.
[82] *Cass* v. *Rudele* (1693) 2 Vern. 280.
[83] *Redmond* v. *Dainton* [1920] 1 K.B. 256.
[84] (1849) 12 Beav. 260.
[85] *Hillingdon Estates Co.* v. *Stonefield Estates Ltd.* [1952] Ch. 627; *Cricklewood Property & Investment Trust Ltd.* v. *Leighton's Investment Trust Ltd.* [1945] A.C. 221; *Amalgamated Investment & Property Co. Ltd.* v. *John Walker and Sons* [1977] 1 W.L.R. 164.
[86] [1981] A.C. 675.

once this has been done the lessor has no further duty to perform ("the estate theory"). Secondly, on the granting of a lease the risk passes to the purchaser ("the risk theory"). The House of Lords dismissed both of these arguments and said there was nothing in the nature of a lease to prevent the doctrine applying. Dicta in the case suggest that although the doctrine is not applicable to a sale of land which has been completed by conveyance it is applicable whilst the contract for sale remains executory. But it must be said that although the House of Lords stated it was not true to say that the doctrine of frustration could never apply to a contract for the sale of land they felt it would hardly ever do so. It seems that their Lordships were endorsing the view of Viscount Simon L.C. that frustration may only occur where there was: "some vast convulsion of nature which swallowed up the property altogether, or buried it in the depths of the sea."[87]

THE PURCHASER SHOULD INSURE FROM CONTRACT

Subject to what has been said above under an open contract the purchaser is obliged to pay the full purchase price to the vendor even if the property is accidentally destroyed between contract and completion.[88] If this occurs the vendor (who will usually continue to insure the property after contract, although he is under no duty to do so) may claim the balance of the purchase price from his insurance company provided he has not been paid by the purchaser.[89] Once the insurance company pays out the policy moneys, the vendor's right to be paid the balance of the purchase price is transferred to the insurance company.[90] The insurance company will recover whatever it paid out to the vendor from the purchaser. The question then arises can the purchaser recoup his loss from anybody? At common law he has no claim to the money received by the vendor from the insurance company.[91] Neither can he go against the vendor's insurance company because he is not a party to that contract (the policy).[92] The loss is with the purchaser— unless he has insured the property himself from the date the contract was made.

Two statutory provisions may improve the position of the uninsured purchaser. Section 83 of the Fires Prevention (Metropolis) Act 1774[93] provides that, following destruction of a building by fire, the insurance company (presuming the vendor has insured) must apply the policy moneys towards reinstating the building at the request of any "person interested" in the property. In *Rayner* v. *Preston*, James L.J. stated *obiter*[94] that: "a purchaser having an equitable interest under a contract of sale is a person having an interest . . . within the meaning of the Act."

---

[87] *Cricklewood Property & Investment Trust Ltd.* v. *Leighton's Investment Trust Ltd.* [1945] A.C. 221 at p. 231.

[88] *Sutherland* v. *Pratt* (1843) 11 M. & W. 296.

[89] *Collingridge* v. *Royal Exchange Assurance Corporation* (1877) 3 Q.B.D. 173.

[90] *Castellain* v. *Preston.* (1883) 11 Q.B.D. 380.

[91] *Rayner* v. *Preston* (1881) 18 Ch.D. 1.

[92] *Beswick* v. *Beswick* [1968] A.C. 58; *Poole* v. *Adams* (1864) 10 L.T. 287.

[93] The section applies to all of England and Wales; *Re Barker, ex p. Gorely* (1864) 4 De.G.J. & S. 477.

[94] (1881) 18 Ch. D. 1 at p. 15.

Despite this some doubt exists whether a purchaser could require his vendor's insurers to use the insurance moneys to reinstate the building. The provision is little used in practice.

The second provision which might afford an uninsured purchaser some relief is section 47 of the Law of Property Act 1925. The section provides: "Where after the date of any contract for sale or exchange of property, money becomes payable under any policy of insurance maintained by the vendor . . . the money shall . . . be held or receivable by the vendor on behalf of the purchaser . . . ."

The section has effect subject to: (a) a term excluding it in the contract between the vendor and the purchaser; (b) obtaining the consent of the vendor's insurance company (many insurance policies covering fire damage contain clauses giving such consent)[95]; (c) the payment by the purchaser of a proportionate part of the premium from the date of the contract.

A purchaser would be ill-advised to rely on section 47. Under the section he is entitled only to policy moneys that "become payable" to the vendor. No money becomes payable if the policy has lapsed or if it is voidable at the option of the insurance company (if, for instance, the vendor is guilty of misrepresentation or non-disclosure in the proposal form). Furthermore, the amount of money payable may be less than the full value of the property or the cost of its reinstatement. Again the section is little used in practice.

Both the National and Law Society Conditions of Sale contain provisions relating to insurance. National Condition 21 provides for the vendor's assistance in bringing section 47 into operation. By Condition 21(3) the purchaser can require the vendor to consent to, or obtain, an endorsement of the purchaser's interest in the property on his insurance policy, thereby obtaining the insurance company's consent for the purposes of section 47. The purchaser, at the vendor's request, must pay a proportionate part of the premium on completion. The purchaser can inspect the vendor's insurance policy at any time to see if the cover provided is adequate; National Condition 21(2). Note that the Condition does not cure the faults of section 47 outlined above. National Condition 21(1) provides that the vendor is under no duty to maintain an insurance policy after contract unless he owes an obligation to a third party to keep the policy on foot. If the vendor has a mortgage he will almost certainly be under such an obligation to his mortgagor. Similarly, if the property is leasehold the vendor will owe an obligation to insure towards his landlord. (If the lease contains a covenant to insure and the vendor has broken it the purchaser may be able to rescind the contract on the ground that the vendor's title is defective.) However, Condition 21(1) further provides that the vendor is; "not bound to give notice to the purchaser of any premium being or becoming due." In other words the vendor can allow the insurance on the property to lapse without telling the purchaser. If the vendor's policy lapses the applicability of section 47 becomes an academic question.

---

[95] Presumably by giving its consent the insurance company would forgo its right to recover the balance of the purchase price from the purchaser.

Law Society Condition 11(3) excludes section 47 altogether. Consequently the purchaser should arrange his own insurance to cover damage to the property. By Condition 11(4) the vendor is only under a duty to maintain insurance where the property is leasehold and he has an obligation to insure. Law Society Condition 11(1) provides: "If the property is destroyed or damaged prior to actual completion and the proceeds of any insurance policy effected by or for the purchaser are reduced by reason of the existence of any policy effected by or for the vendor, the purchase price shall be abated by the amount of such reduction." 11(1) attempts to resolve the problem which sometimes arises when both the vendor and the purchaser have insurance policies covering damage to the property. If the purchaser's insurance company only pay a fraction of the value of the property in the event of it being damaged the purchaser is allowed to pay a reduced sum in satisfaction of the purchase price. The vendor's insurance company will make up the difference. Law Society Condition 11(1) does not apply if the proceeds of the vendor's policy are applied towards reinstating the property pursuant to any statutory or contractual obligation, (Law Society Condition 11(2)). Under Law Society Condition 18(4)(c) a purchaser who is let into occupation pending completion must "insure the property in a sum not less than the purchase price against all risks in respect of which premises of the like nature are normally insured."

It is standard practice in conveyancing transactions to make sure that the purchaser insures the property from the date of the contract. If the purchaser is buying with the aid of a mortgage, insurance can be effected by arrangement with the building society (or other lender). They will insure the premises with their nominated insurance company and deduct the premium from the mortgage advance. The purchaser's solicitor should always discuss the matter of insurance with his client and make him fully aware of his position.

(4) Letting the Purchaser into Occupation Pending Completion

It sometimes happens that a purchaser wishes to go into occupation of the premises before actual completion. The vendor, who retains the right to possession of the property, may agree to this, but there are two dangers in his doing so. First, allowing the purchaser into occupation may encourage him to delay actual completion. Secondly, if the sale goes off the vendor may find it difficult to regain possession of the property because of legislation relating to security of tenure.

The terms on which a purchaser may go into occupation pending completion is a matter for agreement between the parties.[96] The open contract rules (described below) are unsatisfactory from the point of view of the vendor and consideration should be given to varying them in all cases. Both sets of standard conditions contain detailed terms dealing with the parties rights and obligations in such a case.

---

[96] *Cantor Art Services Ltd.* v. *Kenneth Bieber Photography Ltd.* [1969] 1 W.L.R. 1226.

STATUS OF THE PURCHASER

Under an open contract the purchaser taking possession of a property pending completion does so as a tenant at will. A tenant at will may be able to claim security of tenure under the Rent Act 1977[97] or, if the property is an agricultural holding, the Agricultural Holdings Act 1948. A tenant at will of business premises is outside the protection afforded by Part II of the Landlord and Tenant Act 1954.[98] If the tenant is able to claim security of tenure the vendor may experience difficulty in regaining possession.

National Condition 8(1)(i) states that the purchaser shall be the licensee and not the tenant of the vendor. Law Society Condition 18(2) is of similar effect, adding that the licence may not be transferred and that only members of the purchaser's immediate family may be authorised to occupy the property. Both Conditions prevent the purchaser from acquiring security of tenure because the statutory provisions do not apply to licensees.[99]

THE PURCHASER MUST PAY INTEREST

Taking possession under an open contract amounts to a notional completion. From the date of entry the purchaser becomes entitled to any income produced by the property. However, he must pay interest on the balance of the purchase price (if any) as soon as he goes into occupation of the property.[1] Sir William Grant M.R. explained why in *Fludyer* v. *Cocker*[2]: "The act of taking possession is an implied agreement to pay interest; for so absurd an agreement, as that the purchaser is to receive the rents and profits, to which he has no legal title, and the vendor is not to have interest, as he has no legal title to the money, can never be implied." The purchaser is liable to pay interest on the balance of the purchase price until actual completion even where it is the vendor who causes a delay in completion.[3] Furthermore, the fact that the purchaser receives no actual benefit from taking possession does not relieve him of his duty to pay interest.[3]

Both sets of standard conditions follow the open contract rule and require the purchaser to pay interest pending completion of the transaction. National Condition 8(1)(ii) obliges the purchaser to pay interest on "the remainder of the purchase money." Law Society Condition 18(4)(*a*) is more onerous in that interest is calculated on "the amount of the purchase money (less any deposit paid)." For example, the purchaser who pays an instalment of the purchase price on being given possession pending completion (having already paid a deposit on exchange of contracts) will suffer a heavier charge to interest under the Law Society

---

[97] *Francis Jackson Developments Ltd.* v. *Stemp* [1943] 2 All E.R. 601; *Dunthorne and Shore* v. *Wiggins* [1943] 2 All E.R. 678; *Chamberlain* v. *Farr* [1942] 2 All E.R. 567.

[98] *Hagee (London) Ltd.* v. *A.B. Erikson and Larsen* [1976] Q.B. 209.

[99] *Heslop* v. *Burns* [1974] 1 W.L.R. 1241.

[1] *Rhys* v. *Dare Valley Railway Co.* (1873) L.R. 19 Eq. 93.

[2] (1806) 12 Ves. 25 at p. 27.

[3] *Ballard* v. *Shutt* (1880) 15 Ch.D. 122.

Conditions than he would have under a sale governed by the National Conditions because he is not credited with the instalment. The purchaser's solicitor may consider an amendment to Law Society Condition 18(4)(a) desirable so that interest is charged only on the outstanding balance of the purchase price.

Law Society Condition 18(6) states that if the purchaser remains in occupation after the contractual completion date he does so "on the other terms of this condition and the further term that the vendor's rights under Condition 22 shall not thereby be affected." Condition 22[4] contains provisions relating to compensation for late completion. When coupled with Condition 18 it means that a purchaser in occupation who is responsible for a delay in completion must make two payments; one of interest under Condition 18(4)(a) and another of interest or compensation under Condition 22. This casts a heavy burden on the purchaser. His solicitor may wish to provide by special condition that no compensation or interest is payable under Condition 22 whilst the purchaser is paying interest under Condition 18. No "double charge" arises under the National Conditions because National Condition 7[5] (provisions relating to interest for delayed completion) provides: "That the vendor shall in no case be or become entitled in respect of the same period of time both to be paid interest and to enjoy income of the property, or to be paid interest more than once on the same sum of money."

The rate of interest is a matter for agreement between the parties. In the absence of an express term in the contract interest will be charged at the general "equitable rate." Following the decision in the case of *Bartlett* v. *Barclays Bank Trust Co. Ltd.*[6] this would be the rate from time to time in force relating to the court's short term investment account.[7] Both the National and Law Society Conditions contain detailed provisions relating to the rate of interest applicable to the contract.[8]

OUTGOINGS AND REPAIRS

At common law a purchaser becomes responsible for the outgoings of the property from the date he takes possession. He is liable not only for general rates, water rates and so on but also any particular outgoings which fall due during the period of his possession, for instance the expense of abating a public nuisance. National Condition 8(1)(iv) and Law Society Condition 18(4)(a) confirm the common law rule by requiring the purchaser to pay and indemnify the vendor against all outgoings.

The vendor's trustee-like duty to take reasonable care to preserve the property before completion ceases if he gives up possession of the property to the purchaser after contract. The standard conditions follow the common law rule. National Condition 8(1)(iii) and Law Society Condition 18(5)(c) require the purchaser to keep the property in as good repair and condition as it was in when he went into occupation.

---

[4] See *post*, pp. 415 et seq.
[5] See *post*, Chap. 8.
[6] [1980] Ch. 515.
[7] Administration of Justice Act 1965, s.6(1).
[8] See *ante*, p. 154.

WAIVER OF THE VENDOR'S TITLE

Under an open contract a purchaser may impliedly waive any objections he has to the vendor's title if he takes possession of the property pending completion.[9] Although merely taking possession may not be sufficient by itself to constitute acceptance of the vendor's title,[10] if the purchaser performs positive acts of ownership such as building on the land he may be deemed to have accepted the vendor's title.[11] The acceptance will only extend to irremovable defects in title of which the purchaser knew when taking up possession.[12]

Acceptance of the vendor's title does not occur where the purchaser goes into occupation under a contractual term, even if that term does not expressly state that the purchaser is taking possession subject to satisfactory replies being given to his requisitions on title.[13] National Condition 8(3) and Law Society Condition 18(3) both expressly state that the purchaser shall not be deemed to have accepted the vendor's title by taking occupation of the premises pending completion.

ALTERATIONS MADE BY THE PURCHASER

Under an open contract the purchaser is free to make such alterations in the physical condition and use of the property as he wishes, subject only to the limitations imposed by the general law, notably the Planning Acts. There are two potential dangers for the vendor in this context. First, if the sale goes off after the purchaser has altered the condition of the premises the vendor may have to carry out works to restore the property to a habitable condition before he is able to put the property back on the market. Although he is able to recover his expense from the purchaser[14] the resultant delay may cause financial hardship if the vendor is buying a new property. Secondly, the purchaser may carry out some "development" on the property within the Town and Country Planning Act 1971. Section 22(1) of that Act defines development as: "the carrying out of building, engineering, mining or other operations in, on, over or under land, or the making of any material change in the use of any building or other land." If he does not obtain any requisite planning permission the vendor may later be put to expense in remedying the breach of planning control. National Condition 8(1)(v) expressly states that the purchaser shall: "not carry out any development." No sanction for breach of this Condition is prescribed but presumably the vendor could exercise his right to serve a seven day notice terminating the licence given by National Condition 8(2). The Condition could usefully be amended to give the vendor an indemnity in respect of expense he may incur in remedying a breach of planning control. Law Society Condition 18 has no provision equivalent to National Condition 8(1)(v).

---

[9] *Bown* v. *Stenson* (1857) 24 Beav. 631.
[10] *Simpson* v. *Sadd* (1854) 4 De G.M. & G. 665.
[11] *Haydon* v. *Bell* (1838) 1 Beav. 337.
[12] *Re Gloag and Miller's Contract* (1883) 23 Ch.D. 320; *Bousfield* v. *Hodges* (1863) 33 Beav. 90.
[13] *Stevens* v. *Guppy* (1828) 3 Russ. 171.
[14] *Crisp* v. *Fox* (1967) 201 E.G. 769.

The purchaser who makes improvements to the property during his period of possession pending completion cannot recover the cost from the vendor if the sale falls through even if it is due to the vendor's breach of contract. Items which are removable without damaging the property may be taken by the purchaser when he leaves. In *Lloyd* v. *Stanbury*[15] the purchaser took possession pending completion. He installed a power circuit, a telephone and a television aerial. He also brought onto the site a caravan for the vendor to live in temporarily. It was held that he could not recover the cost of installing the power circuit, the telephone, or the television aerial because it was not contemplated by the parties that these improvements would be made. The caravan was brought onto the site pursuant to an agreement and so the purchaser could recover the expenses he incurred in providing it for the use of the vendor. The purchaser was allowed to remove only the television aerial when he left. Neither set of standard conditions attempts to define the parties rights in the event of improvements being made to the property by the purchaser before the sale goes off.

Finally it should be remembered that the purchaser under both Conditions is required to deliver up the premises in as good repair as when he entered. Any unfinished alterations to the premises may result in a breach of this term of the licence.

ADVERSE POSSESSION?

If a purchaser is let into occupation pending completion it is conceivable that he could acquire title to the vendor's land by adverse possession. If the purchaser's licence (or tenancy at will under an open contract) to occupy the property is terminated *and* the contract comes to an end by repudiation (by either party) time will begin to run against the vendor for the purposes of section 15 of the Limitation Act 1980. After 12 years the vendor's title will be extinguished.[16] However, it has recently been held in *Hyde* v. *Pearce*[17] that if the purchaser's licence to go into occupation is terminated but the contract remains on foot the purchaser cannot acquire a title by virtue of his occupation; it is not adverse possession as the contract gives him an equitable interest in the property.

TERMINATING THE PURCHASER'S OCCUPATION

If the purchaser takes occupation under an open contract as a tenant at will either party may terminate the tenancy at any time by giving notice. The purchaser may, however, be entitled to security of tenure under the Rent Acts in which case the vendor would have to seek a court order.[18]

Under National Condition 8(2) the vendor may terminate the purchaser's licence by giving seven working days (or longer) notice to the purchaser or his solicitor. Similarly, upon the discharge or rescission of the contract the purchaser's licence will terminate forthwith. The purchaser is

---

[15] [1971] 1 W.L.R. 535.
[16] *Bridges* v. *Mees* [1957] Ch. 475.
[17] [1982] 1 W.L.R. 560.
[18] See *ante*, p. 251; note also the Protection From Eviction Act 1977.

then obliged to give up the property in as good condition as it was in at the time he took possession National Condition 8(2) contains no provision allowing the purchaser to give notice to terminate the licence. Under Law Society Condition 18(5)(c) either party may terminate the licence by giving five days notice to the other. The purchaser's licence to occupy the property will also come to an end on the contractual completion date or on termination of the contract (18(5)(a) and (b)). Thereupon the purchaser is obliged to leave the property in as good repair as when he took possession.

If the purchaser's licence (or tenancy at will) is terminated by the vendor his obligations to pay interest, outgoings and so on come to an and.

SITUATIONS IN WHICH THE STANDARD CONDITIONS DO NOT APPLY

National Condition 8 and Law Society Condition 18 do not apply in the following situations:

(i) Sales to tenants already in occupation of the premises (National Condition 8(1)). Law Society Condition 18(1)(a) "where the purchaser is already lawfully in possession of any part of the property."

(ii) Where the purchaser is allowed access to the property for the purpose of carrying out works or installations; National Condition 8(4). The Law Society Condition 18(1)(b) is more limited in scope. It only exempts purchasers of dwellinghouses who are given authority to occupy "for the purpose of effecting works of decoration, repair or improvement agreed by the vendor," from the obligations imposed by Condition 18.

7: Contract to Conveyance

In this chapter three matters will be considered:

(1) The proving, examining and verifying of the title to the property to be sold;

(2) The raising of requisitions (questions) on the title shown; and

(3) The drafting of the deed appropriate to pass the title in the property to the purchaser.

I. TITLE

Under an open contract for the sale of land the vendor is under a duty to show good title.[1] The National and Law Society Conditions do not alter the open contract rule. Once it transpires that the vendor has no title, the purchaser can rescind the contract without affording the vendor the opportunity to make good his title on the date set for completion.[2]

Whether or not the vendor has fulfilled his obligation to make good title depends very much on what he has contracted to give. Unless the contract states otherwise in the case of unregistered land there is a presumption that the vendor is selling and is entitled to the fee simple absolute in possession free from incumbrances.[3] In the case of registered land the presumption is that the vendor is selling title absolute.[4]

A. DEDUCING TITLE—UNREGISTERED LAND

(1) FREEHOLD LAND

Root of Title

THE FIFTEEN YEAR RULE

Broadly speaking a vendor deduces good title by giving an historical account of the ownership of the property being sold. The account will end with the document vesting the property in the vendor.[5] The period of time

---

[1] *Lysaght* v. *Edwards* (1876) 2 Ch.D. 499 at p. 507.

[2] *Pips (Leisure Productions) Ltd.* v. *Walton* (1980) 260 E.G. 601.

[3] *Timmins* v. *Moreland Street Property Co. Ltd.* [1958] Ch. 110.

[4] *Re Brine and Davies' Contract* [1935] Ch. 388.

[5] In the case of a sub-purchaser the final document may be the contract to sell to his vendor.

covered by the vendor's account is a matter for agreement between the parties. The earlier this account commences the less risk there will be of the title later proving to be defective. This risk, however, can never be fully eliminated because the title to land is inherently uncertain.[6] In other words to make title certain "the proof would have to start with the grant to Adam and Eve, but even this was save and except the Garden of Eden and one is not even sure whether they took as joint tenants or tenants in common."[7]

If the parties fail to agree the period of title to be shown by the vendor the open contract rule will apply. The period prescribed under an open contract was at one time 60 years.[8] This has been gradually reduced in line with conveyancing practice; first to 40 years by section 1 of the Vendor and Purchaser Act 1874; then to 30 years by section 44(1) of the Law of Property Act 1925; and finally by section 23 of the Law of Property Act 1969 to 15 years. The section provides:

"Section 44(1) of the Law of Property Act 1925 (under which the period of commencement of title which may be required under a contract expressing no contrary intention is thirty years except in certain cases) shall have effect, in its application to contracts made [after January 1, 1970] as if it specified fifteen years instead of thirty years as the period of commencement of title which may be so required."

A purchaser of property under an open contract may, therefore, require the vendor to trace the ownership of the property back to a good root of title[9] which is at least 15 years old. If the vendor wishes to give his purchaser a title less than 15 years old he must stipulate for this in the contract. Furthermore, in cases where the vendor restricts the length of title a purchaser is entitled to presume that the document forming the root evidences a transaction where the title was fully investigated; that is one made for valuable consideration, a conveyance on sale or mortgage for instance.[10] Good conveyancing practice dictates that a vendor should always fully disclose the nature of the root of title where the document forming the same is not 15 years old. If the vendor does not, a court will not force the purchaser to accept the vendor's title unless the root was made for valuable consideration. In *Re Marsh and Earl Granville*[11] a vendor offered a short title describing the root document as a "conveyance." In fact it was a voluntary conveyance. The court held that the description of the root was not adequate to warn a purchase that the title might not have been looked at critically at that time. It was further held that the purchaser could not be forced to complete unless the vendor showed title for the full statutory period.

---

[6] *St. Marylebone Property Co. Ltd.* v. *Fairweather* [1962] 1 Q.B.498 at 513; *Wyld* v. *Silver* [1963] Ch. 243.

[7] Farrand, *Contract and Conveyance* (4th ed.) p. 85.

[8] *Barnwell* v. *Harris* (1809) 1 Taunt. 430

[9] See *post*, p. 260.

[10] *Re Marsh and Earl Granville* (1883) 24 Ch.D. 11.

[11] *Ibid.*

A vendor must not hide a defect in his title by requiring a purchaser to accept less than 15 years title. If a vendor misleads a purchaser by commencing title with a document (less than 15 years old) which is subsequent to an earlier document revealing a flaw in the title he will not be able to enforce the contract if the purchaser later discovers the defect by some other means.

In sales governed by the National or Law Society Conditions of Sale the parties rights in this respect are the same as under an open contract. However, both forms contain special conditions on the back (National Special Condition "B," Law Society Special Condition "E") which allow the vendor to state the date and nature of the document which is to form the root of title. These special conditions are invariably filled in; either the purchaser gets 15 years or contracts for less than this period.

The 15 year rule does not apply on a sale of any of the following:

(a) Leasehold estates; these are discussed at page 283.
(b) Advowsons; an advowson is an incorporeal right of presenting a clergyman to a living. Title must be shown by the Vendor for 100 years.
(c) Reversionary interests; a purchaser is entitled to have the instrument creating the interest whatever the date of its creation and then title for a period of 15 years back from the date of the purchase.

SHOULD A PURCHASER ACCEPT SHORT TITLE?

Before advising a purchaser to accept a vendor's offer of a title less than 15 years old consideration should be given to the following points.

(1) The shorter the period for which the vendor is required to deduce title, the less convincing the evidence of his ownership of the property will be. Consequently, the risk of the purchaser's title to the property being upset by a person with a better title is increased. In practice a purchaser's solicitor will usually accept less than 15 years title if within the period of title offered there has been a conveyance on sale on the occasion of which the title will have been fully investigated.

(2) Section 44(8) of the Law of Property Act 1925 provides:

"A purchaser shall not be deemed to be or ever to have been affected with notice of any matter or thing of which, if he had investigated the title or made enquiries in regard to matters prior to the period of commencement of title fixed by this Act, or by any other statute, or by any rule of law, he might have had notice, unless he actually makes such investigation or enquiries."

For instance a purchaser will not have constructive knowledge of any equitable interest prior to the statutory period of title (15 years and then back to a good root) which he could only have discovered by investigating the earlier title. He will be deemed to have notice of such an equitable interest if he actually investigates the earlier title or if it is registered as a land charge[12] or if it could have been discovered on an inspection of the

---

[12] Law of Property Act 1925, s.198

property being made and it is not an interest capable of registration as a land charge.[13] As most equitable interests are registrable as land charges the protection afforded by section 44(8) is limited mainly to surviving pre–1926 equitable interests or equitable interests arising under constructive trusts, for instance where there is a sale of trust property to a trustee.

A purchaser who accepts a short title will be bound by equitable interests which he would have discovered had he contracted for the full statutory period of title. Accepting less than 15 years title will not extend the protection afforded by section 44(8). As North J. explained in *Re Cox and Neve's Contract*[14] accepting short title "cannot relieve him [the purchaser] from all knowledge of the prior title, or, it would come to this—that if a man was content to purchase property on the condition that he should not inquire into the title, he would acquire a title free from any existing restrictions and would not have constructive notice of any incumbrance."

(3) The system of registering land charges against the name of the legal estate owner means that it is in a purchaser's interest to obtain as many of the post 1925 legal estate owners' names as possible.[15] He can then check that he has a clear land charges search certificate for each of them and so ensure that there is no undisclosed land charge affecting the title. By accepting a short title the purchaser will receive less names than would otherwise have been the case. The possibility of him taking the property subject to the rights of an undisclosed chargee is, therefore, increased.

(4) It has been said that one of the problems with the land charges system is that of "names behind the root of title."[16] Land charges may have been registered against owners of the legal estate right back to January 1, 1926. The purchaser, whose vendor's root of title is dated after 1925 may therefore be unable to discover the names of all the relevant estate owners and so ensure that he knows of all registered land charges affecting he vendor's property. However, whether he knows of a charge or not, he takes the property subject to any third party interest protected by registration. The purchaser is not protected by section 44(8) because section 198 prevails. A purchaser who discovers an undisclosed land charge before completion may rescind the contract.[17–18] His position on discovering a land charge after completion is less satisfactory. The only remedy available to him is a claim for compensation if he suffers loss by reason of the charge, under section 25 of the Law of Property Act 1969. Compensation is payable under the section to the purchaser by the Chief Land Registrar (that is the state) provided the three conditions set out below are satisfied:

(i) completion takes place on or after January 1, 1970;

(ii) at the time of completion the purchaser had no actual knowledge (as opposed to "deemed" knowledge under section 198 of the Law of Property Act 1925) of the registered land charge; and

---

[13] *Hunt* v. *Luck* [1902] 1 Ch. 428.
[14] [1891] 2 Ch. 109 at 117.
[15] See *ante*, p. 31.
[16] See *ante*, p. 30.
[17–18] Law of Property Act 1969, s.24.

(iii) the charge was registered against the name of an owner of an estate in the land who did not appear on the title which the purchaser was entitled to under an open contract, that is 15 years and then back to a good root of title.

The danger to a purchaser lies in the fact that if he accepts less than 15 years title condition (iii) above will not be satisfied. If he later discovers an undisclosed land charge, registered against an estate owner whose name he would have obtained had he called upon the vendor to deduce title for the full statutory period, he will not be able to claim compensation out of public funds. He will, of course, remain bound by the charge. Compensation is payable to a purchaser despite his acceptance of a short title if the land charge would not have been revealed even on an investigation of title back to a good root at least 15 years old.

ESSENTIALS OF A GOOD ROOT OF TITLE

A "root of title" is the document with which the vendor begins his historical account showing the devolution of the ownership of the property. As we have seen under an open contract the root of title must be at least 15 years old. However, the root must also be a "good root of title." In practice, therefore, the vendor will usually be required to show more than 15 years title. North J. explained the position in *Re Cox and Neve's Contract*[19]; "and when I say a (fifteen)[20] years' title, I mean a title deduced for (fifteen) years and for so much longer as it is necessary to go back in order to arrive at a point at which the title can properly commence. A title cannot commence in nubibus at the exact point which is represented by 365 days multiplied by (fifteen). It must commence at or before the (fifteen) years with something which is in itself, or, *which is agreed shall be*, a proper root of title."

The words in italics show that a vendor may stipulate in the contract that the title will commence with some document which does not qualify as a "good root" under an open contract. A purchaser who contracts on this basis cannot later complain that the vendor has not commenced title with a good root. A purchaser's solicitor must use his judgment in deciding whether or not to accept as a root of title a document which does not constitute a "good root." If an undisclosed land charge is discovered after completion and that land charge would have been discovered by the purchaser if he had insisted on having a good root of title, the purchaser will be unable to claim compensation under section 25 of the Law of Property Act 1969. If there has been a recent transaction involving a critical investigation of the title (for example a conveyance on sale accompanied by a mortgage) the solicitor acting for the purchaser will generally accept as a root some document which is not as a matter of law a "good root of title." If so before accepting it the purchaser's solicitor should make his client aware of the situation.

There is no statutory or judicial definition of what amounts to a "good root" under an open contract. The Law Commission, in its Interim Report

---

[19] [1891] 2 Ch. 109 at p. 118.
[20] The period of title to be shown at the time the case was decided was 40 years.

on Root of Title to Freehold Land,[21] considered a statutory definition of a "good root" to be undesirable. They thought it would restrict practitioners in exercising their judgment in accepting on behalf of their client's a document which was not strictly a "good root" but which was acceptable in the circumstances. To define a "good root" would result in a valuable degree of flexibility (necessary in modern conveyancing) being lost. This area of conveyancing is one in which "the legal adviser must always be prepared to exercise his judgment on behalf of his client rather than try to apply any mechanical set of rules for his own protection."[22]

The definition of what amounts to a "good root" most often referred to by conveyancers is that given in *Williams on Vendor and Purchaser*[23]; "an instrument of disposition dealing with or proving on the face of it (without the aid of extrinsic evidence) the ownership of the whole legal and equitable estate in the property sold, containing a description by which the property can be identified and showing nothing to cast any doubt on the title of the disposing parties."

The first requirement is that the document forming the root must deal with the whole legal and equitable estate. The definition was formulated before the property legislation of 1925 was conceived and does not take into account the overreaching provisions contained therein. After 1925 a purchaser of property is generally only concerned with the legal estate. Equitable interests in the property being sold which are capable of being overreached under the provisions of the Law of Property Act 1925 or the Settled Land Act 1925 need not be dealt with by the document forming the good root.

A lease or an equitable mortgage of a property cannot constitute a "good root" under an open contract to sell the freehold estate. Neither document deals with the whole legal estate which is the subject matter of the sale. Again a conveyance subject to a legal mortgage, dated prior to 1926, cannot form a "good root" at common law. Before 1926 property was mortgaged by conveying the legal estate to the mortgagee. The mortgagor retained only an equitable interest in the property and so such a conveyance would necessarily only transfer the vendor's equitable interest. A conveyance subject to a legal mortgage after 1925 can constitute a good root because the legal estate remains vested in the mortgagor.

The second requirement, that the root of title must contain a description of the property sufficient to identify it, is usually illustrated by the fact that before 1926 a general devise in a will could not form a "good root." A pre–1926 general devise does not describe the property with the required particularity. If a testator leaves all his "freehold land" to his son by will, extrinsic evidence is required to identify that property. In practice this requirement causes little problem. If the vendor's root refers to a plan or other description in an earlier deed the purchaser may require it to be abstracted.

---

[21] Law Comm No 9.
[22] (1975) 28 C.L.P., 125 A.M. Pritchard.
[23] (4th ed.) Vol 1, p. 124.

If the proposed root casts doubt on the title it will not be a "good root." In *Re Duce and Boots Cash Chemists (Southern) Ltd.'s Contract*[24] recitals in an assent set out the details of a will. They showed that the land was in fact settled land. However, the correct conveyancing procedure had not been used in relation to the property. The purchaser could not take the assent as "sufficient evidence" of its own propriety within section 36(7) of the Administration of Estates Act 1925. An assent containing such a recital would cast doubt on the title and could not form a good root. Similarly, a document which relies for its validity and effectiveness on an earlier document's existence may not be a good root under an open contract; for example a conveyance executed under a power of appointment or attorney.[25] Another example of a document casting doubt on the vendor's title would be a conveyance of trust property to a trustee. The conveyance would be liable to be set aside in equity at the instance of the beneficiaries.

EXAMPLES OF GOOD ROOTS

(i) **Conveyances on Sale.** This will be the type of root most often offered by a vendor. As valuable consideration is involved it is likely that, on the occasion of the sale, the title will have been fully investigated. This makes the present vendor's evidence of ownership more convincing. In practice a conveyance on sale is regarded as the "best" type of "good root".

(ii) **Mortgages.** A mortgage made prior to 1926, and effected by a conveyance of a fee simple from the mortgagor to the mortgagee, can form a "good root" because it deals with the whole legal estate. Mortgages by demise and equitable mortgages do not and so are not good roots under open contracts.

After 1925 all legal mortgages are either by demise (or sub-demise) or by way of a legal charge.[26] Strictly speaking they are not "good roots" under an open contract because they do not deal with the whole legal estate. Even if the mortgage contains a recital of the mortgagor's seisin it is still a bad root.[27] Another difficulty with legal mortgages made after 1925 is the fact that they tend not to mention incumbrances, such as restrictive covenants, which affect the land. Acceptance of a title, consisting merely of a 15 year old legal mortgage, may therefore increase the risk of the purchaser being bound by an undisclosed land charge and he may not be able to claim compensation under section 25 of the Law of Property Act 1969.[28]

In practice legal mortgages made after 1925 are readily accepted as good roots if stipulated for in the contract by the vendor. The reason for this is that a mortgagee is often less willing to accept a defective title than an ordinary purchaser and therefore will have ensured that it was flawless.

---

[24] [1937] Ch. 642.

[25] *Re Copelin's Contract* [1937] 4 All E.R. 447; *Re W. & R. Holmes and Cosmopolitan Press Ltd.'s Contract* [1944] Ch. 53.

[26] Law of Property Act 1925, s.85.

[27] But see *Williams on Vendor and Purchaser (4th ed.)* Vol. 1, p. 124 for the contrary view; and *Re Wallis and Grout's Contract* [1906] 2 Ch. 206.

[28] See *ante*, p. 259.

(iii) **Wills.** It has been said that a general devise in a will is not a good root because it does not contain a description sufficient to identify the property.[29] A specific devise in the will of a testator dying before 1898 is a "good root" under an open contract. The devise operated to pass the property to the beneficiary under the will. Between 1898 and 1926 it is arguable that a specific devise in a will was not a "good root." During that period an assent was necessary to make the devise operative and so pass the legal estate to the beneficiary.[30] The will itself dealt only with the equitable estate. Since 1926 it is the assent itself which transfers the legal estate. As a result a specific devise in the will of a testator dying after 1925 is not a "good root."

(iv) **Assents.** A written assent made after 1925 naming the party in whose favour it is made, signed by the deceased's personal representatives and describing the property with sufficient particularity is a "good root" under an open contract. The date of the will and date of death of the testator are irrelevant. Although an assent complies with the three limbs of the definition it must be said that in practice the best roots of title are those for which valuable consideration has been given. It is unlikely that any investigation of the title will have taken place when the assent was made. An assent should not be confused with a grant of probate (or letters of administration). A grant of representation, although a necessary link in the vendor's chain of title, is not a "good root" under an open contract. The grant does not, for example, describe the property as required by Williams' definition.

(v) **Vesting Deeds.** When dealing with settled land a distinction must be made between the trust instrument and the vesting deed. The trust instrument will detail the trusts affecting the land, appoint the trustees of the settlement and set out the various powers conferred in connection with the administration of the settled property.[31] The trust instrument should not appear in the vendor's title because it is the policy of the Settled Land Act 1925 to keep the equities off the title—"behind the curtain" as it is sometimes referred to. The vesting deed is a necessary link in the vendor's title and should be abstracted. The vesting deed will describe the settled land, state the names of the tenant for life, trustees of the settlement (and the persons empowered to appoint new trustees) and state any additional powers conferred by the trust instrument.[32] The vesting deed acts as a conveyance to the tenant for life (or where the same person is settlor and tenant for life as a declaration of the change of capacity)[33] It is therefore capable of constituting a good root of title under an open contract.

(vi) **Voluntary Conveyances.** It is not essential that a conveyance be made for valuable consideration for it to be a good root of title under an

---

[29] See *ante*, p. 261.
[30] *Attenborough* v. *Solomon* [1913] A.C. 76.
[31] See Settled Land Act 1925, ss.4, 6 and 9.
[32] *Ibid.* s.5.
[33] In which case it could be argued the vesting deed does not "dispose" of the legal estate and so is not technically a good root.

open contract. A voluntary conveyance over 15 years old can constitute a "good root."

Pre-Root of Title

SECTION 45 OF THE LAW OF PROPERTY ACT 1925

The section provides by subsection (1):

"A purchaser of any property shall not—

(*a*) require the production, or any abstract or copy, of any deed, will, or other document, dated or made before the time prescribed by law, or stipulated, for the commencement of the title, even though the same creates a power subsequently exercised by an instrument abstracted in the abstract furnished to the purchaser; or

(*b*) require any information, or make any requisition, objection, or inquiry, with respect to any such deed, will, or document, or the title prior to that time, notwithstanding that any such deed, will, or other document, or that prior title, is recited, agreed to be produced, or noticed;"

This provision, which will apply in the absence of any contrary intention shown in the contract,[34] prevents a purchaser[35] from seeing or making any enquiries or requisitions about documents prior to the vendor's root of title. It applies both to open contracts and contracts where the root is expressly stated to be a certain document (that is where the root would not be a good root under an open contract).

Section 45(1) does not deprive a purchaser of the right to require the production, or an abstract or copy of the following:

"(i) any power of attorney under which any abstracted document is executed; or

(ii) any document creating or disposing of an interest, power or obligation which is not shown to have ceased or expired, and subject to which any part of the property is disposed of by an abstracted document; or

(iii) any document creating any limitation or trust by reference to which any part of the property is disposed of by an abstracted document."

Where any abstracted document has been executed by an attorney it is vital that a purchaser should be able to see the instrument creating the power of attorney. He will want to ensure that at the time the abstracted document was made the power was subsisting and also that the attorney

---

[34] Law of Property Act 1925, s.45(10).

[35] *i.e.* "a lesee, mortgagee or other person who for valuable consideration acquires an interest in property." Law of Property Act, s.205(1)(xxi).

was acting within the scope of the power.[36] Section 45(1)(i) allows a purchaser to require the power of attorney to be abstracted whenever it was created.[37] Furthermore by section 125(2)[38] of the Law of Property Act 1925 a purchaser of any interest in, or charge over, land is entitled to have any instrument creating a power of attorney or a copy of it handed over on completion free of expense. If a copy of the power of attorney is to be handed over it must be a photocopy of the original, certified as being a true copy by a solicitor or a stockbroker.[39] The purchaser's right to production under section 45(1)(i) cannot be excluded by the vendor.

Section 45(1)(ii) is expressed in wide terms and would allow a purchaser to call for leases, mortgages and restrictive covenants created prior to the root of title and subject to which the property is sold. Also within the scope of this provision would be a plan in a pre-root conveyance by reference to which the property is to be described.[40]

Neither section 45(1)(ii) or (iii) makes it necessary for the vendor to produce details to the purchaser of any equitable interests under a trust which will be overreached by the sale. Indeed, section 10 of the Law of Property Act 1925 states that where title is shown to the legal estate in the property it is "not necessary or proper to include in the abstract of title an instrument relating only to interests or powers which will be overreached by the conveyance." Both section 45(1)(ii) and (iii) may be ousted by an express term in the contract to the contrary. Neither set of standard conditions exclude the operation of the above provisions. National Condition 12(1) which provides for the vendor to supply copies of a document, containing a plan or covenants, created pre-root but referred to in a post root document would seem to modify section 45. Under the condition the vendor is only required to furnish copies of such documents if they are in his possession (or power) or that of his trustees or mortgagee. The Law Society Conditions contain no such provision.

PRE-ROOT DEFECTS

Section 45(11) provides:

> "Nothing in this section shall be construed as binding a purchaser to complete his purchase in any case where, on a contract made independently of this section, and containing stipulations similar to the provisions of this section . . . specific performance of the contract would not be enforced against him by the court."

In other words because the provisions of section 45 take effect as though they were express terms of the contract the purchaser is not prevented from showing the vendor's title to be defective, if he should actually

---

[36] See *post*, p. 291.
[37] *Re Copelin's Contract* [1937] 4 All E.R. 447.
[38] As amended by Law of Property (Amendment) Act 1926 and Powers of Attorney Act 1971.
[39] Powers of Attorney Act 1971, s.3(1).
[40] *Emmet on Title (18th ed.)* J.T. Farrand, p. 140.

discover a pre-root of title defect. Therefore, if the purchaser is given the earlier title deeds by the vendor, or if he discovers from a third party that the vendor's title is defective, he (the purchaser) can produce evidence of the defect in court. If the defect makes the vendor's title bad, as for instance where it rests upon some forged deed, the court will not grant the vendor specific performance of the contract. He will be left to pursue his remedy at common law; damages for breach of contract and forfeiture of the deposit.[41] The vendor will be able to obtain specific performance where the defect merely makes the vendor's title doubtful.[42] This could occur where the vendor's title depends for instance upon a particular construction being placed upon a deed or will prior to the root of title.[43]

PURCHASER'S NOTICE OF EARLIER TITLE

The rule contained in section 44(8) of the Law of Property Act 1925, that a purchaser has no notice of any matter prior to the root of title unless he actually investigates that prior title has already been dealt with at page 258. It should be remembered that section 198 of the Act of 1925 overrides section 44(8) and therefore a purchaser may be bound by a land charge registered against an estate owner prior to the root of title.[44]

Post-Root of Title: The Chain of Title

Having begun with the estate owner named in the root of title the vendor must trace the legal estate through the intermediate estate owners, ultimately showing how the legal estate became vested in him (or some person whom he can compel to convey). Every document after the root of title which deals with or affects the estate agreed to be sold must be abstracted. These documents form the links in the vendor's "chain of title." The purchaser, by investigating these documents, tests "the chain" to ensure the vendor's title is not defective.

Although a document may form the root of title the vendor's title need not be derived directly from that document. Occasionally the vendor's documentary evidence of title may turn out to be defective. Nevertheless the vendor's title may still be indefeasible because of his adverse possession of the property. In *Re Atkinson and Horsell's Contract*[45] a vendor contracted to sell property the title to which was to commence with a will of 1838 (the testator dying in 1842). In fact the vendor derived title by adverse possession of the property from 1874. The purchaser objected that the vendor had not shown a good title. Under an open contract a purchaser can have forced upon him a title depending upon adverse possession.[46] However, the purchaser in this case argued that where the

---

[41] Subject to the court's discretion under s.49(2) of the Law of Property Act 1925 to order repayment of the deposit.

[42] *Re Scott and Alvarez's Contract* [1895] 2 Ch. 603; *Re National Provincial Bank of England and Marsh* [1895] 1 Ch. 190; *Smith* v. *Robinson* (1879) 13 Ch.D. 148.

[43] *Re Hollis Hospital Trustees and Hague's Contract* [1899] 2 Ch. 540.

[44] See *ante*, p. 30.

[45] [1912] 2 Ch. 1.

[46] *Games* v. *Bonner* (1884) 54 L.J. Ch. 517.

contract specified a document as a root of title the vendor had to show a good title through the deeds and other documents without reliance upon any intervening period of adverse possession. The Court of Appeal held that it is open to a vendor to show a documentary title up to a certain point (the defect in his title) and then show a good possessory title.[47] Buckley L.J. explained the purchaser's position [48]; "though you cannot in a contract of this kind get away from the proposition that the title to be shewn is to be such as stipulated, there is nothing which entitles the purchaser to say that the contract is that he is not to have a possessory title, but is to have some other title, namely, a title commencing with the root of title and shewing title therefrom by devolution."

In a case such as that described above it should not be thought that the title deeds and other documentary evidence dealing with the title prior to the period of adverse possession are irrelevant. The deeds will be relevant to show that at the date when the adverse possession commenced there were no persons under a disability who could defeat the title by possession. In other words, these deeds will enable the vendor to show that his adverse possession has barred all other interests which would otherwise subsist in the land.

Finally, before embarking upon a description of how the vendor fulfills his obligation to show good title to freehold land in practice, it must be remembered that a vendor may be obliged to produce documentary evidence of the devolution of the title, rather than relying on parol evidence of adverse possession if he expressly contracts to prove his title in a specified manner.[49] A vendor who agrees to do this may not later rely on the more lenient open contract rule which allows him to fill the gaps in his title with periods of adverse possession.

How the Vendor Shows Good Title to Freehold Land

In practice a vendor shows good title (or more particularly the title he has contracted to show) to his property by first delivering to the purchaser an abstract or an epitome of title, together with copies of the deeds, and subsequently producing evidence that the statements in the abstract or the copies in the epitome are true.

ABSTRACTS OF TITLE

An abstract of title is a written or typed summary of all the documents and events affecting the vendor's title. Each relevant document or event is set out chronologically in an abbreviated form using a type of legal shorthand.[50] Brief-sized paper is used, the contents of the documents being divided amongst a number of columns. This is supposed to make reference to a particular part of a document easier.

---

[47] Following *Douglas* v. *London & North Western Railway Company* (1857) 3 Kay. & J. 173.

[48] [1912] 2 Ch. 1 at p. 20.

[49] *George Wimpey & Co. Ltd.* v. *Sohn* [1967] Ch. 487.

[50] Drafting abstracts is highly skilled work. This is one of the reasons why epitomes are becoming increasingly popular.

In the first column is found the date of the document or event together with details of any stamp duty and particulars delivered stamp in appropriate cases.[51] A space is left for anybody studying the abstract to make notes in the rest of the first column. The second column contains the description of the documents abstracted (conveyance, assent and so on), the names and addresses of the parties, the testatum (IN WITNESS WHEREOF . . .) covenants, conditions, declarations, acknowledgments for production and so on. Events abstracted, for instance deaths of trustees, also appear here. Recitals are the preserve of the third column whilst the habendum (TO HOLD . . .) occupies the fourth. The final column contains the parcels clause (ALL THAT . . .) and a note of the execution and attestation of documents. The abstract is headed at the top of the first page with the vendor's name and a description of the property to which title is being shown.

The abbreviations used in abstracts are a source of great confusion to the uninitiated.[52] For example "purchaser" becomes "pchsr," trustee becomes "tree" and "receipt whereof the Vendor hereby acknowledges" is shortened to "rect ackned." To add to the confusion the abstract is drafted using the past tense and the passive voice. For example, "Now this deed witnesseth" becomes "It was witnessed." A simple abstract, much shorter than is usually received in practice, is shown on the facing page to give the reader an idea of what to expect.

The use of abstracts of title by vendors is becoming less popular. Nowadays, conveyancers prefer to send facsimile copies of the title deeds accompanied by an epitome of title. This is quicker and cheaper. Old style abstracts will remain in circulation for some time to come, only because vendors are forced to deliver them in cases where they have not been given the relevant title documents when they acquired the property. In these circumstances their only evidence of title may be an abstract examined against the original title deeds on completion of their purchase.

EPITOMES OF TITLE

With the advent of modern copying machines it has become increasingly common for a vendor to deduce title by supplying the purchaser with an epitome of title accompanied by copies of the title documents. The epitome is for the convenience of the purchaser, forming an index of the copy documents furnished by the vendor, each of which is given a number. It lists the number of each document, the date and nature of the document and the parties to it. Also the epitome states which of the original documents (if any) are to be handed over by the vendor on completion.

Particulars of events such as the death of estate owners must be reduced to writing and put in with the rest of the documents so they read in a logical order. Merely giving particulars on the epitome itself (that is the index sheet) is not sufficient.

The practice of supplying epitomes has been sanctioned by the Council of the Law Society with the caveat, that the copy documents must be of

---

[51] For stamping of documents see *post*, p. 429.
[52] See Cosway, *Abstracting and Deducing Title*.

ABSTRACT OF THE TITLE
— of —
Patricia Rose to the freehold
property 8 Pane Street in the
County of Avon.

1 Feb 1960   Land Charges search against Stanley Hope revealg no substg entries

4 Feb 1960   BY CONVCE of this dt md betn Stanley Hope of 8 Pane Street in Coy of Avon

Stamp   (thrinar cld "Vdr") of the 1 pt and Joseph Danby of The Cave, Adswood Rd in

£1,700 P.D.   the Coy of Avon (thrinar cld "Pchsr") of or pt

After rectg seisin of Vdr in fee simple free from incumbs and
agmt for sale at price of £85,000.

IT WAS WITNESSED that in psce of sd agmt and in conson of £85,000 pd by
Pchsr to Vdr (rect ackned) Vdr as Benfl Owner convd to Pchsr

ALL THAT pcl of ld known
as 8 Pane Street in Coy of
Avon Togr with the dwllg hse
thron and for ppse of identon
only shwn edgd red on plan
annxd thrto

TO HOLD same unto Pchsr in fee simple

Exctd by bth pties and attstd

4 June 1960   BY MTGE of this dt md betn the sd Joseph Danby (thrinar cld "Mtgor") of
the 1 pt and Chowood Bldg Society of Ham Buildings Avondale Rd Avon afsd
(thrinar cld Mtgee) of the or pt

After rectg seisin of Mtgor in fee simple free from incumbs

IT WAS WITNESSED that in conson of £20,000 pd by Mtgee to Mtgor (rect
ackned) Mtgor as Benfl Ownr thrby demisd to Mtgee

ALL THAT bfre abstd ppty

TO HOLD the same unto Mtgee for term of 3,000
yrs sbjt to cesser as thrinar provdd

PROVISO for cesser and other usual clauses

Exctd by Mtgor and attstd

14 Dec 1981   Land Charges search against Joseph Danby and Chowood Bldg Society revealg
no subsistg entries

18 Dec 1981   BY CONVCE of this dt md betn said Chowood Bldg Society (thrinar cld "Vdrs")

Stamp   of 1 pt and Patricia Rose of 10 Wellington Street, Seamdown in the Coy of Kent

£3,000 P.D.   (thrinar cld "Pchsr") of or pt

After rectg bfre abstd mtge of 4 June 1960 (thrinar cld "the
Mtge")

And rectg that sd Joseph Danby hd default in pymt of ppl intt
and or moys due thrunder and that Vdrs had agd to sell the ld
thrinar descbd to Pchsr for sum of £150,000

IT WAS WITNESSED that in conson of sum of £150,000 pd by Pchsr to Vdrs
(rect ackned) Vdrs in exercise of pwr of sale arising under Mtge or by statute as
Mtgees thrby convd unto Pchsr

ALL THAT bfre abstd ppty

TO HOLD same unto Pchsr in fee simple dischgd
from Mtge and to the intent that the term substg
thrunder shd to extent of ld thrby convd merge and
be extingshd in fee simple throf

Exctd by bth pties and attstd

satisfactory quality to meet the essential requirements of deducing title.[53] The copies must be clear, legible and, as they may have to be retained for a considerable period of time as evidence of title by subsequent owners, durable. For this reason the Council has specified[54] that copy documents produced by a photographic or sensitised paper process cannot be used by a vendor to deduce title in place of the traditional abstract, unless the originals of all the documents copied are to be given to the purchaser on completion. Copy documents which are either typewritten or copied by an electro-static, gelatine–transfer or dual spectrum process and which are otherwise satisfactory may be used to deduce title where the original documents are to be retained by the vendor.

Care must be taken when copying plans. They must be coloured to conform with the original. Where the colouring of the original appears so dark on the copy as to render correct colouring impossible, the Council has stated that the copy should not be offered or accepted.[55]

Subject to the copies being of satisfactory quality the vendor can require the purchaser to accept an epitome of title in lieu of the traditional form of abstract. Apart from being quicker and cheaper to produce, the epitome has the added advantage of reducing the risk of mistakes being made in the details given to a purchaser.

VENDOR'S DUTY TO FURNISH AN ABSTRACT OR EPITOME

The vendor's duty to supply an abstract or epitome has its origins in the conveyancing practice of days long gone. It was formerly the case, that the vendor would hand his title deeds to the purchaser who in turn would pass them to conveyancing counsel for investigation. A custom arose whereby the purchaser's solicitor would draw up an abstract of the documents in the hope of saving counsel's time (and no doubt client's money). In time the practice developed whereby the vendor's solicitor drew up the abstract at his own expense. The practice soon crystallised into a hard and fast rule of common law, adopted by academics and judges alike.[56]

Thus a vendor under an open contract is obliged to supply the purchaser with an abstract of title.[57] Giving the purchaser the title deeds to investigate is no longer regarded as being satisfactory.[58] To the layman taking the trouble to prepare an abstract may seem ludicrous. The rule serves two purposes. First, it allows a vendor to retain his title deeds until completion. (Frequently they will be in the hands of his mortgagee who would be loathe to part with them before repayment of the money due under the mortgage.) Secondly, as has been said, abstracts or epitomes will in some circumstances be the vendor's only documentary evidence of

---

[53] Law Soc. Dig., Opinion No. 94 in 4th (Cumulative) Supp.

[54] *Ibid.* para. 5.

[55] Law Soc. Dig., Opinion No. 95, a rule heeded more frequently in the breach than the observance.

[56] *Sugden on Vendors and Purchasers* (14th ed.) p. 406; *Re Johnson and Tustin* (1885) 30 Ch.D. 42.

[57] Even if no valuable consideration is involved; *Re Pelly and Jacob's Contract* (1899) 80 L.T. 45.

[58] *Horne* v. *Wingfield* (1841) 3 M. & G. 33.

ownership. This will be the case, for example, where the vendor originally bought part of a larger estate and his vendor retained the title deeds.

Even where the vendor and purchaser (or mortgagor and mortgagee) are represented by the same solicitor the purchaser is still entitled to an abstract or epitome of title.[59]

The vendor's common law duty in this respect is expressly confirmed by National Condition 9 and Law Society Condition 12. Additionally under the latter Condition the abstract or epitome must bear the "original markings of examination of all relevant documents of title or of examined abstracts thereof." This refers to an abstract which has been certified by a solicitor as an accurate representation of the original title deeds.

WHO PAYS FOR PREPARING THE ABSTRACT OR EPITOME?

Under an open contract the vendor must bear the expense of compiling an abstract or epitome of title.[60] For example, he must pay the costs of obtaining the deeds from his mortgagee, copying the documents and so forth. Contracts for sale incorporating the National or Law Society Conditions do not change the vendor's position. On a sale of any property in lots, a purchaser of two or more lots, held under the same title is entitled to only one abstract free of charge. If he wants more than one he must pay for its preparation himself.[61]

DELIVERY OF THE ABSTRACT OR EPITOME

Delivery of the abstract or epitome must be unconditional.[62] The Council of the Law Society has said that the purchaser should not be asked to hold it to the order of the vendor pending completion of the contract. If the sale eventually goes off the purchaser will have to return all the documents supplied by the vendor.

When should the vendor deliver the abstract or epitome? Under an open contract the vendor must do so within a reasonable time after exchange of contracts.[63] What amounts to "a reasonable time" depends upon the particular facts of the case. Conveyancers normally prefer the certainty of stipulating for delivery to take place within a specified period or by a specified date. Both sets of standard conditions reflect this. In sales governed by the National Conditions of Sale the vendor is required to deliver an abstract not later than 11 working days after the date of the contract.[64] Although the Condition does not expressly state that an epitome may be delivered instead of an abstract, in practice no objection would be made by a purchaser to a vendor who supplied an epitome. The Law Society Conditions require the delivery of an abstract or epitome "forthwith" upon exchange of contracts (Condition 12(1)).

---

[59] Law Soc. Dig., Opinion No. 95(*b*).
[60] *Re Stamford, Spalding & Boston Banking Co. and Knight's Contract* [1900] 1 Ch. 287; *Re Ebsworth and Tidy* (1889) 42 Ch.D. 23.
[61] Law of Property Act 1925, s.45(5).
[62] Law Soc. Dig., Opinion No. 95(*b*).
[63] *Compton* v. *Bagley* [1892] 1 Ch. 313.
[64] Condition 9(1).

In some cases the vendor may send the abstract or epitome to the purchaser together with the draft contract. This would be especially appropriate where the contract contains many references to incumbrances in the various title deeds. Both parties may benefit from the practice where time is pressing and the investigation of title at an early stage would allow completion to take place sooner than usual. Where the sale is governed by the Law Society Conditions and the vendor supplies an abstract or epitome before exchange of contracts, the purchaser is not fixed with notice of any defect in the vendor's title discoverable on inspection of it (Condition 12(3)). This preserves the right of the purchaser to raise requisitions on any such defects after the contract has become binding. Similarly the purchaser's right to rescind in respect of those defects (not disclosed in the contract) is preserved. There are two exceptions to the rule stated in the Condition. Where the property is leasehold and/or sold subject to an existing tenancy or tenancies, the purchaser is fixed with notice, prior to exchange, of defects disclosed in any copy leases which have been supplied. He loses the right to requisition or rescind in respect of any defects contained there, once contracts have been exchanged unless the defect is removable.[65] The National Conditions contain no equivalent to Law Society Condition 12(3).

LATE DELIVERY OF AN ABSTRACT OR EPITOME

Section 41 of the Law of Property Act 1925 provides that stipulations as to time shall not be of the essence in contracts for the sale of land. The provision does not prevail over an express contractual term making time of the essence. However, neither the National nor the Law Society Conditions make time of the essence of the vendors obligation to deliver an abstract. Consequently the purchaser cannot refuse to complete on the ground that the vendor has not delivered an abstract by the date specified in the contract (or in the case of an open contract within a reasonable time of the contract becoming binding).[66] If the vendor does delay the purchaser can put pressure on him by serving a notice fixing a date by which delivery must be made. Provided the vendor is given a further, reasonable, opportunity to fulfill his obligation, his continued delay will entitle the purchaser to terminate the contract. In *Compton* v. *Bagley*[67] a purchaser was held justified in rescinding after giving the vendor 14 days to furnish an abstract. The vendor had contracted one and a half months earlier no time having been set for delivery. There is good reason for a vendor to be wary of postponing delivery of the abstract for too long. Apart from the above the vendor's sluggishness may result in him being penalised should completion be delayed. Most professionally drafted contracts contain provisions which require the party at fault in holding up completion to pay damages or interest to the other party; for example Law Society Condition 22(2).

---

[65] See *ante*, p. 201.
[66] He can rescind if he proves the vendor is withholding the abstract or epitome deliberately; *Compton* v.*Bagley* [1892] 1 Ch. 313.
[67] *Ibid.*

WHAT SHOULD BE INCLUDED IN THE ABSTRACT OR EPITOME?

It is not possible to state a universal rule as to what should and what should not be abstracted. Each title is unique and in any particular case special considerations may require the abstraction of a particular type of document. Generally speaking every document after the root of title which affects the estate being sold should be included in the abstract or epitome.[68]

Each document that is material to the title must be set out separately. It is not permissible to give details of a material document by introducing it as a recital in other abstracted documents.[69] Permitting such a practice would enable a vendor to minimize suspicious matters on the title. As North J. once remarked[70]: "The omission to abstract a document in chief might proceed from a desire to avoid noticing matters of a suspicious character occurring in such a document, but which is not noticed in the recital." The purchaser is entitled to form his own opinion of the effect of a document and to do this he must have the full contents of the document in front of him. A recital would contain only the vendor's opinion of the effect of that document. This is not what the purchaser wants—he wants the facts. In a traditional abstract it is only necessary to abstract the material part of the various documents. For example, the parties must be identified, certificates of value mentioned and full details of any endorsements on probates and conveyances given. Other matters need to be mentioned in the abstract but not in so much detail. These include *inter alia*, the covenants for title and details of the trusts (if any) upon which the proceeds of sale are to be held.

Obviously everything which has just been said about abstracts in the traditional form can be ignored as far as epitomes of title are concerned. As long as each material document is copied and sent to the purchaser no question arises as to which parts are material. Note that where a copy of the conveyance to the vendor is being sent to the purchaser before contract, it is quite proper for the vendor to cut out the price he paid for the property. This will frequently be done by builder vendors who do not wish to disclose the price they paid for the land on which the purchaser's new house is to be built. It might encourage him to renegotiate the price he has agreed to pay.

Some of the documents most frequently requiring inclusion in abstracts and epitomes of title are discussed below.

(i) **Conveyances.** Conveyances of the property must be abstracted because they form links in the vendor's "chain of title." The purchaser will need to see them to trace the ownership of the estate which is the subject matter of the contract.

It may be necessary for the purchaser to check that a conveyance appearing on the face of the abstract or epitome cannot be set aside under

---

[68] *Williams on Vendor and Purchaser* (4th ed.) p. 48.
[69] *Re Stamford, Spalding & Boston Banking Co and Knight's Contract* [1900] 1 Ch. 287.
[70] *Ibid.* at p. 290.

some statutory provision. A very brief outline of some of these provisions is given below.

(a) *Section 42 Bankruptcy Act 1914.* A trustee in bankruptcy may avoid a "voluntary settlement" (which term includes a transfer or a conveyance) if the settlor becomes bankrupt within two years of making it. Furthermore, if the settlor becomes bankrupt within 10 years of the conveyance, and the beneficiaries (transferees and so on) claiming under the settlement cannot prove that the settlor could have paid all his debts (that is those he had at the time of making the settlement) without the aid of the property settled the disposition is again voidable by the trustee in bankruptcy. However, the trustee in bankruptcy cannot claim the property once it falls into the hands of a bona fide purchaser for valuable consideration[71] without notice of an available act of bankruptcy[72] on the part of the settlor.[73] Where a bankruptcy petition or receiving order has been registered at the Land Charges Department it should be remembered that section 198 of the Law of Property Act 1925 will have fixed any subsequent purchaser with notice.[74] A purchaser who searches against all estate owners on the title and obtains clear certificates of search can be satisfied that there is no possibility of his title to the property being disturbed under the section.

Normally the purchaser should not be worried if there is a voluntary conveyance on the title dated less than 10 years ago. But:

(b) *Section 172(1) of the Law of Property Act 1925.* "Save as provided in this section, every conveyance of property made . . . with intent to defraud creditors, shall be voidable at the instance of any person thereby prejudiced." The section applies to all conveyances whether voluntary or not.

The necessary intent must be proved by the person seeking to have the conveyance set aside. Inferences drawn from the surrounding circumstances may be strong enough to establish a prima facie case.[75] It follows that the fact that a particular conveyance was voluntary (or not made for full consideration) will weigh heavily in favour of the person asking the court to set the disposition aside. There is no need to establish that the person making the conveyance acted dishonestly or deceitfully. As was said in *Lloyds Bank Ltd.* v. *Marcan,* "all that needs to be proved is that it was intended to prevent creditors from "timely recourse to property which would otherwise have been applicable for their benefit.""[76-77]

The defendant and his wife had a horticultural business on property owned by the defendant alone. The premises were mortgaged to the plaintiff bank. He defaulted and the bank sought possession. The

---

[71] *Re Windle* [1975] 1 W.L.R. 1628; *Re Densham* [1975] 1 W.L.R. 1519.

[72] An "available" act of bankruptcy is one of the statutory acts listed in the Bankruptcy Act 1914, s.1(1), committed within the last three months.

[73] *Re Hart, ex. p. Green* [1912] 3 K.B. 6.

[74] See *ante*, p. 26.

[75] *Reese River Co.* v. *Attwell* (1869) L.R. 7 Eq. 347; *Crossley* v. *Elworthy* (1871) L.R. 12 Eq. 158.

[76-77] [1973] 1 W.L.R. 339 at p. 344, *per* Pennycuick V.-C. Confirmed on appeal [1973] 1 W.L.R. 1387.

defendant, on the advice of counsel, purported to grant a 20 year lease at a rack rent to his wife. In the meantime the bank had already started its action for possession to enable them to realise their security. The court held that the lease could be set aside under the provisions of section 172(1) despite the honest belief of Marcan that he had acted in accordance with the law.

Section 172(3) states that sub-section (1) does not apply; "to any estate or interest in property conveyed for valuable consideration and in good faith or upon good consideration and in good faith to any person not having, at the time of the conveyance, notice of the intent to defraud creditors." The section is not happily drafted. Despite the reference to "good consideration" the protection afforded by section 172(3) can only be claimed by a purchaser for valuable consideration (which term includes marriage consideration). It does not protect persons who acquire interests in property in consideration of the donors "natural love and affection".[78]

The person acquiring the interest must act in "good faith." He must have no actual or constructive notice of the donor/transferor's intent to defraud creditors. Knowledge that the transferor is in financial difficulty would not be enough to fix a donee with notice for this purpose.

Once again a purchaser is in no danger of having his title upset by someone claiming under the section where he is, or the property has been purchased by, a bona fide purchaser for valuable consideration.

Reference may also be made to section 173 of the Act of 1925. This renders voidable voluntary dispositions of land made with intent to defraud subsequent purchasers.

(c) *Section 37 Matrimonial Causes Act 1973.* The court has wide powers under this Act to readjust the property rights of parties to a divorce. Clearly if the parties were free to dispose of property in any way before the question of ancillary relief was decided it could lead to injustice. Under section 37 the court may set aside any *inter vivos* disposition by the person against whom a claim for ancillary relief is being made, if it is made with the intention of defeating the other party's claim to the property. Again there is a provision preventing a disposition made in good faith for money or money's worth without notice of the disponor's intention to defeat the claim to the property by the other party to the divorce, from being attacked under the section.

(d) *Fiduciaries.* One other case where a conveyance may be set aside in Equity is where there is a sale of trust property to a trustee or estate property to a personal representative.[79] If a trustee purchases trust property the disposition can be set aside by the beneficiaries no matter how fair the price paid by the trustee. Equity imposes the rule to prevent a trustee from being put in a position where his own interests as a purchaser (to obtain a low price) are in conflict with his duties as a manager of the trust property (to obtain a high price).[80]

If a conveyance to a trustee or personal representative appears in the

---

[78] *Re Eicholz* [1959] Ch. 708.
[79] *Fox* v. *Mackreth* (1788) 2 Bro. Ch. 400.
[80] *Keech* v. *Sandford* (1926) 2 Eq.Cas.Abr. 741.

abstract or the copy documents supplied with the epitome, the purchaser should make further enquiry of the vendor to satisfy himself that the conveyance is not voidable at the instance of the beneficiaries. In the following circumstances the purchase by a trustee or personal representative of trust or estate property cannot be impeached:—

(1) Where the trust instrument authorises the trustee to buy the trust property. In this case it will be necessary for the vendor to produce to the purchaser the will or other trust instrument, so proving that the disposition cannot be set aside in equity.[81]

(2) Where the trustee/personal representative has obtained approval of the court to proceed with the purchase.

(3) Where all the beneficiaries being of full age and capacity (or their respective parents, guardians and so on) have given their written consent to the sale.[82] The trustee must make full and frank disclosure of all the relevant facts to the beneficiaries so that they have all the necessary information to enter into an agreement for sale on a sound commercial basis.[83] It will again be necessary for the vendor to produce the trust instrument so that the purchaser can check that all the necessary consents have been obtained. Where there is a gift or settlement in favour of a class of beneficiaries the problems presented in confirming that all consents have been obtained may prove to be insurmountable.

(4) Where the trustee or personal representative purchased under a contract made before the fiduciary relationship arose.[84]

(5) The beneficiaries can only have the sale set aside if they assert their right to do so within a reasonable time of the conveyance being made. There is unfortunately no yardstick by which to judge what amounts to a reasonable time. A purchaser relying on this equitable doctrine of laches is therefore running a risk. He may consider asking the vendor to take out an insurance policy to indemnify the purchaser against loss caused in the event of the conveyance being set aside.

(6) Where the sale is made to a trustee who retired from office some time ago the beneficiaries will only be able to avoid the disposition if there is some evidence that the trustee influenced the price at which the property was sold to him because of his past links with the beneficiaries.[85]

(ii) **Leases.** It has already been pointed out that a vendor must supply the purchaser with particulars of any leases subject to which the property is sold.[86] Any subsisting leases must be abstracted even though they were created before the date of the root of title.[87] Leases which have expired need not be abstracted or included in the epitome of title.

Leases which have been surrendered should be included so that the pur-

---

[81] *Allen* v. *Taylor* (1880) 16 Ch.D. 355.

[82] *Saunders* v. *Vautier* (1841) 4 Beav. 115.

[83] *Wright* v. *Carter* [1903] 1 Ch. 27.

[84] *Re Mulholland's Wills Trusts* [1949] 1 All E.R. 460.

[85] *Re Boles and British and Company's Contract* [1902] 1 Ch. 244; *Holder* v. *Holder* [1968] Ch. 353.

[86] See *ante*, p. 203.

[87] Law of Property Act 1925, s.45(1); See *ante*, p. 203.

chaser can form his own view of whether the surrender was effective. If it was not the lease may revive in which case it would bind the purchaser.

If a tenant is holding over under statute the lease even though expired is in practice often abstracted.

(iii) **Mortgages.** The abstract or epitome must contain all legal mortgages affecting the property during the period of title to be shown. Mortgages which are no longer subsisting must still be included in the abstract or epitome so that the purchaser can ensure that they have been duly discharged.[88] This he does by checking that a receipt has been endorsed on the mortgage. Any receipts should be checked to see that they are not dated after the mortgagor purported to convey the property free from the mortgage. Section 115(2) of the Law of Property Act 1925 provides that;

> "when by the receipt the money appears to have been paid by a person who is not entitled to the immediate equity of redemption, the receipt shall operate as if the benefit of the mortgage had by deed been transferred to him; unless—
>
> (a) it is otherwise expressly provided; or
> (b) the mortgage is paid off out of capital money, or other money in the hands of a personal representative or trustee properly applicable for the discharge of the mortgage, and it is not expressly provided that the receipt is to operate as a transfer."

Suppose a vendor contracts to sell property free from a mortgage in favour of X. On Monday he purports to convey the property to the purchaser free from the mortgage but in fact as we shall see what he does is transfer the land to the purchaser subject to a subsisting mortgage. On Wednesday (receipt dated Wednesday) the vendor pays off the mortgage to X. This operates as a transfer of the mortgage from X. to the vendor under section 115(2) so that the vendor becomes his purchaser's mortgagee. However, the vendor may be estopped from enforcing repayment of the mortgage according to *Cumberland Court (Brighton) Ltd.* v. *Taylor.*[89]

A receipt in the form specified by section 115(1) of the Law of Property Act 1925 will discharge the mortgage. Under the section the receipt must be signed by the mortgagee and state the name of the person paying the money. A receipt by a Building Society does not have to name the payer to be effective.[90] Law Society Condition 14 states:

> "Where the title includes a mortgage or legal charge in favour of trustees on behalf of a friendly society, a building society or a society registered under the Industrial and Provident Societies Acts, the purchaser shall assume that any receipt given on discharge of any such mortgage or legal charge and apparently duly executed was in fact duly executed by all proper persons and is valid."

---

[88] *Heath* v. *Crealock* (1874) 10 Ch.App. 22.
[89] [1964] Ch. 29.
[90] Building Society Act 1962, s.37.

The Condition relieves the purchaser from finding out whether any particular mortgagees rules have been complied with, as far as executing the receipt is concerned.[91] Note, however, that the provision does not entitle a purchaser to assume due execution of the receipt, for example, where the mortgage is in favour of a bank or an individual. The National Conditions contain no equivalent to Law Society Condition 14.

Equitable mortgages which are protected by deposit of the title deeds are normally not abstracted where the mortgage is going to be discharged and the deeds handed over to the purchaser on completion.[92] If the charge is not protected by deposit of the deeds but by registration as a land charge,[93] the purchaser should be given details of the mortgage because he will discover it anyway when making his land charges search. He would ask for details of it at this stage. If the title deeds including the equitable mortgage are not going to be given to the purchaser because the charge relates to other property and the deeds are to be retained by the mortgagee a letter of release signed by the mortgagee should be obtained.[94]

(iv) **Certificates of Search.** There is no rule of law requiring a vendor to include in the abstract or epitome of title, certificates of search of the land charges register made by previous purchasers of the property. If it comes to light that a search has not been made against an estate owner it is the purchaser who must make the search.[95] However, any certificate of search which the vendor has should be copied and included in the epitome or referred to in the abstract.[96] This is normally done in practice. It helps the purchaser's solicitor in his investigation of title and relieves him of the task of requisitioning another search. For his part the purchaser's solicitor should ensure that the relevant purchase was completed within the period of priority conferred by the search.[97] If not he should make another search of the register himself.

Certificates of searches of the local land charges register are not frequently abstracted in practice. They confer no protection on purchasers and only speak for the date on which they are made.[98] The purchaser will require more up to date information and will make his own search.

(v) **Planning Permissions.** In practice the purchaser's solicitor will ask for copies of all relevant planning permissions when he makes his preliminary enquiries. If not the vendor's solicitor should supply them at this stage of the transaction.

The purchaser's solicitor should check the copy permissions to see that any conditions contained in them have been complied with. He should also

---

[91] See further *post*, p. 339.

[92] *Drummond* v. *Tracy* (1860) John 608 suggests that details of such mortgages should be given to the purchaser.

[93] Class C(iii), Land Charges Act 1972, s.2(4). See *ante*, p. 20.

[94] J.T. Farrand, *Emmet on Title* (18th ed.) p. 144.

[95] At his own expense, Law of Property Act 1925, s.45(4)(*b*).

[96] Law Soc. Dig., Opinion No. 90.

[97] See *ante*, p. 35.

[98] See *ante*, p. 13.

ensure that the local planning authority has given its approval to any matters which were "reserved matters" in the planning permissions.

(vi) **Facts.** Sometimes a vendor's ownership of the property will depend upon the proof of certain facts. An example frequently met in practice is where a vendor company has changed its name after it acquired property. The company when selling would have to prove this fact to the purchaser's satisfaction. It would supply him with a copy of the new certificate of incorporation showing the change to have occurred.[99] Another example would be where the vendor had changed his name by deed poll. The deed poll would have to be furnished to the purchaser.

Details of other facts should be set out in the abstract or typed on a separate sheet of paper and sent to the purchaser with the epitome.

(vii) **Grants of Representation.** Probates and letters of administration must be abstracted where an estate owner has died during the period of title being shown. On the estate owner's death the legal estate vests in the deceased's personal representatives.[1-2] The grant of representation is therefore a necessary link in the "chain of title." Any endorsements on the grants of representation relating to assents and conveyances of the property should be copied or mentioned in the abstract.

The probate or letters of administration is sufficient proof of the estate owner's death although the death certificate is often asked for in practice. Since 1925 the deceased's will need not be abstracted because it operates in Equity only.[3]

DOCUMENTS WHICH NEED NOT BE ABSTRACTED

One of the objectives of the 1925 property legislation was to keep equitable interests off the face of the title documents a purchaser of the legal estate needs to see. Therefore, documents relating to equitable interests which will be overreached on sale need not be abstracted.[4] For example, the tenant for life of a strict settlement may sell the legal estate. The remaindermen's equitable interests in the settled land conferred by the trust instrument will be transferred to the sale proceeds paid by the purchaser to the trustees of the settlement. The trust instrument need not be abstracted or included in the epitome of title.[5]

Expired leases do not need to be abstracted. They do not affect the purchaser of a freehold interest. It might be thought appropriate to give details of any lease after the expiry of which the tenant is holding over by virtue of statute.

Were a mortgagee is selling in exercise of an express, or statutory, power of sale he need not abstract any mortgage which will not bind his purchaser. Generally speaking a mortgagee may sell free from all

---

[99] Companies Act 1981, s.24(6).
[1-2] Administration of Estates Act 1925, ss.1 and 3.
[3] See J.T. Farrand, *Emmet on Title* (18th ed.) p. 148.
[4] Law of Property Act 1925, s.10.
[5] See *Re Duce and Boots Cash Chemists (Southern) Ltd's. Contract* [1937] Ch. 642.

subsequent mortgages whether they have been protected by registration as a land charge or not.

THE PURCHASER MUST VERIFY THE ABSTRACT

The vendor has a duty to prove the abstract or epitome is a true account of the state of the title.[6] To do this he must produce his title documents so that the purchaser can establish the truth of the statements made in the abstract or the accuracy of the copy documents supplied with the epitome. It has been said[7]: "It is only when we turn away from the abstract to the verification of it that the real proof of title begins." For example, the purchaser must be given an opportunity to inspect the deeds to ensure the vendor did not omit any endorsements on them.[8] The endorsement may relate to a previous sale of part of the property.

PRODUCTION OF THE TITLE DEEDS

So far as abstracted documents are concerned verification consists of producing the original documents, for comparison with the abstract or epitome by the purchaser's solicitor. He can then certify that the abstract or epitome has been examined against the original documents. By doing this he will also make the abstract better evidence of title for the purposes of any subsequent sale by the purchaser.

Ideally the examination of the title deeds should be carried out before completion.[9] This will avoid any last minute problems which can prove inconvenient or expensive for the purchaser who has already sold his own house. However, in practice the abstract is frequently only examined against the deeds on the day of completion. This does save time (and consequently clients' money) in the majority of cases.

As a matter of strict law the vendor should prove that the documents produced were duly executed. It is not, however, the practice to require this of the vendor unless there are circumstances present which make proof of due execution desirable.[10] The presumption of due execution only applies if the documents are produced from proper custody. This means from anywhere they might reasonably have been expected to be found.[11]

Section 45(4) of the Law of Property Act 1925 puts the expense of producing and inspecting all documents, not in the possession of the vendor, his mortgagee or trustee, for the purpose of verifying the abstract (or epitome) on the purchaser. The section would appear to give a purchaser the right to require a vendor to produce all his title documents regardless of in whose custody they should be, if he is prepared to meet the expense. This could prove to be inconvenient for the vendor where he does not know who has the original title deeds. Under National Condition

---

[6] *Southby* v. *Hutt* (1837) 2 My. & Cr 207.

[7] *Williams on Vendor and Purchaser* (3rd ed.) p. 131.

[8] For example the back of the original was not photocopied and so omitted from the epitome.

[9] Law Soc. Dig., Opinion 95(*a*) 4th Cumulative Supplement suggest it should be done before the time for requisitions expires.

[10] Law Soc. Dig., Opinion No. 125; see also Evidence Act 1938, s.4.

[11] *Croughton* v. *Blake* (1843) 12 M. & W. 205.

12(3) the vendor cannot be required to procure the production of any title document not in his possession or the possession of his mortgagee or trustee. The Condition also prevents a purchaser from requiring the vendor to trace the person who has custody of the original documents. The Law Society Conditions do not alter the open contract rule. Law Society Condition 12(2)[12] seems to relate only to the delivery of an abstract not to production of the deeds for verification of the abstract.

At common law the proper place for production of the deeds is at the vendor's own residence, the property being sold or in London.[13] If the vendor produces the documents elsewhere he has to reimburse the purchaser for any extra expense incurred.[14] In practice production will take place at the offices of the vendor's solicitor, or those of his mortgagee, in the majority of cases. Although neither is strictly a "proper place" the purchaser does not usually ask the vendor to meet his additional expenses (if any).

Proof of Events Affecting the Vendor's Title

Events may be proved by production of a certificate or other document of record evidencing the event. Probates, letters of administration, marriage certificates, certificates of incorporation and so on are all adequate proof of the appropriate event.

Section 45(6) of the Law of Property Act 1925 eases the potential burden on the vendor in this respect:

> "Recitals, statements, and descriptions of facts, matters and parties contained in deeds, instruments, Acts of Parliament, or statutory declarations, twenty years old at the date of the contract, shall, unless and except so far as they may be proved to be inaccurate, be taken to be sufficient evidence of the truth of such facts, matters and descriptions."

For example, a recital in a conveyance 20 years old stating that an estate owner had married would be sufficient evidence of the marriage; the marriage certificate need not be produced.

Failing either of the above sources of evidence the vendor may satisfy the purchaser by means of a statutory declaration. In the last resort the purchaser will be required to presume the truth of events where a judge would direct a jury to presume the truth of the event on the strength of the evidence produced by the vendor.[15] The rule would prevent a purchaser from making unmeritorious objections to the vendor's evidence as to events where conclusive proof could only be obtained at disproportionate expense.[16]

---

[12] See *ante*, p. 271.
[13] Williams', *Sale of Land*, p. 42.
[14] *Sharp* v. *Page* (1815) Sug. V. & P. 430.
[15] *Williams on Vendor and Purchaser* (3rd ed.) p. 122.
[16] *M.E.P.C. Ltd.* v. *Christian-Edwards* [1981] A.C. 205.

Section 45(4) above applies equally to the expenses incurred by proving events as it does to producing documents. National Condition 12(3) will again limit the vendor's obligation to obtain proof where this consists of a document not in his custody, or that of his trustee or mortgagee.

Position where the Deeds have been Lost

A purchaser cannot refuse to complete a contract where the vendor has lost the original title deeds if the vendor can produce sufficient secondary evidence of their contents. The purchaser can however, require the vendor to explain the circumstances surrounding their loss. A statutory declaration made by the vendor (at the purchaser's expense under an open contract) will usually suffice. The evidence may also consist of copies of the document (but not copies of a copy)[17] first drafts or even parol evidence. Due execution of documents allegedly lost is not presumed.[18] He need not, however, positively prove that the document was stamped.[19] Neither the National nor the Law Society Conditions deal with the situation where the title deeds are lost.

If the deeds are lost before the contract is made the vendor should deal with the matter in the special conditions. In some cases the vendor may also consider voluntary registration of his title as a prelude to a sale. Where some only of the title deeds have been lost the Land Registry may grant title absolute so solving any problems in deducing title in the future.

The Vendor Must Hand Over the Deeds on Completion

Under an open contract a vendor has a duty to obtain the title deeds and hand them over on completion. This is the so-called rule in *Re Duthy and Jesson's Contract*.[20] It is doubtful whether National Condition 12(3) affects this obligation on the vendor's part.[21] Any expense involved in obtaining the deeds for this purpose falls upon the vendor.

The vendor is not required to hand over title documents where he retains any part of the land to which they relate or where the document relates to a subsisting trust, for example a will or deed appointing a trustee.[22] It is especially important for the purchaser's solicitor to examine the abstract or epitome (and mark it in such cases) as compared against the originals. An acknowledgment for production and an undertaking for the safe custody of the retained deeds should be taken from the vendor.[23]

---

[17] *Re Halifax Commercial Banking Co. and Wood* (1898) 79 L.T. 536.
[18] *Bryant* v. *Busk* (1872) 4 Russ. 1.
[19] *Hart* v. *Hart* (1841) 1 Hare. 1.
[20] [1898] 1 Ch. 419.
[21] H.W. Wilkinson; *Standard Conditions of Sale of Land* (3rd ed.) p. 66.
[22] Law of Property Act 1925, s.45(9).
[23] See *post*, p. 383.

(2) LEASEHOLD LAND

Some points relevant to deducing title to leasehold land were discussed in the preceding chapter. The vendor's obligation to disclose unusually onerous covenants,[24] to reveal breaches of covenants in the lease (or superior leases)[25] and to obtain consent to the assignment or grant of the underlease[26] are all facets of the duty to show good title in the case of leasehold property. Also discussed were the statutory presumptions arising out of the production of the last receipt for rent by the vendor.[27] It is not proposed to go over this ground again.

The present section is concerned with the extent to which a purchaser of leasehold land can require his vendor to deduce good title. The open contract rules will be looked at first followed by a discussion of how these may be altered in favour of the purchaser.

Purchaser's Position Under an Open Contract

The rules regulating the purchaser's entitlement in respect of the title he can require of the vendor are contained in section 44 of the Law of Property Act 1925. As with so many other open contract rules the principles developed out of conveyancing practice. A vendor of leasehold land formerly had to produce the lease however old[28] and then title back from the date of the contract for 60 years.[28a] If a lease was being assigned which was only 10 years old at the date of the contract the vendor would have had to produce evidence of title as to superior leases and maybe even the freehold for the 50 years prior to the grant of the lease.[29] This position was not tolerated by vendors too long. They would provide by special condition that the purchaser should not call for the superior title.[30] Conveyancing practice became conveyancing law.[31]

Section 44(2)–(4) provides:

> "(2) Under a contract to grant or assign a term of years, whether derived or to be derived out of freehold or leasehold land, the intended lessee or assign shall not be entitled to call for the title to the freehold.
>
> (3) Under a contract to sell and assign a term of years derived out of a leasehold interest in land, the intended assign shall not have the right to call for the title to the leasehold reversion.

---

[24] See *ante*, p. 207.

[25] See *ante*, p. 210.

[26] See *ante*, p. 178.

[27] Law of Property Act 1925, ss.45(2) and (3); *ante*, p. 000.

[28] *Frend* v. *Buckley* (1870) L.R. 5 Q.B. 213.

[28a] Reduced to 40 years by s.1 of the Vendor and Purchaser Act 1874; to 30 years by s.44(1) of the Law of Property Act 1925; to 15 years by s.23 of the Law of Property Act 1969.

[29] *Souter* v. *Drake* (1834) 5 B. & Ad. 992.

[30] Vendors could not deduce the superior title sometimes because of the lack of co-operation from the superior landlords.

[31] First Rule Vendor and Purchaser Act 1874, ss.1 and 2; Conveyancing Act 1881, s.3.

(4) On a contract to grant a lease for a term of years to be derived out of a leasehold interest, with a leasehold reversion, the intended lessee shall not have the right to call for the title to that reversion."

The rules all negative a purchaser's rights in some respect. Following the precedent set by most other textbook writers these rules will be illustrated by means of an example.

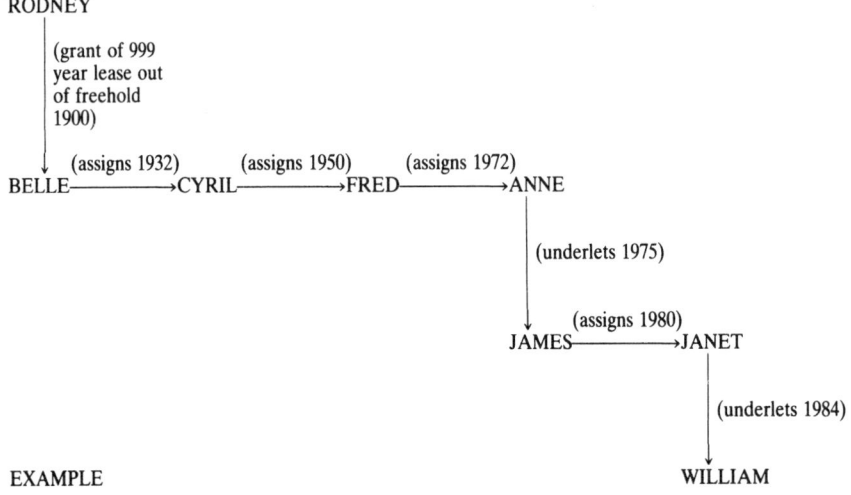

RODNEY

(grant of 999 year lease out of freehold 1900)

(assigns 1932)   (assigns 1950)   (assigns 1972)
BELLE———————→CYRIL———————→FRED———————→ANNE

(underlets 1975)

(assigns 1980)
JAMES———————→JANET

(underlets 1984)

EXAMPLE   WILLIAM

NOTES ON THE EXAMPLE

(i) **Rodney to Belle.** Belle cannot call for Rodney to deduce title to his freehold; section 44(2). She, therefore, has no way of knowing that Rodney is in a position to validly grant her a lease. If the lease is at a ground rent with Belle paying a substantial premium (of say £70,000) Belle's position under an open contract is most unsatisfactory. It is possible that she is paying £70,000 for nothing.

(ii) **Belle to Cyril.** Cyril can require Belle to produce the lease made between her and Rodney. However, section 44(2) again prevents Cyril from seeing the freehold title of Rodney. He is in a slightly better position than Belle only in that possession under the lease has been undisturbed for thirty two years. This is fairly strong evidence that the lease was validly granted.

(iii) **Cyril to Fred.** Fred can require Cyril to produce the lease (Rodney to Belle) even though it is 50 years old. Fred can also require Cyril to produce the assignment to him of the lease by Belle. Fred is entitled to see all assignments, mortgages and so on affecting the lease under which Cyril holds from a deed at least 30 years old[32] at the date of the contract (now reduced by section 23 of the Law of Property Act 1969 to 15 years).

---

[32] *Williams* v. *Spargo* [1893] W.N. 100; Law of Property Act 1925, s.44(1).

(iv) **Fred to Anne.** Again Anne may call for the lease (Rodney to Belle). As the Law of Property Act 1969 (which reduced to 15 years the period of title a purchaser could call for under an open contract) came into operation on January 1, 1970, Anne is entitled to see all assignments, mortgages and so on affecting the lease for a period of at least 15 years and then back to a good root of title. Here Anne can require the assignment made in 1950 (Cyril to Fred) to be produced. She cannot require production of the 1932 assignment (Belle to Cyril). This is behind the 15 year "curtain" drawn by section 23 of the Act of 1969. Section 44(2) again operates to prevent Anne from calling for title to be shown to the freehold estate.

(v) **Anne to James.** Anne grants an underlease to James in 1975. Section 44(2) prevents James from calling for the freehold title. However, James is entitled to see the lease out of which his underlease is to be carved and title to the lease going back at least 15 years from the date of the contract. James will be able to see the lease (Rodney to Belle), the assignments of 1950 (Cyril to Fred) and 1972 (Fred to Anne) and any mortgages and so on made during the period from 1950 to the grant of the underlease. Considering the length of time which has elapsed since the original lease was granted James' position is fairly satisfactory.

(vi) **James to Janet.** James assigns his underlease to Janet in 1980. The reversion to the underlease is a leasehold reversion. Section 44(3) prevents Janet from seeing the title to the leasehold reversion. Section 44(2) prevents her from seeing the freehold title. All Janet can call for is the underlease (Anne to James). She is not allowed to go back beyond 1975 (even though this is only five years ago) under an open contract. She has no way of knowing whether Anne could validly grant the underlease. Janet cannot be sure that the headlease (Rodney to Belle) does not contain a covenant preventing her from using the property in the way in which she wants to because she has no right to see it.[33] Yet if the headlease contained a covenant forbidding the premises from being used as a restaurant and Janet opened one, in ignorance of the covenant, the headlandlord (the freeholder) could re-enter and forfeit the headlease[34]— so terminating the underlease. The open contract rule is seen to be unsatisfactory. Note the crucial difference in the extent of title a grantee of an underlease can call for (that is what James saw) and the extent of title an assignee of an underlease can call for.

(vii) **Janet to William.** Janet grants to William a sub-underlease in 1984. William is entitled to call for the title to the interest out of which his sub-underlease is to be carved. He can call for the 1975 underlease (Anne to James). He can also call for the 1980 assignment (James to Janet). He is entitled to go back 15 years from the date of the contract to the deed under which the interest, out of which his "sub-underlease" is carved, has

---

[33] *Hill* v. *Harris* [1965] 2 Q.B. 601.
[34] The court has discretion to grant relief against forfeiture under s.146(4) of the Law of Property Act 1925.

been held. If, as here, the "sub-underlease" is to be derived from an underlease less than 15 years old the sub-underlessee is not allowed to go back any further under an open contract. Section 44(4) prevents William from calling for the title to "the leasehold reversion"—that is the headlease (Rodney to Belle and the assignments of that lease). It was decided in *Gosling* v. *Woolf* [35] that the term "leasehold reversion" as used in section 44(4) of the Law of Property Act 1925 means the reversion to the leasehold interest out of which the term of years being granted or assigned is derived. This interpretation of section 44(4) has been endorsed by the Court of Appeal; *Becker* v. *Partridge*.[36]

The basic rule to remember on the grant or assignment of a leasehold interest is that the purchaser will be entitled to see the lease under which his vendor holds. Anything else he might have a right to see, for example assignments depends upon how old the lease under which the vendor holds is.

Changing the Open Contract Rules

Transactions in which leasehold interests are assigned or granted sometimes involve millions of pounds being paid as a premium. When a premium is paid the assignee or grantee in practice hardly ever relies upon the open contract rules. He will try to extend his rights to investigate the superior title by inserting a special condition in the contract.[37]

The National Conditions of Sale contain no provisions extending the rights of a purchaser of leasehold property to investigate superior titles. The purchaser under sales governed by these conditions has to persuade his vendor to agree to a special condition extending his rights.

The Law Society Conditions do contain a condition which in certain circumstances improves the position of the purchaser. Law Society Condition 8(2) provides:

> "In all cases the immediate title to the property shall begin with the lease. Where the lease, unless registered with absolute title, is dated not more than fifteen years before the date of the contract and was granted for a term exceeding twenty-one years, the freehold title and all other titles superior to the lease shall be deduced for a period beginning not less than fifteen years prior to the date of the contract and ending on the date of the lease."

Condition 8(2) does not operate on the *grant* of a lease or underlease. In such cases a special condition is needed to extend the purchaser's rights, otherwise section 44 of the 1925 Act (as amended) will regulate the position. Similarly, the Condition will not operate unless:
  (i) the lease is less than 15 years old at the date of the contract;
  (ii) the lease was granted for a term of over 21 years; and

---

[35] [1893] 1 Q.B. 39 (better reported in 68 L.T. 89).
[36] [1966] 2. Q.B. 155 at p. 169.
[37] s.44(11) provides: "This section applies only if and so far as a contrary intention is not expressed in the contract."

(iii) the lease is not registered with title absolute at H.M. Land Registry.[38]

Under the Condition a purchaser of an existing leasehold interest is entitled to see:

(i) the lease (or underlease) being sold no matter how old it is; and

(ii) if the lease (or underlease) is less than 15 years old at the date of the contract the superior title back to a good root at least 15 years old at the time the contract is made.

Again an example may make the operation of Condition 8(2) clearer.

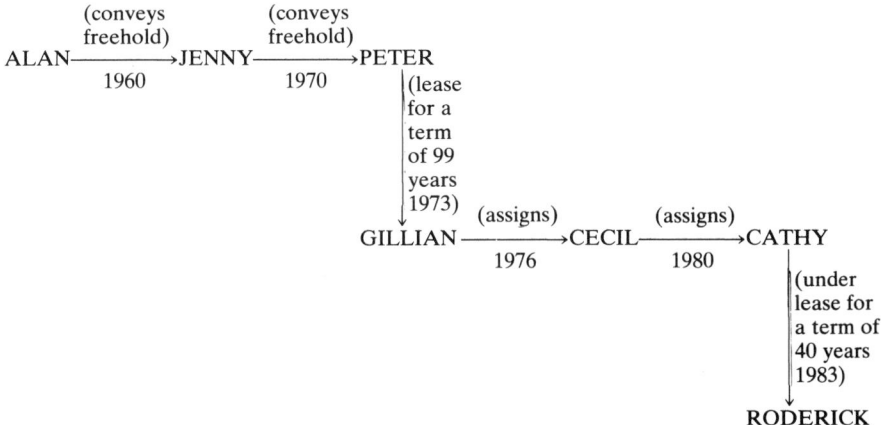

All transactions are governed by the Law Society Conditions. Cathy can call for the 1973 lease (Peter to Gillian) and the 1976 (Gillian to Cecil) assignment—this she could also call for under an open contract.[39] Her position is improved by Condition 8(2) because the lease granted in 1973 is only seven years old (in 1980, the date of the contract to assign). Cathy is entitled under the Condition to call for title to be deduced for 15 years back from the date of the contract (ie. to 1965) and then further back to a good root of title. She will not only see the 1970 conveyance of the freehold but also the conveyance from Alan to Jenny in 1960. Condition 8(2) would not improve Roderick's position on Cathy granting him an underlease—it does not operate on the grant of a lease or underlease.

It has already been pointed out that Condition 8(2), or any other term extending the purchaser's rights, will not help the purchaser if his vendor originally bought without contracting to see the superior title. In such cases the vendor must exclude Condition 8(2) or similar term because he could not comply with its terms. Similarly, if the lease or underlease is more than 15 years old at the date the contract is made, the purchaser in the absence of a special condition to the contrary, is debarred from investigating the superior title. He will have no way of finding out whether the lease was validly granted in the first place.

Finally, whether the purchaser's rights to investigate the superior title are limited by the operation of section 44 of the 1925 Act or by some

[38] See *post*, p. 328.
[39] See *ante*, p. 284.

express provision in the contract, the purchaser who finds out about a defect in the superior title will be entitled to rescind if the vendor does not produce evidence to show his title to be a good one.[40] In this respect the purchaser's claim must be founded on more than general allegations of, for instance, "some covenant" in a superior lease being objectionable.

Notice and Leasehold Interests

Before statute imposed restrictions on the extent to which a purchaser of a leasehold interest could investigate the superior title, a purchaser was only fixed with notice of matters affecting the title discoverable on an investigation of the 60 year title he could call for under an open contract. If he allowed his entitlement to be cut down by special condition he was still fixed with notice of equitable interests and so on appearing on the title prior to the contractual period but within the period he could have called for in the absence of the special condition.[41] This was fair as the purchaser had to face the consequences of submitting to a special condition which restricted his rights. When the statutory restrictions on a purchaser's right to see the superior title were introduced it might have been expected that the rule fixing him with notice of all matters affecting the title within the former period he had been able to call for under an open contract, would be amended. This was not the case. Notwithstanding that he was prevented by statute from seeing the superior title the purchaser continued to be fixed with notice of defects, equitable interests and other matters he could not hope to discover under an open contract.[42] In other words he now had to face the consequences of not persuading his vendor to extend his rights by excluding the open contract rules by means of a special condition enabling him to see the superior title. The injustice of such a rule is illustrated by the pre–1926 case of *Patman* v. *Harland*.[43] The defendant was granted a lease out of a freehold which was subject to a restrictive covenant. The lessee broke the covenant. Whether or not the restrictive covenant was enforceable against her depended upon whether she had notice of the covenant.[44] It was argued for her that because statute prevented her from calling for the freehold title she should not be fixed with constructive notice of the covenant. The Court of Appeal rejected this argument; the covenant could be enforced against her. The injustice created by this rule was removed by section 44(5) of the Law of Property Act 1925. The section provides:

> "Where by reason of [s.44(2)–(4)] an intending lessee or assign is not entitled to call for the title to the freehold or to a leasehold reversion, as the case may be, he shall not, where the contract is made after the commencement of this Act, be deemed to be affected with notice of any matter or thing of which, if he had contracted that such title should be furnished, he might have had notice."

---

[40] *Jones* v. *Watts* (1890) 43 Ch.D. 574.
[41] See *ante*, p. 257, his position was similar to that of a purchaser of a freehold.
[42] *Patman* v. *Harland* (1881) 17 Ch.D. 353; *Imray* v. *Oakshette* [1897] 2 Q.B. 218.
[43] (1881) 17 Ch.D. 353.
[44] At that time enforceability depended not on registration but on the doctrine of notice.

So—if the facts of *Patman* occurred today and pursuant to an open contract a lease was granted out of a freehold subject to a pre–1926 restrictive covenant the lessee by virtue of section 44(5) could not have the covenant enforced against him unless he actually knew of it's existence.[45]

The operation of section 44(5) is limited by the provisions of section 198(1) of the 1925 Act.[46] Registered land charges, for example a post–1926 restrictive covenant, will bind a lessee or assignee even though he could not discover them because of the statutory restrictions on the length of title he can call for.[47] The reason why a lessee or assign will not be able to discover the interest protected by registration of a land charge is that the land charge will be registered not against the property but against the name of the person who owned the legal estate at the time. To make an effective search the lessee/assignee has to know the name to search against. He cannot discover the name because he is debarred from seeing the superior title by sections 44(2)–(4). Furthermore, the right to statutory compensation under section 25 of the Law of Property Act 1969 for loss caused by an undisclosed land charge is only available to a purchaser of a leasehold interest in very limited circumstances. As the following example shows compensation may be available to an underlessee in respect of undisclosed land charges registered against the immediately superior title.[48]

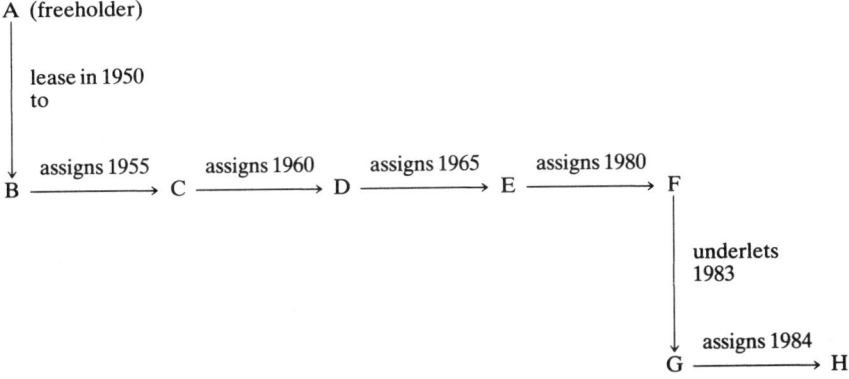

G can call for the lease made between A and B. He can also call for the assignments made in 1965 (D to E) and 1980 (E to F). He will therefore be able to search against the names of A, B, D, E and F. He cannot search against C because the title will not reveal his name. He does not obtain C's name because of the operation of the "fifteen year rule."[49] If there is

---

[45] *Shears* v. *Wells* [1936] 1 All E.R. 832; the same would apply to an equitable mortgage protected by deposit of the title deeds.
[46] See *ante*, p. 26.
[47] *White* v. *Bijou Mansions Ltd.* [1938] Ch. 351.
[48] Law of Property Act 1969, ss.25(1)(9) and (10).
[49] *Ibid.* s.23; see *ante*, p. 256.

a land charge registered against C and the chargee subsequently asserts his right causing G loss G can obtain compensation under section 25 of the 1969 Act.

No compensation is available to the grantee of a lease out of a freehold where there are undisclosed land charges registered against the freehold estate owner. In our example B could not obtain compensation if there was an undisclosed land charge registered against A. Similarly, in any other case where section 44(2)–(4) prevent the purchaser of a leasehold interest from discovering a registered land charge he will not be entitled to compensation under section 25. Thus, returning to our example, H cannot claim compensation in respect of an undisclosed land charge registered against A, B, C, D or E.

(3) CAPACITY

Discussed below are some matters particularly relevant to investigating title where the sale is made by a person other than an individual entitled to the full legal and beneficial ownership of the property. It is not possible in a book of this size to embark upon an examination of the detailed rules relating to every type of vendor. It is hoped that what follows is a useful outline guide. Readers who require more detailed information on this subject are urged to consult *Emmet on Title* (18th ed.) or *Williams on Title* (4th ed.), which provide a more detailed analysis of the relevant principles.

Charities

Charities are not free to dispose of their land in any manner they desire. Under section 29 of the Charities Act 1960 the consent of either the court or the Charity Commissioners must be obtained before any sale, lease, mortgage or any other disposition of land forming part of a charity's permanent endowment can be made. A disposition within section 29 is made when a binding contract is concluded, not when a conveyance is executed. Land forms part of a "permanent endowment" when a charity is restricted from selling it, even in pursuance of its charitable objectives.[50] The consent should be obtained before the contract becomes binding.[51] Alternatively the contract should be made conditional on the consent being obtained.[52] If the contract is not made conditional, and no consent is forthcoming, the contract will be unlawful and the purchaser will be entitled to rescind and recover all moneys already paid to the vendor. A purchaser from a charity must make sure that the requisite consent has been obtained. If it is not the disposition will remain liable to being set aside.

---

[50] Charities Act 1960, s.45(3).
[51] *Milner* v. *Staffordshire Congregational Union* [1956] Ch. 275.
[52] *Michael Richards Properties Ltd.* v. *Corporation of Wardens of St. Saviours Parish, Southwark* [1975] 3 All E.R. 416.

If a purchaser proposes to buy land from a charity which is not part of its permanent endowment but which has been occupied for the purposes of the charity, section 29 again requires the consent of the court or the Charity Commissioners to the disposition. However, in this case the disposition cannot be avoided after the property has been acquired by a bona fide purchaser for money or money's worth without notice that consent was required.[53]

No consent to a disposition is needed if the charity is one of certain exempt charities,[54] on the grant of a lease for a term ending in under 22 years from the date of grant and not being made in consideration of a fine,[55] and where the land is neither part of the permanent endowment nor land which has been occupied for the purposes of a charity.

Attorneys

WHAT IS A POWER OF ATTORNEY?

A power of attorney is a formal document by which the donor of the power gives a second person, the attorney, a power to dispose of his property (either generally or in relation to a specific piece of property) or otherwise act on his behalf, for example to sue for recovery of rent due under a lease. The document must be signed by, or by the direction and in the presence of the person conferring the power.[56] It may be convenient for a vendor (or a purchaser) to grant a power of attorney where he is due to leave the country for a long time and wishes in the meantime to proceed with a contract for sale already entered into.

POINTS A PURCHASER MUST CHECK

The purchaser's starting point must be to verify that the proposed sale is within the scope of the power given to the attorney. For example in *Re Dowson and Jenkins' Contract*[57] an attorney was given power "to sell any real or personal property . . . belonging to me." It was held that this did not authorise the attorney to dispose of the property in mortgage to the donor in exercise of a power of sale. Nowadays the donor of a power may opt to confer a general power of attorney by using the form set out in Schedule 1 of the Powers of Attorney Act 1971. This will empower the attorney "to do on behalf of the donor anything which he can lawfully do by an attorney."[58] Note, however, that a trustee may not appoint a sole co-trustee his attorney,[59] therefore in the common case where a husband and wife hold the legal estate as trustees for sale the husband could not grant a power of attorney to his wife enabling her to sell the property (or vice versa).

---

[53] Charities Act 1960, s.29(2).
[54] *Ibid.* Sched. 2.
[55] *Ibid.* s.29(2).
[56] Powers of Attorney Act 1971, s.1
[57] [1904] 2 Ch. 219.
[58] Powers of Attorney Act 1971, s.10.
[59] *Ibid.* s.10(2).

The next point a purchaser should verify is that the power of attorney is still operative and that it has not been validly revoked. Broadly speaking, a power of attorney may be expressly revoked, orally or in writing, or impliedly revoked by the death of the donor of the power. If it is revoked, the attorney has no authority to sell the property on behalf of the vendor and consequently any contract entered into with the attorney would not bind the donor (the vendor). Certain provisions of the 1971 Act help a purchaser in this respect. Section 4(1) states:

> "Where a power of attorney is expressed to be irrevocable and is given to secure—
> (a) a proprietary interest of the donee of the power; or
> (b) the performance of an obligation owed to the donee,
> then, so long as the donee has that interest or the obligation remains undischarged, the power shall not be revoked—
> (i) by the donor without the consent of the donee; or
> (ii) by the death, incapacity or bankruptcy of the donor or, if the donor is a body corporate, by its winding up or dissolution."

For instance, a power of attorney contained in an equitable mortgage authorising the mortgagee to sell the legal estate remains valid and subsisting as long as the mortgage remains undischarged despite the death of the mortgagor. A purchaser can safely buy from the mortgagee as far as the power of attorney is concerned. The section applies to powers of attorney whenever created.[60]

Section 5(2) of the Act provides:

> "Where a power of attorney has been revoked and a person, without knowledge of the revocation, deals with the donee of the power, the transaction between them shall, in favour of that person, be as valid as if the power had then been in existence."

The protection afforded by the section cannot be claimed by a person who knew of some event which in fact has the effect of revoking the power, such as the death of the donor (even though that person did not know the occurrence of the event had the effect in law of revoking the power).[61]

A purchaser of property may find that his vendor's title depends upon a document having been validly executed by an attorney some time in the past—a prior sale by a vendor (through his attorney) to a previous purchaser of the property, for example. How can the present purchaser be sure the power had not been revoked, or that the person buying from the attorney in the past could claim the benefit of section 5(2) of the Act? Section 5(4) states that it shall be conclusively presumed in favour of (the present) purchaser that the person dealing with the attorney (in the past) did not know of the revocation of the power in two cases. First, where the transaction involving the attorney and the previous purchaser was completed within 12 months of the date on which the power came into

---

[60] *Ibid.*, s.4(3).
[61] *Ibid.*, s.5(5).

operation and second where the purchaser from the attorney (in the past) makes a statutory declaration that he did not know of the revocation of the power at the time of the transaction with the attorney. The statutory declaration however must be made within 3 months of the completion of the transaction between the person who bought from the attorney and the present purchaser (that is the purchase in hand). If it is not the statutory presumption will not arise. For the convenience of future purchasers a purchaser who has bought from an attorney should make a statutory declaration as soon after the transaction with the attorney is completed. After all, if he should die before selling, there will not be anybody else capable of making it!

Tenant for Life under a Settlement

Every settlement of land is effected by two deeds.[62] These deeds—the trust instrument and the vesting deed—have already been briefly described.[63] The vesting deed conveys the legal estate to the tenant for life.[64] The tenant for life although having the legal estate vested in him holds it on trust for the beneficiaries under the settlement. The Settled Land Act 1925 confers upon the tenant for life wide powers of disposition. These may be added to expressly by the trust instrument; their exercise cannot be limited by a provision in it.[65]

In exercising his powers the tenant for life must act in a trustee like manner. The powers include *inter alia*, a power to sell the settled land or any part of it,[66] a power to lease the land or any part subject to the following restrictions on the length of the term granted:

(i) building or forestry leases must not exceed 999 years;
(ii) mining leases must not exceed 100 years; and
(iii) any other type of lease (for example a lease of a dwelling) must not exceed a term of 50 years[67];

and a power to exchange the settled land.[68] A tenant for life has no power to mortgage the legal estate in the settled land for his own (or their own) benefit. A mortgage of the legal estate can be made only for certain purposes set out in section 71 of the Settled Land Act 1925. These purposes include paying for authorised improvements or the discharge of an incumbrance on the settled land or any part thereof. If the tenant for life is to mortgage the property for his own benefit it is essential for the mortgagee to ensure an express power enabling the tenant for life to do so was included in the trust instrument. Any disposition by the tenant for life, which is not made in the exercise of either the powers given to him

---

[62] Settled Land Act 1925, s.4.
[63] See *ante*, p. 263.
[64] Settled Land Act 1925, ss.19 and 20 for statutory definition of "tenant for life."
[65] *Ibid.* s.106.
[66] *Ibid.* s.38; see, *e.g. Wheelwright* v. *Walker (No. 2)* (1883) 31 W.R. 912.
[67] Settled Land Act 1925, s.41.
[68] *Ibid.* ss.39 and 40.

by the statute or conferred upon him expressly by the trust instrument is void,[69] as far as the legal estate in the settled land is concerned.

If a tenant for life sells the legal estate all the equitable interests of the other beneficiaries are overreached; that is they are transferred to the purchase money. The purchase money is "capital money" and must be paid to the trustees of the settlement (who are named in the vesting deed) being at least two in number or a trust corporation.[70] It is vital for a purchaser from a tenant for life to ensure that he gets a receipt from the trustees of the settlement otherwise he will take subject to the other beneficiaries' equitable interests. A purchaser must assume that the details as to the identity of the tenant for life and the trustees of the settlement are correctly stated in the vesting deed. He is not entitled to go behind the "curtain" created by the vesting deed to check the particulars contained in the trust instrument.[71] This document is of no concern to a purchaser in keeping with the general policy of the property legislation to keep the equities off the title.

Trustees for Sale

Under section 2 of the Law of Property Act 1925 a conveyance of a legal estate to a purchaser will overreach the equitable interests of the beneficiaries under the trust provided that the conveyance is made by *trustees* for sale and the requirements as to the payment of capital money are satisfied. These requirements contained in section 27(2) of the same Act are that the money be paid to no fewer than two trustees for sale except where the trustee is a trust corporation. It should be remembered that although the trust is "for sale" trustees for sale have a power to postpone sale. Selling is a duty and can be forced on an unwilling trustee at the court's discretion under section 30 of the Law of Property Act 1925. Postponing is a power which the trustees must exercise unanimously.[72]

The reader will recall that since 1925 concurrent ownership of land exists behind a statutory trust for sale; sections 34–36 of the Law of Property Act 1925. The case of *Bull* v. *Bull* [73] first brought to light the problem which can arise where the legal estate is vested in a sole owner but the beneficial interest is concurrently owned due to one or more other persons contributing towards the purchase price. Section 2 above states that the interests of the beneficiaries under a trust for sale can only be overreached where the conveyance was made by trustees for sale, implying that a sale by a sole trustee (except a trust corporation) would be ineffective to overreach the beneficial interests. *Bull* v. *Bull* [74] itself suggests that the proper procedure is for a second trustee to be appointed and for the

---

[69] *Ibid.* s.18(1)(a).
[70] *Ibid.* s.18(1)(b).
[71] *Ibid.* s.110(2), except where the current vesting deed was made pursuant to an "imperfect" trust instrument under s.9 of the Act.
[72] *Re Mayo* [1943] Ch. 302.
[73] [1955] 1 Q.B. 234.
[74] [1955] 1 Q.B. 234.

interests of the beneficiaries to be consulted as per section 26(3) of the 1925 Act. The recent case of *First National Securities Ltd.* v. *Hegerty*[75] is also consistent with this view. However, other cases,[76] notably *Williams & Glyn's Bank Ltd* v. *Boland* [77] have glossed over this point and suggest that a sale by a sole trustee would be effective to transfer the legal estate to the purchaser. The decision does not however, make clear what happens to the interests of the beneficiaries; whether they attach to the proceeds of sale or what? Following *Boland* practitioners also seem to have assumed that a sale by a sole trustee can be effective even though the purchaser is alerted to the existence of a trust for sale by replies to preliminary enquiries and so on. It is suggested that instead of, as is common, obtaining a beneficiary's consent to the sale a second trustee should always be appointed.

Personal Representatives

A testamentary disposition of real property, whether freehold or leasehold, does not operate to vest the legal estate in the beneficiary. A will operates in Equity only; the beneficiary obtains the equitable estate in the property.[78] The legal estate in the deceased's freehold and leasehold land vests in his or her personal representatives on death.[79] While they have the legal estate the personal representatives hold the property on trust for sale. Section 39 of the Administration of Estates Act 1925 gives them wide powers of management for the purpose of administering the deceased's estate. These powers include *inter alia*, the power to overreach the equitable interests of the beneficiaries, for instance, by selling the property to raise money to settle debts owed by the deceased. In fact the powers given to personal representatives are the same as those given to a tenant for life under a strict settlement.[80]

There is no need to have two personal representatives in order to give a valid receipt for purchase money on the sale of estate property. Section 27(2)[81] of the Law of Property Act 1925 does not affect the right of a sole personal representative to give a valid receipt for the proceeds of the sale of land. If, however, more than one person takes out a grant of probate, or letters of administration, all of the personal representatives must be made parties to the sale. Personal representatives authority is joint where land is concerned.[82]

There are two methods by which personal representatives can transfer the legal estate in property forming part of the estate of the deceased to

---

[75] [1984] 1 All E.R. 139. But see *Thames Guaranty Ltd.* v. *Campbell* [1984] 1 All E.R. 144.
[76] See, *e.g. Caunce* v. *Caunce* [1969] 1 W.L.R. 286.
[77] [1981] A.C. 487.
[78] See *ante*, p. 263.
[79] Administration of Estates Act 1925, ss.1 and 3.
[80] See *ante*, p. 293.
[81] See *ante*, p. 294.
[82] Administration of Estates Act 1925, s.21. There is a maximum of four proving personal representatives in respect of any one piece of property; Supreme Court Act 1981, s.114.

a third party. The legal estate may be transferred to a beneficiary under the will by an assent. The assent must be in writing (it does not have to be a deed) signed by the personal representatives and name the person in whose favour it is given.[83] If the assent is not in writing or if it does not name the beneficiary it is not effective; the legal estate does not pass. As a matter of pure logic it might be thought that a personal representative (who has the legal estate vested in him on the testator's death) who is also to take the property under the will, whether as beneficial owner or trustee, need not assent to himself in that capacity because no legal estate is to pass. However, in the much criticised[84] case of *Re King's Will Trusts*[85] it was held that a personal representative, entitled to the property as trustee at the end of the administration, had to assent in writing to effectually vest the legal estate in himself in that capacity. In other words an assent in writing is necessary not only in cases where a legal estate is to "pass" but also in cases where the legal estate is to remain with the personal representative but in a different capacity, such as beneficial owner or trustee. The decision in *King's* case was not called into question by the Court of Appeal in the recent case of *Re Edward's Will Trusts*[86] where it was said that it might be possible for an administrator to pass the legal estate to a beneficiary under the intestacy rules by means of an implied assent. As the authorities stand at present a purchaser who finds a personal representative on the vendor's title selling as beneficial owner must ensure that the personal representative assented in writing to the legal estate vesting in himself as beneficial owner.

The second method by which a personal representative may transfer the legal estate in land forming part of the estate is by a means of a conveyance. This will be the method used when the personal representatives are selling the property to raise money to pay taxes and so forth.

There are three dangers for a purchaser of property who finds that personal representatives appear on the vendor's abstract or epitome, or where he is buying from personal representatives:

(1) A grant of representation may be revoked if, for example, the probate or letters of administration is issued to the wrong person. A purchaser may make a search of the Probate Registry to ensure the grant has not been revoked. A postal search facility is available on payment of a fee (currently £1.00). Note, however, that if contracts have been exchanged before the grant of representation is revoked, the contract will be enforceable against any subsequent personal representative provided it was made in pursuance of the powers conferred by section 39 of the Administration of Estates Act 1925.[87]

(2) The personal representatives might have disposed of the property to somebody other than their purchaser by a prior conveyance or assent.

---

[83] Administration of Estates Act 1925, s.36(4).

[84] (1964) 108 S.J. 698 and p. 717; (1964) Conv (N.S.) 298; (1976) 29 *C.L.P.* 60.

[85] [1964] Ch. 542; see *Re Cockburn's Will Trusts* [1957] Ch. 438, where it seems no assent was necessary to empower P.R.s as trustees to exercise the power of appointing new trustees under Trustee Act 1925, s.36.

[86] [1982] Ch. 30.

[87] See Administration of Estates Act 1925, s.204 and (1982) 126 S.J. 107.

(3) As has already been explained any will on the title need not be abstracted or included in the epitome. It does not form a link in the vendor's "chain of title" because it operates in Equity only. A purchaser from an assentee, therefore, has no way of checking that the personal representatives assented to the correct person to comply with the terms of the will.

Certain statutory provisions improve a purchaser's position in this respect.

PROTECTION FOR PURCHASERS

Section 36(5) of the Administration of Estates Act 1925 gives any person in whose favour an assent or conveyance is made by personal representatives the right to require a notice of that assent or conveyance to be endorsed on the probate or letters of administration. This must be done at the expense of the estate of the deceased. This right forms the basis of the statutory provisions enacted for the protection of purchasers.

Section 36(6) of the Act states that a statement in writing by the personal representatives that they have not made a previous assent or conveyance of the legal estate is sufficient evidence in favour of a purchaser that no prior assent or conveyance has been made. The statement will usually take the form of a recital in the conveyance to the purchaser. If buying from a personal representative he should be asked to give such a statement in the conveyance. The purchaser can then be satisfied that the property has not already been disposed of by the personal representative to somebody else. A conveyance of the legal estate to a purchaser by a personal representative accepted on the faith of such a statement is effective to pass the legal estate to that purchaser even though there has been a previous assent or conveyance. This protection cannot be claimed in the two following circumstances:[88]

(1) Where a memorandum of that previous assent or conveyance has been endorsed on the probate or letters of administration. This is why the right given by section 36(5) is so important. An endorsement should be put on the grant of representation after every disposition has been made by a personal representative. This will prevent the personal representative from mistakenly selling the same property again. The purchaser should in the first instance ask the vendor whether there are any endorsements on the grant of representation and then check at completion (when the grant is produced) that there are none for himself.

(2) Where there has been in the period since the disposition by the personal representative a disposition for money or moneys worth in favour of another purchaser. In this case there need not be any endorsement relating to the conveyance on the grant.

The combined effect of the above provisions is to make it essential for a donee (for example a beneficiary in whose favour an assent is made) to endorse a note of the assent or conveyance to him, on the probate or letters of administration. If he does not a subsequent conveyance for value by the personal representative will operate to divest the donee of the legal estate.[89]

---

[88] Administration of Estates Act 1925, s.36(6).   [89] *Ibid.* s.36(5).

The importance of endorsing the grant of representation is again emphasised by section 36(7) of the Act. This is the second provision affording a purchaser a measure of protection where there are personal representatives on the title. The sub-section provides that an assent or conveyance by a personal representative shall, in favour of a purchaser, be taken as sufficient evidence that the person in whose favour the assent or conveyance is given or made is the person entitled under the will or intestacy rules. There is, therefore, no need for a purchaser to raise a requisition to confirm the legal estate was transferred to the correct person. Again the purchaser must ensure that no notice of a previous assent or conveyance affecting the legal estate has been endorsed on the grant of representation. If there is an endorsement of a previous assent or conveyance on the grant the purchaser must then require the vendor to prove that the assent or conveyance detailed in the abstract or epitome, was made to the proper person; the person entitled to take under the will or the rules relating to the devolution of property on intestacy.

Finally on the subject of dispositions by personal representatives section 37 of the Administration of Estates Act 1925 provides:

> "All conveyances of any interest in real or personal estate made to a purchaser either before or after the commencement of his Act by a person to whom probate or letters of administration have been granted are valid, notwithstanding any subsequent revocation or variation, either before or after the commencement of this Act, of the probate or administration."

The protection extends only to purchasers; that is a lessee, mortgagee or other person who in good faith acquires an interest in property for valuable consideration. "Valuable consideration" includes marriage consideration but does not include a nominal consideration in money.[90]

POSITION WHERE THE PERSONAL REPRESENTATIVE DIES BEFORE DISPOSING OF THE PROPERTY

Where an executor appointed by "the deceased" dies before disposing of the property forming part of the deceased's estate and himself appoints somebody by his will to be his personal representative that person also becomes executor of "the deceased."[91] The chain of executors may, therefore be built up, the last executor in the chain being the executor of every preceding testator with the same powers of disposition as if he had been the original proving executor. If the chain is broken by an intestacy, failure to appoint an executor in the will, or failure on the part of an appointed executor to prove the will, a grant *de bonis non administratis* will be needed.[92]

---

[90] *Ibid.* s.55.
[91] *Ibid.* s.7.
[92] Non Contentious Probate Rules, rr. 19 and 21.

Mortgagees

THE POWER OF SALE

A mortgagee needs a power of sale so that he can realise his security and discharge the debt owed by the mortgagor. The power of sale may be included as an express term of the mortgage. More commonly, however, mortgagees will rely on the statutory power of sale contained in section 101(1)(i) of the Law of Property Act 1925. A mortgagee has a statutory power of sale where the mortgage was created by deed and no contrary intention is shown in the terms of the mortgage.[93] The mortgagee may sell either the whole or part of the mortgaged property by public auction or by private treaty.

A legal mortgagee may sell the whole legal estate of the mortgagor. He sells the property subject to any legal mortgages having priority to the mortgage under which the sale is made. The purchaser, however, takes free from all subsequent mortgages and, of course, the mortgage in right of which the sale is made.[94] Although the sale may be made in the name of the mortgagor in practice the mortgagee frequently sells in his own name.

Although an equitable mortgagee may have a statutory power of sale (provided his mortgage is by deed) it is doubtful whether he has the power to transfer the mortgagor's legal estate to a purchaser.[94a] Unless the mortgage deed contains a power of attorney or declaration of trust [94b] an order of the court under section 90 of the Law of Property Act 1925 is necessary to do this.

WHEN DOES THE POWER OF SALE ARISE

The power of sale arises once the mortgage money has become due, that is as soon as the legal date for redemption has passed.[95] If the mortgage contains a covenant on the part of the mortgagor to repay by instalments the power will arise when the first instalment has become due.[96]

A purchaser buying property from a vendor mortgagee must ensure that the legal date for redemption has passed. Similarly, if a sale by a mortgagee appears on the face of the abstract or epitome of title delivered by the vendor the purchaser should raise a requisition to check that the power of sale had arisen. Until the legal date for redemption has passed the mortgagee has no power of sale and, therefore, cannot vest the property in a purchaser.

WHEN DOES THE POWER OF SALE BECOME EXERCISABLE

The power of sale does not become exercisable until[97]:

> "(i) Notice requiring payment of the mortgage money has been served on the mortgagor or one of two or more mortgagors, and

---

[93] Law of Property Act 1925, s.101(4).
[94] *Ibid.* s.88, even if subsequent mortgages are registered.
[94a] *Re White Rose Cottage* [1965] Ch. 940.
[94b] See *post*, p. 461.   [95] *Ibid.* s.101(1).
[96] *Payne* v. *Cardiff R.D.C.* [1932] 1 K.B. 241.   [97] Law of Property Act 1925, s.103.

default has been made in payment of the mortgage money, or part thereof, for three months after such service; or

(ii) Some interest under the mortgage is in arrear and unpaid for two months after becoming due; or

(iii) There has been a breach of some provision contained in the mortgage deed or in this Act, or in an enactment replaced by this Act, and one the part of the mortgagor, or of some person concurring in making the mortgage, to be observed or performed, other than and besides a covenant for payment of the mortgage money or interest thereon."

Frequently the terms of the mortgage will make the power of sale exercisable in circumstances other than those mentioned above.[98] For example, it may make the power exercisable if the mortgagor enters into a deed of arrangement with his creditors or, if the mortgagor is a company, if it goes into liquidation other than for the purposes of amalgamation or reconstruction. The power is treated as having been exercised as soon as there is a concluded contract for the sale of the property.[99] If a mortgagee enters into a contract before the power of sale is exercisable any person damnified by the improper exercise of the power will be able to sue the mortgagee for damages.[1]

A purchaser is not concerned to see that the power of sale has become properly exercisable.[2] Provided he is acting in good faith, he will obtain a good title as long as the power of sale has arisen. However, should a purchaser investigate the circumstances in which the sale is taking place and actually discover that the power of sale has not become exercisable (for instance because notice has not been given to the mortgagee as required) he will not obtain a good title. A sale by a mortgagee is bad if the purchaser has actual notice of some impropriety in the exercise of the sale.[3] The mortgagor may be able to have the sale set aside.

B. DEDUCING TITLE—REGISTERED LAND

Introductory

"It is a truism to say that the law of conveyancing (unregistered) is complementary to the law of real property and vice versa and similarly the law of registered conveyancing is based upon both unregistered conveyancing and real property law."[4] The reader will have appreciated that the principal defect in the unregistered system of conveyancing is the "wearisome and intricate task of investigating title"[5] which must be undertaken each and every time the land changes hands. In pursuance of

---

[98] *Ibid.* s.101(3).
[99] *Property & Bloodstock Ltd.* v. *Emerton* [1968] Ch. 94.
[1] Law of Property Act 1925, s.104(1).
[2] *Ibid.* s.104.
[3] *Nutt* v. *Easton* [1900] 1 Ch. 29.
[4] F.R.Crane (1937) 2 Conv. (N.S.) 42.
[5] *Williams & Glyn's Bank Ltd.* v. *Boland* [1980] 3 W.L.R. 138, *per* Lord Scarman at p. 149.

its aim "to give certainty to the title to real estates and to facilitate the proof thereof and also to render the dealing with land more simple and economical"[6] the registered system substitutes a title guaranteed by the state (in the sense that compensation is payable for mistakes and omissions made by H.M. Land Registry) for the separate investigation of title. However, except where absolutely necessary it leaves the substantive principles of Land Law intact.

Title to registered land is examined once only—by the Chief Land Registrar (or more accurately, his legal staff)—on an application for first registration of title. An authoritative record of the title is prepared (the register) describing the land with the rights it enjoys, naming the current owner and detailing most of the incumbrances to which the land is subject. Thereafter the register is kept accurate by a regular updating of the information kept in it. In theory the result is that an intending purchaser of registered land need not concern himself with the history of his vendor's title; he need not even inspect the actual conveyance or transfer to the vendor. By a simple inspection of the register he can verify that the vendor has the power to sell the land and the majority of the incumbrances affecting it. However buying registered land is often not as simple as it looks, and can involve investigations on a scale equal to those that must be undertaken on the purchase of unregistered land, especially in connection with what are known as "overriding interests."

Land registration was introduced into England and Wales over a century ago. The Land Registry Act 1862 and the Land Transfer Act 1875 provided for voluntary registration of title, but it was not until the Land Transfer Act 1897 made registration of title compulsory on dealings with land in the County of London, that an appreciable number of titles became registered. On January 1, 1926, the Land Registration Act 1925 repealed the earlier Acts and consolidated and extended the statute law relating to registered land. The modern system is governed by the Land Registration Acts 1925–1971 (the Land Registration Acts 1925, 1936 and 1966 and the Land Registration and Land Charges Act 1971, as amended by the Administration of Justice Acts 1977 and 1982). The Acts are supplemented by the Land Registration Rules 1925, as amended, and various other rules made under the auspices of the 1925 Act.

At present 73 per cent. of the population of England and Wales are covered by the compulsory registration system, some 36,000,000 people. In the, as yet, non-compulsory areas there are approximately 5,000,000 dwellings, 700,000 of which have voluntarily registered titles and a further 1,400,000 also brought within the compulsory registration system by the Housing Act 1980.[7] In February this year the government [7a] announced their intention to "speed up" the spread of compulsory registration. They predict that by 1987 compulsory registration will cover areas containing 85 per cent of the population. This will be the first extension in the system (apart from the provisions in the Housing Act relating to former council

---

[6] Land Registry Act 1862, see preamble.

[7] Housing Act, s.20.

[7a] (1984) 81 L.S.Gaz. 683.

houses) since 1978. Nevertheless it seems unlikely that the prophecy expressed at the time of the passing of the 1862 Act, that all land in England and Wales would one day be within the registration system, will come true in the near future. Shortly before taking office, the new Chief Land Registrar, Mr. E. J. Pryer, expressed the view that this goal could never be achieved by compulsory registration alone.[8] Broadly speaking even after an area is made an area of compulsory registration, title to property within it only has to be registered the next time it is sold. In London, where compulsory registration on sale was introduced nearly 100 years ago, there are still plenty of titles which are unregistered because they have remained in the same ownership. Many of them belong to ancient universities, the City's livery companies, the Church Commissioners, nationalised boards and corporations, including the City corporation. Mr. Pryer feels it "inevitable that at some time consideration will have to be given to securing the ultimate objective of ensuring that every parcel of land in England and Wales is registered. . . . The prospect of registered and unregistered systems continuing to exist side by side indefinitely is a daunting one."[9]

Even though registration of title is not "all-embracing" it remains a fact that over 8 million titles are presently recorded on the register and that the greater part of most solicitors' conveyancing business will appertain to registered land. Last year Her Majesty's Land Registry received over 500,000 enquiries from practitioners relating to normal day to day transactions with registered land. This suggests that the profession is still not as conversant with the principles of registered conveyancing as they are with those of unregistered conveyancing.

Therefore to enable the less well informed reader to understand fully the process of deducing and examining title to registered land, we shall endeavour to explain the machinery of land registration insofar as it applies to the more straightforward cases likely to be met in practice.[10] Readers who encounter more intricate problems are referred to Ruoff and Roper, *Registered Conveyancing* (4th ed.). We do not apologise for not having included this description of the registered system, as some authors do, at the beginning of this book. We are of the opinion that it is at "title stage" that the conveyancer needs to have this information at hand.

What can be Registered?

There are three classes of interest in registered land in respect of which a proprietor can be registered;

Registrable interests, minor interests and overriding interests.

REGISTRABLE INTERESTS

Section 2(1) of the Land Registration Act 1925 states that the only estates in respect of which a proprietor may be registered are estates capable of

---

[8] (1983) 127 S.J. 46.   [9] *Ibid.* at p. 47.

[10] See also T.B. F. Ruoff and C. West, *Concise Land Registration* Practice (3rd ed.), and Registered Land Practice Notes (1982/83 ed.).

subsisting as legal estates. "Legal Estates" are defined in section 3(xi) as "the estates, interests and charges in or over land subsisting or created at law which are by the Law of Property Act 1925 authorised to subsist or to be created at law." Thus registrable estates and interests are:

(1) An estate in fee simple absolute in possession.

(2) A term of years absolute. As will be seen not all leases are registrable.

(3) An easement right or privilege in or over land for an interest equivalent to an estate in fee simple absolute in possession or a term of years absolute. These cannot be registered on their own with a separate title. They are registered with the dominant tenement[11] (the land with the benefit of the right) and assume the same class of title as that land. Essentially they are treated as part of it.[12]

(4) A rentcharge in possession issuing out of or charged on land being either perpetual or for a term of years absolute. The importance of this category has diminished since the passing of the Rentcharges Act 1977 which came into force on August 22, 1977. The Act prohibited the creation of most new rentcharges after that date[13] and provided for the extinguishment of most existing rentcharges after 60 years[14]. Four classes of rentcharges were excepted[13] those arising under settlements, estate rentcharges, certain rentcharges created under statutory provisions and those created pursuant to agreements entered into before July 22, 1977. Of the four excepted classes estate rentcharges[15] are most likely to be met in practice. They are now quite commonly used as a device to circumvent the rule that the burden of positive covenant is not enforceable against successive owners of freehold land. It is highly probable that the creation of new estate rent charges will soon be prohibited, their role being fulfilled by the positive land obligation (see below).

(5) A charge by way of legal mortgage. The normal way of mortgaging registered land is by registered charge. Section 27(1) of the Land Registration Act 1925 provides that "a registered charge shall, unless made or taking effect by demise or subdemise . . . take effect as a charge by way of legal mortgage."[16] The charge is "registered" by entering the charge and the name of the proprietor of the charge in the register of the charged title.[17]

(6) Rights of entry exerciseable over or in respect of a legal term of years absolute or annexed for any purpose to a legal rentcharge. These cannot be registered separately from the estate to which they belong.

(7) If the Law Commissions proposals set out in their report "Transfer of Land—The Law of Positive and Restrictive Covenants"[17a] become law, a

---

[11] Land Registration Act 1925, ss.5, 9, 19(2) and 22(2); Land Registration Rules 1925, r. 257.

[12] Land Registration Act 1925, s.3(xxiv); *Re Evans' Contract* [1970] 1 W.L.R. 583.

[13] Rentcharges Act 1977, s.2.

[14] *Ibid.* s.3.

[15] For a definition, see Rentcharges Act 1977, s.2(4) and (5).

[16] *Grace Rymer Investments Ltd.* v. *Waite* [1958] 1 Ch. 831.

[17] Land Registration Act 1925, s.26(1).

[17a] Law Com. No. 127.

new registrable interest will be added to the list—the land obligation—an interest in land "which . . . imposes a burden on one piece of land either—

> (a) for the benefit of another piece of land; or
> (b) in pursuance of a development scheme. . . . "[17b]

It is intended that the land obligation be registrable in the same manner as an easement, that is with the dominant tenement.

It will be seen from the above that only fees simple absolute in possession, certain terms of years absolute and rentcharges can be registered independently with separate titles.

Once registered a registrable interest can only be dealt with by means of the machinery of the Act.[18]

MINOR INTERESTS[19]

This is an omnibus category embracing all those interests in registered land which are not registrable interests. They must be protected by an entry on the register otherwise they will not bind a purchaser for value under a registered disposition.[20] Actual notice of the interest is irrelevant for this purpose.[21] Minor interests may be legal but are mainly equitable. Amongst the equitable ones is the same type of division which exists in unregistered land. First there are those interests like restrictive covenants, estate contracts, equitable easements and a spouse's rights of occupation under the Matrimonial Homes Act 1983, corresponding to matters registrable under the Land Charges Act 1972, which if protected on the register will not normally be overridden but will continue to bind the land in the hands of a purchaser. Second are beneficial interests under a trust which, if the formalities prescribed by the protecting entry are complied with (for example, payment of the purchase money to two trustees), will normally be overridden, and the beneficial interests will attach to the proceeds of sale.

However, once registrable interests have been listed it is impossible to make a clear-cut division of interests in registered land in the same way as in unregistered land (legal or equitable). This is because the next category (overriding interests) may alter the status of a minor interest and enable it to be independent of an entry on the register. This is best illustrated by example. In *Bridges* v. *Mees*[22] a purchaser failed to protect his minor interest under a contract for sale by registering a caution. Nevertheless because he was in actual occupation of the land he also had an overriding interest entitling him to the relief claimed. And in *Williams*

[17b] See s.1 of draft bill.

[18] Land Registration Act 1925, s.69(4).

[19] For the statutory definition see Land Registration Act 1925, s.3(xv).

[20] Land Registration Act 1925, ss.5, 9, 20 and 23; *Miles* v. *Bull* (*No.* 2) [1969] 3 All E.R. 1585.

[21] Land Registration Act 1925, s.59(6); *De Lusignan* v. *Johnson*; (1973) 230 E.G. 499; *Williams & Glyn's Bank Ltd* v. *Boland* [1981] A.C. 487. But see *Peffer* v. *Rigg* [1977] 1 W.L.R. 285 and *Lyus* v. *Prowsa Developments Ltd.* [1982] 1 W.L.R. 1044.

[22] [1957] Ch. 475.

& *Glyn's Bank* v. *Boland*[23] the House of Lords held that a subsequent registered chargee was bound by a wife's beneficial interest in the matrimonial home of which her husband was the sole registered proprietor. She had an overriding interest by virtue of her occupation of the home; her failure to protect her interest as a minor interest by an entry on the register was immaterial.

OVERRIDING INTERESTS

"Overriding Interests" are "all the incumbrances, interests, rights and powers not entered on the register but subject to which registered dispositions are by [the Land Registration] Act to take effect."[24]

Overriding interests are usually spoken of as burdens adversely affecting the land over which they operate. But every burden has a corresponding benefit and the owner of an overriding interest possesses an invaluable benefit—his interest binds the whole world, even a purchaser for value, irrespective of notice.[25] In unregistered land the quality of binding "all the world" is restricted to legal interests. However overriding interests may be equitable as well as legal. They all have one characteristic in common. Although they are not mentioned on the register they are usually discoverable on a careful inspection of the property and by making the usual conveyancing searches and enquiries. The present list of overriding interests is set out in section 70(1) of the Land Registration Act 1925 (although this has been added to by the 1925 rules and later statutes).[26] The more important ones are legal easements and legal or equitable profits, rights acquired or in the course of acquisition under the Limitation Act 1980, rights of occupiers, short leases and local land charges. The following can never be overriding interests, they are minor interests only; the rights of a beneficiary under a Settled Land Act settlement,[27] a spouse's rights of occupation under the Matrimonial Homes Act 1983,[28] the rights of a tenant arising from a notice under the Leasehold Reform Act 1967 of his request to have the freehold or an extended lease,[29] and the rights of a mortgagee other than under a registered charge.[30] The land obligation (if it comes into being) will not be capable of being an overriding interest, because (unlike most easements) it will not be readily visible on inspection.[30a]

The fact that the register fails to record overriding interests and is not therefore a complete record of all matters affecting land, is an oft-used ground for criticism of the registered system. But it must be remembered that the register was intended to replace the separate investigation of title,

---

[23] [1981] A.C. 487.
[24] Land Registration Act 1925, s.3(xvi).
[25] See, for example, *Webb* v. *Pollmount Ltd.* [1966] Ch. 584; *Williams & Glyn's Bank Ltd.* v. *Boland* [1981] A.C. 487.
[26] A list also appears on the inside cover of every Land and Charge Certificate.
[27] Land Registration Act 1925, s.86(2).
[28] Matrimonial Homes Act 1983, s.2(8).
[29] Leasehold Reform Act 1967, s.5(5).
[30] Land Registration Act 1925, s.106(2).
[30a] See cl.5(1) of the Draft Bill, Law Com. No. 127.

not physical inspection of the property. Furthermore it would probably be impossible and certainly impracticable (bearing in mind Land Registry resources) to record every piece of relevant information on the register and to keep that information up to date. Recently however the former and present Chief Land Registrars[31] expressed the view that the present list of overriding interests needed revision and that "the types of such interest should be clearly identifiable and their number kept to a minimum." The Law Commission is expected to make recommendations on this in the near future.

Reference to overriding interests may, however, appear on the register in three ways:

(1) The Registrar may make an entry of the existence of an overriding interest on the register of the dominant tenement,[32] but in the case of easements, rights and privileges only where they are appurtenant to the land and capable of existing as legal interests.[33]

(2) The Registrar must enter a note of any easement, right, privilege or benefit created by instrument and adversely affecting the land which appears on the title at the time of first registration.[34]

(3) The Registrar may make an entry of any kind of overriding interest against the title of the servient land, provided that its existence is proved to his satisfaction or is admitted by the owner of the servient land.[35] No claim to an easement right or privilege not created by instrument may be noted against the title to the servient land if the servient owner shows sufficient cause to the contrary.

Once an overriding interest is entered on the register it ceases to be such, because the definition of overriding interests excludes those interests entered on the register.

The entry of overriding interests on the register in some cases has led two authors to comment that "a wide gulf divides interests which are capable of being overriding (that is, those set out in the statutory list) from interests which are in fact overriding because they have not been set out on the register. The latter are relatively rare."[36] Nevertheless the present writers respectfully submit that the hazard of overriding interests (especially rights of occupiers) to potential purchasers is very real and should not be understated.

First Registration and Registered Dispositions—Compulsory and Voluntary Registration

So that the Land Registry could work smoothly, economically and efficiently towards the eventual goal of bringing the whole country within

---

[31] Messrs. R. Roper C.B. and J. Pryer, (1983) L. S. Gaz. 77.
[32] Land Registration Act 1925, s.70(3).
[33] Land Registration Rules 1925, r. 257.
[34] Land Registration Act 1925, s.70(2); *Re Dances Way* [1962] Ch. 490.
[35] Land Registration Rules 1925, r. 41.
[36] T.B.F. Ruoff and C. West *Concise Land Registration Practice* (3rd ed.) p. 42.

the registration system, registration of title was systematically made compulsory by reference to the situation of land. Explanatory Leaflet Number 9 (issued by the Land Registry free of charge) sets out the areas in which registration is compulsory and the particular district land registry which serves each county and London Borough. A supplement to leaflet 9 is also available on request giving the dates on which each particular area became a compulsory area. The compulsory areas include all the large urban parts of the country like Manchester and West Yorkshire (accounting for 73 per cent of the population) but huge sparsely populated areas (about one half of the land) remain outside the system.

Section 123 of the Land Registration Act 1925 deals with the effect of an area being declared a compulsory area and requires registration on certain dispositions on *sale* (which expression includes an exchange where equality money is paid though not a bare exchange.[37]) Thus, until there is a disposition on sale, titles will not be registered even in compulsory areas. Under section 4 of the 1925 Act any estate owner could apply for registration voluntarily whether or not the area was compulsory but from January 13, 1967, the voluntary first registration of land in non-compulsory areas was suspended except in those limited classes of cases as the Registrar may by notice specify.[38] The latest notice (with effect from May 4, 1983) is published in [1983] Conv. 172. The exception for building estates comprising 20 or more plots has been extended to include industrial and commercial as well as residential developments, otherwise the previous exceptions, where title deeds have been lost or destroyed and where council houses are sold to tenants under the Housing Act 1980[39] remain substantially the same. It seems that it is still possible to apply voluntarily for registration in a compulsory area, independently of any disposition on sale.

In order to give a subsequent purchaser notice of the registration of title the Registry stamp the title number on certain documents before they are returned on completion of an application for first registration.[40] For example in the case of a freehold title the stamp would be placed on the conveyance to the applicant. Occasionally the documents will not have been stamped on first registration because some of the deeds are missing or lost and the application for first registration has been supported by statutory declaration. In these circumstances the applicant is required to undertake to produce the documents if they are later recovered, whereupon they will be duly stamped. But where this is not done a subsequent purchaser would not be able to discover the fact of registration from the title deeds and a fraud or mistake might ensue (for instance the subsequent purchase might be completed by unregistered conveyance

---

[37] Land Registration Act 1925, s.123(3).
[38] Land Registration Act 1966, s.1(2).
[39] Housing Act 1980, s.20.
[40] Registered Land Practice Notes (1982/3 ed.) Note A6.

which is not authorised by the 1925 Act). A search of the Public Index Map[41] is the sure way of preventing this occurring.

Once an area has become compulsory two rather separate activities will be going on at the same time. First, "new titles" will be coming onto the register for the first time and secondly dispositions will be taking place in respect of land which is already registered. The two must be looked at independently because the legislature settled on different criteria for dispositions which will bring land onto the register for the first time and for dispositions which must be registered once a particular parcel of land has been brought onto the register.

However before proceeding any further, consideration should be given to three legal estates that are *always* incapable of registration. These are:

(i) a lease for 21 years or under[42];
(ii) a mortgage term where there is a subsisting right of redemption[43]; and
(iii) "a lease containing an absolute prohibition against all dealings therewith inter vivos."[44]

It has recently been asked[45] whether the last prohibition precludes a lease which contains an unqualified covenant "not to assign underlet or part with possession of the demised premises," from registration. "Dealings" is not defined by the 1925 Act but it is argued that it should be interpreted as including the powers of disposition given by the Act[46] to the registered proprietor of leasehold land. If so the covenant does not prevent all dealings and the lease is registrable (unless for a term of 21 years or less). However if as some authors suggest[47-48] the prohibition refers to "inalienable" leases, the lease would appear not to be registrable. The importance of knowing whether it is registrable or not will emerge from the following discussion.

COMPULSORY REGISTRATION ON SALE

Section 123(1) provides that in compulsory areas a grantee must apply for first registration of his title within two months, on

(i) every conveyance on sale of freehold land;
(ii) every grant of a term of years absolute not being less than 40 years from the date of delivery of the grant whether or not a fine or premium is taken, and

---

[41] See *ante*, Chap. 2, p. 15.
[42] Land Registration Act 1925, ss.8(1)(*a*) and 19(2) proviso (*a*).
[43] *Ibid.* ss.8(1) and 19(2) proviso (*b*).
[44] *Ibid.* s.8(2).
[45] [1983] Conv. 173.
[46] Land Registration Act 1925, s.21.
[47-48] Ruoff and Roper, *Registered Conveyancing* (4th ed.) p. 186, D.J. Hayton *Registered Land* (3rd ed.) p. 44; Registered Land Practice Notes (1982/3 ed.) Note D.1.(*d*).

(iii) every assignment on sale of leasehold land held for a term of years having not less than 40 years to run from the date of delivery of the assignment.

Unless the disposition is registered within the two months it is void insofar as the legal estate is concerned.[49] Oddly enough the grantee does initially get the legal estate under the deed which requires to be registered (and this may affect his position since the validity of his interest will be governed by the rules relating to unregistered land) but he loses it after the two month period. Thereafter he has an equitable interest only, and apparently the legal estate revests in the grantor who holds it on bare trust for the grantee. Although there is little risk of the grantee's interest being defeated by a subsequent purchaser of the legal estate,[50] because that purchaser would have notice of the grantee's interest from the lack of title deeds,[51] the grantee by failing to register his title makes the property virtually unmarketable. A purchaser from him would also fail to get a legal estate and he could not be forced to accept title notwithstanding any stipulation to the contrary.[52] Fortunately the matter can be put right quite easily. The Registrar may, upon application by any person interested showing sufficient cause, extend the period for first registration.[53] In case of refusal by the Registrar provision is made for appeal to the High Court. So far no appeals have been made because "the Chief Land Registrar is always willing to make an order whenever some quite ordinary but reasonable excuse for the delay is put forward by the applicants' solicitors and the proper fee is paid."[54]

COMPULSORY REGISTRATION OF DISPOSITIONS

Once the title to land has been registered, whether it is situate in a compulsory or non-compulsory area, it is necessary to register dispositions of that land. If inferior estates are carved out of it and are themselves registrable interests then they too must be registered. This is provided for by section 19 (freeholds) and section 22 (leaseholds) of the 1925 Act. The reader will be well aware of the fact that in unregistered land the legal estate passes to the grantee immediately the deed is signed, sealed and delivered. However the disponee under a disposition of land that is already registered only gets the legal estate once the "statutory magic" of registration is completed, that is when his application for registration is received by the land registry.[55] Until the disposition is completed by registration it takes effect as a minor interest only, dependent on entry in the register, unless it qualifies as an overriding interest, if protected by

---

[49] Land Registration Act 1925, s.123(1).

[50] *Le Neve* v. *Le Neve* (1747) Amb. 436.

[51] See *Hewitt* v. *Loosemore* (1851) 9 Hare. 449 and *Agra Bank* v. *Barry* (1874) L.R. 7 H.L. 135.

[52] Law of Property Act 1925, s.42.

[53] Land Registration Act 1925, s.123(1) proviso.

[54] Ruoff and Roper, *Registered Conveyancing* (4th ed.) p. 179.

[55] Land Registration Rules 1925, r. 83(2).

occupation, which is likely. There is no prescribed time limit within which the disponee must apply for registration but delay is obviously not in his best interests.

If the subject of the disposition is the grant of a lease for more than 21 years or a perpetual rentcharge then it must be completed by registering the lease or rentcharge with a separate title and by noting the interest against the burdened title. Formerly it was necessary to lodge the superior land certificate with the registry for the application to be duly made. This could cause problems in the case of leaseholds because in the absence of contrary stipulation, an intending lessee has no right to call for his lessor's title or land certificate. Since the decision in *Strand Securities Ltd.* v. *Caswell*,[56] where the Court of Appeal held that the Registrar could not insist on production of the land certificate and that an application for first registration was complete without it, the Registrar has changed his practice. Production of the lessor's land certificate is only demanded where the lease is granted at a premium, not a rent.[57] Easements, charges and rights of re-entry are completed by noting the interest against the burdened title. Where an easement over registered land is created by an instrument of transfer which is presented for registration the Registrar automatically makes the appropriate entries on both the dominant and servient titles. But where an easement is created by deed of grant the onus is on the grantee to apply for registration. If no application is made by him for his interest to be noted against the servient title, then it will not bind a subsequent purchaser of that land. The easement will not be an overriding interest under section 70(1)(*a*) of the Land Registration Act 1925. Because it has not been completed by registration[58] it will not be a legal easement and will not be "subsisting" for the purposes of the section.

An overlap between section 123 and sections 19 and 22 occurs where a lease is granted out of registered land in a compulsory area for a term of more than 40 years. Does the two month time limit for first registration applications apply? The preferred view seems to be that such a lease is a disposition requiring registration without time limit,[59] but this is contrary to the only relevant decision, *British Maritime Trust Ltd.* v. *Upsons Ltd.*,[60] where Clauson J. actually treated the first registration provisions as governing the grant of a sub-lease of registered land.

CONVEYANCING PENDING REGISTRATION

One question that arises from the foregoing discussion is whether a person who is entitled to be registered under section 123 or sections 19 or 22 can deal with the land before he becomes the registered proprietor.[61] The

---

[56] [1965] Ch. 958.
[57] Registered Land Practice Notes (1982/3 ed.) Note D1.
[58] Under Land Registration Act 1925, ss.19 and 22.
[59] Ruoff and Roper, *Registered Conveyancing* (4th ed.) p. 448; Registered Land Practice Notes (1982/3 ed.) Note DI; [1983] Conv. 175.
[60] [1931] W.N.7. Criticised by D.J. Hayton, *Registered Land* (3rd ed.) p. 193.
[61] See [1979] Conv. 1 and R. Dixon [1980] Conv. 168.

question is clearly answered in the affirmative by rule 72 of the 1925 Rules in the case of a person entitled to apply for first registration and section 37 of the 1925 Act in the case of a person entitled under a disposition of registered land. The provisions appear to say that such a vendor may transfer the land to a purchaser and complete the sale prior to being registered as proprietor, his only obligation being that of proving his entitlement to be registered to the satisfaction of the purchaser.[62] However Messrs. Ruoff and Roper in their work on registered conveyancing suggest that the vendor should necessarily always procure the registration of himself as proprietor of the land "some time before completion" and add "it would appear to be no answer to a requisition under these provisions for the vendor to offer to prove that he is in a position to execute a transfer as a person entitled to be registered."[63] It is certainly true that where the land is already registered the purchaser is entitled to insist that the vendor "procure the registration of himself as proprietor of the land . . . or procure a disposition from the proprietor to the purchaser," notwithstanding any stipulation to the contrary. (s.110(5), Land Registration Act 1925). But it is not clear whether the vendor should procure his own registration before completion of the contract or completion of the purchaser's registration. Neither is it clear who should make the choice between the vendor's own registration and procuring a disposition from the registered proprietor. Furthermore section 110(5) cannot apply where the land is unregistered[64] and the vendor is entitled to apply for registration under the first registration provisions, although rule 81[65] provides that no registration of the vendor's transfer to the purchaser should be made until the vendor "has been registered as proprietor or his right to be so registered has been shown to the satisfaction of the purchaser."

The conclusion must be that the vendor need only procure his own registration (or a transfer from the registered proprietor) if the purchaser insists sometime before registration of the purchaser's transfer, otherwise his only obligation is to prove his entitlement to be registered under section 123 or section 19 or 22.

Proof of Title

INTRODUCTORY

A purchaser of registered land is (with certain exceptions)[66] not concerned with the history of his vendor's title and therefore abstracts of the type required in unregistered land are as a rule unnecessary. Indeed section 110(3) of the 1925 Act states "notwithstanding any stipulation to the contrary, it shall not be necessary for the vendor to furnish the purchaser

---

[62] J.T. Farrand, *Emmet on Title* (18th ed.) p. 150.
[63] *Registered Conveyancing* (4th ed.) p. 315.
[64] *Re Evans' Contract* [1970] 1 W.L.R. 583.
[65] Land Registration Rules 1925.
[66] For example, plans on earlier deeds in *Lee* v. *Barrey* [1957] Ch. 251 or where the vendor is not registered with absolute title. See *post*, p. 327.

with any abstract or other written evidence of title, or any copy or abstract of the land certificate, or of any charge certificate." A purchaser is however very much concerned with the register of the vendor's title. The cardinal rule of registered land is that a purchaser for value takes the land subject to subsisting entries on the register and overriding interests but free from everything else. In *Williams & Glyn's Bank Ltd.* v. *Boland*[67] Lord Wilberforce referring to the position of a purchaser of registered land, said:

> "In place of the lengthy and often technical investigation of title to which a purchaser (of unregistered land) was committed, all he has to do is consult the register; from any burden not entered on the register, with one exception [overriding interests], he takes free. Above all, the system is designed to free the purchaser from the hazards of notice, real or constructive, which in the case of unregistered land, involved him in inquiries, often quite elaborate. . . . . The only kind of notice recognised is by entry on the register. The exception just mentioned consists of 'overriding interests' listed in section 70. As to these all registered land is stated to be deemed to be subject to such of them as may be subsisting in reference to the land. The land is so subject regardless of notice actual or constructive. In my opinion, therefore, the law as to notice as it may affect purchasers of unregistered land has no application even by analogy to registered land."

Further since the rule only operates when the purchaser acquires the legal estate,[68] he remains interested in the state of the register right up until he becomes the new registered proprietor.

The register is kept at the appropriate district land registry. It is divided into three parts which are kept together on one index card which will bear the title number. These, together with the filed plan, contain "complete" particulars of one estate owner's title. Rather confusingly the term "register" is also used to describe the entire card index system[69] operated by the land registry through its 13 district land registries.

When a title to land is first registered the registered proprietor is issued with a Land Certificate containing office copies of the register and filed plan. If the land is subject to a registered charge the Land Certificate is kept at the land registry and the proprietor of the charge is given a Charge Certificate which further contains the original deed of charge (the estate owner gets nothing). A rentowner is issued with a Rentcharge Certificate. These certificates are admissible as evidence of the matters they contain, but only at the date they were issued, and for this purpose a date is stamped on their inside cover. Although the land, charge or rentcharge certificate must be produced to the land registry on any dealing with the

---

[67] [1981] A.C. 487 at p. 503.

[68] *Re Boyle's Claim* [1961] 1 W.L.R. 339; Land Registration Act 1925, ss.5, 9, 20, 23 and 59(6).

[69] Under Land Registration Act 1925, s.1(1). Preparations are being made to computerise the system, Administration of Justice Act 1982.

land, charge or rentcharge and will as a matter of course be updated to correspond with the register (and a new stamp affixed showing the latest date on which the certificate was compared with the register) some entries can be made on the register without such production, and discrepancies may occur. It is important to realise that the register is the registered proprietor's proof of title, the certificate is evidence only.

VENDOR'S OBLIGATION

With the above in mind section 110 of the Land Registration Act 1925 provides that on a sale or disposition of registered land (other than to a lessee or chargee) the vendor shall furnish the purchaser with the following documents: (This statutory obligation is recognised by National Construction (11) and Law Society Condition 12(1)(b)).

    1. "notwithstanding any stipulation to the contrary:"[70]

        (a) an authority to inspect the register.

The register is private and without this authority the purchaser would not be able to inspect the vendor's title.[71] The authority also entitles the purchaser to take pencil copies,[72] to obtain office copies of all the entries and documents he is permitted to see and to make official searches with the protection afforded by the 1981 Official Searches Rules.[73] In practice the authority is only used for this latter purpose. The authority to inspect must contain the title number and a short description of the property.[74] It does not allow the purchaser to give a similar authority to his prospective mortgagee (or his solicitor) and is therefore generally worded to cover the purchaser and his prospective mortgagees as follows[75]:

> Title No. . . . . . .
> Property . . . . . .
> As solicitors for [registered proprietor] of . . . . . . the registered proprietor of the land above described we, hereby authorise Messrs . . . . . . of . . . . . . who are the solicitors acting for [purchaser] a purchaser [and Messrs . . . . . . of . . . . . . who are solicitors acting for his mortgagees] to inspect the register of the above-mentioned title and any documents referred to therein.
> [Date]
>   [Signature of solicitors]
>   Solicitors for the registered proprietor

Law Society Condition 12(b)(ii) contains a new provision that the vendor shall supply additional authorities to inspect the register for "any sub-purchaser or prospective mortgagee or lessee." His duty is limited by the words "as the purchaser shall reasonably require." The National Condi-

---

[70] Land Registration Act 1925, s.110(1).

[71] *Ibid.* s.112.

[72] Land Registration Rules 1925, rr. 287–295.

[73] See *ante*, Chap. 2, p. 37.

[74] Schedule to Land Registration Rules 1925, Form 80.

[75] See Concise Land Registration Practice (3rd ed.) p. 88.

tions have no equivalent provision. It will be remembered that under the 1981 Official Searches Rules solicitors need no longer lodge an authority to inspect at the land registry; he must just certify that such an authority is held. The ruling is recognised by Law Society Special Condition E.

    (b) if required[76]—

        (i) a copy of the subsisting entries on the register. This is always required.

        (ii) a copy of the filed plan. Sometimes this is not required where the whole of the land in a title is being transferred or the sale is of a plot on a building estate.

        (iii) copies or abstracts of any documents or any part thereof noted on the register (but not set out in full)

Office copies of the above can be obtained from the land registry. The fee for an office copy of the entries or the filed plan is £1 and for an office copy of a document referred to on the register as being filed, £2.[77] In practice most solicitors bespeak (on form A44) and give the purchaser a full set of office copies, the fee for which is £3 irrespective of the number of documents on the register. As between the vendor and purchaser, filed abstracts or copies referred to by the register are to be deemed to be complete and correct without production of the original.

The practice of supplying office copies has been thoroughly endorsed by the Council of the Law Society. In their opinion[77a] a photocopy of the land or charge certificate should not be supplied by way of deduction of title, as it may not show all the entries on the register and does not provide the protection conferred on an office copy by section 113 of the 1925 Act. Section 113 states that office copies are admissible in evidence to the same extent as the originals and if a person suffers loss by reason of any inaccuracy in them he is entitled to be compensated by the land registry. A solicitor is not liable for loss incurred by his client, through his reliance on these documents. Following the Council's recommendation Law Society 12(1)(b)(i) provides that "copies of the entries on the register, the filed plan and any documents noted on the register and filed in the registry shall be office copies." The National Conditions are silent on the matter.

The above-mentioned copies need only be supplied insofar as they relate to the land sold.[78] Copies of filed settlements need not be supplied,[79] nor copies of charges or incumbrances that will be discharged or overriden on completion.[80] If the purchase price does not exceed £1000 the purchaser must pay for the copies he requires, otherwise the vendor bears the expense in the absence of any contrary stipulation.[81]

Law Society Condition 12(1) provides that the vendor shall deliver the office copies to the purchaser "forthwith upon exchange of contracts."

---

[76] Land Registration Act 1925, s.110(1).
[77] All these can be bespoken on Form A44.
[77a] (1973) 70 L.S. Gaz. 1281.
[78] Land Registration Act 1925, s.110(1).
[79] *Ibid.* s.110(1), proviso (b).
[80] *Ibid.* s.110(1).
[81] *Ibid.* s.110(1), proviso (a).

Under National Condition 9(1) copies must be delivered within 11 working days of the contract and under an open contract, within a reasonable time. Failure to supply them within these limits does not entitle the purchaser to rescind the contract (time is not of the essence). But since office copies can be obtained fairly rapidly it is likely that the court would find that a much shorter period of delay in this case than in unregistered land (where the abstract might take longer to prepare) would justify a purchaser serving notice giving the vendor a further set reasonable period in which to supply the copies, non-compliance with which would entitle the purchaser to rescind.[82]

Frequently the office copies are sent to the purchaser along with the draft contract and in view of the decision in *Faruqi* v. *English Real Estates Ltd.*[83] this would appear to be the wiser course. The brief facts of the case were that property was sold at auction, "subject to all entries on the register." The register showed that the property was subject to restrictive covenants contained in a deed dated 1883, which had not been produced on first registration. The vendors in reply to requisitions could not produce a copy of the deed. Walton J. held that the purchaser was not bound in Equity because the vendors had failed to disclose their defective title "fully and frankly in the particulars or in the conditions." The purchaser was entitled to repayment of his deposit. Had copies of the register been sent with the draft contract then the difficulty would have been discovered and settled before the parties became bound.

By Law Society Condition 12(3) if the purchaser is supplied with these copies before contract, he is not deemed to have had notice of any matter of title thereby disclosed and can still requisition on it after contract.

2. "Subject to any stipulation to the contrary, at his (the vendor's) own expense"[84]

(a) copies, abstracts and evidence of any subsisting rights and interests appurtenant to the registered land as to which the register is not conclusive. An example would be where the registry has entered notice that the registered proprietor merely claims that some right is appurtenant to his land, as would be the case where the title to the servient land had not been proved to the satisfaction of the Registrar.

(b) copies, abstracts and evidence of such matters excepted from the effect of registration as the purchaser would have been entitled to if the land had not been registered. This applies mainly to the pre-registration position of possessory title,[85] overriding interests and incumbrances entered on the register as subsisting at first registration.

SPECIAL POSITION VIS Á VIS LEASES

(a) **Grant of a Lease out of Registered Title.** It has always been the rule that when granting a lease a freeholder is never obliged to prove his title to the freehold, unless otherwise agreed. Similarly when a leaseholder

---

[82] *Compton* v. *Bagley* [1892] 1 Ch. 313 and see H.W. Wilkinson, *Standard Conditions of Sale of Land* (3rd ed.) p. 58.

[83] [1979] 1 W.L.R. 963.

[84] Land Registration Act 1925, s.110(2).

[85] See *post*, p. 327.

grants an underlease he is bound to produce his own title (the lease he holds) but not to prove title to the freehold or any superior lease (s.44 of the Law of Property Act 1925). Strangely, this archaic rule is rather unnecessarily perpetuated in relation to registered land.

Thus on the grant of a lease out of a registered freehold title, the lessee gets nothing; section 110 is expressly excluded. If he wishes to inspect the register of the lessors title he must reserve himself this right in the contract. Apart from the obvious reason of checking that the lessor has the power to grant the lease (especially important where a premium is paid) the wisdom of contracting to investigate the freehold title is illustrated by the case of *White* v. *Bijou Mansions Ltd.*[86] There a proprietor registered with a freehold absolute title subject to a restrictive covenant, notice of which was given on the register, granted a lease without disclosing the restrictive covenant. The lease was subsequently registered. On an action being brought to enforce the covenant against the lessee, Simmonds J. rejected the argument that section 44(5)[87] of the Law of Property Act 1925 protected the lessee and held that he was bound by the covenant, because by section 20 of the Land Registration Act 1925 a disposition, including a lease of registered land, takes effect subject to the entries on the register.

Where an underlease is granted out of a registered leasehold, by analogy with the unregistered land position, one would expect section 110 to oblige the underlessor to provide details of his title. However section 110 expressly excludes "lessee" and "lease" is defined in the Act to include "underlease," although the section does apply to a "disposition" which otherwise includes an underlease. Since the position is unclear the title to be shown should be expressly mentioned in the contract. The underlessee should also contract for the right to investigate any superior title, especially the freehold, unless the underlessor is registered with title absolute (when this will already have been done). Again this is to check that an underlease can validly be granted, and that there are no adverse interests which are likely to affect the underlessee. Further where the freehold title is unregistered and the adverse interest is registered as a land charge, the underlessee will not be entitled to claim compensation under section 25 of the Law of Property Act 1969 (but will be bound by the charge).

(b) **Assignment on Sale of a Lease the Title to which is Registered.** Section 110 does apply. The vendor is under the same obligations as if he was selling a registered freehold except that he must also supply the purchaser with a copy of his lease, which although an essential part of his title remains in his possession after registration.[88] Section 110 does not alter the rule that under an open contract the purchaser is not entitled to call

---

[86] [1938] Ch. 351.

[87] "Where . . . an intending lessee or assign is not entitled to call for the title to the freehold or leasehold reversion, as the case may be, he shall not . . .be deemed to be affected with notice of any matter or thing of which, if he had contracted that such title should be furnished, he might have had notice."

[88] See *post,* p. 433.

for any superior title. Therefore unless the vendor is registered with an absolute leasehold title[89] this should be expressly contracted for, for the reasons given above. Where however the contract is governed by the Law Society Conditions of Sale, the lease being sold is not registered with title absolute and is dated not more than 15 years prior to the date of the contract, the freehold and all other titles superior to the registered lease must be deduced for a period of not less than 15 years prior to the date of the contract and ending on the date of the grant of the lease; Condition 8(2). The National Conditions leave the open contract rule unaltered.

Examining the Title

To ease the process of explaining what the office copies will (or will not) reveal to the purchaser we have included on pages 318–321 two fictitious titles; one freehold, one leasehold. By commenting on these it is hoped to cover most of the problems likely to be encountered in a normal conveyancing transaction.

"Like all Gaul"[90] the register is divided into three parts:
1. The property register,
2. The proprietorship register, and
3. The charges register.

The first and last registers are sometimes described as the "credit" and "debit" sides of the register.[91] The first shows the estate and the benefit of any rights it enjoys, the last shows the burden of any incumbrances affecting it.

THE PROPERTY REGISTER

The property register states whether the land is freehold or leasehold, but the quality of the title is dealt with in the proprietorship register. The land is usually described verbally and by reference to a filed plan,[92] which is a separate individual plan drawn up for the particular title, and which shows the registered property outlined in red. Sometimes, land comprised in older titles is described by reference to a section of the General Map, which is the title plan for all the properties shown on it which are registered and also the index map for these properties. However, experience showed that use of the General Map, as both an index map and title plan, although economical, had serious disadvantages, chiefly inflexibility, and today filed plans are almost always used both on first registration of title and subsequent sales of part of registered land. The land or charge certificate contains an office copy of the filed plan (or section of the General Map).

"The provision, for every registered title, of an accurate plan, based upon the ordnance survey map, revised to date"[93] is an important and

---

[89] The superior titles will have already been investigated by the Registrar; see *post*, p. 328.
[90] F.R. Crane (1937) 2 Conv. (N.S.) 46.
[91] D.J. Hayton, *Registered Land* (3rd ed.) p. 30; T.B.F. Ruoff and C. West, *Concise Land Registration Practice* (3rd ed.) p. 8.
[92] Land Registration Act 1925, s.76(*a*).
[93] Ruoff and Roper, *Registered Conveyancing* (4th ed.) p. 43.

H.M. LAND REGISTRY   Map Reference ST6789L
                          TITLE NUMBER AV12345
Edition 1 opened 14.7.60   This register consists of 2 pages

A. PROPERTY REGISTER
containing the description of the registered land and the estate comprised in the Title

COUNTY	DISTRICT
AVON	TABOCK

The Freehold land shown and edged with red on the plan of the above Title filed at the Registry registered on July 14, 1960 known as 4 The Avenue.

NOTE: The land coloured brown on the plan is subject to rights of way created by a Conveyance of the land in this title dated June 26, 1960 made between (1) Charles Reid (Vendor) and (2) Aubrey Fiddle (Purchaser).

B. PROPRIETORSHIP REGISTER
stating nature of the Title, name, address and description of the proprietor of the land and any entries affecting the right of disposing thereof

TITLE ABSOLUTE

Entry number	Proprietor etc
1	~~AUBREY FIDDLE, Lecturer, Price paid £900 of 17 York Crescent, Tabock, Avon registered on July 14, 1960~~
2	BERTIE LITTMAN, Chef, and JOYCE LITTMAN, his wife both of 92 Russell Street, Tabock, Avon registered on November 23, 1977
3	RESTRICTION registered on November 23, 1977:—No disposition by one proprietor of the land (being the survivor of joint proprietors and not being a trust corporation) under which capital money arises is to be registered except under an order of the registrar or of the Court.

Register Model   Any entries struck through are no longer subsisting

Demand No.

Page 2   TITLE NUMBER AV12345

	C. CHARGES REGISTER containing charges, incumbrances etc., adversely affecting the land and registered dealings therewith	
Entry number	The date at the beginning of each entry is the date on which the entry was made on this edition of the Register	Remarks
1	July 14, 1960 – A conveyance of the land in this title dated June 26, 1960 and made between (1) Charles Reid (Vendor) and (2) Aubrey Fiddle (Purchaser) contains the following covenants: "The Purchaser hereby covenants with the vendor for the benefit of his adjoining land known as 3 The Avenue aforesaid to observe and perform the stipulations specified in the First Schedule hereto. The First Schedule 1. No further buildings shall be erected on the said land. 2. The land is not to be used for the purpose of carrying on the trade or business of an innkeeper or licensed victualler nor for a beer or spirit shop, or for the retail of any liquors and nothing is to be done or permitted on the land which may be or become a nuisance or annoyance to the adjoining houses or to the neighbourhood.	
2	November 23, 1977 – CHARGE dated November 7, 1977 registered on November 23, 1977 to secure the monies therein mentioned.	
3	PROPRIETOR: THE TABOCK BUILDING SOCIETY of 100 City Lane, Tabock, Avon registered on November 23, 1977.	

Any entries struck through are no longer subsisting

H.M. LAND REGISTRY   Map Reference ST9876L
TITLE NUMBER AV54321
Edition 1 opened 16.11.82   This register consists of 2 pages

---

A. PROPERTY REGISTER

containing the description of the registered land and the estate comprised in the Title. Unless the contrary is indicated below, any subsisting legal easements granted by the undermentioned lease(s) for the benefit of the land in this title are included therein. The registration takes effect subject to any rights excepted and reserved by the said lease(s) so far as such rights are subsisting and affect the land in this title.

COUNTY	DISTRICT
AVON	TABOCK

The Leasehold land shown and edged with red on the plan of the above Title filed at the Registry on November 16, 1982 known as 50 Luckingham Place, Tabock.

NOTE 1: As to the part tinted blue on the filed plan only the ground floor flat is included in the title.

SHORT PARTICULARS OF THE LEASE(S)
UNDER WHICH THE LAND IS HELD.
(The word lease includes an under-lease)

DATE	PARTIES	TERM		RENT
		YEARS	FROM	£10
22.10.82	1. OLIVE JOAN ADAMS	999	24.6.82	PREMIUM
	2. HORACE GORDON			£24,750

NOTE A: There are excepted from the effect of registration all estates, rights, interests, powers and remedies under the lease at any time arising from any alienation prohibited or restricted by the lease.

Demand No.

Register Model   Any entries struck through are no longer subsisting

TITLE NUMBER AV54321

B. PROPRIETORSHIP REGISTER

stating nature of the Title, name address and description of the proprietor of the land and any entries affecting the right of disposing thereof.

TITLE ABSOLUTE	
Entry number	Proprietor etc.
1	HORACE GORDON of Ground Floor Flat, 50 Luckingham Place, Tabock, Avon, registered on November 16, 1982.

C. CHARGES REGISTER

containing charges (and registered dealings therewith), adverse easements, restrictive covenants under-leases and other incumbrances.

Entry number	The date at the beginning of each entry is the date on which the entry was made on this edition of the register	Remarks
1	November 16, 1982 – A Conveyance dated June 24, 1840 made between (1) Sam Cook and Charles Ede (2) Hilary Ede (3) Ham Wallace and (4) Frederick Cook contains covenants of which the following are particulars:— COVENANTS by the said Ham Wallace for himself his heirs executors administrators and assigns with the said Hilary Ede her heirs and assigns and also a separate covenant with the said Sam Cook and Charles Ede their heirs and assigns . . . . Not to do or permit or suffer anything upon either of said plots of ground which might be in any wise noisome injurious or offensive or be or grow to be the annoyance damage or inconvenience of the said Sam Cook and Charles Ede their heirs or assigns or to owners or occupiers of any houses intended to be built on other part of said ground or to neighbourhood it being the intent and agreement of said parties that said premises should be used as private residences only – To stein in and complete with proper materials before December 21, 1841 a carriage road and paved footway the road and way marked out along front of said eight pieces of ground and keep same in repair – To permit inspection either during erection of said messuages or after and to make amendments if necessary – Not to alter elevation of said messuages without consent in writing of said Cook and Ede, their heirs or assigns.	
2	October 11, 1983 – Contract for Sale dated October 3, 1983 in favour of Peter Pocock.	

distinctive feature of registered land and theoretically replaces the need for a plan on the instrument of transfer, which may arise in unregistered conveyancing.[94] Despite the 'great clarity and exactitude'[95] of these plans it is possible to envisage a conflict arising between the verbal description and the filed plan,[96] particularly in view of the rule that (except when there is a note in the property register that the boundaries are fixed) the filed plan (or General Map) denotes the general boundaries only[97] leaving the exact line undetermined. Indeed the 1925 Rules provide for any such conflict: the Registrar "shall decide any question arising on a conflict between the verbal particulars and the filed plan"[98] However since "the filed plan, if any . . . shall be used for assisting the identification of the land"[99] and is not included "by way of identification only" it seems that the principle in unregistered conveyancing, that in cases of conflict a clear verbal description overrides a plan,[1] does not apply to registered conveyancing. If on inspection of the property the accuracy of the filed plan is doubted, the purchaser's solicitor should make a search of the index map to check that the two correspond.

The case of *Lee* v. *Barrey*[2] illustrates that in certain circumstances the purchaser may not be able to rely on the filed plan but may have to refer to a plan attached to a document of title. An owner of a plot divided it into five separate plots. Plot 4 was sold to a purchaser by reference to a transfer plan instead of to the official filed plan. There was a discrepancy between the two plans as to the boundaries of Plot 4. Relying on the filed plan the purchaser built a house on his plot, which according to the transfer plan (but not the filed plan) encroached onto the land of Plot 3. The owner of Plot 3 claimed damages for trespass and an injunction, and succeeded. The court held that the filed plan showed general boundaries only and could not be used to override the plain effect of the bargain between the parties—the dispute had to be determined by reference to the transfer plan.

It may be useful to add a few words about the colours the registry use on filed plans and the relevance of "T" marks thereon.

First the colours[3]:

Red edging denotes the extent of the registered land.

Green edging indicates land removed from a title.

Green tinting shows excluded islands of land within the land edged red.

Brown tinting shows land over which the registered land has the benefit of a right of way.

---

[94] J.T. Farrand, *Contract and Conveyance* (4th ed.) p. 291.

[95] Ruoff and Roper, *Registered Conveyancing* (4th ed.) p. 43 and see criticisms [1981] Conv. 260–268.

[96] [1979] Conv. 316–319.

[97] Land Registration Rules 1925, rr. 278 and 279.

[98] *Ibid.* 1925, r. 285. The rule confers jurisdiction but gives no principle by which he should resolve the conflict.

[99] Land Registration Act 1925, s.76.

[1] *Wiggington-Milner Ltd.* v. *Winster Engineering Ltd.* [1978] 1 W.L.R. 1462.

[2] [1957] Ch. 251.

[3] Registered Land Practice Notes (1982/3 ed.) Note F.I.

Blue tinting indicates part of the registered land which is subject to a right of way.

When land is added to an existing title a note is entered that the land edged and lettered "A" in red on the filed plan was added on a given date. If land is removed from a title (for example on a sale of part) a note is entered stating that the land edged and numbered in green on the filed plan has been removed from the title and registered under the title number shown in green on the plan.

"T" marks:

If "T" marks are referred to in a deed which is presented for registration and the contents of the deed are set out on the register, then the registry will copy the "T" marks from the deed plan onto the filed plan. Further, if the schedule of restrictive covenants on the charges register includes a fencing covenant, the "T" marks regulating the fencing obligation may be shown on the filed plan. Otherwise, "T" marks on a deed plan which are not referred to in the body of the deed are not reproduced by the registry (because they have no legal significance) unless an applicant specifically so requests, in which case the origin of the "T" marks is noted on the filed plan.

The description of the property may be followed by the date of the first registration of the land, notes and rules dealing with the ownership of mines and minerals,[4] a note that the property is exempt from certain overriding interests[5] and more commonly details of any appurtenant easements, profits à prendre, rights and privileges. It will be remembered that only the benefit of those rights which are (1) appurtenant to the estate and (2) capable of subsisting in themselves as legal estates may be entered on the register.[6] Usually the easement or other like right is recorded either by referring to the instrument creating it or by setting out on the register an extract from it.[7] If the easement can be described simply and accurately a verbal description is entered onto the register without reference to any instrument. Where an instrument both creates and reserves easements or other rights a statement will be included to the effect that the land is held together with the rights granted by, but subject to the exceptions and reservations contained in the deed. If the terms of the easement or right are not set out fully on the register (as with our specimen freehold title where the property register refers to rights of way created by a conveyance dated June 26, 1960) the purchaser will need to see the instrument creating it to ascertain the exact nature and extent of the right. The filed original or copy of the instrument held at the registry may be inspected by any person interested in the land.[8] It should be added that even though an appurtenant easement or the like is not noted on the register it does not lapse, because "the registration of a person as proprietor of land shall vest in him together with the land, all rights, privileges, and appurtenances

---

[4] Land Registration Rules 1925, rr. 195 and 196.
[5] Land Registration Act 1925, s.70(1), proviso. Land Registration Rules 1925, r. 197.
[6] Land Registration Rules 1925, r. 257.
[7] *Ibid.* r. 255.
[8] *Ibid.* r. 288(1).

appertaining or reputed to appertain to the land or any part thereof, or, at the time of registration, demised, occupied or enjoyed therewith, or reputed or known as part or parcel of or appurtenant to the land or any part thereof, including the appropriate rights and interests which, had there been a conveyance of the land . . . would under section 62 of the Law of Property Act 1925 have passed therewith."[9]

Mention should also be made of the benefit of restrictive covenants. The registry do not generally note the benefit of restrictive covenants.[10] This is mainly because the benefit of a restrictive covenant is not a legal estate; it is an equitable interest. Another reason given is "that many modern restrictive covenants suffer from the inherent defect that the land to be benefitted by their imposition is identified insufficiently or not at all."[11] However if specifically requested to do so, the Registrar may enter a note that the benefit of restrictive covenants is claimed under a certain document, but he will not guarantee their enforceability.[12] Although the proposed new land obligation will eventually be registered like an easement[12a], initially and to avoid manpower difficulties at the registry, it will be noted in the same way as a restrictive covenant; the benefit will be entered on a non-guaranteed basis only.[12b]

Where the registered land is leasehold short particulars of the lease are given together with the description of the property. The lease itself is returned to the registered proprietor as he will need to refer to it in the future.[13] It therefore remains an essential part of the vendor's title and notice of its contents must be given to the purchaser as in unregistered conveyancing.[14] As a general rule, the registry do not supply office copies of leases. They need only supply office copies when a document is filed at the registry and referred to on the register.[15] Otherwise the supply of copies of documents in the registrar's custody is within his discretion.[16] The property register refers to the lease itself, which is rarely retained by the registry. Often they will not even have a copy. An original lessee must supply a certified copy of his lease when he applies for first registration[17] but an assignee need only supply an office copy of the assignment to him (not the lease). Usually this causes no problem as the vendor-lessee will have the lease (or a marked abstract or copy of it, if he bought and was registered in respect of part only of leasehold land) which he is willing to

---

[9] *Ibid.* r. 251 and r. 3(2)(c); *Re Evans' Contract* [1970] 1 W.L.R. 583.

[10] Registered Land Practice Notes, (1982/3 ed.) Note J.5. No more restrictive covenants will be capable of being created if the Law Commissions Report No. 127 becomes law.

[11] Ruoff and Roper, *Registered Conveyancing* (4th ed.) p. 17. The criticism may not be of such importance since *Federated Homes Ltd.* v. *Mill Lodge Properties Ltd.* [1980] 1 W.L.R. 594.

[12] Registered Land Practice Notes (1982/3 ed.) p. 36. Note J.5.

[12a] Except development obligations which will only be entered against the servient title.

[12b] Law. Com. No. 127, para. 9.

[13] Land Registration Rules 1925, rr. 5 and 21.

[14] See *ante*, p. 207.

[15] Land Registration Act 1925, s.112; Land Registration Rules 1925, r. 287.

[16] Land Registration Rules 1925, r. 290(1).

[17] *Ibid.* r. 21.

let the purchaser inspect. However the registry will help in cases of difficulty provided they have a copy of the lease in their possession.[18]

If the lease contains a qualified covenant against assignment, underletting or parting with possession (as Horace Gordon's lease of 50 Luckingham Place does) the property register will contain a statement that all estates, rights, interests, powers and remedies under the lease at any time arising from a prohibited alienation are excepted from the effect of registration.[19] This means that the Registrar does not have to involve himself in questions relating to the giving of the lessor's consent. If the superior title is registered then the lessor's title number will also be stated. Normally no mention is made of appurtenant easements and the like in the case of a leasehold interest, as they will be set out in the lease, which forms part of the register even though it remains in the lessee's possession. In the context of easements, a solicitor acting for a lessee who is intending to purchase the reversion, should remember that the merger of a term of years in the reversion has the effect of terminating easements granted by the lease for the benefit of the demised premises because they cannot then become appurtenant to a different estate, the reversion.[20] The same applies to the benefit of restrictive covenants annexed to a lease.[21] The client should be advised not to apply to have his lease merged.

In describing a registered rentcharge the property register of the rentowner's title will refer to the instrument creating it.

THE PROPRIETORSHIP REGISTER

The proprietorship register contains details of[22]:
  1. The nature of the registered title;
  2. The name, address and description of the present owner of the land;
  3. Any restraints that exist against the proprietor's powers of disposition of the land;
  4. Cautions registered to protect a claim adverse to the title of the registered proprietor; and
  5. Miscellaneous matters including creditors' notices and bankruptcy inhibitions.

The nature of the registered title. On an application for first registration, in addition to investigating an applicant's title the Chief Land Registrar awards the title a class depending on its legal value. The title is then issued with that class. The intended result is that a purchaser can tell from the register whether he is buying a "perfect" title or, if less than perfect, the type of defects that are likely to exist therein. "Whereas the quality of an unregistered title is a matter of opinion about which differing views may be held, the quality of a registered title is one of hard fact."[23]

---

[18] T.B. Ruoff and C. West, *Concise Land Registration Practice* (3rd ed.) p. 147.
[19] Land Registration Rules 1925, r. 45. In older titles this statement may appear in the proprietorship register.
[20] Registered Land Practice Notes (1982/3 ed.) Note I.3.
[21] *Golden Lion Hotel (Hunstanton) Ltd.* v. *Carter* [1965] 1 W.L.R. 1189.
[22] Land Registration Rules 1925, r. 6.
[23] Ruoff, *Torrens System*, 1957.

(A) A freehold title may be (i) absolute (ii) possessory or (iii) qualified.

(i) *Absolute freehold title.* This is the best title the Registrar can grant and means that he is satisfied with the title adduced. The term "absolute" is slightly misleading as the Registrar is entitled to accept within this class what would be described as "good holding title" in unregistered land.[24] The award of "Title Absolute" lies completely within the discretion of the Registrar, without appeal (although an order for mandamus would lie in the High Court).[25] In practice it is nearly always granted in respect of freehold land even though not applied for.[26] It is sometimes described as "indefeasible" in that only the Registrar's power to order rectification can affect the registered proprietor and save in exceptional cases, the title cannot be rectified against a registered proprietor who is in possession of the land.[27] Such an order would dispossess him, subject to his receiving compensation.

Rectification apart, an absolute freehold title gives to the registered proprietor an estate in fee simple in possession with all rights privileges and appurtenances belonging thereto, subject to any entries on the register and overriding interests but otherwise free from all other estates and interests.[28] A first proprietor who is not entitled to the land for his own benefit also takes subject to any minor interest of which he has notice.[29] Furthermore where a disposition is made without valuable consideration the disponee takes the registered title subject to any minor interest the disponor held it subject to.[30] Noteworthy minor interests which would bind a volunteer would be interests under a trust, the right of a subsequent purchaser to have the proprietor's title set aside on the ground that the transfer to the volunteer was made with intent to defraud the purchaser,[31] the right of a trustee in bankruptcy to have a voluntary settlement avoided under section 42 of the Bankruptcy Act 1914 or the right of "any person thereby prejudiced" to have a voluntary conveyance or transfer made with intent to defraud set aside under section 172 of the Law of Property Act 1925.[32] In these circumstances if the register is rectified in favour of someone who is entitled to the land, aggrieved or defrauded, the volunteer will not be entitled to compensation.

A point of interest that arises from the provisions of the 1925 Act dealing with the effect of registration with title absolute, is that by virtue of section 20(1) a proprietor whose title is subject to a defect can transmit to a purchaser for value under a registered disposition a better title than he himself possesses.[33] The section states that "the disposition shall

---

[24] Land Registration Act 1925, s.13(c); C.T. Emery (1976) 40 Conv. (N.S.) 122.
[25] *Dennis* v. *Malcolm* [1934] Ch. 244; R.S.C. 1981 Ord. 53.
[26] Land Registration Act 1925, s.4 proviso (iii).
[27] Land Registration Act 1925, s.82(3) (as amended); see *post*, p. 342.
[28] Land Registration Act 1925, ss.5 and 20.
[29] *Ibid.* s.5.
[30] *Ibid.* s.20(4).
[31] Law of Property Act 1925, s.173; Land Registration Act 1925, s.114.
[32] Applied to registered land by Land Registration Act 1925, s.114.
[33] *Morelle Ltd.* v. *Wakeling* [1955] 2 Q.B. 379 at p. 411.

operate in like manner as if the registered transferor or grantor were . . . entitled to the registered land in fee simple in possession for his own benefit." However according to two recent first instance decisions the section presupposes good faith[34] or lack of actual knowledge[35] of the defect on the part of the purchaser.

(ii) *Possessory freehold title*. Registration with a possessory title does not affect the enforcement of any adverse rights existing or capable of arising at the time of first registration, but otherwise has the effect of absolute title.[36] As the name implies the title depends on actual occupation of the land or receipt of the rents and profits[37] and it is the title granted where a squatter claims land. It is also granted to an applicant whose lawful possession of the land is beyond doubt, but whose documentary evidence of title is lacking in some material respect.

When possessory title is sold this must be disclosed to the purchaser otherwise he can rescind the contract.[38] As the vendor's title is not guaranteed before first registration, the purchaser will need to investigate the pre-registration title in the normal unregistered way (this he is entitled to do under s.110(2) of the 1925 Act). Where however possessory title to freehold land has been held for 15 years or more, it is capable of being converted into absolute title on the occasion of sale.[39] Such being the case, the vendor will usually provide in the contract that no title beyond that afforded by the register shall be deduced. If the title has not been held for 15 years the vendor may insert a condition restricting the title to the evidence that is available.

It should be added that an application for conversion of possessory title can be made at any time should the circumstances warrant it,[40] for example, if missing deeds are found.

(iii) *Qualified freehold title*. This is wholly exceptional—*a rara avis*.[41] A qualified title is equivalent to an absolute title, but the effect of some right or interest, arising either before a particular date or under a particular instrument is excepted from registration.[42] It arises where absolute title is asked for but the Chief Land Registrar decides that the title can only be established for a limited period or subject to certain reservations. The applicant then has to apply for a qualified title; the Registrar cannot grant it of his own accord. Unlike possessory title, particulars of the defect are entered on the register. Under section 110(2) the vendor must supply an abstract as to the part of his title excepted from the effect of registration. This is usually covered by a condition in the contract.

---

[34] *Peffer* v. *Rigg* [1977] 1 W.L.R. 285.
[35] *Lyus* v. *Prowsa Developments Ltd.* [1982] 1 W.L.R. 1044.
[36] Land Registration Act 1925, s.6.
[37] *Ibid.* s.3(xviii).
[38] *Re Brine and Davies' Contract* [1935] Ch. 388.
[39] Land Registration Act 1925, s.77(2) and (3)(*b*).
[40] *Ibid.* s.77(2) and (3)(*a*).
[41] T.B.F. Ruoff and C. West, *Concise Land Registration Practice* (3rd ed.) p. 27.
[42] Land Registration Act 1925, s.7.

Qualified title is difficult to convert[43] because the defect (invariably serious) must be remedied.

(B) A leasehold title may be (i) absolute (ii) good leasehold (iii) possessory or (iv) qualified.

(i) *Absolute leasehold title.* An absolute leasehold title can only exist when the Registrar has investigated not only the title desired to be registered, but also the title to the freehold and any intermediate leases.[44] The title used to be comparatively rare most leases being registered with good leasehold title (see below) because of the rules which, in the absence of contrary stipulation, prevented a lessee from investigating his lessor's freehold and leasehold reversion.[45] Registration with title absolute has two important advantages over good leasehold title, as far as a purchaser is concerned. First, the Registrar guarantees that the lease was validly granted, and secondly the register reveals any restrictive covenants affecting the reversion and hence the lessee. A further practical advantage lies in the fact that many institutional lenders are only willing to advance money on an absolute leasehold title. It must be said that where the freehold or an intermediate reversion is registered with title absolute, the Registrar will normally register an applicant for registration with good leasehold title with title absolute, noting any charges on the register of the new title. In other words although the lessee cannot look at the register of the superior title the Registrar can. As more and more titles come onto the register the need for a "good leasehold" category will diminish. The effect of registration with absolute leasehold title is the same as for registration with absolute freehold title, except of course that the registered proprietor will also hold subject to all the conditions contained in the lease.[46]

In our fictitious leasehold title Horace Gordon expressly contracted to see the freehold title to 50 Luckingham Place, which was unregistered, and could therefore apply for registration of his lease with title absolute. The office copy of the register of his title shows that Olive Joan Adams validly granted the lease. It also reveals certain restrictive covenants affecting the freehold and hence the leasehold title.

(ii) *Good leasehold title.* A good leasehold title has the same effect as an absolute title except that any matters derogating from the power of the lessor to grant the lease are not affected.[47] The title does not guarantee that the lease was validly granted nor will it reveal adverse interests affecting any superior title; in other words it corresponds to the case in unregistered conveyancing where the title of the lessor has not been investigated.

Although a good leasehold title excepts from the effects of registration all matters arising under the superior title or titles, section 110(2) of the

[43] *Ibid.* s.77(2).
[44] *Ibid.* s.8(1), proviso (i).
[45] Law of Property Act 1925, s.44; see *ante*, p. 283.
[46] Land Registration Act 1925, s.9.
[47] *Ibid.* s.10.

Land Registration Act 1925 only entitles a purchaser under an open contract to investigate the superior titles permitted by section 44 of the Law of Property Act 1925, as interpreted in *Gosling* v. *Woolf* [48] A purchaser can of course bargain for more, although his vendor will not always be in a position to comply with his request (because he himself had no access to the superior title(s)).[48a]

Provided the freehold and any leasehold reversion are registered with absolute title, the lessee may at any time apply for his title to be converted into title absolute. Where the reversion(s) is not registered conversion is more difficult:[49]

(iii) *and* (iv) *Possessory and qualified leasehold title*. The former is uncommon, the latter virtually unknown. Both have the same effect as such titles in the case of freeholds with the added qualification that the lessor's title has not been investigated.[50] A purchaser of either title must, in the absence of contrary agreement, be provided with proof of the vendor's pre-registration title within the bounds of section 44 of the Law of Property Act 1925.[51]

Where the possessory title is more than 10 years old it is usually converted into a good leasehold title on sale—otherwise conversion is within the discretion of the Registrar. Conversion of a qualified leasehold title is only possible if it can be proved that the defect in the earlier pre-registration title has been removed.

Title to a rentcharge. The statutory provisions are silent as to the effect of the grant of the different classes of title to a rentcharge. Rule 50 of the Land Registration Rules 1925 just states that

> "Application for registration of rentcharges . . . shall be proceeded with in the same manner (as freeholds and leaseholds) subject only to such modifications as the nature of the case may require and the Registrar may approve."

Ruoff and Roper therefore conclude that absolute, possessory or qualified title will be granted to a rentcharge in similar circumstances and with a similar effect, as registration of corporeal land with that title.

Description of the Present Owner. The proprietorship register will give the full name, address and occupation of the registered proprietor. This address is his address for service unless he directs otherwise. A registered proprietor may have up to three addresses entered in the register including that of his solicitor.

Restraints Against the Proprietor's Powers of Disposition of the Land. The reader will recall that under the general law a landowner's powers to

---

[48] [1893] 1 Q.B. 39 and see *ante*, p. 286.

[48a] A vendors solicitor should remember to exclude Law Society Condition 8(2) where necessary.

[49] For details see T.B. Ruott and C. West, *Concise Land Registration Practice* (3rd ed.) pp. 31–33.

[50] Land Registration Act 1925, ss.11 and 12.

[51] *Ibid.* s.110(2).

deal with the land may be limited to a greater or lesser degree (a tenant for life, for example) and that in unregistered coneyancing this necessitates careful inquiry into what powers the vendor possesses.[52] In registered conveyancing a registered proprietor is deemed to have full plenary powers of disposition, unless an entry on the proprietorship register states otherwise[53] The investigations of the purchaser's solicitor are thereby made easier.

One way in which limitations on a proprietor's powers of disposition are reflected on the register is by the entry of a restriction.[54] A restriction is a "friendly" registration made with the concurrence of the registered proprietor. The advantages of a restriction are that its operation can be limited to a particular type of transaction and that it endures until modified or withdrawn. It tells a prospective purchaser whether or not his vendor (the registered proprietor) has the ability to enter into the transaction contemplated and usually the steps he must take to ensure that the transaction is effective (for instance, payment of the purchase money to two trustees).

The most common general examples of restrictions are in relation to settled land or land held on trust for sale. Thus where settled land is registered in the name of the tenant for life, the restriction would read:

> "No disposition by the proprietor of the land under which capital money arises is to be registered unless the money is paid to A. B. of . . . . . . and C. D. of . . . . . . (the trustees of the settlement of whom there must be not less than two or more than four unless a trust corporation is the sole trustee) or into court.
>
> Except under an order of the registrar no disposition by the proprietor of the land is to be registered unless authorised by the Settled Land Act 1925."[55]

A purchaser is informed that provided his transaction is one authorised by the Settled Land Act and he pays the purchase money to the persons named in the restriction, his transaction will be duly registered and the interests of the beneficiaries overreached.

Alternatively if the land was held on trust for sale the restriction would read:

> "No disposition by one proprietor of the land (being the survivor of joint proprietors and not being a trust corporation) under which capital money arises is to be registered without an order of the registrar or of the court."[56]

Although in unregistered conveyancing it is necessary to see that the trustees for sale have the same unrestricted powers of an absolute owner (if appropriate), in registered conveyancing this is assumed (because the

---

[52] See *ante*, p. 290.
[53] Land Registration Act 1925, ss.18(1), 21(1) and 34(1).
[54] *Ibid.* s.58.
[55] Form 9.
[56] Form 62.

trustees are the registered proprietors) unless the restriction contains further words limiting those powers. Where concurrent owners (for example husband and wife) are holding land on trust for themselves beneficially, this restriction indicates that they are beneficially interested as tenants in common. The absence of the restriction informs the purchaser that they are beneficial joint tenants and that the survivor can give a valid receipt for capital money. The provisions of the Law of Property (Joint Tenants) Act 1964 are thus made redundant.

A restriction will also be used where the registered proprietor is a company whose articles or memorandum limit its powers in relation to land, or where certain land cannot be transferred without the consent of the Charity Commissioners or Church Commissioners.[57] Again, provided the terms of the restriction are complied with, the disposition in favour of the purchaser will be valid.

A restriction will continue in force even after a dealing takes place in accordance with its provisions.[58] Therefore a purchaser should insist on his vendor obtaining its withdrawal on completion, unless of course he is to continue to be bound by its terms.

In addition dispositions by the following persons should be noted:

(i) *A minor.*[59] A minor cannot hold a legal estate in land[60] and is not capable of being registered as proprietor thereof under the Land Registration Act.[61] If a transfer is executed in his favour the transferor holds the land on trust for the infant transferee until he attains majority,[62] and an appropriate restriction is entered on the register.[63] Should a minor accidentally be registered as proprietor, the register is subject to rectification.

Since a minor cannot hold a legal estate in land, he cannot transfer it, although he may dispose of his equitable interest but the transaction may be repudiated during his minority or within a reasonable time of his attaining majority. There is a presumption in favour of a purchaser that parties to a conveyance or transfer are of full age[64] but should a minority be suspected it would be wise for the purchaser to ask to see his vendor's birth certificate.

(ii) *A mental patient.* A person suffering form a mental disorder may be registered as proprietor; a disposition may be effected by his duly appointed receiver and no note of the incapacity will appear on the

---

[57] For the forms see T.B.F. Ruoff and C. West, *Concise Land Registration Practice* (3rd ed.) pp. 215–219.

[58] Land Registration Act 1925, s.58.

[59] Since January 1, 1970, the age of majority has been 18. Family Law Reform Act 1969, s.1.

[60] Law of Property Act 1925, s.1(6).

[61] Land Registration Act 1925, s.4.

[62] The land is settled land. Settled Land Act 1925, s.1(2) and s.27. Land Registration Act 1925, s.111(1).

[63] Form 10 restriction.

[64] Law of Property Act 1925, s.15.

register.[65] If a registered proprietor later becomes insane, then under the Mental Health Act 1959 a receiver may be appointed by the Court of Protection and the receiver may then exercise the powers of a registered proprietor. On a dealing in either case the Registrar will require evidence of the receiver's power to act. Alternatively, should the receiver apply for registration himself, a restriction appears on the proprietorship register that no disposition by the proprietor of the land is to be registered unless made pursuant to an order of the court.

(iii) *A personal representative.* The position of a purchaser of registered land from a personal representative is completely different to that of a purchaser of unregistered land. Because of the conclusive nature of the register sections 36(6) and 36(7) of the Administration of Estates Act (discussed earlier[66]) are irrelevant. On the death of a registered proprietor (entitled for his own benefit) his personal representative may adopt one of two courses. First he may procure his registration as proprietor in place of the deceased.[67] The grant of probate or letters of administration must accompany his application[68] and the Registrar can treat a grant lodged with him as conclusive that it has been properly granted and not revoked.[69] Once registered as proprietor the personal representative has vested in him the deceased's legal estate[70] and a transfer by him is effective to pass it to a purchaser. Alternatively, a personal representative need not be registered as proprietor to be able to sell the property (although a purchaser may require him to do so under section 110(5)).[71] He may simply transfer the property to a purchaser who will become the new registered proprietor on production of the transfer deed and grant of representation.[72] Again the Registrar is under no duty to investigate the grant.[73] The somewhat surprising result is that in neither case is the Registrar concerned with the contents of the will or to see that the personal representative is acting correctly.

To ensure the greatest possible protection for his client, a purchaser's solicitor in either case is advised to make a search at the Probate Registry (at the cost of £1) to ensure that the grant has not been revoked. Should this be the case the register may subsequently be rectified against the purchaser[74] and his entitlement to compensation will depend on whether or not he contributed to his loss by lack of proper care.[75] Actual or constructive knowledge of revocation may constitute lack of proper care on his part, disentitling him to compensation. A search at the Probate

---

[65] Ruoff and Roper, *Registered Conveyancing* (4th ed.) p. 136. The Registrar does have power to enter a restriction. Land Registration Rules 1925, r. 39.

[66] See *ante*, p. 295.

[67] Land Registration Act 1925, s.41, (on form 82).

[68] Land Registration Rules 1925, r. 168(1).

[69] *Ibid.* r. 170(5).

[70] Land Registration Act 1925, s.69.

[71] See *ante*, p. 311.

[72] Land Registration Rules 1925, rr. 170(1) and (4).

[73] *Ibid.* r. 170(5).

[74] Land Registration Act 1925, s.82.

[75] *Ibid.* s.83(5)(*a*).

Registry, whether or not it revealed a revocation would combat any problem of this nature.

(iv) *A mortgagee.* Section 34(1) of the 1925 Act provides that subject to any entry on the register to the contrary the proprietor of a registered charge has all the powers of a legal mortgagee, including the power of sale. The Act does not obviate the need to ensure that the power of sale has arisen,[76] although the purchaser can acquire good title even if the power has not become exerciseable.[77]

(v) *An attorney.* The position is really complementary to that in unregistered conveyancing and is governed by the Powers of Attorney Act 1971 and the Land Registration (Powers of Attorney) Rules 1971. When the Registrar is presented with an application for registration of a disposition that has been executed by a donee under a power of attorney, he must protect himself against a possible claim for indemnity should in fact the power have been revoked at the time of its purported exercise, because after registration the fact that the disposition was executed by an attorney will not be apparent to a subsequent purchaser. He will rely on the entries on the register and will not investigate the earlier title. If the disposition presented for registration was completed within 12 months of the coming into operation of the power, the Registrar will register it on production of the power of attorney or a certified copy of it. This is because he, the applicant and any subsequent purchaser will be shielded by the statutory protection afforded by section 5(2) and 5(4) of the Powers of Attorney Act 1971. Should, by chance, the applicant have known of the revocation the register may be rectified against him but not against any subsequent purchaser (who is protected as above). Where the disposition was not completed within 12 months of the grant of the power, to qualify for the statutory protection, the Registrar will require evidence usually in the form of a statutory declaration by the applicant for registration, that the principal was alive at the time of completion of the disposition and that the power had not been revoked. A subsequent purchaser is again protected.

Cautions Registered to Protect a Claim Adverse to the Title of the Registered Proprietor. These consist of two types; cautions against dealings and cautions against conversion.

(i) *Cautions against dealings.* Entry of a caution against dealings is essentially a "hostile action" (the consent of the registered proprietor is unnecessary) and a temporary expedient. It prevents a dealing in the registered land being effected without the knowledge of the cautioner (the person lodging the caution) and acts as a warning to a prospective purchaser to "beware" before completing his transaction. It may be lodged by anyone interested as a judgment creditor or otherwise in any land or charge that is registered, unless their right or interest is already

---

[76] Law of Property Act 1925, s.101(1).
[77] *Ibid.* s.104(2).

protected on the register by a notice or restriction in which case the express consent of the Registrar is required.[78] Once a caution against dealings has been entered on the register, no dealing with the property concerned on the part of the registered proprietor will be registered until the cautioner has been served with notice of it.

Examples of interests protected by a caution against dealings are a claim to be the beneficial owner in fee simple, or to be beneficially entitled to a registered lease or to be a tenant for life under the Settled Land Act 1925, a purchaser under a contract for sale (the usual form of protection is by entering a notice) or a plaintiff in an action relating to land.[79]

(ii) *Cautions against conversion.* Such a caution can be entered to prevent a possessory, qualified or good leasehold title being converted into an absolute title.[80]

The person lodging a caution must show that he has a cautionable interest.[81] Even if a caution is registered it does not affect the proprietor's title; it merely entitles the cautioner to notice of any proposed dealing or conversion so that he can challenge it if he wants to.[82] "It heralds a possible dispute."[83] An intending purchaser need not inquire into its cause. He should require the vendor to procure its removal before completion[84] or that the cautioner's consent to the intended disposition is obtained.

Miscellaneous matters including creditors' notices and bankruptcy inhibitions

(i) *Creditors' notices.* After a petition in bankruptcy is presented, it is registered in the register of pending actions in the Land Charges Department. The Registrar (who is also the head of the Land Charges Department) is then under a duty to register a creditor's notice against the title to any registered land or charge which appears to him to be affected.[85] The notice is entered in the proprietorship register, if the debtor is the proprietor of registered land, (and in the charges register if the proprietor of a charge). Section 61(1) of the Land Registration Act 1925 states that the effect of the entry of a creditor's notice is to "protect the rights of all creditors, and unless cancelled by the registrar . . . such notice shall remain in force until a bankruptcy inhibition is registered or the trustee in bankruptcy is registered as proprietor." Needless to say, a purchaser should not complete if the register reveals a creditor's notice (unless it is cancelled). If regardless of this, a purchaser does take a transfer from the debtor-proprietor and then lodges it for registration, a note will be entered

---

[78] Land Registration Act 1925, s.54(1).

[79] T.B.F. Ruoff and C. West, *Concise Land Registration Practice* (3rd ed.), see table on p. 220.

[80] Land Registration Act 1925, s.54(1).

[81] Land Registration Rules 1925, r. 66.

[82] Land Registration Act 1925, s.54(1); Land Registration Rules 1925, rr. 67–69.

[83] Lewis and Holland, *Principles of Registered Land Conveyancing*, p. 191.

[84] For how to get rid of a caution see T.B.F. Ruoff and C. West, *Concise Land Registration Practice* (3rd ed.) p. 211.

[85] Land Registration Act 1925, s.61(1); Form—Land Registration Rules 1925, r. 179.

after his name as the new proprietor to the effect that the disposition is registered subject to the rights of all creditors protected by the creditors notice which remains on the register.[86]

(ii) *Bankruptcy inhibitions.* "From and after the entry of a bankruptcy inhibition . . . no dealing affecting the registered land or charge of the proprietor, other than the registration of the trustee in bankruptcy, shall be entered on the register until the inhibition is vacated . . . . "[87] The inhibition reads as follows[88] "Bankruptcy inhibition registered on . . . . No disposition or transmission is to be registered until a trustee in bankruptcy is registered." Its registration follows the making of a receiving order which is registered in the register of writs and orders kept under the Land Charges Act. Obviously the purchaser cannot proceed with his purchase.

(iii) *Miscellaneous.* At one time the price paid by the proprietor on so becoming was entered on the proprietorship register. If an office copy of the entries on the register was supplied before exchange of contracts, the price paid was usually cut out to prevent a purchaser from discovering the profit his vendor hoped to make on the sale. For property sold after 1976 the Land Registry have followed this practice and now omit the price paid.

Burdens of positive covenants are by concession sometimes entered on the proprietorship register "for the practical reason that when such covenants are contained in a transfer of registered land which is filed in the Registry, they can easily be overlooked so that on a sale the registered proprietor's solicitor might omit to take an indemnity from the purchaser."[89]

THE CHARGES REGISTER

Broadly speaking this register gives details of those incumbrances and charges affecting a vendor's property, which in unregistered conveyancing a purchaser would discover from the abstract of title, the latest conveyance or other deed or from a search of the land charges register. More specifically rule 7 of the Land Registration Rules 1925 provides that the charges register shall contain:–

"(i) incumbrances subsisting at the date of first registration;
(ii) subsequent charges and other incumbrances (including notices of leases and other notices of adverse interests permitted by the Act [to be entered]);
(iii) such notes as have to be entered relating to covenants conditions and other rights adversely affecting the land;
(iv) all such dealings with registered charges and incumbrances as are capable of registration."

---

[86] Land Registration Act 1925, s.61(5).
[87] *Ibid.* s.61(4).
[88] Land Registration Rules 1925, r. 180.
[89] Registered Land Practice Notes, (1982/83 ed.) Note 0.1. This will only apply to the burden of existing positive covenant if the Law Commissions proposals as to Land Obligations are enacted, Law Com. No. 127.

At the start a distinction must be drawn between "registering" and "noting" an incumbrance. Earlier we saw that a charge by way of legal mortgage is a registrable interest but that title thereto cannot be registered independently of the estate that is charged.[90] If and when that estate is brought onto the register, the interest of the chargee may be protected by registration of his title as proprietor of the charge in the charges register of the charged title, whether or not the charge was created before[91] or after[92] the date of first registration. The chargee's title *must* be registered if he wishes to enjoy the powers of a legal mortgagee.[93]

"Noting", or the entry of a notice of a deed or right is the method of recording incumbrances other than registered charges which will continue to bind the registered land. It may be helpful to sub-divide the interests capable of protection by notice[94] into (1) interests which are themselves capable of substantive registration or of being registered charges (for example, where a lease of over 21 years is granted out of registered land it will be registered with a separate title and a note of its grant entered in the charges register of the superior title), and (2) those interests which would be land charges in the case of unregistered land.[95] By section 49(1) of the 1925 Act it is not possible to enter a notice in respect of a beneficial interest under a settlement or a trust for sale. Usually the entry of a notice requires the collaboration of the registered proprietor because the Registrar will not enter a notice unless the land certificate is sent to the registry for amendment. Even if the land certificate happens to be lodged at the registry because the land is subject to a mortgage, the Registrar will give the proprietor an opportunity to object before entering a notice.[95] Notice of a lease[96] (unless a premium is paid) and of a spouses' rights of occupation under the Matrimonial Homes Act 1983[97] are the chief examples of entries that can be made without the production of the land certificate. Finally, it should be mentioned that although a registered proprietor of the land takes it subject to incumbrances and entries appearing on the register including those rights and interests protected on the register by a notice, this is only true if the right or interest protected by the notice is a valid one and not overridden by the disposition.[98] In *Kitney* v. *M.E.P.C. Ltd.*[99] an option to renew contained in a lease was void for non-registration as a land charge against the lessor's successors in title. It was not subsequently re-vitalised when notice of the lease was entered in the charges register of the lessor's title on first registration.

A purchaser for value will take free from all matters which are capable of being protected by notice on the register but which are not so protected.[1]

---

[90] See *ante*, p. 303.
[91] Land Registration Rules 1925, r. 160.
[92] Land Registration Act 1925, s.26.
[93] *Ibid.* s.34(1).   [94] *Ibid.* ss.48–51.
[95] Land Registration Rules 1925, rr. 186, 190, 194, 197, 198 and 239.
[96] *Strand Securities Ltd.* v. *Caswell* [1965] Ch. 958.
[97] Matrimonial Homes Act 1983, s.2(8).
[98] Land Registration Act 1925, s.52.
[99] [1977] 1 W.L.R. 981.
[1] Land Registration Act 1925, ss.20, 23 and 59(6).

The type of information disclosed by the charges register will now be examined in more detail.

Incumbrances Subsisting at First Registration. On first registration the Registrar takes steps to ensure that all burdens then affecting the land are noted in the register either directly, by setting out extracts from them, or by reference to the instruments by which they were created.[2] A legal mortgagee would normally apply for substantive registration of his title, but if for some reason this was not done, his interest could be protected by a notice on the register. Apart from this all leases that are not overriding interests,[3] restrictive covenants,[4] notices of intended deposit of the land certificate (when issued) as security for money,[5] rentcharges, and burdens imposed by instruments[6] such as a right of way or right of drainage are entered.

Where several leases affect the land they are often tabulated in a separate schedule. The terms of restrictive covenants are also usually set out in a separate schedule, and short particulars of the deed imposing them entered in the charges register.

Entries After First Registration. The most likely entry that will be made in the charges register after first registration will be the substantive registration of a charge. All subsequent leases[7] that are not overriding interests, new restrictive covenants[8] and other classes of landcharge,[9] rights of a spouse to occupy the matrimonial home,[10] and all other burdens that come into effect after first registration, including any overriding interest[11] proved to the satisfaction of the registrar or admitted by the servient owner (and which is not trivial) may be noted.

Notes Relating to Rights Adversely Affecting the Land. These mainly relate to restrictive covenants. Under the provisions of section 110(4) of the 1925 Act all copies and extracts of restrictive covenants that are set out on the register are assumed to be correct and any person who suffers loss by reason of any error or omission in the matter set out is liable to be indemnified. Often applications for first registrations include unexamined particulars of restrictive covenants contained in old deeds. If the Registrar cannot vouch for the accuracy of such covenants he will merely note that the relevant deed contained restrictive covenants but that neither the

---

[2] Land Registration Rules 1925, r. 40.
[3] Land Registration Act 1925, s.70(1)(*k*) and see *post*, p. 347.
[4] *Ibid*. s.50(1).
[5] Land Registration Rules 1925, rr. 240–241.
[6] Land Registration Act 1925, s.70(2); Land Registration Rules 1925, r. 41; *Re Dances Way* 1962] Ch. 490.
[7] Land Registration Act 1925, s.48. Land Registration Rules 1925, rr. 186–189.
[8] Land Registration Act 1925, s.50(1).
[9] *Ibid*. s.59(2).
[10] Under Matrimonial Homes Act 1983.
[11] See *ante*. p. 344.

original instrument nor a certified copy or examined abstract has been produced.[12]

Similarly, if on first registration it is thought that the land may be subject to undisclosed restrictive covenants the Registrar may enter a note to the effect that the land is subject to such restrictive convenants as may have been imposed before a certain date, so far as the same are subsisting and capable of being enforced.[13] This is to protect himself from any possible claim for rectification of the register and indemnification. However the Registrar only makes such a note when he considers that there is a real risk of such a claim being made, for example where an application for registration is founded on adverse possession and no documentary title is shown.[14]

Dealings with Incumbrances. These relate to charges in respect of which there is a registered proprietor, that is, registered charges.[15] Restrictions, creditor's notices and bankruptcy inhibitions may be registered against the chargee where appropriate.[16] It is not possible to register any devolution or dealing with a mortgage or other interest protected by a notice only.[15] When a lease, rentcharge, easement, or other interests determines, the Registrar usually cancels the original entry if he is satisfied as to the proof of its determination.[17] An entry relating to restrictive covenants is not as a rule cancelled if the covenants are released, due to the uncertainties in the law in this area. The deed of release is noted instead.[18] Of course if the Lands Tribunal discharges a restrictive covenant the entry is cancelled.

Position of a Purchaser. A purchaser will continue to be bound by most of the incumbrances mentioned in the charges register on becoming the new registered proprietor. It is therefore important for him to know the extent of any rights or interests claimed and where this is not apparent from the register the vendor should be asked to provide a copy of the instrument creating it. Further enquiries may also be necessary where a note has been entered on the register relating to unverified or undisclosed restrictive covenants or to ascertain whether or not restrictive covenants have been effectively released.[19] In *Re Stone and Saville's Contract*[20] the purchaser contracted to buy registered land the charges register of which

---

[12] Registered Land Practice Notes (1982/3 ed.) Note J.2. Alternatively on special request the covenants may be fully set out but accompanied by a statement that their accuracy is not guaranteed. It should be noted that even if the Law Commissions Report (Law Com. 127) is given statutory recognition the law and registry practice regarding existing restrictive covenants will remain unchanged.

[13] Registered Land Practice Notes (1982/3 ed.) Note J.3.

[14] A squatter is bound by covenants affecting the land even if he is unaware of their existence *Re Nisbet and Potts' Contract* [1906] 1 Ch. 386. If no such entry was made in the charges register he could dispose of the land free from them. Later a claim for rectification of the register might be made and the registered proprietor would prima facie be entitled to indemnification.

[15] Land Registration Act 1925, s.26; Land Registration Rules 1925, r. 160.

[16] Land Registration Act 1925, ss.58(1), 61(1) and 61(4).

[17] Land Registration Rules 1925, r. 203.

[18] *Ibid.* r. 212.

[19] It may be decided to refer the matter to the court.

[20] [1963] 1 W.L.R. 163.

revealed a covenant not to use the property other than as a private dwelling house. The covenant had in fact ceased to be enforceable. The purchaser intended another use for the property and his solicitors raised a requisition as to the enforceability of the covenant. The vendor's solicitors ignored this and when the purchaser failed to complete on the due date served a notice to complete. The purchasers solicitors referred to the requisition and rescinded the contract. It was held that the purchaser had validly rescinded the contract and was entitled to the return of his deposit. The vendor had failed to make good title.

If the charges register reveals a notice protecting a spouse's rights of occupation the purchaser should insist on its cancellation on or before completion or rescind the contract.

The parties will generally have agreed that the vendor should discharge all monetary charges on completion. It might be useful to both sides to mention briefly the various ways in which these charges are discharged. When a mortgage of registered land is discharged it will be deleted from the register and the purchaser's solicitor is therefore not concerned with the proper discharge of prior mortgages. However, in ensuring that the vendor's mortgage(s) will be properly discharged it should be remembered that when a mortgage, legal or equitable, has been protected by a notice, no devolution of title to it will be shown on the register.[21] When it is discharged the title to it must be deduced as in unregistered conveyancing.

(i) *Discharge of a Registered Charge.* The form prescribed by statute for use when a registered charge is discharged wholly or in part is form 53 and 53(CO) for corporations.[22] It must be signed by the chargee, or executed under seal in the case of discharge by a trading company. The procedure relating to the lodgement of form 53 is described in the next chapter.[23]; If however this lodged unaccompanied by a transfer (though of course with the charge certificate) and the appropriate form (A4), the charge will be cancelled and the land certificate returned to the registered proprietor if applied for.

Form 55 can be used to effect a transfer and discharge of the whole of the registered land in one form. Form 55A should be used where the transaction involves part only of the land. The subsequent application for registration must be accompanied by the charge certificate.

Where the chargee is a building society, friendly society or industrial or provident society Form 53 (duly sealed) is usually used,[24] but the registry will accept a statutory receipt[25] endorsed on the original charge and sealed and attested by the duly authorised officer of the society, as satisfactory evidence of discharge. If Form 53 is used and the society is unincorporated signature by the trustees (or other proper officers) acting on behalf of the society should be witnessed by the secretary of the society.[26]

---

[21] See *ante*, p. 319.
[22] Land Registration Rules 1925, r. 151.
[23] See *post*, p. 434.
[24] Land Registration Rules 1925, r. 152(1).
[25] Law of Property Act 1925, s.115; Building Societies Act 1962, Sched. 6, s.37(1).
[26] Land Registration Rules 1925, r. 152(2).

(ii) *Discharge of Legal or Equitable Mortgages Protected by Notice.* These are discharged in the same way as if the land was unregistered, that is by statutory receipt.[27] The title (if any) of the mortgagee's power to give a receipt must be deduced to the Registrar when an application is made for removal of the notice.

(iii) *Withdrawal of Notices of Deposit or Intended Deposit.* A notice of deposit or notice of intended deposit may be withdrawn from the register on the written request or consent of the person entitled to the lien created by the deposit or notice of intended deposit. The request or consent must be signed by the depositee, personally if an individual or by a responsible officer if the depositee is an institutional lender, and be accompanied by the land or charge certificate.[28] Form 86 is usually used for this purpose, which is on the reverse side of Form 85A, B or C, the printed notice of deposit.

Notices of deposit or intended deposit cannot be registered in respect of part only of land comprised in a title,[29] similarly they cannot be withdrawn as to part. But the depositee may by letter consent to a dealing with part. Again the land or charge certificate must accompany the application.

Verification of Title

Earlier we saw that a vendor proves his title to registered land by supplying his purchaser with an authority to inspect the register together with copies of the entries in the register and other documents noted on it.[30] Armed with the authority to inspect, a purchaser or his solicitor could verify the title by personally comparing the information he has been given with the register. In practice purchasers rely on seeing the land or charge certificate or office copies, both of which constitute admissible evidence of the matters they contain,[31] and making an official search to ensure that the state of the register has not changed since the date noted as being when the land or charge certificate was last officially made to correspond with the register or since the date the office copies were issued from the registry.[32] The official search procedure was fully explained in Chapter 2.[33] Verification by personal search would have been more advantageous in *Parkash* v. *Irani Finance Co. Ltd.*[34] A purchaser's certificate of official search failed to reveal a caution entered on the vendor's register of title. He nevertheless took the land subject to the cautioners' interest which had been correctly protected on the register.

---

[27] Law of Property Act 1925, s.115.
[28] Land Registration Rules 1925, r. 246.
[29] *Ibid.* r. 243.
[30] Land Registration Act 1925, s.110 and see *ante*, p. 313.
[31] *Ibid.* ss.68 and 113.
[32] This practice has the approval of the Chief Land Registrar and Council of the Law Society. 56 L.S.Gaz. 395.
[33] See *ante*, p. 37. For official searches in the case of developing building estates see Registered Land Practice Notes (1982/83 ed.) Note B6.
[34] [1970] Ch. 101.

Stamping the Title

In practice all questions of the stamping of earlier title are left to the Registrar who is under a statutory duty to satisfy himself in this respect.[35]

How Far can a Purchaser Rely on the Register?

In assessing a vendor's ownership of unregistered land few would quarrel with the statement quoted earlier[36] that "ownership in English land law is rarely absolute and generally relative." Conversely adherents to the present system would refute the applicability of this statement to registered land; "the quality of a registered title is one of hard fact."[37] It has been said[38] of title "absolute," the title most commonly registered, that the register is "a conclusive and complete record of title" to which no objection is possible. Such categorical statements prompt the observer to enquire, how far can a purchaser trust the register, how far can he be sure of the vendor's ownership, how absolute is "absolute?" The answer lies in a consideration of the pregnability of two of the three principles underlying the registered system; the mirror principle and the curtain principle. Only if these two principles are strictly adhered to, can the purchaser's position be completely assured. If not he gets the "consolation prize," the third principle, insurance.

THE MIRROR PRINCIPLE

" . . . involves the proposition that the register is a mirror which reflects accurately and completely and beyond all argument the current facts that are material to a man's title. This mirror does not reveal the history of the title, for disused facts are obliterated. It does not show matters (such as trusts) that are incapable of substantive registration. In addition it does not allow anyone to view and consider facts and events which are capable of being registered and ought to have been registered. In other words a title is free from all adverse burdens rights and qualifications unless they are mentioned on the register."[39]

The mirror image is defective in two important respects. Firstly as previously mentioned it fails to reveal the existence of overriding interests, which although not mentioned on the register will bind a purchaser. Secondly, it does not take account of the possibility that the register may be rectified even in the case of title "absolute," "the most reliable and marketable title that exists."[40] Overriding interests constitute an exception both to the mirror and next principle to be discussed and it is more

---

[35] Land Registration Act 1925, s.14(3); Stamp Act 1891, s.17.
[36] See *ante*, p. 257.
[37] Ruoff, *Torrens system*, 1957.
[38] Ruoff and Roper, *Registered Conveyancing* (3rd ed.) p. 346.
[39] Ruoff, *The Torrens System*, p. 8.
[40] Ruoff and Roper, *Registered Conveyancing* (4th ed.) p. 74.

convenient to deal with them under a separate heading. Here the principles of rectification and indemnity will be briefly described.[41]

Rectification. Under section 82[42] of the 1925 Act the court and Registrar have wide powers to rectify (correct) the register where any error or omission has been made. Examples would be, where a legal estate has been registered in the name of a person who is not the true owner, where an entry has been obtained by fraud, where by mistake two or more persons are registered as proprietors of the same estate or charge, or where a mortgagee is registered as proprietor of the land instead of a charge and there is a subsisting right of redemption, section 82(3)[43] adds a qualification to these powers in that the register shall not be rectified except for the purpose of giving effect to an overriding interest or an order of the court so as to affect the title of the proprietor who is *in possession*, unless:

(i) he has caused or substantially contributed to the error or omission by fraud or lack of proper care; or

(ii) for some other reason, in any particular case it is considered that it would be unjust not to rectify the register against him.

Possession is defined in the Act, (unless the context otherwise requires) as including the receipt or right to receive rents and profits (if any).[44] In *Strand Securities Ltd.* v. *Caswell*[45] the meaning of possession arose. It is clear that it encompasses actual occupation but in this case it was held that it did not include a proprietor not in actual occupation who allowed a licensee to occupy premises rent free. A person can be deemed to be in possession however, where it is not he but a licensee (a caretaker for instance), who is in occupation as an agent of the proprietor.

Indemnification. A claim for rectification can have one of two results. Either the register will be rectified, in which case the registered proprietor will suffer loss, or the claimant for rectification will be turned away, in which case he will suffer loss. Provided that the loss is caused by the rectification or non-rectification[46] and the applicant (or a person through whom he claims otherwise than by a disposition for value which is registered or protected on the register) has not caused or substantially contributed to the loss by fraud or lack of care,[47] compensation will be payable in respect of actual loss suffered in either case. The compensation is payable out of public funds, hence the phrase "State guaranteed title."

---

[41] For a full discussion, see Ruoff and Roper, *Registered Conveyancing,* (4th ed.) pp. 783–810.

[42] And Land Registration Rules 1925, rr. 13 and 14.

[43] As amended by Administration of Justice Act 1977.

[44] Land Registration Act 1925, s.3(xviii).

[45] [1965] Ch. 958.

[46] Land Registration Act 1925, s.83(1) and (2); In *Re Chowood's Registered Land* [1933] Ch. 574 the registered proprietor bought land with a squatter in possession of part. The register was subsequently rectified to exclude that part from the title. Because the rectification just gave recognition to the existing state of affairs by giving effect to the squatter's overriding interest, no compensation was payable.

[47] Land Registration Act 1925, s.83(5), as amended by the Land Registration and Land Charges Act 1971, s.3(1).

No indemnity is payable if a claim is made more than six years after the date that the land was registered with an absolute title or with good leasehold title.[48]

THE CURTAIN PRINCIPLE

"The curtain principle is one which provides that the register is the sole source of information for proposing purchasers, who need not and, indeed must not concern themselves with trusts and equities which lie behind the curtain."[49]

The curtain principle is promulgated in the 1925 Act by section 74, which provides that no person "dealing with a registered estate or charge shall be affected with notice of a trust express implied or constructive," and sections 20(1) and 23(1) which provide that registration should confer the legal estate on the transferee subject to entries on the register and overriding interests "but free from all other estates and interests whatsoever." Bridge L.J. in *Miles* v. *Bull* (No. 2) said that these words "embrace prima facie not only all kinds of legal interests but all kinds of equitable interests."[50] These sections make it quite clear that there is no room for the doctrine of notice in registered conveyancing. To quote Lord Wilberforce in *Williams & Glyn's Bank Ltd.* v. *Boland*[51] "In my opinion therefore the law as to notice as it may affect purchasers of unregistered land, whether contained in decided cases or in a statute (*e.g.* the Conveyancing Act 1882, s.3 and the Law of Property Act 1925, s.199) has no application even by analogy to registered land."[52]

Yet note must be taken of two recent first instance decisions which seem to have re-introduced notice into the registered system and made an unwelcome inroad into the curtain principle. In *Peffer* v. *Rigg*,[53] P. and R. bought a house in R.'s name, to provide a home for R.'s wife's mother. P. and R. agreed that R. should hold the house on trust for them as beneficial tenants in common. R. and his wife were subsequently divorced and R. transferred the whole beneficial ownership in the house to her for £1. She knew of the arrangement between P. and R. but claimed that as a transferee for value within section 20(1), she took free from P.'s interest which was not protected by an entry on the register. "Transferee" is undefined by the Act but section 3(xxi) provides that a "purchaser" is someone who acts in good faith and gives valuable consideration. Graham J. felt that it could not possibly have been the intention of section 20(1) to allow a transferee for value to take free from an unprotected interest of which he was fully aware. He therefore linked section 20(1) with section 59(6) which provides that fraud and bankruptcy apart ". . . a purchaser acquiring title under a registered disposition shall not be concerned

---

[48] Land Registration Act 1925, s.83(11); *Epps* v. *Esso Petroleum Co. Ltd.* [1973] 1 W.L.R. 1071.
[49] Ruoff, *The Torrens System*, p. 11.
[50] [1969] 3 All E.R. 1585 at p. 1589.
[51] [1981] A.C. 487 at p. 504.
[52] See also *Bridge L. J. Miles* v. *Bull* (*No. 2*) [1969] 3 All E.R. 1585 at p. 1590 and Cross J. in *Strand Securities* v. *Caswell* [1965] Ch. 373 at p. 390.
[53] [1977] 1 W.L.R. 285.

with . . . " in effect, any matter not protected by an entry on the register, and held that a transferee claiming to take free from an unprotected minor interest within section 59(6) must be a transferee in good faith. Mrs. R. was bound by P.'s interest. If the case is followed it means that a transfer will not be in good faith and the transferee will not take free from an unprotected minor interest where he has at least actual knowledge of the interest. In other words a purchaser with notice cannot rely on the register. This said, *Peffer* v. *Rigg* will probably be confined to its own particular set of facts.[54]

In the other case, *Lyus* v. *Prowsa Developments Ltd.*[55] the defendants contracted to buy a plot of registered land subject to the plaintiff's contract to purchase, so far, if at all, as it might be enforceable. The plaintiff's contract was not mentioned in the transfer to the defendants. The plaintiff was not in occupation, so did not have an overriding interest, nor had he protected his contract by an entry on the register. Nonetheless Dillon J. held that the contract was binding on the defendants on the basis that a statute, the Land Registration Act 1925, should not be used as an instrument of fraud. Because the sale was subject to the contract, a constructive trust arose in the plaintiff's favour.[56]

Finally it should be added that a purchaser may be bound by "trusts and equities which lie behind the curtain" because they constitute overriding interests, considered next.

OVERRIDING INTERESTS

These interests constitute an exception both to the mirror and the curtain principle. They will bind a purchaser for value even though not mentioned on the register, and their number may comprise "equities" which otherwise the Land Registration Acts strive to keep off the title. It has been explained[57] that the registration system was designed to replace the process of title investigation by perusal of title documents. It was not intended to replace the other equally important side of the process, namely an inspection of the property to see what was actually happening "on the ground." This side of the process was preserved by creating a separate class of interests in registered land, of a type (seemingly) discoverable on personal inspection and which would bind a purchaser for value irrespective of notice. Thus the introductory words of section 70 of the 1925 Act, which sets out the list of overriding interests, state that

> "all registered land shall, unless under the provisions of this Act the contrary is expressed on the register, be deemed to be subject to such of the following overriding interests as may be for the time being subsisting in reference thereto, and such interests shall not be treated as incumbrances within the meaning of this Act."

---

[54] T.B. Ruoff and C. West, *Concise Land Registration Practice* (3rd ed.) Appendix B, p. 257.

[55] [1982] 1 W.L.R. 1044; C.T. Emery and B. Smythe (1983) 133 New L.J. 798–801.

[56] Following *Binions* v. *Evans* [1972] Ch. 359.

[57] See *ante*, p. 300.

We must now look at Section 70 in rather more detail. There are a considerable number of rights listed in the section many of which are of limited practical importance.[58] Due to the confines of this book we shall deal only with those most likely to be encountered by a purchaser in a normal conveyancing transaction. First however, it should be remembered that under a contract for the sale of registered land the vendor is under a duty to disclose any overriding interests which come within the meaning of latent defects in title, but need not disclose any which amount to patent defects. Furthermore where the Law Society's contract of sale is used, Condition 5(1) probably requires him to disclose all overriding interests of which he knows or ought to know (including patent ones) unless the purchaser actually knows of them or should have discovered them.

The classes of overriding interests of importance to a purchaser now follow. The rights of those in actual occupation probably constitute the greatest hazard and these will be dealt with last.

Section 70(1)(a). " . . . profits . . . and easements not being equitable easements required to be protected by notice on the register."

The purpose and scope of his provision is far from clear.[59] It seems that it would give protection to legal easements in the unlikely event of their not having been noted on the charges register of the title to the servient land. The better view is that equitable easements, for example an agreement to grant a right of way over a road until it is adopted by the local authority are not overriding interests.[60]

Section 70(1)(f). "Subject to the provisions of this Act rights acquired or in the course of being acquired under the Limitation Acts."

Squatters rights are overriding interests until the successful adverse possessor has the register rectified in his favour. The Limitation Act 1980 applies to registered land, but the estate of the registered proprietor is not extinguished like that of an estate owner of unregistered land. Instead section 75(1) of the Land Registration Act 1925 provides that the proprietor "squatted against" holds his estate as a trustee for the squatter. Section 75(2) and (3) further provides that any person claiming to have acquired title by adverse possession may apply to be registered as proprietor and that the Registrar shall, if satisfied as to the applicant's title enter the applicant as proprietor with absolute, good leasehold, qualified or possessory title as appropriate, but without prejudice to any estate or interest protected by an entry on the register which may not have been extinguished under the Limitation Act. The registration has the same effect as the registration of a first proprietor. Thus an approximation of the equivalent position in unregistered land is achieved. Indeed section 75 begins: "The Limitation Acts shall apply to registered land in the same manner and to the same extent as those Acts apply to land not registered."

---

[58] For a full consideration see J.T. Farrand, *Emmet on Title* (18th ed.) pp. 200–213 and Ruoff and Roper, *Registered Conveyancing* (4th ed.) pp. 93–116.

[59] J.T. Farrand, *Emmet on Title* (18th ed.) p. 202; D. Hayton, *Registered land* (3rd ed.) p.83.

[60] Ruoff and Roper, *Registered Conveyancing* (4th ed.) p. 97.

Nevertheless in *Spectrum Investment Co.* v. *Holmes*[61] at least one substantive distinction in the application of the Limitation Act[62] to registered and unregistered land, was brought to light. In unregistered land the effect of limitation by a squatter against a tenant is to leave the relationship between the landlord and tenant unimpaired. So if the tenant surrenders his lease to his landlord thereby entitling him to possession, the landlord can recover possession from the squatter. (*Fairweather* v. *St. Marylebone Property Co. Ltd.*)[63] Taking the equivalent factual situation in registered land, the squatter only remains vulnerable until he registers his possessory title, although it has been suggested[64] that a surrender by the tenant in the interim would amount to breach of the tenant's trust under section 75(1). Once, however, the squatter registers his title he is immune, according to the court's decision in *Spectrum*. The tenant's register to the lease having been closed (properly in the court's view) he is no longer in a position to surrender the lease because section 69(4) of the Land Registration Act states: "The estate for the time being of the registered proprietor shall only be capable of being disposed of or dealt with by him in the manner authorised by the Act." The landlord therefore cannot recover possession until the lease comes to an end.

A squatter is entitled to have the register rectified even against a proprietor with title absolute, and without indemnification being paid to that proprietor.[65] Although the idea of making squatters' rights overriding interests, thus binding future purchasers, may bring the registered land position into line with that in unregistered land, it does produce inconsistencies in the statutory provisions. Section 70(1)(*f*) begins with the words: "Subject to the provisions of this Act . . . ." As we have already seen in connection with the curtain principle, section 74 of the Act provides that no person dealing with registered land "shall be affected with notice of a trust express implied or constructive." The effect of the Limitation Act on registered land is that the proprietor becomes a trustee for the squatter. Should a purchaser for value be bound by this trust, or in other words should squatters' rights be overriding interests? A clear answer in the affirmative was given by Harman J. in *Bridges* v. *Mees*.[66] The plaintiff agreed to buy registered land from a company and went into possession. The company later sold the same land to the defendant who became registered as proprietor of it. It was held that the plaintiff had acquired title by adverse possession and was entitled to rectification of the defendant's register in his favour. Failure to protect his contract by entering a caution was of no consequence; his rights were adequately protected by virtue of his having an overriding interest within section 70(1)(*f*).[67]

---

[61] [1981] 1 W.L.R. 221; C. Sydenham [1981] Conv. 157.

[62] In *Spectrum* the Limitation Act 1939.

[63] [1963] A.C. 510.　　[64] P.H. Kenny, [1982] Conv. 201.

[65] *Chowood* v. *Lyall (No. 2)* [1930] 2 Ch. 156; *Re Chowood's Registered Land* [1933] Ch. 574.

[66] [1957] Ch. 475.

[67] Or in the alternative s.70(1)(*g*). In *Hyde* v. *Pearce* [1982] 1 W.L.R. 560 a case with similar facts the point was not argued. See [1983] 127 S.J. 210; M. P. Thompson, who

Section 70(1)(k). "Leases for any term or interest not exceeding twenty-one years, granted at a rent without taking a fine."

These leases are not capable of being registered in their own right,[68] or of being the subject of a registered disposition,[69] or of being noted on the register.[70] Their protection lies in being accorded the status of overriding interests. A lease cannot be an overriding interest if no rent is payable, if the original term granted exceeded 21 years (however little time it has left to run) or if a premium is paid. Cases[71] have arisen involving lump sum payments expressed to be of rent in advance but the courts have given no clear indication whether these are to be treated as rent or premiums for the purposes of paragraph (*k*). Agreements for lease do not constitute overriding interests within this head.[72]

Section 70(1)(g). "The rights of every person in actual occupation of the land or in receipt of the rents and profits thereof, save where inquiry is made of such person and the rights are not disclosed."

This is the most important class of overriding interests, if volume of litigation is any test. In *National Provincial Bank Ltd.* v. *Ainsworth*,[73] Lord Wilberforce stated that section 70(1)(*g*) amounts to "a statutory application to registered land of the well known rule protecting the rights of persons in occupation." In fact it would seem to do more than that. The "well known" rule was formulated in *Hunt* v. *Luck*[74] as follows:

(i) a tenant's occupation is notice of all that tenant's rights but *not* of his lessor's title or rights;

(ii) *actual* knowledge that the rents are paid by the tenant to some person whose receipt is inconsistent with the title of the vendor *is* notice of that person's rights.

The court rejected the argument that a purchaser would be fixed with constructive notice if he found that there was a tenant in the property and did not bother to make sure that the tenant paid rent to the vendor. But under section 70(1)(*g*) if there is a tenant and he is paying rent to someone other than the vendor the purchaser will take subject to that other person's interest, because, whether the purchaser is aware of it or not that person is in receipt of the rents and profits.

This extension of the rule in *Hunt* v. *Luck* in relation to registered land seems strange when it is remembered that it was inadvertently excluded in relation to unregistered land. Section 33 of the Law of Property Act 1922 limited the operation of the part of that Act dealing with land charges by providing that it should not prejudicially affect the rights of persons in possession or actual occupation of the land. When the 1922 Act was divided up in 1925, section 33 became section 14 of the Law of Property

---

suggests this may have been because the full purchase price had not been paid to the vendor; in *Bridges* v. *Mees* [1957] Ch. 475 it had.

[68] Land Registration Act 1925, s.8(1)(*a*).

[69] *Ibid.* ss.19(2)(*a*) and 22(2)(*a*).   [70] *Ibid.* s.48(1).

[71] *City Permanent Building Society* v. *Miller* [1952] Ch. 840; *Grace Rymer Investments Ltd.* v. *Waite* [1958] Ch. 831.

[72] *City Permanent Building Society* v. *Miller* [1952] Ch. 840.

[73] [1965] A.C. 1175.

[74] [1902] 1 Ch. 428.

Act 1925 and although it nominally preserved the rule in *Hunt* v. *Luck* it failed to qualify the harsh rules in the Land Charges Act 1925 (now the Land Charges Act 1972) which rendered void registrable but unregistered interests. As a result the application of the rule in registered conveyancing produces a considerable difference in the two systems. To take an example: Suppose A the fee simple owner agrees to grant a 10 year lease to B, who enters into possession. B then agrees to grant a 5 year underlease to C who is also allowed into possession. Neither transaction is formally completed. A then sells the fee simple to D. In the case of registered land D is bound by both B and C's interests; C's because he is in actual occupation and B's because he is entitled to the receipt of rents.[75] In the equivalent unregistered land situation, D would take free from B and C's interests unless they were registered as estate contracts under the Land Charges Act 1972, even if D actually knew of them.[76]

Section 70(1)(g) makes an even further extension in the rule in that being so widely drawn, it probably protects more rights than did *Hunt* v. *Luck*. *Hunt* v. *Luck* was limited, insofar as the purchaser would only be bound by rights of which he had express, constructive or imputed notice. The rights covered by section 70(1)(g) are not limited to those of which the purchaser knows, or ought to know. The section states quite categorically that the purchaser will take subject to the rights of persons in actual occupation or in receipt of rents *unless* inquiry is made and the rights are not disclosed; however difficult those rights may be to discover.

> "What is involved is a departure from an easy-going practice of dispensing with inquiries as to occupation beyond that of the vendor and accepting the risks of doing so. To substitute for this a practice of more careful inquiry as to the fact of occupation, and, if necessary, as to the rights of occupiers, cannot, in my view of the matter, be considered as unacceptable . . . "[77]

But perhaps the greatest anomaly of section 70(1)(g) is that the recipient of rent appears to be protected even if the payer is not in actual occupation. It is unlikely that the legislature even considered this possibility and drafted the section on the assumption that the presence of a tenant would alert a purchaser to someone in receipt of rents and profits. Nevertheless the section as worded contains no such limitation.

Finally whilst on the subject of 'rents and profits' it should be added that in *E.S. Schwab & Co. Ltd.* v. *McCarthy*[78] the Court of Appeal indicated[79] that for the purposes of section 70(1)(g) there must be actual receipt of rent from a tenant. However in other cases[80] it has been assumed that a person can be 'in receipt' if they are entitled to receive rent.

---

[75] *Strand Securities* v. *Caswell* [1965] Ch. 958.
[76] *Hollington Bros. Ltd.* v. *Rhodes* [1951] Ch. 578.
[77] *Per* Lord Wilberforce in *Williams & Glyn's Bank Ltd.* v. *Boland* [1981] A.C. 487 at p. 508.
[78] (1975) 31 P. & C.R. 196.
[79] Sir John Pennycuick and Buckley L.J.
[80] *Strand Securities* v. *Caswell* [1965] Ch. 958; *Sheridan* v. *Dickson* [1970] 1 W.L.R. 1328.

The Proviso to Section 70(1)(g). Although it is clear that the usual considerations of actual or constructive notice have no part to play in relation to the validity of the rights of those in actual occupation or in receipt of rents and profits, such rights will only be valid "save where inquiry is made (of such person) and the rights are not disclosed." Unless some guidance is sought from the old doctrine of notice, in the sense of the sort of requirements that would be included if notice was the test, it is difficult to ascertain the precise meaning of the proviso.

It is clear that inquiry must be made of the person in occupation or in "receipt." Thus Russell L.J. remarked in *Hodgson* v. *Marks*[81]: "Reliance upon the untrue *ipse dixit* of the vendor will not suffice." Despite this it is usual to direct the purchaser's inquiries relating to section 70(1)(g) in Enquiries before Contract and Requisitions on Title to the vendor, or in the case of institutional lenders to the borrower. Some doubts are felt on the efficacy of these enquiries.[82] If a company is involved inquiry of an officer of the company, but not some other employee, would seem to suffice.[83]

According to the case of *London and Cheshire Insurance Company* v. *Laplagrene Property Co. Ltd.*,[84] to come within the proviso the relevant enquiry must have been demonstrably made "by or on behalf of the intending transferee or grantee for the purposes of the intended disposition."[85]

Furthermore it seems that the proviso can be modified by adding "if the rights are not disclosed within a reasonable time."[86] What amounts to a reasonable time would of course depend on the facts of each particular case, but it is hardly likely that a person claiming rights of occupation or "receipt" could rely on a prolonged refusal to disclose his rights on being asked. Bearing this in mind it might be thought useful to accompany a purchaser's enquiries with a stipulated time limit for reply. If an ambiguous reply is received, presumably the onus is on the purchaser to make further enquiries. Not so much because the ambiguous reply would constitute constructive notice, but rather because the purchaser will be bound (irrespective of notice) unless he can prove that there had been no disclosure after a proper enquiry.

Finally, it should be remembered that a purchaser takes subject to overriding interests affecting the purchased estate at the date of registration of the purchaser as the new proprietor[87] (the date of the delivery of his application for registration at the registry[88]). Care must therefore be taken to protect a purchaser during the period in between completion and registration if he does not take possession immediately after his purchase.

---

[81] [1971] Ch. 892.
[82] J.T. Farrand, *Emmet on Title* (18th ed.) p. 210.
[83] *Panorama Developments (Guildford) Ltd.* v. *Fidelis Furnishing Fabrics Ltd.* [1971] 2 Q.B. 711.
[84] [1971] Ch. 499.
[85] *Ibid.* at p. 505.
[86] *Panorama Developments (Guildford) Ltd.* v. *Fidelis Furnishing Fabrics Ltd.* [1971] 2 Q.B. 711.
[87] *Re Boyle's Claim* [1961] 1 W.L.R. 339.
[88] Land Registration Rules 1925, r. 83(2).

Another, but allied problem arising from the proviso is knowing who to ask; who is in actual occupation or in receipt of rents and profits? Guidelines can only be gleaned from past cases. In *Epps* v. *Esso Petroleum Co. Ltd.*[89] the regular parking of cars of a strip of land was held not to amount to an overriding interest; it did not amount to actual occupation either in whole or in respect of any defined part or time. In *Strand Securities Ltd.* v. *Caswell*[90] a lessee allowed his daughter and her family to occupy a flat as a favour without receiving even a token rent. It was held that he was not a person in receipt of rents or profits for the purposes of section 70(1)(g). However it is clear that a person can be in actual occupation[91] or in receipt of rents and profits[92] through the agency of another person. And in *Hodgson* v. *Marks*[93] the Court of Appeal held that a person could be in actual occupation of land even though the vendor was also in occupation. Finally this question has become even more difficult since the House of Lords, in *Williams & Glyn's Bank Ltd.* v. *Boland*,[94] recognised that equitable interests under a trust for sale could be overriding interests.

Rights Within Section 70(1)(g). It might be useful at this stage to consider what sort of rights are within section 70(1)(g). Here the reader will be pleased to know that some limit has been placed on its scope. It follows from *Hunt* v. *Luck* that the rights protected by occupation are not merely rights of occupation. If the occupier had other rights the fact of his occupation gave any prospective purchaser constructive notice of those rights. This is no longer so in unregistered land if those rights are registrable as land charges. In registered land the protection of the rights is no longer dependent upon the constructive notice given by occupation, the fact of occupation is enough in itself.[95] Nevertheless, apparently the ordinary principles of property law (supposedly unaltered by the registered system) will limit the rights capable of being protected under section 70(1)(g), to those which, under the old law could have been protected by constructive notice, that is proprietary as opposed to purely personal rights. In *National Provincial Bank Ltd.* v. *Ainsworth*,[96] Lord Wilberforce said:

> "To ascertain what rights come within [paragraph *g*] one must look outside [the Land Registration Act 1925] and see what rights affect purchasers under the general law . . . there is no warrant in the terms of this paragraph or elsewhere in the Act for supposing that the nature of the rights which are to bind a purchaser is to be different, excluding personal rights in one case, including them in another."

---

[89] [1973] 1 W.L.R. 1071.
[90] [1965] Ch. 958.
[91] *National Provincial Bank Ltd.* v. *Ainsworth* [1965] A.C. 1175.
[92] *Strand Securities* v. *Caswell* [1965] Ch. 958.
[93] [1971] Ch. 892.
[94] [1981] A.C. 487.
[95] See Lord Wilberforce in *Williams & Glyn's Bank Ltd.* v. *Boland* [1981] A.C. 487 at p. 507.
[96] [1965] A.C. 1175 at p. 1261.

All the Lords in that case agreed with the view of Russell L.J. (dissenting) in the Court of Appeal[97]: "It seems to me that [section 70 of the Land Registration Act 1925] in all its parts is dealing with rights in reference to land which have the quality of enduring through different ownerships of the land according to the normal conceptions of title to real property."

The range of rights is also narrowed by the fact that certain rights (enumerated earlier)[98] such as the rights of a spouse to occupy the matrimonial home under the Matrimonial Homes Act 1983, can only be minor interests. On the other hand it will be remembered that the mere fact that an interest may be registrable or a minor interest, does not preclude it from being an overriding interest, provided that it is not mentioned on the register.

Here are examples of just a few of the rights that (when coupled with *actual* occupation) have been recognised by the courts as overriding interests within section 70(1)(*g*):

(1) The right of occupation and specific performance under a contract to purchase a freehold or leasehold interest; *Bridges* v. *Mees*[99]; *Woolwich Equitable Building Society* v. *Marshall.*[1]

(2) The right of a tenant to purchase the freehold reversion of a lease; *Webb* v. *Pollmount Ltd.*[2]

(3) The right to an unpaid vendor's lien (where there has been a "sale and leaseback"); *London and Cheshire Insurance Company* v. *Laplagrene Property Co. Ltd.*[3]

(4) The right of a tenant and his successors under a waiver of rights by the landlord; *Brikom Investments* v. *Carr.*[4]

(5) A right of rectification anciliary to an equitable estate or interest in land; *Blacklocks* v. *J. B. Developments (Godalming) Ltd..*[5]

(6) The rights of a beneficiary under a bare trust; *Hodgson* v. *Marks.*[6]

(7) The rights of a beneficiary under a trust for sale; *Williams & Glyn's Bank Ltd.* v. *Boland.*[7]

This last case deserves further comment. A husband was registered as the sole proprietor of the matrimonial home in which he lived with his wife. She had made substantial contributions to the acquisition of the home entitling her to an equitable interest therein. The husband mortgaged the home to the bank, without his wife's knowledge to secure the debts of his faltering business. The Bank failed to make inquiries regarding her interest, which she had not protected by entering a caution. The combined result of the Court of Appeal and House of Lords decisions was that the husband held the home on trust for sale for himself and his

---

[97] [1964] 1 Ch. 665 at p. 684.
[98] See *ante*, p. 304.
[99] [1957] Ch. 475.
[1] [1952] Ch. 1.
[2] [1966] Ch. 584.
[3] [1971] Ch. 499.
[4] [1979] 2 W.L.R. 737.
[5] [1981] 3 W.L.R. 554.
[6] [1971] Ch. 892.
[7] [1981] A.C. 487.

wife as tenants in common,[8] and that because the wife was in actual occupation she had an overriding interest within section 70(1)(g) which was binding on the Bank.

One problem with this decision is that where there is a trust for sale (whether the co-owners be legal or equitable) the doctrine of conversion operates to convert the interests of the beneficiaries into personalty, that is a share of the proceeds of sale, and this is not an interest in land. In *Boland* itself the point was evaded by saying that a trust for sale was a matter of convenience imposed on the parties and not in accordance with their real intentions, which were to occupy the property. Therefore it was illusory to describe their interests as interests in the proceeds of sale, when sale was probably the last idea that entered their head. Fair enough, but it does mean that where the true purpose of a trust for sale is sale, which is the case with most express trusts for sale created to provide for several members of a family, and one of the beneficiaries happens to be in occupation, then he will not be able to claim an overriding interest.

Another problem arising out of *Boland* and the procedure (enquiries, obtaining of consents and so on) now adopted in practice as a result of it, is that if an inquiry reveals an equitable interest in land registered in the name of a sole proprietor, the purchaser is alerted to the existence of a trust for sale, and to the fact that the vendor alone cannot give a valid receipt for the purchase money. Furthermore since his powers of mortgaging are limited by statute any mortgage he purports to grant must surely be void. Merely obtaining the consent of the person entitled to the overriding interest (so recognising that the person does have an equitable interest, but allows priority) "must be defective conveyancing."[9] It seems that the better practice would be to secure the appointment of a second trustee, so that full advantage can be taken of the overreaching machinery.

Licensees. Despite the fact that the Court of Appeal, notably Lord Denning, has in several cases[10] taken the contrary view, the orthodox position[11] is that contractual licences which are irrevocable as between the licensee and licensor are merely personal rights, incapable of being protected under section 70. Thus, unless a licensee with an irrevocable licence has also acquired an equity in the form of an estoppel arising from the expenditure of money on the property in the expectation of the licence continuing,[12] it is unlikely that their occupation would entitle them to an overriding interest.[13]

Conclusion

We should like to conclude this section with a passage from Harman L.J.'s judgment in *Re White Rose Cottage*[14]:

---

[8] Following *Bull* v. *Bull* [1955] 1 Q.B. 234.
[9] J.T. Farrand, *Emmet on Title* (18th ed.) p. 210; J. Martin, [1980] Conv. 316–387.
[10] *Binions* v. *Evans* [1972] Ch. 359; *Bendall* v. *McWhirter* [1952] 2 Q.B. 466.
[11] *National Provincial Bank Ltd.* v. *Ainsworth* [1965] A.C. 1175.
[12] *Inwards* v. *Baker* [1965] 2 Q.B. 29; *Pascoe* v. *Turner* [1979] 1 W.L.R. 431.
[13] But see *Midland Bank Ltd.* v. *Farmpride Hatcheries Ltd.* [1980] 260 E. G. 493.
[14] [1965] Ch. 940 at p. 951.

"The system of land registration was introduced into our law in response to the lay demand that dealings with land should be assimilated to dealings with chattels and should cease to be a mystery understood only by conveyancers. The process of reform began as long ago as Lord Cairns' Act of 1875 and was enlarged by Lord Halsbury's Act of 1897. When the great change in the law of real property was brought about by Lord Birkenhead's Acts of 1925, it was of course necessary to reform radically the land registration system to match the new régime. At the same time the reformers proposed to introduce various improvements. The preface to Brickdale and Steward-Wallace's Land Registration Act 1925, (4th ed., 1939) claims in its first chapter, among other things, that the system of land registration 'provides plain and simple methods for effecting transfers and charges.' It cannot be said that either of these policies emerge from the facts of the present case. No doubt the system has worked very well since 1925 by the efforts of the land registrars and the practice of the office, but the present case shows that there are difficulties and pitfalls in the way of comparatively simple transactions which would not have arisen with unregistered land . . . ."

II. REQUISITIONS ON TITLE

Raising Requisitions

After the purchaser has completed his examination of the abstract, he will compile and send to the vendor a list of additional questions about the property "In principle requisitions are appropriate only to matters arising from the perusal of the abstract of title, being confined to stating the purchaser's objections and requirements in respect of such matters. In practice however, the requisitions on title so-called will almost always be found to include many other statements and enquiries."[15] Requisitions therefore often arise out of the purchaser's pre-completion searches[16] or involve matters "of conveyance," for instance the discharge of a mortgage,[17] which "are clearly unnecessary in theory (see *Bain* v. *Fothergill* (1874) L.R. 7 H.L. 158) but clearly convenient as reminders in practice."[18]

The standard printed form of 'Requisitions on Title" (Con 28B) used by most purchasers' solicitors combines questions of conveyance with purely administrative matters. The form incorporates by reference the preliminary enquiries made before exchange of contracts (any change in the replies thereto are required to be detailed by Requisition 1), so

---

[15] J.T. Farrand, *Emmet on Title* (18th ed.) p. 150.

[16] *G. & K. Ladenbau (U.K.) Ltd.* v. *Crawley & de Reya* [1978] 1 W.L.R. 266.

[17] *Re Jackson and Oakshott* (1880) 14 Ch.D. 851.

[18] J.T. Farrand, *Emmet on Title* (18th ed.) p. 151.

shortening the list of enquiries that have to be made. In the rare case of no preliminary enquiries having been made Con 28A (long form) should be used. A completion statement is asked for together with confirmation that receipts for outgoings to be apportioned, and for rent and insurance where leasehold property is being sold, will be produced on completion. If the sale is of unregistered land an enquiry is made whether any abstracted document will not be handed over on completion and for confirmation that an acknowledgment and undertaking will be given in respect of any original documents retained. In the case of registered land where the purchaser has merely been supplied with a photocopy of the vendor's land or charge certificate, the date on which the certificate was last examined with the register is asked for, to enable the purchaser to carry out his official search of the register. On a sale of part of registered land the vendor is asked whether his land certificate is on deposit with the registry and if so for the deposit number. Where the purchaser is buying a plot on a registered building estate, the developer is required to state whether an estate lay-out plan has been approved by the registry; again for the purposes of the purchaser's official search. Requisition 4 relates to mortgages; confirmation must be given that all subsisting mortgages will be discharged on completion, entitling the purchaser to take the property freed therefrom, and if the receipted mortgage deed or Form 53, in the case of a registered charge, will not be handed over on completion the terms of the undertaking that will be given to discharge the mortgage and forward the receipted deed and Form 53. Then follows a statement that vacant possession must be given on completion and the question: "Has every person in occupation of all or any part of the property agreed to vacate on or before completion?" This question is aimed at avoiding the problems highlighted by the case of *Williams & Glyn's Bank Ltd.* v. *Boland*.[19] Although the decision relates to registered land only it is probable that the interests of those in occupation pose similar hazards to purchasers of unregistered land by virtue of the doctrine of constructive notice.[20] Arrangements for the delivery of keys to the purchaser and, or an authority for tenants to pay their rent to the purchaser in the future are also required to be detailed. Requisition 6 asks for the name(s) and address(es) of any person(s) to whom notice of the purchase must be given. Requisition 7 concerns the actual arrangements for completion. The form concludes with a note that "The Requisitions founded on the Abstract of Title or Contract must, of course, be added to the above."

It would be unusual for a vendor's solicitor not to answer the requisitions on Con 28B, although it seems that he would be well within his rights in so doing. *Williams on Vendor and Purchaser* say that "the vendor is, as a rule, bound to answer all questions relevant to the abstracted title, that is the title he is offering for the purchaser's acceptance"[21] but not any others. *Emmet on Title* feels that "it would appear to be more consistent with authority if (the rule) were stated to be

---

[19] [1981] A.C. 487.
[20] *Midland Bank Ltd.* v. *Farmpride Hatcheries Ltd.* (1980) 260 E.G. 493.
[21] At p. 123.

that the vendor must answer all specific questions relevant to the abstracted title."[22] The authority referred to is the case of *Re Ford and Hill*[23] where the Court of Appeal held that the vendor was not bound to answer the whole or any part of the purchaser's question: "Is there to the knowledge of the vendors or their solicitors any settlement, deed, fact, omission, or any incumbrance affecting the property not disclosed by the abstract?" The question was too wide and amounted to an insinuation that the vendor had improperly failed to abstract a material matter known to him.

The rule is however qualified where the sale is governed by the National Conditions of Sale. Condition 9(2) (introduced in the wake of *Boland*) provides:

"Subject always to the rights of the purchaser under the Law of Property Act 1925, s.42(1), the vendor may be required by the purchaser to deal with requisitions and observations concerning persons who are or may be in occupation or actual occupation of the property, so as to satisfy the purchaser that the title is not, and that the purchaser will not be, prejudicially affected by any interests or claims of such persons."

Section 42(1) of the Law of Property Act 1925, it will be remembered, renders void a stipulation in a contract that a purchaser shall accept a title made with the concurrence of a person entitled to an equitable interest if a title can be made discharged from the interest without such concurrence.

Additionally to be noted is National Condition 15(2) which entitles the purchaser to raise requisitions on the authorised use of the property for the purposes of the Planning Acts. This is a limited exception to the open contract rule that a purchaser cannot make requisitions on planning matters.

The Law Society Conditions of Sale have no equivalent to either National Condition 9(2) or 15(2).

Registered Land

In their chapter "Procedure on the Sale of Registered Land"[24] Ruoff and Roper include the heading "Requisitions on title are unnecessary."[25] However, the preceding section has shown that requisitions should be made in the following cases *inter alia*:

1. Where the contract states or implies that the vendor is selling an absolute title but he is in fact registered with a possessory title, as in *Re Brine and Davies' Contract*.[26]

2. Where the charges register of the title refers to an incumbrance which has not been disclosed in the contract; a restrictive covenant in *Re Stone*

---

[22] At p. 151.
[23] (1879) 10 Ch.D. 365.
[24] Ruoff and Roper, *Registered Conveyancing* (4th ed.), Chap. 18.
[25] At p. 320.
[26] [1935] Ch. 388.

and Saville's Contract[27] and an option to renew an underlease in *Kitney* v. *M.E.P.C. Ltd.*[28]

3. Where the property or charges register refers to a right the full extent of which is not detailed; for example an "overriding interest" noted on the register.

4. Where, as occurred in *Faruqi* v. *English Real Estates Ltd.*[29], the vendor tries to disclose his defective title behind a condition in the contract that the sale is "subject to all entries on the register."

5. In the case of matters excepted from registration, that is where the vendor is registered with possessory, good leasehold or qualified title, and, most importantly, overriding interests.

Time for Raising Requisitions

The time limit within which the purchaser is to submit his requisitions on title is usually directly linked to the delivery of the abstract. Thus under an open contract the purchaser has a reasonable period from the date of delivery of the abstract within which to submit his requisitions. The National Conditions 9(3) give the purchaser 11 working days from the delivery of the abstract, whereas Law Society Condition 15(2) gives him 6 working days from the receipt of the abstract or from the date of the contract if later. Time is of the essence for the making of requisitions under both sets of conditions,[30] the day of delivery or receipt of the abstract being excluded.[31] If the vendor fails to deliver the abstract within the time set in the contract, then the purchaser also does not have to comply with time limits for the making of requisitions. The purchaser has a reasonable time even though the contract makes time of the essence in that respect.[32] But this must be read subject to National Condition 9(4) which makes time of the essence for the delivery of requisitions whether or not the abstract was delivered within due time. Law Society Condition 12(1) says that the abstract shall be delivered "forthwith" upon exchange of contracts and it is difficult to know precisely when the vendor will have failed to comply with this requirement.

Under an open contract time only begins to run when the vendor has delivered a "perfect" abstract.[33] A "perfect" abstract is one as complete in content as the vendor can possibly manage at the time of its delivery. It is not necessary for a "perfect" abstract to show that the vendor has good title.[34] There is a presumption in the vendor's favour that an abstract is "perfect." The onus of proving the vendor has not provided all the

---

[27] [1963] 1 W.L.R. 163.
[28] [1977] 1 W.L.R. 981.
[29] [1979] 1 W.L.R. 963.
[30] National Condition 9(4); Law Society Condition 15(5).
[31] *Blackburn* v. *Smith* (1848) 2 Ex. 783.
[32] *Upperton* v. *Nickolson* (1871) L.R. 6 Ch. 436.
[33] *Hobson* v. *Bell* (1839) 2 Beav. 17.
[34] *Pryce-Jones* v. *Williams* [1902] 2 Ch. 517.

information that he could have done is on the purchaser.[35] The standard conditions of sale vary the open contract position. Both National Condition 9(5) and Law Society Condition 15(4) require the purchaser to requisition on the abstract as delivered, *provided* it is deficient only in regard to matters which are unimportant. The proviso (not stated in either condition) is implied by the general law. As Graham J. stated in *Ogilvy* v. *Hope-Davies*,[36] the justification for requiring a purchaser to requisition on an incomplete abstract is

> "that a solicitor investigating the title would, or ought to, assume that the gaps could be and would be likely to be filled in a way which he would expect from the information supplied in the abstract. In such a case, he ought to get on with it, raise what requisitions he can on the abstract submitted and at some time call for the obvious gaps to be filled."

As regards any outstanding parts of the abstract, time only begins to run for the purposes of National Condition 9(3) and Law Society Condition 15(4) when those parts are delivered to the purchaser.

As a rule only those requisitions arising out of the abstract are subject to time limits imposed by the contract.[37] The National Conditions[38] expressly entitle the purchaser to make requisitions about persons in occupation and the authorised use of the property but do not make it clear whether time is of the essence for so doing. Under the general law (not altered by the standard conditions) the following requisitions may be raised out of time:

1. An objection showing that the vendor cannot convey what he has contracted to convey.[39] Even if the contract provides that the purchaser shall accept the title offered and make no requisition or objection to it, that does not stop the purchaser objecting if the vendor does not possess the title he has contracted to sell.[40]

2. An objection to a matter of conveyance.[41]

3. An objection to a matter affecting the title which the vendor has not disclosed but which the purchaser discovers in some other way, for example a search. In *Re Cox and Neve's Contract*[42] a purchaser discovered the existence of restrictive covenants affecting the land by enquiring of an adjoining landowner. He was entitled to object to them, even though his objection was made out of time.

Often a purchaser is supplied with an abstract or copy documents of matters affecting a vendor's title before contracts are exchanged. Can the purchaser still requisition on these matters after contract? If the contract is governed by the Law Society Conditions of Sale (and in the absence of a special condition) the answer is, yes. Condition 12(3) provides: "Where

---

[35] *Gray* v. *Fowler* (1873) L.R. 8 Ex. 249.

[36] [1976] 1 All E.R. 683 and see also H. W. Wilkinson (1976) 126 New L.J.

[37] *Re Cox and Neve's Contract* [1891] 2 Ch. 109.

[38] National Conditions 9(2) and 15(2).

[39] *Re Scott and Eave's Contract* (1902) 86 L.T. 617; *Re Brine and Davies' Contract* [1935] Ch. 388.

[40] *Becker* v. *Partridge* [1966] 2 Q.B. 155.

[41] *Leominster Properties Ltd.* v. *Broadway Finance Ltd.* (1981) 42 P. & C.R. 372.

[42] [1891] 2 Ch. 109.

before the date of the contract any abstract, epitome or document has been delivered to the purchaser, he shall not, . . . be deemed to have had notice before the date of the contract of any matter of title thereby disclosed." The National Conditions are silent on the matter, therefore the general law applies. Provided the contract expressly or impliedly provides that a good title shall be shown, the purchaser may raise requisitions on documents delivered to him before exchange of contracts and insist on a good title, even though he contracted with notice of defects in the vendor's title.[43]

Time for Replies and Observations

Law Society Condition 15(2) imposes time limits on the vendor as well as the purchaser; the vendor must deliver his replies to the purchaser's requisitions, in writing, within four working days of their delivery. The purchaser must then deliver his observations on the replies within a further four days (15(3)). Time is of the essence in both cases. The National Conditions impose no time limit on the vendor to deliver his replies. Under the general law he has a reasonable time in which to reply, whereupon the purchaser can serve a notice on him stipulating a time within which he must reply, time being of the essence.[44] By National Condition 9(3) the purchaser has six working days to deliver his observations on the vendor's replies once they have been delivered, time being of the essence. Time does not begin to run against a purchaser for making objections, if the vendor's reply to a requisition hides the truth. In *Pratt* v. *Betts*[45] the vendor gave a non-specific reply to the purchaser's requisition as to the statutory acknowledgments regarding documents of title, so concealing the fact that there was no valid acknowledgment for an earlier conveyance. The purchaser was entitled to object outside the contractual period. If the contract does not place a time limit on the purchaser within which to make objections to the vendors replies to requisitions, he apparently[46] has the same time as he had within which to raise requisitions.

If the vendor refuses to answer a proper requisition or does not answer to the purchaser's satisfaction, a summary remedy is provided by section 49 of the Law of Property Act 1925. The court can make such order as it thinks fit to settle the dispute and can direct payment of costs. Alternatively the purchaser can rescind the contract.[47]

Waiver

A vendor who replies to a purchaser's requisitions made out of time, may be taken to have waived his right to rely on the contractual time-limits.[48]

---

[43] *Re Gloag and Miller's Contract* (1883) 23 Ch.D. 320.
[44] *Re Stone and Saville's Contract* [1963] 1 W.L.R. 163.
[45] (1973) 27 P & C.R. 398.
[46] J.T. Farrand, *Emmet on Title* (18th ed.) p. 154.
[47] *Re Stone and Savilles Contract* [1963] 1 W.L.R. 163.
[48] *Cutts* v. *Thodey* (1842) 6 Jur. 1027.

Emmet on Title.[49] advises a vendor's solicitor that "to avoid any liability the client's authority should be sought before replying although it might be sufficient to state in replying that the time-limits are not to be taken as waived." Similarly, the purchaser's submission of the draft transfer or conveyance for approval may amount to an acceptance of the vendors' title and a waiver of his right to raise further objections.[50] Law Society Condition 17(3) specifically deals with this problem by stating: "The purchaser shall not, by delivering the draft conveyance or the engrossment, be deemed to accept the vendor's title or to waive any right to raise or maintain requisitions." The National Conditions have no such provision.

Rescission for Insistence on a Requisition

Both standard contracts for sale contain conditions allowing the vendor to rescind if the purchaser refuses to withdraw a requisition. National Condition 10(1) limits the vendor's right to "any objection to the title." The vendor cannot make use of the Condition where the purchaser persists in a requisition as to conveyance; in *Leominster Properties Ltd.* v. *Broadway Finance Ltd.*[51] that a prior mortgage be paid off before completion. The Condition probably also does not apply to a requisition about persons in occupation which the purchaser is entitled to make under National Condition 9(2). Law Society Condition 16(1) permits rescission for "any requisition or objection made by the purchaser." Although apparently wider than its National counterpart, it is thought[52] that Condition 16(1) should be read subject to Condition 15(2) which allows the purchaser to make "requisitions or objections relating to the title, evidence of title or the abstract." Neither Condition (nor any other contractual condition of this nature) can affect a purchaser's right to insist by requisition that the vendor fulfill certain statutory obligations; for example obtain a vesting order at his own expense under section 42(1) of the Law of Property Act 1925, or produce a power of attorney (or copy) affecting his title under section 125 of the same Act.

National Condition 10(1) provides that the vendor can serve notice to withdraw if the purchaser "shall *persist* in any objection to the title which the vendor shall be unable or unwilling, on reasonable grounds, to remove." Law Society Condition 16(1) states that notice may be served "if the vendor is unable, or on some reasonable ground unwilling, to satisfy any requisition or objection *made* by the purchaser." *Emmet on Title*[53] comments:

> "If the contract contains the words 'should the purchaser *make* any requisition,' etc. the right of the vendor to rescind arises directly the requisition is made, without giving the purchaser any locus poeniten-

---

[49] At p. 153.

[50] *Clearbrook Property Holdings Ltd.* v. *Verrier* [1974] 1 W.L.R. 243.

[51] (1981) 42 P. & C.R. 372 and see *Re Jackson and Oakshott* (1880) 14 Ch.D. 851.

[52] J.T. Farrand, *Emmet on Title* (18th ed.) p. 253 *cf. Leominster Properties Ltd.* v. *Broadway Finance Ltd.* (1981) 42 P. & C.R. 372 at p. 386.

[53] At p. 253.

tiae (*Re Starr-Bowlett Building Society and Sibun's Contract* (1889) L.R. 2 Ch. 375). But if the words are 'should the purchaser *insist*' (*Duddell* v. *Simpson* (1886) L.R. 2 Ch. 102) or 'persist,' a vendor cannot refuse to answer reasonable requisitions (*Re Dames and Wood* (1885) 29 Ch.D. 626; *Procter* v. *Pugh* [1921] 2 Ch. 256); in such cases the vendor cannot rescind if the purchaser at once withdraws his objection."

But as H.W. Wilkinson points out in his book *Standard Conditions of Sale of Land*[54] this distinction is inapplicable in the case of National Condition 10(1) and Law Society 16(1), because both give the purchaser time to withdraw his requisition once notice has been served. It does seem however that under the former condition the purchaser needs to repeat his objection but not under the latter condition.

No condition providing for rescission in these circumstances can be used by a vendor to evade his contractual obligations at will. The relevant principles were summarised by Viscount Radcliffe in *Selkirk* v. *Romar Investments Ltd.*[55]:

> "a vendor in seeking to rescind, must not act arbitrarily, or capriciously, or unreasonably. Much less can he act in bad faith. He may not use the power of rescission to get out of a sale '*brevi manu*,' since by doing so he makes a nullity of the whole elaborate and protracted transaction. Above all, perhaps, he must not be guilty of 'recklessness' in entering into his contract, a term frequently resorted to in discussion of the legal principle and which their lordships understand to connote an unacceptable indifference to the situation of a purchaser who is allowed to enter into a contract with the expectation of obtaining a title which the vendor has no reasonable anticipation of being able to deliver. A vendor who has so acted is not allowed to call off the whole transaction by resorting to the contractual right of rescission."

National Condition 10(1) and Law Society 16(1) both state that the vendor must be unable or, on reasonable grounds unwilling, to comply with the purchaser's requisitions; the test of reasonableness only appearing to qualify the word "unwilling." However case-law goes against a vendor being able to rescind for unreasonable inability to comply. In *Baines* v. *Tweddle*[56] the vendor contracted (Law Society Conditions of Sale, 1953 ed.) to sell property which together with other property he owned, was in mortgage. The vendor was in arrears with his mortgage payments. His mortgagees refused to join in the conveyance to the purchaser. The vendor could not rescind the contract on the ground that he was unable to comply with the purchaser's objection to taking the land burdened by the mortgage. He had acted recklessly in not obtaining the mortgagees concurrence to the sale before contract.

---

[54] (3rd ed.) p. 97.
[55] [1963] 1 W.L.R. 1415 at p. 1422.
[56] [1959] Ch. 679 and see *Re Jackson and Haden's Contract* [1906] 1 Ch. 412.

Both sets of conditions provide that if the vendor gives notice to the purchaser to withdraw his objection or requisition and the purchaser fails to do so within the time specified (time not being of the essence[57]), rescission may follow. By National Condition 10(1) the purchaser has 10 working days to withdraw his requisition after being required to do so. Presumably verbal notice to withdraw suffices. If the purchaser refuses to comply the vendor may rescind "by notice in writing." Law Society Condition 16(1) states that the vendor may give the purchaser notice to withdraw and that the purchaser has seven working days from service of the notice in which to do so. The Condition clearly contemplates notice in writing by its reference to "service." The notice must specify the reason why the vendor is unable or unwilling to comply with the requisition. If the purchaser does not withdraw his requisition, *either party* may rescind the contract. Giving the purchaser the right to rescind was a new change introduced by the 1980 edition of the Law Society Conditions of Sale. It seems (although not expressly stated) that the same principles are applicable to rescission by the purchaser as to rescission by the vendor; the purchaser must act reasonably in rescinding.

The right to rescission under either condition is "notwithstanding any intermediate negotiation or litigation." These words are designed to exclude from operation the rule that if a vendor, being entitled to rescind because of a requisition, negotiates upon it, he looses his right to rescind.[58] But they do not prevent the rule operating if the vendor expressly or impliedly chooses not to rescind.[59]

Upon rescission the vendor must return the purchaser's deposit and the purchaser must return the abstract and other documents supplied to him under the contract. (National Condition 10(2), Law Society 16(2)). Law Society Condition 16(2) provides for the vendor to pay interest at the contract rate on the deposit (whether it is he or the purchaser who rescinds) from four working days after rescission until payment.

Finally it should be noted, that National Condition 15(3) gives the purchaser the right to rescind the contract by notice in writing and avail himself of National Condition 10(2), "if it appears before actual completion of the purchase that the specified use is not an authorised use of the property for the purposes of the Planning Acts . . . ."

---

[57] Law of Property Act 1925, s.41.
[58] *Tanner* v. *Smith* (1840) 10 Sim. 401.
[59] *Gardom* v. *Lee* (1865) 3 H. & C. 651.

III. THE CONVEYANCE OR TRANSFER

General Points

In the absence of contrary agreement[60] the conveyance[61] is prepared by the purchaser at his own expense. National Condition 19(2) and Law Society Condition 17(1) reaffirm this general rule. Where the interest sold is leasehold for a term of years to be granted by the vendor, National Condition 19(1) states that the vendor's solicitor shall prepare the lease or underlease and counterpart in accordance, "as nearly as the circumstances admit," with the draft annexed to the contract. The Law Society form has no similar provision and if it is the vendor who is to prepare the lease, a special condition must be included in the contract, otherwise the task will fall on the purchaser under the general provisions of Law Society Condition 17(1). By section 48(1) of the Law of Property Act 1925 a vendor is entitled to reserve the right to furnish a form of conveyance to a purchaser from which the draft can be prepared and charge a reasonable fee for it, but such practice is uncommon except in the case of building estates. In the opinion of the Council of the Law Society,[62] a draft conveyance should be complete in itself and should not require reference to any other document to prepare an engrossment.

A timetable for the preparation of the conveyance is set up by both sets of standard conditions. The Law Society Conditions state that the purchaser must deliver the draft conveyance at least 12 working days before the contractual completion date, and that the vendor must return it approved or revised within four working days of delivery.[63] The purchaser must then "engross" the approved or revised draft (prepare the final copy) and re-deliver it to the vendor at least five working days before completion.[64] Non-compliance by either party with these time-limits, leading to late completion, will be "a failure to perform an obligation of the contract"[65] and compensation may be payable for any loss caused by the delay.[66] It is expressly provided that "the purchaser shall not, by delivering the draft conveyance or the engrossment, be deemed to accept the vendor's title or to waive any right to raise or maintain requisitions."[67] Under the National Conditions the draft must be delivered at least six working days before the contractual completion date and the engrossment within three working days of the return of the approved draft.[68] No time-limit is set for approval of the draft but bearing the other time-limits in mind, the vendor's solicitor could be liable for delayed completion if he

---

[60] *Poole* v. *Hill* (1840) 6 M. & W. 835.

[61] Law of Property Act 1925, s.205(i)(ii) " 'Conveyance' includes a mortgage, charge, lease, assent, vesting declaration, vesting instrument, disclaimer, release and every other assurance of property or of an interest therein by any instrument, except a will." Law Society Condition 1(d), " 'conveyance' includes an assignment and a transfer under the Land Registration Acts."

[62] Law Society's Digest, Supp. 160(c).   [63] Law Society Condition 17(1).

[64] Law Society Condition 17(2).   [65] Law Society Condition 22(1)a.

[66] Law Society Condition 22(2).   [67] Law Society Condition 17(3).

[68] National Condition 19(3).

does not approve it within three days. The engrossment must be "left" at the vendor's solicitors office. It is thought[69] that the word does not connote physical delivery but that the time-limit is calculated with reference to the receipt of the engrossment. The National Conditions do not speak of the effect of submitting the draft conveyance and engrossment an outstanding objections to title. The general law therefore applies and the purchaser may be taken to have waived his right to object to the vendor's title.[70]

Section 52(1) of the Law of Property Act 1925 provides: "All conveyances of land or of any interest therein are void for the purpose of conveying or creating a legal estate unless made by deed." Certain limited exceptions are listed in section 52(2), like vesting assents and leases for a term not exceeding three years.[71] Apart from the requirement that it must be by deed, a conveyance of unregistered land can be in any form. However an estate vested in a registered proprietor can only be disposed of or dealt with in the manner authorised by the Land Registration Acts.[72] The deed must be in the form prescribed by rule 74 of the Land Registration Rules 1925 and set out in the Schedule thereto, "with such alterations and additions, if any, as are necessary or desired and the Registrar allows." If an improper form is used the Registrar may decline to complete the transaction by registration,[73] and the legal estate will not pass to the purchaser. A lease of registered land need not be in any particular form.[74] Apart from provisions relating to indemnities,[75] neither set of standard conditions prescribe the form the conveyance must take. The rest of this part of the chapter is devoted to a discussion of the contents of the conveyance or transfer. Here a few more general points remain to be mentioned.

A deed is "writing in paper or parchment" which is signed, sealed and delivered.[76] Interestingly although a land registry transfer is a deed,[77] the legal estate in the land does not pass until registration.[78] The purchaser only executes the deed if he covenants therein. Sometimes execution by a third party is necessary; where a mortgagee joins in to release his mortgage on the property for example. Any stipulation in a contract that an outstanding legal estate shall be traced or got in at the purchaser's expense is void,[79] the cost of obtaining execution by the third party must be borne by the vendor. The execution of a deed is usually attested (witnessed). Attestation is strictly unnecessary for a conveyance of unregistered land but since the various forms of disposition for registered land contain attestation clauses it is arguably necessary here.[80]

---

[69] H.W. Wilkinson, *Standard Conditions of Sale of Land* (3rd ed.) p. 109.
[70] *Clearbrook Property Holdings Ltd.* v. *Verrier* (1974) 1 W.L.R. 243.
[71] Law of Property Act 1925, s.54(2).
[72] Land Registration Act 1925, ss.39(1) and 69(4).
[73] Land Registration Rules 1925, r. 78.
[74] Land Registration Act 1925, ss.18(1)(*e*) and 21(1)(*d*).
[75] See *post*, p. 382.
[76] *Goddard's case* (1584) 2 Co. Rep. 4; Law of Property Act 1925, s.73(1).
[77] *Chelsea and Walham Green Building Society* v. *Armstrong* [1951] Ch. 853.
[78] Land Registration Act 1925, ss.19(1) and 22(1).
[79] Law of Property Act 1925, s.42(3).
[80] J.T. Farrand, *Emmet on Title* (18th ed.) p. 576.

A deed can still be duly executed even though not formally sealed. In *First National Securities Ltd.* v. *Jones*,[81] the Court of Appeal held that a document which had no wax or wafer seal attached to it, but which the party had signed at the end over the printed words "L.S." (*locus sigilli*) in a circle and which bore an attestation clause in standard form duly signed by a witness, was capable of being a deed.

The third essential characteristic of a deed is delivery. Where requisite a purchaser will often execute the engrossment of the conveyance, before delivering it to the vendor. He must do so if the sale is governed by the Law Society Conditions of Sale.[82] The executed deed is usually handed over by the purchaser "in escrow" meaning that it is not to take effect until completion. But as H.W. Wilkinson points out in his *Standard Conditions of Sale of Land*[83]: "cases have made it clear that there is a serious variance between theory and practice on the topic of escrows." Once a deed has been delivered in escrow it is beyond recall and becomes binding on performance of the condition.[84] Furthermore the Court of Appeal have recently held that a document delivered in escrow takes effect from the date of delivery of the deed and not from the date when the conditions are satisfied.[85]

Co-purchasers

After 1925 all concurrent ownership must exist behind a trust for sale, implied by statute or express.[86] The co-owners hold the legal estate as joint tenants (the joint tenancy of the legal estate being unseverable[87]) on trust for themselves as beneficial joint tenants or tenants in common. Co-purchasers should decide at an early stage exactly how they wish to share the beneficial ownership of the property. A joint tenancy is a difficult concept to explain to a layman. In essence it means that the whole interest in all of the land is vested in one and all of the joint tenants simultaneously. Neither joint tenant(s) has a specific or defined interest in the land, because each owns the whole jointly with the other(s). The main characteristic of a joint tenancy is that it is governed by the rule of survivorship. When one of the joint tenants dies, his interest in the land automatically vests in the other(s). The last surviving joint tenant eventually has the whole interest in the property and like any other absolute owner, has full power to deal with it as he wishes, including the power to sell it, and can give to a subsequent purchaser a valid receipt for the purchase money. Spouses usually take property as beneficial joint tenants. On the other hand, where land is held so that when one partner dies his share passes under his will or on his intestacy, and not necessarily

---

[81] [1978] Ch. 109.
[82] Condition 17(2).
[83] (3rd ed.) p. 110 where he refers the reader further to (1967) 117 New L. J. 1287.
[84] *Beesly* v. *Hallwood Estates Ltd.* [1961] Ch. 105.
[85] *Alan Estates Ltd.* v. *W.G. Stores Ltd.* [1981] 3 W.L.R. 892.
[86] Law of Property Act 1925, s.1(6) and ss.34–36; *Bull* v. *Bull* [1955] 1 Q.B. 234.
[87] Law of Property Act 1925, s.36(2).

to the surviving partner(s), a tenancy in common exists. A tenant in common does have an ascertainable share in the land, whether it be one half, a third or whatever, and can deal with that share as he wishes. Because it is impossible to say, without further evidence, that on the death of one tenant in common the survivor is entitled to the whole interest in the property, he cannot give a valid receipt to a subsequent purchaser. A beneficial joint tenancy can be severed to form a beneficial tenancy in common.[88]

Co-purchasers have in the past relied on the implied statutory trust for sale to indicate the nature of their beneficial ownership of the land. Recently in the case of *Bernard* v. *Josephs*,[89] Griffiths L.J. giving a minority judgment in the Court of Appeal said: "I wish more heed had been paid to the advice to solicitors given by Bagnall J. in *Cowcher* v. *Cowcher* [1972] 1 All E.R. 943 in which he pointed out the wisdom of making an express declaration of the beneficial interests at the time it is bought." *Bernard* v. *Josephs,* like a multitude of cases heard by the courts of late, involved a dispute between co-habitees as to their respective shares in a property, which had been conveyed into their joint names without any express declaration of trust. In cases other than divorce, where, under sections 23 to 25 of the Matrimonial Causes Act 1973, the Family Division has wide powers to do what it considers "fair and reasonable" having regard to "all the circumstances of the case," all disputes concerning the property rights of cohabitants must be decided by the Chancery Division[90] according to the law of trusts.[91] If the conveyance or other deed of transfer contains an express declaration of trust as to the beneficial ownership of the property, this is conclusive. If however there is no such declaration in the document, then oral evidence is admissible to show what the intention of the parties was at the time they bought the property. The court may infer this intention from the conduct of the parties. If no such evidence exists then the presumptions of resulting trust and advancement come into play.[92] Under the classic exposition of the doctrine of resulting trust the parties' shares are deduced from actual contributions to the purchase price.[93] The courts have however extended the doctrine, both in husband and wife[94] and man and mistress cases[95] to encompass more indirect contributions to the purchase price, like mortgage repayments. But these indirect contributions can only be taken into account if it was the parties' intention at the time of acquisition that they should result in some share in the property.[96] However despite a clear ruling by the House of Lords in *Pettitt* v. *Pettitt*,[97] that the court cannot

---

[88] *Ibid.*
[89] [1982] Ch. 391; [1982] 2 W.L.R. 1052; R.E. Annand [1983] 133 New L.J. 613.
[90] Supreme Court Act 1981, s.61(1) and Sched. 1.
[91] 38 Halsbury's Laws (3rd ed.) p. 868, para 1462; *Pettitt* v. *Pettitt* [1970] A.C. 777 (H.L.); *Gissing* v. *Gissing* [1971] A.C. 886; [1970] 2 All E.R. 780 (H.L.).
[92] Lord Upjohn, *Pettitt* v. *Pettitt* [1969] 2 All E.R. 385 at 405–6.
[93] *Dyer* v. *Dyer* (1788) 30 E.R. 42.
[94] *Pettitt* v. *Pettitt* [1969] 2 All E.R. 385; *Hazell* v. *Hazell* [1972] 1 W.L.R. 301.
[95] *Cooke* v. *Head* [1972] 1 W.L.R. 518.
[96] *Re Nicholson* [1974] 1 W.L.R. 476; *Cooke* v. *Head* [1972] 1 W.L.R. 518.
[97] *Per* Lord Upjohn [1969] 2 All E.R. 385 at p. 408.

look backwards and say that what the parties decided at the date of acquisition is now unfair at the date of the hearing, there has lately been a definite trend by the court to do what it considers "fair and reasonable" by assessing the shares of the parties at the date of separation[98] or when the property is sold.[99]

Griffith L.J.'s plea stems from the fact that in cases like *Bernard* v. *Josephs* the parties are usually legally aided and the charges greatly diminish if not exhaust, their respective shares in the property.

When acting for co-purchasers of unregistered land, it is usual to extend their powers to those of an absolute owner. Otherwise, as trustees for sale, they only enjoy the limited powers of a tenant for life and the trustees of the settlement under the Settled Land Act 1925.[1] A typical clause would read as follows:

"The Purchasers agree that:
(a) they are in equity tenants in common in equal shares (or . . . joint tenants)
(b) the trustees for sale of the property shall have powers of dealing with it equal to those of a sole beneficial owner."

In the case of registered land such a clause is unnecessary, because the proprietors of registered land enjoy full and unrestricted powers of disposition unless there is some entry to the contrary on the register.

A. THE CONVEYANCE

Description and Date	This Conveyance is made the 3rd day of June 1984 BETWEEN RUPERT FERRY and LESLEY FERRY both of 18 Fosse Way Boddington in the County of Avon (hereinafter called "the Vendors") of the
Parties	first part HALFORD BUILDING SOCIETY of 34 Shakespeare Road Boddington in the said County of Avon (hereinafter called "the Society") of the second part and DAVID WHEELER and JENNIFER WHEELER both of 16 Landrock Rise, Hasham in the County of Kent (hereinafter called "the Purchasers") of the third part
	WHEREAS:
	(1) The Vendors are seised of the property hereinafter described for an estate in fee simple in possession subject (a) to the Mortgage next
Recitals	mentioned and (b) as hereinafter mentioned but otherwise free from incumbrances.
	(2) By a Mortgage dated the 31st day of December 1979 and made between the Vendors of the one part and the Society of the other part the property hereby conveyed was with other property charged

---

[98] *Bernard* v. *Josephs* [1982] Ch. 391; *Hall* v. *Hall* (1982) 3 F.L.R.. 379.
[99] *Gordon* v. *Douce* [1983] 2 All E.R. 228. But see now *Burns* v. *Burns* [1984] 1 All E.R. 244 (C.A.) which reaffirms the traditional approach.
[1] Law of Property Act 1925, s.28(1).

by the Vendors in favour of the Society by way of legal mortgage for securing the principal sum of Fifteen Thousand Pounds (£15,000.00) and interest thereon as therein mentioned.

(3) The principal sum of £15,000.00 remains owing on the security of the said Mortgage.

(4) The Vendors have agreed with the Purchasers for the sale to them for the sum of Twenty Eight Thousand One Hundred Pounds of the fee simple of the property hereby conveyed subject as hereinafter mentioned but otherwise free from incumbrances.

(5) The Society being satisfied that the other property comprised in the said Mortgage is a sufficient security for all moneys thereby secured by the said Mortgage has agreed to join in this Deed for the purpose and in the manner hereinafter appearing

Testatum	Now This Deed Witnesseth as follows:
Consideration	1. In consideration of the sum of Twenty Eight Thousand One Hundred Pounds (£28,100.00)
Receipt Clause	paid by the Purchasers to the Vendors (the receipt whereof the Vendors hereby acknowledge) the
Capacity	Vendors as Beneficial Owners Hereby
Operative Words	Convey and the Society as mortgagee Hereby Surrenders and Releases unto the Purchasers All That piece of land situate at Fosse Way Boddington in the County of Avon and forming part of No. 18 Fosse Way Boddington aforesaid
Parcels	which said piece of land is for the purpose of identification only delineated on the plan annexed hereto and thereon edged in red Together With the right to pass and repass along the road hatched green on the said plan at all times and for all purposes Except and Reserving to the Vendors
Exceptions and Reservations	and their successors in title the owners and occupiers, for the time being of the land retained by the Vendors and which is edged in blue on the said plan (hereinafter called "the retained property") the right to use for all proper purposes connected with the retained property any sewers drains watercourses pipes cables wires conduits or other channels now laid in under or over the land hereby conveyed To Hold the same unto the
Habendum	Purchasers in fee simple Discharged from all principal moneys and interest secured by and from all claims and demands under the said Mortgage Subject To the covenants and conditions con-
Existing Restrictions	tained in a Conveyance dated 4th June 1959 and

made between BERTRAM BODIE of the one part and
DUDLEY PETERSHAM of the other part so far as the
same are still subsisting and capable of being
enforced in relation to the property hereby
conveyed UPON TRUST to sell the same with power
to postpone the sale thereof and to hold the net
proceeds of sale and other money applicable as
capital and the net rents and profits thereof until
sale upon trust for themselves as joint tenants
AND IT IS HEREBY DECLARED THAT the trustees for
the time being of this deed shall have the power to
sell mortgage charge lease or otherwise dispose of
all or any part of the said property with all the
powers in that behalf of an absolute owner.

Declaration of Trust and Extention of Trustees powers

2. The Purchasers with the intent to afford to the
Vendors a full and sufficient indemnity but not
further or otherwise HEREBY COVENANT with the
Vendors that they the Purchasers and their
successors in title will henceforth observe and
perform the covenants and conditions aforesaid
so far as the same are still subsisting and capable
of being enforced in relation to the land hereby
conveyed and will at all times effectually
indemnify the Vendors against all actions
proceedings costs claims and demands in respect
thereof so far as aforesaid.

Indemnity Covenant

3. The Society HEREBY ACKNOWLEDGES the right
of the Purchasers to the production of the documents specified in the Schedule hereto (possession
of which is retained by the Society) and to
delivery of copies thereof AND the Vendors for
themselves and their successors in title hereby
covenant with the Purchasers that they the
Vendors or their successors in title shall so soon as
the said documents come into their possession
give to the Purchasers or their successors in title
when requested by them at their cost an undertaking for the safe custody thereof and in the
meantime and until such undertaking has been
given that every person for the time being having
the possession or control of the said documents
shall keep the same safe whole uncancelled and
undefaced unless prevented from so doing by fire
or other inevitable accident.

Acknowledgement and Undertaking

4. IT IS HEREBY CERTIFIED that the transaction
hereby effected does not form part of a larger
transaction or of a series of transactions in respect
of which the amount or value or the aggregate

Certificate of Value

amount or value of the consideration exceeds THIRTY THOUSAND Pounds (£30,000.00).

Testimonium

IN WITNESS whereof the parties hereto have executed this Deed the day and year first before written.

THE SCHEDULE

Date	Document	Parties
4th June 1959	Conveyance	Bertram Bodie (1)
		Dudley Petersham (2)
1st March 1965	Conveyance	
		Dudley Petersham (2)
		The Vendors (2)
31st December 1979	Mortgage	The Vendors (1)
		The Society (2)

Attestation

SIGNED SEALED AND DELIVERED
by the said RUPERT FERRY   *Rupert Ferry* L.S.
in the presence of:—
  K. Deatty
    7 Fox Place

SIGNED SEALED AND DELIVERED
by the said LESLEY FERRY   *L. Ferry*   L.S
in the presence of:—
  K. Deatty
  As above.

THE COMMON SEAL OF HALFORD
BUILDING SOCIETY was affixed   L.S
hereto in the presence of:-
  B. Stoneybroke
  F. Rose
    Authorised Sealing Officers

SIGNED SEALED AND DELIVERED
by the said DAVID WHEELER   *D. Wheeler* L.S
in the presence of:—
  A. Brennan
    18 Slim Road
    Hightown

SIGNED SEALED AND DELIVERED
by the said JENNIFER WHEELER *J. Wheeler*   L.S.
in the presence of:—
  A. Brennan
    As above.

Commentary

DESCRIPTION

The document begins by stating the type of deed which is being made.[2] The opening words will be "This Conveyance," "This Assignment," "This Lease" and so on. What if the document is described incorrectly? In *Re Stirrup's Contract*[3] a bank conveyed property to a person by an assent under seal when it should have used a conveyance. As the assent was under seal, and therefore a deed,[4] the effect of the document was to transfer the legal estate just as if the document had been described as a conveyance. The court held that the manifest intention of the document, to pass the legal estate, should not be defeated by the fact that a technically incorrect description of the type of deed had been used.

THE DATE

The date from which a deed takes effect is the date upon which it is unconditionally delivered.[5] Dating the deed with some date other than the date of its unconditional delivery does not change the effective date. Although there is a presumption that a deed is effective from the date appearing on its face[6] the presumption can be rebutted by adducing evidence of unconditional delivery on some other date.

The effective date of a deed is important as it determines *inter alia*; the rights which pass under section 62 of the Law of Property Act 1925, whether the purchaser retains protection from any land charges search made prior to completion[7], the priority of the estate or interest created *vis à vis* other legal estates and interests in the same property, and the time within which stamping of the document must take place.

The practice of backdating a conveyance, usually in the hope of retaining protection under a land charges search, is not recommended. The protection conferred by an official certificate of search is effective only if the transaction is actually completed within the priority period.[8]

THE PARTIES

The vendor and purchaser are obviously going to be parties to the deed. Also joined as parties should be persons with an interest in the property which will not be overreached, but which it is intended will not bind the purchaser; persons necessary to give a valid receipt for purchase money, persons undertaking burdens, and persons acquiring interests which they may need to enforce subsequently.

---

[2] Law of Property Act 1925, s.57.

[3] [1961] 1 W.L.R. 449; *Cholmondeley (Marquis)* v. *Clinton* (1820) 2 Jac. & W. 1.

[4] Law of Property Act 1925, s.52.

[5] *Goddard's Case* (1584) 2 Co. Rep. 46.

[6] *Browne* v. *Burton* (1847) 17 L.J.Q.B. 49.

[7] See *ante*, p. 35.

[8] Land Charges Act 1972, s.11, speaks of the purchase being "completed" before the expiration of the relevant number of days after the date of the certificate, see also Forgery and Counterfeiting Act 1981, s.9; *Barnsley Conveyancing Law and Practice* (2nd ed.) p. 435.

On the sale of part of a property, which has been mortgaged, the mortgagee should be joined, to release the part from the mortgage.[9] If the vendor is a tenant for life under a strict settlement he should join as parties the trustees of the settlement (who must be at least two in number or a trust corporation) so that they can give a valid receipt.[10] All persons who are to undertake burdens must be made a party to the deed. This would include, for example, a surety under a lease. A surety is a third party who guarantees that the tenant will pay the rent and observe and perform the covenants in the lease. Should the tenant default in some way the surety must make good any loss sustained by the landlord.

Section 56(1) of the Law of Property Act 1925 states that "a person may take an immediate or other interest in land . . . or the benefit of any condition, right of entry, covenant or agreement over or respecting land . . . although he may not be named as a party to the conveyance or other instrument." On a literal reading this provision would seem to be in conflict with the doctrine of privity of contract.[11] However, it appears that a person can only claim the benefit of a covenant (and so on) under the section if he is a person who is intended to fall within the benefit of the covenant on a proper construction of the deed.[12] For the avoidance of doubt it is, therefore, desirable for persons acquiring interests or rights under the deed to be made parties to it.

Sometimes the purchaser will have sub-sold to his own sub-purchaser shortly after exchanging contracts with his vendor. Under an open contract where the purchaser sells on before taking a conveyance himself, he can require his vendor to convey directly to the sub-purchaser.[13] The purchaser must, however, meet any additional expenses of the vendor in complying with his request. Law Society Condition 17(6) provides:

"The vendor shall be entitled on reasonable grounds to decline to convey the property to any person other than the purchaser, by more than one conveyance, at more than the contract price or at a price divided between different parts of the property."

This provision restricts the purchasers right at common law to require his vendor to convey to a sub-purchaser (or other nominee of the purchaser). The vendor must have reasonable grounds for refusing his purchaser's request. The explanatory notes issued by the Council of the Law Society with the 1980 edition of the Conditions suggested that one case where it might be reasonable for the vendor to refuse to convey to a sub-purchaser, was where the conveyance is to contain an indemnity by the purchaser in respect of liability for breaches of restrictive covenants. The National Conditions of Sale contain no provision equivalent to Law Society Condition 17(6).

---

[9] Alternatively a seperate Deed of Discharge could be executed by the mortgagee.
[10] Settled Land Act 1925, s.18; see *ante*, p. 293.
[11] *Drive Yourself Hire Co.* v. *Strutt* [1954] 1 Q.B. 250 at p. 271.
[12] *Beswick* v. *Beswick* [1968] A.C. 58.
[13] Unless the purchaser's personality is material; see also *Curtis Moffat Ltd.* v. *Wheeler* [1929] 2 Ch. 224.

Still on the topic of sub-sales it is the opinion of the Council of the Law Society that the purchaser should join in a conveyance by his vendor to his sub-purchaser.[14] The reason for this is that unless the purchaser is a party to the deed, directing the vendor to convey to the purchaser, no covenants for title will be implied on the part of the purchaser *vis á vis* his sub-purchaser.

The incapacity of the vendor may make it necessary to join (or substitute) a person as a party to the deed. If the vendor is bankrupt the correct procedure is to substitute the trustee in bankruptcy as a party (the vendor) to the deed. The bankrupt need not be a party because the trustee in bankruptcy has the legal estate vested in him by the adjudication order. If the vendor is a company in liquidation then the position is slightly more complicated. If an order has been made under section 244 of the Companies Act 1948 vesting the property in the liquidator, he should be the vendor; the company should not. If no order has been made under section 244 the company should convey (or assign etc.) and the liquidator should be joined in order to give a valid receipt and state that he has not incumbered the property in any manner.[15]

The parties to the deed should be described by giving their full christian names, surnames and addresses.[16] Although there is no rule requiring the occupation of parties to be given this may be helpful in identifying a party in cases of doubt. It is important that the correct name is given as this may be relied on subsequently to make a land charges search.[17-18] It is extremely useful after listing a party to define him in brackets afterwards for the sake of brevity. This also saves confusion when a party appears in the body of the deed more than once in different capacities.

RECITALS

There are two different types of recital, narrative recitals and introductory recitals. Generally speaking the former set out the history of the title, whilst the latter explain the circumstances in which the deed is made. Neither type of recital is strictly necessary and the modern practice is to keep recitals to a bare minimum, frequently reciting only the agreement for sale and the price. However, in conveyancing transactions other than a sale[19] it is useful to incorporate a recital setting out the purpose of a particular deed. Thus, a Deed of Variation of a lease will recite the parties' intention to alter the terms of the particular lease (giving the date of the lease and so on) in whatever manner as appropriate.[20] A deed relating to a party wall agreement (governing rights as to repair and so on) will recite

---

[14] Law Soc. Dig., Opinion 1266.

[15] A liquidator still has power to deal with the company's property even though no order has been made under s. 244 of the Companies Act 1948.

[16] In the case of a company the full company name and registered office should be used.

[17-18] See, *e.g. Diligent Finance Co. Ltd.* v. *Alleyne* (1972) 23 P. & C.R. 346 for possible consequences.

[19] Recitals are not usually found in a lease.

[20] The Deed of Variation would be made "supplemental" to the lease and under s.58 of the Law of Property Act 1925 this would make the Deed take effect as if the lease had been fully recited.

the reason why each party wishes to regulate his rights in relation to the wall to be built along the boundary line of each others property.

Recitals may also be desirable because:

(1) Section 45(6) of the Law of Property Act 1925[21] provides that a recital in a deed over 20 years old is sufficient evidence of the facts recited. Recitals may be included in a conveyance with a view to them acquiring this useful evidential value and so making a subsequent vendor's task of proving good title easier. For example a recital, in a deed dated 1963, that an estate owner had died, probate being granted to A and B would, in the absence of any contrary evidence, remove the need to produce the probate to prove the death.[22] As the period for which title needs to be shown has been reduced to 15 years the 20 year rule has become less useful in practice.

(2) A recital by a personal representative that he has not made a previous assent or conveyance of the property confers on a purchaser the protection afforded by section 36(6) of the Administration of Estates Act 1925.[23]

(3) A party who makes a clear and unambiguous[24] statement of fact in a recital may be estopped from denying the truth of that statement.[25] The estoppel will bind the successors of the person making the statement and it enures for the benefit of the successors to the person to whom it was made originally. For example if A conveys to B reciting in the purchase deed that he is the owner of the estate in fee simple he will be estopped from denying that fact as against B or B's successors. If A in fact occupied the land under a licence at the date of the conveyance (purporting to deal with the fee simple) but subsequently became entitled to the fee simple, the estate would vest in B as soon as A became entitled to it.[26]

(4) A recital may assist in the construction of the operative part of the deed (that is the part appearing after the words NOW THIS DEED WITNESSETH). If the operative part of the deed is expressed in unambiguous terms then those terms will prevail over the terms of the recitals. However, if the operative part of the deed is unclear or ambiguous a recital, provided it is clear, could be used as an aid in construing the operative part.[27] If the recitals contain a promise by the parties to do a certain act, yet there is no express covenant in the operative part of the deed, it is possible that the court will construe a covenant to do that act from the recital. For example, if there was a conveyance of part of a property to adjust the boundary line between two properties a failure to

---

[21] See *ante*, p. 264.

[22] The purchaser may wish to check the probate for endorsements; see *ante*, p. 297.

[23] See *ante*, p. 297; see also s.38 of the Trustee Act 1925.

[24] *District Bank Ltd.* v. *Webb* [1958] 1 W.L.R. 148; *Wight* v. *Bucknell* (1837) 9 L.J.K.B. 304; *Heath* v. *Crealock* (1874) 10 Ch. App. 22.

[25] *Cumberland Court (Brighton) Ltd.* v. *Taylor* [1964] Ch. 29.

[26] *Partridge* v. *Ward* [1910] 2 Ch. 342.

[27] *Ex p. Dawes, Re Moon* (1886) 17 Q.B.D. 275 particularly p. 286.

impose a covenant to fence may be cured by a recital of an agreement that a fence should be erected along the new boundary.[28]

THE CONSIDERATION

Section 5 of the Stamp Act 1891 requires all facts and circumstances affecting the liability of any instrument to stamp duty to be fully and truly stated. The price paid for the property (excluding the price of any chattels included in the sale) must always be stated. This determines the amount of stamp duty payable. Failure to state the purchase price accurately may be a fraud on the Inland Revenue. In some cases there will be no monetary consideration and some phrase such as "in consideration of the donor's natural love and affection for the donee" will take the place of the purchase price.

THE RECEIPT CLAUSE

When there is a monetary consideration the words, "the receipt whereof the vendor hereby acknowledges," should always be inserted into the deed. A receipt clause in the body of a deed brings Sections 67 to 69 of the Law of Property Act 1925 into operation.

Section 67 states that the receipt is sufficient discharge for the person paying the money; no further receipt is necessary. Section 68 provides that a receipt clause shall:

"in favour of a subsequent purchaser, not having notice that the money or other consideration thereby acknowledged to be received was not in fact paid or given, wholly or in part, be sufficient evidence of the payment or giving of the whole."

Note, however, that a subsequent purchaser will take the property subject to an unpaid vendor's lien, despite the inclusion of a receipt clause acknowledging payment, if the unpaid vendor registered the lien as a Class C (iii) land charge.[29] The section confers no protection on a donee. Section 69 is self explanatory. It states:

"Where a solicitor produces a deed, having in the body thereof or indorsed thereon a receipt for consideration money or other consider-ation, the deed being executed, or the indorsed receipt being signed, by the person entitled to give a receipt for that consideration, the deed shall be a sufficient authority for the person liable to pay or give the same for his paying or giving the same to the solicitor, without the solicitor producing any separate or other direction or authority in that behalf from the person who executed or signed the deed or receipt."

Although the section requires the deed containing the receipt clause to be produced by a "solicitor" payment is often made in practice to an articled clerk or agent. There is no judicial guidance as to whether section 69 would operate in such circumstances.[30]

---

[28] *Aspdin* v. *Austin* (1844) 5 Q.B. 671; *Mackenzie* v. *Childers* (1889) 43 Ch.D. 265; see *Dawes* v. *Tredwell* (1881) 18 Ch.D. 354 for the position where there is also an express covenant in the operative part of the purchase deed.

[29] The lien is not registrable if protected by deposit of the title deeds.

[30] See however, Law Soc. Dig., Opinion Nos. 163/4.

THE CAPACITY OF THE VENDOR: IMPLIED COVENANTS FOR TITLE

Following the receipt clause is a statement of the capacity in which the vendor conveys. The capacity in which the vendor conveys determines which covenants for title are implied into the conveyance.

(a) **Beneficial Owner.** Section 76(1)(A) of the Law of Property Act 1925 provides that where a person conveys and is expressed to convey as "beneficial owner" in a conveyance for valuable consideration, other than a mortgage, the following covenants will be implied[31]:

    (i) that the grantor has full power to convey;
    (ii) that the grantee shall quietly enjoy the property;
    (iii) that the grantee shall receive the property free of all undisclosed incumbrances;
    (iv) that the grantor will do anything reasonably required of him to further assure the title, that is to cure any defect in the title.

Two further covenants are implied on the assignment for value of a leasehold interest in land. These are dealt with below at page 378. Before embarking upon a discussion of the covenants something must first be said about the extent of the implied covenants for title.

By giving the beneficial owner covenants the grantor does not guarantee that the title is free from all imperfections. The covenantor (the vendor) is only liable for the acts and ommissions of a qualified list of people. There are four such groups:

(1) The vendor himself and anyone conveying by his direction. Thus, if Mr. Joe Soap, being the controlling shareholder of Joe Soap Limited, directed that company to convey land held by it to a purchaser and the company subsequently disturbed the purchaser's enjoyment of the property, Mr. Joe Soap would be liable for breach of the implied covenant for quiet enjoyment.

(2) Any person through whom the vendor claims otherwise than for value. In this context "value" means money or money's worth not marriage. For example, A obtains "Blackacre" by means of a gift from B. A as beneficial owner then sells the property to C. After completion C discovers that the property is subject to an incumbrance created by B. C may sue A for breach of the implied covenants for title. A is responsible for the acts of B because B *gave* the property to A. Had A purchased the property from B, A would not have been liable. In this latter case C's remedy would be against B direct. The benefit of B's implied covenants for title runs with the land under section 76(6) of the Law of Property Act 1925.

(3) Any person claiming through or under a person from whom the vendor took otherwise than for value. This category would include the acts and omissions of, for instance, a donor's tenants.

(4) Any person claiming through, under, or in trust for the vendor. Falling within this category would be the acts and omissions of the vendor's tenants mortgagees and anybody who held the legal estate as

---

[31] Law of Property Act 1925, Sched. 2, Pt. II.

trustee for the vendor. Thus, in the case of *David* v. *Sabin*[32] the vendor granted a lease to T who sub-let to ST. Subsequently T surrendered his lease. The sub-lease was not affected by the surrender of the lease and continued to subsist. The vendor conveyed to T who sold on to X who, having discovered the property was subject to an incumbrance (the sub-lease) successfully sued the vendor on his implied covenants for title. The incumbrance was created by T, a person claiming under the vendor.

The basic rule on an ordinary conveyance on sale by a vendor who conveys as "beneficial owner," is that he is liable for all acts and omissions, except those occurring prior to the preceding conveyance for valuable consideration.

Where a mortgagor mortgages land as beneficial owner he gives the same covenants for title set out above on page 375. However, in this case the covenants are not qualified. The mortgagor is liable for the acts and omissions of all his predecessors even those through whom he claims for value.[33]

Having looked at the extent of the covenantor's liability a brief look at the operation of the actual covenants may be found useful.

(i) *Full power to convey.* This is a covenant that the vendor (or a person for whom he has to accept liability) has not "made, done, executed, or omitted, or knowingly suffered" anything to be done which limits his power to convey the property as detailed in the conveyance. In *Eastwood* v. *Ashton*[34] the defendant Ashton, as beneficial owner, conveyed certain property to the plaintiff Eastwood. Title to a part of the land had been acquired by an adjoining landowner by virtue of his adverse possession. Ashton did not therefore have power to convey that part of the property. Eastwood discovered the true position when he subsequently tried to sell the property. He sued on the implied covenant for title. Ashton was held liable because he had omitted throughout the limitation period to take steps to prevent the adjoining owner from acquiring title by adverse possession. It makes no difference that the purchaser knows of the defect in title. In *Page* v. *Midland Railway Co.*[35] AP conveyed property to the railway company as beneficial owner. AP derived title under the will of X and her ability to make good title depended upon the construction of that will. The will was fully recited in the deed conveying the property. After the railway company had paid the purchase price AP died. Some children, claiming under the will of X, obtained judgment against the railway company for the purchase money paid to AP. The company sued AP's personal representatives on the covenants for title. It was held that defects in title falling within the scope of the covenants for title were not excluded from their operation on the ground they appear on the face of the conveyance or are otherwise known to the purchaser. The railway company recovered damages from AP's personal representatives.

---

[32] [1893] 1 Ch. 523.
[33] Law of Property Act 1925, Sched. 2, Pt. III.
[34] [1925] A.C. 900.
[35] [1894] 1 Ch. 11.

(ii) *Quiet enjoyment.* This is a covenant that the purchaser shall not be lawfully[36] disturbed in his enjoyment of the property by the vendor or someone for whom the vendor is responsible. For a breach of the covenant to occur the disturbance must actually take place; the fact that there is a person entitled to disturb the purchaser's enjoyment of the property with nothing more is not sufficient. Thus in *Howard* v. *Maitland*[37] P bought a piece of former waste land in Epping Forest. V gave a covenant for quiet enjoyment. Seven years later there was a court decision that the land was subject to rights of common. Nobody had exercised the right and nobody had entered onto the purchaser's land. It was held that no breach of the covenant had taken place.

The fact that a breach of the covenant for quiet enjoyment only occurs when the purchaser's enjoyment of the property is actually disturbed could in some circumstances, work in favour of the purchaser. For example, in *Conodate Investments Ltd.* v. *Bentley Quarry Engineering Co. Ltd.*[38] V as beneficial owner conveyed 6,900 square yards of land to P in 1962. In 1967 P laid out a housing development on the land and a third party established title to part of the land. There were breaches of two of the covenants for title. The "full power to convey" covenant was broken in 1962 when V conveyed without having good title. The "quiet enjoyment" covenant was broken in 1967 when the third party actually established his claim. In 1962 the "lost" land was worth approximately £1,000 whilst in 1967 it was worth £5,000. The purchaser suing on the quiet enjoyment covenant recovered £5,000 in damages.[39]

(iii) *Freedom from incumbrances.* Although listed above as a separate covenant this is in fact regarded by most commentators as part of the second covenant.[40] Whether separate or not it is a covenant by the vendor that the title is free from all "estates, incumbrances, claims and demands." The vendor must indemnify the purchaser in the event of any incumbrance being enforced. In *Stock* v. *Meakin*[41] the vendor, giving the beneficial owner covenants for title, conveyed property to the purchaser on November 22. Street works had been carried out the previous year but the final apportionment of costs to each frontager was made after completion on December 29. The court held that the cost of doing the works became a charge on the property when the works were done, that is before completion took place. The property was, therefore, subject to an incumbrance when the vendor conveyed it to the purchaser. The covenant relating to freedom from incumbrances had been broken and the vendor was liable to indemnify the purchaser. The situation which occurred in *Stock* v. *Meakin* is now covered by the standard conditions of sale. Law Society Condition 3 and National Condition 16[42] would ensure that the

---

[36] *Malzy* v. *Eichholz* [1916] 2 K.B. 308, tortious remedies would be available if the disturbance was unlawful.

[37] (1883) 11 Q.B.D. 695.   [38] (1970) 216 E.G. 1407.

[39] See also [1978] Conv. 418. *Bunny* v. *Hopkinson* (1859) 27 Beav. 565.

[40] Farrand, *Contract and Conveyace* (4th ed.) p. 265; *Williams on Title* (4th ed.) p. 755; *Williams on Vendor and Purchaser* (4th ed.) Vol II, p. 1080. *cf. Turner* v. *Moon* [1901] 2 Ch. 825, *per* Joyce J. at p. 828

[41] [1900] 1 Ch. 683.   [42] See *ante*, p. 245.

purchaser indemnified the vendor in respect of any local authority charge paid by him after contracts became binding. The covenant does not just relate to financial incumbrances. "Claims and demands" would be wide enough, for instance, to make a vendor liable if he was to sell property which was subject to an enforcement notice in respect of a breach of planning law committed by the vendor or someone for whom he is responsible. Obviously if the sale is made subject to some incumbrance, claim or demand the purchaser can have no remedy in respect of that particular matter under the implied covenants for title.

(iv) *Further assurance.* The provisions of this covenant for title require the vendor (and anybody for whom he is responsible) to execute any further document or do any other act reasonably required of him to perfect the title of the purchaser or his successors in title. If a personal representative conveyed as beneficial owner without first formally assenting to himself in writing[43] the purchaser could require him to do so under this covenant.

(b) **Settlor.** A person who conveys and is expressed to convey as "settlor" gives only an implied covenant for further assurance.[44] He is responsible only for his own acts and those of persons deriving title under him.

(c) **Mortgagee, trustee, personal representative or conveyance under an order of the court.** Where a person conveys and is expressed to convey as "mortgagee," "trustee," "personal representative" or the conveyance is made "under an order of the court," s.76(1)(F) of the Law of Property Act 1925 implies just one covenant for title into the conveyance. The covenant is one by the grantor that he has not personally incumbered the land.[45] The trustee, mortgagee and so on is responsible only for his own acts or omissions.

ADDITIONAL COVENANTS FOR TITLE ON ASSIGNMENT OF LEASEHOLD INTEREST

Section 76(1)(B) and Part II of the Second Schedule to the Act imply an additional covenant into a conveyance of leasehold property for valuable consideration where the vendor conveys and is expressed to convey as beneficial owner. As well as the four beneficial owner covenants set out above there is implied a covenant (sometimes said to be two separate covenants) that the lease was validly granted and is still subsisting and that the covenants and other obligations on the part of the lessee have been complied with up to the time of the conveyance.[46]

Where leasehold property is mortgaged there is yet another covenant for title implied in addition to those mentioned already. The mortgagor impliedly covenants to pay the rent and perform the covenants in the lease

---

[43] See *Re Kings Wills Trusts* [1964] Ch. 542.

[44] Law of Property Act 1925, s.76(1)(*E*), Sched. 2, Pt. V.

[45] *Wise* v. *Whitburn* [1924] 1 Ch. 460.

[46] Both Standard Conditions of Sale modify the effect of the statutory implied covenants for title; see *ante,* p. 209. National Condition 11(7); Law Society Condition 8(5).

for the period during which the mortgage subsists. This covenant is obviously necessary for the protection of the security.

THE PARCELS CLAUSE

The parcels clause must contain a completely accurate description of the property. The description must be in accordance both with the description of the property contained in the contract and the vendor's title.[47] Describing the property in the contract has already been dealt with at page 194 above. Frequently, the conveyance will contain both a plan and a verbal description. If the verbal description differs from the plan the question arises, which description is to prevail. This is a matter of construction of the particular deed. If the parcels clause states, "which said property is more particularly delineated on the plan annexed hereto and thereon edged red," the plan will prevail if it is at variance with the verbal description.[48] Conversely if the plan is said to be "for the purposes of identification only" the verbal description contained in the operative part of the deed will prevail over the plan in the event that they differ. Thus in *Wiggington and Milner* v. *Winster Engineering*[49] it was decided that a plan referred to as being "for the purpose of identification only" could not be used to determine the identity of the property conveyed where the verbal description was clear and unambiguous. If the verbal description is unclear and yet the plan is stated to be for the "identification only" the court will refer to the plan in an attempt to resolve the difficulty and give effect to the deed as a whole. For example, in *Truckell* v. *Stock*[50] the vendor conveyed "a dwellinghouse" to the purchaser. The conveyance contained a verbal description of the property and a plan showing the property's boundaries at ground level. The eaves and footings of the property projected further than the boundaries shown on the plan. The court in construing the deed looked at the parcels clause as a whole. They found that the subject-matter of the conveyance was *a dwelling-house* and although the plan would have prevailed in the event of a conflict they reconciled the two descriptions to achieve the right result—the eaves and footings passed to the purchaser despite the plan.

EASEMENTS GRANTED BY THE VENDOR

Any easements to be granted to a purchaser, over the vendors retained land for example on a sale of part, are introduced by the words "Together with." The following points should be borne in mind when drafting this part of the conveyance:

(a) **The Identification of the Dominant Tenement.** Although it is not strictly essential for the dominant tenement to be identified in the conveyance creating the easement, good conveyancing practice dictates that this should be done in every case. This can be done simply by edging

---

[47] See *ante*, p. 194.
[48] *Neilson* v. *Poole* (1969) 20 P. & C.R. 909; *Wallington* v. *Townsend* [1939] Ch. 588.
[49] [1978] 1 W.L.R. 1462.
[50] [1957] 1 W.L.R. 161.

the dominant tenement on the deed plan and defining the dominant land in the body of the deed, by reference to the coloured edging.

If the dominant tenement is not identifiable from the deed extrinsic evidence can be adduced to establish its identity. Obviously, during the course of time establishing the indentity of the dominant land may become more difficult.[51]

(b) **The Parties To Be Benefited.** Often an easement, for example a right of way, is granted to the owner of the dominant tenement, his successors in title and the owners and occupiers for the time being of any part of the dominant tenement. If the dominant land is broken up and sold off in parts the owners of each part obtain the benefit of the easement. In the case of a right of way traffic over the servient tenement would increase, possibly to the detriment of the owner of the property over which the right of way is enjoyed. In some cases it may be appropriate to limit the category of persons benefited.

(c) **Scope of the Right.** The most frequently encountered easement in practice is the right of way. When granting the right consideration should be given to the type of user to be allowed. It may be appropriate to limit the right of way to passage on foot rather than with vehicles.[52] The purpose for which the right of way is to be enjoyed and the times at which it may be exercised should also be considered.[53] Any contributions towards the expense of maintaining the path or road over which the right is enjoyed should also be set out in the deed granting the right. Different considerations may apply to the various types of right capable of forming the basis of a grant. For example, the grant of a right to use drains running under the servient land should include the right to enter that land for the purposes of executing repairs to the drains.

(d) **The Rule Against Perpetuities.** This rule operates on rights which are expressed to arise at some future date. If the right is not limited in its exercise to within a valid perpetuity period as expressed in the grant and is not actually exercised within the "wait and see" period allowed by section 3 of the Perpetuities and Accumulations Act 1964 the right becomes invalid.

The rule does not apply to future rights granted in connection with roads or drains *which already exist.*

SECTION 62 OF THE LAW OF PROPERTY ACT 1925

Under section 62 certain rights pass automatically on the conveyance of land. These include *inter alia,* all easements, rights, privileges and advantages "appertaining or reputed to appertain to the land or any part thereof." The section applies to all rights appertaining to the property sold whether their enjoyment was previously by permission or not. The section

---

[51] *The Shannon Ltd.* v. *Venner Ltd.* [1965] Ch. 682.

[52] *Hurt* v. *Bowmer* [1937] 1 All E.R. 797.

[53] *Jelbert* v. *Davis* [1968] 1 W.L.R. 589.

applies only insofar as a contrary intention is not expressed in the conveyance.[54]

The effect of section 62 and the provisions contained in the standard conditions of sale have already been discussed.[55]

EXCEPTIONS AND RESERVATIONS

An exception is any right or interest in existence at the time the conveyance is made, which is not to pass to the purchaser. For instance, the owner of a large estate may sell part of it to the purchaser and prevent the purchaser from extracting minerals by excepting mining and mineral rights from the grant. This would obviously be advantageous to the running of a large scale mining operation for the benefit of the whole estate.

A reservation occurs when the vendor creates in the conveyance a new right for his benefit, over the land he is selling. For example on the sale of part of his property the vendor may reserve a right of way out of the part sold for the benefit of the retained land.

The distinction between an "exception" and a "reservation" was once of vital importance. In the latter case it was necessary for the purchaser to execute the conveyance because the reservation operated by way of a regrant by the purchaser of the new right to the vendor. Since 1926 the purchaser's execution has no longer been necessary because section 65(1) of the Law of Property Act 1925 provides that a reservation of a legal estate by a vendor shall operate without any execution of the conveyance by the grantee or any regrant by him so as to create the legal estate reserved. However, for the purposes of applying the *contra proferentem* rule the "grantor" (against whom any ambiguity is construed) is the purchaser because of the doctrine that an easement lies in grant.[56]

THE HABENDUM

Strictly speaking the habendum is not an essential part of the purchase deed. If it is left out section 60 of the Law of Property Act 1925 provides:

"A conveyance of freehold land to any person without words of limitation, or any equivalent expression, shall pass to the grantee the fee simple or other the whole interest which the grantor had power to convey in such land . . . ."

In practice an habendum should be included for two reasons. First, if it is omitted the covenants for title will not be implied. Second, section 60 applies only in so far as a contrary intention does not appear in the conveyance. If the habendum is missing and such a contrary intention did appear the results for the purchaser would obviously be disastrous.

EXISTING RESTRICTIONS

Immediately after the habendum and usually introduced by the words "SUBJECT TO" are detailed the restrictions already in existence and to

---

[54] Law of Property Act 1925, s.62(4).

[55] See *ante.* p. 182.

[56] See *St. Edmundsbury and Ipswich Diocesan Board of Finance* v. *Clarke (No. 2)* [1975] 1 W.L.R. 468; *Johnstone* v. *Holdway* [1963] 1 Q.B. 601.

which the property will remain subject after the conveyance. For example, any restrictive covenants burdening the land.

DECLARATION OF TRUST

The reader is referred to the previous section on co-purchasers.[57]

NEW COVENANTS

Following the declaration of trust (if any) are any new covenants made between the parties. A positive covenant such as one to contribute towards the cost of maintaining a private road serving the property[57a] will only be binding between the parties to the deed creating the obligation. It may become binding on a subsequent owner of the purchaser's land if the purchaser takes an indemnity covenant when he sell on.

As every student of land law will be aware the benefit and burden of a restrictive covenant will in limited circumstances run with the land. A detailed discussion of the rules as to enforcement of restrictive covenants is outside the scope of this book.[58]

INDEMNITY COVENANTS

Frequently a vendor who sells land subject to existing covenants, whether positive or negative in nature, will remain liable for their breach notwithstanding that he has parted with his interest in the property. The vendor may, for instance, be the original covenantor or one of his successors in title who has given a covenant to indemnify his predecessors in title; there being an unbroken chain of indemnity covenants stretching back to the original covenantor. If this is the case the vendor must insist on his purchaser giving an indemnity covenant similar to that contained in clause 2 of the conveyance above.[58a]

Where land is expressed to be sold subject to existing covenants the contract should specify the form of indemnity to be given by the purchaser. In the absence of any contractual provision there is, however, an obligation implied at common law on the part of the purchaser to indemnify the vendor against breach of the covenants.

National Condition 19(5)(6) and (7) give the vendor a right to require the purchaser to give an indemnity clause. Under National Condition 19(6) the purchaser is obliged in the conveyance to covenant to observe and perform the covenants and to indemnify the vendor against actions and claims in respect thereof. The form of covenant provided for by Law Society Condition 17(4) is less satisfactory from the vendor's viewpoint because it does not oblige the purchaser to observe and perform the

---

[57] See *ante*, p. 364.

[57a] But remember *Halsall* v. *Brizell* [1967] Ch. 169. And see "Transfer of Land. The Law of Positive and Restrictive Covenants" Law Com. No. 127 for proposals that positive covenants should in future be binding (*per se*) on subsequent purchasers.

[58] See further Preston and Newsom; *Restrictive Covenant to Affecting Freehold Land* (7th ed.)

[58a] This will still be necessary as far as existing covenants are concerned even if the Law Commission's proposals for "land obligations" are given statutory force (see Law Com. No. 127). The legislation will not be retrospective.

covenants. Whilst a vendor might be able to obtain an injunction restraining a breach of covenant under the National Conditions; he could not do so under the Law Society Conditions.

Finally, on the assignment of a leasehold property section 77(1)(C) and Part IX of the Second Schedule of the Law of Property Act 1925 imply a covenant on the part of the assignee to:

(a) pay the rent reserved;
(b) perform the covenants and other conditions contained in the lease;
(c) to indemnify the assignor in respect of any liability he retains after completion under the lease.

Where there is an assignment of part of a leasehold property the implied covenant relates to the apportioned rent only but is in other respects the same.[59]

THE ACKNOWLEDGMENT AND UNDERTAKING

By section 45(9) of the Law of Property Act 1925 a vendor is entitled to retain documents of title where:

(a) he retains any part of the land to which the documents relate; or
(b) the document consists of a trust instrument or other instrument creating a trust which is still subsisting, or an instrument relating to the appointment or discharge of a trustee of a subsisting trust.

Under an open contract if a vendor retains title deeds the purchaser is entitled to an acknowledgment of his right to production and to take copies at the expense of the person requesting them.[60] The vendor can also be required to undertake for the safe custody of the deeds.

An acknowledgment and undertaking can only be given by the person with possession of the deeds. If the title deeds are in the hands of a mortgagee it is the mortgagee who must give the acknowledgment. A mortgagee, trustee or personal representative will not give an undertaking for the safe custody of the deeds. Commonly, the vendor will agree to give an undertaking for safe custody when the title deeds come into his possession. It must also be remembered that an acknowledgment for production must be given to another.[61] A personal representative who assents to himself as beneficial owner cannot give an acknowledgment for production to himself. If he later conveys the property to a purchaser (as beneficial owner) he should give the acknowledgment for production at that time.

The acknowledgment gives a right to production to all reasonable times for the purpose of inspection, comparison with abstracts and in relation to court proceedings and so on engaged in to prove or support title. The undertaking for safe custody gives a right to damages if the documents are not kept, "whole, uncancelled and undefaced" unless this is prevented by fire or other inevitable accident.

---

[59] Law of Property Act 1925, s.77(1)(*D*), Sched. 2, Pt. X.
[60] *Ibid.* s.64(5).
[61] *Ibid.* s.64(1).

The burden of the acknowledgment and undertaking runs with the deeds; any person having possession of them is required to perform the obligations imposed by section 64 of the Act. The benefit of the acknowledgment and undertaking runs with the land and passes to the original purchaser's successors in title automatically under section 62 of the Law of Property Act 1925. The benefit does not, however, vest in a lessee at a rent.

If documents of title are being retained by the vendor it might be necessary to ensure that some note or memoranda of the transaction is endorsed on those documents. For instance, on the sale of part of a property the conveyance to the vendor should be endorsed to put a subsequent purchaser of the retained land on notice.

The National Conditions do not deal with the question of acknowledgments and undertakings, the open contract rule therefore applies. Law Society Condition 17(5) confirms the open contract rule expressly. This Condition does, however, additionally provide that where documents of title are retained "by a mortgagee, trustee or personal representative, the vendor shall procure that such person shall given an acknowledgment for production, and the vendor, unless in a fiduciary capacity, shall covenant that if and when he receives any such document he will, to the cost of the person requiring it, give an undertaking for safe custody."

CERTIFICATE OF VALUE

A certificate of value (usually in the form shown in the conveyance above) must always be included in the purchase deed where the consideration is £30,000 or less. This brings into operation the nil rate of stamp duty chargeable on such conveyances. If no certificate of value is included, or the consideration for the purchase exceeds £30,000, stamp duty at the rate of 1 per cent. of the total consideration is payable.[62] There is therefore no point in including a certificate of value in the conveyance for purchases over £30,000.

The certificate of value refers to the transaction effected by the instrument not forming "part of a larger transaction or series of transactions in respect of which the amount or value or aggregate amount or value of the consideration exceeds thirty thousand pounds." If, for example, the vendor and purchaser negotiate several conveyances at the same time the certificate of value must reflect this fact.[63] If the total consideration exceeded £30,000 duty would be levied at 1 per cent.

In the case of voluntary dispositions stamp duty at 1 per cent. is levied on the value of the property.[64] The value is ascertained by the Inland Revenue, the instrument being sent to them for adjudication. Where the value of the gifted property does not exceed £30,000 a certificate of value must again be included in the deed of gift, to claim exemption from duty.

---

[62] Finance Act 1984.
[63] *Att. Gen.* v. *Cohen* [1936] 2 K.B. 246; see also [1937] 1 K.B. 478; *Kimbers & Co.* v. *I.R.C.* [1936] 1 K.B. 132.
[64] Finance Act 1910, s.74.

TESTIMONIUM AND TESTATUM

The testimonium and testatum may be dealt with together because they both serve the same function, that is to link the various parts of the deed together so that they read logically. Both clauses are purely formal.

ATTESTATION: EXECUTING THE DEED

(a) **Individuals.** Section 73(1) of the Law of Property Act 1925 provides where, "an individual executes a deed, he shall either sign or place his mark upon the same and sealing alone shall not be deemed sufficient." It has been held that stamping a document with a facsimile of a parties signature is sufficient provided there is an intention to authenticate the document.[65] Placing an "X" at the end of the deed would also be sufficient to satisfy the requirements of section 73 for instance, if one of the parties were unable to write. By analogy with the cases on section 9 of the Wills Act 1837 "signature" is likely to be fairly widely construed by the courts.

In addition to being signed the deed must also be sealed. A small paper-wax seal is commonly used nowadays. The courts are reluctant to insist on strict compliance with this particular requirement. In *First National Securities Ltd* v. *Jones*[66] a mortgagor signed the mortgage deed across the circle containing the printed letters LS, which stands for *locus sigilli*—"the place of the seal." No wafer seal was attached to the mortgage. Despite this the mortgage was held to have been validly executed. Danckwerts J. in *Stromdale and Ball Limited* v. *Burden*[67] even suggested that a signature along the words "now this deed witnesseth . . . [the parties] set their hands and seals" would amount to an estoppel in respect to sealing.

(b) **Corporations.** Section 74 of the Law of Property Act 1925 contains provisions relating to the execution of instruments by or on behalf of corporations. In favour of a purchaser a deed is to be presumed duly executed "if its seal be affixed thereto in the presence of and attested by its clerk, secretary or other permanent officer or his deputy, and a member of the board of directors, council or other governing body of the corporation." Provided the seal purports to be the seal of the company and the persons witnessing the sealing purport to be the secretary, director and so on the requirements of the section are satisfied. In *D'Silva* v. *Lister House Developments Ltd.*[68] a lease was sealed by a corporation without a resolution of the board of directors to authorise the sealing. It was held that the lease had been effectively sealed and therefore bound the company.

Wherever the deed is executed in accordance with section 74 the purchaser need not ensure that the execution is in accordance with the articles of association. A corporations constitution only becomes relevant

---

[65] *Goodman* v. *Eban* [1954] 1 Q.B. 550; *Jenkins* v. *Gaisford* (1863) 3 Sw. & Tr. 93.
[66] [1978] Ch. 109.
[67] [1952] Ch. 223; see also *Re Smith* (1892) 67 L.T. 64 where a document stated to be "sealed with my seal" but no seal was affixed was held validly sealed.
[68] [1971] Ch. 17.

when the seal is not attested by any of the persons mentioned in the section.

(c) **Who Must Execute The Deed.** The basic rule is that anybody who is granting or releasing rights should execute the deed. Thus, in the conveyance reproduced above the building society executed the purchase deed to effectually release the property conveyed from the mortgage. The purchasers in a straightforward conveyance containing no covenants or declaration of trust need not execute the conveyance. If the purchasers give any covenants or the conveyance contains a declaration of trust the purchasers must execute the conveyance. Obviously the vendor must execute the purchase deed in all cases because he is always transferring some estate or interest.

B. THE TRANSFER

The Form

The printed form (obtainable from all branches of H.M. Stationery Office) for use where the whole of land comprised in a registered title is being transferred is form 19; form 20 for a transfer of part. Most solicitors employ forms 19 and 20 whether the land concerned is freehold or leasehold although special printed forms are available for the transfer of leaseholds (forms 32A (whole) and 32B (part)). In the case of a sale to joint purchasers, form 19 (JP) is the appropriate form. This includes a declaration indicating whether the survivor of them can (joint tenancy) or cannot (tenancy in common) give a valid receipt for capital money. In the latter event the Registrar will enter a restriction on the register preventing the registration of dispositions for value by one trustee[69] Form 19 (JP) must be executed by the purchasers as well as the vendor. Special forms, printed and statutory,[70] are available for other transactions, like a transfer in exercise of a registered chargee's power of sale (printed form 31A), a transfer to a company (printed form 35) or a transfer for charitable uses (statutory form 36). The forms can be altered to suit the particular transaction, but if the basic principles of the registration system are infringed, by referring to a trust for example, the Registrar may refuse to register the transaction.[71] In cases of doubt a solicitor can obtain the Registry's prior approval to a proposed draft on payment of a £5 fee.

Here is a specimen completed form 19:

---

[69] Land Registration Act 1925, s.58(3).
[70] Land Registration Rules 1925, Sched.
[71] *Ibid*. r. 78.

Form 19

H.M. Land Registry   Land Registration Acts, 1925 to 1971

TRANSFER OF WHOLE
(Rule 98 or 115 Land Registration Rules 1925)

County and district ⎱
(or London borough) ⎰ .... AVON, TABOCK

Title Number AV98765

Property .... 17 YORK ROAD, TABOCK.

Date .... 1st June 1984. In consideration of thirty-eight thousand pounds (£38,000.00) the receipt whereof is hereby acknowledged I, SHEILA BYRON of 10 KING'S PLACE, HAMPTON, SOMERSET, SCHOOLTEACHER, as beneficial owner hereby transfer to:

> GLYN THOMAS of 17 YORK ROAD, TABOCK, AVON
> ENGINEER

the land comprised in the title above mentioned.

Signed, sealed and delivered by the said ⎫
   SHEILA BYRON   ⎬   *Sheila Byron*   (SEAL)
in the presence of   ⎭   ....

Name .... *Herbert Smith*

Address .... Barclands Bank, High Street, Hampton

Occupation .... Bank Manager

Commentary

HEADING

The office copy of the vendor's title will provide the name of the county and district, a short description of the property and the title number.

DATE

The transfer must be dated. It is effectual between the parties when signed, sealed and delivered, but the legal estate in the land does not pass until the purchaser's application for registration as proprietor is received by the Registry.[72]

RECITALS

Form 19 leaves no space for recitals. The Registry discourages the use of recitals in transfers because they are inconsistent with the principles on which the register is kept. Recitals are redundant in a transfer by a beneficial owner of the whole of land registered with title absolute, but their inclusion may be necessary in other cases for the same reasons as in unregistered conveyancing. If recitals are made in the transfer it should be remembered that the transfer does not form part of the Register and is filed at the Registry after registration of the purchaser as proprietor. A certified copy of the transfer should therefore be made and kept with the land or charge certificate.

CONSIDERATION AND RECEIPT CLAUSE

These serve the same purpose as in unregistered conveyancing. If a gift of registered land is contemplated, form 19[73] may be adapted by substituting the words: "In consideration of my natural love and affection for . . . ."[74] The registration of the donee as proprietor will be subject to any minor interests subject to which the donor held the land, but such interests are not entered on the register because they do not affect a subsequent purchaser for value.[75]

THE VENDOR "AS BENEFICIAL OWNER HEREBY TRANSFERS"

It must be re-noted that the legal estate is not transferred until completion of the disposition by registration.[76] The words "as beneficial owner" are designed to import into the transfer the usual covenants for title. The importation of covenants for title into dispositions of registered land is complex and the reader will forgive a brief foray into the subject.

 For the purpose of introducing the covenants for title implied under section 76 of the Law of Property Act 1925, rule 76 of the Land Registration Rules 1925 states that a person may in a registered disposition

---

[72] Land Registration Act 1925, ss.19(1) and 22(1); Land Registration Rules 1925, r. 83(2); *Grace Rymer Investments Ltd.* v. *Waite* [1958] Ch. 831.

[73] Or forms 20, 32A or B.

[74] Ruoff and Roper, *Registered Conveyancing*, (4th ed.) p. 324.

[75] Land Registration Act 1925, ss.20(4) and 23(5); see *ante*, p. 304.

[76] *Ibid.* ss.19(1) and 22(1); Land Registration Rules 1925, r. 83(2).

be expressed to execute, transfer or charge as "beneficial owner" (or as "settlor," "mortgagee," "trustee" and so on as the case may be). Thus where a vendor, as "beneficial owner" transfers a registered freehold for valuable consideration, he impliedly covenants:

(a) that he has the power to transfer the land;
(b) that the purchaser will have quiet enjoyment of the land;
(c) that the land is free from incumbrances; and
(d) that he will execute any necessary further deed of assurance.[77]

Where he transfers a registered leasehold for valuable consideration as "beneficial owner," he further covenants:

(e) that the lease is valid and subsisting; and
(f) that the rent and covenants and conditions have respectively been paid and observed.[78]

No reference to these covenants may appear on the register.[79] Furthermore rule 77[80] provides that the covenants take effect as though the disposition was expressly made subject to:

> "(a) all charges and other interests appearing or protected on the register at the time of the execution of the disposition and affecting the title of the covenantor;
>
> (b) any overriding interests of which the purchaser has notice and subject to which it would have taken effect, had the land been unregistered."

The benefit of any covenant implied under section 76 of the Law of Property Act is annexed to the interest for the benefit of which it is given and is capable of being enforced by the registered proprietor of that interest for the time being.[81] Rule 77 goes on to provide that its provisions are in addition to, not in substitution for, the other provisions in the Land Registration Acts relating to covenants.

The desirability of importing the usual covenants for title into a registered transfer is obvious where the title is non-absolute. The purchaser needs protection against interests and rights subsisting prior to first registration if he buys a possessory title[82]; against matters excepted from registration if he buys a qualified title.[83] Although registration with absolute leasehold title shows that the lease was validly granted, registration with good leasehold title does not affect the enforcement of any interest or right adversely affecting the lessor's title.[84] Finally in the case of a gift, the donee will take subject to any minor interests subject to which the donor holds the land.[85]

---

[77] Law of Property Act 1925, s.76(1)(A) and Sched. 2, Pt. I.
[78] Law of Property Act 1925, s.76(1)(B), Sched. 2, Pt. II.
[79] Land Registration Rules 1925, r. 76.
[80] *Ibid.* r. 77(1).
[81] *Ibid.* r. 77(2).
[82] Land Registration Act 1925, ss.6, 20(3) and 23(4).
[83] *Ibid.* ss.7, 20(2) and 23(3).
[84] *Ibid.* s.23(2).
[85] *Ibid.* ss.20(4) and 23(5).

Ruoff and Roper demonstrate[86] that the usual covenants for title are of very little value to a purchaser of an absolute title, except in connection with overriding interests of which the purchaser is ignorant. We have already seen that the covenants for title take effect as if the disposition had been expressly made subject to "overriding interests" noted on the register and any overriding interests of which the purchaser has notice. Ruoff and Roper are of the opinion that the covenants for title implied into a transfer by the use of the words "beneficial owner," do give the purchaser some protection against undisclosed overriding interests. Of course the purchaser must take subject to any such interests,[87] but he has the benefit of the vendor's covenant to transfer the land free from them, and may sue on it for damages. This is so even though the Land Registration Act states that overriding interests are not to be treated as incumbrances.[88]

Emmet on Title;[89] however points to "academic controversy" as to whether the usual covenants for title are "effective protection in the case of undisclosed overriding interests," in which case "the mere insertion of the words "as beneficial owner" in a transfer for value of freehold land registered with absolute title is probably pointless."[90] They comment that it is doubtful, even if this view is correct, that a vendor should be advised to extend his covenants for title to cover undisclosed overriding interest and say that in any event the vendor cannot be compelled to do so in the absence of an express term in the contract. They conclude: "The practical view seems to be that overriding interests are outside the protection [of the usual covenants for title] and inquiries should be made, for instance by preliminary inquiries, inspection and questions to tenants and others."

Before we depart this area something should be said about covenants relating to a registered lease. In a transfer of registered leasehold land (otherwise than by underlease) section 24 of the Land Registration Act 1925 automatically (that is without use of special words) implies certain covenants. Where the demised premises is transferred in whole or in part, the purchaser covenants to pay the rent, perform the covenants and observe the conditions affecting the land (or the relevant part) and to indemnify the vendor against any action arising out of the purchasers failure to perform and observe the covenants and conditions.[91] In other words the position is the same as in unregistered land, where the purchaser impliedly (and again automatically) covenants in similar terms by virtue of section 77 of the Law of Property Act 1925.[92] However section 24 also automatically implies a covenant on the part of the vendor that the rents and covenants have been paid and performed, and where the vendor retains part that he will pay the rent and observe and perform the

---

[86] *Registered Conveyancing* (4th ed.) pp. 286–288.

[87] Land Registration Act 1925, s.70(1).

[88] *Ibid*. s.70(1).

[89] (18th ed.) p. 470.

[90] (1960) 105 S.J. 800.

[91] Land Registration Act 1925, ss.24(1)(*b*) and (2).

[92] Law of Property Act 1925, s.77(1)(*C*), Sched. 2, Pt. IX, and s.77(1)(D)(i), Sched. 2, Pt. X, para. (i).

conditions and covenants relevant to his part.[93] In unregistered land such covenants are only implied if the vendor conveys "as beneficial owner,"[94] in which case the purchaser gets the benefit of the additional covenant that the lease was validly granted.[95] (which is not automatically implied under section 24). Furthermore in the case of unregistered land the covenants are only implied if the conveyance is for valuable consideration; section 24 appears to apply even if the transfer is voluntary. The covenants in section 24 may be modified or negatived in the transfer.[96] If it is wished to exclude section 24 and rely instead on section 77, that section or the Parts of the Second Schedule to the Law of Property Act in which the covenants are set out must be referred to expressly.[97] The benefit of a covenant implied under section 77 is annexed to the interest for the benefit of which it is given and is capable of being enforced by the registered proprietor for the time being thereof.[98] Finally in this connection it should be mentioned that if a personal representative is selling leasehold land under an open contract, the covenant implied on his part under section 24 must be excluded, because he cannot be required to give covenants for title more onerous than those he would be required to give, if the land were unregistered.[99]

Where unregistered freehold land is sold subject to a rentcharge section 77(1)(A) of the Law of Property Act 1925 automatically implies covenants on the purchaser's part to pay the rentcharge, perform and observe the covenants and conditions contained in the deed which created the rentcharge and indemnify the vendor. Where part only of land affected by a rentcharge is sold, the purchaser's covenants are the same, only limited to his part, and section 77(1)(B)(ii) additionally implies covenants on the part of a vendor who conveys "as beneficial owner" to pay the balance of the rentcharge and perform and observe the covenants and conditions relating to his part.

Where registered freehold land is transferred subject to a rentcharge, rule 109 of the Land Registration Rules 1925 provides that: "covenants (similar to those implied by section 24 of the (Land Registration) Act on a transfer of leasehold land) shall be implied under section 77 of the Law of Property Act 1925 . . . ." Rule 109 appears to conflict with rule 77(4) which requires express reference to section 77 in the transfer. Ruoff and Roper advise[1]: "In view of these inconsistencies, it appears to be normally desirable to state in the instrument of transfer that the covenants implied under section 77 of the Law of Property Act 1925 are to be implied in the deed." The covenants should be limited to those implied on the part of the purchaser where a fiduciary owner is transferring. It will be

[93] Land Registration Act 1925, ss.24(1)(a) and (2).
[94] Law of Property Act 1925, s.76(1)(B), Sched. 2, Pt. II and s.77(1)(D)(ii), Sched. 2, Pt. X, para. (ii).
[95] *Ibid*. s.76(1)(B), Sched. 2, Pt II.
[96] Land Registration Rules 1925, r. 115.
[97] *Ibid*. r. 77(4).
[98] *Ibid*. r. 77(2).
[99] *Re King* [1962] 1 W.L.R. 632.
[1] *Registered Conveyancing* (4th ed.) p. 567.

remembered that apart from certain limited exceptions rentcharges can no longer be created, and that existing ones only have a set period to run.[2]

Finally the reader is re-referred to National Conditions 19(7) and Law Society Condition 17(4): the vendor may not insist on an express covenant from the purchaser to cover the same matters as the implied statutory covenants.[3]

THE DESCRIPTION OF THE PROPERTY

If the sale is of the whole of the land (freehold or leasehold) comprised in the vendor's title, a description by reference to the title number suffices. The wording prescribed by form 19 is, "the land comprised in the title above mentioned"; by form 32A, "the land comprised in the title abovementioned for the residue of the term granted by the registered lease."[4] If only part of the land in the title is to be sold, the description should normally refer to a plan[5] on which the land is shown edged in red, give a brief description of the property (usually the postal address) and conclude with the words "being part of the land comprised in the title above referred to."[6] The Registry recommend that the plan be an extract from or based upon, the vendor's filed plan. The plan must be signed by the vendor and the purchaser or by his solicitor on his behalf. However, where the part to be sold can be clearly defined by a verbal reference to the filed plan or general map, often the case in built up areas, a transfer plan can be dispensed with.[7]

Where the part of the registered title is a flat or maisonette the Registry invariably insist on compliance with rule 54 of the Land Registration Rules 1925[8]:

> "on the registration of a proprietor of a flat or floor or part of a flat or floor, of a house or of a cellar or tunnel or other underground space apart from the surface, a plan shall be furnished of the surface under or over which the tenement to be registered lies, and such verbal or other description as the Registrar may deem necessary, together with notes of any appurtenant rights of access, whether held in common with others or not, or obligations affecting other tenements for the benefit of the tenement the title to which is being registered."

The insistence on a plan is despite the proviso to rule 54 that "if the applicant leaves in the registry a reference to the General Map showing with sufficient accuracy the land affected by his application it shall not be necessary for him to leave, deposit or furnish any plan."

Parties frequently attach their own plans to the transfer. As a general rule the registry does not bind such plans into the land or charge

---

[2] Rentcharges Act 1977; see *ante*, p. 303.
[3] See *ante*, p. 375.
[4] Land Registration Rules 1925, r. 98.
[5] *Ibid.* r. 79.
[6] *Ibid.* rr. 98 and 117; forms 20 and 32B.
[7] *Ibid.* r. 79.
[8] Registered Land Practice Notes (1982/3 ed.) Note C2.

certificate; they are often of an informal nature. However in cases such as those of overlapping floors or party walls, where solicitors and their clients have gone to the trouble of having detailed transfer plans prepared on large scales which approximate almost to architectural drawings, the Registrar will, on request consider using them either as an adjunct to or in substitution for the filed plan.[9]

For reasons mentioned earlier,[10] no plan is acceptable to the registry, whether in fulfillment of the statutory requirements or otherwise, if the plan is described in the body of the transfer as being "for the purposes of identification only."[11]

HABENDUM

No habendum is included in form 19. The purchaser gets "the land comprised in the title above mentioned," in other words the freehold or leasehold interest owned by the vendor described in the register.

APPURTENANCES

Rule 251 of the Land Registration Rules 1925 states that "the registration of a person as proprietor of land shall vest in him together with the land all rights, privileges and appurtenances appertaining or reputed to appertain to the land or any part thereof, or at the time of registration demised, occupied, or enjoyed therewith, or reputed or known as part or parcel of or appurtenant to the land or any part thereof including the appropriate rights and interest which had there been a conveyance of the land or manor, would under section 62 of the Law of Property Act 1925 have passed therewith." Rule 251 renders it unnecessary to include in the transfer a clause stating that it includes all such rights, easements, quasi-easements and so on as have hitherto been enjoyed as if the land transferred and the land adjoining had previously belonged to different owners.

NEW EASEMENTS AND RESTRICTIVE COVENANTS[11a]

There is space at the bottom of form 19 for the inclusion of clauses granting or reserving easements and imposing new restrictive covenants. If the space is insufficient the purchaser's solicitor will draft his own form of transfer based on form 19.

Where a transfer creates new easements the Registry automatically makes the appropriate entries of the benefit and burden when the application for registration of the transfer is made. However if the easements are created by a separate deed of grant the onus is on the

---

[9] Registered Land Practice Notes (1982/83 ed.) Note F.3.

[10] See *ante*, p. 322.

[11] Registered Land Practice Notes (1982/83 ed.) Note C1.

[11a] It should be remembered that if the recent Law Commission's Report (Law Com. No. 127) is given statutory force, the creation of new restrictive covenants will be impossible. The "land obligation" will be used instead.

grantee to apply for registration.[12] If he fails to do so the grant will not bind a subsequent purchaser for value.[13]

New restrictive covenants imposed by the transfer will either be set out in full in the charges register of the purchaser's title or the original document creating them (or a copy thereof) bound up in the land or charge Certificate. The benefit of restrictive covenants is not usually noted on the vendor's title unless a special request is made and is never noted where there are several transfers of part imposing restrictive covenants.[14]

INDEMNITY COVENANTS

A vendor at registered land will need to insist on his purchaser[15] giving an indemnity covenant in the transfer in similar circumstances to those in unregistered conveyancing. The most common cases will be where the vendor is to remain liable on restrictive covenants after he has parted with the land, either because he was the original covenantor or because when he purchased he promised to indemnify his vendor, or where it is desired to perpetuate the enforceability of positive covenants. A positive covenant is personal to the original covenantor and does not run against the land unless the original covenantor takes an indemnity covenant from his purchaser and successive vendors do likewise. The vendor will be able to tell whether he entered into an indemnity covenant on his purchase by looking at the proprietorship register of his title. Positive covenants (including of course indemnity covenants) are noted by the registry as a concession,[16] "because the Chief Land Registrar appreciates that when positive covenants are contained in the transfer which is filed in the registry, they tend to be overlooked, or their exact nature forgotten, so that a vendor's solicitor might omit to take an indemnity covenant from the purchaser on a transfer of the land."[17]

We have already seen that National Condition 19(5), (6) and (7) and Law Society Condition 17(4) give the vendor the right to insist on such an indemnity clause being included in the transfer. The form of covenant stipulated for by National Condition 19(6), that the purchaser observe and perform the covenants and indemnity the vendor is to be preferred to one providing for indemnity only, as required by Law Society 17(4). An injunction to restrain a breach might be obtainable under the former[18] but not under the latter type of covenant.

No express indemnity covenant is required[19] in a transfer of registered leasehold land in respect of positive or restrictive covenants contained in

---

[12] Land Registration Act 1925, ss.19(2) and 22(2). Registered Land Practice Notes (1982/3 ed.) Note I.1.

[13] Land Registration Act 1925, ss.20(1) and 23(1).

[14] T.B. Ruoff and C. West, *Concise Land Registration Practice* (3rd ed.) p. 111. The same procedure will initially be followed for the "land obligation".

[15] The covenant would be joint and several, if more than one purchaser.

[16] Not by virtue of any statutory provision.

[17] T.B. Ruoff and C. West *Concise Land Registration Practice* (3rd ed.) p. 111.

[18] *Re Poole and Clarke's Contract* [1904] 2 Ch. 173 and see *ante*, Chap. 6, p. 166. This will be unnecessary in the future in respect of "land obligation", but such a clause will still remain important in respect of existing covenants.

[19] Nor can they be insisted upon under National Condition 19(7), or Law Society 17(4).

the registered lease. Such covenants are automatically implied into the transfer by section 24 of the Land Registration Act 1925, unless negatived wholly or in part.

ACKNOWLEDGMENT AND UNDERTAKING

Since the whole idea of the registration system is to dispense with the history of past ownership of land and to record all matters relevant to a particular title on the register, an acknowledgment or undertaking for the production of documents is, as a rule, unnecessary. Indeed Ruoff and Roper[20] describe the inclusion of an acknowledgment or undertaking in a transfer of land registered with absolute or good leasehold title as "mere verbiage." However an acknowledgment and undertaking should be obtained where the vendor only has a possessory or qualified title in respect of pre-registration deeds (as in unregistered conveyancing) and where part only of registered leasehold land is being sold, in respect of the lease itself.

CERTIFICATE OF VALUE

This serves the same purpose as in unregistered conveyancing, namely to enable the purchaser to claim an exemption from stamp duty where the consideration for his purchase does not exceed £30,000.[21] No certificate of value is included in the specimen transfer to Glyn Thomas because the purchase price is £38,000. Stamp duty at the ordinary rate of 1 per cent. is payable; £380. A gift bears duty according to the value of the property.[22] If the value is £30,000 or less a certificate of value should be included, the word "consideration" being replaced by the word "property," so that the donee is not charged duty. Once the transfer has been duly stamped, the registry can assess their fees for registration.[23]

EXECUTION

The transfer should be executed in the same way as in unregistered conveyancing. The party or parties' signatures should be attested by a witness. The registry "having no discrimination on the grounds of sex"[24] do not object to the husband or wife of a party to a deed being an attesting witness. Remember that if the transfer incorporates a plan, the plan must be signed by the vendor and the purchaser or a solicitor on his behalf. A company "signs" plans in the same way as deeds; by use of the company's seal attested by its officers.

---

[20] *Registered Conveyancing* (4th ed.) p. 327.
[21] Finance Act 1984.
[22] Finance Act 1910, s.74.
[23] See Land Registration Fee Order 1981 (S.I. 1981 No. 54).
[24] T.B. Ruoff and C. West, *Concise Land Registration Practice* (3rd ed.) p. 77.

8: Completion

I THE FINANCIAL SIDE OF COMPLETION

The aim, one hopes of any conveyancing transaction, and indeed this book, is "having all its parts entire,"[1] so that the vendor receives his money and the purchaser obtains the property—"completion." The "moves" necessary to achieve this aim have been plotted in previous chapters. Now so near to its actual realisation, the financial side of completion must be looked at.

Completion Statements

Here is a simple completion statement, concocted on the basis that rates are to be apportioned between the parties:

COLE to PORTER

8 ROYAL DRIVE, TABOCK, AVON

Completion Statement made up to 1st March, 1984

	£	£
Purchase price		40,000.00
Less Deposit		4,000.00
		36,000.00
Add:		
Proportion of general rates from 1st March to 31st March, 1984 (31 days) at £472.00 p.a.	40.09	
Proportion of water rate for same period (31 days) at £49.00 p.a.	4.16	
Proportion of water services charge for same period (31 days) at £51.00 p.a.	4.33	
		48.58
Balance payable on completion		£36,048.58

Please provide the above sum in two drafts in favour of:
(1) Tabock Building Society for £7,100.18.
(2) Ourselves (Gate and Son) for £28,948.40.

---

[1] Definition of "complete," Concise Oxford Dictionary.

The object of a completion statement is to inform the purchaser of the exact amount of money he requires to complete his purchase and to whom it should be paid. The final sum will represent the purchase price, less any deposit paid, plus or minus an apportionment of the income and outgoings of the property, depending on whether they are payable in advance or in arrear, plus any amount to be paid for chattels and fittings and where appropriate a figure representing interest on the balance of the purchase price. The statement is normally sent by the vendor's solicitors to the purchaser's solicitors about a week to 10 days before completion, to give the purchaser time to make the necessary financial arrangements. A request for a completion statement is included in the standard form of requisitions on title.[2]

Apportionments

Irrespective of whether a purchase is completed at the contractual time or subsequently, some financial adjustment of the income and outgoings of the property is usually desirable, to prevent one party benefiting at the expense of the other from payments made. The vendor may, for example, pay the water rate in advance and wish to recoup from the purchaser the amount paid for the future, or the vendor may have been paid rent in advance by a tenant in which case the purchaser will want deducted from the purchase price, that proportion of the rent to which he is entitled. Both sets of standard conditions contain provisions for the apportionment of income and outgoings. The calculations are normally carried out on a daily basis and included in the completion statement as part of the purchase price. The necessity for contractual apportionment provisions was seen as early as the late 19th century, when practical difficulties were encountered in making a final settlement on completion of the parties' financial rights and liabilities under the open contract rules, especially in connection with rents. To appreciate the modern apportionment provisions a brief look must be taken at the parties' entitlement to the rents and profits of the property and liability for outgoings under an open contract.

THE OPEN CONTRACT POSITION

(a) **Rent.** Under an open contract completion should take place at the date on which good title is first shown.[3] The vendor is entitled to the rents and profits of the property down to this date, the purchaser thereafter. If completion is delayed, any rents received by the vendor must be held by him as a trustee and he must account for them to the purchaser on completion. If the parties agree a completion date but the contract is

---

[2] See *ante*, p. 354.
[3] *Re Highett and Bird's Contract* [1903] 1 Ch. 287.

otherwise open, the fixed date is substituted for the date on which good title is first shown.[4] There are two exceptions to this general rule:

(i) Where delay is due to default on the part of the vendor, he may have to continue receiving rents until actual completion, instead of interest on the balance of the purchase price from the purchaser[5]; and

(ii) If the purchaser is in possession as a tenant of the vendor, his entitlement to rent runs from the date of the contract or where the purchaser otherwise takes possession, from the date of possession.[6] In either case the purchaser compensates the vendor by paying interest.

The main problem with these rules occurs when rent is payable in arrears. In the absence of express stipulation, the vendor cannot require the purchaser to pay him an apportioned part of rent accruing at completion until the purchaser actually receives it. This could (and did) lead to vendors having to send their purchasers rent demands well after completion had taken place.

(b) **Outgoings.** The vendor is responsible for all expenses and outgoings which are a *charge* on the property to the time when good title is first shown, or the contractual completion date in an otherwise open contract. Thereafter such outgoings must be borne by the purchaser. Thus in *Stock* v. *Meakin,*[7] the vendor was held liable to pay the cost of street works completed but not assessed until after the contractual completion date. The cost became a charge on the property on completion of the works. By contrast the purchaser in *Egg* v. *Blaney*[8] was unsuccessful in recovering the amount of paving works which had been billed to the vendor before he had contracted to sell the property to the purchaser. The cost of the works did not constitute a charge on the property, it was a sum recoverable personally from the owner of the property for the time being and the vendor was therefore not in breach of his implied covenant of freedom from incumbrances. Under an open contract a purchaser should insist that such sums are paid by the vendor before completion, otherwise when he has to pay them he will be left without recourse.

Rates are yet another creature of expense. They are not charged on the property but are payable by the occupier.[9] As *Liverpool Corporation* v. *Hope*[10] illustrates, a purchaser cannot be held liable to pay arrears of rates unpaid by his vendor. However in the absence of express apportionment provisions problems can arise where the contractual completion date falls between the end of one rating period and the fixing of a new rate, or where the vendor has paid the rate in advance or by instalments and so on. In practice such problems can always be overcome by asking the local authority to assess the vendor and purchaser separately.

---

[4] *Esdaile* v. *Stephenson* (1822) 1 Sim. & St. 122.
[5] *Re Hewitt's Contract* [1963] 1 W.L.R. 1298.
[6] *Fludyer* v. *Cocker* (1806) 12 Ves. 25.
[7] [1900] 1 Ch. 683.
[8] [1888] Q.B. 107.
[9] General Rate Act 1967 s.16.
[10] [1938] 1 K.B. 751.

APPORTIONMENTS UNDER THE STANDARD CONDITIONS OF SALE

(a) **"Income and Outgoings."** National Condition 6 and Law Society Condition 19(3) provide for the "income and outgoings" of the property to be apportioned. "Income and outgoings" has in practice been generally thought of as including rent, general rate, water rate, sewerage charge and ground rent or rent charge. However under Law Society Condition 19(2), where applicable, the vendor is not entitled to require apportionment of liabilities for which the purchaser is not accountable, for example general rate, nor any outstanding sums the purchaser has no power to collect. Neither the National nor the Law Society Condition allows the apportionment of a capital sum. In *Re Jacobs and Stedman's Contract*[11] Farwell J. held that an instalment of war damage contribution payable on a property by the owner, was not an "outgoing" so as to be liable to apportionment between him and a purchaser from him; the vendor had to pay the whole amount.

The Council of the Law Society have stated that fire insurance premiums are also not "outgoings" within the conditions.[12] With the ruling in mind difficulty is seen in the provisions of National Condition 21(3), which provides that in a case where the vendor keeps his insurance policy on foot after exchange of contracts, the purchaser may require him to have his (the purchaser's) interest endorsed thereon. Provided that the purchaser also pays a proportionate part of the premiums, he will be able to make a claim under the vendor's policy in the event of damage occurring to the property in between contract and completion by virtue of section 47 of the Law of Property Act 1925. The condition further provides that "in such case the vendor (keeping the policy on foot) may require the purchaser to pay on completion a proportionate part of the premium from the date of the contract." Two questions spring to mind. First, can the purchaser use section 47 if he has not actually paid his part of the premiums, but is merely willing to pay them? Secondly, are insurance premiums capable of apportionment on completion? If the answer to these questions is no, National Condition 21(3) has very little meaning. A similar problem does not arise with Law Society Condition 11. Section 47 is expressly excluded. The vendor need only maintain his insurance policy in between contract and completion in limited circumstances[13] and in any event the purchaser is not entitled to ask for his interest to be endorsed on the policy, nor can he be required to pay a proportion of the premiums.

(b) **When are Apportionments to be Made.** Apportionments under the National Conditions are to be made as from the contractual completion date[14] unless:

(i) Completion is delayed and the vendor elects, before actual completion, to take the income of the property instead of interest on the purchase money (under Condition 7(1)(i)) when apportionments are made as at the date of actual completion.[15]

---

[11] [1942] Ch. 400. [12] Law. Soc. Dig. Supp. 73(*a*).
[13] See *ante*, p. 248. [14] National Condition 6(3). | [15] National Condition 6(1).

(ii) The purchaser is in possession of the whole of the property as a lessee or a tenant at a rent.[16] Apportionments are made as at the date of actual completion, but if a delay in completion is not the purchaser's fault and the purchaser has elected to place his purchase money on deposit in a designated bank (under Condition 7(1)(ii)) the apportionments are made as at the date of the purchaser's notice to the vendor informing him of the deposit.[17]

(iii) Completion is delayed because of the vendor's failure to obtain the reversioner's licence where necessary, or the vendor remains in beneficial occupation after the contractual completion date and the purchaser by notice in writing before actual completion elects that the apportionments shall be made as at the actual completion date.[18]

In each case the day of completion (contractual or actual) is treated as the vendor's responsibility.

Under Law Society Condition 19(1) on a sale with entire vacant possession the apportionment is at the actual date of completion, whether delayed or not. Otherwise the calculation is at the contractual completion date. Again the day of completion (contractual or actual) is apportioned to the vendor.

(c) **Calculation of Apportionments.** National Condition 6(4) says that rates are to be apportioned according to the period for which they are intended to provide and rents (whether payable in advance or in arrear) according to the period in respect of which they have been paid or are payable. The provision is advantageous in that normally all financial matters can be settled on completion, but can be disadvantageous to a purchaser of tenanted property where rent is payable in arrears. On completion he will have to account to the vendor for a proportion of rent which he will not actually receive until some time thereafter. Condition 6(4) further provides that in the interest of simplicity, yearly items are to be apportioned on a daily basis, irrespective of the fact that the payments are actually made by instalments relating to a shorter period (quarterly, monthly or otherwise).

Apportionments under Law Society Condition 19 are generally made on a daily basis.[19] However if a complete payment period is attributable to one party the instalment is to be charged or allowed to that party as a whole.[20]

(d) **Service Charges.** Both sets of conditions contain provisions designed to ease the problem of apportioning liability for service charges under leases. The difficulty is that the amount of such charges is often unknown before the end of the period to which they relate. Unforeseen expenses render their assessment on previous charges undesirable.

---

[16] For the position where a purchaser otherwise goes into possession see Chap. 6 p. 250.
[17] National Condition 6(2).
[18] National Condition 6(3).
[19] Law Society Condition 19(4)(b) and (5)(b).
[20] Law Society Condition 19(5)(a).

National Condition 6(5) provides that if a service charge under a lease is unknown or not readily ascertainable then it shall be apportioned according to the best estimate available at the time of completion, the vendor making the appropriate payment. Both parties then remain bound under the terms of the contract to compensate the other for any under-or over-payment made within 15 days of being informed of the actual amount of the charge. Law Society Condition 19(6) is wider in that it applies to "any sum payable in respect of any period following wholly or partly prior to the apportionment day, the amount of which is not notified to either party before actual completion." It therefore covers service charges (or other payments) under a lease and similar charges in respect of freehold property. Again a provisional apportionment of such sums is to be made on the best estimate available and a final apportionment made when the exact amount of the charge is known.

National Condition 6(5) does not cater for service charges on freehold property. A special condition will have to be drafted to cover the situation.

TAXATION

In effect the parties income tax liability is apportioned in the same way as the income and outgoings of the property.[21] The Board of the Inland Revenue have stated that because of the trustee–like relationship that exists between a vendor and purchaser under a specifically enforceable contract "due account shall be taken for income tax purposes of the apportionment of rents and other receipts and outgoings between vendor and purchaser on the sale of an estate or interest in land."[22]

Interest

Equity deems done what ought to be done. If completion is delayed the parties' financial rights and liabilities must, *inter alia,* be adjusted on actual completion, in order to place the parties, as far as possible, in the position they would have been in had completion taken place on the due date. As Wilberforce J. said in *Re Hewitt's Contract,*[23] "on general principle, it is not right that (the purchaser) should have the income of the property as from the date of the contract [*sic*] and in addition, should be relieved from paying interest on the purchase money." In other words the whole idea of the purchaser paying interest is to compensate the vendor for his loss of the income of the property (or the use of the purchase money) from the contractual completion date until actual completion. As we shall see this "compensation" idea inspired in 1980 the introduction of a revolutionary new condition in the Law Society's contract. Departing from the traditional contractual provision for payment of interest by the purchaser, it makes the party in default in completing compensate the other for loss caused by his default. The position under an open contract and the

---

[21] Income and Corporation Taxes Act 1970, s.86.
[22] For further details see 61 L.S.Gaz. 701; 108 S.J. 752.
[23] [1963] 1 W.L.R. 1298 at p. 1302.

National Conditions will be looked at first; the Law Society Condition contrasted.

INTEREST UNDER AN OPEN CONTRACT

Under an open contract if there is a delay in completion, the purchaser must pay to the vendor interest on the balance of the purchase price from the date on which good title is first shown (or in an otherwise open contract, the date fixed for completion) until actual completion.[24] Since this is also the date on which the purchaser becomes entitled to the income of the property, the parties' financial positions are seemingly maintained, but for the fact that the rate of interest payable under an open contract is the "equitable rate"—a derisory four per cent.[25] However two recent cases indicate that the courts may imply a more realistic rate today. In *Wallersteiner* v. *Moir*[26] (No. 2), W., who had improperly profited from his position as company director, was ordered to pay interest on the judgment sum at one per cent. per annum above the official bank rate or minimum lending rate, "in order to give adequate compensation"[27] to the company. And in *Bartlett* v. *Barclays Bank Trust Co. Ltd.* (*No. 2*) Brightman L.J. said of the four per cent. rule: "In these days of huge and constantly changing interest rates (the movement being usually upwards so far) I think it would be unrealistic for a court of equity to abide by the modest rate of interest which was current in the stable times of our forefathers."[28] In his judgment, the proper rate of interest to be awarded following a breach of trust was that allowed from time to time on the courts' short term investment account, established under section 6(1) of the Administration of Justice Act 1965.

Except where the delay is caused by the purchaser and the vendor remains in occupation of the property to protect it and not for his own benefit, a vendor who remains in possession must pay his purchaser a fair occupation rent from the date when the purchaser has to pay interest until actual completion.[29] In *Singh* (*Sudagar*) v. *Nazeer*[30] Megarry V.-C. calculated a fair occupation rent on the basis of two and a half times the gross annual value of the property for rating purposes.

Provided that the purchaser is not at fault in delaying completion, he may place his purchase money on deposit at a bank and on giving notice to the vendor pay him the interest earned on deposit, rather than interest at the equitable rate.[31] Furthermore if the delay is the vendor's fault, and the amount of interest would exceed the income of the property the purchaser may insist "that the vendor, instead of getting the interest, must be satisfied with the interim rents and profits; but he does not lose both ways."[32]

---

[24] *Esdaile* v. *Stephenson* (1822) 1 Sim. & St. 122.
[25] *Esdaile* v. *Stephenson* (1822) 1 Sim. & St. 122; *Halkett* v. *Dudley* [1907] 1 Ch. 590.
[26] [1975] 1 Q.B. 373.
[27] *Per* Lord Denning M.R.
[28] [1980] 2 All E.R. 92 at pp. 97–98.
[29] *Metropolitan Railway Company* v. *Defries* (1877) 2 Q.B.D. 387.
[30] [1979] Ch. 474.
[31] *Regents Canal Co.* v. *Ware* (1857) 23 Beav. 575.
[32] *Re Hewitt's Contract* [1963] 1 W.L.R. 1298 at p. 1302.

A purchaser who goes into possession before completion is entitled to the income of the property from the date he takes possession, and he must accordingly pay interest from that date until actual completion,[33] even if delay is caused by the vendor. A purchaser in possession as a tenant or lessee of the vendor must similarly pay interest, but as from the date of the contract. Finally, a purchaser in possession cannot by depositing his purchase money at a bank, avoid his liability to pay interest at the equitable rate.[34]

INTEREST UNDER NATIONAL CONDITION 7

National Condition 7 adopts the traditional approach of making the purchaser pay interest in most cases of delayed completion. Thus National Condition 7(1) states: "If the purchase shall not be completed on the completion date then (subject to the provisions of paragraph (2) of this condition) the purchaser shall pay interest on the remainder of his purchase money[35] at the prescribed rate from that date until the purchase shall actually be completed . . . ." It will be noticed that this is one of the few instances where calculations are not to be made by reference to "working days;" the purchaser must pay interest for each day of delay. The "prescribed rate" is either the rate of interest specified in the contract or the rate payable by an acquiring authority on entry under compulsory powers.[36]

By Condition 7(1)(i) the vendor may elect by notice in writing before actual completion to take the income of the property (less outgoings) instead of interest. This, a vendor will only do if the actual income of the property exceeds the amount of interest, and may only do if he would otherwise be entitled to interest. In *Re Hewitt's Contract*,[37] completion was delayed because the vendors, former shareholders of a company in voluntary liquidation, were tardy in registering certain transfers of their title to the bank which was acting on their behalf in the sale[38] of the property to the purchaser. The vendors failed in their attempt to claim the income of the property for the period of the delay. The delay was their fault, they had no right to interest and therefore no right to take income instead.

If the delay in completion is not attributable to the purchaser's default, he may lodge the balance of his purchase money in a deposit account in a designated bank[39] and on giving notice to the vendor, need only pay him the interest actually earned on the deposit, rather than interest at the "prescribed rate."[40] In this case the vendor is not entitled to elect to take income under Condition 7(1)(i).[41]

---

[33] *Fludyer* v. *Cocker* (1806) 12 Ves. 25.
[34] *Re Priestley's Contract* [1947] Ch. 469.
[35] The purchase price less any deposit paid.
[36] National Construction (4) and see *ante*, Chap. 6, p. 166.
[37] [1963] 1 W.L.R. 1298.
[38] Under the 17th ed. of the National Conditions of Sale.
[39] Defined in National Construction (7) and see *ante*, Chap. 6, p. 166.
[40] National Condition 7(1)(ii).
[41] Law Soc. Dig. 4th Supp. 70(*d*).

A purchaser who goes into occupation of the property pending completion under National Condition 8 (*i.e.* not as a lessee or tenant of the vendor), must pay interest at the "prescribed rate" from the date of his going into occupation until actual completion,[42] even if the delay is caused by the vendor. He cannot avoid paying interest at the "prescribed rate," by depositing his purchase money.[43] One allied question is, does a purchaser who goes into possession before completion which is delayed have to pay interest twice, once under National Condition 8(1)(ii) and again under Condition 7(1) for the delay. The answer is no. Condition 7(1)(iii) provides: "That the vendor shall in no case be or become entitled in respect of the same period of time both to be paid interest and to enjoy income of the property, or to be paid interest more than once on the same sum of money."

No interest is payable by the purchaser where the "delay in completion is attributable to any act or default of the vendor or his mortgagee or Settled Land Act trustees."[44] Wilberforce J. had to consider a similar provision[45] in the 17th edition of the National Conditions of Sale in *Re Hewitt's Contract.*[46] He favoured the definition of "default" enunciated by Lindley L.J. in *Re Hetling and Merton's Contract,*[47] where one of two mortgagees, whose consent was needed to release the mortgage, was, to the knowledge of the vendors, going to be abroad until after the contractual date of completion. Lindley L.J. said:

> "If a vendor knows the material facts—knows that there are difficulties which it is his duty to overcome—knows that he may not be able to overcome them by the time fixed for completion, and he fails to overcome them by that time, although no fresh unforeseen occurrence prevents him from doing so, the delay caused by such failure on his part is attributable to wilful default in the sense in which the expression is used in contracts of this description; and his right to interest during such delay is excluded."

Wilberforce J. added in the present case, that it was probably necessary to show more if the condition (as here) only refers to "default." Nevertheless he found that the vendors were in default in not registering the transfers of their title before the contractual completion date. The "default" in question must be the reason for the delay.[48] If not, the purchaser still has to pay interest.

National Condition 7(2)(ii) further relieves the purchaser from his liability to pay interest, "in case the property is to be constructed or converted by the vendor, so long as the construction or conversion is unfinished."

The National Conditions make no provision for the case where a vendor remains in occupation of the property during the delay. The open contract

---

[42] National Condition 8(1)(ii).
[43] *Re Priestley's Contract* [1947] Ch. 469.
[44] National Condition 7(2)(i).
[45] Condition 6.   [46] [1963] 1 W.L.R. 1298.
[47] [1893] 3 Ch. 269 at p. 281.
[48] *Re Mayor of London and Tubb's Contract* [1894] 2 Ch. 524.

rule therefore applies and the vendor may have to pay the purchaser a "fair occupation rent."[49]

LAW SOCIETY CONDITION 22

The financial consequences of late completion are treated entirely differently by Law Society Condition 22. According to Condition 22(2): "If the sale shall be completed after contractual completion date, the party in default (if any) shall be liable to compensate the other for loss occasioned to the other by reason of that default." In the Explanatory Notes which accompanied the 1980 Edition of the conditions, the Council of the Law Society described their new condition as providing "a concept of comparative default." They stated: "This means that if each party has been in default, as defined in the condition, then the period of default for the purposes of compensation is the length of the excess of the greater total over the smaller." The 1984 revision of Condition 22 has made it clear that the "period of default" cannot exceed the period from contractual completion date to the date of actual completion.

A party is "in default" if, and to the extent that the period of his "delay" exceeds that of the other.[50] "Delay" is defined as "failure to perform or lateness in performing any obligation of the contract which causes or contributes to lateness in completion."[51] "Delay," whether in completing or performing any other obligation under the contract is calculated by reference to ordinary days, not "working days." Either party's entitlement (if any) to compensation for late completion is, in other words, directly linked to the timetable[52] laid down by the conditions for the steps to be taken in between contract and completion. Thus, suppose the purchaser is 10 days late in completing, but the vendor was six days late in replying to the purchaser's requisitions on title. The purchaser is "in default" and must compensate the vendor for delay to the tune of four days.

Condition 22 is simple at face-value but more complicated to operate in practice. "Delay" means a failure to perform or lateness in performing an obligation under the contract. Presumably where a party fails to do or is late in doing something which is not an "obligation," his omission or lateness does not count against him, even though the result is that the other party is then late in fulfilling one of his obligations. Thus if the purchaser delivers his requisitions out of time and the vendor gives his replies (which he is therefore under no obligation to give) out of time, the vendor's delay must be ignored in the calculation, notwithstanding the fact that the purchaser as a result cannot deliver the draft conveyance in time. The "delay" in question must cause or contribute to the lateness in completion. One can foresee arguments as to "delays" which count, and those which do not. Condition 22 states that a party is "in default" by reason of "*his* delay." Suppose that delay is caused by events outside a party's control? To take an example specifically provided for in the National Conditions the vendor cannot finish the building work to a new

---

[49] See *ante*, p. 398.
[50] Law Society Condition 22(1)(*b*).
[51] Condition 22(1)(*a*).
[52] See Chap. 6, p. 184 *et seq.*

bungalow because of bad weather[53] and completion is delayed for 10 days. The only party "in default" is the purchaser, for completing late and he must seemingly pay compensation to the vendor. Yet in the equivalent situation governed by the National Conditions[54] the purchaser is relieved from his liability to pay interest.

It is further felt that the Law Society may have been a trifle idealistic in measuring "delay" by reference to a rigid timetable of events. Parties frequently desire shorter or longer completion dates. No problem arises in the latter case if the parties are careful not to adjust the time limits set by the conditions too drastically, but it has been suggested[55] that where a short date for completion is set, then the time limits under the conditions are inoperative, and are replaced by shorter periods under a "reasonableness" approach. This could present problems in deciding whether or not a party had performed his obligations under the contract on time.

Law Society Condition 22 does not apply if neither party is in default and this could work to the detriment of a vendor. Take a sale of tenanted property. Completion is delayed for one week due to the fault of neither party. The purchaser is entitled to the rents for that week but the vendor gets no compensation.

A party entitled to compensation has the choice of suing for damages for his loss[56] or taking a sum equal to interest at the contract rate for the period of delay[57] (liquidated damages[57a]). The second alternative was introduced "to provide a way to finalise the position quickly."[58] He must notify his election to take interest to the other party before actual completion or within five working days thereafter (as to which period time is of the essence). The "contract rate" is defined by the conditions[59] as the rate specified in the special conditions or if none the rate payable by an acquiring authority on entry under compulsory powers. Opting for interest can work to the advantage of the purchaser. Provided that he can show some loss, however small, he can elect to receive interest at the "contract rate" instead of damages and this may well exceed his actual loss. Where however it is the purchaser "in default" the vendor has the further choice of taking the net income of the property instead of damages, provided that he notifies the purchaser before actual completion.[60] The right to compensation (or alternatives) is preserved even though completion has taken place.[61]

Law Society Condition 22 does not relieve a purchaser who goes into possession before completion under Condition 18 from his liability[62] to pay the vendor interest at "the contract rate," from the time of his taking

---

[53] Given as an example by H.W. Wilkinson, *Standard Conditions of Sale of Land* (3rd ed.) at p. 158.

[54] National Condition 7(2)(ii), see *ante*, p. 404.

[55] H.W. Wilkinson, *Standard Conditions of Sale of Land* (3rd ed.) at p. 92.

[56] Accomodating the decision in *Raineri* v. *Miles* [1981] A.C. 1050.

[57] Law Society Condition 22(3).

[57a] The notes to the 1984 revision state: "However the Revenue may be able to treat it as in the nature of interest in the circumstances of a particular case and taxable accordingly."

[58] See explanatory notes accompanying the 1980 Edition.

[59] Law Society Condition 1(*b*).   [60] Law Society Condition 22(4).

[61] Law Society Condition 22(5).   [62] *Re Priestley's Contract* [1947] Ch. 469.

possession until actual completion. Furthermore such a purchaser may have to pay interest twice if completion is delayed due to "his default"[63] under Condition 18(4)(a) and under Condition 22(2). Purchasers' solicitors may wish to avoid this harsh possibility by including in the contract the following special condition: "Interest payable by the purchaser under Condition 18 for any period after contractual completion date shall be allowed as a deduction from any compensation payable by him under Condition 22."[64]

ODD POINTS

In connection with interest it remains to mention a couple of odd points. First, in *Re Debenham and Mercer's Contract*[65] the contract expressly provided that if completion was delayed the purchaser was to pay interest at five per cent. on the balance of the purchase price. Nothing was stated as to whose fault should make interest payable. The contract incorporated the Law Society's Conditions of Sale 1934 edition "so far as they are not varied by or inconsistent with" the terms of the contract. Condition 7 provided that no interest was payable if completion was delayed due to the vendor's default. It was held that the express provision in the contract did no more than fix the rate of interest; it did not exclude Condition 7 of the standard conditions. Since the delay was caused by the vendor no interest was payable. Secondly, in most cases interest on the balance of the purchase money should on completion be paid gross[66]; tax should not be deducted. A purchaser of a dwelling-house who pays gross interest, is entitled to tax-relief thereon.[67] Thirdly, even though a purchaser may dispute the amount of interest he is charged with, once time for completion has been made of the essence of the contract by the serving of a completion notice, he should pay over what he considers to be the proper amount required to complete, by the time the notice expires.[68] If he does not, the vendor may be able to treat the contract as repudiated.

Payment of the Purchase Money

It is usual practice between solicitors for the purchase money to be paid by banker's draft. Although a banker's draft resembles a cheque in appearance, signed on behalf of a bank rather than an individual customer, it is not one,[69] the bank being both the drawer and the drawee. And because it is virtually inconceivable that it would not be met on presentation a banker's draft is treated as the equivalent of cash.

However unless the contract provides for other modes of payment, a vendor can technically insist that he be paid in cash[70]; he may refuse to

---

[63] Reaffirmed by Condition 18(6).
[64] Suggested by Professor J.E. Adams.
[65] [1944] 1 All E.R. 364.
[66] Income and Corporation Taxes Act 1970, ss.52–6.
[67] Finance Act 1972, s.75(3) and Sched. 9 as amended by the Finance Acts 1974 and 1975.
[68] *Schindler* v. *Pigault* (1975) 30 P. & C.R. 328.
[69] *Capital and Counties Bank Ltd.* v. *Gordon* [1903] A.C. 240.
[70] *Johnston* v. *Boyes* [1899] 2 Ch. 73.

accept a cheque or other negotiable instrument, including a banker's draft. A vendor's solicitor should be wary of accepting a cheque for the purchase money, without his client's express authority. If he parts with the title deeds before the cheque is paid and it is subsequently dishonoured, he will be personally liable for any loss incurred by his client. "The ordinary course is, I do not say not to take a cheque but not to part with the deeds until the cheque is paid."[71] In the opinion of[72] The Council of the Law Society a vendor's solicitor should not be asked to accept a purchaser's solicitor's cheque: "His duty to his client is clearly to receive cash or its equivalent . . . if he accepts the cheque without his client's authority he will be in breach of that duty and will be personally responsible for making good the amount immediately if anything should by chance go wrong. That risk is not necessarily limited to the rare case of the other solicitor being in financial difficulties. It could also arise from some unnoticed error in making out the cheque or from the death of the drawer before clearance in the case of a one man practice. Paying by cheque might even prove an embarrassment to the purchaser's solicitor, if, for example his own client found something seriously wrong immediately after completion and specifically instructed him to stop payment of the cheque." They advise that "in the absence of a special arrangement either cash or a banker's draft should be produced."

Both the National and Law Society Conditions give recognition to the practice of paying completion moneys by banker's draft.[73] Under the National Conditions the draft must be issued by a designated bank,[74] which includes most clearing and merchant banks and some foreign banks. The Law Society Conditions limit acceptable drafts to those drawn by and upon a settlement bank for the purposes of the Clearing House Automated Payments System or other bank specified in a special condition. A list of present CHAPS banks was given in Chapter Six. National Condition 5(3) provides the purchaser with several other methods of paying the purchase money: authority to a stakeholder to release a deposit, a cheque guaranteed by a designated bank, telegraphic or other direct transfer (as requested or agreed to by the vendor's solicitor), legal tender or any other method agreed to by the vendor's solicitor. Of these alternative modes of payment, telegraphic transfer is perhaps the most often used. It provides a means of achieving a contemporaneous sale and purchase where the parties live at some remove. The procedure is as follows: the vendor's solicitor gives the purchaser's solicitor details of his bank and the number of the client account before completion. The purchaser's solicitor arranges for the completion money to be paid direct to that account, by credit transfer from the client account at his own bank. The vendor's solicitor's bank is requested to notify its customer as soon as the credit is received. One criticism levelled at this method of transmitting funds is that it can cause

---

[71] *Pape* v. *Westacott* [1894] Q.B.D. 272.
[72] (1969) L.S.Gaz. 406.
[73] National Condition 5(3), Law Society Condition 21(2).
[74] See *ante*, Chap. 6, p. 166.

a delay in completion if an account is credited later than the time (usually 2.0–2.30 p.m.) set for completion. It should be noted that under National Condition 5(3) the vendor's solicitor must either request or agree to payment by telegraphic transfer.

Law Society Condition 21(2) gives as alternative methods of payment, legal tender and unconditional release of any deposit held by a stakeholder. The CHAPS service provides for the immediate transfer of funds and so a reference to telegraphic transfer is unnecessary. If however the purchaser's solicitor needed to pay by telegraphic transfer (a special condition in the contract may provide for the completion draft to be drawn on a non-CHAPS bank), this would be permissible under Law Society Condition 21(2)d "otherwise as the vendor shall have agreed before actual completion."

Stamp Duty

The purchaser will not need informing that *ad valorem* stamp duty is payable on a conveyance or transfer on sale of freehold or leasehold property.[75] The ordinary rate of duty charged is one per cent. of the purchase price. If the purchase price is £30,000 or less and the purchase deed contains a certificate of value the purchaser will be able to take advantage of the nil rate band.[76] No stamp duty is payable where the consideration is not more than £30,000. Duty is payable on a gift in the same way but charged on the value of the land,[77] instead of the consideration, and the duty must be adjudged by the Inland Revenue.[78] Generally speaking, *ad valorem* duties[79] are also charged on the grant of a lease. Conveyance on sale duty at the ordinary rate of one per cent. is payable on any premium but the lessee can take advantage of the nil rate band provided that the lease contains a certificate of value and the rent does not exceed £300 per annum. Duty is also payable on the amount of rent. The rate depends on the length of the term.

Land Registry Fees

A purchaser of registered land or unregistered land which requires to be registered for the first time, will also have to pay land registry fees to have his purchase completed by registration. The current fees are tabled in the Schedules to the Land Registration Fee Order 1981. On an application for first registration of title to freehold or leasehold land, the fees are based on the value of the land, usually the purchase price, Where the applicant for first registration is an original lessee, fees are payable in respect of the amount of rent reserved by the lease, as well as any premium paid. Fees for the registration of gifts are based on the actual value of the land, those for the registration of dealings, on the consideration.

---

[75] Stamp Act 1891, s.1 and Sched. 1.
[76] Budget and Finance (No. 2) Bill 1984.
[77] Finance Act 1910, s.74.
[78] The liability to and amount of stamp duty determined.
[79] Stamp Act 1891, s.1 and Sched. 1; Finance Act 1963, s.55; Finance Act 1982, s.128.

II REMEDIES AVAILABLE IN THE EVENT OF DELAY

The proliferation of rules in this area tends to complexity. The reader will therefore tolerate the rather military style in which it is presented.

(1) Where time is of the essence of a contract for the sale of land, the completion date must be strictly adhered to. If one party fails to complete on time the other may treat the contract as at an end, and in the case of a purchaser, recover his deposit or a vendor, sell elsewhere and sue for the difference. This rule is unaffected by the standard conditions of sale.

The parties may make the time for completion of the essence expressly. The contract in *Harold Wood Brick Co. Ltd.* v. *Ferris*[80] stated that completion should be on August 31, 1933 and "if for any reason the actual completion of the purchase is delayed beyond August 31, 1933, then nevertheless on that date the purchase money . . . shall be placed on deposit . . . but the purchase shall in any event actually be completed not later than September 15, 1933 . . . ." The Court of Appeal held that the date, September 15, fixed for completion was of the essence and since the purchaser had failed to complete on that date, the vendor was entitled to treat himself as discharged from the contract and claim damages for the breach.

Or it may be implied from the nature of the property or the circumstances of the transaction. The agreement in the *Ferris* case was for the sale of a brickfield. Had the parties not expressly made time of the essence, Slesser L.J. thought that there was "sufficient evidence contained in the agreement itself that the property, the subject of the contract was not merely a freehold piece of land but was land with kilns, etc. . . . , thereon. Being thus a property intended to be used for trade purposes it would be inequitable to treat the time for completion otherwise than as of the essence of the contract."[81] Similarly, time would impliedly be of the essence for the purchase of a farm,[82] or a cafe or shop as a going concern.[83] Time will also be of the essence for the purchase of a wasting asset, a lease for example. *Pips (Leisure Productions) Ltd.* v. *Walton*[84] concerned an open contract for the sale of a 21 year lease with approximately 15 years left to run. The vendors could not complete on the agreed date, Monday December 3, because their lease had been previously forfeited by the landlords, although the vendors did hope to re-open the forfeiture. Sir Robert Megarry V.-C. held that time was of the essence of the contract. "The principle, I think is that time is of the essence where what is sold is property "which by delay will not be of the same value as at the time of sale:" *Withy* v. *Cottle* (1823) Turn R. 78 at 80 *per* Lord Eldon L.C."[85] The fact that the parties had contracted to "use their best endeavour" to complete the purchase by December 3, did not negative time being of the essence.

---

[80] [1935] 1 K.B. 198.   [81] *Ibid.* at p. 208.
[82] *Stickney* v. *Keeble* [1915] A.C. 386 *per* Ld Atkinson at p. 401.
[83] *Vasilou* v. *Metz* (1960) 176 E.G. 260.
[84] (1981) 260 E.G. 601.   [85] *Ibid.* at p. 602.

Some controversy exists as to the effect of agreeing to complete "on or before" a certain date. In *Lock* v. *Bell*[86] the parties agreed that completion should take place "on or about" November 10. Maugham J. equated the words "on or about" with the words "on or before" and held that time was of the essence of the contract; the purchaser had failed to complete "on or about" November 10 and the vendor was therefore entitled to forfeit his deposit. However, in *James Macara Ltd.* v. *Barclay*[87] the Court of Appeal thought (*obiter*) that the words "on or before" did not make time of the essence of the contract. And in *Raineri* v. *Miles*[88] the point was not argued, for despite the fact that the contract provided for completion "on or before July 12, 1977": "It is common ground that time was not of the essence of the original contract between the appellants and the respondents."[89] The key to the controversey lies perhaps in the fact that in *Lock* v. *Bell* the subject matter of the sale was a public house, whereas *James Macara Ltd.* v. *Barclay* and *Raineri* v. *Miles* both involved the sale of a private dwelling-house with vacant possession, and "it would need very special circumstances to make time of the essence of the contract on a sale of an ordinary private dwelling-house with vacant possession."[90] Nevertheless, in *Tilley* v. *Thomas*[91] time was found to be essential where the purchaser had already sold his house at the date of the contract, and, to the knowledge of the vendor, needed another quickly. And in *Raineri* v. *Miles,* Lord Edmund-Davies suggested[92] that if the purchaser had argued that time was of the essence of the contract because his purchase was part of a chain transaction, he might have been successful.

(2) Whether time is of the essence of the contract or not, either party may apply to the court for an order of specific performance, if the contractual completion date has not been met, or even before it has arrived if one party has reasonable cause to suspect that the other will not complete on time.[93]

In *Marks* v. *Lilley,*[94] Vaisey J. explained this rule by referring to a passage from T. Cyprian William's book, *A Contract of Sale of Land:*[95] "The cause of action (specific performance) therefore, is not a breach of the contract, such as alone gives rise to an action at law for damages, but is the duty considered in Equity to be incumbent on the defendant of actually doing what he promised by the contract to perform. It follows that a breach of the contract by one party thereto is not necessarily a condition precedent to the other party's obtaining an order for its specific performance." In *Marks* v. *Lilley,* the purchaser who had issued his writ for specific performance after the contractual completion date, was

---

[86] [1930] 1 Ch. 35.
[87] [1945] K.B. 148.
[88] [1980] 2 W.L.R. 847; [1980] Conv. 238.
[89] [1980] 2 W.L.R. 847 *per* Lord Fraser of Tullybelton at p. 864.
[90] *Smith* v. *Hamilton* [1951] Ch. 174 *per* Harman J. at p. 179.
[91] (1867) L.R. 3 Ch. App. 61.
[92] [1980] 2 W.L.R. 847 at p. 859.
[93] *Hasham* v. *Zenab* [1960] A.C. 316.
[94] [1959] 1 W.L.R. 749 at p. 753.
[95] (1930) at p. 132.

allowed his costs, even though time had not been made of the essence and the vendor had completed within one week of the issue of the purchaser's writ.

A party's right to apply for an order of specific performance is undisturbed by the standard conditions of sale.[96]

(3) In ordinary domestic conveyancing transactions time is not usually of the essence of the contract. This does not mean that the contract is not broken by delay (see paragraph 5 below). It simply means that in certain circumstances, the innocent party cannot treat the contract as repudiated at the contractual completion date. He must allow the "delayor" a reasonable time thereafter within which to complete. And should the innocent party insist on treating the contract as at an end, the "delayor" may succeed in obtaining an order of specific performance, and as a necessary adjunct to that relief, an order restraining the innocent party from repudiating the contract and suing accordingly.[97]

In deciding whether or not to grant an order of specific performance to the "delayor" the court will look at all the circumstances of the case.[98] The court would not have considered exercising their discretion in the vendor's favour in *James Macara Ltd.* v. *Barclay;*[99] the vendor had contracted to but could not give, vacant possession on completion. The purchaser could rescind the contract and recover his deposit. Specific performance would not have been available to the vendor in *Pips (Leisure Productions) Ltd.* v. *Walton,*[1] he had no title to sell on completion and it made no difference that he might have had subsequently. Furthermore a "delayor" may loose his right to apply for an order of specific performance if he delays unreasonably.[2] What amounts to unreasonable delay in any particular case is a matter of fact. In *Stickney* v. *Keeble*[3] taking into account the legal work to be done, the previous delay of the vendor and the attitude of the purchaser, six months delay was clearly unreasonable. The conveyancing business left to be attended to was small in *Inns* v. *D. Miles, Griffiths, Piercy & Co.*[4] and a month's delay by the purchaser was considered unreasonable. But, in *Re Barr's Contract,*[5] 28 days was not considered time enough for the purchaser to find £50,000.

In an attempt to pin-point the date at which delay became unreasonable, the innocent party would serve on the "delayor" a "notice to complete." This practice has now been refined and incorporated into both sets of standard conditions and is considered below.

---

[96] National Condition 22(1) and *Woods* v. *Mackenzie Hill Ltd.* (1975) 1 W.L.R. 613.
[97] *Stickney* v. *Keeble* [1915] A.C. 386; *Raineri* v. *Miles* [1981] 1 A.C. 1050. This is the true meaning of the Law of Property Act 1925, s.41 and see C.T. Emery [1978] 42, Conv. 144.
[98] *Stickney* v. *Keeble* [1915] A.C. 386.
[99] [1945] K.B. 148.
[1] (1981) 260 E.G. 601.
[2] *Stickney* v. *Keeble* [1915] A.C. 386.
[3] *Ibid.*
[4] (1980) 255 E.G. 624.
[5] [1956] Ch. 551.

(4) "Even where the date for completion was not originally of the essence (either by express provision or in accordance with the above mentioned rules) if delay has been unreasonable, the other party can treat the contract as broken (at an end)[6] without first giving notice. . . . "[7]

Although this proposition may seem self-evident from the rule in paragraph three, it has been suggested that it is often lost sight of in practice.[8] It was cited with approval by Goff J. in *Accuba Ltd.* v. *Allied Shoe Repairs,*[9] where a landlord's delay in serving a notice under an underlease, was held not to be unreasonable in the context of a seven year term. And, it was applied in *Inns* v. *D. Miles, Griffiths, Piercy & Co.*[10] where Sir Douglas Frank Q.C. said, that "the crucial question to be considered is not the validity and effect of the notice to complete but whether a reasonable time has passed in which the purchaser could have completed . . . if so, the plaintiff was entitled to treat the contract as at an end . . . ."

The proposition stands, even where the transaction is governed by the standard conditions of sale, and regardless of whether the innocent party avails himself (effectively or ineffectively) of the "notice to complete" procedures set out therein. In *Woods* v. *Mackenzie Hill,*[11] Megarry J. rejected the argument that years could go by without the delayor ever being in breach of contract (repudiating the contract[12]), if the innocent party did not serve a notice to complete under the standard conditions. In his judgment the standard conditions added to the remedies available against a delayor under the general law. More support can be drawn from the case of *Cole* v. *Rose.*[13] The vendors, having served an ineffective notice to complete under the Law Society Conditions (1970 ed.) sought to rely on the proposition to evade returning the deposit to the purchaser. Mervyn Davies Q.C. accepted the validity of the vendors' submission but found that the purchaser had not been guilty of any unreasonable delay.

(5) Whether time is of the essence of the contract or not, a party is in breach of contract, if he fails to complete on the due date, unless his failure is due to some failure by the other party (for example, to make good title). He will be liable in damages to the other party for his delay. Neither the reasonableness of his delay, the service of a notice to complete nor the subsequent completion of the transaction excuse him. Damages for a vendor's delay in completing the contract will only be nominal, where the delay is caused by the vendor's inability, without fault on his part, to make good title.[14]

---

[6] Writers' own words.
[7] J.T. Farrand, *Emmet on Title* (16th ed.) p. 214, citing *Farrant* v. *Olver* [1922] W.N. 47 as authority. Repeated in (18th ed.) at p. 240.
[8] A. Sydenham [1980] Conv. 19.
[9] [1975] 1 W.L.R. 1565.
[10] (1980) 255 E.G. 624 at p. 626.
[11] [1975] 1 W.L.R. 613.
[12] Writers' own addition.
[13] [1978] 3 All E.R. 1121.
[14] *Bain* v. *Fothergill* (1874) L.R. 7 H.L. 158.

The above was recently confirmed by the House of Lords in *Raineri* v. *Miles*.[15] The case involved two properties in an ordinary chain transaction. The appellants had agreed to sell their house to the respondents, who had in turn agreed to sell their house to C. Both contracts were to be completed on July 12. On July 13, the appellants informed the respondents that they could not complete. As a result, the respondents could not give vacant possession to C. who was, by this time, "on the road" with his furniture and family. The respondents gave the appellants 28 days notice to complete. Both sales and purchases were completed on August 11. C. recovered damages from the respondents for the expense of providing himself and his family with living accomodation from July 12, to August 11. The respondents tried to claim an indemnity from the appellants because of their failure to give vacant possession of their house on July 12.

The appellants resisted the claim by denying that they had broken their contract. Their primary argument was that although they had contracted to complete on July 12, time was not of the essence of the contract and their obligation was therefore to complete on July 12 or within a reasonable time thereafter. There was therefore no breach until that reasonable time had elapsed. The appellants argument reflected a commonly held fallacy (stemming from our third paragraph), that where time is not of the essence of the contract: "it is only on failure to complete within a reasonable time after that (fixed) day that the contract is broken."[16] And a fallacy it was: "several cases are cited as authority but the appellants' counsel concede that they do not support the statement in the text."[17] The House of Lords finally rejected the idea that a contractual completion date can be regarded as a "mere target": "A promise to do something on a certain date is not implemented by doing the thing within a time, reasonable or otherwise, after that date."[18] Even if time is not of the essence of the contract, failure to complete on the agreed date is a "breach of contract which in appropriate cases would give rise to a claim for damages."[19] The appellants had broken their contract and must compensate the respondents for their loss. And the fact that the appellants failure to complete was due to their inability to raise the necessary money, was no defence: "It is axiomatic that, in relation to claims for damages for breach of contract, it is in general, immaterial why the defendant failed to fulfil his obligation, and certainly no defence to plead that he had done his best."[20]

The appellants second argument was that when the respondents served their notice to complete, the contract was varied by the substitution of a

---

[15] *Raineri* v. *Miles* [1981] A.C. 1050.

[16] *Williams on Vendor and Purchaser* (4th ed.) Vol. 2, p. 991, followed by Whitford J. at first instance in *Raineri* v. *Miles* and Goff J. in *Babacomp* v. *Rightside Properties Ltd.* [1973] 3 All E.R. 873. Accepted as correct by Megarry J. in *Woods* v. *Mackenzie Hill Ltd.* [1975] 1 W.L.R. 613.

[17] *Per* Lord Fraser of Tullybelton [1980] 2 W.L.R. at p. 865. See also Viscount Dilhome at p. 853 and Lord Edmund Davies at p. 860.

[18] Lord Fraser of Tullybelton *ibid* at p. 865.

[19] Lord Fraser of Tullybelton following *Phillips* v. *Lamdin* [1949] 2 K.B. 33.

[20] Delay within the rule of *Bain* v. *Fothergill* (1874) L.R. 7 H.L. 158 is the exception.

new date for completion. As they, the appellants, had completed by that date, there was no breach of contract. This argument was also rejected by the House of Lords. The service of a notice adds to the remedies available against a delayor, it does not negative existing ones.[21]

At this point it may help the reader, to bring together the rules set out in paragraphs 3 and 5. This, Lord Fraser of Tullybelton did for us in *Raineri* v. *Miles*, at the end of his consideration of the House of Lords decision in *Stickney* v. *Keeble:*[22] "All these statements show that the noble learned Lords who made them regarded any breach of stipulation as to time in a contract for the sale of land as unquestionably a breach of contract, although they said that a party in breach of that stipulation might be relieved of the full consequences of his breach to the extent of allowing him to obtain specific performance of the contract. There is no suggestion that he would be relieved from any liability for damages."

Three further points must be made before we leave damages. First, it has been suggested[23] that any damages awarded may include a sum for vexation, distress and disappointment suffered by the innocent party and his family. *Emmet on Title* accordingly advises the inclusion of a special condition in the contract, limiting the measure of damages under the general law for delay. Secondly, it was said by Templeman L.J. in the Court of Appeal in *Raineri* v. *Miles*,[24] that if the innocent party is given advance warning that completion will be delayed, he may be able to mitigate or prevent damage, and he is under a duty to do so. Clearly it is in the delayor's best interests to give an early warning of delay, but practical difficulties can be seen in ascertaining what steps it is reasonable to expect the innocent party to take to mitigate or prevent damage.

Thirdly, reference should be made to the standard conditions of sale. National Condition 5(2) leaves the decision in *Raineri* v. *Miles* to operate fully. It states: "Unless the Special Conditions otherwise provide, in respect of the completion date time shall not be of the essence of the contract, but this provision shall operate subject and without prejudice to (ii) the rights of either party to recover from the other damages for delay in fulfilling his obligations under the contract." Law Society Condition 22, we have seen, tries to accomodate the decision in *Raineri* v. *Miles*[24] by providing that a party "in default" in completing is liable to compensate the other for loss occasioned by "his delay." However the condition modifies *Raineri* v. *Miles*, in that (where appropriate) delay by the other before completion, may lessen the amount of damages the defaulting party has to pay.

(6) The usual course of action adopted by a party in the event of delay, time not being of the essence of the contract, is to serve upon the delayor a notice to complete, fixing a reasonable date and stating that if the

---

[21] *Woods* v. *Mackenzie Hill Ltd* [1975] 1 W.L.R. 613.

[22] [1915] A.C. 386.

[23] [1978] 42 Conv. 325 citing *Buckley* v. *Lane Herdman & Co.* [1977] C.L.Y. 3143 and *Jackson* v. *Horizon Holidays Ltd.* [1975] 1 W.L.R. 1468.

[24] [1980] 2 W.L.R. 189.

purchase or sale is not completed by that date then the party serving the notice will regard the contract as at an end, except for the purpose of pursuing such contractual remedies as he may have.

Under the general law the service of a notice to complete is thought to involve a "two stage approach."[25] First, before the innocent party can serve a notice, the delayor must have been guilty of unreasonable delay, and secondly, the notice itself must give a reasonable time for performance.[26] The reason for the "two stage approach" was explained by Lord Simon of Glaisdale in *United Scientific Holdings Ltd.* v. *Burnley Borough Council*:[27]

> "In equity, and now in the fused system, performance had or has, in the absence of time being made of the essence, to be within a reasonable time. What is reasonable time is a question of fact to be determined in the light of all the circumstances. After the lapse of a reasonable time the promisee could and can give notice fixing a time for performance. This must itself be reasonable notwithstanding that *ex hypothesi* a reasonable time for performance has already elapsed in the view of the promisee. The notice operates as evidence that the promisee considers that a reasonable time for performance has elapsed by the date of the notice and as evidence of the date by which the promisee considers it reasonable for the contractual obligation to be performed. The promisor is put on notice of these matters. It is only in this sense that time is made of the essence of a contract in which it was previously non-essential. The promisee is really saying, 'Unless you perform by such-and-such a date, I shall treat your failure as a repudiation of the contract. . . . ' To say that 'time can be made of the essence of a contract by notice,' except in the limited sense indicated above, would be to permit one party to the contract unilaterally by notice to introduce a new term into it."

The "two stage approach" was accepted as valid in *Inns* v. *D. Miles Griffiths, Piercy & Co.*[28] An open contract for the sale of a small holding was due for completion on November, 9. A notice was served on November 19, giving 21 days for completion. Sir Douglas Frank Q.C. considered that a reasonable time for performance had elapsed before November 19; the notice was validly served.

It is submitted that the theortical basis for the "two stage approach" is wrong. The original purpose of serving a notice to complete was to inform the delayor when he would lose his right to apply for specific performance, that is when his delay would become unreasonable. The notice was "an ultimatum threatening recission;"[29] unquestionably the period specified by the notice had therefore to be reasonable. But, what if a notice was not served? The court would decide whether a delayor's failure to complete was unreasonable with reference to the contractual completion date. Why

---

[25] For discussion see C.T. Emery [1978] 42 Conv. 144–160.
[26] *Green* v. *Sevin* (1879) 13 Ch.D. 589.   [27] [1978] A.C. 904 at p. 946.
[28] (1980) 255 E.G. 624.

then the necessity of the first stage; waiting a reasonable time before serving a notice? Mr C.T. Emery, suggested in 1978[29] that the "two stage approach" reflects the formerly held fallacy, that a contract in which time is not of the essence may be completed on the fixed day or within a reasonable time thereafter. In *Raineri* v. *Miles*,[30] the House of Lords put an end to the "or reasonable time thereafter" idea. A contract is broken, when the contractual completion date is not met. Did not the decision also impliedly end the necessity of the first stage in the "two stage approach"?

In any event the problem is academic, where the contract is governed by either set of standard conditions. By National Condition 22(1) either party may serve a notice to complete "at any time on or after the completion date"; by Law Society Condition 23(2), "if the sale shall not be completed on contractual completion date."

The notice itself must give a reasonable time for performance. Under the general law, what is a reasonable time is a matter of fact: "Regard must be had to all the circumstances of the case, and to the practical considerations of the ability in the circumstances of the purchaser to find the money, having regard to reasonable behaviour as well as to mere conveyancing matters."[31] Thus in *Re Barr's Contract*,[32] a notice requiring completion within 28 days gave insufficient time for the purchaser to find £50,000. In *Smith* v. *Hamilton*,[33] 14 days was unreasonable. Harman J. said he could find, "no instance where a delay as short as a fortnight has been held to entitle either a vendor or a purchaser to rescind." Nevertheless, in *Ajit* v. *Sammy*,[34-35] a notice giving the purchaser six days to complete was held valid by the Privy Council; the purchaser had no money and no prospects.

If the notice to complete is served under National Condition 22(2) "it shall become and be a term of the contract, *in respect of which time shall be of the essence thereof,* that the party to whom the notice is given shall complete the contract within 16 working days after service of the notice (exclusive of the day of service)." Law Society Condition 23(3) is in similar terms, except that "the transaction shall be completed within fifteen working days of service." Because both parties agree that time shall automatically become of the essence of the contract when a completion notice is served under the conditions, no question of the reasonableness of the period allowed by the notice can arise.[36] This certainty has however been somewhat sullied by an *obiter* finding of Goulding J. in *Pagebar Properties Ltd.* v. *Derby Investment Holdings Ltd.*[37] A notice requiring completion on August 11, was served upon the purchaser by the vendor under National Condition 22, 18th edition (in similar terms to the current National Condition 22). On August 11 the purchaser's solicitors' managing

---

[29] C.T. Emery, (1978) 42 Conv. 144.
[30] [1981] 1 A.C. 1050.
[31] *Re Barr's Contract* [1956] Ch. 551 at p. 558.
[32] [1956] 1 Ch. 551.
[33] [1951] Ch. 174 at p. 182.
[34-35] [1967] A.C. 255.
[36] As to National Conditions of Sale, see *Cumberland Court (Brighton) Ltd.* v. *Taylor* [1964] 1 Ch. 29; Law Society Conditions of Sale, see *Hooker* v. *Wyle* [1974] 1 W.L.R. 235.
[37] [1973] 1 All E.R. 65.

clerk attended the vendor's solicitors' office to effect completion, but
discovered that part of the property to be purchased was subject to an
undisclosed tenancy. He did not complete, deciding to take instructions
over the weekend. The vendor then refused to complete on the ground
that the notice had expired and purported to forfeit the purchaser's
deposit. In fact the vendor's notice had been ineffectively served, so that
the purchaser could get specific performance of the contract. But
Goulding J. also saw fit to accept counsel for purchaser's contention that
even if the notice had been valid and the purchaser without any fault on
his part only discovered the existence of a defect in title on the last day
for completion, he should have a reasonable time to consider the matter.

Ideally a notice to complete served under National Condition 22 or Law
Society Condition 23 as the case may be, should refer specifically to that
Condition. However in *Babacomp* v. *Rightside Properties Ltd,*[38] the
purchaser sent a letter giving: "Notice to complete the contract in
accordance with its terms." The contract incorporated the National
Conditions of Sale, 18th edition. The Court of Appeal held that the letter
was sufficient to activate National Condition 22. *Babacomp's* case also
shows that it is possible, by special condition, to reduce the time allowed
for completion by the conditions. There a period of 14 days was effectively
substituted.

In computing the date fixed for completion by the notice regard should
be had to Walton J.'s comment in *Rightside Properties Ltd.* v. *Gray*[39] that
Saturday is not a normal working day for most solicitors.

By Law Society Condition 23(7) where the period of a completion notice
had been extended by agreement or implication, either party may invoke
the provisions of the condition again and serve a seven working day notice
to complete, instead of 15 working days. The National Conditions contain
no equivalent and the general law applies. It is possible under the general
law to extend the period of a notice to a fixed date or for a specified
period, time remaining of the essence.[40] Care must however be taken not
to waive the original notice, otherwise a fresh notice will have to be served
making time of the essence. In *Luck* v. *White*[41] the parties negotiated a
new completion date at the expiration of the vendor's notice to complete.
Completion did not take place on the new date, because the purchaser
disputed the amount of interest payable. The vendor claimed that the
contract was ended. Goulding J. said:[42] "If the party who is in the right
allows the defaulting party to try to remedy his default after an essential
date has passed, he cannot then call the bargain off without first warning
the defaulting party by fixing a fresh limit reasonable in the circumstances." The vendor had not done this and could not rely on the fact
that at one time he had, by notice, made time of the essence. The purchaser

---

[38] [1974] 1 W.L.R. 235.

[39] [1975] 1 Ch. 72.

[40] *Buckland* v. *Farmar & Moody* [1979] 1 W.L.R. 221 and see H.W. Wilkinson (1979)
New.L.J. 185.

[41] (1973) 26 P. & C.R. 89.

[42] *Ibid.* at p. 96. *Luck* v. *White* was distinguished in *Prosper Homes Ltd.* v. *Hambros Bank
Executor and Trustee Co. Ltd.* (1979) 39 P. & C.R. 395.

was entitled to specific performance. The moral of the story is, when extending a notice to complete under the general law, expressly state that time remains of the essence.

It is possible that an oral extension of a notice to complete is invalid for offending the provisions of section 40(1) of the Law of Property Act 1925.[43]

An effective notice to complete cannot be served (under the general law or the standard conditions) after a decree of specific performance has been obtained, unless the decree specifically so provides.[44]

"It is not only Scouts who must 'be prepared.' The party who serves on the other a notice to complete must be in a state of readiness and willingness."[45] The common law rule is restated in the standard conditions. National Condition 22(1) provides that "either party, being ready and willing to fulfil his own outstanding obligations under the contract, may . . . give to the other party or his solicitor notice in writing requiring completion of the contract in conformity with this condition." Law Society Condition 23(2) states that the party serving the notice to complete must be "ready, able and willing to complete."

A vendor will not be "ready and willing" if he is not in a position to convey the title he has contracted to sell. In *Pagebar Properties Ltd.* v. *Derby Investment Holdings Ltd.*[46] the vendor failed to disclose the existence of a tenancy affecting part of the property he was selling. He had broken his obligation to disclose existing tenancies and was not "ready and willing" when he served his notice to complete. The notice was ineffective. In *Horton* v. *Kurzke*[47] the vendor contracted to sell her farm with vacant possession, and served a notice to complete on the purchaser at a time when a third party was claiming a grazing tenancy over part of the land and an arbitration award was pending. The arbitrator subsequently found that there was no tenancy claim. Nevertheless Goff J. held that the vendor was not "ready and willing" when she served her notice; she was not then able to prove her title. Further, in *Jneid* v. *Mirza*[48] where the contract was conditional on the landlords licence to assign being obtained before completion, the vendors were not "ready and willing" when they served their notice to complete because the licence had not been obtained by them. The notice was invalid.

In deciding whether a party is "ready and willing" to complete, it appears to be necessary to draw a distinction between "matters of substance" and "administrative arrangements." In *Cole* v. *Rose,*[49] the purchaser did not complete on the agreed completion date because he was unable to raise the money. The vendors served a notice to complete and on failure by the purchaser to comply, resold the property and forfeited the purchaser's deposit. The purchaser sought the return of his deposit and

---

[43] *Clearbrook Property Holdings Ltd.* v. *Verrier* [1974] 1 W.L.R. 243.
[44] *Singh* v. *Nazeer* [1979] Ch. 474.
[45] H.W. Wilkinson (1973) New.L.J. 229, and see Danckwerts J. in *Re Barr's Contract* [1956] Ch. 551 at p. 556.
[46] [1972] 1 W.L.R. 1500.
[47] [1971] 1 W.L.R. 769.
[48] (1981) 131 New.L.J. 472.
[49] [1978] 3 All E.R. 1121.

Mervyn Davies Q.C. held that he was entitled to it. At the time the notice to complete was served, the vendor's solicitor did not know what a registered charge revealed by the purchaser's search related to, and could not then give an undertaking to discharge it on completion. The judge held that the solicitor was therefore not "ready" to complete, he was only "ready in the sense that it was later confirmed that the entries did indeed relate to the charges that he supposed that they did relate to." And for the purposes of serving an effective notice to complete, the vendor or his solicitor must have satisfied himself as to every "matter of substance," so that he is "merely in a position of having to set up the necessary administrative arrangements respecting completion."[50] Examples the judge gave of "administrative arrangements" were: "a completion statement may have to be prepared and agreed or arrangements made for the discharge of mortgages (in the ordinary case[51]), or the time and place of completion agreed."[52] Other examples may include, where it is the purchaser serving the notice, obtaining mortgage monies or making a land charges or land registry search.

Following the decision in *Cole* v. *Rose,* Professor J.T. Farrand[53] pointed out that, "according to the ordinary usage of words, a vendor seems hardly 'ready' (or able) to complete a sale free from incumbrances so long as any mortgages actually remain undischarged," and asks, "can vendors of dwelling-houses subject to a mortgage ever serve effective notices to complete?" He goes on to say, that the answer in most cases is, that the purchaser's solicitor will have assented to particular arrangements for the discharge of a mortgage on completion, by not objecting to the reply to his standard requisition on title asking for the details of such arrangements. The purchasers solicitor is therefore unable to complain of the vendor not being ready. But what if no requisition is made about discharging the mortgage? Law Society Condition 23(2)(*b*) was intentionally drafted to cover any problems arising out of *Cole* v. *Rose:* "A party shall be deemed to be ready, able and willing to complete—(b) notwithstanding that any mortgage on the property is unredeemed when the completion notice is served if the aggregate of all sums necessary to redeem all such mortgages (to the extent that they relate to the property) does not exceed the sum payable on completion." Law Society Condition 23(2)(*a*) provides that a party is also to be deemed ready, able and willing to complete, "if he could do so but for some default or omission of the other party." The National Conditions contain no equivalent provision to Law Society Condition 23(2)(*a*) or (*b*).

When an effective notice to complete is served, time becomes of the essence of the contract for *both* parties. If the server does not complete the party served can take advantage of his notice. In *Finkielkraut* v. *Monohan*[54] the vendor served a notice to complete on the purchaser. It

---

[50] *Ibid.* at p. 1128.
[51] Writers' own words.
[52] [1978] 3 All E.R. 1121 at p. 1128.
[53] [1979] Conv. 161.
[54] [1949] 2 All E.R. 234, applied in *Quadrangle Development and Construction Co. Ltd.* v. *Jenner* [1974] 1 W.L.R. 68.

was not realised until the notice had started to run that there were mistakes in the engrossed conveyance, which could not be corrected by the time the notice expired. The vendor did not complete and the purchaser (who was by this time "ready and willing") gave the vendor three days notice to complete. Still the vendor could not complete and the purchaser was entitled to rescind the contract.

Revised Law Society Condition 9 newly provides for payment of less than the normal 10 per cent. deposit. If the purchaser has paid a reduced deposit and the *vendor* serves a completion notice under Condition 23, the purchaser must pay the vendor the amount requisite to bring his deposit up to 10 per cent.[54a]

III ACTUAL COMPLETION

Meaning of the term "completion"

In *Killner* v. *France*,[55] Stable J. had to determine the precise date on which the purchase of an inn was completed. The purchaser had paid over his purchase money and been let into possession of part, but the inn was destroyed by enemy bombing before the contractual completion date. The judge held that the purchase had not been completed by the date of the bombing. Since there was nothing in the contract to suggest that the parties intended otherwise, he adopted the words of Turner V.-C. in *Lewis* v. *South Wales Railway Co.*[56] that "completion" means "the complete conveyance of the estate and final settlement of the business." Here the lease had not been formally transferred to the purchaser, no apportionments had been made and the purchaser had not been let fully into possession.

There was no "final settlement of the business" and no "completion" in *Maktoum* v. *South Lodge Flats Ltd.*[57] The purchaser of four underleases of flats at the price of £1,250,000, who had paid the purchase money in full and who had been let into possession, was held not to have complied with the vendor's notice to complete. She had "left the vendor in doubt whether she or a company was to be the underlessee," and no counterpart leases had been executed. "Final settlement included constituting the purchaser as owner of the legal estate, by the vendor executing and the purchaser accepting the appropriate deed of assurance."[58] The decision is not however wholly consistent with that in the earlier case of *D'Silva* v. *Lister House Development Ltd.*[59] where the lessor company became bound by affixing its seal to the lease; exchange of the lease and counterpart being unnecessary to complete the grant.

[54a] Condition 9(2).
[55] [1946] 2 All E.R. 83.
[56] (1852) 10 Hare. 113 at p. 119.
[57] The Times April 22, 1980; see [1982] Conv. 1.
[58] *Per* Judge Mervyn Davies.
[59] [1971] Ch. 17.

Undertakings

To facilitate a sale and purchase, a solicitor will often give, on completion, undertakings to attend to outstanding matters; such undertakings given by the client being unacceptable to the other side. If the solicitor does not wish to incur personal liability, he should make this clear in the undertaking itself. In the opinion[60] of the Council of the Law Society an undertaking given "on behalf of my client," or "on behalf of the vendor," without any further qualification involves the solicitor in personal liability. Should he fail to implement his undertaking promptly, the Council will take action to compel him so to do. The Council are also of the view[61] that "solicitors should not give undertakings which they are not in a position to implement personally, or in a matter where circumstances beyond the control of the solicitor may well supervene to make implementation impossible, *e.g.* where there is a possibility of bankruptcy." Perhaps the most common undertakings given in practice are, by the vendor's solicitor, to use the purchase money to redeem the vendor's outstanding mortgage and to forward the receipted deed, and, in the case of a postal completion, on receiving the purchase money to send back all the necessary documents, including, where appropriate, a discharge of the vendor's mortgage. We shall see that a recent Privy Council decision[62] has cast doubts on the advisability of the purchaser's solicitor accepting such undertakings in their current form, and has prompted a new Law Society code of procedure for postal completions.

Completion date and time

These received detailed consideration in Chapter 6. To recap under an open contract it is implied that completion shall take place within a reasonable time, taking into account the legal business yet to be carried out. Where one of the standard forms of contract is used the parties will usually fix a date for completion and insert it in the appropriate place on the contract form. If no date is agreed, by National Condition 5(2), completion shall be on the 26th working day after the date of the contract or the date of delivery of the abstract, whichever is the later, and by Law Society Condition 21(1) on the 25th working day after the date of the contract. To ease the banking arrangements of the parties, Law Society Condition 21(5)(*a*) and (*b*) provide that if completion does not take place before 2.30 pm (or such other as is stated by special condition) then completion is deemed to have taken place on the next working day, for the purposes of claiming compensation for late completion under Condition 22. However the purchaser is only liable to account to the vendor for a deemed late completion under Condition 21(5)(*a*) and (*b*) if the vendor gives him notice within five working days after completion, requiring payment, time being of the essence for the notice. The purchaser

---

[60] 45 L.S. Gaz. 56.
[61] 54 L.S. Gaz. 215.
[62] *Edward Wong Finance Co. Ltd.* v. *Johnson Stokes and Master* [1984] 2 W.L.R. 1.

must then pay the compensation within 5 working days of the receipt of the notice. National Condition 5(5)(*i*) less stringently states that if completion day falls on a Friday, the purchaser must complete before 2.15 p.m. Otherwise for the purpose of calculating apportionments and interest under Conditions 6, 7 and 8, completion is deemed to take place on the first working day thereafter.

Place and Manner of Completion

If the contract is silent as to the venue for completion, the common law rule will apply. The person tendering the money, the purchaser, must seek out his tenderee, the vendor.[63] The vendor may choose to complete at his home, the property or anywhere else, provided that the place lies within England or Wales.[64] However, in practice, the proper place for completion is at the vendor's solicitor's office, or where the same solicitor is not acting for both the vendor and his mortgagee, the office of the vendor's mortgagee's solicitor. Thus National Condition 5(4) provides that completion may be carried out at such office or place as the vendor's solicitor shall reasonably require. Law Society Condition 21(1) says: "Completion shall take place in England or Wales either at the office of the vendor's solicitors or, if required by the vendor at least five working days prior to actual completion, at the office of the vendor's mortgagee or his solicitors." Reference should also be made to the proviso to National Condition 5(4)[65] to the effect that where the sale is with vacant possession, the purchaser may require, on giving reasonable notice to the vendor, that possession of the property be handed over to the purchaser or his representative at the property.

National Condition 5(4) and Law Society Condition 21(1) both contemplate what has lately been described as a "proper English-style settlement;"[66] namely the delivery of a banker's draft against the simultaneous handing over of deeds. This method of completing is usually adopted where both parties reside in the same town. But it should be said that a simultaneous handing over of *all* the deeds does not occur, even in this type of completion, where the vendor's property is subject to a mortgage which is to be discharged. Mortgagees rarely execute their discharges at completion (even if they attend personally) and the purchaser has to content himself with an undertaking given either by the vendor's or his mortgagee's solicitor, to account to the mortgagee and forward form 53 (duly executed) or the receipted mortgage.

If the parties live in different parts of the country, attendance by the purchaser's solicitor at the office of the vendor's or his mortgagee's solicitor, is inconvenient and expensive, if not impossible. One way of overcoming the problem is for the purchaser's solicitor to appoint local

---

[63] *Reading Trust Ltd.* v. *Spero* [1930] 1 K.B. 492.
[64] *Re Young and Harston's Contract* (1885) 31 Ch.D. 168.
[65] Introduced to counteract the decision in *Williams & Glyn's Bank Ltd.* v. *Boland* [1981] A.C. 487.
[66] *Edward Wong Finance Co. Ltd.* v. *Johnson Stokes and Master* [1984] 2 W.L.R. 1.

agents to act on completion. The agent solicitor receives the main draft and attends completion, acting in all respects as if he were acting personally for the purchaser as above. The main disadvantage, apart from the extra cost in fees to the client, of appointing local agents is that the purchase money must be found well in advance; particularly unattractive to the client especially if it involves him in bridging finance. Hence the now common practice has evolved of completing with the vendor's solicitor by post. The purchaser's solicitor advances the purchase money to the vendor's solicitor (often by telegraphic transfer) against the latter's simple undertaking to forward the documents of title.

Both sets of standard conditions provide for completion by post.[67] National Condition 5(4) permits completion "by post, or by means of solicitors' undertakings concerning the holding of documents or otherwise." Law Society Condition 21(3) gives more indirect recognition to postal completions by providing that if a completion other than by personal attendance is agreed, completion shall take place on the date when "the vendor's solicitor holds to the order of the purchaser all the documents to which he is entitled on completion."

HONG KONG-STYLE?

The recent decision of the Privy Council in *Edward Wong Finance Co. Ltd.* v. *Johnson Stokes and Master*[68] is persuasive authority for the proposition that a purchaser's solicitor who completes by post in the above manner and/or relies on the standard undertaking to discharge outstanding mortgages lays himself open to the possibility or a claim for negligence. The appeal from Hong Kong arose out of what their Lordships described as a "Hong Kong-style completion;" remitting the whole of the purchase money, advanced on mortgage to the purchaser, to the vendor's solicitor against the latter's undertaking to forward the documents of title, which would include discharge of the vendor's mortgage—very like our procedure on postal completions. Expert evidence was adduced to the court to show that this was the normal method of completing in Hong Kong. The vendor's solicitor ran off with the purchase money leaving the vendor in possession of the property and the vendor's mortgagee in the possession of the deeds. The Privy Council held that the loss of the money must be borne by the purchaser's solicitors for failing to take the necessary steps to protect their client's interests. Their Lordships said that the purchaser's solicitors should have insisted on a normal "proper English-style completion" by which they meant the purchaser's solicitor handing over a banker's draft in exchange for *all* the necessary documents, including where appropriate a discharge of the vendor's mortgage. Not only did their Lordships betray their ignorance of the common practice in this country of completing by post but also seemed unaware of the standard procedure (adopted on formal and postal completions) of accepting the

---

[67] But not on an agency basis as in the new Law Society code for completion by post.
[68] [1984] 2 W.L.R. 1 ; see T. Aldridge *Property Law Bulletin*, Vol. 4, No. 6, p. 45; M. Brahams 80 L.S.Gaz., 3135.

vendor's solicitor's undertaking that the money handed over will be used to pay off the mortgage debt.

Concern felt amongst the profession led the Council of the Law Society to ask its Land Law and Conveyancing Committee to report on the implications of the *Wong* case. The report has resulted in a new practice code for completion by post, which owing to its importance we set out in full, with accompanying notes.

THE LAW SOCIETY'S CODE FOR COMPLETION BY POST (1984) EDITION.[69]

Preamble

The code provides a procedure for postal completion which practising solicitors may adopt by reference.

First, each solicitor must satisfy himself that no circumstances exist that are likely to give rise to a conflict between this code and the interests of his own client (including where applicable a mortgagee client).

The code, where adopted, will apply without variation except so far as recorded in writing beforehand.

The Code

1. Adoption hereof must be specifically agreed by all the solicitors concerned and preferably in writing.
2. On completion the vendor's solicitor will act as agent for the purchaser's solicitor without fee or disbursements.
3. The vendor's solicitor undertakes that on completion, he:
(1) will have the vendor's authority to receive the purchase money; and
(2) will be the duly authorised agent of the proprietor of any charge upon the property to receive the part of the money paid to him which is needed to discharge such charge.
4. The purchaser's solicitor shall send to the vendor's solicitor instructions as to:
(1) documents to be examined and marked;
(2) memoranda to be endorsed;
(3) deeds, documents, undertakings and authorities relating to rents, deposits, keys, *etc.* and
(4) any other relevant matters.

In default of instructions, the vendor's solicitor shall not be under any duty to examine, mark or endorse any documents.
5. The purchaser's solicitor shall remit to the vendor's solicitor the balance due on completion specified in the vendor's solicitor's completion statement or with written notification; in default of either, the balance shown due by the contract. If the funds are remitted by transfer between banks, the vendor's solicitor shall instruct his bank to advise him by

---

[69] (1984) L.S. Gaz. 858.

telephone immediately the funds are received. The vendor's solicitor shall hold such funds to the purchaser's solicitor's order pending completion.

6. The vendor's solicitor, having received the items specified in paras 4 and 5, shall forthwith, or at such later times as may have been agreed, complete. Thereupon he shall hold all documents and other items to be sent to the purchaser's solicitor as agent for such solicitor.

7. Once completion has taken place, the vendor's solicitor shall as soon as possible thereafter on the same day confirm the fact to the purchaser's solicitor by telephone or telex and shall also as soon as possible send by first class post or document exchange written confirmation to the purchaser's solicitor, together with the enclosures referred to in para 4 hereof. The vendor's solicitor shall ensure that such title deeds and any other items are correctly committed to the post or document exchange. Thereafter, they are at the risk of the purchaser's solicitor.

8. If either the authorities specified in para 3 or the instructions specified in para 4 or the funds specified in para 5 have not been received by the vendor's solicitor by the agreed completion date and time, he shall forthwith notify the purchaser's solicitor and request further instructions.

9. Nothing herein shall override any rights and obligations of parties under the contract or otherwise.

10. Any dispute or difference which may arise between solicitors that is directly referable to a completion agreed to be carried out in accordance herewith, whether or not amended or supplemented in any way, shall be referred to an arbitrator to be agreed, within one month of any such dispute or difference arising between the solicitors who are party thereto, and, in default of such agreement, on the application of any such solicitor, to an arbitrator to be appointed by the President of The Law Society.

11. Reference herein to vendor's solicitor and purchaser's solicitor shall, where appropriate, be deemed to include solicitors acting for parties other than vendor and purchaser.

Notes:

1. The object of the code is to provide solicitors with a convenient means for completion, on an agency basis, that can be adopted for use, where they so agree beforehand, in completions where a representative of the purchaser's solicitors is not attending at the office of the vendor's solicitors for the purpose.

2. As with The Law Society's formulae for exchange of contracts by telephone/telex (republished in [1984] *Gazette*, 18 January, 82), the code embodies professional undertakings and is, in consequence, only recommended for adoption between solicitors.

3. Cl 2 of the code expressly provides that the vendor's solicitor will act as agent for the purchaser's solicitor without fee or disbursements. It is envisaged that, in the usual case, the convenience of not having to make a specific appointment on the day of completion for the purchaser's solicitor to attend for the purpose will offset the agency work that the vendor's solicitor has to do and any postage he has to pay in completing under the code, and on the basis that most solicitors will from time to time

act both for vendors and purchasers. If, nevertheless, a vendor's solicitor does consider that charges and/or disbursements are necessary in a particular case, as such an arrangement represents a variation in the code, it should be agreed in writing beforehand.

4. Having regard to the decision in *Edward Wong Finance Co Ltd v Johnson, Stokes & Master*, cl 3(2) of the code requires the vendor's solicitor to confirm, before he agrees to use the code, that he will be the duly authorised agent of the proprietor of any charge upon the property (typically but not exclusively the vendor's building society) to receive that part of the money paid to him which is needed to discharge such charge.

5. Cl 9 of the code expressly provides that nothing therein shall override any rights and obligations of parties under the contract or otherwise.

As the Notes indicate Clause 3 will protect a purchaser's solicitor who completes by post under the auspices of the Code. Since the vendor's solicitor undertakes that he has the express authority of the vendor and, if need be, the vendor's mortgagee, to receive the purchase moneys on their behalf, if the vendor's solicitor absconds with the moneys they bear the loss. But it has been suggested that the *Wong* case also undermines the standard undertaking given by a vendor's solicitor at a *formal* completion involving the discharge of a mortgage. Surely this too should be extended to show that the vendor's solicitor has the express authority of the vendor's mortgagee to receive the sum necessary to discharge the mortgage.

Receipts

Section 69(1) of the Law of Property Act 1925 states:

> "Where a solicitor produces a deed, having in the body thereof or indorsed thereon a receipt for consideration money or other consideration, the deed being executed, or the indorsed receipt being signed, by the person entitled to give a receipt for that consideration, the deed shall be sufficient authority to the person liable to pay or give the same for his paying or giving the same to the solicitor, without the solicitor producing any separate or other direction or authority in that behalf from the person who executed or signed the deed or receipt."

The section is self-explanatory and needs little further comment. In the opinion of the Council of the Law Society,[70] section 69(1) does not extend to payment to an articled clerk, but this opinion seems to be ignored in practice. Nor does it cover other money payable under the contract for the sale of furniture and fittings. Theortically the vendor's solicitor should be given a separate authority to receive payment of this money, but this is rarely done in practice.

---

[70] Law Soc. Dig., Opinion 163.

Endorsement of memorandum

Law Society Condition 20 provides: "Where the vendor does not hand over all the documents of his title, he shall at completion endorse a memorandum of the sale to the purchaser on the last such document in each relevant title and thereupon produce the endorsed documents for inspection." The National Conditions of Sale have no equivalent provision; the general law therefore applies.

Section 200(1) of the Law of Property Act 1925 gives a purchaser (other than a lessee or mortgagee) of part of land a non-excludable right to require the endorsement of certain rights which he holds over the retained land, on one of the documents of title (of his choosing) kept by the vendor. These rights are "those contained in the disposition to him restrictive of user of, or giving rights over, any other land comprised in the common title." Failure to require such an endorsement does not prejudice the purchaser's title,[71] nor does it relieve him of the necessity to register his rights in the Land Charges Register.[72] Section 200(1) does not apply to the sale of part of a registered title.[73] Endorsement is unnecessary because documents of title are redundant to the registration system. The Registrar automatically notes these rights against the servient title on the presentation of the purchaser's transfer for registration.[74]

Ensuring that a memorandum of sale-off is endorsed on the relevant deed where only part of unregistered land is being dealt with, is considered good conveyancing practice.[75] "In our view, a memorandum should always be endorsed, and be seen to have been endorsed, and a copy of the memorandum handed over and placed with the deeds, duly marked as examined."[76] Not only does it protect the purchaser against a subsequent resale of his property, but averts the possibility of a suit against the vendor for breach of his implied covenants of title should he inadvertently sell the land again to another purchaser.

In the absence of an express contractual provision, the purchaser cannot insist on a memorandum of sale-off being endorsed on the vendor's retained deeds,[77] except in the limited circumstances provided for by section 200(1). Hence the necessity for Law Society Condition 20. Where appropriate, the National Conditions should be extended to include such a provision.

---

[71] Law of Property Act 1925, s.200(2).
[72] *Ibid.* s.200(4).
[73] *Ibid.* s.200(3).
[74] See *ante*, Chap. 7.
[75] H.W. Wilkinson *Standard Conditons of Sale of Land* (3rd ed.) p. 172.
[76] (1983) 127 S.J. 73.
[77] Law Soc. Dig., Opinion 198.

IV AFTER COMPLETION

Stamping the Purchase Deed

Where the conveyance, assignment, transfer or lease to the purchaser attracts ad valorem stamp duty,[78] it must be stamped within 30 days of its execution.[79] If the chargability to or amount of stamp duty payable has to be adjudicated, the deed must be lodged for adjudication by the Inland Revenue within the same time. A deed submitted for adjudication must be stamped within the 14 days following notice of the assessment.[80] Stamping is possible after these time-limits but penalties may be payable as a pre-condition to stamping and a small fine imposed on the purchaser. Any penalty paid is denoted on the deed.

In addition, whether or not stamp duty is payable, certain instruments must be produced to the Inland Revenue within 30 days of their execution, together with a statement of particulars about the instrument.[81] The instrument will be stamped with a stamp denoting that it has been so produced.[82] The instruments are:

(a) any conveyance or transfer on sale of the fee simple in land,
(b) any lease of land for a term of seven or more years, and
(c) any conveyance or transfer on sale of any such lease.

A fine of up to £50 is payable by the purchaser for non-compliance. The standard method of supplying the particulars required by the Inland Revenue is to use form Stamps L(A) 451, commonly referred to as a "P.D. Form" and perhaps the easiest of all conveyancing forms to fill in.

Stamping and payment of stamp duty is usually done in person at one of the various Inland Revenue stamp offices. It is also possible to send deeds for stamping through the post to The Controller of Stamps, Inland Revenue (D), (Direct Post Section), West Block, Barrington Road, Worthing, West Sussex. A completed form Stamps 61 and payment (if any) for the correct amount of stamp duty should be included.

Apart from the levying of fines, the real sanction against non-stamping is that the instrument cannot be produced in evidence in court proceedings[83] and therefore is not a good root or link in a chain of title to unregistered land. A subsequent purchaser would be entitled to insist on the instrument being duly stamped, and this right cannot be excluded by the contract.[84] In the case of instruments relating to registered titles, the Registrar will refuse to complete the transactions by registration unless they are duly stamped.[85]

---

[78] See *ante*, p. 409.
[79] Stamp Act 1891, s.15(2).
[80] *Ibid*.
[81] Finance Act 1931, s.28 as amended by Land Commission Act 1967.
[82] Known as a "P.D." stamp.
[83] Stamp Act 1891, s.14; Finance Act 1931, s.28.
[84] Stamp Act 1891 s.117.
[85] Land Registration Act 1925, s.14(3).

What if an instrument needs to be adjudicated and registered? The process of adjudication can be lengthy and the purchaser needs to lodge his application for registration either within the period allowed for first registration or in the case of a dealing, before the 30 day priority period conferred by his official certificate of search has expired. The procedure is as follows.[86] The purchaser's solicitor should send to the registry the instrument, a certified copy of the instrument and the application for registration, accompanied by a written request for the immediate return of the instrument coupled with an undertaking to return it to the registry, once it has been adjudicated upon. The application for registration is then held over by the registry until the instrument is returned, whereupon it is completed as of the date it was first lodged.

First Registration of Title

A purchaser of unregistered land within a compulsory registration area, must apply for first registration of his title *within two months of completion,* if his purchase is one of the following:[87]

(i) a conveyance on sale of freehold land;
(ii) a grant of a term of years absolute not being less than 40 years from the date of the grant, whether or not a premium is paid;
(iii) an assignment on sale of leasehold land held for a term of years absolute having not less than 40 years to run from the date of the assignment.

The grant of a lease out of registered land (whether in a compulsory area or not) for a term of more than 21 years, also necessitates first registration of title,[88] but the two month time limit does not apply. It should be remembered that no lease is registrable if it contains an absolute prohibition against alienation *inter vivos*[89] or is a mortgage term where there is a subsisting right of redemption.[90]

The current Notes[91] issued by the Joint Advisory Committee of the Law Society and H.M. Land Registry, glibly inform practitioners that there are 18 different forms for use in applying for first registration of title. They soften the blow by adding that use of the wrong form does not result in the application being cancelled, just delay.

The three forms most likely to be relevant to ordinary domestic conveyancing are:

Form 1B   Application by solicitors for first registration on behalf of a recent purchaser (other than a company or corporation) of freehold land.

---

[86] Land Registration Rules 1925, r. 95.
[87] Land Registration Act 1925, s.123(1).
[88] *Ibid.* s.20 and 23.
[89] *Ibid.* s.8(2).
[90] *Ibid.* s.8(1) and s.19(2) proviso (*b*).
[91] Registered Land Practice Notes (1982/3 ed.) Note A.1. A list is set out in Appendix (ii) pp. 58–59.

Form 2F Application by solicitors for first registration on behalf of a recent purchaser (other than a company or corporation) of leasehold land, with absolute leasehold title (Form 2B should be used in applying for good leasehold title)

Form 3F Application by solicitors for first registration, on behalf of an original lessee (not being a company or corporation) with absolute leasehold title (Form 3B should be used in applying for good leasehold title).

On the few occasions where possessory title is sought forms 1B and 2B should be amended to ask for possessory title. Each application form contains a certification that the title has been properly investigated by the purchaser's solicitor. This must be signed by a practising solicitor. Neither a rubber stamp, nor the signature of an unqualified person is acceptable to the registry. The purchaser's solicitor is required (*inter alia*) to disclose all incumbrances affecting the land and explain any land charge registrations. Since the Registrar has to approve the title applied for himself, certain deeds and documents must be included in support of the application for first registration.

APPLICATION FOR FIRST REGISTRATION WITH ABSOLUTE FREEHOLD TITLE

The following should be sent to the *appropriate* district land registry:

(1) Form 1B duly completed and signed by the applicant or his solicitor.

(2) *All* the deeds and documents relating to the title (including of course the purchase deed), that the applicant has in his possession or under his control, including a normal abstract, marked "examined."[92] The abstract should include every deed containing restrictive covenants which affect the land. The registry should not only be supplied with full particulars of restrictive covenants (unexamined particulars are not much good) but also the exact wording of covenants to observe and perform the restrictions.[93] It is a mistake to assume that only the deeds constituting a 15 year title need to be lodged at the registry. Exceptionally, for example, where there are a huge number of old deeds, the registry may accept a schedule of every available deed, coupled with an undertaking by the purchaser's solicitor to lodge any of the deeds on request. All the deeds lodged must be scheduled as individual items. The registry do not like the description "a bundle of old deeds," and will charge the applicant a fee, if a schedule has to be prepared. The contract requisitions on title and official certificates of search of the local land charges and land charges registers should also be included.[94] Omission may lead to registry requisitions and delay.

---

[92] Land Registration Rules 1925, r. 20(i).
[93] Registerd Land Pratice Notes (1982/3 ed.) Note J.1.
[94] *Ibid.* Note A.5.

(3) A certified copy of the conveyance (or transfer, where this has been used instead of conveyance under Rule 72) to the purchaser. The certification must be in the firm name.[95]

(4) Sufficient particulars by plan or otherwise to enable the land to be fully identified on the Ordnance Survey Map.[96] In urban areas the verbal description in the purchase deed usually suffices, otherwise the land should be described with reference to an adequate plan[97] outlining the land to be registered in red.

(5) If the land has been mortgaged by the purchaser, the original mortgage or charge and a certified copy of it.[98]

(6) A list in triplicate of all documents delivered. The first list is returned to the applicant as a receipt at the time the documents are lodged. Another is returned to him on completion of the registration to show which documents the registry has retained.

(7) A cheque for the appropriate fees.

Where possessory freehold title is applied for the applicant need only send those deeds he has (if any) in support of his application. To account for the "hole" in his title he should include a statutory declaration[99] made by him or, if necessary, others, proving the fact of his possession and accounting for the lack of title deeds.

APPLICATION FOR FIRST REGISTRATION WITH ABSOLUTE LEASEHOLD TITLE

Where the purchaser is applying for absolute leashold title, he must lodge, with the appropriate completed application form, the lease, if it is in his possession or under his control, and if he is the original lessee, a certified copy of it.[1] If the applicant does not have the lease, he must produce a certified copy of it or examined abstract. Then, in addition to supplying all the other deeds and documents relating to the leasehold title he must supply normal conveyancing proof of the title to the freehold and all superior leaseholds. If the reversionary titles are registered with title absolute, it is no longer necessary[2] to lodge their land or charge certificates at the registry for this purpose, unless the lease was granted at a premium.[3] Whether or not the reversion is registered the applicant must establish the following (*inter alia*):

(a) if at the date of the grant of the lease there was a subsisting mortgage or charge which curtailed the leasing powers of the lessor, that the consent of the mortgagee or chargee was obtained to the grant;

---

[95] Land Registration Rules 1925, rr. 20(ii) and 309.

[96] Land Registration Rules 1925, r. 20(iii).

[97] The plan must be signed by the vendor and the purchaser (or by his solicitor on his behalf). See *ante*, p. 000.

[98] Land Registration Rules 1925, rr. 92 and 139.

[99] Land Registration Rules 1925, r. 37. The declaration should be in form 4.

[1] Land Registration Rules 1925, r. 41.

[2] Registered land Practice Notes (1982/3 ed.) note D.1 and see *ante*, p. 326.

[3] Land Registration Act 1925, s.64(1)(*c*).

(b) if the lease was granted out of leasehold land, that where requisite his lessor gained the consent of the superior lessor to the grant of the underlease.

Apart from the above, the items which must accompany the application are the same as for an application for first registration with absolute freehold title.

If good leasehold title is sought proof of the title to the freehold and any superior leaseholds is of course not required.

AFTER REGISTRATION

After completion of the application for first registration the land or charge certificate (if there is a new mortgage) will be issued to the purchaser's or chargee's solicitors, and the deeds will be returned.[4] Title thereafter will be deduced in accordance with section 110 of the Land Registration Act 1925, so that the deeds will not often be needed. However, certain deeds remain part of the purchaser's title, for example the lease or pre-registration deeds in the case of possessory and qualified titles, and must obviously be kept. Even in the case of absolute freehold title retention of the deeds is desirable for a variety of reasons, for example to check indemnity covenants. The proprietor of a registered charge has no right to dispose of old deeds; he must return them to the registered proprietor on the redemption of his mortgage. Old deeds may, with the consent of the registered proprietor, be deposited on permanent loan with an approved Archives Repository. Enquiries should be directed to, the British Records Association, Records Preservation Section, Charterhouse, Charterhouse Square, London EC1M 6AU.

An application for first registration of title takes approximately 12 to 14 working weeks to process.

Registration of Dealings

As we have seen, one of the basic principles of registered conveyancing is that a registered disposition must be completed by registration to be effective at law. A purchaser of registered freehold or leasehold property will not obtain the legal estate in the land until the application to register his dealing is lodged with the appropriate district land registry. There is no statutory compunction to register a dealing within a certain time, but in practice a purchaser needs to lodge his application before the 30 days priority period conferred by his official certificate of search of the register runs out.

One of two forms should be used; Form A4 to register dealings with the whole of land comprised in a registered title or Form A5 to register dealings with part of the land in a registered title (other than the grant of a lease). Most purchases in domestic conveyancing involve more than one

---

[4] The registration dates from the lodging of the application. Land Registration Rules 1925, r.42.

dealing with the same land, all of which require registration, usually the discharge of the vendor's mortgage, the transfer to the purchaser, and the creation of a new mortgage by him. The beauty of Forms A4 and A5 is that applications for registration of all these dealings can be made on the same form.

All the dealings should be entered, according to the order in which they are to take priority, in the panel headed "Nature and priority of applications," on page 1 of Form A4 or 5. For example:

Nature and priority of applications	Value	Fee scale para or abatement	£ . p
Discharge of mortgage	—	—	
Transfer	£40,000	4	98.00
Mortgage	£32,000	abatement	
		Total fees paid	98.00

No fee is payable for the discharge of a mortgage. Fees on dealings are assessed on Scale 4 (Schedule 4).[5] Where a transfer and mortgage are registered simultaneously, the normal registry fee is abated.

Then the documents which support the application must be listed; the land certificate, or Form 53 (where there is a mortgage to be discharged), the transfer to the purchaser, and the new mortgage, if any. Certified copies must be supplied of all charges and mortgages and also of the transfer, if it imposes new restrictive covenants.[6] If the transfer is of part, a plan[7] should accompany it.

Panels are then provided for the names and addresses of solicitors to whom requisitions arising from the applications should be sent and to whom the documents should eventually be returned to.

If acting for joint purchasers, the solicitor should remember to indicate (on the back of Form A4 or A5) whether the survivor of the joint purchasers will have the power to give a valid receipt for capital moneys arising. This will enable the registry to enter a restriction on the register, if necessary.

Finally the appropriate fee must accompany the application.

The land or charge certificate will be issued to the purchaser's or chargee's solicitor within approximately four to five working weeks.

Office Copies?

It is recommended that office copy entries[8] of the register, showing the purchaser and any mortgagee as correctly registered, be obtained before any purchase involving title registration is regarded as completed.[9]

---

[5] See *ante*, p.409.

[6] Land Registration Rules 1925, rr. 135 and 309.

[7] This must be signed by the vendor and the purchaser (or a solicitor on his behalf) and see *ante*, p. 317.

[8] Apply on Form A44.

[9] (1980) 124 S.J. 745; (1983) 127 S.J. 73.

The Contract is merged in the Conveyance

Neither the National nor the Law Society Conditions expressly provide that there shall be no merger of any terms to which effect is not given by the conveyance. Therefore the general law applies: "All the provisions of the contract which the parties intend should be performed by the conveyance are merged in the conveyance, and all the rights of the purchaser in relation thereto are thereby satisfied."[10] In other words the contract merges with the conveyance and the purchaser's only remedy is an action for damages for breach of those covenants of title which are implied into his conveyance. The doctrine of merger applies equally to a contract followed by a registered land transfer, although the merger probably does not operate until the transfer is registered.[11] In *Greswolde-Williams* v. *Barneby*[12] the agreement contained a warranty that the drains of a mansion house were sound. The purchaser could not sue for damages for breach of this warranty after completion; the agreement had been superseded by the conveyance.

It is however, only those provisions in the contract which the parties intend to be performed by the conveyance, that become merged. If a provision is intended to survive the conveyance then it is treated as a separate contract, on which the vendor remains liable.[13] The parties may indicate this intention expressly in the contract. For example, National Condition 6(5) provides that the parties shall remain, after completion mutually bound under the terms of the contract, to account to each other in respect of service charges payable under the terms of a lease. The equivalent Law Society Condition 19(6) applies to any sums payable in respect of freehold or leasehold property which cannot be quantified until after completion. Or this intention may be gleaned from the wording of the contract itself. In *Palmer* v. *Johnson*[14] Bowen L.J. said: "When one is dealing with a deed by which the property has been conveyed, one must see if it covers the whole ground of the preliminary contract. One must construe the preliminary contract by itself, and see whether it was intended to go on to any and what extent after the formal deed has been executed." In *Lawrence* v. *Cassel*[15] a builder contracted to sell a house in the course of erection to the purchaser and to complete it in accordance with certain plans and specifications. After completion the purchaser sued the builder for failure to complete the work in a proper and workmanlike manner. It was held that the terms of the contract as to building had not become merged in the conveyance; the purchaser was entitled to recover damages. Again, in *Hissett* v. *Reading Roofing Co. Ltd.*[16] after completion the purchaser found that there was a protected tenant in part of his

---

[10] *Knight Sugar Company Ltd.* v. *The Alberta Railway & Irrigation Company* [1938] 1 All E.R. 366 at p. 269.

[11] J.T. Farrand, *Emmet on Title* (18th ed.) p. 247.

[12] (1900) 83 L.T. 708.

[13] *Barclays Bank Ltd.* v. *Beck* [1952] 2 Q.B. 47.

[14] (1884) 13 Q.B.D. 351 at p. 357.

[15] [1930] 2 K.B. 83.

[16] [1969] 1 W.L.R. 1757.

property. He was able to sue the vendor for damages for breach of a term in the contract to give vacant possession.

Emmet on Title advises:[17] "If it is intended that any obligation contained in a contract should continue to have effect after completion, then, unless it is clearly collateral to the main contract which is carried out by the conveyance, the safest course is the repeat the provision in the conveyance in the form of a covenant."

V NON-COMPLETION

It remains here to consider the rights of the vendor or the purchaser, being the innocent party in one of the following factual situations:

(1) Time is of the essence of the contract. One party fails to complete. The other terminates the contract.

(2) Time has become of the essence of the contract, after the service of a notice to complete. One party fails to comply with the notice. The other terminates the contract.

(3) Time is not of the essence of the contract, but there has been unreasonable delay in completing the sale and purchase. The innocent party terminates the contract.

(4) An order of specific performance has been applied for and made but not complied with. The innocent party applies to the court for permission to terminate the contract.

(5) Time is not of the essence of the contract. There is a delay in completion. One party refuses to complete without having given proper notice and before the delay becomes unreasonable. His refusal is wrongful and amounts to a repudiation of the contract.[18] The other party[19] accepts his repudiation, thereby terminating the contract.[20] It is only in this sense, that is a wrongful refusal to perform the contract, that the term "repudiation"[21] is used in this section.

Although in all five cases, the contract is terminated and the parties are discharged from further performance of it, the rights under the contract remain intact and damages for non-performance can be recovered by the innocent party.

Damages

Theoretically the breach of a contract for the sale of land, should be no different from the breach of any other contract for sale. "The law should

---

[17] 18th ed. p. 247.

[18] As occurred in *Cole* v. *Rose* [1978] 3 All E.R. 1121.

[19] *Howe* v. *Smith* (1884) 27 Ch.D. 89.

[20] This situation can be distinguished from the case of *Woodar Investment Development Ltd.* v. *Wimpey Construction U.K. Ltd.* [1980] 1 W.L.R. 277 because there the purchaser's attempted recission did not amount to a repudiation, which is why the vendors could not terminate the contract.

[21] This being its true meaning. *Johnson* v. *Agnew* [1979] 2 W.L.R. 487; [1980] A.C. 367.

be able to accomodate such matters without indigestion."[22] It does however, seem to have had attacks of hiccups in the past.

In the law of contract, damages are the vehicle used to place the innocent party, as far as money can, in the position he would have been in had the contract been completed. A simple example,[23] well-known to students of contract law is as follows: X buys a manuscript for £10. Had the manuscript been genuine it would have been worth £30. However, due to the vendor's breach of contract, it is valueless. In assessing the damages payable to X, the aim is to put him in the position he would have been in but for the breach of contract; namely owning a manuscript worth £30. The quantum of damages is the difference between the actual value of the manuscript and the amount necessary to purchase the genuine manuscript—£30. Contractual damages are compensatory, not punitive.

In *Johnson* v. *Agnew*[23a], Lord Wilberforce, delivering the judgment of a unanimous House of Lords, made it clear that the innocent party has a right to damages *at common law*[24] where he terminates a contract for the sale of land in any one of our five situations. In the case of a breach of a contract for the sale of goods, the innocent party can normally be adequately compensated by assessing the damages to which he is entitled, at the date of the breach: "But this is not an absolute rule; if to follow it would give rise to injustice, the court has power to fix such other date as may be appropriate in the circumstances."[25] In *Raineri* v. *Miles*[26] it was finally established that a contract for the sale of land is broken at the time agreed for completion if that date is not met. Therefore, it is difficult to see how an assessment of damages made at the date of the breach, could ever do justice to the innocent party in the event of non-completion, except possibly, in one circumstance. That is, where, time being of the essence of the contract, the innocent party elects to terminate the contract immediately the breach occurs. Where time is not of the essence of the contract, even if the innocent party does not wish to continue to try and have the contract completed, he must wait a certain time after the breach has occurred (until the expiry of a notice to complete or until delay becomes unreasonable) before he is allowed to terminate the contract and sue for damages for its non-performance. In *Johnson* v. *Agnew,* Lord Wilberforce took the view that "where a breach of contract of sale has occurred, and the innocent party reasonably continues to try to have the contract completed, it would to me appear more logical and just rather than tie him to the date of the original breach, to assess damages as at the date when (otherwise than by his default) the contract is lost."[27] The vendors in that case had obtained an order for specific performance, which

---

[22] *Johnson* v. *Agnew* [1979] 1 All E.R. 883 at p. 888.

[23] Professor Ogus, *The Law of Damages* at pp. 286–287.

[23a] [1979] 1 All E.R. 883.

[24] So ending the idea that where the court awarded damages in lieu of specific performance under the Chancery Amendment Act 1858, they were ordering a different "species" of damages, with a different basis of assessment.

[25] *Johnson* v. *Agnew* [1979] 1 All E.R. 883 at p. 888.

[26] [1981] A.C. 1050.

[27] *Johnson* v. *Agnew* [1979] 1 All E.R. 883 at p. 888.

subsequently became impossible to enforce because their mortgagees stepped in and sold the property. It was held that the vendors were entitled in substitution, to an order for damages at common law, to be assessed at the date when the mortgagees first contracted to sell the property. The "contract lost" approach was applied to an assessment of the purchasers' damages in *Domb* v. *Isoz*.[28] They had at first claimed specific performance of a contract to sell a house to them, but before the appeal was heard they bought another house to live in. At the hearing of the appeal they successfully elected to have damages instead of specific performance; the date for the assessment of their damages to be the date of their election.

However it is clear, that the "contract lost" approach is not an inflexible rule for the assessment of damages, especially in view of the variability of today's property market. The object of awarding damages is to compensate the victim of the breach; the correct date for assessing damages must depend on what is "just and logical" in any particular case. Thus in *Wroth* v. *Tyler*[29] the appropriate date was the date of judgment. The date of judgment was again found to be the correct one in *Malhotra* v. *Choudhury*,[30] although the date for valuing the property was moved back one year to take account of the plaintiff's delay in pursuing his claim. In *Techno Land Improvements Ltd.* v. *British Leyland (U.K.) Ltd.*[31] the defendants broke their contract to take a long-term lease at a rent of £61,000 per annum in 1974. The plaintiffs sought an order of specific performance. In 1976 they elected to have damages instead because they found short-term tenants. In 1977 they managed to find long-term tenants paying an annual rent of £52,000. The plaintiffs claimed that the contract was "lost" when they found short-term tenants, and that damages should be assessed in that year (which of course meant that they would be higher). It was held that the proper date for assessing damages was 1977; the plaintiffs were under a continuing duty to mitigate their loss and had done so by reletting in 1977.

What type of losses are recoverable? Again the answer lies in the ordinary law of contract. In *Hadley* v. *Baxendale*[32] it was decided that the innocent party may claim for: (i) losses arising naturally from the breach, and (ii) losses which ought reasonably to have been forseen by the party in breach.

In advising the innocent party, sight should not be lost of the decision in *Raineri* v. *Miles*[33]. An amount can be claimed for expenditure, inconvenience and possibly mental distress resulting from the contract not being completed on the due date. The second limb of *Hadley* v. *Baxendale,* is perhaps best explained by example. In *Diamond* v. *Campbell-Jones,*[34] the purchaser wanted the property for development.

---

[28] [1980] Ch. 548.
[29] [1974] Ch. 30.
[30] [1980] Ch. 52.
[31] (1979) 252 E.G. 805.
[32] (1854) 9 Ex. 341.
[33] [1980] 2 W.L.R. 847.
[34] [1961] Ch. 22.

He was not awarded damages for loss of development value, because the vendor was not aware of his intention to develop at the time the contract was made. By contrast, in *Cottrill* v. *Steyning & Littlehampton Building Society*,[35] the vendor knew of the purchaser's development plans. The vendor had to pay damages assessed by reference to the profits both parties contemplated that the purchaser would make. And in *Wadsworth* v. *Lydall*,[36] a purchaser who had delayed in completing was held liable to pay the interest and legal costs incurred by his vendor in borrowing money to complete his own purchase. Any reasonable person could forsee that these type of losses were a probable result of the purchase not being completed on time.

These general principles must now be applied more particularly to the respective positions of the vendor and purchaser as the innocent party.

The Vendor as the Innocent Party

The rule is that the vendor is entitled to the full loss which he has sustained from the purchaser's breach. If the vendor resells the property he may recover as damages, the difference between the contract price of the property and the lower sum on resale, plus the expenses of the resale, provided that the resale is soon enough after the breach for the loss to be attributable to it.[37] If the vendor does not resell he will be entitled to the difference between the contract price and the market value of the property, taken at such date as the court deems "just and logical."[38] A further sum might be recoverable for any loss sustained by him by reason of any delay. In *Bruce* v. *Waziri*[39] the vendor was able to recover, in addition to his loss on the resale, the interest on money borrowed to complete a purchase of which the original purchaser was aware, and the costs of maintaining insurance on the property and keeping it staffed. The vendor must give credit for any deposit paid by the purchaser.[40]

The case of *Cuckmere Brick Co. Ltd.* v. *Mutual Finance Ltd.*[41] is indirect authority for the proposition that the vendor must be careful to obtain the proper market price of the property on a resale, if he wishes to recover his full loss from the purchaser.

What if the vendor suffers no loss or makes a profit on the resale? Irrespective of any loss and even if the contract is silent on the matter, the vendor has an implied right to forfeit any deposit paid by the purchaser.[42] In 1883, Baron Pollock said:[43] "According to the law of vendor and purchaser, the inference is that such deposit is paid as a guarantee for the

---

[35] [1966] 1 W.L.R. 753.
[36] [1981] 1 W.L.R. 598.
[37] *Noble* v. *Edwardes* (1877) 5 Ch.D. 378.
[38] *Johnson* v. *Agnew* [1979] 2 W.L.R. 487.
[39] (1983) 46 P. & C.R. 81.
[40] *Ockenden* v. *Henly* (1858) El. Bl. & El. 485.
[41] [1971] Ch. 949.
[42] *Hall* v. *Burnell* [1911] 2 Ch. 551.
[43] *Collins* v. *Stimson* (1883) 11 Q.B.D. 142 at p. 143.

performance of the contract, and where the contract goes off by the default of the purchaser, the vendor is entitled to retain the deposit." This was reiterated by Cotton L.J. in *Howe* v. *Smith*:[44] "The deposit is as I understand it . . . a guarantee that the contract shall be performed. If the sale goes on, of course, not only in accordance with the contract, but in accordance with the intention of the parties in making the contract, it goes in part payment of it; but if in default of the purchaser, the contract goes off, that is to say, if he repudiates the contract then . . . he can have no right to recover the deposit."

A distinction must be drawn between money paid as a deposit and money paid in part payment of the purchase price. The vendor cannot forfeit the latter.[45] A vendor does not have to return a forfeited deposit, if the purchaser later discovers a defect in his title.[46]

The courts have in the past shown a marked reluctance to interfere with a vendor's right to forfeit the purchaser's deposit. This right has undergone much criticism as being in the nature of a penalty.[47] However in *Stockloser* v. *Johnson*[48] Denning L.J. did indicate (*obiter*) that relief may be granted against the forfeituue of a 50 per cent. deposit. And in *Starside Properties Ltd.* v. *Mustapha*[48a] the Court of Appeal found that the particular provision was penal in nature and gave the purchaser relief in the form of an extension of time within which to complete. But in *Windsor Securities Ltd.* v. *Loreldal and Lester Ltd.*[48b] Oliver J. spectacularly refused to order the vendor to return to the purchaser his 10 per cent. deposit of £235,000 even though the vendor had resold the property for £150,000 more than the original contract price.

RETURN OF THE PURCHASER'S DEPOSIT[49]

The courts have only recently found out, that they *do* have the power to order the return of the purchaser's deposit, under section 49(2) of the Law of Property Act 1925. Section 49(2) provides: "Where the court refuses to grant specific performance of a contract, or in any action for the return of the deposit, the court may, if it thinks fit, order the repayment of any deposit."

Until 1979 there was some confusion as to the circumstances in which a court could order the return of a deposit under section 49(2). In *Schindler* v. *Pigault* (1975)[50] Megarry J. took the wide view that repayment could be ordered "when justice required it" and in the absence of any fault on the vendor's part. He said that in exercising its discretion under section 49(2)

---

[44] (1884) 27 Ch.D. 89 at p. 95.
[45] *Harris* v. *Holland* [1922] 1 K.B. 211.
[46] *Soper* v. *Arnold* (1889) 14 App.Cas. 429.
[47] M.P. Thompson (1981) 125 S.J. 405; J.E. Adams (1983) L.S.Gaz. 2811, H.W. Wilkinson (1984) L.S.Gaz. 1268.
[48] [1954] 1 Q.B. 476.
[48a] [1974] 1 W.L.R. 816.
[48b] *The Times*, September 10, 1975.
[49] H.W. Wilkinson (1980) 130 New.L.J. 668.
[50] (1975) 30 P. & C.R. 328.

the court should have regard to, "a general consideration of the conduct of the parties (especially the applicant), the gravity of the matters in question, and the amounts at stake." In *Cole* v. *Rose*[51] Mervyn Davies Q.C. took this to mean that, "one can contemplate an order under section 49(2) only if there are some special circumstances in the particular matter, being circumstances that suggest that it is perhaps unfair or inequitable that the purchaser should lose his deposit." However Buckley L.J. approved Megarry J.'s wide view in *Universal Corporation* v. *Five Ways Properties Ltd.*[52] He said that the jurisdiction under section 49(2) should be used "in any circumstances which make this the fairest course between the two parties," but he added that the court's discretion should be "exercised judicially and with regard to all the relevant considerations including the very important consideration of the terms of the contract into which the parties have chosen to enter." Thus in this case there was a triable issue as to whether the vendor should be able to forfeit the deposit or return it under section 49(2) and pursue such remedy in damages as may be available to him. Return of the purchaser's deposit (10 per cent. of £1,250,000) was considered to be "the fairest course between the two parties," in *Maktoum* v. *South Lodge Flats Ltd.*[53] The fact that the value of the flats had risen since the termination of the contract by £250,000 and the vendors were expected to make a large profit on resale, may well have been the persuasive reason.

It has been held that although the court may order repayment of the whole of the deposit, they may not order repayment of part.[54] There is authority[55] for the view that the operation of section 49(2) can be excluded by express agreement.

The Purchaser as the Innocent Party

Where the purchase falls through due to the vendor's inability to make good title, the purchaser's right to damages is limited by the rule in *Bain* v. *Fothergill*.[56] He is only entitled to the return of his deposit[57] (if any) with interest and any expenses incurred in investigating the vendor's title. This applies even though the vendor knew that he could not make good title. In Chapter 6[58] we saw that the courts will not allow a vendor to take advantage of the rule in *Bain* v. *Fothergill*, unless he has done all that he can to make good title.[59] Also his inability to make good title because of the presence of a Class F land charge or a notice protecting his spouse's rights of occupation under the Matrimonial Homes Act 1983, does not fall

---

[51] [1978] 3 All E.R. 1121.
[52] [1979] 1 All E.R. 552 at p. 555.
[53] *The Times*, April 22, 1980.
[54] *James Macara Ltd.* v. *Barclay* [1945] K.B. 148.
[55] *Michael Richards Properties Ltd.* v. *Corpn. of Wardens of St. Saviour's Parish, Southwark* [1975] 3 All E.R. 416.
[56] (1874) L.R. 7 H.L. 158.
[57] For which he has a lien over the land *Whitbread & Co. Ltd.* v. *Watt* [1902] 1 Ch. 835.
[58] See *ante*, p. 223.
[59] *Malhotra* v. *Choudhury* [1980] Ch. 52.

within the rule.[60] If however the rule does apply in any particular case, the purchaser can still recover substantial damages by framing his action in misrepresentation,[61] even perhaps, where the vendor has not expressly contracted to give good title free from incumbrances.[62]

If the vendor repudiates the contract for any other reason, the purchaser can recover his deposit with interest, and damages for loss of bargain.[63] In the absence of special circumstances known to the vendor, this head of damages will be limited to the difference between the contract price and the market price of the property; the valuation to be made at such date as the court deems "just and logical."[64] Damages for loss of bargain will not include the purchaser's conveyancing costs[65] but will include his pre-contract expenditure.[66] Any costs incurred in buying another house and the cost of temporary accommodation pending the purchase of the new house may also be recovered.[67]

The purchaser should also claim damages for the vendor's delay (if any) in completing; covering storage costs, temporary accommodation and so on.[68]

In *Cole* v. *Rose*,[69] the vendor repudiated the contract by reselling the property. Although not attempted by the purchaser in that case, it seems that he could have "gone for" the vendor's gain on resale relying on a beneficiary's remedy in rem of "tracing" the land or trust property in the trustee-vendor's hands in its new form of money.[70] *Emmet on Title*[71] suggests "tracing" as a useful alternative to damages in two situations:

"(i) if the vendor has become insolvent, any trust property which can be 'traced' (*i.e.* the proceeds of the sale in breach) would not vest in his trustee in bankruptcy; and (ii) the measure of damages might be less, especially if the sale in breach was at a price substantially above the market value."

The Standard Conditions of Sale

National Condition 22(3) only deals with the rights and remedies of a vendor who terminates the contract on failure by the purchaser to comply with a notice to complete served under the condition: "In case the purchaser refuses or fails to complete in conformity with this condition, then (without prejudice to any other right or remedy available to the vendor) the purchaser's deposit may be forfeited (unless the court

---

[60] Wroth v. *Tyler* [1974] Ch. 30.
[61] *Watts* v. *Spence* [1976] Ch. 165.
[62] *Errington* v. *Martell-Wilson* (1980) 130 New.L.J. 545.
[63] *Engell* v. *Fitch* (1869) L.R. 4 Q.B. 659.
[64] *Johnson* v. *Agnew* [1979] 2 W.L.R. 487.
[65] *Re Daniel* [1917] 2 Ch. 405.
[66] *Lloyd* v. *Stanbury* [1971] 1 W.L.R. 535.
[67] *Beard* v. *Porter* [1948] 1 K.B. 321.
[68] *Raineri* v. *Miles* [1981] A.C. 1050.
[69] [1978] 3 All E.R. 1121.
[70] *Lake* v. *Bayliss* [1974] 1 W.L.R. 1073, [1979] Conv. 326.
[71] 18th ed. p. 250.

otherwise directs) and, if the vendor resells the property within twelve months of the expiration of the said period of sixteen working days, he shall be entitled (upon crediting the deposit) to recover from the purchaser hereunder the amount of any loss occasioned to the vendor by expenses of or incidental to such resale, or by diminution in the price."

Two very recent decisions illustrate that if the vendor resells the property at a loss within a year, it is better to claim damages at large under the general law than to rely rights under National Condition 22(3). In both cases the contracts were governed by the 19th edition of the National Conditions of Sale, Condition 22 of which was in similar terms as the current Condition 22. In *Wallace-Turner* v. *Cole*,[72] the vendor included in his claim for damages under Condition 22(3) an amount in respect of costs incurred in an abortive intermediate resale. He failed to recover this extra sum. The sub-condition only entitled him to recover the liquidated damages therein defined; the costs of the intermediate resale had nothing to do with the actual resale. By contrast, in *Bruce* v. *Waziri*,[73] the vendor's claim for damages at large included items in respect of interest on money borrowed to complete a purchase of which the original purchaser was aware and the expense of maintaining insurance and keeping maintenance staff on the property. It was held that he was entitled to these special damages and was not limited by Condition 22(3) to forfeiting the purchaser's deposit and claiming his loss on the resale. Condition 22(3) operates "without prejudice to any other right or remedy available to the vendor."

Law Society Condition 23 covers the position of either party in the event of their terminating the contract for non-compliance with a notice to complete served under the condition.

Law Society Condition 23(4) states:

"If the purchaser does not comply with a completion notice—
  (a) the purchaser shall forthwith return all documents delivered to him by the vendor and at his own expense procure the cancellation of any entry relating to the contract in any register
  (b) without prejudice to any other rights and remedies available to him the vendor may—
      (i) forfeit and retain any deposit paid and/or
      (ii) resell the property by auction, tender or private treaty.

The vendor's right to forfeit the deposit is subject to the court's jurisdiction to order its return under section 49(2) of the Law of Property Act 1925.

Condition 23(5) then goes on to state:

"If on any such re-sale contracted within one year after contractual completion date the vendor incurs a loss *and so elects by notice to the purchaser within one month after the contract for such re-sale*, the purchaser shall pay to the vendor liquidated damages. The amount

[72] (1983) 46 P. & C.R. 164.
[73] (1983) 46 P. & C.R. 81.

payable shall be the aggregate of such loss, all costs and expenses reasonably incurred in any such re-sale and any attempted re-sale and interest at the contract rate on such part of the purchase money as is from time to time outstanding (giving credit for all sums received under any re-sale contract on account of the re-sale price) after contractual completion date".

The words in italics[73a] emphasise that if the re-sale is caused by the original purchaser's default, the vendor must choose either to sue at common law for damages at large or take liquidated damages under the condition. The latter course may not always be as lucrative but will result in a quicker settlement. The liquidated damages provided for by Condition 23(5) are wider those under National Condition 22. They include interest at the contract rate on the balance of the purchase price until the re-sale moneys are received,[74] and the costs of any attempted re-sale.

Where a vendor sells outside the one year period specified in both sets of conditions, the general law applies.

In view of the harshness of Law Society Condition 23(5) to a purchaser, Condition 23(6) tries to redress the balance in his favour, by providing that if he terminates the contract he may serve notice on the vendor to repay his deposit. The vendor is then liable to pay the purchaser interest on the deposit at the contract rate from four working days after service of the notice until payment.

Apart from the above-mentioned provisions, the standard conditions leave the general law outlined in this section to operate freely.

[73a] Added by the 1984 revision.

[74] In *Talley* v. *Wolsey-Neech* (1979) 38 P. & C.R. 45 it was held that as the conditions (1973 rev.) provided for liquidated damages, no interest could be claimed for the delayed receipt of capital moneys. Condition 23 was accordingly redrafted in 1980 to give the vendor this right.

9: Mortgages

"No one . . . by the light of nature ever understood an English mortgage of real estate." (Lord Macnaughten, *Samuel* v. *Jarrah Timber and Wood Paving Corpn. Ltd.* [1904] A.C. 323 at p. 326.)

INTRODUCTORY

In today's house market a purchase and a mortgage are like love and marriage—they go together like a horse and carriage. No book on conveyancing would be complete without some reference to the chief types of mortgage available to a house buyer, the forms of modern mortgage, the rights of the lender (the mortgagee) and the borrower (the mortgagor) and the procedure to be followed by a solicitor acting for a mortgagee.

For present purposes a mortgage is defined as the transfer of a legal or equitable interest in land as security for a loan.

TYPES OF MORTGAGE

Usually a purchaser will not have the resources to fund his purchase himself. Finance must frequently be sought from an institutional lender; a building society, bank or insurance company. Where this is the case the purchaser will ordinarily have little say in the terms upon which the loan is made. The mortgage will be in standard form. The task of the purchaser's solicitor is then merely to explain to his client the terms of the mortgage and his obligations under it. Generally speaking mortgages fall into four broad categories:

(a) Ordinary Repayment Mortgages;
(b) Fixed Instalment Mortgages;
(c) Interest Only or Standing Mortgages;
(d) Endowment Mortgages.

(a) Ordinary Repayment Mortgages

Along with endowment mortgages this is the type of mortgage most commonly encountered in domestic conveyancing transactions.

The characteristic feature of this type of mortgage is the fact that the repayments are constant throughout the period of the loan. A principal sum is advanced at a rate of interest which is variable. Each month during the term of the mortgage (which is usually a period of between 15 and 25 years) a specified sum is repaid by the mortgagor. This will consist partly of interest and partly of principal. As the mortgage term progresses the amount of the monthly instalment allocated towards repayment of the principal sum will increase until the mortgage is finally discharged.

(b) Fixed Instalment Mortgages

Under this type of mortgage a fixed amount of principal is repaid by the mortgagor each year. In addition the mortgagor pays a sum representing interest calculated on the balance of the principal sum left outstanding, at the rate of interest from time to time in force. For example, A borrows £10,000 from the Stoneybroke Building Society to be repaid over 10 years with interest at the Stoneybroke Home Loan Rate from time to time in force. His repayments[1] for the first four years would be:—

Year	Principal Outstanding	Rate of Interest	Repayment
1	£10,000	10%	£2,000
2	£9,000	10%	£1,900
3	£8,000	15%	£2,200
4	£7,000	10%	£1,700

Although the total (*i.e.* principal and interest) repayment will normally decrease throughout the mortgage term a large increase in the interest rates will lead to a rise in the annual repayment.

(c) Interest Only or Standing Mortgages

As the name suggests in this type of mortgage, only interest is paid during the mortgage term. The principal sum is left outstanding to be repaid as a lump sum at the end of the mortgage term.

(d) Endowment Mortgages

This type of mortgage is effectively not one mortgage but two. First, there is a mortgage of the property. Secondly, there is a mortgage of an approved endowment policy—by way of assignment of the benefit of the policy to the mortgagor.

During the mortgage term the mortgagor only pays interest. However, it is a term of the mortgage of the property, that he shall take out and maintain, so long as the mortgage subsists, an endowment policy. The endowment policy, usually for an amount equal to the principal sum advanced (perhaps with profits) matures at the end of the mortgage term

---

[1] Ignoring any tax consequences.

or on the death of the mortgagor and pays off the mortgage. The mortgagor makes two payments each month; interest on the loan to the mortgagee and the premium on the endowment policy to the insurance company.

Endowment mortgages have become increasingly popular because of their once privileged tax treatment. Furthermore, should the "breadwinner" die the mortgagor's family is at least spared the financial worry of maintaining mortgage repayments.

A mortgage linked to an endowment policy must be distinguished from the "mortgage protection policy" scheme. Under this arrangement an insurance policy is taken out at a fairly low premium to cover the balance of the principal sum outstanding *from time to time* (not the amount of the original advance). If the "breadwinner" dies the principal sum is paid off by the insurance company. The policy is a form of guarantee for the mortgagor's family. If the mortgagor survives the whole of the mortgage period he obtains no pecuniary benefit from the scheme.

(e) Index Linked Mortgages

Recently the Nationwide Building Society has tested the validity of its index-linked mortgage scheme. In *Nationwide Building Society* v. *Registrar of Friendly Societies*[2] the society asked the court to decide whether an arrangement whereby the capital outstanding on a mortgage was increased to reflect any movement in the retail prices index infringed the Building Societies Act 1962.[3] By varying the amount of capital outstanding the Nationwide could offer mortgages at a much lower rate of interest than was usual. The court held that index linked mortgages did not infringe the provisions of the 1962 Act provided the capital treated as due from time to time never fell below the amount of the original advance. This type of mortgage, where the amount repayable in the first years of the mortgage term are low in comparison to ordinary mortgages, would be especially suited to first-time buyers.

Mortgage Interest: Tax Relief

A solicitor acting for a purchaser who is taking a mortgage should advise his client on the tax relief available on mortgage interest.

Tax relief is available to a mortgagor in respect of interest paid on the loan. Currently, relief is confined to interest on the first £30,000 of any mortgage advance or other qualifying loan.[4] Under the old system interest on the loan was added to the mortgagor's personal allowances and his P.A.Y.E. code or tax assessment adjusted accordingly. This system

---

[2] [1983] 3 All E.R. 296. See also *Multiservice Bookbinding Ltd.* v. *Marden* [1979] Ch. 84.

[3] Particularly ss.1(1) and 4(1)(g).

[4] See Finance Act 1972, s.75 and Sched. 9; Sched. 1 to Finance Act 1974 (as amended by Finance Act 1982). Basically loans to improve dwelling houses.

presented problems for the Inland Revenue as interest rates fluctuated wildly in the late 1970s and early 1980s. Each change in the interest rate necessitated a review of tax coding. The Finance Act 1982[5] introduced a system that gives instant tax relief for most mortgagors. From April 1983 the Mortgage Interest Relief at Source (MIRAS) system of tax relief has been in operation.

Under the MIRAS system the tax relief still relates to the interest payable on the mortgage. Borrowers, whose mortgages fall within the scope of the scheme,[6] deduct basic rate income tax from payments of mortgage interest. Therefore, a borrower who used to pay £100 gross interest to a building society would now pay £70 (assuming basic rate income tax at 30 per cent.). The building society claims the balance of £30 from the Inland Revenue.

The MIRAS system is particularly advantageous where the mortgage repayments consist solely of interest, as for instance with endowment mortgages. Where the monthly instalments paid by the mortgagor comprise interest and capital the element representing interest will decrease as the mortgage term progresses. The tax relief available will therefore also diminish causing the amount of the monthly repayment (after deduction of basic rate tax) to increase. Some building societies and other lenders require that the net mortgage repayments remain constant rather than rise as the tax relief diminishes. Some mortgagors will therefore find that their capital repayments will be rescheduled to keep the net monthly payments the same.

Mortgagors who pay income tax at the higher rates will obtain certificates of interest paid from their lenders and can obtain higher rate tax relief through their P.A.Y.E. code or assessment.

Finally, where the mortgage or other qualifying loan exceeds £30,000 the lender is given the choice of whether or not to bring the loan within the MIRAS system. It is likely that many lenders will opt to keep such loans outside the ambit of the new provisions, if only for administrative reasons.

MODERN FORMS OF MORTGAGE

(a) Legal Mortgages of Unregistered Land

Before 1926 a legal mortgage of freehold land was made by conveying the fee simple to the mortgagee with a proviso for reconveyance on redemption (repayment). A legal mortgage of leasehold land took a similar form, namely an assignment of the residue of the term subject to a proviso for reassignment on redemption. In keeping with the policy of the 1925 legislation to vest the legal estate in its true owner, the fee simple or term of years absolute now remains vested in the mortgagor, the

---

[5] ss.26–29 and Sched. 7.
[6] As to which see below.

mortgagee being given a lesser legal estate. Section 85(1) of the Law of Property Act 1925 provides that:

"A mortgage of an estate in fee simple shall only be capable of being effected at law either by a demise for a term of years absolute subject to a provision for cesser on redemption, or a charge by deed expressed to be by way of legal mortgage."

Section 86(1) of that Act similarly provides that the only two ways of creating a legal mortgage of leasehold land are by sub-demise or legal charge. No requirement as to the length of the demise or sub-demise is mentioned in either sub-section. Solicitors usually follow the example set by section 85(2) or 86(2). By section 85(2):

"Any purported conveyance of an estate in fee simple by way of mortgage made after the commencement of this Act shall (to the extent of the estate of the mortgagor) operate as a demise of the land to the mortgagee for a term of years absolute, without impeachment for waste, in manner following, namely:
(a) A first or only mortgagee shall take a term of three thousand years from the date of the mortgage:
(b) A second or subsequent mortgagee shall take a term (commencing from the date of the mortgage) one day longer than the term vested in the first or other mortgagee whose security ranks immediately before that of such second or subsequent mortgage."

In the case of an attempted assignment of a term of years absolute by way of mortgage after 1925, section 86(2) states that the mortgagee in fact obtains a sub-lease and that:

"(a) The term to be taken by a first or only mortgagee shall be ten days less than the term expressed to be assigned:
(b) The term to be taken by a second or subsequent mortgagee shall be one day longer than the term vested in the first or other mortgagee whose security ranks immediately before that of the second or subsequent mortgagee, if the length of the last mentioned term permits, and in any case for a term less by one day at least than the term expressed to be assigned."

The effects of sections 85(2) and 86(2) is illustrated by *Grangeside Properties Ltd.* v. *Collingwood*.[7] The mortgagors executed an assignment of their entire leasehold interest in favour of the mortgagees. The landlord company subsequently claimed forfeiture of the lease for breach of certain covenants and the mortgagees obtained relief as *sub-lessees* under section 146(4) of the Law of Property Act 1925.

A legal mortgage of unregistered land by demise or sub-demise is however rare, the alternative method of the charge by deed expressed to be by way of legal mortgage being preferred. This gives the mortgagee "the same protection, powers and remedies (including the right to take proceedings to obtain possession from the occupiers and the persons in

---

[7] [1964] 1 W.L.R. 139.

receipt of rents and profits, or any of them)" as if the mortgage had been created by demise or sub-demise,[8] but has the advantage, from a drafting point of view, of being much neater in form and capable of embracing freehold and leasehold property at one time. Its use for a mortgage of leasehold property also ensures that no breach of a normal covenant against assignment or sub-letting is committed; although a legal charge gives the chargee the same rights and remedies as if he held a term of years, he does not actually hold such a term.[9] Nevertheless such "protection, powers and remedies" are not confined to "protection, powers and remedies merely as between the mortgagor and mortgagee; it extends to protections, powers and remedies against all persons."[10]

(b) Legal Mortgages of Registered Land

A legal mortgage of registered land, freehold or leasehold, may be created in the same way as of unregistered land, that is by demise or sub-demise or by charge by deed expressed to be by way of legal mortgage.[11] Originally such a mortgage could only be protected by a caution "in a specially prescribed form."[12] Now, by virtue of amendments made to section 106 of the Land Registration Act 1925 by section 26 of the Administration of Justice Act 1977,[13] it is registrable as a registered charge (which is not necessarily the same as a charge by deed expressed to be by way of legal mortgage under the Law of Property Act 1925). Unless and until it becomes a registered charge, it takes effect in equity only and is capable of being overridden as a minor interest unless protected by an ordinary notice or caution.[14] If the mortgage remains a protected minor interest (that is it is not registered as a registered charge) then it is discharged by means of a normal statutory receipt.[15]

The more usual way of creating a legal mortgage of registered land is by registered charge.[16] The charge may be in any form provided that it is by deed and the registered land comprised in it is described by reference to its title number or in some other manner sufficient for the registry to identify it.[17] The charge will be invalid if it contains a clause which purports to take away from the chargee the power of transferring it by registered disposition or deprive the chargor of his right to have the cessation of the charge noted on the register.[18] The prescribed statutory

---

[8] Law of Property Act 1925, s.87(1).

[9] *Weg Motors Ltd.* v. *Hales* [1962] Ch. 49.

[10] *Per* Upjohn J. in *Grand Junction Co. Ltd.* v. *Bates* [1954] 2 Q.B. 160 at p. 168 approved in *Regent Oil Co. Ltd.* v. *J.A. Gregory (Hatch End) Ltd.* [1966] Ch. 402.

[11] Law of Property Act 1925, ss.85(3) and 86(3) and Land Registration Act 1925, s.106.

[12] Land Registration Act 1925, s.106(2).

[13] Introduced as a result of the decision in *Barclays Bank Ltd.* v. *Taylor* [1974] Ch. 137, where a legal mortgage not protected by mortgage caution was nevertheless given priority over a subsequent equitable interest.

[14] Under s.49 or s.54 of the Land Registration Act 1925.

[15] See *ante*, Chap. 7, p. 277.

[16] In accordance with Land Registration Act 1925, s.25(1).

[17] *Ibid.* s.25(2).

[18] *Ibid.* s.25(3).

form of charge is form 45.[19] For the legal estate to pass to the chargee, the charge must be completed by registration,[20] until then it is only effective inter partes.[21] The chargee must therefore guard against the interests of persons in actual occupation right up until the time he lodges his application for registration at the registry; there is always a danger that someone, for example, a tenant under an agreement for lease with the chargor made prior to the charge, may acquire an overriding interest[22] by taking possession of the property in between the making and registration of the charge.

(c) **Equitable Mortgages of Unregistered Land**

The creation of a legal mortgage of unregistered land entails two things; the mortgagor must possess a legal estate in the land and there must be a deed. If there is insufficient interest or formality, or both, the mortgage is necessarily equitable. Writing will however be required under section 53(1)c of the Law of Property Act 1925 (a disposition of an equitable interest in land) or section 40(1) of the same Act (a contract to dispose of an interest in land). Neither of these statutory provisions affects the law relating to part performance, and one act that is invariably regarded as sufficient to partly perform an equitable mortgage is the deposit by the mortgagor with the mortgagee of his title deeds backed up by evidence that the deposit of the deeds was intended as security for a loan.[23] An equitable mortgage protected by the deposit of title deeds is commonly used by banks to secure overdrafts and personal loans. But because of the limited powers possessed by an equitable mortgagee, banks usually insist that the deposit is accompanied by a memorandum of the agreement under seal, which gives them approximately the same rights as a legal mortgagee. Since the apparent object of an equitable mortgage is to cut the cost and time involved in the creation of a formal legal mortgage, it is hard to see why banks continue to prefer equitable mortgages in this form, to legal charges.

An equitable mortgage, which is not protected by the deposit of title deeds, does not arise or affect an interest under a trust for sale or a settlement, and is not included in any other class of land charge is registrable as a general equitable charge under the Land Charges Act 1972.[24] An interesting problem arises in connection with an equitable mortgage in the form of a contract to create a legal mortgage. Is it registrable under the Land Charges Act as an estate contract,[25] or a general equitable charge? If it is registrable as an estate contract it would

---

[19] Land Registration Rules 1925, r. 139.
[20] Land Registration Act 1925, ss.19(2) and 22(2); *Re Boyle's Claim* [1961] 1 W.L.R. 339.
[21] *Grace Rymer Investments Ltd.* v. *Waite* [1958] Ch. 831.
[22] *Woolwich Equitable Building Society* v. *Marshall* [1952] Ch.1; contrast *City Permanent Building Society* v. *Miller* [1952] Ch.840.
[23] *Dixon* v. *Muckleston* (1872) L.R. 8 Ch. App. 155 at p. 162.
[24] Land Charges Act 1972, s.2(4)(iii).
[25] *Ibid.* s.2(4)(iv).

seem to be precluded from registration as a general equitable charge, by the definition of that term. Yet equitable mortgages of this type are registered (if at all) as general equitable charges. Furthermore the effect of not registering a general equitable charge differs from that of not registering an estate contract; the former is void for non-registration against a purchaser for value of any interest in the land, the latter is void only against a purchaser of the legal estate for money or money's worth.[26]

An equitable mortgage of a beneficial interest under a trust should be notified to the trustees to ensure priority.[27]

(d) Equitable Mortgages of Registered Land

Section 106(1) of the Land Registration Act 1925 states that instead of using a registered charge, a proprietor of registered land may mortgage his land in any of the ways permissible for unregistered land. Unless and until that mortgage becomes a registered charge, and only *legal* mortgages and charges are capable of becoming registered charges,[28] it takes effect as a minor interest in equity only. Thus "equitable mortgages" in registered land can comprise both legal and equitable mortgages in the unregistered land sense. As minor interests they need to be protected by the entry of a notice or caution on the register. It is possible for a proprietor of registered land to create the equivalent of a mortgage by deposit of title deeds of unregistered land, by depositing his land certificate with the mortgagee, only for some strange reason the mortgage is called a "lien."[29] The "lien" should be protected by the entry of a notice of deposit or intended deposit on the register. It is worth remarking that the entry of a notice of deposit on the register, prevents the subsequent registration of a legal charge as a registered charge until the notice is withdrawn.

(e) Discharge of Mortgages

The discharge of mortgages of unregistered and registered land was considered in Chapter 7.[30]

(f) "Regulated Agreements" Under the Consumer Credit Act 1974

Whether a mortgage is legal or equitable, of unregistered or registered land, if it is a "regulated agreement" under the Consumer Credit Act 1974 certain requirements must be met. The agreement must be in the form prescribed by section 60; it must be executed in the manner set out in section 61; copies must be supplied under section 62 and 63. Before the

---

[26] Land Charges Act 1972, ss.4(5) and (6).
[27] Under the rule in *Dearle* v. *Hall* (1828) 3 Russ. 1.
[28] *Per* Lord Denning M.R. in *Re White Rose Cottage* [1965] Ch. 940.
[29] Land Registration Act 1925, s.66.
[30] See *ante*, p. 277.

agreement is entered into the mortgagor must be given a copy of the unexecuted agreement and informed (by notice) of his right to withdraw and the method of so doing. He must then be given a "cooling off" period of seven days.[31] If these formalities are not complied with the agreement is "improperly executed" and unenforceable without a court order.

Generally speaking, a mortgage of land will be a "regulated agreement" provided that the mortgagor is an "individual," the loan does not exceed £5,000 and is not made by an exempt lender. Building societies and local authorities are exempt lenders, banks and finance companies are not.

THE RIGHTS OF A LEGAL MORTGAGEE, INCLUDING A REGISTERED CHARGEE[32]

The more important rights possessed by a legal mortgagee are:

(a) to sue for the debt;
(b) to sell the property;
(c) foreclosure;
(d) to take possession;
(e) to appoint a receiver;
(f) to possession of the title deeds.

These rights are cumulative, not mutually exclusive. Insurance and leasing will be dealt with under the heading "Rights common to both parties."

(a) To Sue for the Debt

Most mortgages contain a covenant[33] by the mortgagor to repay the loan on a fixed date, known as "the legal date of redemption." The legal date of redemption will normally be six months after the mortgage is made, to "activate" the mortgagee's rights at an early stage in case of default (although in the interests of both parties, the mortgage deed will usually provide for repayment over a much longer period). Once the legal date of redemption has passed, the mortgagee like any unsecured creditor can sue for the money lent. The right may be of particular use to a mortgagee who has exercised his power to sell the property but the proceeds of sale are insufficient to cover his debt. In *Rudge* v. *Richens*,[34] £1,500 was lent and £1,243 realised on sale. The mortgagee could recover the balance by suing the mortgagor on the personal covenant to repay.

---

[31] Consumer Credit Act 1974, s.58.

[32] Land Registration Act, s.34(1), provides "Subject to any entry on the register to the contrary, the proprietor of a charge shall have and may exercise all the powers conferred by law on the owner of a legal mortgage."

[33] This is implied into a registered charge by Land Registration Act 1925, s.28(1). Form 45 therefore contains no such covenant.

[34] (1873) L.R. 7 C.P. 358.

(b) **To Sell the Property**

Sale[35] by a mortgagee extinguishes the borrower's right to redeem. A distinction must be drawn between the right to sell arising, and it becoming exercisable.

Section 101(1) of the Law of Property Act 1925 states that:

> "A mortgagee, where the mortgage *is made by deed*, shall . . . have the following powers . . .
>
> (i) A power, when the mortgage money has become due, to sell, or to concur with any other person in selling, the mortgaged property, or any part thereof, either subject to prior charges or not, and either together or in lots, by public auction or by private contract, subject to such conditions respecting title or evidence of title, or other matter, as the mortgagee thinks fit, with power to vary any contract for sale, and to buy it in at an auction, or to rescind any contract for sale, and to re-sell without being answerable for any loss occasioned thereby."

The power of sale arises when the mortgage money "has become due," that is when the legal date of redemption has passed. Where no date for repayment is stated in the deed but the loan is to be paid off by instalments, the power arises as soon as any instalment is in arrear.[36] If the power of sale has not arisen, the mortgagee cannot sell the property to a purchaser; the most he can sell is his mortgage.[37]

Even though the power of sale has arisen, it does not become exercisable unless and until:

> (i) Notice requiring payment of the mortgage money has been served on the mortgagor . . . and default has been made in payment of the mortgage money, or part thereof for three months after such service; or
>
> (ii) Some interest under the mortgage is in arrear and unpaid for two months after becoming due; or
>
> (iii) There has been a breach of some provision contained in the mortgage deed or in this Act, or in an enactment replaced by this Act, and on the part of the mortgagor, or of some person concurring in making the mortgage, to be observed or performed, other than and besides a covenant for payment of the mortgage money or interest thereon."[38]

A purchaser from a mortgagee is only concerned to see that the power of sale has arisen; "the title of the purchaser shall not be impeachable on

---

[35] Including a contract for sale, *Waring* v. *London and Manchester Assurance Co.* [1935] Ch. 310; *Property & Bloodstock Ltd.* v. *Emerton* [1968] Ch. 94.

[36] *Payne* v. *Cardiff R.D.C.* [1932] 1 K.B. 241. This case should be distinguished from *Twentieth Century Banking Corpn. Ltd.* v. *Wilkinson* [1977] Ch. 99. A charge made in 1973 contained a covenant for repayment in 1988 and for payment of interest in the meantime. The statutory power of sale could not arise until 1988 even though default occurred with interest payments. However the court did order sale instead of foreclosure.

[37] *First National Securities Ltd.* v. *Hegerty* [1984] 1 All E.R. 139.

[38] Law of Property Act 1925, s.103.

the ground" that none of the events just mentioned have occurred or that the power of sale has been "otherwise improperly or irregularly exercised."[39] But if the purchaser knows that the power has not become exercisable or that there has been some impropriety or irregularity, then he cannot obtain good title.[40] "Any person damnified (usually the mortgagee) by an unauthorised, or improper, or irregular exercise of the power shall have his remedy in damages against the person exercising the power."[41]

In the case of unregistered land the effect of a sale by a mortgagee under the statutory power is to vest, in the purchaser, the freehold or leasehold title of the mortgagor, subject to prior mortgages but free from the rights of the vendor and any subsequent mortgagees.[42] A similar effect for registered land is achieved by section 34(4) of the Land Registration Act 1925:

> "A sale . . . under the power of sale shall operate and be completed by registration in the same manner . . . as a transfer for valuable consideration by the proprietor of the land at the time of the registration of the charge would have operated or been completed, and, as respects the land transferred, the charge and all incumbrances and entries inferior thereto shall be cancelled."

A mortgagee is not, strictly speaking, a trustee of his power of sale. Nevertheless it is clear "both on principle and authority, that the mortgagee in exercising his power of sale does owe a duty to take reasonable precautions to obtain the true market value of the mortgaged property"[43] and that this duty is owed not only to the mortgagor but also to any guarantor.[44] Whether a mortgagee has taken "reasonable precautions" in any particular case is a question of fact. In *Cuckmere Brick Co. Ltd.* v. *Mutual Finance Ltd.*[45] the mortgagees failed to advertise the property as having the benefit of planning permission for flats. They were liable to account to the mortgagor for the difference between the sale price of the property and the higher amount it would have fetched had it been advertised properly. On the other hand in *Bank of Cyprus (London) Ltd.* v. *Gill*[46] the mortgagees were not in breach of their duty to take reasonable care when they sold a hotel without informing the purchaser that it had the benefit of planning permission for an extension. The steep rise in the value of the property after the sale was due to the "jubilee boom"; not a forseeable factor. The question recently arose again in a slightly different context, in *Tse Kwong Lam* v. *Wong Chit Sen and Others*.[47] The

---

[39] *Ibid.* s.104(2).
[40] *Jenkins* v. *Jones* (1860) 66 E.R. 43.
[41] Law of Property Act 1925, s.104(2).
[42] *Ibid.* ss.88(1) and 89(1).
[43] *Per* Salmon L.J. *Cuckmere Brick Co. Ltd.* v. *Mutual Finance Ltd.* [1971] Ch. 949 at p. 968.
[44] *Standard Chartered Bank* v. *Walker* [1982] 1 W.L.R. 1410.
[45] [1971] Ch. 949.
[46] [1979] 2 Lloyd's Rep. 508.
[47] [1983] 1 W.L.R. 1394.

mortgagee in the exercise of his power of sale, auctioned a 15 storey
building in Hong Kong with "Centrepoint" trouble. It was bought by a
company financed by the mortgagee and owned by him and his family. His
wife made the only bid at the auction (on behalf of the company) and it
was knocked down to her at the reserve price of $1·2 m. The Privy Council
said that although a mortgagee could sell the mortgaged property to a
company in which he had an interest, "the sale . . . can only be supported
if the mortgagee proves that he took reasonable precautions to obtain the
best price reasonably obtainable at the time of the sale."[48] The present
mortgagee could not prove that he had taken such precautions; the auction
was badly advertised, the reserve price had been arrived at by the
mortgagee alone without consulting the auctioneer, and any purchaser
would have had to have paid a 20 per cent. deposit at the date of the
auction. The fact that only one bid was made at the auction was no
indication that the proper market value of the property had been
obtained. The mortgagor had been guilty of undue delay in bringing his
action and could not therefore upset the sale. He was however, entitled
to damages to the tune of $950,000 being the difference between $1·2m
and the proper market value of the property.

Although the mortgagee is not a trustee of his power of sale, he is a
trustee of the proceeds of sale. Section 105 of the Law of Property Act
1925 provides:

> "The money which is received by the mortgagee, arising from the
> sale, after discharge of prior incumbrances to which the sale is not
> made subject, if any, . . . shall be held by him in trust to be applied
> by him, first, in payment of all costs, charges, and expenses properly
> incurred by him as incident to the sale or any attempted sale, or
> otherwise; and secondly, in discharge of the mortgage money,
> interest, and costs, and other money, if any, due under the mortgage;
> and the residue of the money so received shall be paid to the person
> entitled to the mortgaged property, or authorised to give receipts for
> the proceeds of sale thereof."

A mortgagee who has a surplus, should therefore make a search in the
land charges register and register of title.[49]

(c) Foreclosure

Foreclosure, like sale, puts an end to the mortgagor's right to redeem. It
is however a much more drastic remedy than sale. The effect of
foreclosure in unregistered land is to transfer the legal estate from the
mortgagor to the mortgagee.[50] In registered land the proprietor of the
charge is registered as the proprietor of the land and the charge is

---

[48] *Ibid.* at p. 60.
[49] For procedure, see Chap. 2, pp. 17 and 37 et seq.
[50] Law of Property Act 1925, ss.88(2) and 89(2).

cancelled.[51] The right to foreclose does not arise until the legal date of redemption has passed, and can only be exercised by court order.

The mortgagor and any mortgagees who rank in priority below the foreclosing mortgagee must be made parties to the action, to ensure that they are given the opportunity to either redeem the mortgage or ask for a judicial sale.[52] A foreclosure decree is usually made in two stages. First, the court makes a foreclosure order nisi, giving the mortgagor a certain period (normally six months) in which to repay the mortgage. After this period has elapsed, repayment not having been made, the order is made absolute. However, even a foreclosure order absolute may be re-opened in special circumstances. Sir G. Jessel. M.R. laid down the relevant principles in *Campbell* v. *Holyland*.[53]

> "An order for foreclosure, according to the practice of the old Court of Chancery, was never really absolute, nor can it be so now . . . [The mortgagor seeking to re-open] must come, as it is said promptly; that is within a reasonable time . . . Was the mortgagor entitled to redeem, but by some accident unable to redeem? Did he expect to get money from a quarter from which he might reasonably hope to obtain it, and was he disappointed at the last moment? Then an element for consideration has always been the nature of the property as regards value. For instance, if an estate were worth £50,000 and had been foreclosed for a mortgage debt of £5,000, the man who came to redeem that estate would have a longer time than when the estate was worth £5,100, and he was foreclosed for £5,000. But not only is there money value; there may be other considerations. It may be an old family estate, or a chattel or a picture, which possesses a special value for the mortgagor, but which possesses not the same value for other people . . . Then it is said you must not interfere against purchasers . . . there are purchasers and purchasers. If the purchaser buys . . . after the lapse of a considerable time from the order of foreclosure absolute, with no notice of any extraneous circumstances which would induce the court to interfere, I for one should decline to interfere with such title as that; but if the purchaser bought the estate within 24 hours after the foreclosure absolute, and with notice of the fact that it was of much greater value than the amount of the mortgage debt, is it to be supposed that a Court of Equity would listen to the contention of such a purchaser that he ought not to be interfered with . . . ?"

The court may grant a stay of a mortgagee's possession claim in an action for foreclosure.[54]

For obvious reasons, foreclosure is a remedy not often sought by mortgagees; an action for possession followed by sale being more popular by far.

---

[51] Land Registration Act 1925, s.34(3).
[52] Law of Property Act 1925, s.91.
[53] (1877) 7 Ch.D. 166.
[54] Administration of Justice Act 1973, s.8(3).

(d) **To Take Possession**

Sale and foreclosure extinguish the mortgagor's rights in the property, possession does not. It is really a remedy to protect the payment of interest, but is now "a very fashionable form of relief because, owing to the conditions now prevailing, if it is desired to realise a security by sale, vacant possession is almost essential. Where therefore, the mortgagor is in occupation, a summons for possession is taken out, and no other relief is sought and where the mortgagee is in a position to exercise his power of sale, that is all the help he requires from the court."[55] If the property is tenanted taking possession is in the form of a direction to the tenant to pay his rent to the mortgagee.

A mortgagee's right to possession arises from the fact that he has a legal term of years in the property or its statutory equivalent (a charge by deed expressed to be by way of legal mortgage[56] or a registered charge.[57]) The right is not dependant on the mortgage money becoming due or on default by the mortgagor; "the mortgagee may go into possession before the ink is dry on the mortgage."[58] However the mortgage deed itself may preclude the mortgagee from taking possession of the mortgaged property, either expressly or by implication. It has been suggested that such a term might be implied into an instalment mortgage where the mortgagor is in possession, "but there must be something upon which to hang such a conclusion in the mortgage other than the mere fact that it is an instalment mortgagee"[59]; the legal mortgagee's right to possession is "a common law right . . . which should not be lightly treated as abrogated or restricted."[60]

But restricted it has been, in the case of mortgaged property which consists of or includes a dwelling-house. Under section 36 of the Administration of Justice Act 1970 the court has power to adjourn a mortgagee's proceedings for possession for a reasonable time or to give judgment for possession but suspend execution for such period as it thinks fit, if it appears that a mortgagor is likely to be able to pay "any sums due" under the mortgage within a reasonable time. "Any sums due" under section 36 does not mean the whole capital sum, where the whole capital sum is expressed to be payable on default in payment of interest or of interest and instalments; it just means those sums due in respect of interest and instalments.[61] In such a case the mortgagor must also be likely to be able to pay interest and instalments accruing during the period of

---

[55] Harman J. in *Four-Maids Ltd.* v. *Dudley Marshall (Properties) Ltd.* [1957] Ch. 317.
[56] Law of Property Act 1925, s.87(1).
[57] Land Registration Act 1925, s.34(1).
[58] Harman J. in *Four-Maids Ltd.* v. *Dudley Marshall (Properties) Ltd.* [1957] Ch. 317. Provided that any tenancy created by an attornment clause has been terminated, *Hinckley and Country Building Society* v. *Henry* [1953] 1 W.L.R. 352.
[59] *Esso Petroleum Co. Ltd.* v. *Alstonbridge Properties Ltd.* [1975] 1 W.L.R. 1474, at p. 1484.
[60] *Western Bank Ltd.* v. *Schindler* [1976] 3 W.L.R. 341 *per* Buckley L.J.
[61] Administration of Justice Act 1973, s.8; reversing the decision in *Halifax Building Society* v. *Clarke* [1973] Ch. 307.

postponement. In *Centrax Trustees Ltd.* v. *Ross*,[62] it was held that the court's power to postpone possession under the Administration of Justice Act is available whether the mortgage is an instalment mortgage or where, as in the present case, the mortgage deed states that the principal sum is to be paid on the legal date of redemption and otherwise only provides for the payment of interest, but the principal is intended to be paid at a later date (as is the case with an endowment mortgage). In *Quennell* v. *Maltby*[63] Lord Denning suggested that the court under its inherent jurisdiction, has discretion to refuse a mortgagee possession of a dwelling house on much wider grounds than those laid down by the Administration of Justice Act 1970.

Section 1(5) of the Matrimonial Homes Act 1983 gives a mortgagor's spouse the right to tender mortgage payments on the mortgagor's behalf, so as to prevent the mortgagee from taking possession and so as to invoke the protection of the Administration of Justice Act. Where a spouse has protected his or her rights of occupation by registering a Class F land charge or entering a notice (or caution)[64] on the register, the mortgagee must notify him or her of his intention to seek an order for possession. A special mortgagees search procedure has been introduced to this end.[65]

Where the mortgage is a "regulated agreement" under the Consumer Credit Act 1974,[66] the mortgagee must serve a default notice[67] on the mortgagor before seeking possession. If the mortgagor complies with the notice, the breach is treated as never having occurred.[68] The agreement is enforceable by court order only[69] and the court has wide powers to postpone and suspend orders for possession.[70]

A mortgagee will very rarely take possession of mortgaged property for more than a short period. He is liable to account to the mortgagor, not only for the actual income of the property during his possession, but also for any income that he would have received if he had managed it properly.[71]

If a mortgagee remains in possession for 12 years without acknowledging the mortgagor's title and without accepting any payment, the mortgagor's right to redeem will be barred; the mortgagee will acquire title to the property by adverse possession.

(e) To Appoint a Receiver

The right to appoint a receiver will be used as an alternative to taking possession, where the real object of the exercise is to control the income

---

[62] [1979] 2 All E.R. 952 distinguished in *Habib Bank Ltd.* v. *Tailor* [1982] 1 W.L.R. 1218.
[63] [1979] 1 W.L.R. 318.
[64] See *ante*, Chap. 2.
[65] See *ante*, Chap. 2.
[66] See generally J.E. Adams, (1975) Conv. 95.
[67] Consumer Credit Act 1974, s.87.
[68] *Ibid.* s.89.
[69] *Ibid.* s.126.
[70] *Ibid.* ss.129 and 135.
[71] *White* v. *City of London Brewery Co.* (1889) 42 Ch.D. 237.

of the property to protect interest payments under the mortgage. The great advantage this remedy has over possession is that the receiver is the *agent of the mortgagor*,[72] the mortgagee therefore only has to account to the mortgagor for income he actually receives from the receiver, not that which he ought to receive. The power to appoint a receiver is statutory, and arises and becomes exercisable in the same way as the power of sale. The receiver must be appointed in writing.[73] A person who pays money to the receiver is not concerned to see that the power to appoint him has become exercisable; only that it has arisen.[74] The function of a receiver is to manage the property. He has power "to demand and recover all the income of which he is appointed receiver, by action, distress, or otherwise, in the name of the mortgagor or the mortgagee to the full extent of the estate or interest which the mortgagor could dispose of, and to give effectual receipts accordingly for the same, and to exercise any powers which may have been delegated to him by the mortgagee pursuant to this Act."[75]

The receiver must use the income, first to discharge outgoings, including payments due under prior mortgages; secondly, to pay his own commission; and thirdly to pay the interest due to the mortgagee appointing him. The mortgagee can then take any surplus towards repayment of capital, otherwise it goes to the mortgagor.[76]

(f) Right to Possession of the Title Deeds

A first legal mortgagee of unregistered land has the right to possession of the title deeds.[77] Title deeds are of course redundant in the system of registration of title. On registration a registered chargee is issued with a charge certificate, and the mortgagor's land Certificate is retained at the registry.

THE RIGHTS OF AN EQUITABLE MORTGAGEE OF UNREGISTERED OR REGISTERED LAND

Here a distinction must be drawn between a mortgage that is made with due formality but is not of the legal estate and a mortgage of the legal estate without formality.

(a) To Sue for the Debt

The suit is on the mortgagor's *personal* covenant to repay. The position is the same as for a legal mortgagee.

---

[72] Law of Property Act 1925, s.109(2).
[73] *Ibid.* s.109(1).
[74] *Ibid.* s.109(4).
[75] *Ibid.* s.109(3).
[76] *Ibid.* s.109(8).
[77] *Ibid.* ss.85(1), 86(1) and 87(1).

(b) To Sell the Property

In the case of unregistered land the statutory power of sale applies in any mortgage made by *deed*.[78] Thus if the equitable mortgage is made by deed, the mortgagee has the power of sale, otherwise a sale through the court under section 91(2) of the Law of Property Act 1925 is necessary. Even though an equitable mortgagee by deed has the power of sale, it is thought that he does not have the power to convey the mortgagor's estate to a purchaser; he can only transfer his mortgage.[79] In practice this difficulty is overcome by one, or both, of two devices:

(i) A power of attorney is given by the equitable mortgagor to the equitable mortgagee in the mortgage deed, empowering him to convey the mortgagor's legal estate. Such a power of attorney is irrevocable.[80]

(ii) The mortgagor declares, in the mortgage deed, that he holds the legal estate on trust for the mortgagee and empowers the mortgagee to appoint someone else (the purchaser) in his place in the case of default.

The result is that the equitable mortgagee can sell the property.

Section 34(1) of the Land Registration Act 1925 only gives the power of sale to a registered chargee, but an equitable mortgagee may use the above devices to sell the registered land to a purchaser.

(c) Foreclosure

This is the primary remedy of an equitable mortgagee, but has the disadvantage of being slow and costly. The court order will direct the mortgagor to convey the legal title to the mortgagee.

(d) To Take Possession of the Property

It is doubtful whether an equitable mortgagee has the right to take possession of the property. To counter this, equitable mortgages often contain a clause empowering the mortgagee to take possession of the property in the event of default.

(e) To Appoint a Receiver

If the mortgaged property is unregistered, the power only exists if the mortgage is by deed[81]; registered, only if the mortgage is a registered

---

[78] *Ibid.* s.101(1).
[79] *Re Hodson and Howes' Contract* (1887) 35 Ch.D. 668.
[80] Powers of Attorney Act 1971, s.4(1).
[81] Law of Property Act 1925, s.109(1).

charge,[82] otherwise an application must be made to the court to appoint a receiver.

THE RIGHTS OF A MORTGAGOR (UNREGISTERED OR REGISTERED LAND)

(a) The Right to Redeem

A mortgagor has a dual right to redeem or repay the mortgage:

(i) at common law, on or before the date when the money becomes due;
(ii) in equity, after the date the money becomes due.

Equity has always jealously guarded the mortgagor's right to redeem, with the result that no fetters or "clogs" on the equity of redemption are permissible; "once a mortgage, always a mortgage." The application of this general principle can be summarised in four academic doctrines, which should be borne in mind when drafting a mortgage deed. But first it should be explained that the phrase "the equity of redemption" refers to the mortgagor's ownership of the property, subject to the mortgage. It originated at a time when the mortgagor conveyed the whole of his estate to the mortgagee, but is now rather misleading as the mortgagor retains the legal estate.

The four doctrines are as follows:

(1) Provisions in a mortgage deed which restrict or prevent redemption will be set aside.

In *Samuel* v. *Jarrah Timber and Wood Paving Corpn. Ltd.*[83] a mortgage of stock contained a clause giving the mortgagee an option to purchase the stock within 12 months: the purchase price was fair and the transaction freely entered into. The mortgagee sought to exercise the option, the mortgagor refused to convey and served notice to redeem. The House of Lords held that the option was invalid. A provision giving the mortgagee the option to purchase the security for his loan was against the principle "once a mortgage, always a mortgage". If the option could be validly exercised the mortgagor would not be able to recover that which he mortgaged. However the earlier decision of *Reeve* v. *Lisle*[84] suggests that if the grant of an option to buy the mortgaged property can be regarded as a separate transaction then it will be valid. These two cases were reconciled in the recent decision of *Lobb (Alex) Garages Ltd.* v. *Total Oil G.B. Ltd.*[85] The Lobbs charged their garage to Total as security for a loan. Later, in an attempt to solve the Lobb's financial difficulties, Total took a lease of the garage and immediately sub-leased it back to the Lobbs. It was held that the lease-back transaction as a whole[86]

---

[82] Land Registration Act 1925, s.34(1).
[83] [1904] A.C. 323.
[84] [1902] A.C. 461.
[85] [1983] 1 W.L.R. 87.
[86] See *post*, p. 465.

was valid. The judge explained that although the equity of redemption under a mortgage cannot be extinguished by any covenant or agreement made at the time of the mortgage and as part of the mortgage transaction, this does not prevent the mortgagee from purchasing the mortgagor's equity of redemption by a later separate and independent transaction. The purchase will be scrutinised by the court because of the danger that the mortgagee may have taken an unfair advantage of the mortgagor, but the transaction will only be set aside in circumstances in which a transaction would be set aside between non-mortgagees and non-mortgagors.

(2) A provision in the mortgage deed postponing the mortgagor's right to redeem *may* be invalid.

The authorities indicate that this is a question of fact, to be decided according to the particular circumstances of the case. The test to be applied is; Is the totality of the transaction harsh or oppressive? If not the provision is valid. Thus in *Knightsbridge Estate Trust Ltd.* v. *Byrne*,[87] freeholds in London were mortgaged to secure a loan of £310,000. The loan was to be repayable over 40 years by six monthly instalments. After six years the mortgagor tried to redeem the mortgage and claimed that the postponment of 40 years was a clog on his equity of redemption. The court held that he was not entitled to redeem. The agreement was "a commercial agreement by two important corporations experienced in such matters, and had none of the features of an oppressive bargain where the borrower [was] at the mercy of an unscrupulous lender."[88]

(3) Where a provision in the mortgage deed confers upon the mortgagee some benefit during the continuance of the mortgage over and above the right to payment of interest and capital, it *may* be void if it is unconscionable or a clog on the equity of redemption.

In *Cityland and Property (Holdings) Ltd.* v. *Dabrah*,[89] Mr. Dabrah had been the tenant of a house owned by the company. When his lease expired he bought the house from them for £3,500; he paid £600 in cash and took the balance of £2,900 on mortgage from the company. The mortgage was to be repaid by paying £63 per month for 6 years; in other words, £4,553, which meant a premium of 57 per cent. over the sum advanced. No provision was made for payment of interest. Goff J. held that this premium was unlawful. Bearing in mind the relative strengths of Mr. Dabrah and Cityland, the size of the premium and the lack of any explanation or justification for it, the premium was unconscionable and unreasonable. *Cityland* was distinguished in *Multiservice Bookbinding Ltd.* v. *Marden*.[90] Marden advanced Multiservice a 100 per cent. loan of £36,000 on business premises. All payments of capital and interest under the mortgage were index-linked by reference to the rate of exchange of the Swiss franc. Because of an excessive fall in the value of the pound

---

[87] [1939] Ch. 441; Contrast *Fairclough* v. *Swan Brewery Co. Ltd.* [1912] A.C. 565.
[88] *Per* Sir Wilfred Greene M.R.
[89] [1968] Ch. 166
[90] [1979] Ch. 84.

against the Swiss franc the amount required by Multiservice, to redeem the loan after 10 years, was £132,000. Browne-Wilkinson J., having decided that an index-linked money obligation was not against public policy, said: "The defendant made a hard bargain. But the test is not reasonableness. The parties made a bargain which the plaintiffs, who are businessmen, went into with their eyes open, with the benefit of independent advice, without any compelling necessity to accept a loan on these terms and without any sharp practice by the defendant. I cannot see that there was anything unfair or oppressive or morally reprehensible in such bargain entered into in such circumstances. The need for the defendant to invest his money in a way which preserved its real purchasing power provides an adequate explanation of all the terms of the mortgage."

Following *Multiservice,* Mr. Justice Peter Gibson recently gave the Nationwide Building Society[91] the "go-ahead" for their new index-linked mortgage repayment scheme.

Note should also be taken of the court's power to interfere with "extortionate credit bargains" under the Consumer Credit Act 1974. The provisions apply to mortgages of land for any amount, but only those made by a private individual.[92] A credit bargain will be extortionate if the payments to be made under it are "grossly exhorbitant" or if it "otherwise grossly contravenes the ordinary principles of fair dealing."[93] In deciding whether a credit agreement is extortionate the court must take into account interest rates prevailing when the bargain was made; in relation to the debtor, his age, experience, health and business capacity and the degree to which he was under financial pressure when he made the bargain; and in relation to the creditor the amount of risk he accepted. In *A. Ketley Ltd.* v. *Scott*[94] Foster J. refused to re-open as extortionate a short-term loan at a rate of interest equivalent to 48 per cent. per annum taken to facilitate the immediate completion of a house purchase.

(4) A collateral advantage to the mortgagee which is to subsist after redemption may be valid, as long as the mortgagee "has not acted unfairly or oppressively, and provided that the bargain does not conflict with . . . the principle . . . that a mortgage cannot be made irredeemable, and that any stipulation which restricts or clogs the equity of redemption is void."[95]

In practice, the modern doctrine of collateral advantages after redemption is inextricably linked with the doctrine of restraint of trade, especially in petrol tie cases, the test being, is the restraint (that is, the collateral advantage) in the public interest. *Esso Petroleum Co. Ltd.* v. *Harper's Garage (Stourport) Ltd.*[96] involved a filling station tied to Esso for petrol supply, under a mortgage. It was held that period of the restraint, 21 years, was too long and could not continue after the mortgage was

---

[91] [1983] 3 All E.R. 296.

[92] Consumer Credit Act 1974, s.137.

[93] *Ibid.* s.138.

[94] [1981] 1 C.R. 241.

[95] *Kreglinger* v. *New Patagonia Meat and Cold Storage Co. Ltd.* [1914] A.C. 25 *per* Viscount Haldane L.C.

[96] [1968] A.C. 269.

redeemed (although it was valid while the mortgage subsisted). The doctrine of restraint of trade was also held to apply to the lease-back transaction in *Lobb (Alec) Garages Ltd.* v. *Total Oil G.B. Ltd.*[97] A 21 year petrol tie was struck out of the agreement.

(b) Other Rights

These include, the right to have the property sold by the court, the right to inspect the title deeds, the right to compel a transfer of the mortgage, and the right to bring actions.

RIGHTS COMMON TO BOTH PARTIES

(a) Insurance

A mortgagee is given a statutory power to insure and keep insured the mortgaged property at the expense of the mortgagor,[98] but it is unusual for a mortgagee to rely on this power and not an express one, because the amount of insurance is not to exceed the amount specified in the mortgage, or, if none, two-thirds of the amount necessary to restore the property after total destruction. The power does not exist:[99]

    (i) Where there is a declaration in the mortgage deed that no insurance is required;

    (ii) Where an insurance is kept up by or on behalf of the mortgagor in accordance with the mortgage deed;

    (iii) Where the mortgage deed contains no stipulation respecting insurance, and an insurance is kept up by or on behalf of the mortgagor with the consent of the mortgagee to the amount to which the mortgagee is by this Act authorised to insure."

In view of the decision in *Halifax Building Society* v. *Keighley*[1] mortgagees are advised[2] that the mortgage should contain a provision that the mortgagor shall not insure himself, but if he does, must hold any money received from the insurers as a trustee for the mortgagee. In that case, there were two separate policies of insurance covering the mortgaged property. One was maintained jointly by the mortgagee and mortgagor, the other by the mortgagor alone. The former contained the usual condition that if there were any other insurance effected on the property the liability of the insurance company was to be limited to a rateable proportion of the damage suffered. The property was damaged by fire. Both insurance companies paid out. The mortgagees then sought to recover the amount paid to the mortgagor. They failed.

---

[97] [1983] 1 W.L.R. 87.
[98] Law of Property Act 1925, s.108(1); Land Registration Act 1925, s.34(1).
[99] Law of Property Act 1925, s.108(2).
[1] [1931] 2 K.B. 248.
[2] See J.T. Farrand, *Emmet on Title* (18th Ed.) p. 764.

Most building society mortgages provide for the property to be insured by the mortgagee and for the premiums to be charged to the mortgagor.

(b) Leasing

Section 99 of the Law of Property Act 1925 gives to both mortgagor and mortgagee, a limited power to create leases which are binding upon each other. The power is excluded in most mortgages for fear that the mortgagor might create a tenancy with Rent Act protection which would be binding on the mortgagee and prevent him from exercising his remedies in the event of default. If the power is excluded, no lease granted after the mortgage is created can bind the mortgagee unless adopted by him.[3]

ACTING FOR A MORTGAGEE

(a) Searches

The following searches should be made when acting for a mortgagee:

LOCAL LAND CHARGES SEARCH[4]

Many of the matters registrable as local land charges could seriously affect the value of a mortgagee's security.

LAND CHARGES SEARCH[5]

A full land charges search should be made against each owner of the legal estate and each borrower. Where the land which is to form the security is registered a bankruptcy only search (form K16) should be made against the name of each borrower. Bankruptcy only searches should also be made in respect of any party guaranteeing the mortgagor's performance of his obligations whether the land is registered or unregistered.

LAND REGISTRY SEARCHES[6]

Where title to the property is registered and the purchase is accompanied by a mortgage, a search made on behalf of the mortgagee will automatically protect the purchaser. An official search of the register of title made on behalf of the purchaser will not extend protection to the mortgagee.[7]

COMPANY SEARCH[8]

When a mortgagee is lending money to a company a search at the companies registry should always be made. The lender will need to know,

---

[3] *Rust* v. *Goodale* [1957] Ch. 33.
[4] See *ante*, p. 7.
[5] See *ante*, p. 17.
[6] See *ante*, p. 37.
[7] Land Registration (Official Searches) Rules 1981, r. 6.
[8] See *ante*, p. 50.

inter alia, that the company has power to charge its property and to borrow, the degree to which the property has already been charged[9] and not least the general financial structure and position of the company.

OTHER SEARCHES AND ENQUIRIES

Other searches, for instance a commons registration search,[10] may be desirable in the particular circumstances. The mortgagee's instructions should be taken if there is any doubt as to whether a particular type of search should be made. Preliminary Enquiries of the Vendor[11] and Enquiries of the Local Authority[12] should be made; in most cases copies of these will be available from the purchaser's solicitor.[13]

A detailed discussion of all these matters can be found in Chapters 2 and 3.

(b) **Persons in Possession of the Property**

The most important power available to a mortgagee in the event of the mortgagor's default is the power of sale.[14] A mortgagee will, therefore, be particularly concerned that his ability to sell the property with vacant possession is not impaired by tenancies or other interests existing in the property to which his rights as a mortgagee are subject. Numerous cases[15] have dealt with the question of a mortgagee's rights *vis à vis* a third party with some interest in the property and it is not proposed to go through them all. Two cases serve as reminders to mortgagees' solicitors to make the fullest possible enquiries as to the possibility of third party interests.

In *Church of England Building Society* v. *Piskor*[16] mortgagors contracted to buy some leasehold property. Their vendor allowed them to go into possession of the property pending completion of the sale. Before actual completion took place the mortgagors purported to sub-let various parts of the property (the mortgagors had no power to grant these tenancies because they had no legal estate). On completion of the purchase the property was immediately mortgaged by way of a legal charge to the Building Society. The mortgagees subsequently claimed possession of the property. Could the sub-tenants prevent this? The court held that there

---

[9] If the property has been charged previously this will often be an end to the matter for institutional lenders.

[10] See *ante*, p. 47.

[11] See *ante*, p. 57.

[12] See *ante*, p. 73.

[13] Assuming both to be separately represented.

[14] See *ante*, p. 454.

[15] *Caunce* v. *Caunce* [1969] 1 W.L.R. 286; *Bird* v. *Syme-Thompson* [1979] 1 W.L.R. 440; *Williams & Glyn's Bank Ltd.* v. *Boland* [1981] A.C. 487; *Hodgson* v. *Marks* [1971] Ch. 892, *Whittingham* v. *Whittingham* [1978] 2 W.L.R. 936.

[16] [1954] Ch. 553; *Jessamine Investment Co.* v. *Schwartz* [1977] 2 W.L.R. 145; contrast *Coventry Permanent Economic Building Society* v. *Jones* [1951] W.N. 218. Where there was an informal agreement to create a tenancy, this did not bind a mortgagee because the tenancy could not exist as a legal estate and could not be fed. Such an agreement should be registered as an estate contract.

was a moment of time in which the mortgagors held the property before they mortgaged it. The estoppel created by the mortgagors when they purported to grant the sub-tenancies was fed during this period; that is when the legal estate vested in the mortgagors. The sub-tenancies therefore had priority over the mortgage because they were effected before the legal charge was made. The mortgagees could not obtain vacant possession of the property. The case shows the necessity of ensuring that the proposed mortgagor has not agreed, or purported, to grant a tenancy of the property.

The second case is *Williams & Glyn's Bank Ltd.* v. *Boland.*[17] Mr. B was the sole proprietor of the property which was registered. Mrs. B, who had contributed to the purchase price and therefore acquired an equitable interest, claimed that as she was in actual occupation of the property when it was mortgaged to the bank, her interest was binding on the bank by virtue of section 70(1)(g) of the Land Registration Act 1925.[18] The House of Lords held in favour of the wife and the bank was prevented from selling with vacant possession.

The principle which emerged from *Boland* (that a purchaser/mortgagee of land *may* be bound by an undisclosed equitable interest of an occupant) is applicable both to registered and unregistered land. However, the problems presented by the case are aggravated with registered land because a mortgage is not perfected until the *charge* is registered at H.M. Land Registry. It is, therefore, possible that some third party with an interest in the property could go into "actual occupation" within section 70(1)(g) after the advance has been made by the mortgagee but before the mortgage is registered; so making the mortgagee's rights subject to those of the third party.[19]

No solution to the problems posed by *Boland* has yet been found. The Law Commission[20] in its "Report on the Implications of *Williams and Glyn's Bank Ltd.* v. *Boland*" has stated that "it is not acceptable in principle that a purchaser should be at risk of being bound by an interest which, however extensive his enquiries, he is unable to discover." It was suggested that rights similar to those enjoyed by Mrs. Boland should be protected by registration and cease to be overriding interests.

(c) Requisitions on Title

A solicitor acting for a mortgagee should raise requisitions on title to ensure that his client obtains a property with a good and marketable title. The purchaser's solicitor may make the replies to his own clients requisitions available for consideration by the mortgagee.

A mortgagee is frequently said to be stricter in his requirements in investigating title than other purchasers. Certainly, any defect in title

---

[17] [1981] A.C. 487; noted [1980] Conv. 361; see also *Blacklocks* v. *J.B. Developments (Godalming) Ltd.* [1981] 3 W.L.R. 554.

[18] See *ante*, p. 347.

[19] See *Re Boyle's Claim* [1961] 1 W.L.R. 339; *London & Cheshire Insurance Co.* v. *Laplagrene Property Co. Ltd.* [1971] Ch. 499.

[20] Cmnd. 8638.

should be brought to the attention of the mortgagee. In practice a defective title indemnity policy taken out to cover the defect may satisfy the mortgagee.

(d) Miscellaneous Matters

Various other matters which a mortgagee's solicitor should bear in mind include:

(i) Insurance: the mortgagor may be asked to insure for a specified amount with an approved insurance company.

(ii) National House-Building Council: where the property has been built within the last 10 years the mortgagee will require it to be covered by the NHBC scheme described in the next Chapter.

(iii) Repair: frequently a mortgagee will specify certain repairs which must be executed before completion.

(iv) Leasehold interests: a mortgagee will usually have its own guidelines as to what terms in a lease are acceptable. A proviso for re-entry and forfeiture in the event of the tenant/mortgagor becoming bankrupt will usually be unacceptable to most institutional lenders.

(v) Endowment mortgages: this type of mortgage involves an assignment of the endowment policy. Notice of the mortgagee's interest should be given to the insurers so that it can be noted on the policy pursuant to section 3 of the Policies of Assurance Act 1867.

(e) After Completion

Once completion has taken place and the mortgage has been executed the mortgagees solicitor must ensure that his clients security is protected in the appropriate manner. The method of protection adopted will depend upon whether the land is registered or unregistered.

REGISTERED LAND

A legal mortgage of registered land must be completed by registration at the appropriate district land registry. The following documents should be sent to the correct district land registry within the 30 day priority period afforded by the official certificate of search:

(1) The original charge and a certified copy of it.

(2) Form A4 (if the charge relates to the whole of the property in a title) or Form A5 (if the charge relates to part).

(3) A cheque for fees calculated in accordance with Scale 4 of the Land Registry (Fees) Order 1981.

(4) The land certificate.

Where the mortgage accompanies a transfer to the mortgagor additional documents must be lodged;

(5) The transfer to the mortgagor.

(6) Where an existing charge is being discharged there will be no land certificate. The existing charge certificate should be lodged together with an application to discharge the transferor's mortgage (form 53). N.B. Where a transfer and a charge are being registered fees are payable on the transfer only.

When the mortgagee has been entered on the register as proprietor of the charge he will be issued with a charge certificate. The land certificate is retained at the registry. The mortgagee's solicitor should send the charge certificate to the mortgagee.

Once registered, mortgages have priority in the order in which they were registered.

UNREGISTERED LAND

There are two ways in which a mortgage of unregistered land may be protected; deposit of title deeds and registration as a land charge.

Where a legal mortgage is protected by the mortgagee having custody of the title deeds the question of priority will seldom arise.[21] In the absence of fraud he will have priority to subsequent mortgagees. Where an equitable mortgage is created by deposit of title deeds and then a legal mortgage is entered into the legal mortgage will prevail if the legal mortgagee can show that he was a bona fide purchaser for value without notice of the prior equitable mortgage.[22] Equitable mortgages rank *vis à vis* one another in the order in which they are created subject to there being some element of fraud.

Where a mortgage is not protected by deposit of title deeds it must be protected by registration of a land charge. A legal mortgage is registrable as a Class C(i) land charge; an equitable mortgage as a Class C(iii) land charge. Registered mortgages rank according to the date upon which they are registered.[23]

(f) Further Advances

Sometimes a mortgagee having made an initial advance under his mortgage will make a further advance. This could be to enable the mortgagor to make improvements to the property. If the mortgagor has taken out a second mortgage in the interval between the making of the initial advance and the further advance under the first mortgage, it may be necessary to ensure the further lending takes priority over the second mortgage. In some circumstances the first morgagee will be able to "tack" the further advance to the original mortgage and so claim priority over the second mortgage.

Section 94(1) of the Law of Property Act 1925 provides:

"After the commencement of this Act, a prior mortgagee shall have

---

[21] But see Hayton, D. *Megarry's Manual of the Law of Real Property* (6th ed.) p. 506.

[22] *Pilcher* v. *Rawlins* (1872) 7 Ch. App. 259; *Oliver* v. *Hinton* [1899] 2 Ch. 264; *Walker* v. *Hinan* [1907] 2 Ch. 104.

[23] Law of Property Act 1925 s.97; Land Charges Act 1972, s.18(6).

a right to make further advances to rank in priority to subsequent mortgages (whether legal or equitable)—

(a) if an arrangement has been made to that effect with the subsequent mortgagees; or

(b) if he had no notice of such subsequent mortgages at the time when the further advance was made by him; or

(c) whether or not he had such notice as aforesaid, where the mortgage imposes an obligation on him to make such further advances."

This subsection applies whether or not the prior mortgage was made expressly for securing further advances."

Section 94(1)(a) and (c) need no further explanation. Section 94(1)(b) allows a prior mortgagee to tack a further advance if he does not have notice of a second (or third and so on) mortgage. Registration of a subsequent, intervening, mortgage will fix a prior mortgagee with notice unless the prior mortgage was made expressly for securing further advances. In this latter case, the prior mortgagee must have made a search after the date upon which the *subsequent* mortgage was registered before he is fixed with notice.[24]

Where a mortgagor of registered land is obliged by the terms of a registered charge to make further advances and this obligation is noted on the register of title, section 30(3) of the Land Registration Act 1925 provides that "a subsequent registered charge shall take effect subject to any further advance made pursuant to the obligation." If a registered proprietor is not obliged to make further advances but his original mortgage is security for such advances a different procedure applies. The Registrar shall

"before making any entry on the register which would prejudicially affect the priority of any further advance . . . give to the proprietor of the charge . . . notice by registered post [or recorded delivery] of the intended entry, and the proprietor of the charge shall not, in respect of any further advance, be affected by such entry, unless the advance is made after the date when the notice ought to have been received in due course of post."[25]

A prior mortgagee will, therefore, receive notification of a second mortgage of the registered land. He will then be able to make arrangements to have the second mortgage postponed to the further lending by agreement before advancing the moneys. Application can then be made to the Registrar to have the priority of the further advance noted on the register. A fee of £3.00 is payable for this service.[26]

---

[24] Law of Property Act 1925, s.94(2).
[25] Land Registration Act 1925. s.30(1).
[26] Land Registration (Fees) Order 1981.

10: The National House-Building Council's Scheme

INTRODUCTORY

The maintenance of high standards in any profession can be ensured in one of two ways; compulsorily, by the Government or voluntarily, by the profession as a whole. Buyers of new homes are protected against "jerry-building" by the building industry itself under the aegis of the National House-Building Council.[1] The Council, which assumed its present form in 1967,[2] has 44 members in England and Wales. Many of the members are builders but the majority represent a multitude of different bodies interested in promoting high building standards, like the Government, the Building Societies' Association, the Greater London Council, the Association of Metropolitan Authorities, the Royal Institute of Chartered Surveyors and the Consumers' Association. These 44 members are responsible for supervising the running of the Council's scheme. One popular misconception is that registered developers and builders are members of the Council. This is not so. The Council keeps a register of developers and builders "who in the opinion of the Council observe and maintain sufficiently high standards of house-building"[3] and it is only these developers and builders who may sell new homes with the benefit of the N.H.B.C. scheme. Once registered they agree to observe and be bound by the Council's Rules,[4] which entails (*inter alia*) meeting certain technical standards. Breach of the rules can lead to disciplinary proceedings and ultimately being struck off the register.

Although registration with the Council is theoretically voluntary, three factors combine to make it the rule rather than the exception. First, a new home offered for sale with the benefit of the scheme is infinitely more attractive to a purchaser, than one without. Secondly, and most importantly, the building societies will only advance a loan on the security of a home that is less than ten years old if it has the protection of the scheme. Thirdly, if developers and builders stopped registering with the Council, the Government might well consider introducing a compulsory scheme of their own.

---

[1] For further reading see Tapping and Rolfe, *Guarantees for New Homes, a guide to the N.H.B.C. Scheme* (2nd ed.)

[2] The Council made its début in 1936 as the Housing Improvement Association. In 1967 it became the National House-Builders Registration Council; in 1973 the National House-Building Council.

[3] The Council's Memorandum of Association.

[4] HB1 (1979) in force from April 1, 1979.

In 1979 the N.H.B.C. scheme underwent substantial changes for homes not started before 1st April 1979. Claims under the previous 1975 scheme are still possible but only for a short time in the future. We shall therefore concentrate our discussion on the present scheme,[5] mentioning the 1975 scheme only where the differences are important. A purchaser's protection under the 1979 scheme revolves around three documents:

(a) The House Purchaser's Agreement, HB5, entered into immediately after the sale contract is exchanged;
(b) The House Purchaser's Insurance Policy, HB7, handed over at the same time; and
(c) The Standard Notice of Insurance Cover, HB6, applied for by the developer or builder before the construction of the home and issued by the Council to him when the home is completed, and handed over to the purchaser when received (but not usually until completion of the sale, if later). The Notice "activates" the major part of the insurance.

The 1979 N.H.B.C. scheme is an approved one under section 2 of the Detective Premises Act 1972.[6] Once a Notice of Insurance Cover is issued and a House Purchaser's Agreement is entered into for a new home, the provisions of that Act are excluded. Also excluded are the provisions of the Unfair Contract Terms Act 1977.[7]

THE HOUSE PURCHASER'S AGREEMENT, HB5[8]

Rule 18 of the Council's Rules provides that a House Purchaser's Agreement must irrevocably be offered to the purchaser at the time of the sale contract or building agreement. The person who must offer and enter into the agreement with the purchaser (and be named in it as "the Vendor") is "the developer who sells[9] the dwelling to that purchaser." "Developer" is defined[10] as "any person partnership company or organisation that arranges for the construction of dwellings or is concerned in or with such arrangements." An agreement should not be offered or entered into by a builder unless he himself is selling the dwelling to the purchaser or is building the dwelling on the purchaser's own land. The inclusion of

---

[5] See J. E. Adams (1980) 130 New.L.J. 171 at pp. 195 and 219.
[6] 1979 SI/381.
[7] Unfair Contract Terms Act 1977, s.29.
[8] House Purchaser's Agreement HB5B and HB5C are used where the vendor is a public authority.
[9] Professor J. E. Adams suggests in (1980) 130 New.L.J. at p. 171, that, especially where group companies are involved, the identity of the vendor would be more certain if it was specified whether "sells" in Rule 18 refers to exchange of the sale contract or conveyance of the estate. A subsidiary building company might make the contract of sale; the parent company convey the estate. Tapping and Rolfe, *Guarantees for New Homes* (2nd ed.) at p. 28 say that in cases of doubt the vendor is the organisation that will derive the bulk of the profit from the sale.
[10] r.47.

the following clause in the contract for sale would satisfy the vendor's obligation under Rule 18:

> "The Vendor undertakes to make an irrevocable offer to enter into the form of Agreement HB5 (1979) prescribed by the National House-Building Council."[11]

Once entered into the Agreement gives the purchaser certain rights against the developer or builder vendor. "Purchaser" is defined by Clause 12(a) of the Agreement as "the First Purchaser and also, where the context so admits, his successors in title and his and their mortgagees in possession."

The protection conferred by the Agreement is intended to start immediately the purchaser pays his deposit. The offer should therefore be taken up and the Agreement entered into immediately after the exchange of the contracts for sale (or building agreement) and the consideration of five pence paid.[12]

Clause 1 of the Agreement needs no comment:

> "The rights conferred upon the Purchaser under this Agreement shall be in addition to any rights he may have against the Vendor under any other agreement relating to the Dwelling."

Clauses 2 to 6 spell out the vendor's obligations to the purchaser. In Clause 2 the vendor warrants:

> "(a) That his name is entered on the Council's Register;
> (b) That he has undertaken to comply with the Council's Rules;
> (c) That he has made to the Council an Application for Inspection of the Dwelling during construction."

Breach of these warranties is unlikely. The N.H.B.C. no longer issues House-Purchaser's Agreements in blank. Every Agreement bears the vendor's name and the address of the dwelling to which it refers and is only issued after an application has been made by the vendor for a Notice of Insurance Cover and the appropriate fee for inspection of the construction, paid. A breach might however occur if the vendor's name was removed from the register in between the issuing and the entering into of the Agreement. In such a case the vendor is liable for breach of contract and is possibly guilty of a criminal offence; either deception or breach of the Trade Description Act. But the purchaser has no remedy against the Council; his insurance policy is invalidated by General Condition 10 of the policy.

The main source of claims arises out of the important warranty given in Clause 3:

> "The Vendor warrants to the Purchaser that the Dwelling has been or will be built in an efficient and workmanlike manner and of proper materials and so as to be fit for habitation."

---

[11] Suggested by the Council in respect of the 1975 Agreement.
[12] Never done in practice.

Clause 3 repeats the vendor's obligations at common law, confirmed by the Court of Appeal in *Hancock* v. *Brazier (Anerly) Ltd.*[13] Breach of Clause 3 is actionable in contract and in the tort of negligence.[14] The vendor's contractual liability for breach is expressly extended by the Agreement,[15] beyond the original purchaser (the only person entitled to sue at common law because of the privity of contract rule) to a second and subsequent purchaser. A claim in contract must be brought within six years of the date of the Agreement.[16] A claim in negligence for breach of the same duty is not however time barred until six years have elapsed from the time the dwelling is damaged[17] (not the time when the damage was or could reasonably have been noticed), thus extending the time within which actions on Clause 3 may be brought. Actual damage to the dwelling is a condition precedent to founding a suit in negligence[18] and this could be important where a purchaser is trying to recover damages from someone other than the vendor with whom he has no contractual relationship, the vendor's architect for example. A further point has been made by the Professor Street in his recent article[19] "Damage by Subsidence: The Conveyancing Problems." A cause of action in negligence vests in the owner of the dwelling at the relevant time[20] (since *Pirelli General Cable Works Ltd.* v. *Oscar Faber & Partners*,[21] when the damage occurs) and does not pass to a purchaser from him. However that purchaser could sue in nuisance[22] (provided of course the damage is still continuing) although the previous owner probably loses his right to sue after the sale, for damage up to that point. Professor Street therefore suggests that the following procedure be adopted where an owner wishes to sell a dwelling which has already suffered actual damage:[23]

1. The dwelling should be sold at a reduced price, and the owner should recover his loss by suing the developer or builder vendor in negligence or nuisance; or
2. If the full price is paid, the purchaser can sue in nuisance but needs an express assignment of the benefit of the claim if he wishes to sue in negligence. Otherwise only his vendor can sue in negligence.

The reader may feel that the purchaser's ability to sue the developer or builder on his "common law" obligations in clause 3 is redundant in view of the 10 year "guarantee" (discussed below) given by the Council to the dwelling. Clause 3 is anything but redundant. The nature of the damage suffered by the purchaser may not be covered by the Council's "guaran-

---

[13] [1966] 1 W.L.R. 1317.
[14] *Batty* v. *Metropolitan Property Realisation Co. Ltd.* [1978] Q.B. 554.
[15] c. 10.
[16] Limitation Act 1980.
[17] *Pirelli General Cable Works Ltd.* v. *Oscar Faber & Partners* [1983] 2 W.L.R. 6.
[18] *Ibid.* Lord Fraser of Tullybelton.
[19] [1979] Conv. 241.
[20] *Dutton* v. *Bognor Regis U.D.C.* [1972] 1 Q.B. 373.
[21] [1983] 2 W.L.R. 6, decided after the article was written.
[22] *Masters* v. *London Borough of Brent* [1978] Q.B. 841.
[23] Slightly amended by the present authors in view of the *Pirelli* case.

tee," nor may it occur within the 10 year limit.[24] And it should be remembered that where defective construction is concealed by fraud (not necessarily involving moral turpitude[25]) time does not begin to run for the purposes of the limitation of an action in contract or tort, until "the fraud, concealment or mistake" is discovered or could with reasonable diligence have been discovered.[26] It is unlikely that a N.H.B.C. inspection of the construction of a dwelling would negate a finding of fraud.

Before proceeding with the other warranties given by the vendor in the Agreement the definition of "Dwelling" should be noted: "Dwelling" means "the house, bungalow, maisonette or flat identified on the front of this Agreement and, if constructed simultaneously therewith, its garage, permanent out-building, driveway, footpath, boundary wall, retaining wall and any drainage pipe, channel, gully or inspection chamber within the curtilage of the premises, but not any lift, fence or any construction of non-permanent materials."[27]

Clause 4 relates HB5 with the other two documents:

> "The vendor warrants to the purchaser:
>
> (a) That a Standard Notice of Insurance Cover (and, if appropriate, a Common Parts Notice of Insurance Cover) has been or will be issued by the Council in relation to the Dwelling;
>
> (b) That upon signing of this agreement he shall forthwith deliver the Insurance Policy to the Purchaser;
>
> (c) That upon the signing of this Agreement or (if later) upon receipt of the Notice or Notices of Insurance Cover he shall forthwith deliver the Notice or Notices of Insurance Cover to the Purchaser."

"Common Parts"[28] are defined as "those parts of the building containing the Purchaser's maisonette or flat (excluding any lift, fence or any construction of non-permanent materials) for which the Purchaser is liable directly or indirectly to share in the cost of repair or reinstatement but which have not been and will not be conveyed or demised into his exclusive possession."

Failure to perform the obligation in Clause 4 would render the vendor liable to the purchaser for breach of contract, and might also involve him in disciplinary proceedings. With regard to Clause 4(a), the Council has a duty to issue a Notice of Insurance Cover when, but only if, the dwelling complies with the Council's Requirements.[29] If the Council refuses to issue the Notice, the vendor (but not the purchaser) has the right to have any dispute as to whether the dwelling satisfies the Council's Requirements, referred to arbitration.

---

[24] As in *Lyons* v. *F. W. Booth Contractors Ltd. and Maidstone Borough Council* (1982) 262 E.G. 981.

[25] *King* v. *Victor Parsons* [1973] 1 W.L.R. 29 and see *Applegate* v. *Moss* [1971] 1 Q.B. 406.

[26] Limitation Act 1980, s.32.

[27] HB5, c. 12(*a*).

[28] *Ibid.*

[29] r. 22.

Next, Clause 5 provides:

"The Vendor shall not be liable to the Purchaser in respect of any breach of the warranty set out in Clause 3 if the defect or damage caused by that breach does not first appear until after the expiry of the Initial Guarantee Period unless and until the Purchaser has made a claim against the Council under Section III of the Insurance Policy in respect of that defect or damage and the Council has disclaimed liability in respect of that claim or any part of it; any relief obtained from the Council shall be taken into account in mitigation of damages against the Vendor."

After the Initial Guarantee Period the purchaser must look first to the Council in respect of defects or damage caused by breach of Clause 3. He can only look to the vendor for loss or excess loss not recoverable under the insurance policy. But as one commentator[30] has pointed out, if the purchaser's claim is for an amount in excess of the council's cover or for defects within Clause 3 but outside Section III of the insurance policy, the Council has no liability; how can they disclaim it? And does clause 5 mean, that if it is obvious that the defects are not covered by the policy, the purchaser still has to go through the charade of making a claim against the Council before suing the vendor?

"Initial Guarantee Period" means "the period of two years from the date of issue of the Notice of Insurance Cover or, where the Dwelling has been unoccupied for 12 months or more from such date, the period of one year from the completion of the first purchase of the Dwelling. In relation to the Common Parts, it means the period of two years from the date of issue of the Common Parts Notice of Insurance Cover or (if later) the period of one year from the completion of the first purchase of the first maisonette or flat in the building.[31]"

Thus the date of the Notice of Insurance Cover on an individual flat or maisonette may differ from that of the Common Parts Notice of Insurance Cover. The Initial Guarantee Period has been used by the Council for determining the point at which the vendor's liability gives way to that of the Council, since 1967. It is also used to apportion liability for defects falling within Clause 6 and will be discussed there.

The vendor's second major obligation (the first being his "common law" obligation in Clause 3) to the purchaser is set out in Clause 6:

"(a) The Vendor shall within a reasonable time and at his own expense remedy any defect in the Dwelling caused by a breach of the Council's Requirements and any damage to the Dwelling caused by such defect provided that such defect or damage first appears and is reported to the vendor in writing within the Initial Guarantee Period: the Vendor's liability under this Clause shall be subject to the provisions of Clause 7 and without prejudice to his liability under Clause 3.

---

[30] J. E. Adams, (1980) 130 New.L.J.
[31] HB5 c. 12(a).

(b) If any work undertaken by the Vendor under Clause 6(a) fails to remedy such defect or damage, the Vendor shall remain under a continuing liability to remedy such defect or damage even after the expiry of the Initial Guarantee Period."

There are several important points to note about Clause 6. The vendor is under an obligation to "remedy" any defect, that is provide a dwelling which complies with the Council's Requirements, but *only* if there has been a breach of the Council's Requirements *and* the breach has resulted in a defect. Assuming such a "defect," the vendor must also remedy "any damage *to the Dwelling* caused by the defect." In other words the purchaser has to bear the cost of any damage to the contents of his home. The vendor is only liable for defects that first appear during the Initial Guarantee Period (defined above). This test of liability can cause difficulties in practice. Professor J. E. Adams gives as an example,[32] "the case of a householder who is away from home for several months, spanning the end of the initial guarantee period, and on his return finds a long crack in the dining-room wall, or the circumstances of the cracked roof-timber fully visible to the naked eye of anyone active enough to climb into the roof-space in the house which is however owned by an elderly widow in poor health." The purchaser must report the defect to the vendor *in writing* within the Initial Guarantee Period. It seems that the Council interpret this requirement widely, where a defect appears near the end of the period and the written report is not made until after the period expires. In *Marchant* v. *Caswell & Redgrave Ltd.*[33] the purchaser reported defects verbally to his builder-vendor, who thereupon carried out remedial works. It was held that the builder had waived his right to require written notice of the defects.

Clause 6(b) emphasises that if the vendor is liable to remedy defects under Clause 6(a) he remains so liable even after the Initial Guarantee Period has expired.

Clauses 7 and 8 list limitations on the vendor's liability under Clause 6. Clause 7 states that:

"The Vendor shall not be liable to the Purchaser under Clause 6:
(a) Unless the Purchaser as soon as practicable gave the Vendor notice in writing of any defect or damage complained of;
(b) (save where the Purchaser is a mortgagee in possession) unless any previous Purchaser as soon as practicable gave the Vendor notice in writing of any defect or damage complained of;
(c) in respect of any defect caused by a breach of the Council's Requirements in relation to central heating boilers or any electrical installation with moving parts (including waste disposal units, extractor fans, and air conditioning units) or in respect of any damage caused by such defect, if such defect or damage first appears after the expiry of 12 months from the commencement of the Initial Guarantee Period;

---

[32] (1980) 130 New.L.J. 172.
[33] (1976) 240 E.G. 127.

(d) in respect of any defect in or caused by anything built into the Dwelling otherwise than pursuant to the building or sale agreement between the First Purchaser and the Vendor, or in respect of any damage caused by such defect;

(e) in respect of any defect or damage caused by defective design where the First Purchaser provided the structural or installation design details which gave rise to such defect or damage."

Clause 7(b) stresses the need, when acting for a subsequent purchaser, to obtain, before contracts are exchanged, a warranty that all defects have been reported in writing and an undertaking to report any defects that appear before completion. Clause 7(c) was introduced because the items therein listed themselves usually only bear a one year manufacturer's guarantee.

Clause 8 adds two more limitations:

"Nothing in this Agreement shall render the Vendor liable to the Purchaser in respect of any defect or damage caused by:

(a) wear and tear or gradual deterioration caused by neglect;

(b) normal dampness, condensation or shrinkage."

The benefit of the vendor's obligations under Clause 6 is extended by Clause 9 to adjoining dwellings also within the Scheme:

"The Vendor shall within a reasonable time and at his own expense remedy any damage to the Dwelling first appearing and reported to him in writing within the Initial Guarantee Period and caused by any defect in an adjoining or adjacent dwelling which he has built or agreed to build and consequent upon a breach of the Council's Requirements; the Vendor shall also remedy (provided that he is granted access to the adjoining or adjacent dwelling) such defect so as to prevent a recurrence of such damage."

One "grey area" within the N.H.B.C. scheme has always been the position of a second or subsequent purchaser. Is an express assignment of the benefit of the Agreement vital to enable him to sue the builder or developer vendor for breach of the Agreement? The Council's Rules have consistently contained a provision prohibiting registered vendors from taking objection in proceedings or otherwise to the fact that the benefit of the Agreement has not been assigned to the purchaser making the claim. Now such provision has been included in the Agreement itself. Clause 10 states:

"This Agreement is made by the First Purchaser on behalf of himself and his successors in title and his and their mortgagees in possession. The Vendor undertakes that he shall not seek to deny liability under this Agreement on the ground that it has not been assigned."

Nevertheless, the cold fact is that the Agreement is only made between the vendor and the first purchaser. Should the vendor plead the lack of assignment as a defence to a purchaser's claim, he would lay himself open to disciplinary proceedings and probably removal of his name from the register, but the possibility of having to meet a large claim might well outweigh the unpleasantness of these sanctions.

However in view of the decision in *Marchant* v. *Caswell Redgrave Ltd.*[34] his defence would probably fail, either on the ground (confirmed in *Federated Homes Ltd.* v. *Mill Lodge Properties Ltd.*[35]) that the benefit of the Agreement runs automatically with the land under section 78 of the Law of Property Act 1925, or that the vendor is estopped from relying on the lack of assignment because of the undertaking he has given in Clause 10.

The penultimate clause of the Agreement, Clause 11, provides that any disputes arising under the Agreement shall be referred to arbitration unless:

(i) Clause 3 is broken (the vendor's "common law" obligations); or
(ii) Either party refuses also to refer to arbitration a dispute under any other agreement, including the sale or building agreement.

Faced with a decision whether to arbitrate or litigate, the purchaser should bear the following in mind:

1. The Arbitrator (appointed by the President (or Vice-President) of the Chartered Institute of Arbitrators[36]) will be an expert on building disputes. The arbitration is conducted entirely independently of the N.H.B.C. and the Arbitrator has "the same power to award damages for any breach of (the) Agreement as a judge of the High Court of Justice."[37] It is uncertain however whether this includes the power to order interest to be paid on awards. A right of appeal lies to the High Court on any point of law arising out of the award.[38]

2. An order for payment of costs lies within the discretion of the Arbitrator, but he usually follows the practice of the courts and awards costs to the successful party. The cost of taking a dispute to arbitration can be considerable in a complex case.

3. Legal Aid is not available for arbitration.

Note shoudl also be taken of the decisions in *Willday* v. *Taylor* [39] and *Purser & Co. (Hillingdon) Ltd.* v. *Jackson.*[40] In *Willday*, a Clause 6 arbitration failed because the purchaser had not given proper notice of the defects during the Initial Guarantee Period. Subsequently, and long after the expiry of the time for any appeal against the award, the purchaser started proceedings for the same defects under his purchase contract, which also contained a binding arbitration clause. The judge held that the purchaser was estopped from doing so; the matter was *res judicata* having once been litigated, and the arbitration clause in the HB5 Agreement over-rode the arbitration clause in the sale contract. By contrast, in

---

[34] *Ibid.*
[35] [1980] 1 W.L.R. 594.
[36] Under Arbitration Act 1950.
[37] HB5, c. 11.
[38] Arbitration Act 1979.
[39] (1976) 241 E.G. 835.
[40] [1977] Q.B. 166.

Purser's case, the purchaser took the builder to arbitration in respect of certain defects and obtained an award against him. It was held that this arbitration was no bar to a second arbitration in respect of other defects.

Clause 12 concludes the House Purchaser's Agreement by defining the terms used in it. The most important of these have already been given.

THE HOUSE PURCHASER'S INSURANCE POLICY, HB7 [41]

The N.H.B.C. have run an insurance based scheme since 1967, the purchaser's insurance cover in prior versions to be found in the first and second schedules to the House Purchaser's Agreement. One of the main objectives of the 1979 revision was to render the scheme more easy to understand by purchasers. To this end, on entering into a House Purchaser's Agreement the vendor must provide the purchaser with a new document, House Purchaser's Insurance Policy HB7 (1979), which sets out fully the insurance cover given to the purchaser by the Scheme. A House Purchaser's Insurance Policy is issued by the N.H.B.C. at the same time as the House Purchaser's Agreement and therefore includes the same details of vendor, purchaser and dwelling as appear on the front of the HB5 Agreement. For reasons that will become apparent, the purchase price of the dwelling and the date of completion should be inserted on the front of both documents. The major part of the insurance given by HB7 is activated by a Standard Notice of Insurance Cover HB6, to be discussed next. The consideration to be paid and received for HB7 is again a nominal five pence.

Before reading the Policy the purchaser is warned that:

"1. Certain words and phrases contained in the Policy have been particularly defined and the Policy must be interpreted in accordance with those Definitions.
2. The cover afforded by each Section of the Policy is subject not only to the Special Conditions applying to that Section but also to the General Exclusions, Limitation on Liability, and General Conditions."

Two definitions should be noted at the outset. "Purchaser" is defined differently on the Policy to the Agreement and means "any person who purchases the Dwelling whether or not from the Vendor bona fide intending that he, his tenants or licensees should occupy it as a residence (but if such person is a Public Authority it shall not qualify as "the Purchaser" if the Dwelling was designed by it, or on its behalf) and such person's mortgagees in possession: no person who purchases other than from the Vendor shall qualify as "the Purchaser" unless the First Purchaser himself so qualified." Thus included is a person or organisation who lets the property to residential tenants, whether on a private or commercial basis. Excluded is the landlord who lets the property for

---

[41] House Purchaser's Insurance Policy HB7B and HB7C are used where the vendor is a public authority.

purely commercial purposes, for example, offices or shops. Also excluded is a person who buys a property solely for resale, and once the first purchaser is denied insurance cover a subsequent purchaser cannot claim the benefit of it. The phrase "to purchase" is elaborately defined. It means:

"(a) to exchange contracts for the acquisition of the freehold or leasehold interest (provided it be for a term exceeding 21 years at the date it is or was acquired by the First Purchaser): in this case completion of the purchase takes place upon legal completion; or

(b) otherwise to acquire such interest: in this case completion of the purchase takes place when such interest is acquired; or

(c) to enter into an agreement with the Vendor for the construction of a dwelling: in this case completion of the purchase takes place when the Council issues the Notice of Insurance Cover."

The only part of this definition that needs further comment is part (c). Completion is set at the date of the issue of the Notice of Insurance Cover for the avoidance of doubt, because many building agreements do not specify a proper completion date.

The Special Conditions governing each section will be discussed with that section; the General Exclusions, Limitations and Conditions at the end. It will be remembered that no test of "reasonableness" can be applied to any of the exclusions contained in the Policy; the provisions of the Unfair Contract Terms Act 1977 do not apply because the N.H.B.C. scheme is an approved one under section 2 of the Defective Premises Act 1972.

The cover given by the Insurance Policy is divided into three sections.

Section I: Loss Before Issue of Notice of Insurance Cover

In this section the Council undertakes to compensate the purchaser for loss incurred before the date of issue of a Notice of Insurance Cover and caused by the vendor's failure due to his bankruptcy, liquidation or fraud to commence or to complete the dwelling in accordance with the Council's Requirements. A claim only arises under Section I if it was caused by the vendor's bankruptcy, liquidation or fraud. If the vendor fails to construct the dwelling in accordance with the Council's Requirements for any other reason, the purchaser must pursue his remedies against the vendor himself.

The risks covered are as follows:

(a) If work on the dwelling has not started the Council will refund any amounts the purchaser has paid *in respect of the dwelling* and which are irrecoverable from the vendor; but the purchaser must have a binding contract with the vendor. Examples would be deposits and reservation fees.

(b) If work on the dwelling has been started but not substantially completed:

(i) Provided that the purchaser has completed the purchase the Council may, at its own choosing, either pay the cost of remedying defects in that part of the dwelling that has been completed and of doing the remaining work, or refund as in (a).

(ii) If the purchaser has exchanged contracts but not yet completed the purchase, he is only entitled to a refund as in (a).

(c) If the dwelling has been substantially completed the Council will pay the costs of remedying any defect or damage. Once the defect or damage has been remedied and the dwelling complies with the Council's Requirements the purchaser will be issued with a Standard Notice of Insurance Cover.

As in Agreement HB5, for the cost of defects or damage to be recoverable under the Policy, the defect must have been caused by a breach of the Council's Requirements and the damage by such defect.

To make a claim under Section I the purchaser must give the Council notice in writing within three months of the adjudication in bankruptcy or winding up of the vendor or the discovery of his fraud (to ensure that claims are made promptly). Even if the purchaser establishes his claim he does not recover the full amount of his loss. Any amounts payable under the section are subject to a deduction of 10 per cent. or 2 per cent. of the purchase price of the dwelling, if less. In the event of a purchase being completed after the vendor's bankruptcy, fraud or liquidation at a price less than the original purchase price the purchaser has to refund any sums paid to him by the Council, but not over and above the difference between the price he has paid and the original purchase price.

Section II: Loss During the Initial Guarantee Period

Here the purchaser is covered for the cost of remedying any defect or damage to the dwelling which first appears and is reported by him in writing within the Initial Guarantee Period but which the vendor fails to remedy under Clause 6 of the House Purchaser's Agreement. Claims under Section II are subject to the following Special Conditions:

(1) The purchaser must have commenced arbitration or legal proceedings within twelve months from the expiry of the Initial Guarantee Period and obtained an award or judgement against the vendor which has not been met. But it is not necessary for the purchaser to have taken these steps against the vendor if his chances of success were remote due to the vendor being bankrupt or in liquidation or having insufficient assets.

(ii) If a Structural Notice of Insurance Cover[42] has been issued in respect of the dwelling, the purchaser can only recover the cost of remedying major defects in the structure.

(iii) If an Endorsed Notice of Insurance Cover[43] has been issued in respect of the dwelling the purchaser cannot recover anything in respect of the endorsed matters.

(iv) Again the claim is not paid in full. A 10 per cent. deduction is made subject to a maximum deduction of 2 per cent. of the purchase price of the dwelling. For the purpose of calculating

---

[42] Described *post*, p. 487.
[43] Explained *post*, p. 487.

the maximum deduction the original purchase price is increased from the date of completion of the first purchase (or Notice of Insurance Cover if later) until the claim in line with the Housing Cost Index or if less at the rate of 15 per cent. per annum compound. In other words the original purchase price is adjusted at the date of the claim to take account of inflation and the maximum deduction calculated from that new figure.

Section III: Loss During the Structural Guarantee Period

In Section III the Council agrees to pay the cost of major damage appearing and reported during the Structural Guarantee Period due to a defect in the structure or subsidence, settlement or heave (provided that major damage has appeared), not covered by other insurance.

"Major Damage" means "Damage to the Dwelling requiring complete or partial rebuilding or extensive repair work. It includes Damage classified as very severe or severe in Appendix A to the Building Research Establishment Current Paper on "Foundations for Low-Rise Buildings (61/78)." The Structural Guarantee Period runs from the end of the Initial Guarantee Period till ten years from the date of the Notice of Insurance Cover.

Special Conditions exclude the Council's liability under Section III for:

   (i) matters for which notice was or should have been given during the Initial Guarantee Period.
  (ii) claims payable under Section II.
 (iii) negligence, other than that of the vendor, his engineer, architect, surveyor, sub-contractor, employee or agent. This represents an extension of the previous cover; responsibility was only accepted for the negligence of the builder and his sub-contractor.
  (iv) loss, where legislation provides compensation.
   (v) defective design when the structural or installation design details were provided by the first purchaser.
  (vi) anything built into the dwelling other than under the original sale or building contract.
 (vii) defects relating to lifts and swimming pools.
(viii) wear and tear.
  (ix) normal dampness, condensation or shrinkage.
   (x) claims by a Public Authority for subsidence, settlement or heave for a dwelling built on its own land.

No deduction is made from sums payable under Section III.

General Exclusions

Four General Exclusions relate to all three sections. The Council is not liable for:

   1. "professional fees, alternative accommodation, removal expenses,

loss of enjoyment, inconvenience, distress or any other consequential loss of any kind or description whatsoever and howsoever arising."

2. common parts, except to the extent that the purchaser is liable to share in the cost of repair.
3. gradual deterioration caused by neglect.
4. defects or damage where prompt written notice was not given to the Council by the previous owner.

The last exclusion emphasises the need for a purchaser's solicitor to ensure before exchange of contracts that the vendor has notified all claims and to obtain an undertaking from him to notify any claims arising before completion.

Limitations on Liability

OVERALL LIMITATION

For dwellings registered (that is, for which applications for inspection were received) between April 1, 1979 and September 31, 1983 the Council's overall liability is £10m, for any year's intake. For dwellings registered from October 1, 1983 the overall annual cover has been increased to £20m.

LIMITATION PER DWELLING

(a) under Section I: £5000.
(b) under Sections II and III: the purchase price of the dwelling up to a maximum of £50,000 or twice the National Average Purchase Price at the date of completion if greater. For the purpose of cover year by year the purchase price (up to the maximum above) is increased in line with the Housing Cost Index or if less at the rate of 15 per cent. per annum compound.

LIMITATION PER VENDOR FOR ANY YEAR ENDING 31ST MARCH

(a) under Section I: £125,000.
(b) under Sections II and III: £500,000 or £200 times the number of dwellings registered by the vendor in that year if greater.

COMMON PARTS

Insurance payments made in respect of Common Parts can be apportioned between all those liable to meet the cost of repair or reinstatement.

LIMITATION PER DEFECT

(a) The Council's liability for the cost of remedying defects is limited to:
    (i) "the amount a reasonable man spending his own money would himself spend for that purpose;" and
    (ii) "the Notional cost increased from the date of completion of the first purchase (or, if later, the date of issue of the Notice of Insurance Cover) until the date of payment of a claim in line with the Housing Cost Index (or, if less, at the rate of 15 per cent. per annum compound)". "Notional Cost" means "the cost of remedying the Defect or Damage at the date of payment

of the claim multiplied by the Housing Cost Index at the date of completion of the first purchase (or, if later, the date of issue of the Notice of Insurance Cover) and divided by the Housing Cost Index at the date of payment of the claim." A formula easily understood by the man on the Clapham omnibus! Thanks to Professor J.E. Adams[44] who explains that it means "payment will be of the actual cost, unless taking the actual cost, reducing it by applying the index in reverse to produce the "back-dated" cost and adjusting that upwards by the mathematical formula of the actual rise in the index or 15 per cent. per annum compound (whichever is the less) produces a lower figure, when only that sum is paid."

(b) If the Council chooses to repair or reinstate the dwelling itself "it shall not be liable to do any more than a reasonable man spending his own money would himself do for that purpose."

Assuming that the reader has managed to struggle his way through the limitations this far, he will have appreciated that the purchaser may derive considerable benefit from the cover being index linked. In 1975 because of galloping rates of inflation and not wishing to deliver another blow to an already struggling building industry by increasing fees, the Council limited the cost of repairs for dwellings registered from October 1, 1975 to the date on which the Certificate (now the Notice) of Insurance Cover was issued. A purchaser could however protect himself by buying "Top up Cover" which effectively achieved the same result at above. But "Top up Cover" was available to first purchasers only, not second or subsequent purchasers, although if taken up by the first purchaser, it was automatically transferred to subsequent owners. If acting for a purchaser of a dwelling protected by HB5 (1975) or (1977) it is important to check whether "Top up Cover" was bought by the first purchaser.

GENERAL CONDITIONS

Eleven General Conditions follow the Limitations. They are conditions precedent to any claim under the Policy and necessitate the following actions by the purchaser; prompt notice to the Council of claims, return of completed claim forms within one month, payment of investigation fees, facilitating inspection, and producing two builder's estimates at his own expense for repairs. The vendor's name must have been on the Council's register at the time the House Purchaser's Agreement was entered into and any disputes arising out of the Policy must be referred to arbitration.

THE STANDARD NOTICE OF INSURANCE COVER, HB6

This is a short but important document. As it explains to the purchaser, it "brings into operation valuable insurance benefits in respect of the

---

[44] (1980) 130 New.L.J. 197.

above Dwelling." Most dwellings will be issued with a Standard Notice of Insurance Cover. This states that the Council's Requirements as to design and construction have or appear to have been substantially complied with in relation to the dwelling, and will entitle the purchaser to the full benefit of the Insurance Policy. Sometimes a Structural or Endorsed Notice of Insurance cover is given. The former states that the Council's Requirements as to the structure of roof coverings have or appear to have been substantially complied with in relation to the dwelling and the insurance cover is modified accordingly. The latter states that most of the Council's requirements have been met in relation to the dwelling but not in respect of the endorsed matters (not the structure and roof coverings). The endorsed matters are not insured. A Common Parts Notice of Insurance Cover states that the Council's Requirements in respect of the Common Parts have been met in relation to the dwelling.

All Notices bear the following exclusion clause (which is not subject to the provisions of the Unfair Contract Terms Act 1977):

> "The Council employs inspectors to assist it in deciding whether to issue this Notice but they are able to make spot-check inspections only. Except in accordance with the Insurance Policy, the Council, its servants or its agents shall not be liable to compensate any person for any loss or damage (including consequential loss) of any kind or description whatsoever, arising out of or in respect of the Dwelling or any inspection of it, and whether caused by the negligence of the Council, its servants or agents or in any other way."

The clause was introduced into the Notice to allay fears that the Council may be held liable in negligence for its inspection procedures in the same way as Local Authorities have been in several cases[45] following the decision in *Anns* v. *Merton London Borough Council*.[46]

NOTE

In the summer of 1983 the N.H.B.C. announced its intention to extend its scheme to conversions of existing properties.

---

[45] See, for example, *Acrecrest Ltd.* v. *W. S. Hattrell & Partners* (1982) 3 W.L.R. 1076; *Eames London Estates* v. *North Hertfordshire District Council* (1980) 259 E.G. 491; *Worlock* v. *Saws* (1982) 260 E.G. 774.
[46] [1978] A.C. 728.

Appendix

The Law Society's General Conditions of Sale (1984 Revision)

Reproduced by kind permission of the Law Society and of the Solicitors' Law Stationery Society, plc.

The National Conditions of Sale (20th edition 1981)

Reproduced by kind permission of the Solicitors' Law Stationery Society, plc.

The Law Society's General Conditions of Sale (1984 Revision)

1 DEFINITIONS
In these conditions—
(a) "completion notice" means a notice served under condition 23 (2)
(b) "the contract rate" means the rate specified in a special condition or, if none is so specified, the rate prescribed from time to time under section 32 of the Land Compensation Act 1961 for interest payable thereunder
(c) "contractual completion date" has the meaning given in condition 21
(d) "conveyance" includes an assignment and a transfer under the Land Registration Acts
(e) "lease" includes underlease
(f) "normal deposit" means the sum which, together with any preliminary deposit paid by the purchaser, amounts to ten per centum of the purchase money (excluding any separate price to be paid for any chattels, fixtures or fittings)
(g) "working day" means any day from Monday to Friday (inclusive) other than—
  (i) Christmas Day, Good Friday and any statutory bank holiday, and
  (ii) any other day specified in a special condition as not a working day
(h) a reference to a statute includes any amendment or re-enactment thereof.

2 SERVICE AND DELIVERY
(1) Section 196 of the Law of Property Act 1925 applies to any notice served under the contract, save that—
(a) a notice shall also be sufficiently served on a party if served on that party's solicitors
(b) a reference to a registered letter shall include a prepaid first class ordinary letter
(c) if the time at which a letter containing a notice would in the ordinary course be delivered is not on a working day, the notice shall be deemed to be served on the next following working day
(d) a notice shall also be sufficiently served if—
  (i) sent by telex or by telegraphic facsimile transmission to the party to be served, and that service shall be deemed to be made on the day of transmission if transmitted before 4 p.m. on a working day, but otherwise on the next following working day
  (ii) when the addressee is a member of a document exchange (as to which the inclusion of a reference thereto in the solicitors' letterhead shall be conclusive evidence) delivered to that or any other affiliated exchange, and that service shall be deemed to have been made on the first working day after that on which the document would, in the ordinary course, be available for collection by the addressee.
(2) Sub-condition (1) applies to the delivery of documents as it applies to the service of notices.

3 MATTERS AFFECTING THE PROPERTY
(1) In this condition—
(a) "competent authority" means a local authority or other body exercising powers under statute or Royal Charter
(b) "requirement" includes (whether or not subject to confirmation) any notice, order or proposal
(c) "relevant matter" means any matter specified in sub-condition (2) whenever arising.
(2) The property is sold subject to—
(a) all matters registrable by any competent authority pursuant to statute
(b) all requirements of any competent authority
(c) all matters disclosed or reasonably to be expected to be disclosed by searches and as a result of enquiries formal or informal, and whether made in person, by writing or orally by or for the purchaser or which a prudent purchaser ought to make
(d) all notices served by or on behalf of a reversioner, a tenant or sub-tenant, or the owner or occupier of any adjoining or neighbouring property.
(3) (a) Notwithstanding sub-condition (2), the vendor warrants that he has informed the purchaser of the contents of any written communication received by, or known to, the vendor on or before the working day preceding the date of the contract relating to any relevant matter. Failure to give such information before the contract is made shall be deemed to be an omission in a statement in the course of the negotiations leading to the contract, but shall give rise to no right to compensation to the extent that the purchaser has a claim for damages against a competent authority

(b) In the event of any conflict or variation between information in fact received from any competent authority relating to any relevant matter and any statement made by the vendor in respect of the same matter, the purchaser shall rely on the information received from the competent authority to the exclusion of that given by the vendor

(c) The vendor shall forthwith inform the purchaser of the contents of any written communication received by him after the working day preceding the date of the contract and before the day of actual completion which if received on or before the former day would have fallen within paragraph (a).

(4) The purchaser (subject to any right or remedy arising under sub-condition (3)) will indemnify the vendor in respect of any liability under any requirement of a competent authority (whether made before or after the date of the contract), including the reasonable cost to the vendor of compliance after reasonable notice to the purchaser of the vendor's intention to comply, such sum to be payable on demand. The provisions of this sub-condition shall prevail in the event of conflict with any other condition.

4 OPPORTUNITY TO RESCIND

(1) This condition only applies if a special condition so provides.

(2) Within such period as is specified in a special condition or, if none is so specified, within twenty working days from the date of the contract (as to which, in either case, time shall be of the essence), the purchaser shall be entitled, notwithstanding condition 3 (2), to rescind the contract by service of notice on the vendor specifying a matter to which this condition applies affecting the property.

(3) This condition applies to any of the following matters of which the purchaser had no knowledge on or before the working day preceding the date of the contract—

(a) a financial charge which the vendor cannot or has not at the purchaser's written request agreed to discharge on or before actual completion

(b) a statutory provision prohibiting, restricting or imposing adverse conditions upon the use or the continued use of the property for such purpose as is specified in a special condition or, if none is so specified, the purpose for which the vendor used it immediately before the date of the contract

(c) a matter which is likely materially to reduce the price which a willing purchaser could otherwise reasonably be expected to pay for the relevant interest in the property in the open market at the date of the contract.

(4) For the purposes of this condition, the purchaser's knowledge—

(a) includes everything in writing received in the course of the transaction leading to the contract by a person acting on his behalf from the vendor, a person acting on the vendor's behalf, or a competent authority (as defined in condition 3 (1) (a))

(b) does not include anything solely because a statute deems that registration of a matter constitutes actual notice of it.

5 EASEMENTS, RESERVATIONS, RIGHTS AND LIABILITIES

(1) The vendor warrants that he has disclosed to the purchaser the existence of all easements, rights, privileges and liabilities affecting the property, of which the vendor knows or ought to know, other than the existence of those known to the purchaser at the date of the contract, or which a prudent purchaser would have discovered by that date.

(2) Without prejudice to the generality of sub-condition (1)—

(a) the purchaser shall purchase with full notice of the actual state and condition of the property and shall take it as it stands, save where it is to be constructed or converted by the vendor

(b) the property is sold, and will if the vendor so requires be conveyed, subject to all rights of way, water, light, drainage and other easements, rights, privileges and liabilities affecting the same.

(3) (a) In this sub-condition "the retained land" means land retained by the vendor—

    (i) adjoining the property, or

    (ii) near to the property and designated as retained land in a special condition.

(b) The conveyance of the property shall contain such reservations in favour of the retained land and the grant of such rights over the retained land as would have been implied had the vendor conveyed both the property and the retained land by simultaneous conveyances to different purchasers.

6   TENANCIES

(1) This condition applies if the property is sold subject to any lease or tenancy and shall have effect notwithstanding any partial, incomplete or inaccurate reference to any lease or tenancy in the special conditions or the particulars of the property.

(2) Copies or full particulars of all leases or tenancies not vested in the purchaser having been furnished to him, he shall be deemed to purchase with full knowledge thereof and shall take the property subject to the rights of the tenants thereunder or by reason thereof. The purchaser shall indemnify the vendor against all claims, demands and liability in respect of such rights, notwithstanding that they may be void against a purchaser for want of registration.

(3) The vendor gives no warranty as to the amount of rent lawfully recoverable from any tenant, as to the effect of any legislation in relation to any lease or tenancy or as to the compliance with any legislation affecting the same.

(4) The vendor shall inform the purchaser of any change in the disclosed terms and conditions of any lease or tenancy.

(5) If a lease or tenancy subject to which the property is sold terminates for any reason, the vendor shall inform the purchaser and, on being indemnified by the purchaser against all consequential loss, expenditure or liability, shall act as the purchaser may direct.

7   ERRORS, OMISSIONS AND MISSTATEMENTS

(1) No error, omission or misstatement herein or in any plan furnished or any statement made in the course of the negotiations leading to the contract shall annul the sale or entitle the purchaser to be discharged from the purchase.

(2) Any such error, omission or misstatement shown to be material shall entitle the purchaser or the vendor, as the case may be, to proper compensation, provided that the purchaser shall not in any event be entitled to compensation for matters falling within conditions 5 (2) or 6 (3).

(3) No immaterial error, omission or misstatement (including a mistake in any plan furnished for identification only) shall entitle either party to compensation.

(4) Sub-condition (1) shall not apply where compensation for any error, omission or misstatement shown to be material cannot be assessed nor enable either party to compel the other to accept or convey property differing substantially (in quantity, quality tenure or otherwise) from the property agreed to be sold if the other party would be prejudiced by the difference.

(5) The purchaser acknowledges that in making the contract he has not relied on any statement made to him save one made or confirmed in writing.

8   LEASEHOLDS

(1) This condition applies if the property is leasehold.

(2) In all cases the immediate title to the property shall begin with the lease. Where the lease, unless registered with absolute title, is dated not more than fifteen years before the date of the contract and was granted for a term exceeding twenty-one years, the freehold title and all other titles superior to the lease shall be deduced for a period beginning not less than fifteen years prior to the date of the contract and ending on the date of the lease.

(3) A copy of the lease and a copy of, sufficient extract from, or abstract of, all superior leases, the contents of which are known to the vendor, having been supplied or made available to the purchaser, he shall be deemed to purchase with full notice of the contents thereof, whether or not he has inspected the same.

(4) Where any consent to assign is necessary—

(a) the vendor shall forthwith at his own cost apply for and use his best endeavours to obtain such consent

(b) the purchaser shall forthwith supply such information and references as may reasonably be required by the reversioner before granting such consent

(c) if any such consent is not granted at least five working days before contractual completion date, or is subject to any condition to which the purchaser reasonably objects, either party may rescind the contract by notice to the other.

(5) Any statutory implied covenant on the part of the vendor shall not extend to any breach of the terms of the lease as to the state and condition of the property and the assignment shall so provide. This sub-condition applies notwithstanding that a special condition provides for the vendor to convey as beneficial owner.

(6) Where the property is sold subject to an apportioned rent specified as such in a special condition, the purchaser shall not require the consent of the reversioner to be obtained, or the rent to be otherwise legally apportioned.

(7) The purchaser shall assume that any receipt for the last payment due for rent under the lease before actual completion was given by the person then entitled to such rent or his duly authorised agent.

9 DEPOSIT

(1) The purchaser shall on or before the date of the contract pay by way of deposit to the vendor's solicitors as stakeholders the normal deposit, or such lesser sum as the vendor shall have agreed in writing. On a sale by private treaty, payment shall be made by banker's draft or by cheque drawn on a solicitors' bank account.

(2) Upon service by the vendor of a completion notice, the purchaser shall pay to the vendor any difference between the normal deposit and any amount actually paid (if less).

(3) If any draft, cheque or other instrument tendered in or towards payment of any sum payable under this condition is dishonoured when first presented the vendor shall have the right by notice to the purchaser within seven working days thereafter to treat the contract as repudiated.

10 OPTIONAL METHODS OF EXCHANGE

(1) Exchange of contracts may be effected by a method authorised by condition 2 for the service of notices. If so effected, the contract shall be made when the last part is, as the case may be, posted or delivered to a document exchange.

(2) Where contracts have not been exchanged, the parties' solicitors may agree by telephone or telex that the contract be immediately effective and thereupon the solicitors holding a part of the contract signed by their client shall hold it irrevocably to the order of the other party.

11 INSURANCE

(1) If the property is destroyed or damaged prior to actual completion and the proceeds of any insurance policy effected by or for the purchaser are reduced by reason of the existence of any policy effected by or for the vendor, the purchase price shall be abated by the amount of such reduction.

(2) Sub-condition (1) shall not apply where the proceeds of the vendor's policy are applied towards the reinstatement of the property pursuant to any statutory or contractual obligation.

(3) This condition takes effect in substitution for section 47 of the Law of Property Act 1925.

(4) The vendor shall be under no duty to the purchaser to maintain any insurance on the property, save where the property is leasehold and the vendor has an obligation to insure.

12 ABSTRACT OF TITLE

(1) Forthwith upon exchange of contracts the vendor shall deliver to the purchaser—

(a) where the title is not registered, an abstract of the title to the property or an epitome of the title together with photocopies of the relevant documents

(b) where the title is registered—

  (i) the documents, particulars and information specified in sub-sections (1) and (2) of section 110 of the Land Registration Act 1925, save that copies of the entries on the register, the filed plan and any documents noted on the register and filed in the registry shall be office copies, and

  (ii) such additional authorities to inspect the register as the purchaser shall reasonably require for any sub-purchaser or prospective mortgagee or lessee.

(2) Where the title is not registered, the vendor shall at his own expense produce the relevant documents of title or an abstract, epitome of title or copy thereof (bearing in each case original markings of examination of all relevant documents of title or of examined abstracts thereof).

(3) Where before the date of the contract any abstract, epitome or document has been delivered to the purchaser, he shall not, save as provided by conditions 6 (2) or 8 (3), be deemed to have had notice before the date of the contract of any matter of title thereby disclosed.

13   IDENTITY AND BOUNDARIES

(1) The vendor shall produce such evidence as may be reasonably necessary to establish the identity and extent of the property, but shall not be required to define exact boundaries, or the ownership of fences, ditches, hedges or walls, nor, beyond the evidence afforded by the information in his possession, separately to identify parts of the property held under different titles.

(2) If reasonably required by the purchaser because of the insufficiency of the evidence produced under sub-condition (1), the vendor shall at his own expense provide and hand over on completion a statutory declaration as to the relevant facts, in a form agreed by the purchaser, such agreement not to be unreasonably withheld.

14   MORTGAGES IN FAVOUR OF FRIENDLY AND OTHER SOCIETIES

Where the title includes a mortgage or legal charge in favour of trustees on behalf of a friendly society, a building society or a society registered under the Industrial and Provident Societies Acts, the purchaser shall assume that any receipt given on the discharge of any such mortgage or legal charge and apparently duly executed was in fact duly executed by all proper persons and is valid.

15   REQUISITIONS

(1) In this condition "abstract" means all the documents, particulars and information required to be delivered by the vendor under condition 12.

(2) Subject to sub-condition (4), the purchaser shall deliver any requisitions or objections relating to the title, evidence of title or the abstract, in writing within six working days of receipt of the abstract (or, in the case of an abstract delivered before the date of the contract, within six working days of the date of contract). Within four working days of such delivery the vendor shall deliver his replies in writing.

(3) The purchaser shall deliver any observations on any of the vendor's replies in writing within four working days of their receipt.

(4) Where some but not all parts of the abstract have been delivered, and defects in title are not disclosed by such parts of the abstract as have been delivered, then in respect only of the undelivered parts or undisclosed defects (as the case may be) the abstract shall be deemed to be received for the purpose of sub-condition (2) at the time or respective times when any previously undelivered part is delivered.

(5) Time shall be of the essence for the purposes of this condition.

16   RESCISSION

(1) If the vendor is unable, or on some reasonable ground unwilling, to satisfy any requisition or objection made by the purchaser, the vendor may give the purchaser notice (specifying the reason for his inability or the ground of his unwillingness) to withdraw the same. If the purchaser does not withdraw the same within seven working days of service, either party may thereafter, notwithstanding any intermediate negotiation or litigation, rescind the contract by notice to the other.

(2) Upon rescission under any power given by these conditions or any special condition—

(a) the vendor shall repay to the purchaser any sums paid by way of deposit or otherwise under the contract, with interest on such sums at the contract rate from four working days after rescission until payment

(b) the purchaser shall forthwith return all documents delivered to him by the vendor and at his own expense procure the cancellation of any entry relating to the contract in any register.

17   PREPARATION OF CONVEYANCE

(1) The purchaser shall deliver the draft conveyance at least twelve working days before contractual completion date, and within four working days of such delivery the vendor shall deliver it back approved or revised.

(2) The purchaser shall deliver the engrossment of the conveyance (first executed by him, where requisite) at least five working days before contractual completion date.

(3) The purchaser shall not, by delivering the draft conveyance or the engrossment, be deemed to accept the vendor's title or to waive any right to raise or maintain requisitions.

(4) Save to the extent that a covenant for indemnity will be implied by statute, the purchaser shall in the conveyance covenant to indemnify the vendor and his estate (and any estate of which the vendor is personal representative or trustee) against all actions, claims and liability for any breach of any covenant, stipulation, provision or other matter subject to which the property is sold and in respect of which the vendor or any such estate will remain liable after completion.

(5) The vendor shall give an acknowledgment for production and, unless in a fiduciary capacity, an undertaking for safe custody of documents of title retained by him. Where any such document is retained by a mortgagee, trustee or personal representative, the vendor shall procure that such person shall give an acknowledgment for production, and the vendor, unless in a fiduciary capacity, shall covenant that if and when he receives any such document he will, at the cost of the person requiring it, give an undertaking for safe custody.

(6) The vendor shall be entitled on reasonable grounds to decline to convey the property to any person other than the purchaser, by more than one conveyance, at more than the contract price or at a price divided between different parts of the property.

18 OCCUPATION BEFORE COMPLETION

(1) This condition applies if the vendor authorises the purchaser to occupy the property before actual completion, except—

(a) where the purchaser already lawfully occupies any part of the property, or

(b) where the property is a dwellinghouse and the authority for the occupation is only for the purpose of effecting works of decoration, repair or improvement agreed by the vendor.

(2) The purchaser occupies the property as licensee and not as tenant. The purchaser may not transfer his licence or authorise any other person save members of his immediate family to occupy any part of the property.

(3) The purchaser shall not, by taking such occupation, be deemed to accept the vendor's title or to waive any right to raise or maintain requisitions.

(4) While the purchaser is in occupation of the whole or any part of the property under this condition, he shall—

(a) pay and indemnify the vendor against all outgoings and any other expenses in respect of the property and pay to the vendor in respect of such occupation a sum calculated at the contract rate on the amount of the purchase money (less any deposit paid)

(b) be entitled to receive any rents and profits from any part of the property not occupied by him

(c) insure the property in a sum not less than the purchase price against all risks in respect of which premises of the like nature are normally insured.

(5) The purchaser's licence to occupy the property shall end—

(a) on contractual completion date, or

(b) upon termination of the contract, or

(c) upon the expiry of five working days' notice given by either party to the other,

and thereupon the purchaser shall give up occupation of the property and leave the same in as good repair as it was in when he went into occupation.

(6) If the purchaser, after his licence has ended under sub-condition 5(a), remains in occupation with the express or implied consent of the vendor, he shall thereafter occupy on the other terms of this condition and on the further term that the vendor's rights under condition 22 shall not thereby be affected.

19 APPORTIONMENTS

(1) In this condition—

(a) "the apportionment day" means—

(i) if the property is sold with vacant possession of the whole, the date of actual completion

(ii) in any other case, contractual completion date

(b) "payment period" means one of the periods for which a sum payable periodically is payable, whether or not such periods are of equal length.

(2) This condition shall not apply to any sum if—

(a) the purchaser cannot, by virtue only of becoming the owner of the property, either enforce payment of it or be obliged to pay it, or

(b) it is an outgoing paid in advance, unless the vendor cannot obtain repayment and the purchaser benefits therefrom or is given credit therefor against a sum that would otherwise be his liability.

(3) On completion the income and outgoings of the property shall, subject to sub-condition (2) and conditions 3 and 22(4) and to any adjustment required by condition 18(4), be apportioned as at the apportionment day.

(4) For the purposes of apportionment only, it shall be assumed—

(a) that the vendor remains owner of the property until the end of the apportionment day, and

(b) that the sum to be apportioned—

(i) accrues from day to day

(ii) is payable throughout the relevant period at the same rate as on the apportionment day.

(5) Sums payable periodically shall be apportioned by charging or allowing—
(a) for any payment period entirely attributable to one party, the whole of the instalment payable therefor
(b) for any part of a payment period, a proportion on an annual basis.
(6) (a) This sub-condition applies to any sum payable in respect of any period falling wholly or partly prior to the apportionment day, the amount of which is not notified to either party before actual completion
(b) A provisional apportionment shall be made on the best estimate available. Upon the amount being notified, a final apportionment shall be made and one party shall thereupon make to the other the appropriate balancing payment.

20   ENDORSEMENT OF MEMORANDUM
Where the vendor does not hand over all the documents of his title, he shall at completion endorse a memorandum of the sale to the purchaser on the last such document in each relevant title and thereupon produce the endorsed documents for inspection.

21   COMPLETION
(1) Contractual completion date shall be as stated in the special conditions but if not so stated shall be the twenty-fifth working day after the date of the contract. Completion shall take place in England or Wales either at the office of the vendor's solicitors or, if required by the vendor at least five working days prior to actual completion, at the office of the vendor's mortgagee or his solicitors.
(2) The vendor shall not be obliged to accept payment of the money due on completion otherwise than by one or more of the following methods—
(a) legal tender
(b) a banker's draft drawn by and upon a settlement bank for the purposes of the Clearing House Automated Payments System or any other bank specified in a special condition
(c) an unconditional authority to release any deposit held by a stakeholder
(d) otherwise as the vendor shall have agreed before actual completion.
(3) If completion is effected otherwise than by personal attendance the time for completion is when on a working day
(a) the money due on completion is paid to the vendor or his solicitors, and
(b) the vendor's solicitors hold to the order of the purchaser all the documents to which he is entitled on completion.
(4) For the purposes of this condition money is paid when the vendor receives payment by a method specified in sub-condition (2). Where the parties have agreed upon a direct credit to a bank account at a named branch, payment is made when that branch receives the credit.
(5) (a) This sub-condition applies if the money due on completion is not paid by 2.30 p.m. on the day of actual completion or by such other time on that day as is specified in a special condition
(b) For the purposes of condition 22 only, completion shall be deemed to be postponed by reason of the purchaser's delay from the day of actual completion until the next working day
(c) The purchaser shall not as a result of the deemed postponement of completion be liable to make any payment to the vendor unless the vendor claims such payment by giving notice at completion or within five working days thereafter (as to which period time shall be of the essence). Payment shall be due five working days after receipt of such notice.

22   COMPENSATION FOR LATE COMPLETION
(1) For the purposes of this condition—
(a) "delay" means failure to perform or lateness in performing any obligation of the contract which causes or contributes to lateness in completion
(b) a party is "in default" if and to the extent that the period, or the aggregate of the periods, of his delay exceeds the period, or the aggregate of the periods, of delay of the other party
(c) "the period of default" means the length of the excess defined in paragraph (b) or, if shorter, the period from contractual completion date to the date of actual completion.
(2) If the sale shall be completed after contractual completion date, the party in default (if any) shall be liable to compensate the other for loss occasioned to him by reason of that default.
(3) Before actual completion, or within five working days thereafter (as to which period time shall be of the essence), the party entitled to compensation may, by notice to the other party, opt to be paid or allowed a sum calculated at the contract rate on the amount of the purchase money (less any deposit paid) for the period of default as liquidated damages in settlement of his claim for compensation.

(4) If the vendor is entitled to compensation, he may, before actual completion, by notice to the purchaser, opt to take the net income of the property for the period of default in lieu of such compensation.

(5) The right to recover any compensation under this condition shall not be prejudiced by completion of the sale, whether before or after the commencement of proceedings.

23 COMPLETION NOTICE

(1) This condition applies unless a special condition provides that time is of the essence in respect of contractual completion date.

(2) If the sale shall not be completed on contractual completion date, either party, being then himself ready able and willing to complete, may after that date serve on the other party notice to complete the transaction in accordance with this condition. A party shall be deemed to be ready, able and willing to complete—

(*a*) if he could be so but for some default or omission of the other party

(*b*) notwithstanding that any mortgage on the property is unredeemed when the completion notice is served if the aggregate of all sums necessary to redeem all such mortgages (to the extent that they relate to the property) does not exceed the sum payable on completion.

(3) Upon service of a completion notice it shall become a term of the contract that the transaction shall be completed within fifteen working days of service and in respect of such period time shall be of the essence.

(4) If the purchaser does not comply with a completion notice—

(*a*) the purchaser shall forthwith return all documents delivered to him by the vendor and at his own expense procure the cancellation of any entry relating to the contract in any register

(*b*) without prejudice to any other rights or remedies available to him, the vendor may—

    (i) forfeit and retain any deposit paid and/or

    (ii) re-sell the property by auction, tender or private treaty.

(5) If on any such re-sale contracted within one year after contractual completion date the vendor incurs a loss and so elects by notice to the purchaser within one month after the contract for such re-sale, the purchaser shall pay to the vendor liquidated damages. The amount payable shall be the aggregate of such loss, all costs and expenses reasonably incurred in any such re-sale and any attempted re-sale and interest at the contract rate on such part of the purchase money as is from time to time outstanding (giving credit for all sums received under any re-sale contract on account of the re-sale price) after contractual completion date.

(6) If the vendor does not comply with a completion notice, the purchaser, without prejudice to any other rights or remedies available to him, may give notice to the vendor forthwith to pay to the purchaser any sums paid by way of deposit or otherwise under the contract and interest on such sums at the contract rate from four working days after service of the notice until payment. On compliance with such notice the purchaser shall not be entitled to specific performance of the contract, but shall forthwith return all documents delivered to him by the vendor and at the expense of the vendor procure the cancellation of any entry relating to the contract in any register.

(7) Where after service of a completion notice the time for completion shall have been extended by agreement or implication, either party may again invoke the provisions of this condition which shall then take effect with the substitution of "seven working days" for "fifteen working days" in sub-condition (3).

24 CHATTELS

The property in any chattels agreed to be sold shall pass to the purchaser on actual completion.

25 AUCTIONS

(1) This condition applies if the property is sold by auction.

(2) The sale is subject to a reserve price for the property and, when the property is sold in lots, for each lot.

(3) The vendor reserves the right—

(*a*) to divide the property into lots and to sub-divide, re-arrange or consolidate any lots

(*b*) to bid personally or by his agent up to any reserve price

(*c*) without disclosing any reserve price, to withdraw from the sale any property or lot at any time before it has been sold, whether or not the sale has begun.

(4) The auctioneer may—

(*a*) refuse to accept a bid

(*b*) in the case of a dispute as to any bid, forthwith determine the dispute or again put up the property or lot at the last undisputed bid.

(5) The purchaser shall forthwith complete and sign the contract and pay, but not necessarily by the means specified in condition 9(1), the normal deposit.

The National Conditions of Sale (20th edition 1981)

Construction of the conditions

In these conditions, where the context admits—

(1) The "vendor" and the "purchaser" include the persons deriving title under them respectively

(2) "Purchase money" includes any sum to be paid for chattels, fittings or other separate items

(3) References to the "Special Conditions" include references to the particulars of sale and to the provisions of the contract which is made by reference to the conditions

(4) The "prescribed rate" means the agreed rate of interest or, if none, then the rate of interest prescribed from time to time under Land Compensation Act 1961, s. 32

(5) "Solicitor" includes a barrister who is employed by a corporate body to carry out conveyancing on its behalf and is acting in the course of his employment

(6) "Working day" means a day on which clearing banks in the City of London are (or would be but for a strike, lock-out, or other stoppage, affecting particular banks or banks generally) open during banking hours Except in condition 19(4), in which "working day" means a day when the Land Registry is open to the public

(7) "Designated bank" means a bank designated by the Chief Registrar under Building Societies Act 1962, s. 59

(8) The "Planning Acts" means the enactments from time to time in force relating to town and country planning

(9) On a sale by private treaty references to the "auctioneer" shall be read as references to the vendor's agent

(10) On a sale in lots, the conditions apply to each lot

(11) "Abstract of title" means in relation to registered land such documents as the vendor is required by Land Registration Act 1925, s. 110, to furnish.

The conditions

1. The Sale: by Auction: by Private Treaty

(1) Paragraphs (2) to (5) of this condition apply on a sale by auction and paragraphs (6) and (7) on a sale by private treaty

(2) Unless otherwise provided in the Special Conditions, the sale of the property and of each lot is subject to a reserve price and to a right for the vendor or any one person on behalf of the vendor to bid up to that price

(3) The auctioneer may refuse any bid and no person shall at any bid advance less than the amount fixed for that purpose by the auctioneer

(4) If any dispute arises respecting a bid, the auctioneer may determine the dispute or the property may, at the vendor's option, either be put up again at the last undisputed bid, or be withdrawn

(5) Subject to the foregoing provisions of this condition, the highest bidder shall be the purchaser and shall forthwith complete and sign the contract, the date of which shall be the date of the auction

(6) Where there is a draft contract, or an arrangement subject to contract, or a negotiation in which there are one or more outstanding items or suspensory matters (which prevent there being yet a concluded agreement of a contractual nature), a solicitor, who holds a document signed by his client in the form of a contract of sale in writing and embodying this condition, shall (unless the other party or his solicitor is informed to the contrary) have the authority of his client to conclude, by formal exchange of contracts, or by post, or by telex or other telegraphic means, or by telephone, and in any case with or without involving solicitors' undertakings, a binding contract in the terms of the document which his client has signed

(7) The date of the contract shall be—

    (i) the date, if any, which is agreed and put on the contract, but if none, then

    (ii) on an exchange of contracts by post (unless the parties' solicitors otherwise agree), the date on which the last part of the contract is posted, or

    (iii) in any other case, the date on which, consistently with this condition, a binding contract is concluded.

2. Deposit
(1) Unless the Special Conditions otherwise provide, the purchaser shall on the date of the contract pay a deposit of 10 per cent. of the purchase price, on a sale by auction, to the auctioneer, or on a sale by private treaty, to the vendor's solicitor and, in either case, as stakeholder
(2) In case a cheque taken for the deposit (having been presented, and whether or not it has been re-presented) has not been honoured, then and on that account the vendor may elect—
either   (i) to treat the contract as discharged by breach thereof on the purchaser's part
or   (ii) to enforce payment of the deposit as a deposit, by suing on the cheque or otherwise.

3. Purchaser's short right to rescind
(1) This condition shall have effect if the Special Conditions so provide, but not otherwise
(2) If the property is affected by any matter to which this condition applies, then the purchaser may by notice in writing (hereinafter referred to as a "Condition 3 Notice") given to the vendor or his solicitor and expressly referring to this condition and the matter in question, and notwithstanding any intermediate negotiation, rescind the contract on the same terms as if the purchaser had persisted in an objection to the title which the vendor was unable to remove
(3) A Condition 3 Notice shall not be given after the expiration of 16 working days from the date of the contract, time being of the essence of this condition
(4) This condition applies to any matter materially affecting the value of the property, other than—
    (i) a matter which was not yet in existence or subsisting at the date of the contract
    (ii) a specific matter to which the sale was expressly made subject, or
    (iii) a matter of which the purchaser had at the date of the contract express notice or actual knowledge, not being notice or knowledge imputed to the purchaser by statute solely by reason of a registration of such matter, or notice or knowledge which the purchaser is only deemed to have had by the conditions
(5) This condition and condition 15 are additional to each other.

4. Chattels, etc., and separate items
If the sale includes chattels, fittings or other separate items, the vendor warrants that he is entitled to sell the same free from any charge, lien, burden, or adverse claim.

5. Date and manner of completion
(1) The completion date shall be the date specified for the purpose in the contract or, if none, the 26th working day after the date of the contract or the date of delivery of the abstract of title, whichever be the later
(2) Unless the Special Conditions otherwise provide, in respect of the completion date time shall not be of the essence of the contract, but this provision shall operate subject and without prejudice to—
    (i) the provisions of condition 22 and
    (ii) the rights of either party to recover from the other damages for delay in fulfilling his obligations under the contract
(3) The purchaser's obligations to pay money due on completion shall be discharged by one or more of the following methods—
    (i) authorisation in writing to release a deposit held for the purposes of the contract by a stakeholder
    (ii) banker's draft issued by a designated bank
    (iii) cheque drawn on and guaranteed by a designated bank
    (iv) telegraphic or other direct transfer (as requested or agreed to by the vendor's

solicitor) to a particular bank or branch for the credit of a specified account
    (v) legal tender
    (vi) any other method requested or agreed to by the vendor's solicitor
(4) Completion shall be carried out, either formally at such office or place as the vendor's solicitor shall reasonably require, or (if the parties' solicitors so arrange) by post, or by means of solicitors' undertakings concerning the holding of documents or otherwise Provided that on a sale with vacant possession of the whole or part of the property, if the conveyance or transfer will not, by overreaching or otherwise, discharge the property from interests (if any) of persons in, or who may be in, actual occupation of the property or such part of it, then (subject always to the rights of the purchaser under Law of Property Act 1925, s. 42 (1)), the purchaser may, by giving reasonable notice, require that on, or immediately before the time of, completion possession of the property or part be handed over to the purchaser or his representative at the property
(5) The date of actual completion shall be the day on which, the contract being completed in other respects, the purchaser has discharged consistently with the provisions of this condition the obligations of the purchaser to pay the money due on completion Provided that—
    (i) for the purposes only of conditions 6, 7 and 8, if but for this proviso the date of actual completion would be the last working day of a week (starting on Sunday) and the purchaser is unable or unwilling to complete before 2.15 p.m. on that day, then the date of actual completion shall be taken to be the first working day thereafter
    (ii) a remittance sent by post or delivered by hand shall be treated as being made on the day on which it reaches the vendor's solicitor's office, unless that day is not a working day in which case the remittance shall be treated as being made on the first working day thereafter.

6. Rents, outgoings and apportionments

    The purchase being completed (whether on the completion date or subsequently), the income and outgoings shall be apportioned as follows (the day itself in each case being apportioned to the vendor) :—
(1) In a case to which proviso (i) to condition 7 (1) applies apportionment shall be made as at the date of actual completion
(2) In a case in which the purchaser is in possession of the whole of the property as lessee or tenant at a rent apportionment shall be made as at the date of actual completion unless proviso (ii) to condition 7 (1) applies, when apportionment shall be made as at the date of the purchaser's notice under that proviso
(3) In any other case apportionment shall be made as from the completion date Provided nevertheless that, if delay is attributable to the vendor's failure to obtain the reversioner's licence, where necessary, or if the vendor remains in beneficial occupation of the property after the completion date, the purchaser may by notice in writing before actual completion elect that apportionment shall be made as at the date of actual completion
(4) Rates shall be apportioned according to the period for which they are intended to provide and rents (whether payable in advance or in arrear) according to the period in respect of which they have been paid or are payable ; and apportionment of yearly items (whether or not the same are payable by equal quarterly, monthly or other instalments) shall be according to the relevant number of days relatively to the number of days in the full year
(5) Service charges under leases, in the absence of known or readily ascertainable amounts, shall be apportioned according to the best estimate available at the time of completion and, unless otherwise agreed, the vendor and the purchaser shall be and remain mutually bound after completion to account for and pay or allow to each other, within 15 working days after being informed of the actual amounts as ascertained, any balances or excesses due.

7. Interest

(1) If the purchase shall not be completed on the completion date then (subject to the provisions of paragraph (2) of this condition) the purchaser shall pay interest on the remainder of his purchase money at the prescribed rate from that date until the purchase shall actually be completed Provided nevertheless—

(i) That (without prejudice to the operation of proviso (ii) to this paragraph) the vendor may by notice in writing before actual completion elect to take the income of the property (less outgoings) up to the date of actual completion instead of interest as aforesaid

(ii) That, if the delay arises from any cause other than the neglect or default of the purchaser, and if the purchaser (not being in occupation of the property in circumstances to which condition 8 applies) places the remainder of his purchase money (at his own risk) at interest on a deposit account in England or Wales with any designated bank, and gives written notice thereof to the vendor or his solicitor, then in lieu of the interest or income payable to or receivable by the vendor as aforesaid, the vendor shall from the time of such notice be entitled to such interest only as is produced by such deposit

(iii) That the vendor shall in no case be or become entitled in respect of the same period of time both to be paid interest and to enjoy income of the property, or to be paid interest more than once on the same sum of money

(2) The purchaser shall not be liable to pay interest under paragraph (1) of this condition—

(i) so long as, or to the extent that, delay in completion is attributable to any act or default of the vendor or his mortgagee or Settled Land Act trustees

(ii) in case the property is to be constructed or converted by the vendor, so long as the construction or conversion is unfinished.

8. Occupation pending completion

(1) If the purchaser (not being already in occupation as lessee or tenant at a rent) is let into occupation of the property before the actual completion of the purchase, then, as from the date of his going into occupation and until actual completion, or until upon discharge or rescission of the contract he ceases to occupy the property, the purchaser shall—

(i) be the licensee and not the tenant of the vendor

(ii) pay interest on the remainder of the purchase money at the prescribed rate

(iii) keep the property in as good repair and condition as it was in when he went into occupation

(iv) pay, or otherwise indemnify the vendor against, all outgoings and expenses (including the cost of insurance) in respect of the property, the purchaser at the same time taking or being credited with the income of the property (if any)

(v) not carry out any development within the meaning of the Planning Acts

(2) Upon discharge or rescission of the contract, or upon the expiration of 7 working days' or longer notice given by the vendor or his solicitor to the purchaser or his solicitor in that behalf, the purchaser shall forthwith give up the property in such repair and condition as aforesaid

(3) A purchaser going into occupation before completion shall not be deemed thereby to have accepted the vendor's title

(4) Where the purchaser is allowed access to the property for the purpose only of carrying out works or installations, the purchaser shall not be treated as being let into occupation within the meaning of this condition.

9. Abstract, requisitions and observations

(1) The vendor shall deliver the abstract of title not later than 11 working days after the date of the contract but, subject and without prejudice as mentioned in condition 5(2), that time limit shall not be of the essence of the contract

(2) Subject always to the rights of the purchaser under Law of Property Act 1925, s. 42(1), the vendor may be required by the purchaser to deal with requisitions and observations concerning persons who are or may be in occupation or actual occupation of the property, so as to satisfy the purchaser that the title is not, and that the purchaser will not be, prejudicially affected by any interests or claims of such persons.

(3) The purchaser shall deliver in writing his requisitions within 11 working days after delivery of the abstract, and his observations on the replies to the requisitions within 6 working days after delivery of the replies

(4) In respect of the delivery of requisitions and observations, time shall be of the essence of the contract, notwithstanding that the abstract may not have been delivered within due time

(5) The purchaser shall deliver his requisitions and observations on the abstract as delivered, whether it is a perfect or an imperfect abstract, but for the purposes of any requisitions or observations which could not be raised or made on the information contained in an imperfect abstract, time under paragraph (3) of this condition shall not start to run against the purchaser, until the vendor has delivered the further abstract or information on which the requisitions or observations arise

(6) Subject to his requisitions and observations, the purchaser shall be deemed to have accepted the title.

10. Vendor's right to rescind

(1) If the purchaser shall persist in any objection to the title which the vendor shall be unable or unwilling, on reasonable grounds, to remove, and shall not withdraw the same within 10 working days of being required so to do, the vendor may, subject to the purchaser's rights under Law of Property Act 1925, ss. 42 and 125, by notice in writing to the purchaser or his solicitor, and notwithstanding any intermediate negotiation or litigation, rescind the contract

(2) Upon such rescission the vendor shall return the deposit, but without interest, costs of investigating title or other compensation or payment, and the purchaser shall return the abstract and other papers furnished to him.

11. Existing leaseholds

(1) Where the interest sold is leasehold for the residue of an existing term the following provisions of this condition shall apply

(2) The lease or underlease or a copy thereof having been made available, the purchaser (whether he has inspected the same or not) shall be deemed to have bought with full notice of the contents thereof

(3) On production of a receipt for the last payment due for rent under the lease or underlease, the purchaser shall assume without proof that the person giving the receipt, though not the original lessor, is the reversioner expectant on the said lease or underlease or his duly authorised agent

(4) No objection shall be taken on account of the covenants in an underlease not corresponding with the covenants in any superior lease

(5) The sale is subject to the reversioner's licence being obtained, where necessary. The purchaser supplying such information and references, if any, as may reasonably be required of him, the vendor will use his best endeavours to obtain such licence and will pay the fee for the same. But if the licence cannot be obtained, the vendor may rescind the contract on the same terms as if the purchaser had persisted in an objection to the title which the vendor was unable to remove

(6) Where the property comprises part only of the property comprised in a lease or underlease, the rent, covenants and conditions shall, if the purchaser so requires, be legally apportioned at his expense, but completion shall not be delayed on that account and in the meantime the apportionment by the auctioneer shall be accepted, or the property may at the option of the vendor be sub-demised for the residue of the term, less one day, at a rent apportioned by the auctioneer and subject to the purchaser executing a counterpart containing covenants and provisions corresponding to those contained in the lease or underlease aforesaid

(7) Any statutory covenant to be implied in the conveyance on the part of a vendor shall be so limited as not to affect him with liability for a subsisting breach of any covenant or condition concerning the state or condition of the property, of which state and condition the purchaser is by paragraph (3) of condition 13 deemed to have full notice, and where Land Registration Act 1925, s. 24, applies the purchaser, if required, will join in requesting that an appropriate entry be made in the register.

12. Vendor's duty to produce documents
(1) If an abstracted document refers to any plan material to the description of the property, or to any covenants contained in a document earlier in date than the document with which the title commences, and such plan or earlier document is in the possession or power of the vendor or his trustees or mortgagee, the vendor shall supply a copy thereof with the abstract
(2) If the property is sold subject to restrictive covenants, the deed imposing those covenants or a copy thereof having been made available, the purchaser (whether he has inspected the same or not) shall be deemed to have purchased with full knowledge thereof
(3) The vendor shall not be required to procure the production of any document not in his possession or not in the possession of his mortgagee or trustees, and of which the vendor cannot obtain production, or to trace or state who has the possession of the same.

13. Identity: boundaries: condition of property
(1) The purchaser shall admit the identity of the property with that comprised in the muniments offered by the vendor as the title thereto upon the evidence afforded by the descriptions contained in such muniments, and of a statutory declaration, to be made (if required) at the purchaser's expense, that the property has been enjoyed according to the title for at least twelve years
(2) The vendor shall not be bound to show any title to boundaries, fences, ditches, hedges or walls, or to distinguish parts of the property held under different titles further than he may be able to do from information in his possession
(3) The purchaser shall be deemed to buy with full notice in all respects of the actual state and condition of the property and, save where it is to be constructed or converted by the vendor, shall take the property as it is.

14. Property sold subject to easements, etc.
Without prejudice to the duty of the vendor to disclose all latent easements and latent liabilities known to the vendor to affect the property, the property is sold subject to any rights of way and water, rights of common, and other rights, easements, quasi-easements, liabilities and public rights affecting the same.

15. Town and Country Planning
(1) In this condition, where the context admits, references to "authorised use" are references to "established use", or to use for which permission has been granted under the Planning Acts, or to use for which permission is not required under those Acts, as the case may be
(2) The purchaser shall be entitled to deliver, with his requisitions in respect of the title, requisitions concerning the authorised use of the property for the purposes of the Planning Acts. The vendor in reply shall give all such relevant information as may be in his possession or power
(3) Where the property is in the Special Conditions expressed to be sold on the footing of an authorised use which is specified, then if it appears before actual completion of the purchase that the specified use is not an authorised use of the property for the purposes of the Planning Acts, the purchaser may by notice in writing rescind the contract, and thereupon paragraph (2) of condition 10 shall apply. But, subject to the foregoing provisions of this condition, the purchaser shall be deemed to have accepted that the specified use is an authorised use of the property for the purposes of the Planning Acts
(4) Save as mentioned in the Special Conditions, the property is not to the knowledge of the vendor subject to any charge, notice, order, restriction, agreement or other matter arising under the Planning Acts, but (without prejudice to any right of the purchaser to rescind the contract under paragraph (3) of this condition) the property is sold subject to any such charges, notices, orders, restrictions, agreements and matters affecting the interest sold
(5) Subject as hereinbefore provided, and without prejudice to the obligations of the vendor to supply information as aforesaid, the purchaser shall be deemed to buy with knowledge in all respects of the authorised use of the property for the purposes of the Planning Acts.

16. Requirements by local authority
(1) If after the date of the contract any requirement in respect of the property be made against the vendor by any local authority, the purchaser shall comply with the same at his own expense, and indemnify the vendor in respect thereof : in so far as the purchaser shall fail to comply with such requirement, the vendor may comply with the same wholly or in part and any money so expended by the vendor shall be repaid by the purchaser on completion
(2) The vendor shall upon receiving notice of any such requirement forthwith inform the purchaser thereof.

17. Errors, mis-statements or omissions
(1) Without prejudice to any express right of either party, or to any right of the purchaser in reliance on Law of Property Act 1969, s. 24, to rescind the contract before completion ,ıd subject to the provisions of paragraph (2) of this condition, no error, mis-statement or omission in any preliminary answer concerning the property, or in the sale plan or the Special Conditions, shall annul the sale, nor (save where the error, mis-statement or omission relates to a matter materially affecting the description or value of the property) shall any damages be payable, or compensation allowed by either party, in respect thereof
(2) Paragraph (1) of this condition shall not apply to any error, mis-statement or, omission which is recklessly or fraudulently made, or to any matter or thing by which the purchaser is prevented from getting substantially what he contracted to buy
(3) In this condition a "preliminary answer" means and includes any statement made by or on behalf of the vendor to the purchaser or his agents or advisers, whether in answer to formal preliminary enquiries or otherwise, before the purchaser entered into the contract.

18. Leases and tenancies
(1) Abstracts or copies of the leases or agreements (if in writing) under which the tenants hold having been made available, the purchaser (whether he has inspected the same or not) shall be deemed to have notice of and shall take subject to the terms of all the existing tenancies and the rights of the tenants, whether arising during the continuance or after the expiration thereof, and such notice shall not be affected by any partial or incomplete statement in the Special Conditions with reference to the tenancies, and no objection shall be taken on account of there not being an agreement in writing with any tenant
(2) Where a lease or tenancy affects the property sold and other property, the property sold will be conveyed with the benefit of the apportioned rent (if any) mentioned in the Special Conditions or (if not so mentioned) fixed by the auctioneer, and no objection shall be taken on the ground that the consent of the tenant has not been obtained to the apportionment and the purchaser shall not require the rent to be legally apportioned
(3) The purchaser shall keep the vendor indemnified against all claims by the tenant for compensation or otherwise, except in respect of a tenancy which expires or is determined on or before the completion date or in respect of an obligation which ought to have been discharged before the date of the contract
(4) Land in the occupation of the vendor is sold subject to the right (hereby reserved to him) to be paid a fair price for tillages, off-going and other allowances as if he were an outgoing tenant who had entered into occupation of the land after 1st March 1948, and as if the purchaser were the landlord, and in case of dispute such price shall be fixed by the valuation of a valuer, to be nominated in case the parties differ by the President of the Royal Institution of Chartered Surveyors.

19. Preparation of conveyance: priority notices: indemnities
(1) Where the interest sold is leasehold for a term of years to be granted by the vendor, the lease or underlease and counterpart shall be prepared by the vendor's solicitor in accordance (as nearly as the circumstances admit) with a form or draft annexed to the contract or otherwise sufficiently identified by the signatures of the parties or their solicitors
(2) In any other case the conveyance shall be prepared by the purchaser or his solicitor and the following provisions of this condition shall apply

(3) The draft conveyance shall be delivered at the office of the vendor's solicitor at least 6 working days before the completion date and the engrossment for execution by the vendor and other necessary parties (if any) shall be left at the said office within 3 working days after the draft has been returned to the purchaser approved on behalf of the vendor and other necessary parties (if any)

(4) Where the property is unregistered land not in an area of compulsory registration and the conveyance is to contain restrictive covenants, and the purchaser intends contemporaneously with the conveyance to execute a mortgage or conveyance to a third party, he shall inform the vendor of his intention and, if necessary, allow the vendor to give a priority notice for the registration of the intended covenants at least 15 working days before the contract is completed

(5) Where the property is sold subject to legal incumbrances, the purchaser shall covenant to indemnify the vendor against actions and claims in respect of them; and the purchaser will not make any claim on account of increased expense caused by the concurrence of any legal incumbrancer

(6) Where the property is sold subject to stipulations, or restrictive or other covenants, and breach thereof would expose the vendor to liability, the purchaser shall covenant to observe and perform the same and to indemnify the vendor against actions and claims in respect thereof

(7) Paragraphs (5) and (6) of this condition shall have effect without prejudice to the provisions of Law of Property Act 1925, s. 77, and Land Registration Act 1925, s. 24, where such provisions respectively are applicable, and in respect of matters covered by a covenant implied under either of those sections no express covenant shall be required.

20. Severance of properties formerly in common ownership

Where the property and any adjacent or neighbouring property have hitherto been in common ownership, the purchaser shall not become entitled to any right to light or air over or in respect of any adjacent or neighbouring property which is retained by the vendor and the conveyance shall, if the vendor so requires, reserve to him such easements and rights as would become appurtenant to such last-mentioned property by implication of law, if the vendor had sold it to another purchaser at the same time as he has sold the property to the purchaser.

21. Insurance

(1) With respect to any policy of insurance maintained by the vendor in respect of damage to or destruction of the property, the vendor shall not (save pursuant to an obligation to a third party) be bound to keep such insurance on foot or to give notice to the purchaser of any premium being or becoming due

(2) The purchaser shall be entitled to inspect the policy at any time

(3) The vendor shall, if required, by and at the expense of the purchaser obtain or consent to an endorsement of notice of the purchaser's interest on the policy, and in such case the vendor (keeping the policy on foot) may require the purchaser to pay on completion a proportionate part of the premium from the date of the contract.

22. Special notice to complete

(1) At any time on or after the completion date, either party, being ready and willing to fulfil his own outstanding obligations under the contract, may (without prejudice to any other right or remedy available to him) give to the other party or his solicitor notice in writing requiring completion of the contract in conformity with this condition

(2) Upon service of such notice as aforesaid it shall become and be a term of the contract, in respect of which time shall be of the essence thereof, that the party to whom the notice is given shall complete the contract within 16 working days after service of the notice (exclusive of the day of service): but this condition shall operate without prejudice to any right of either party to rescind the contract in the meantime

(3) In case the purchaser refuses or fails to complete in conformity with this condition, then (without prejudice to any other right or remedy available to the vendor) the purchaser's deposit may be forfeited (unless the court otherwise directs) and, if the vendor resells the property within twelve months of the expiration of the said period of 16 working days, he shall be entitled (upon crediting the deposit) to recover from the purchaser hereunder the amount of any loss occasioned to the vendor by expenses of or incidental to such resale, or by diminution in the price.

Index